Wal e in
My Muu-Muu

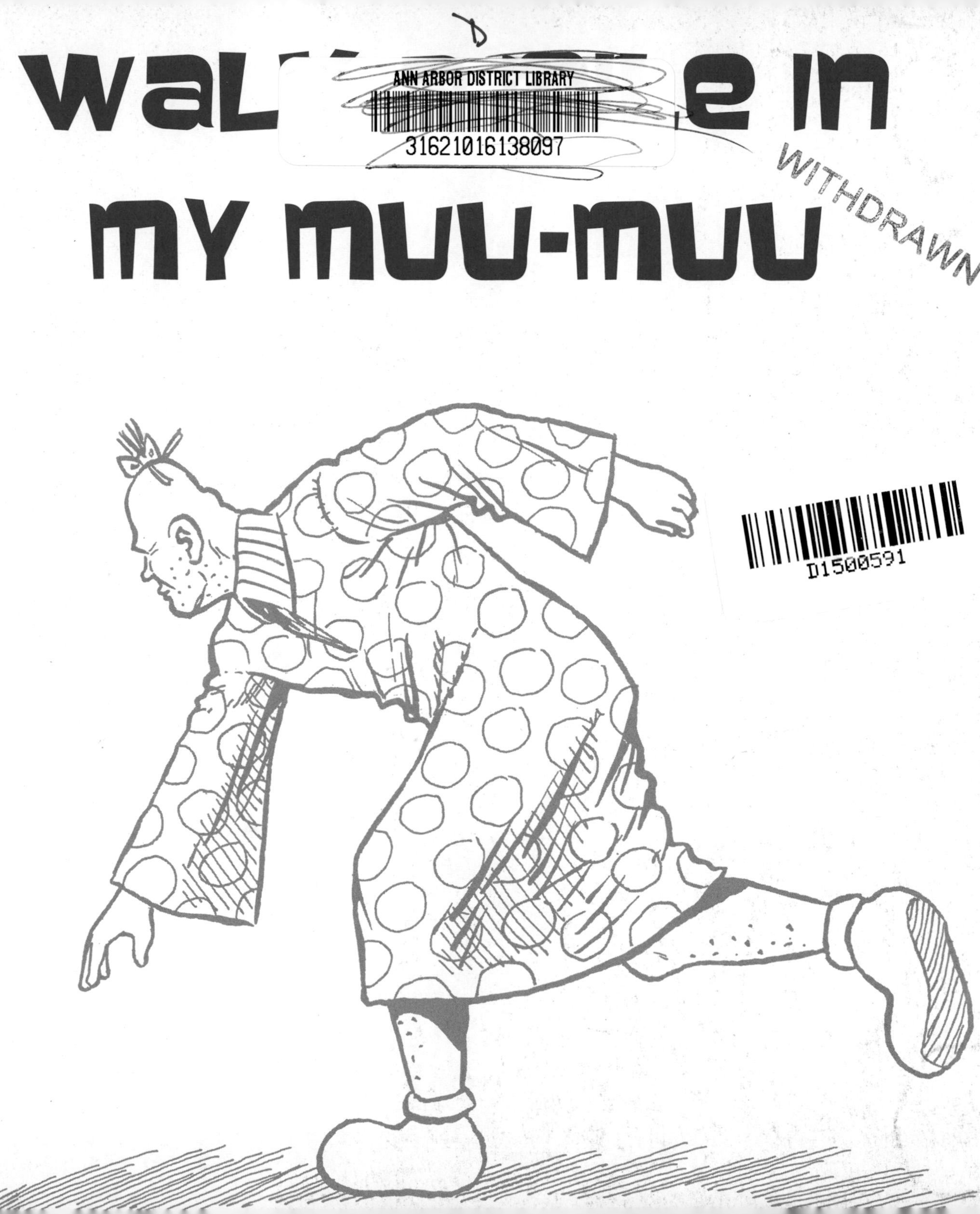

ZIPPY

WALK A MILE IN MY MUU-MUU

AUGUST 2006 - AUGUST 2007

BILL GRIFFITH

ANTAGRAPHICS BOOKS

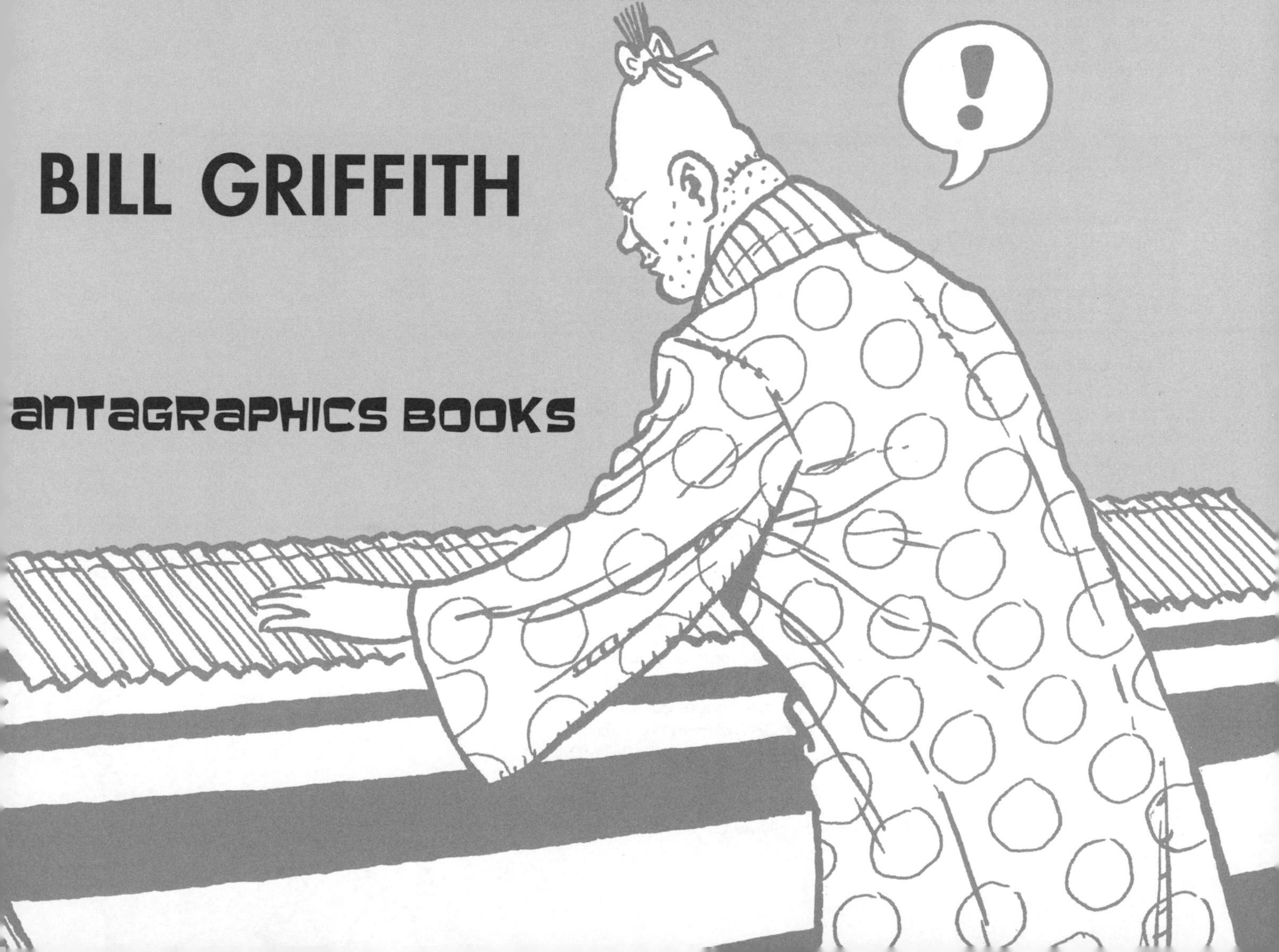
!

ZIPPY / Walk A Mile In My Muu-Muu
Zippy Annual – Volume 8

FANTAGRAPHICS BOOKS

7563 Lake City Way NE, Seattle WA 98115
www.fantagraphics.com
Call 1-800-657-1100 for a full color catalog of fine comics publications.
First Edition: October 2007
Designed by Bill Griffith
Production managed by Kim Thompson
Production by Paul Baresh
Cover production by Paul Baresh
Published by Gary Groth and Kim Thompson
Promotion by Eric Reynolds

Printed in Malaysia
ISBN: 978-1-56097-877-0

The comic strips in this book have appeared in newspapers in the
United States and abroad, distributed by King Features Syndicate,
300 W. 57th St., New York NY 10019.
www.kingfeatures.com

For more on Zippy (including the Zippy Storefront, Zippy Strip Search and extensive free
Zippy Archives), visit:
www.zippythepinhead.com

Thanks and a tip o' th' pin to: American Color, Gary Groth, Kim Thompson, Jon Buller,
Diane Noomin and all the roadside field researchers who continue to send in Zip-worthy
photos and location information.

Books by Bill Griffith:
Zippy Stories • *Nation of Pinheads* • *Pointed Behavior* • *Pindemonium*
Are We Having Fun Yet? • *Kingpin* • *Pinhead's Progress* • *Get Me A*
Table Without Flies, Harry • *From A To Zippy* • *Zippy's House Of Fun*
Griffith Observatory • *Zippy Annual #1* • *Zippy Annual 2001*
Zippy Annual 2002 • *Zippy Annual 2003* • *ZIPPY: From Here To*
Absurdity • *ZIPPY: Type Z Personality* • *ZIPPY: Connect The Polka Dots*

To contact Bill Griffith:
Pinhead Productions, LLC, P.O. Box 88, Hadlyme CT 06439
Griffy@zippythepinhead.com

The **PINDEX**

THE PINHEAD LIFESTYLE

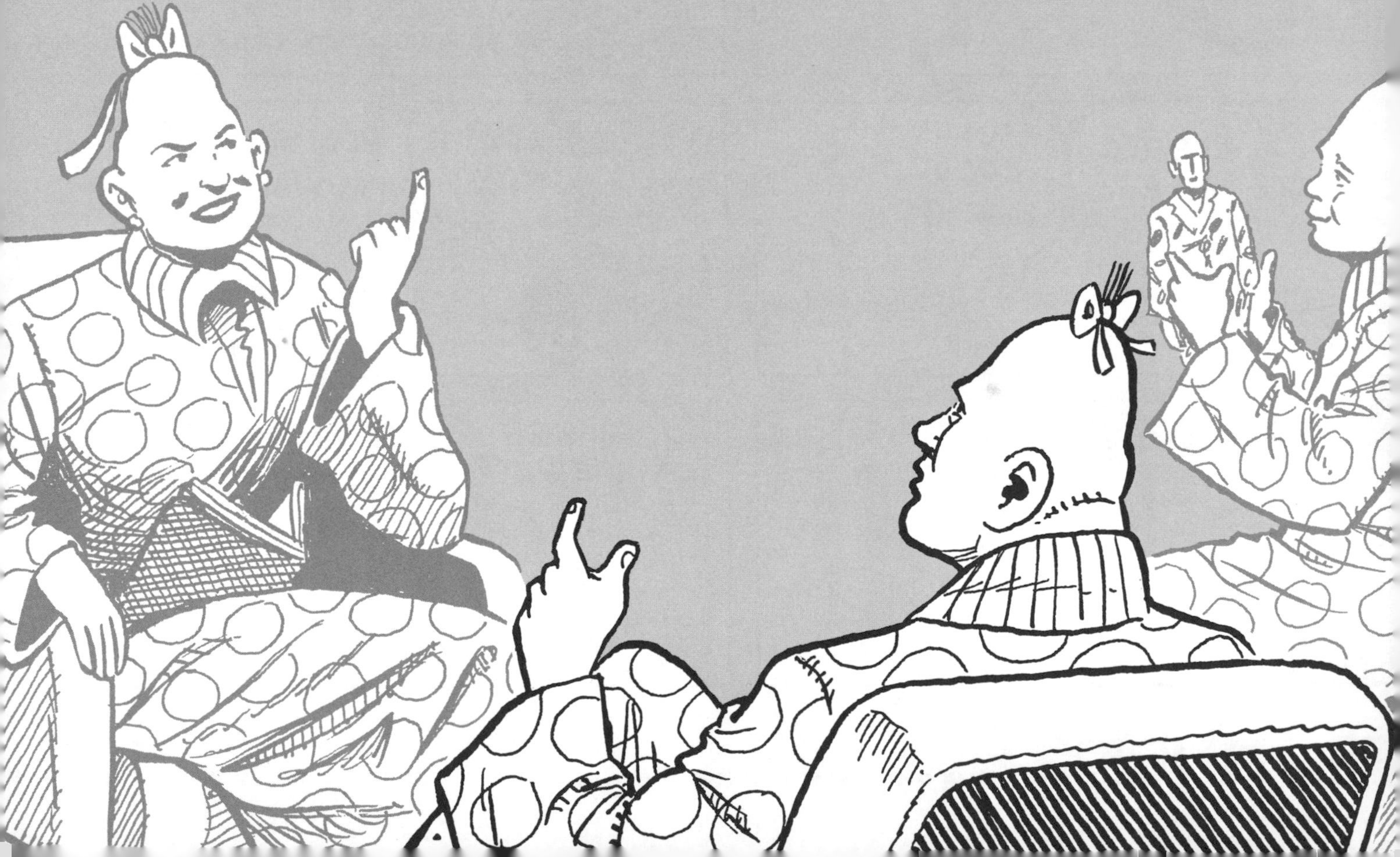

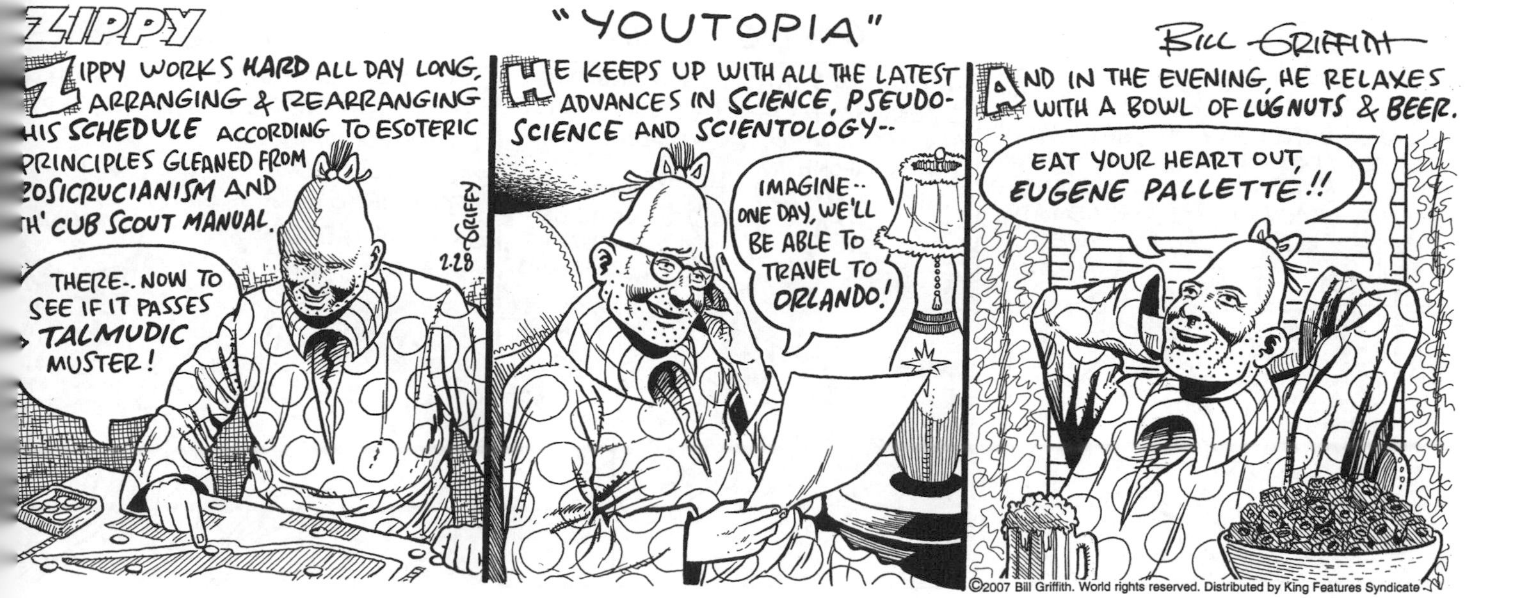
ZIPPY
"YOUTOPIA"
BILL GRIFFITH
ZIPPY WORKS HARD ALL DAY LONG, ARRANGING & REARRANGING HIS SCHEDULE ACCORDING TO ESOTERIC PRINCIPLES GLEANED FROM ROSICRUCIANISM AND TH' CUB SCOUT MANUAL.
THERE.. NOW TO SEE IF IT PASSES TALMUDIC MUSTER!
GRIFFY 2.28
HE KEEPS UP WITH ALL THE LATEST ADVANCES IN SCIENCE, PSEUDO-SCIENCE AND SCIENTOLOGY--
IMAGINE.. ONE DAY, WE'LL BE ABLE TO TRAVEL TO ORLANDO!
AND IN THE EVENING, HE RELAXES WITH A BOWL OF LUGNUTS & BEER.
EAT YOUR HEART OUT, EUGENE PALLETTE!!
©2007 Bill Griffith. World rights reserved. Distributed by King Features Syndicate

1

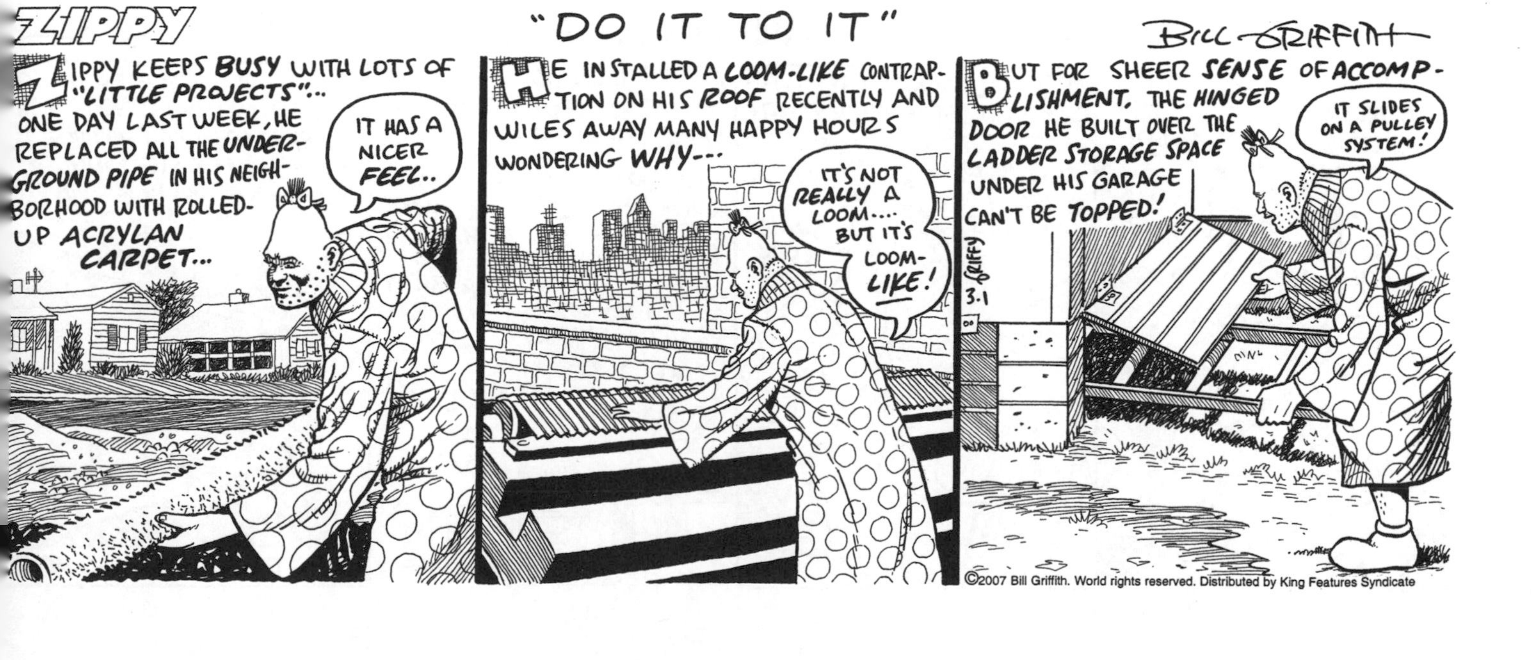
ZIPPY
"DO IT TO IT"
BILL GRIFFITH
ZIPPY KEEPS BUSY WITH LOTS OF "LITTLE PROJECTS".. ONE DAY LAST WEEK, HE REPLACED ALL THE UNDERGROUND PIPE IN HIS NEIGHBORHOOD WITH ROLLED-UP ACRYLAN CARPET...
IT HAS A NICER FEEL..
HE INSTALLED A LOOM-LIKE CONTRAPTION ON HIS ROOF RECENTLY AND WILES AWAY MANY HAPPY HOURS WONDERING WHY---
IT'S NOT REALLY A LOOM.... BUT IT'S LOOM-LIKE!
GRIFFY 3.1
BUT FOR SHEER SENSE OF ACCOMPLISHMENT, THE HINGED DOOR HE BUILT OVER THE LADDER STORAGE SPACE UNDER HIS GARAGE CAN'T BE TOPPED!
IT SLIDES ON A PULLEY SYSTEM!
©2007 Bill Griffith. World rights reserved. Distributed by King Features Syndicate

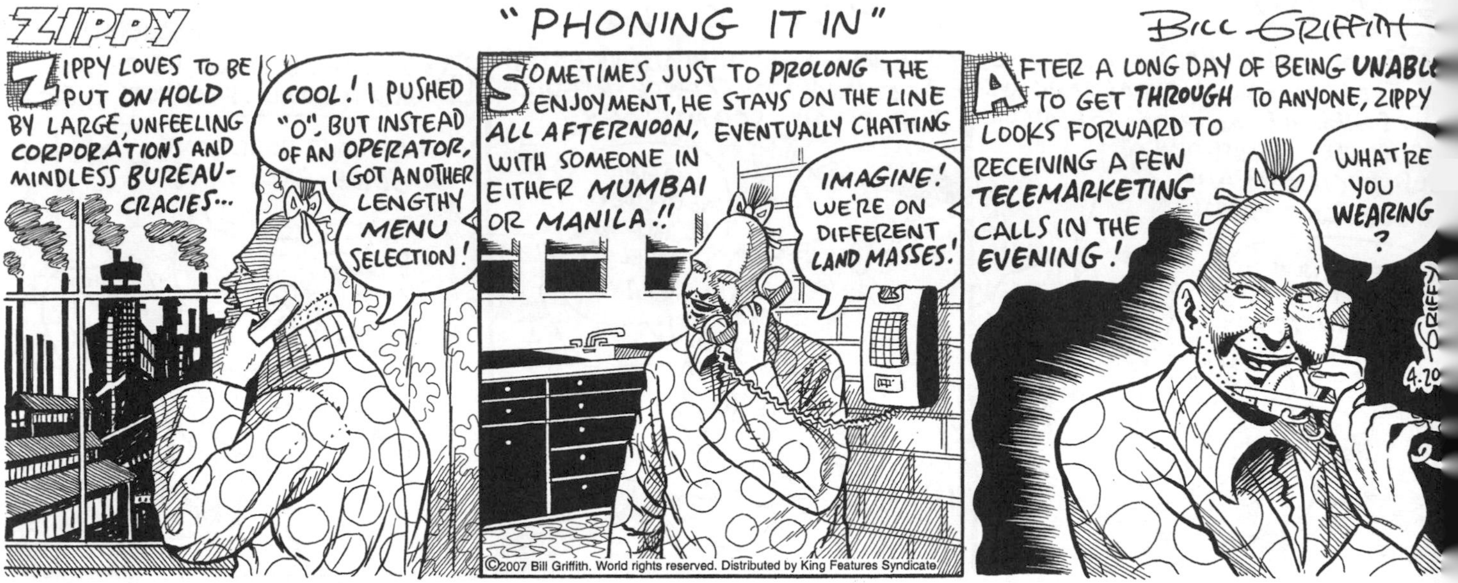
ZIPPY
"PHONING IT IN"
BILL GRIFFITH
ZIPPY LOVES TO BE PUT ON HOLD BY LARGE, UNFEELING CORPORATIONS AND MINDLESS BUREAUCRACIES...
COOL! I PUSHED "0" BUT INSTEAD OF AN OPERATOR, I GOT ANOTHER LENGTHY MENU SELECTION!
SOMETIMES, JUST TO PROLONG THE ENJOYMENT, HE STAYS ON THE LINE ALL AFTERNOON, EVENTUALLY CHATTING WITH SOMEONE IN EITHER MUMBAI OR MANILA!!
IMAGINE! WE'RE ON DIFFERENT LAND MASSES!
©2007 Bill Griffith. World rights reserved. Distributed by King Features Syndicate
AFTER A LONG DAY OF BEING UNABLE TO GET THROUGH TO ANYONE, ZIPPY LOOKS FORWARD TO RECEIVING A FEW TELEMARKETING CALLS IN THE EVENING!
WHAT'RE YOU WEARING?
GRIFFY 4.20

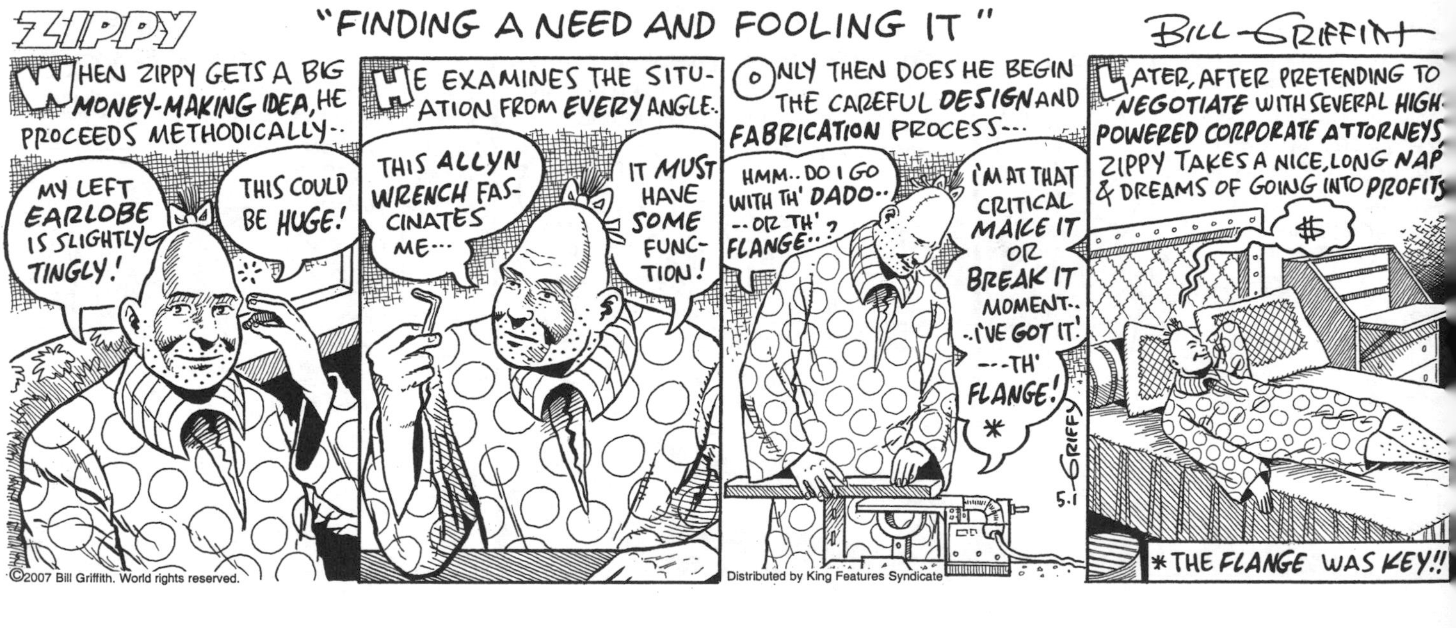
ZIPPY
"FINDING A NEED AND FOOLING IT"
BILL GRIFFITH
WHEN ZIPPY GETS A BIG MONEY-MAKING IDEA, HE PROCEEDS METHODICALLY..
MY LEFT EARLOBE IS SLIGHTLY TINGLY!
THIS COULD BE HUGE!
HE EXAMINES THE SITUATION FROM EVERY ANGLE.
THIS ALLYN WRENCH FASCINATES ME...
IT MUST HAVE SOME FUNCTION!
ONLY THEN DOES HE BEGIN THE CAREFUL DESIGN AND FABRICATION PROCESS...
HMM.. DO I GO WITH TH' DADO.. --OR TH' FLANGE..?
I'M AT THAT CRITICAL MAKE IT OR BREAK IT MOMENT.. ..I'VE GOT IT! --TH' FLANGE! *
GRIFFY 5.1
LATER, AFTER PRETENDING TO NEGOTIATE WITH SEVERAL HIGH-POWERED CORPORATE ATTORNEYS, ZIPPY TAKES A NICE, LONG NAP & DREAMS OF GOING INTO PROFITS
$
* THE FLANGE WAS KEY!!
©2007 Bill Griffith. World rights reserved.
Distributed by King Features Syndicate

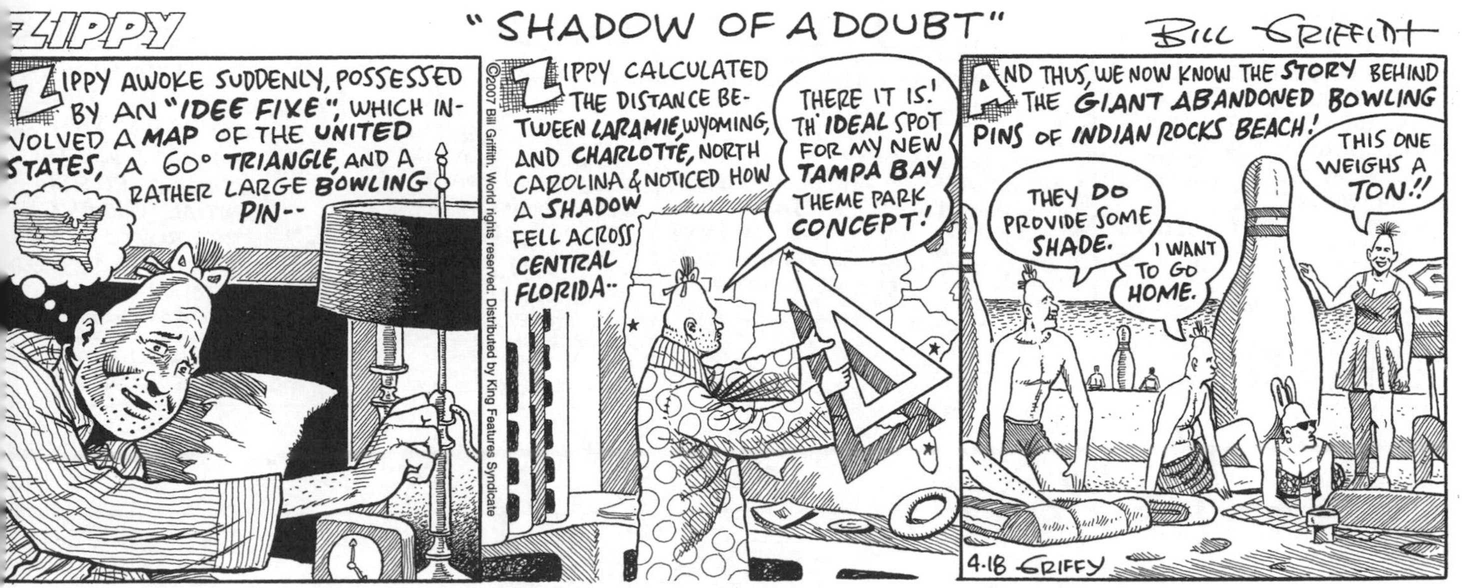

ZIPPY
"SHADOW OF A DOUBT"
BILL GRIFFITH
ZIPPY AWOKE SUDDENLY, POSSESSED BY AN "IDEE FIXE", WHICH INVOLVED A MAP OF THE UNITED STATES, A 60° TRIANGLE, AND A RATHER LARGE BOWLING PIN--
©2007 Bill Griffith. World rights reserved. Distributed by King Features Syndicate
ZIPPY CALCULATED THE DISTANCE BETWEEN LARAMIE, WYOMING, AND CHARLOTTE, NORTH CAROLINA & NOTICED HOW A SHADOW FELL ACROSS CENTRAL FLORIDA..
THERE IT IS! TH' IDEAL SPOT FOR MY NEW TAMPA BAY THEME PARK CONCEPT!
AND THUS, WE NOW KNOW THE STORY BEHIND THE GIANT ABANDONED BOWLING PINS OF INDIAN ROCKS BEACH!
THEY DO PROVIDE SOME SHADE.
I WANT TO GO HOME.
THIS ONE WEIGHS A TON!!
4.18 GRIFFY

2

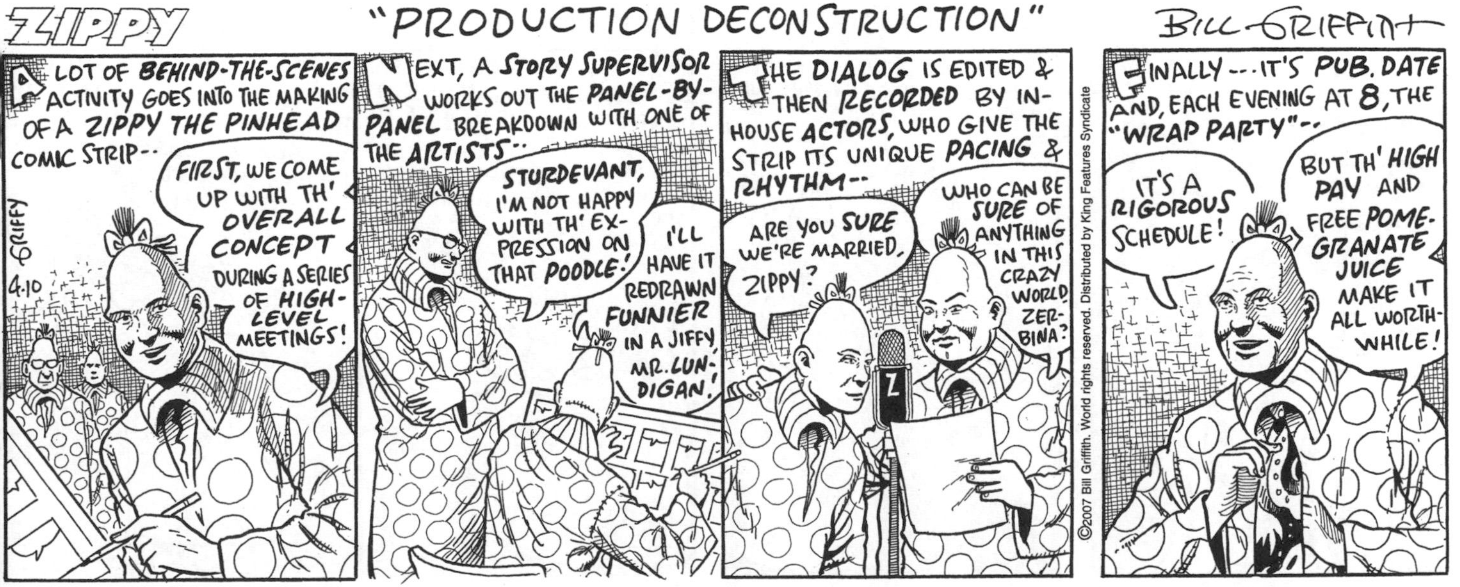

ZIPPY
"PRODUCTION DECONSTRUCTION"
BILL GRIFFITH
A LOT OF BEHIND-THE-SCENES ACTIVITY GOES INTO THE MAKING OF A ZIPPY THE PINHEAD COMIC STRIP--
FIRST, WE COME UP WITH TH' OVERALL CONCEPT DURING A SERIES OF HIGH-LEVEL MEETINGS!
GRIFFY 4.10
NEXT, A STORY SUPERVISOR WORKS OUT THE PANEL-BY-PANEL BREAKDOWN WITH ONE OF THE ARTISTS..
STURDEVANT, I'M NOT HAPPY WITH TH' EXPRESSION ON THAT POODLE!
I'LL HAVE IT REDRAWN FUNNIER IN A JIFFY, MR. LUNDIGAN!
THE DIALOG IS EDITED & THEN RECORDED BY IN-HOUSE ACTORS, WHO GIVE THE STRIP ITS UNIQUE PACING & RHYTHM--
ARE YOU SURE WE'RE MARRIED, ZIPPY?
WHO CAN BE SURE OF ANYTHING IN THIS CRAZY WORLD, ZERBINA?
©2007 Bill Griffith. World rights reserved. Distributed by King Features Syndicate
FINALLY---IT'S PUB. DATE AND, EACH EVENING AT 8, THE "WRAP PARTY"--
IT'S A RIGOROUS SCHEDULE!
BUT TH' HIGH PAY AND FREE POMEGRANATE JUICE MAKE IT ALL WORTHWHILE!

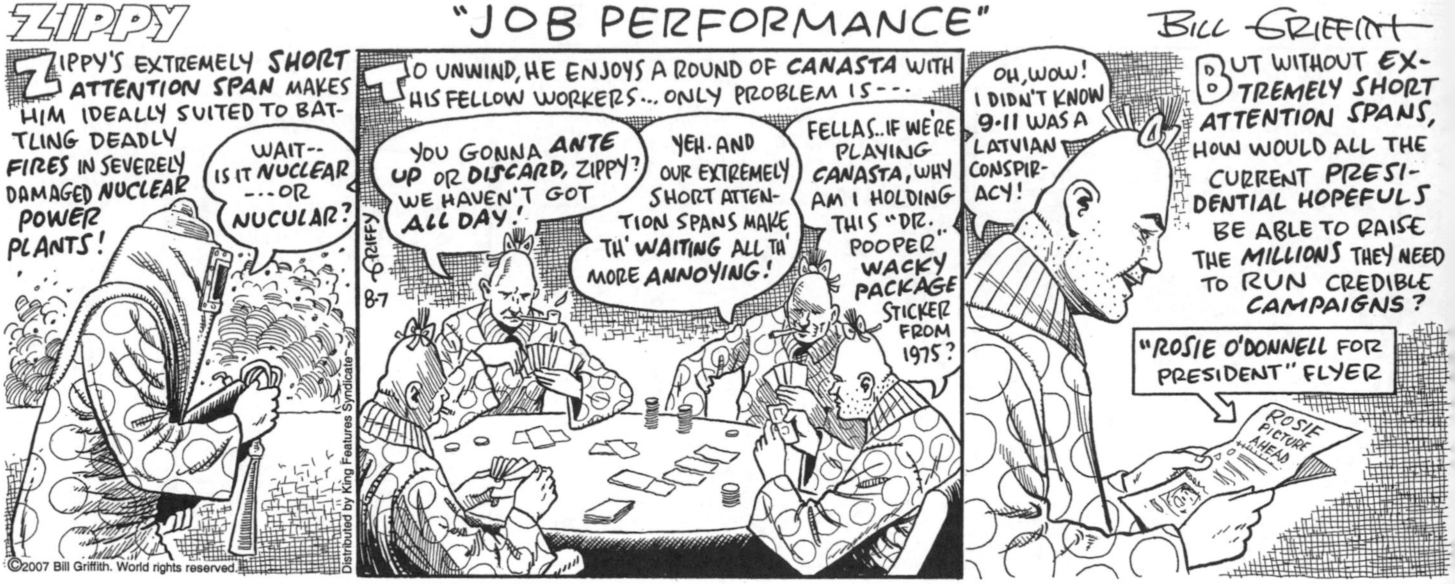
ZIPPY
"JOB PERFORMANCE"
BILL GRIFFITH
ZIPPY'S EXTREMELY SHORT ATTENTION SPAN MAKES HIM IDEALLY SUITED TO BATTLING DEADLY FIRES IN SEVERELY DAMAGED NUCLEAR POWER PLANTS!
WAIT-- IS IT NUCLEAR ---OR NUCULAR?
©2007 Bill Griffith. World rights reserved.
TO UNWIND, HE ENJOYS A ROUND OF CANASTA WITH HIS FELLOW WORKERS... ONLY PROBLEM IS---
YOU GONNA ANTE UP OR DISCARD, ZIPPY? WE HAVEN'T GOT ALL DAY!
YEH. AND OUR EXTREMELY SHORT ATTENTION SPANS MAKE TH' WAITING ALL TH' MORE ANNOYING!
FELLAS.. IF WE'RE PLAYING CANASTA, WHY AM I HOLDING THIS "DR. POOPER" WACKY PACKAGE STICKER FROM 1975?
Distributed by King Features Syndicate
GRIFFY 8-7
OH, WOW! I DIDN'T KNOW 9-11 WAS A LATVIAN CONSPIRACY!
BUT WITHOUT EXTREMELY SHORT ATTENTION SPANS, HOW WOULD ALL THE CURRENT PRESIDENTIAL HOPEFULS BE ABLE TO RAISE THE MILLIONS THEY NEED TO RUN CREDIBLE CAMPAIGNS?
"ROSIE O'DONNELL FOR PRESIDENT" FLYER
ROSIE PICTURE AHEAD

3

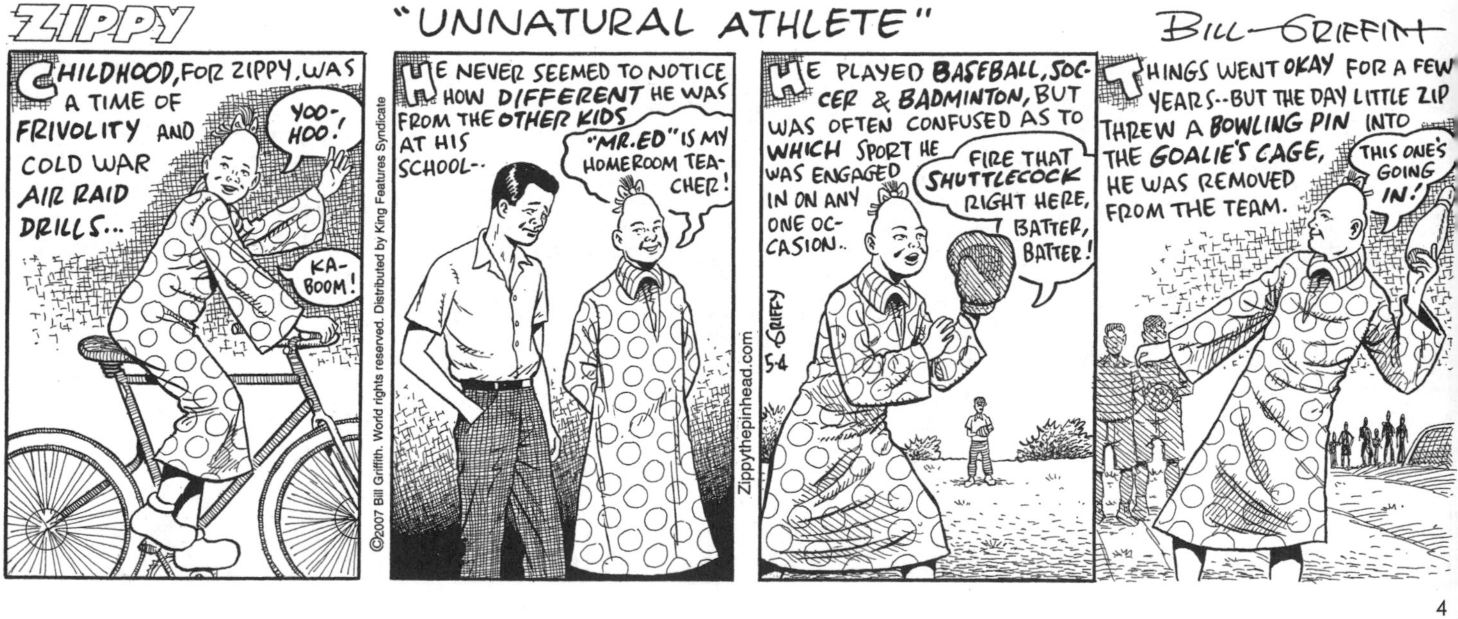
ZIPPY
"UNNATURAL ATHLETE"
BILL GRIFFITH
CHILDHOOD, FOR ZIPPY, WAS A TIME OF FRIVOLITY AND COLD WAR AIR RAID DRILLS...
YOO-HOO!
KA-BOOM!
©2007 Bill Griffith. World rights reserved. Distributed by King Features Syndicate
HE NEVER SEEMED TO NOTICE HOW DIFFERENT HE WAS FROM THE OTHER KIDS AT HIS SCHOOL..
"MR. ED" IS MY HOMEROOM TEACHER!
Zippythepinhead.com
GRIFFY 5-4
HE PLAYED BASEBALL, SOCCER & BADMINTON, BUT WAS OFTEN CONFUSED AS TO WHICH SPORT HE WAS ENGAGED IN ON ANY ONE OCCASION..
FIRE THAT SHUTTLECOCK RIGHT HERE, BATTER, BATTER!
THINGS WENT OKAY FOR A FEW YEARS.. BUT THE DAY LITTLE ZIP THREW A BOWLING PIN INTO THE GOALIE'S CAGE, HE WAS REMOVED FROM THE TEAM.
THIS ONE'S GOING IN!

4

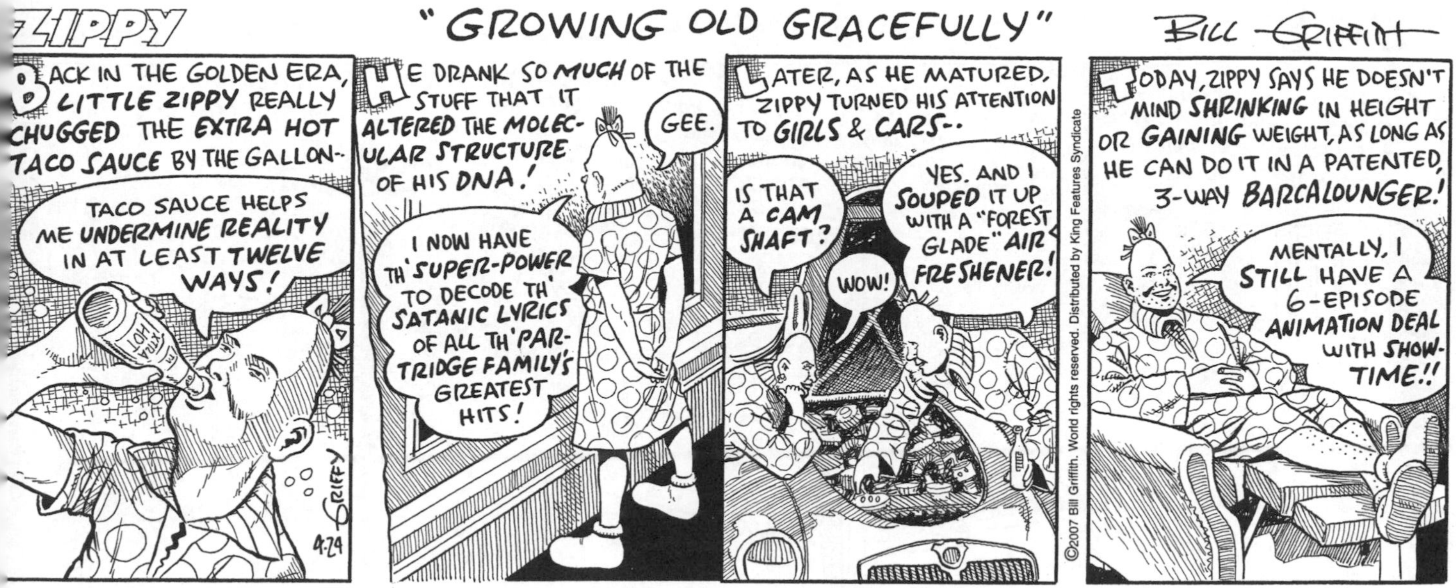
ZIPPY
"GROWING OLD GRACEFULLY"
BILL GRIFFITH
BACK IN THE GOLDEN ERA, LITTLE ZIPPY REALLY CHUGGED THE EXTRA HOT TACO SAUCE BY THE GALLON..
TACO SAUCE HELPS ME UNDERMINE REALITY IN AT LEAST TWELVE WAYS!
GRIFFY 4-24
HE DRANK SO MUCH OF THE STUFF THAT IT ALTERED THE MOLECULAR STRUCTURE OF HIS DNA!
GEE.
I NOW HAVE TH' SUPER-POWER TO DECODE TH' SATANIC LYRICS OF ALL TH' PARTRIDGE FAMILY'S GREATEST HITS!
LATER, AS HE MATURED, ZIPPY TURNED HIS ATTENTION TO GIRLS & CARS..
IS THAT A CAM SHAFT?
YES. AND I SOUPED IT UP WITH A "FOREST GLADE" AIR FRESHENER!
WOW!
©2007 Bill Griffith. World rights reserved. Distributed by King Features Syndicate
TODAY, ZIPPY SAYS HE DOESN'T MIND SHRINKING IN HEIGHT OR GAINING WEIGHT, AS LONG AS HE CAN DO IT IN A PATENTED, 3-WAY BARCALOUNGER!
MENTALLY, I STILL HAVE A 6-EPISODE ANIMATION DEAL WITH SHOWTIME!!

5

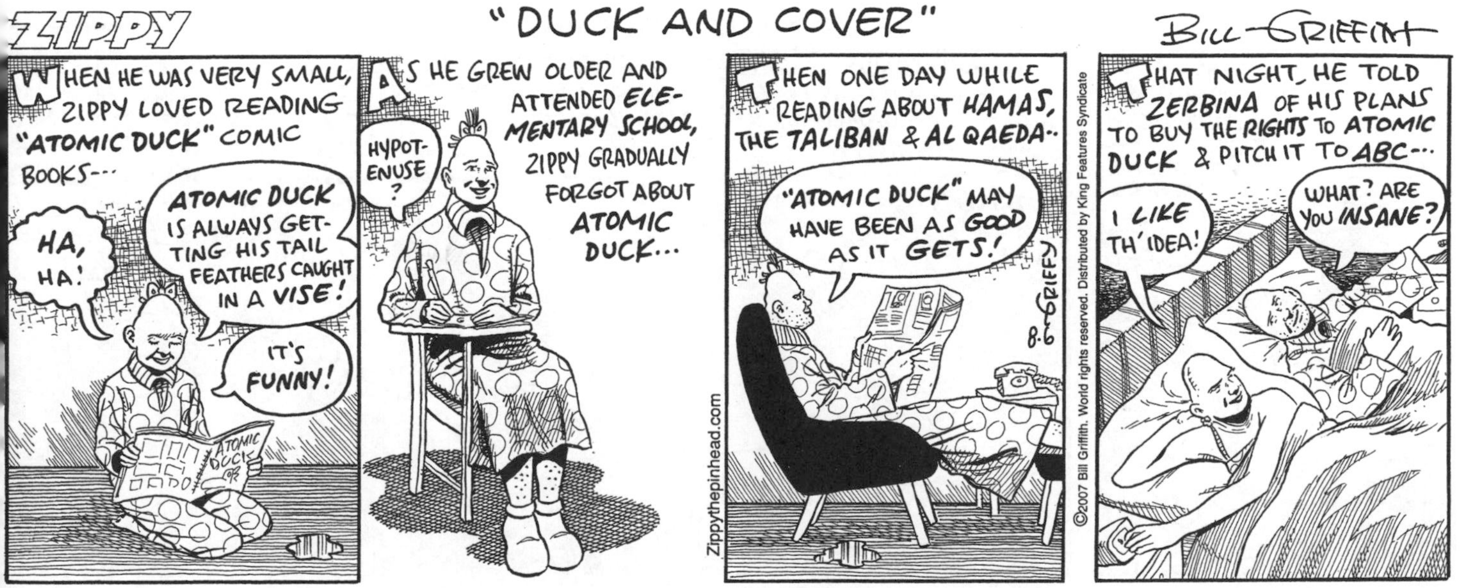
ZIPPY
"DUCK AND COVER"
BILL GRIFFITH
WHEN HE WAS VERY SMALL, ZIPPY LOVED READING "ATOMIC DUCK" COMIC BOOKS...
HA, HA!
ATOMIC DUCK IS ALWAYS GETTING HIS TAIL FEATHERS CAUGHT IN A VISE!
IT'S FUNNY!
ATOMIC DUCK
AS HE GREW OLDER AND ATTENDED ELEMENTARY SCHOOL, ZIPPY GRADUALLY FORGOT ABOUT ATOMIC DUCK...
HYPOTENUSE?
Zippythepinhead.com
THEN ONE DAY WHILE READING ABOUT HAMAS, THE TALIBAN & AL QAEDA..
"ATOMIC DUCK" MAY HAVE BEEN AS GOOD AS IT GETS!
GRIFFY 8-6
©2007 Bill Griffith. World rights reserved. Distributed by King Features Syndicate
THAT NIGHT, HE TOLD ZERBINA OF HIS PLANS TO BUY THE RIGHTS TO ATOMIC DUCK & PITCH IT TO ABC...
I LIKE TH' IDEA!
WHAT? ARE YOU INSANE?

6

ZIPPY "OUT OF THE DARK" BILL GRIFFITH

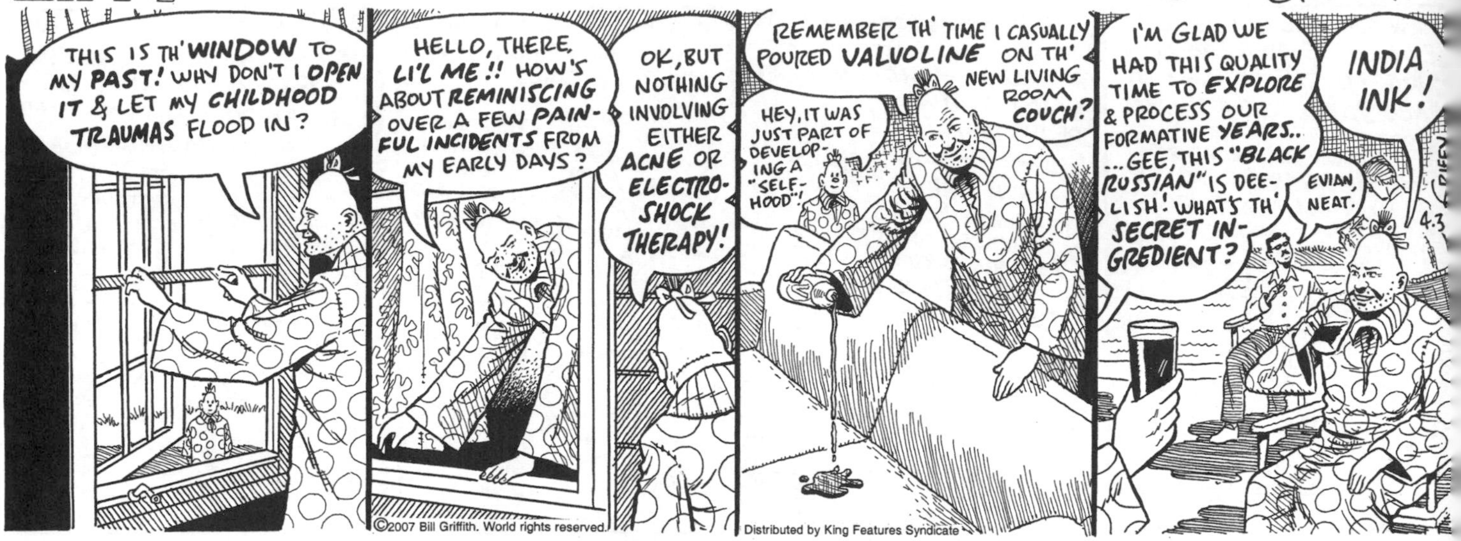
THIS IS TH' WINDOW TO MY PAST! WHY DON'T I OPEN IT & LET MY CHILDHOOD TRAUMAS FLOOD IN?
HELLO, THERE, LI'L ME!! HOW'S ABOUT REMINISCING OVER A FEW PAIN-FUL INCIDENTS FROM MY EARLY DAYS?
OK, BUT NOTHING INVOLVING EITHER ACNE OR ELECTRO-SHOCK THERAPY!
REMEMBER TH' TIME I CASUALLY POURED VALVOLINE ON TH' NEW LIVING ROOM COUCH?
HEY, IT WAS JUST PART OF DEVELOP-ING A "SELF-HOOD"!
I'M GLAD WE HAD THIS QUALITY TIME TO EXPLORE & PROCESS OUR FORMATIVE YEARS.. ...GEE, THIS "BLACK RUSSIAN" IS DEE-LISH! WHAT'S TH' SECRET IN-GREDIENT?
INDIA INK!
EVIAN, NEAT.
©2007 Bill Griffith. World rights reserved.
Distributed by King Features Syndicate

7

ZIPPY "COFFEE BREAK" BILL GRIFFITH

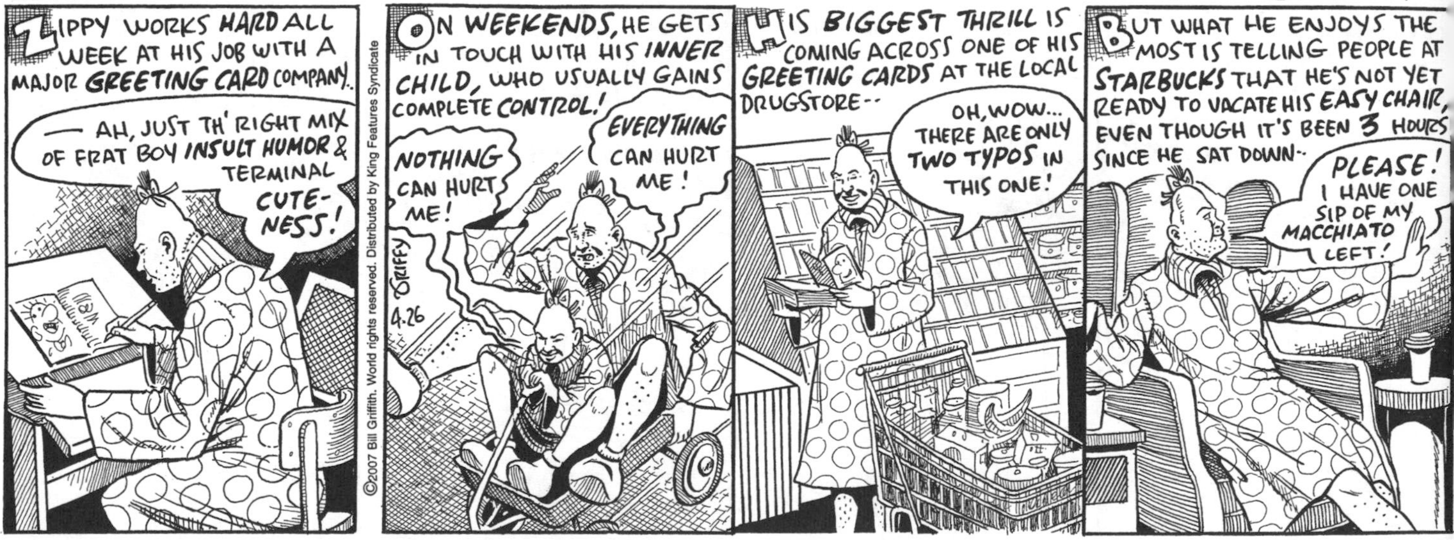
ZIPPY WORKS HARD ALL WEEK AT HIS JOB WITH A MAJOR GREETING CARD COMPANY..
— AH, JUST TH' RIGHT MIX OF FRAT BOY INSULT HUMOR & TERMINAL CUTE-NESS!
ON WEEKENDS, HE GETS IN TOUCH WITH HIS INNER CHILD, WHO USUALLY GAINS COMPLETE CONTROL!
NOTHING CAN HURT ME!
EVERYTHING CAN HURT ME!
©2007 Bill Griffith. World rights reserved. Distributed by King Features Syndicate
HIS BIGGEST THRILL IS COMING ACROSS ONE OF HIS GREETING CARDS AT THE LOCAL DRUGSTORE--
OH, WOW... THERE ARE ONLY TWO TYPOS IN THIS ONE!
BUT WHAT HE ENJOYS THE MOST IS TELLING PEOPLE AT STARBUCKS THAT HE'S NOT YET READY TO VACATE HIS EASY CHAIR, EVEN THOUGH IT'S BEEN 3 HOURS SINCE HE SAT DOWN--
PLEASE! I HAVE ONE SIP OF MY MACCHIATO LEFT!

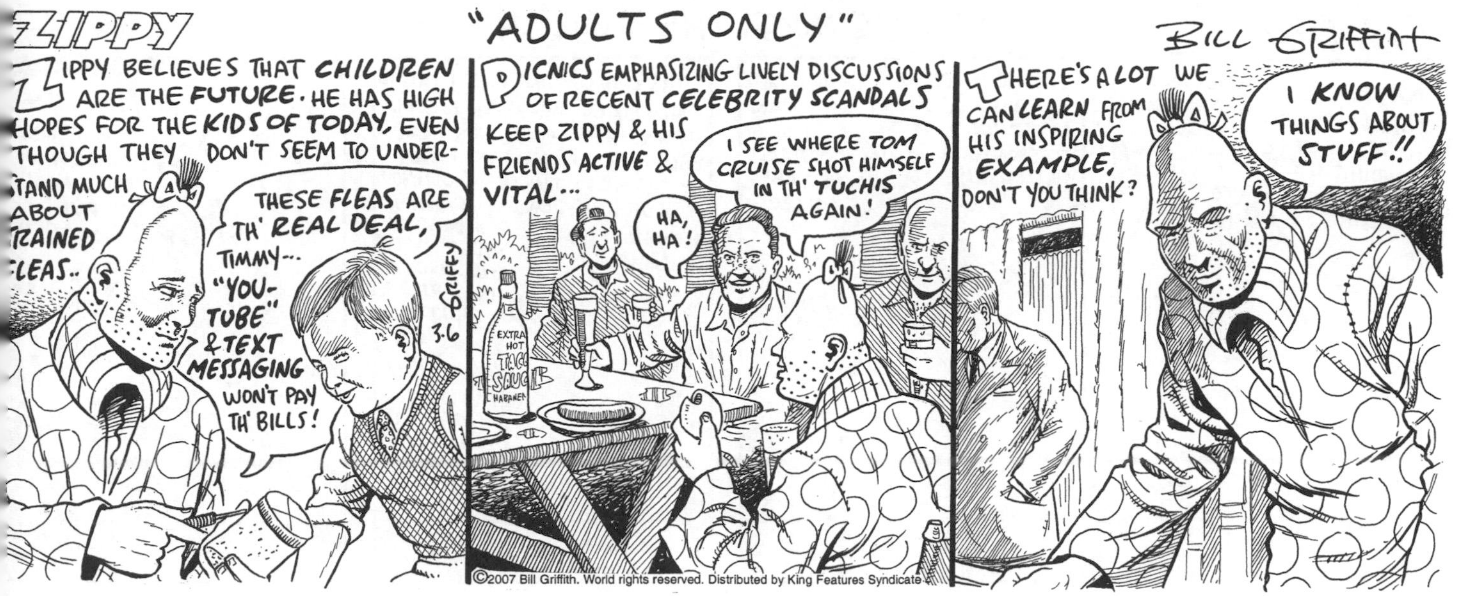
ZIPPY
"ADULTS ONLY"
BILL GRIFFITH
ZIPPY BELIEVES THAT CHILDREN ARE THE FUTURE. HE HAS HIGH HOPES FOR THE KIDS OF TODAY, EVEN THOUGH THEY DON'T SEEM TO UNDERSTAND MUCH ABOUT TRAINED FLEAS..
THESE FLEAS ARE TH' REAL DEAL, TIMMY... "YOU-TUBE" & TEXT MESSAGING WON'T PAY TH' BILLS!
GRIFFY 3.6
PICNICS EMPHASIZING LIVELY DISCUSSIONS OF RECENT CELEBRITY SCANDALS KEEP ZIPPY & HIS FRIENDS ACTIVE & VITAL...
I SEE WHERE TOM CRUISE SHOT HIMSELF IN TH' TUCHIS AGAIN!
HA, HA!
EXTRA HOT TACO SAUCE
©2007 Bill Griffith. World rights reserved. Distributed by King Features Syndicate
THERE'S A LOT WE CAN LEARN FROM HIS INSPIRING EXAMPLE, DON'T YOU THINK?
I KNOW THINGS ABOUT STUFF!!

8

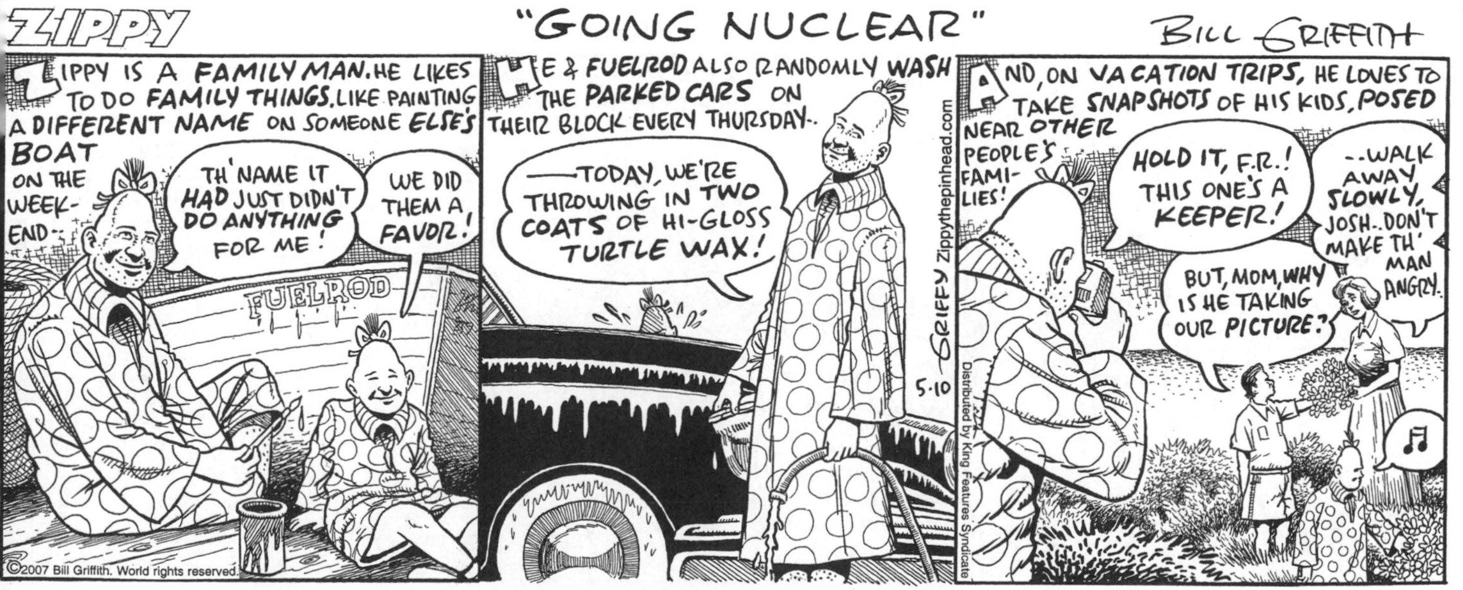
ZIPPY
"GOING NUCLEAR"
BILL GRIFFITH
ZIPPY IS A FAMILY MAN. HE LIKES TO DO FAMILY THINGS. LIKE PAINTING A DIFFERENT NAME ON SOMEONE ELSE'S BOAT ON THE WEEK-END--
TH' NAME IT HAD JUST DIDN'T DO ANYTHING FOR ME!
WE DID THEM A FAVOR!
FUELROD
©2007 Bill Griffith. World rights reserved.
HE & FUELROD ALSO RANDOMLY WASH THE PARKED CARS ON THEIR BLOCK EVERY THURSDAY..
——TODAY, WE'RE THROWING IN TWO COATS OF HI-GLOSS TURTLE WAX!
GRIFFY 5.10
Zippythepinhead.com
Distributed by King Features Syndicate
AND, ON VACATION TRIPS, HE LOVES TO TAKE SNAPSHOTS OF HIS KIDS, POSED NEAR OTHER PEOPLE'S FAMILIES!
HOLD IT, F.R.! THIS ONE'S A KEEPER!
--WALK AWAY SLOWLY, JOSH.. DON'T MAKE TH' MAN ANGRY.
BUT, MOM, WHY IS HE TAKING OUR PICTURE?

9

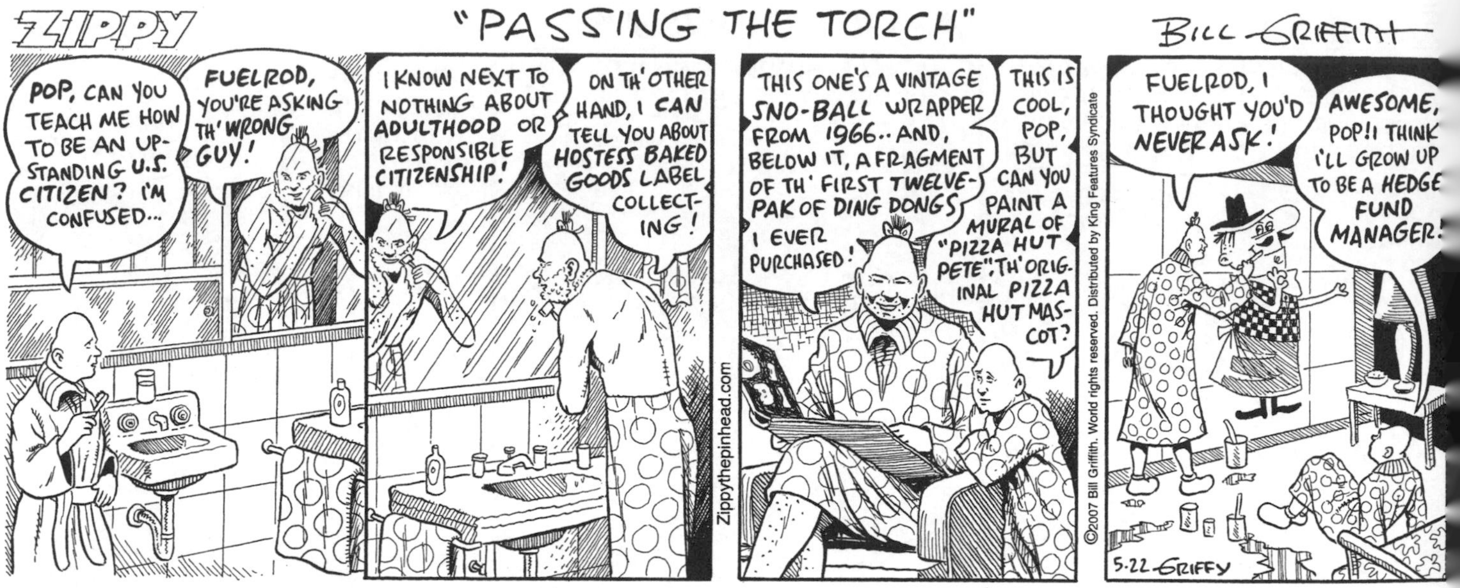
ZIPPY
"PASSING THE TORCH"
BILL GRIFFITH
POP, CAN YOU TEACH ME HOW TO BE AN UP-STANDING U.S. CITIZEN? I'M CONFUSED...
FUELROD, YOU'RE ASKING TH' WRONG GUY!
I KNOW NEXT TO NOTHING ABOUT ADULTHOOD OR RESPONSIBLE CITIZENSHIP!
ON TH' OTHER HAND, I CAN TELL YOU ABOUT HOSTESS BAKED GOODS LABEL COLLECT-ING!
Zippythepinhead.com
THIS ONE'S A VINTAGE SNO-BALL WRAPPER FROM 1966.. AND, BELOW IT, A FRAGMENT OF TH' FIRST TWELVE-PAK OF DING DONGS I EVER PURCHASED!
THIS IS COOL, POP, BUT CAN YOU PAINT A MURAL OF "PIZZA HUT PETE", TH' ORIG-INAL PIZZA HUT MAS-COT?
©2007 Bill Griffith. World rights reserved. Distributed by King Features Syndicate
FUELROD, I THOUGHT YOU'D NEVER ASK!
AWESOME, POP!! I THINK I'LL GROW UP TO BE A HEDGE FUND MANAGER!
5.22 GRIFFY

10

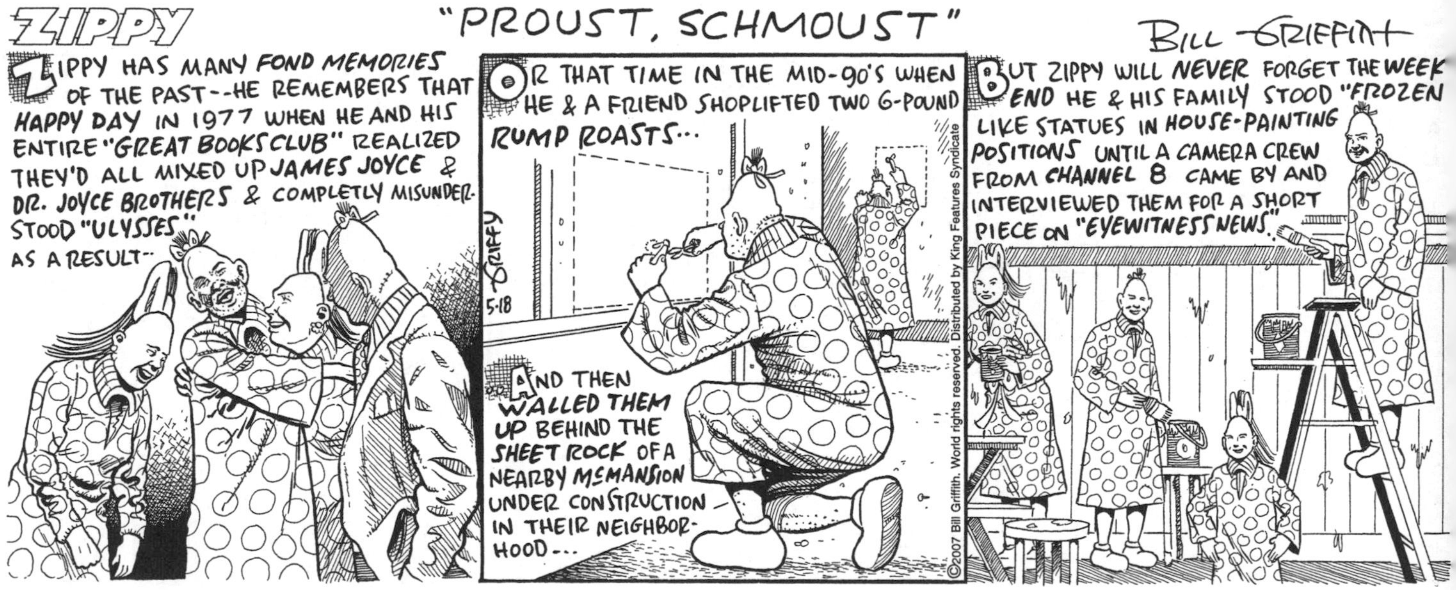
ZIPPY
"PROUST, SCHMOUST"
BILL GRIFFITH
ZIPPY HAS MANY FOND MEMORIES OF THE PAST--HE REMEMBERS THAT HAPPY DAY IN 1977 WHEN HE AND HIS ENTIRE "GREAT BOOKS CLUB" REALIZED THEY'D ALL MIXED UP JAMES JOYCE & DR. JOYCE BROTHERS & COMPLETLY MISUNDER-STOOD "ULYSSES" AS A RESULT--
OR THAT TIME IN THE MID-90'S WHEN HE & A FRIEND SHOPLIFTED TWO 6-POUND RUMP ROASTS...
GRIFFY 5-18
AND THEN WALLED THEM UP BEHIND THE SHEET ROCK OF A NEARBY McMANSION UNDER CONSTRUCTION IN THEIR NEIGHBOR-HOOD...
©2007 Bill Griffith. World rights reserved. Distributed by King Features Syndicate
BUT ZIPPY WILL NEVER FORGET THE WEEK END HE & HIS FAMILY STOOD "FROZEN" LIKE STATUES IN HOUSE-PAINTING POSITIONS UNTIL A CAMERA CREW FROM CHANNEL 8 CAME BY AND INTERVIEWED THEM FOR A SHORT PIECE ON "EYEWITNESS NEWS".

11

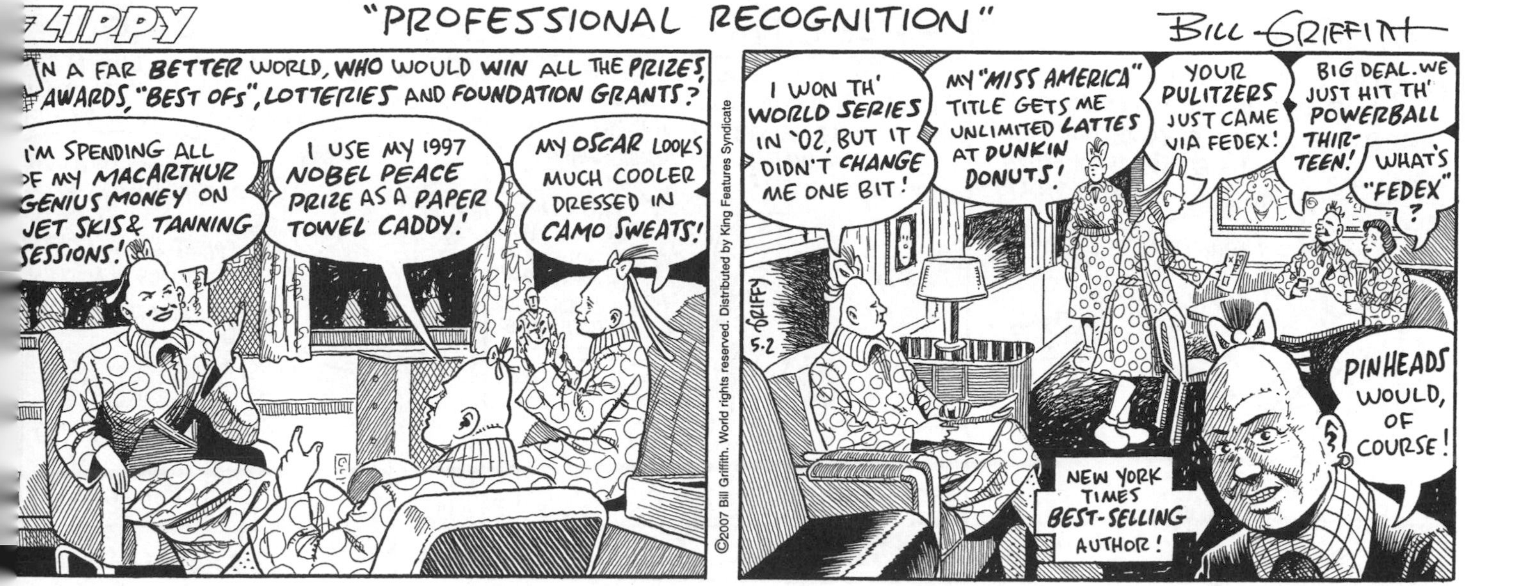
ZIPPY
"PROFESSIONAL RECOGNITION"
BILL GRIFFITH
IN A FAR BETTER WORLD, WHO WOULD WIN ALL THE PRIZES, AWARDS, "BEST OFS", LOTTERIES AND FOUNDATION GRANTS?
I'M SPENDING ALL OF MY MACARTHUR GENIUS MONEY ON JET SKIS & TANNING SESSIONS!
I USE MY 1997 NOBEL PEACE PRIZE AS A PAPER TOWEL CADDY!
MY OSCAR LOOKS MUCH COOLER DRESSED IN CAMO SWEATS!
©2007 Bill Griffith. World rights reserved. Distributed by King Features Syndicate
I WON TH' WORLD SERIES IN '02, BUT IT DIDN'T CHANGE ME ONE BIT!
MY "MISS AMERICA" TITLE GETS ME UNLIMITED LATTES AT DUNKIN DONUTS!
YOUR PULITZERS JUST CAME VIA FEDEX!
BIG DEAL. WE JUST HIT TH' POWERBALL THIRTEEN!
WHAT'S "FEDEX"?
PINHEADS WOULD, OF COURSE!
NEW YORK TIMES BEST-SELLING AUTHOR!
GRIFFY 5-2

12

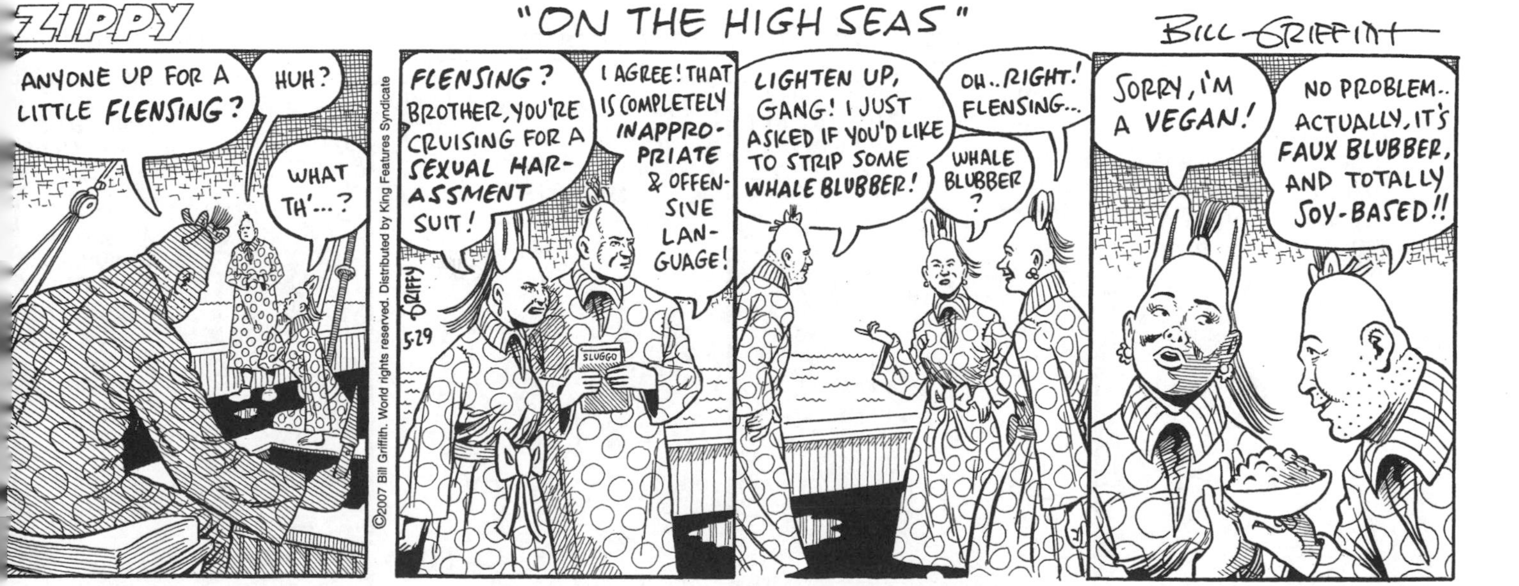
ZIPPY
"ON THE HIGH SEAS"
BILL GRIFFITH
ANYONE UP FOR A LITTLE FLENSING?
HUH?
WHAT TH'...?
©2007 Bill Griffith. World rights reserved. Distributed by King Features Syndicate
FLENSING? BROTHER, YOU'RE CRUISING FOR A SEXUAL HARASSMENT SUIT!
I AGREE! THAT IS COMPLETELY INAPPROPRIATE & OFFENSIVE LANGUAGE!
SLUGGO
GRIFFY 5-29
LIGHTEN UP, GANG! I JUST ASKED IF YOU'D LIKE TO STRIP SOME WHALE BLUBBER!
OH.. RIGHT! FLENSING...
WHALE BLUBBER?
SORRY, I'M A VEGAN!
NO PROBLEM.. ACTUALLY, IT'S FAUX BLUBBER, AND TOTALLY SOY-BASED!!

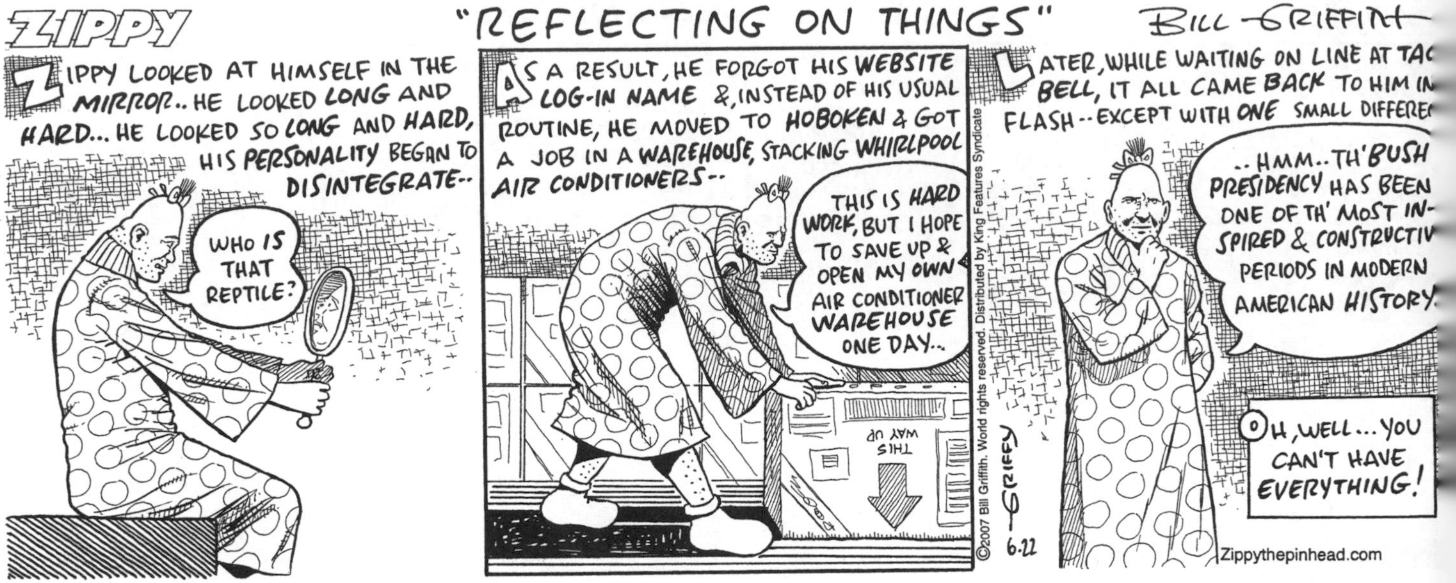
ZIPPY
"REFLECTING ON THINGS"
BILL GRIFFITH
ZIPPY LOOKED AT HIMSELF IN THE MIRROR.. HE LOOKED LONG AND HARD... HE LOOKED SO LONG AND HARD, HIS PERSONALITY BEGAN TO DISINTEGRATE--
WHO IS THAT REPTILE?
AS A RESULT, HE FORGOT HIS WEBSITE LOG-IN NAME &, INSTEAD OF HIS USUAL ROUTINE, HE MOVED TO HOBOKEN & GOT A JOB IN A WAREHOUSE, STACKING WHIRLPOOL AIR CONDITIONERS--
THIS IS HARD WORK, BUT I HOPE TO SAVE UP & OPEN MY OWN AIR CONDITIONER WAREHOUSE ONE DAY..
THIS WAY UP
LATER, WHILE WAITING ON LINE AT TAC BELL, IT ALL CAME BACK TO HIM IN FLASH -- EXCEPT WITH ONE SMALL DIFFERE
..HMM.. TH' BUSH PRESIDENCY HAS BEEN ONE OF TH' MOST IN-SPIRED & CONSTRUCTIV PERIODS IN MODERN AMERICAN HISTORY
OH, WELL... YOU CAN'T HAVE EVERYTHING!
©2007 Bill Griffith. World rights reserved. Distributed by King Features Syndicate
GRIFFY 6-22
Zippythepinhead.com

1

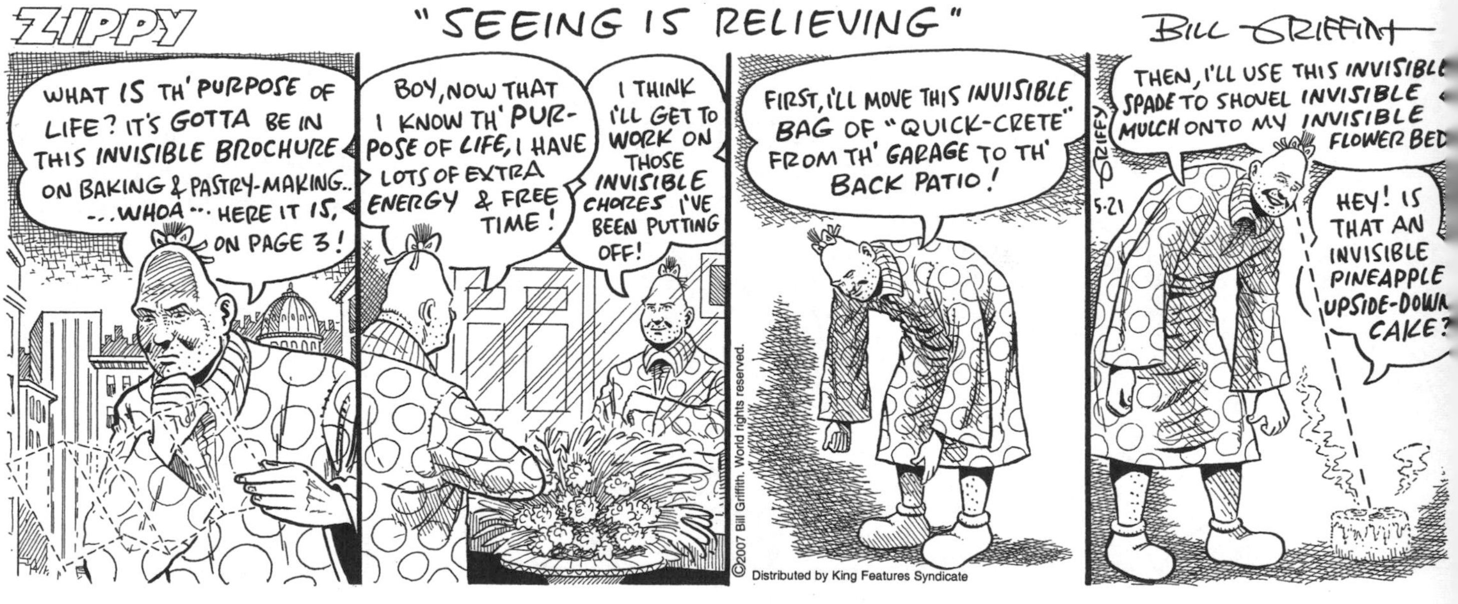
ZIPPY
"SEEING IS RELIEVING"
BILL GRIFFITH
WHAT IS TH' PURPOSE OF LIFE? IT'S GOTTA BE IN THIS INVISIBLE BROCHURE ON BAKING & PASTRY-MAKING.. --..WHOA -- HERE IT IS, ON PAGE 3!
BOY, NOW THAT I KNOW TH' PURPOSE OF LIFE, I HAVE LOTS OF EXTRA ENERGY & FREE TIME!
I THINK I'LL GET TO WORK ON THOSE INVISIBLE CHORES I'VE BEEN PUTTING OFF!
©2007 Bill Griffith. World rights reserved.
FIRST, I'LL MOVE THIS INVISIBLE BAG OF "QUICK-CRETE" FROM TH' GARAGE TO TH' BACK PATIO!
Distributed by King Features Syndicate
GRIFFY 5-21
THEN, I'LL USE THIS INVISIBLE SPADE TO SHOVEL INVISIBLE MULCH ONTO MY INVISIBLE FLOWER BED
HEY! IS THAT AN INVISIBLE PINEAPPLE UPSIDE-DOWN CAKE?

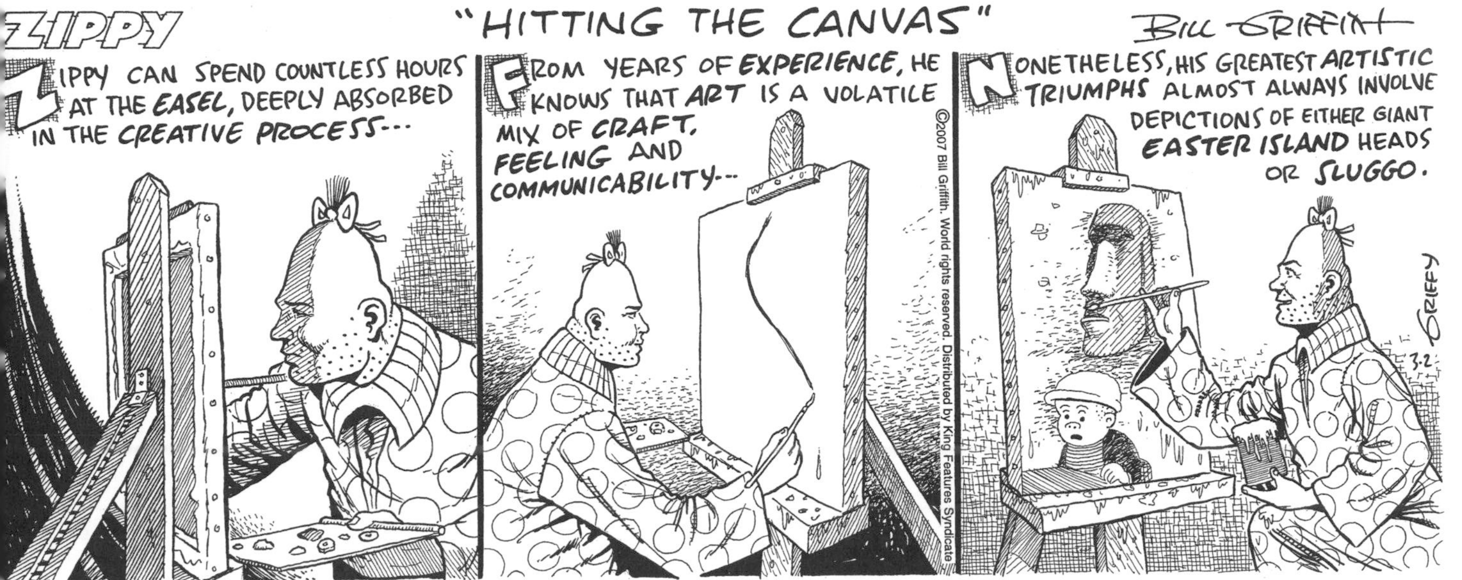
ZIPPY
"HITTING THE CANVAS"
BILL GRIFFITH
ZIPPY CAN SPEND COUNTLESS HOURS AT THE EASEL, DEEPLY ABSORBED IN THE CREATIVE PROCESS---
FROM YEARS OF EXPERIENCE, HE KNOWS THAT ART IS A VOLATILE MIX OF CRAFT, FEELING AND COMMUNICABILITY--
©2007 Bill Griffith. World rights reserved. Distributed by King Features Syndicate
NONETHELESS, HIS GREATEST ARTISTIC TRIUMPHS ALMOST ALWAYS INVOLVE DEPICTIONS OF EITHER GIANT EASTER ISLAND HEADS OR SLUGGO.
GRIFFY
3-2

14

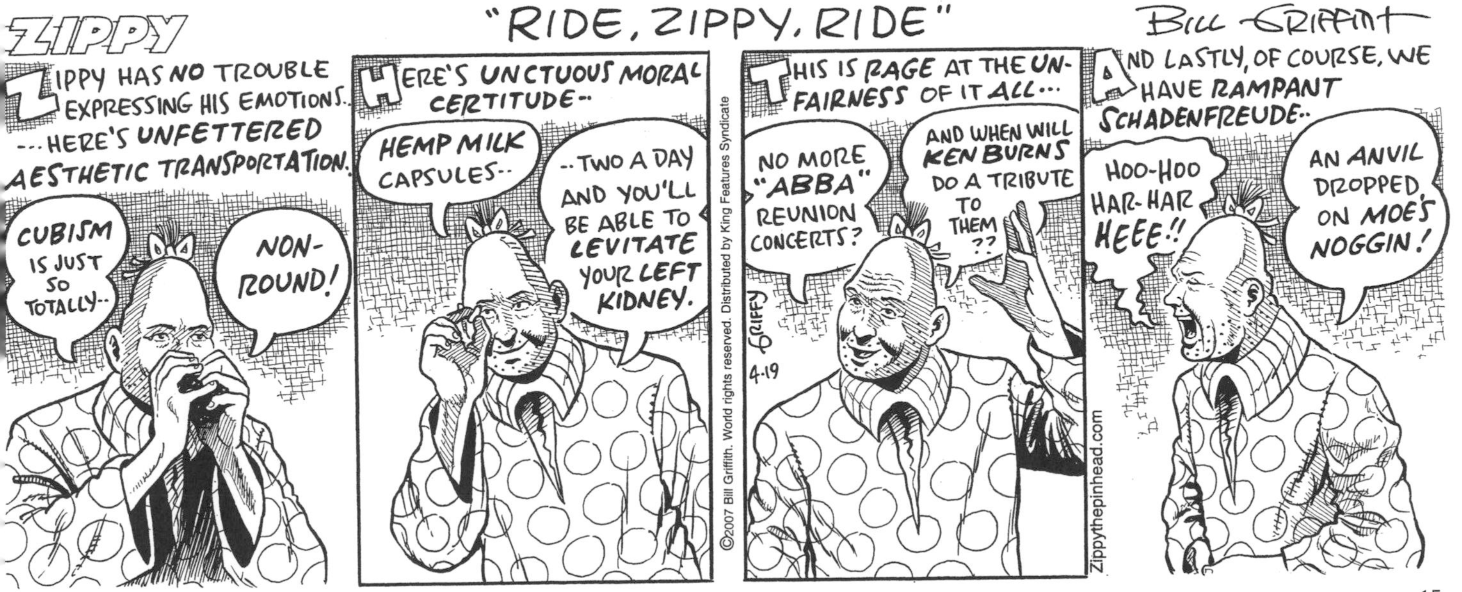
ZIPPY
"RIDE, ZIPPY, RIDE"
BILL GRIFFITH
ZIPPY HAS NO TROUBLE EXPRESSING HIS EMOTIONS.. ---HERE'S UNFETTERED AESTHETIC TRANSPORTATION.
CUBISM IS JUST SO TOTALLY--
NON-ROUND!
HERE'S UNCTUOUS MORAL CERTITUDE--
HEMP MILK CAPSULES--
--TWO A DAY AND YOU'LL BE ABLE TO LEVITATE YOUR LEFT KIDNEY.
©2007 Bill Griffith. World rights reserved. Distributed by King Features Syndicate
GRIFFY
4-19
THIS IS RAGE AT THE UNFAIRNESS OF IT ALL---
NO MORE "ABBA" REUNION CONCERTS?
AND WHEN WILL KEN BURNS DO A TRIBUTE TO THEM ??
Zippythepinhead.com
AND LASTLY, OF COURSE, WE HAVE RAMPANT SCHADENFREUDE--
HOO-HOO HAR-HAR HEEE!!
AN ANVIL DROPPED ON MOE'S NOGGIN!

15

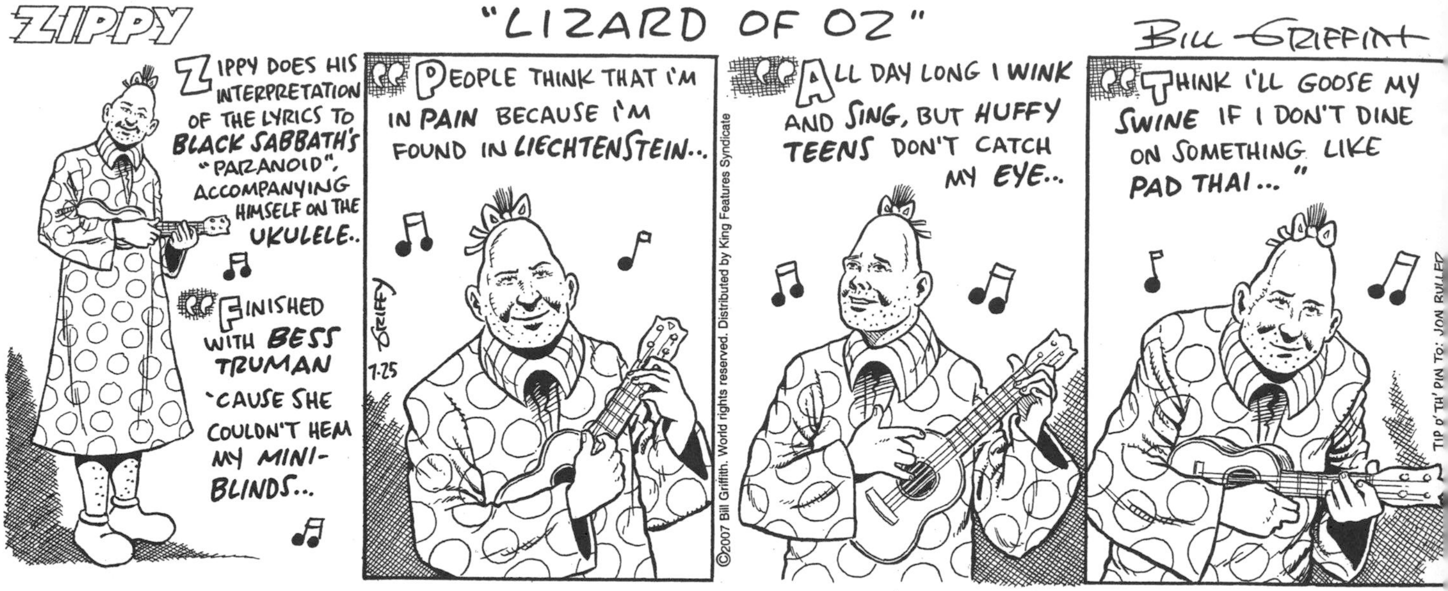
ZIPPY
"LIZARD OF OZ"
BILL GRIFFITH
ZIPPY DOES HIS INTERPRETATION OF THE LYRICS TO BLACK SABBATH'S "PARANOID", ACCOMPANYING HIMSELF ON THE UKULELE..
"FINISHED WITH BESS TRUMAN 'CAUSE SHE COULDN'T HEM MY MINI-BLINDS...
"PEOPLE THINK THAT I'M IN PAIN BECAUSE I'M FOUND IN LIECHTENSTEIN...
GRIFFY 7-25
©2007 Bill Griffith. World rights reserved. Distributed by King Features Syndicate
"ALL DAY LONG I WINK AND SING, BUT HUFFY TEENS DON'T CATCH MY EYE...
"THINK I'LL GOOSE MY SWINE IF I DON'T DINE ON SOMETHING LIKE PAD THAI..."
TIP O' TH' PIN TO: JON RULLER

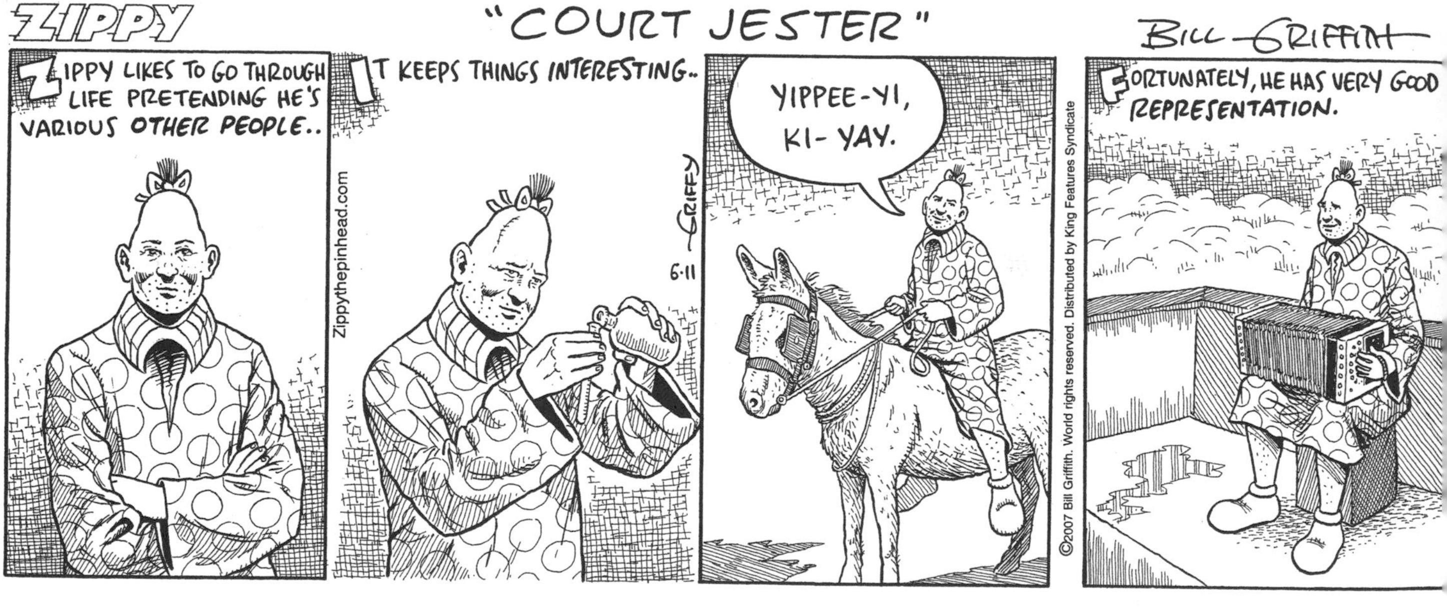
ZIPPY
"COURT JESTER"
BILL GRIFFITH
ZIPPY LIKES TO GO THROUGH LIFE PRETENDING HE'S VARIOUS OTHER PEOPLE..
Zippythepinhead.com
IT KEEPS THINGS INTERESTING..
GRIFFY 6-11
YIPPEE-YI, KI-YAY.
©2007 Bill Griffith. World rights reserved. Distributed by King Features Syndicate
FORTUNATELY, HE HAS VERY GOOD REPRESENTATION.

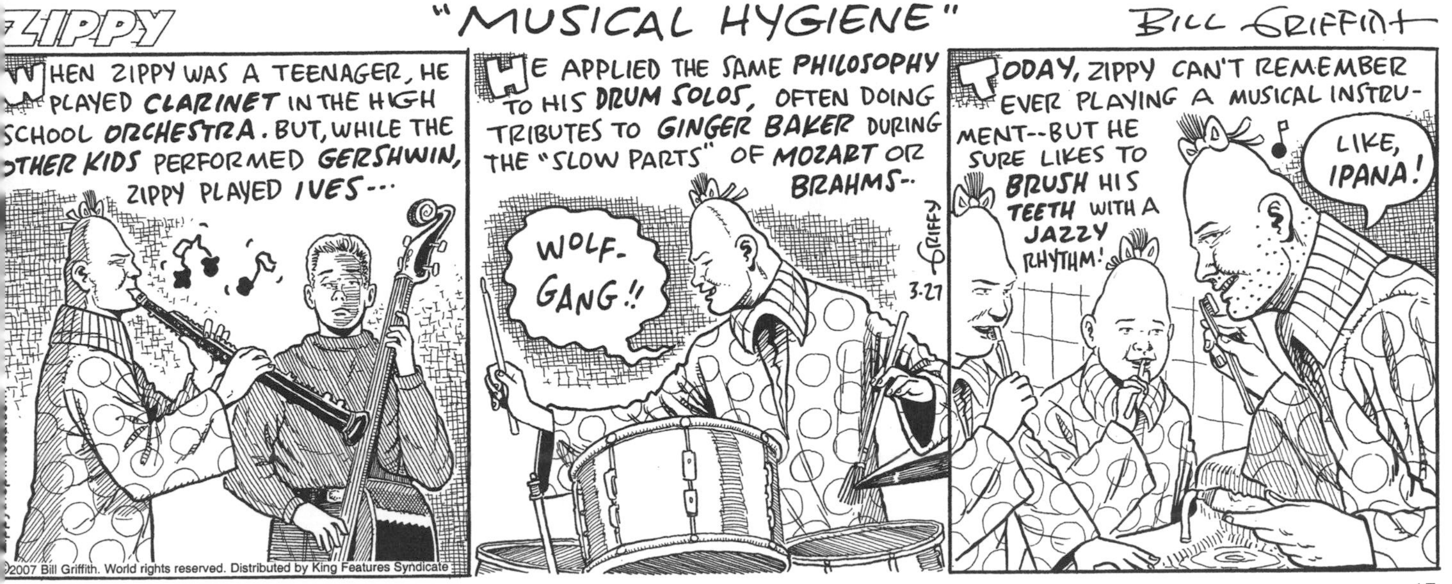
ZIPPY
"MUSICAL HYGIENE"
BILL GRIFFITH
WHEN ZIPPY WAS A TEENAGER, HE PLAYED CLARINET IN THE HIGH SCHOOL ORCHESTRA. BUT, WHILE THE OTHER KIDS PERFORMED GERSHWIN, ZIPPY PLAYED IVES---
HE APPLIED THE SAME PHILOSOPHY TO HIS DRUM SOLOS, OFTEN DOING TRIBUTES TO GINGER BAKER DURING THE "SLOW PARTS" OF MOZART OR BRAHMS--
WOLF-GANG!!
GRIFFY
3-27
TODAY, ZIPPY CAN'T REMEMBER EVER PLAYING A MUSICAL INSTRU-MENT--BUT HE SURE LIKES TO BRUSH HIS TEETH WITH A JAZZY RHYTHM!
LIKE, IPANA!
©2007 Bill Griffith. World rights reserved. Distributed by King Features Syndicate

17

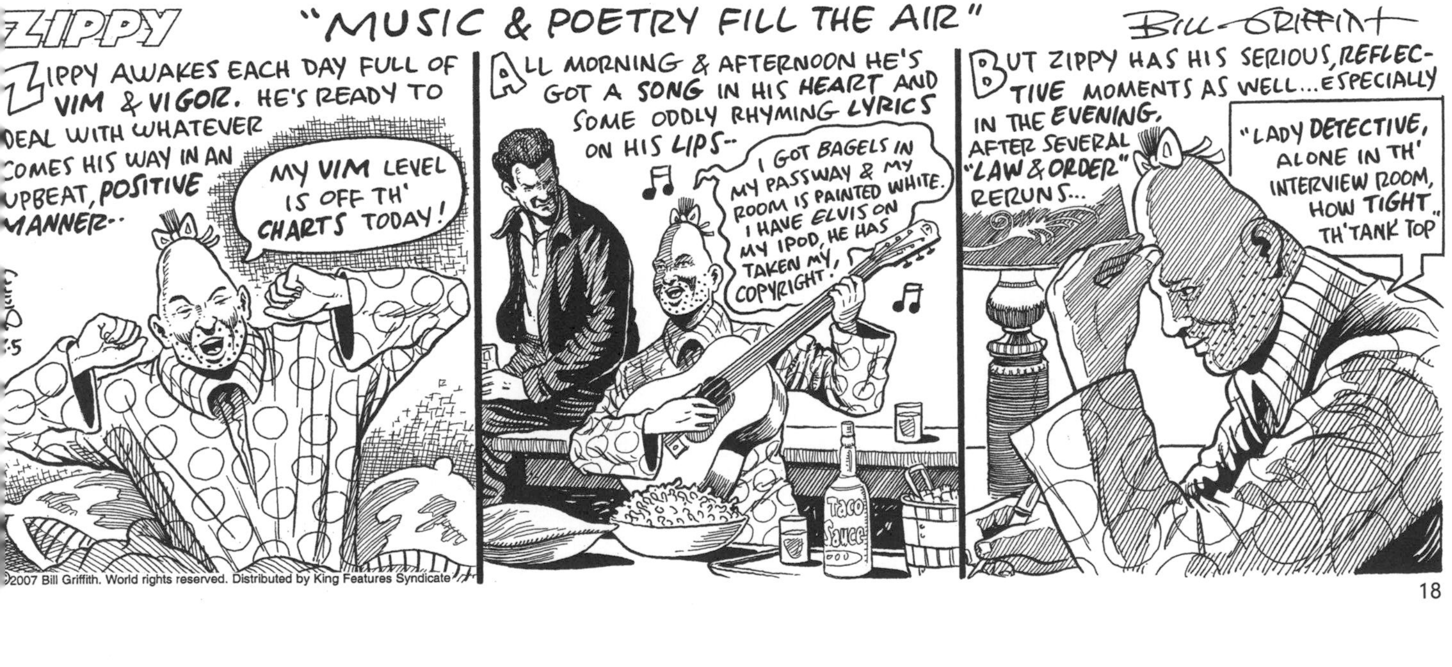
ZIPPY
"MUSIC & POETRY FILL THE AIR"
BILL GRIFFITH
ZIPPY AWAKES EACH DAY FULL OF VIM & VIGOR. HE'S READY TO DEAL WITH WHATEVER COMES HIS WAY IN AN UPBEAT, POSITIVE MANNER--
MY VIM LEVEL IS OFF TH' CHARTS TODAY!
ALL MORNING & AFTERNOON HE'S GOT A SONG IN HIS HEART AND SOME ODDLY RHYMING LYRICS ON HIS LIPS--
I GOT BAGELS IN MY PASSWAY & MY ROOM IS PAINTED WHITE. I HAVE ELVIS ON MY IPOD, HE HAS TAKEN MY COPYRIGHT!
Taco Sauce
BUT ZIPPY HAS HIS SERIOUS, REFLEC-TIVE MOMENTS AS WELL...ESPECIALLY IN THE EVENING, AFTER SEVERAL "LAW & ORDER" RERUNS...
"LADY DETECTIVE, ALONE IN TH' INTERVIEW ROOM, HOW TIGHT TH' TANK TOP"
©2007 Bill Griffith. World rights reserved. Distributed by King Features Syndicate

18

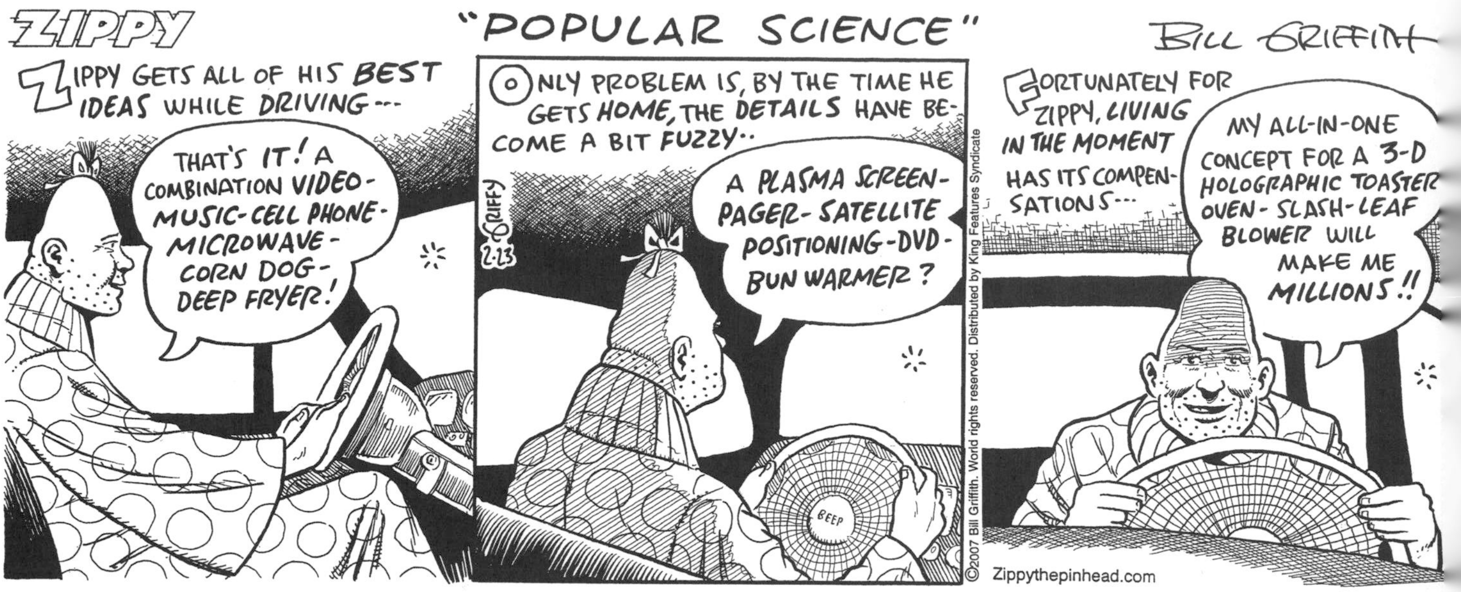
ZIPPY
"POPULAR SCIENCE"
BILL GRIFFITH
ZIPPY GETS ALL OF HIS BEST IDEAS WHILE DRIVING---
THAT'S IT! A COMBINATION VIDEO-MUSIC-CELL PHONE-MICROWAVE-CORN DOG-DEEP FRYER!
ONLY PROBLEM IS, BY THE TIME HE GETS HOME, THE DETAILS HAVE BECOME A BIT FUZZY..
A PLASMA SCREEN-PAGER-SATELLITE POSITIONING-DVD-BUN WARMER?
BEEP
GRIFFY 2-23
FORTUNATELY FOR ZIPPY, LIVING IN THE MOMENT HAS ITS COMPENSATIONS---
MY ALL-IN-ONE CONCEPT FOR A 3-D HOLOGRAPHIC TOASTER OVEN-SLASH-LEAF BLOWER WILL MAKE ME MILLIONS!!
©2007 Bill Griffith. World rights reserved. Distributed by King Features Syndicate
Zippythepinhead.com

19

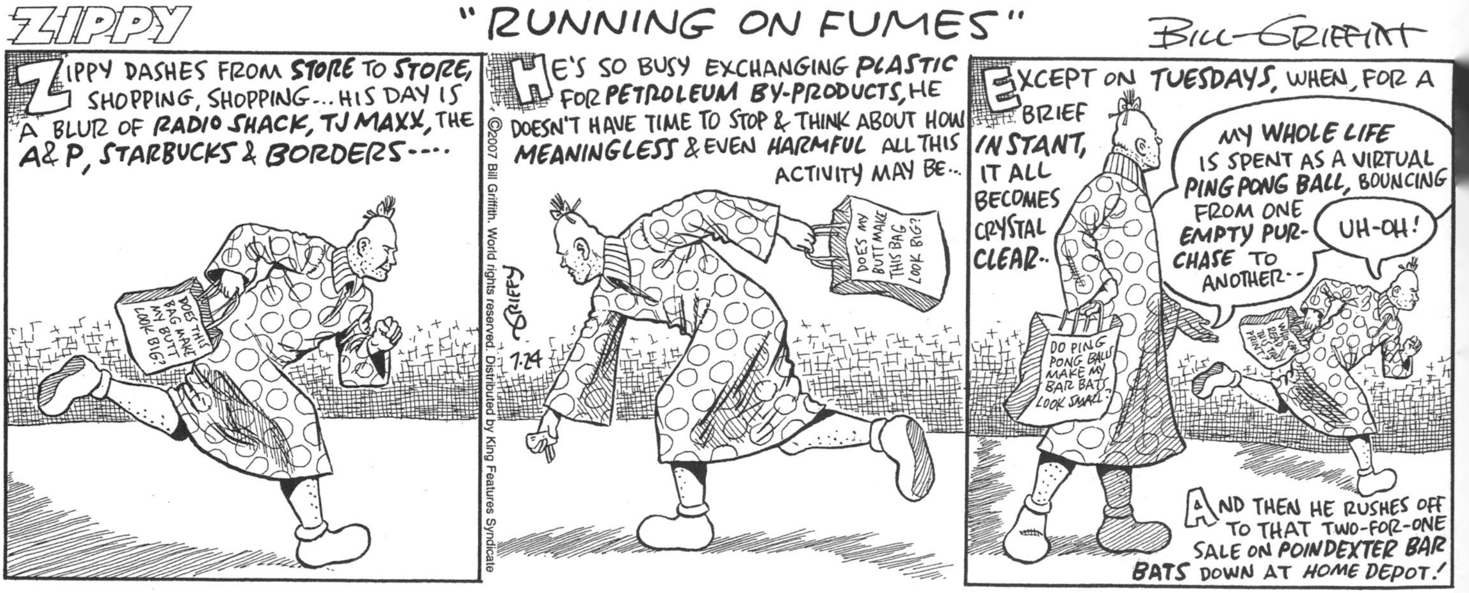
ZIPPY
"RUNNING ON FUMES"
BILL GRIFFITH
ZIPPY DASHES FROM STORE TO STORE, SHOPPING, SHOPPING... HIS DAY IS A BLUR OF RADIO SHACK, TJ MAXX, THE A&P, STARBUCKS & BORDERS----.
DOES THIS BAG MAKE MY BUTT LOOK BIG?
©2007 Bill Griffith. World rights reserved. Distributed by King Features Syndicate
HE'S SO BUSY EXCHANGING PLASTIC FOR PETROLEUM BY-PRODUCTS, HE DOESN'T HAVE TIME TO STOP & THINK ABOUT HOW MEANINGLESS & EVEN HARMFUL ALL THIS ACTIVITY MAY BE..
DOES MY BUTT MAKE THIS BAG LOOK BIG?
GRIFFY 7-24
EXCEPT ON TUESDAYS, WHEN, FOR A BRIEF INSTANT, IT ALL BECOMES CRYSTAL CLEAR..
MY WHOLE LIFE IS SPENT AS A VIRTUAL PING PONG BALL, BOUNCING FROM ONE EMPTY PURCHASE TO ANOTHER--
UH-OH!
DO PING PONG BALLS MAKE MY BAR BAT LOOK SMALL?
AND THEN HE RUSHES OFF TO THAT TWO-FOR-ONE SALE ON POINDEXTER BAR BATS DOWN AT HOME DEPOT!

20

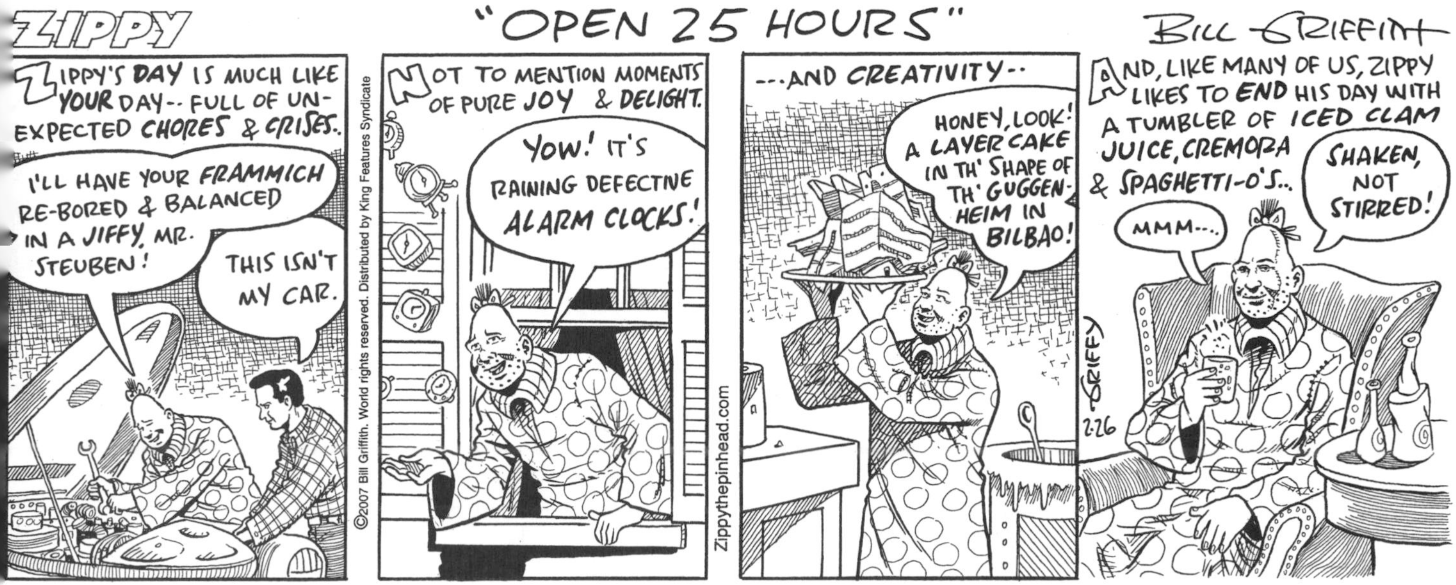
ZIPPY
"OPEN 25 HOURS"
BILL GRIFFITH
ZIPPY'S DAY IS MUCH LIKE YOUR DAY-- FULL OF UNEXPECTED CHORES & CRISES..
I'LL HAVE YOUR FRAMMICH RE-BORED & BALANCED IN A JIFFY, MR. STEUBEN!
THIS ISN'T MY CAR.
©2007 Bill Griffith. World rights reserved. Distributed by King Features Syndicate
NOT TO MENTION MOMENTS OF PURE JOY & DELIGHT.
YOW! IT'S RAINING DEFECTIVE ALARM CLOCKS!
Zippythepinhead.com
---AND CREATIVITY--
HONEY, LOOK! A LAYER CAKE IN TH' SHAPE OF TH' GUGGENHEIM IN BILBAO!
GRIFFY 2-26
AND, LIKE MANY OF US, ZIPPY LIKES TO END HIS DAY WITH A TUMBLER OF ICED CLAM JUICE, CREMORA & SPAGHETTI-O'S...
MMM--..
SHAKEN, NOT STIRRED!

21

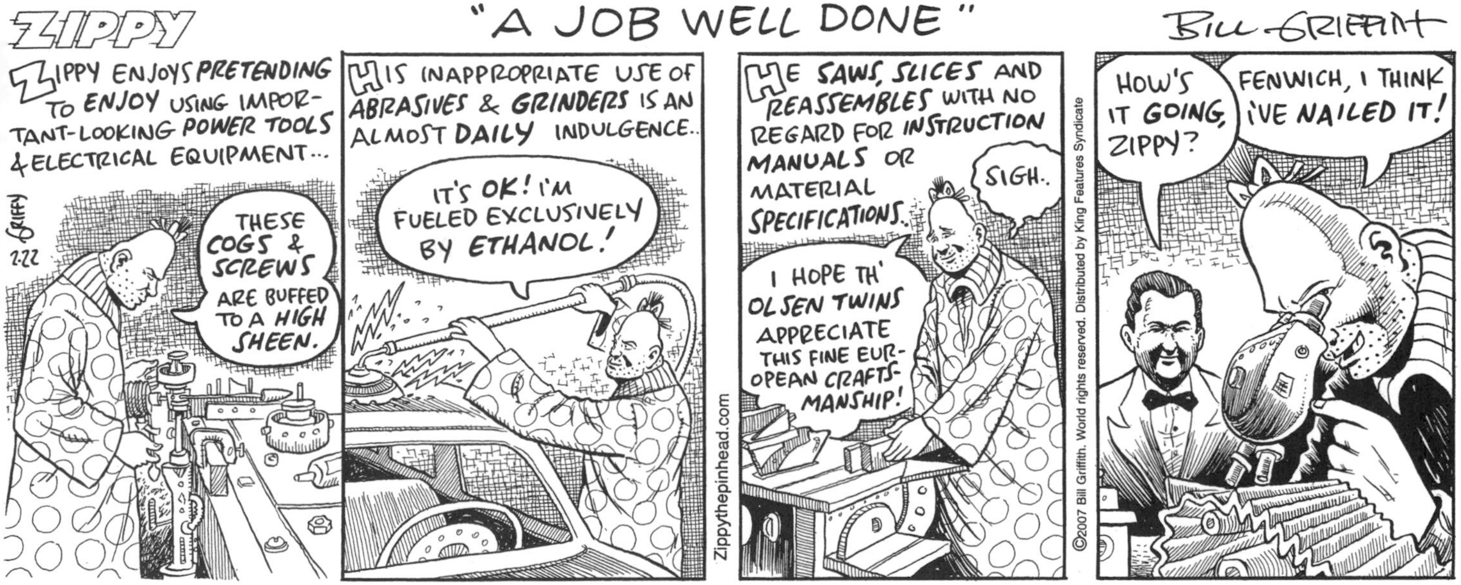
ZIPPY
"A JOB WELL DONE"
BILL GRIFFITH
ZIPPY ENJOYS PRETENDING TO ENJOY USING IMPORTANT-LOOKING POWER TOOLS & ELECTRICAL EQUIPMENT...
GRIFFY 2-22
THESE COGS & SCREWS ARE BUFFED TO A HIGH SHEEN.
HIS INAPPROPRIATE USE OF ABRASIVES & GRINDERS IS AN ALMOST DAILY INDULGENCE..
IT'S OK! I'M FUELED EXCLUSIVELY BY ETHANOL!
Zippythepinhead.com
HE SAWS, SLICES AND REASSEMBLES WITH NO REGARD FOR INSTRUCTION MANUALS OR MATERIAL SPECIFICATIONS..
SIGH..
I HOPE TH' OLSEN TWINS APPRECIATE THIS FINE EUROPEAN CRAFTSMANSHIP!
©2007 Bill Griffith. World rights reserved. Distributed by King Features Syndicate
HOW'S IT GOING, ZIPPY?
FENWICH, I THINK I'VE NAILED IT!

22

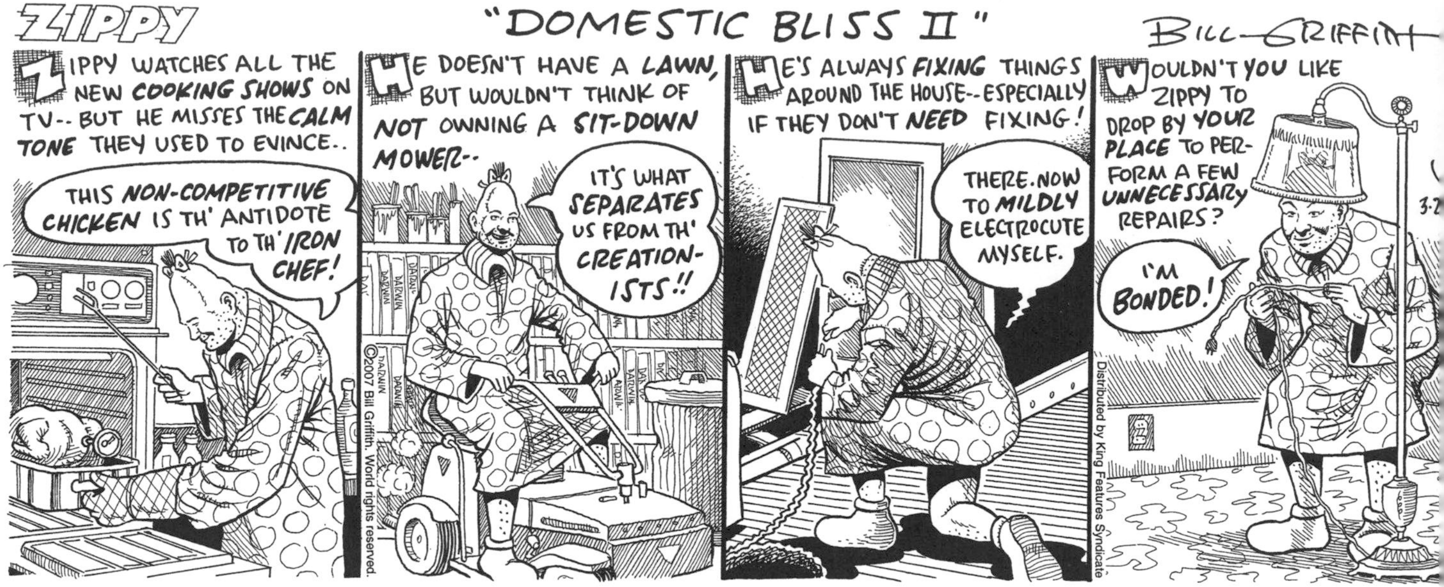
ZIPPY
"DOMESTIC BLISS II"
BILL GRIFFITH
ZIPPY WATCHES ALL THE NEW COOKING SHOWS ON TV-- BUT HE MISSES THE CALM TONE THEY USED TO EVINCE..
THIS NON-COMPETITIVE CHICKEN IS TH' ANTIDOTE TO TH' IRON CHEF!
HE DOESN'T HAVE A LAWN, BUT WOULDN'T THINK OF NOT OWNING A SIT-DOWN MOWER--
IT'S WHAT SEPARATES US FROM TH' CREATIONISTS!!
©2007 Bill Griffith. World rights reserved.
HE'S ALWAYS FIXING THINGS AROUND THE HOUSE--ESPECIALLY IF THEY DON'T NEED FIXING!
THERE. NOW TO MILDLY ELECTROCUTE MYSELF.
Distributed by King Features Syndicate
WOULDN'T YOU LIKE ZIPPY TO DROP BY YOUR PLACE TO PERFORM A FEW UNNECESSARY REPAIRS?
I'M BONDED!

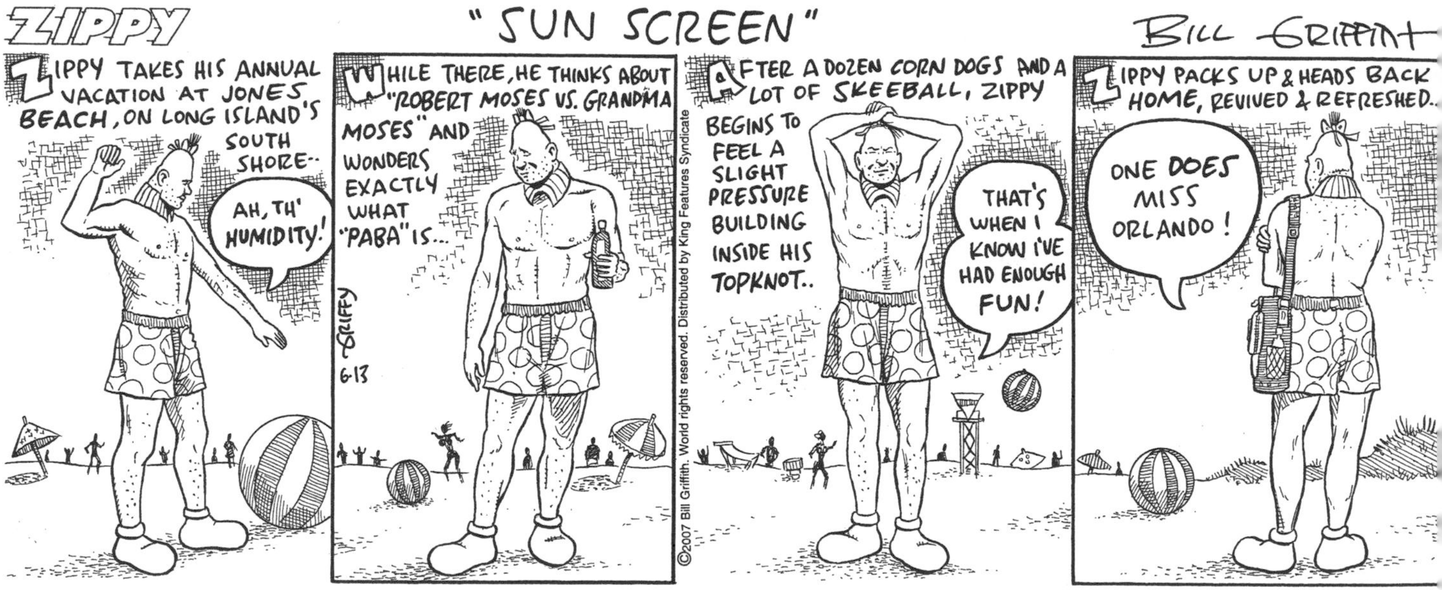
ZIPPY
"SUN SCREEN"
BILL GRIFFITH
ZIPPY TAKES HIS ANNUAL VACATION AT JONES BEACH, ON LONG ISLAND'S SOUTH SHORE--
AH, TH' HUMIDITY!
WHILE THERE, HE THINKS ABOUT "ROBERT MOSES VS. GRANDMA MOSES" AND WONDERS EXACTLY WHAT "PABA" IS...
GRIFFY 6-13
©2007 Bill Griffith. World rights reserved. Distributed by King Features Syndicate
AFTER A DOZEN CORN DOGS AND A LOT OF SKEEBALL, ZIPPY BEGINS TO FEEL A SLIGHT PRESSURE BUILDING INSIDE HIS TOPKNOT..
THAT'S WHEN I KNOW I'VE HAD ENOUGH FUN!
ZIPPY PACKS UP & HEADS BACK HOME, REVIVED & REFRESHED..
ONE DOES MISS ORLANDO!

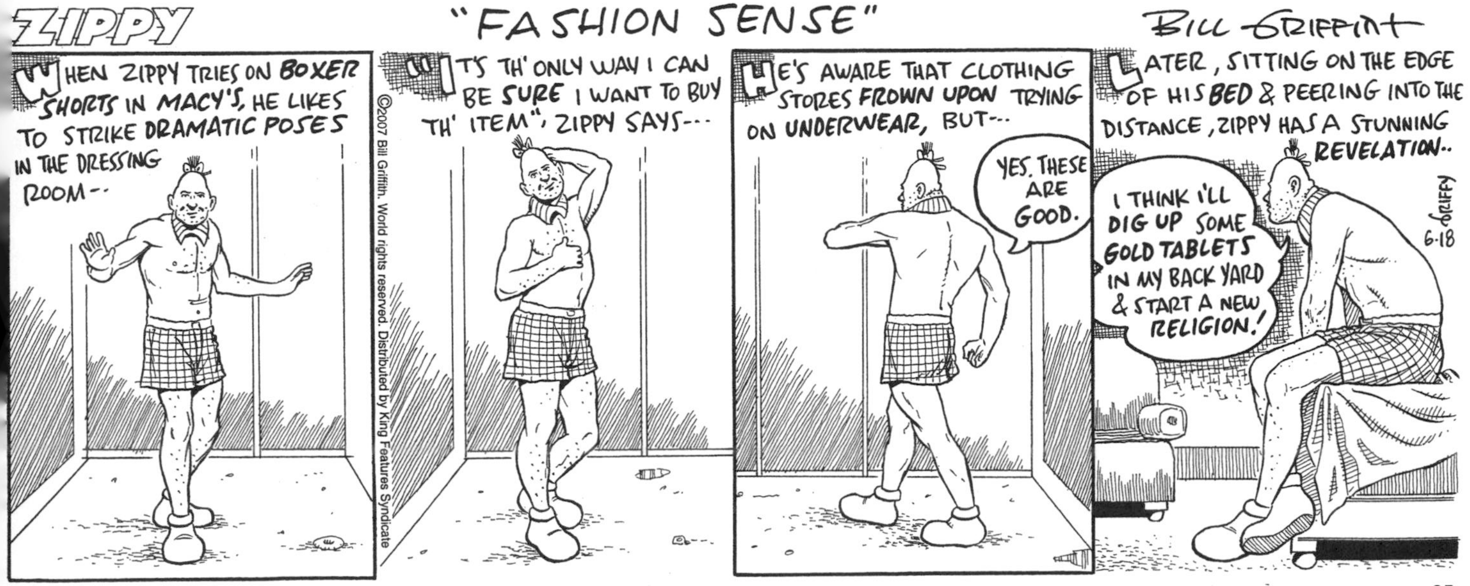
ZIPPY
"FASHION SENSE"
BILL GRIFFITH
WHEN ZIPPY TRIES ON BOXER SHORTS IN MACY'S, HE LIKES TO STRIKE DRAMATIC POSES IN THE DRESSING ROOM--
©2007 Bill Griffith. World rights reserved. Distributed by King Features Syndicate
"IT'S TH' ONLY WAY I CAN BE SURE I WANT TO BUY TH' ITEM", ZIPPY SAYS---
HE'S AWARE THAT CLOTHING STORES FROWN UPON TRYING ON UNDERWEAR, BUT--
YES, THESE ARE GOOD.
LATER, SITTING ON THE EDGE OF HIS BED & PEERING INTO THE DISTANCE, ZIPPY HAS A STUNNING REVELATION..
I THINK I'LL DIG UP SOME GOLD TABLETS IN MY BACK YARD & START A NEW RELIGION!
GRIFFY
6-18

25

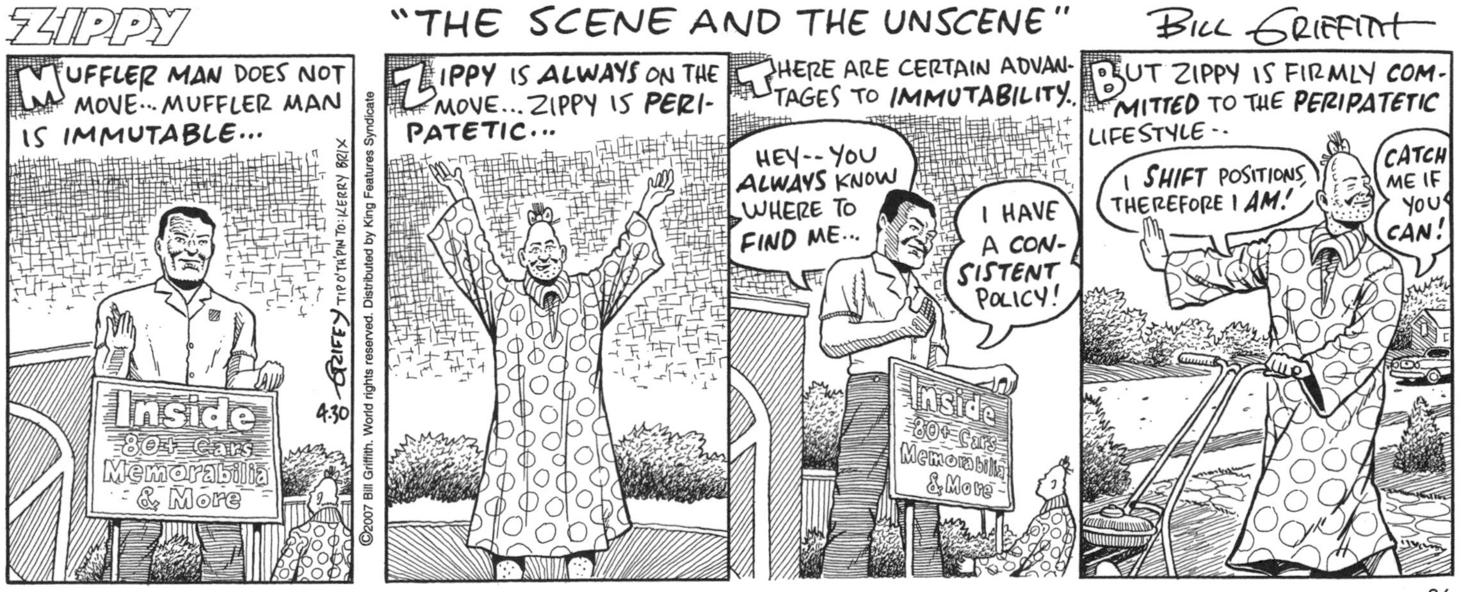
ZIPPY
"THE SCENE AND THE UNSCENE"
BILL GRIFFITH
MUFFLER MAN DOES NOT MOVE... MUFFLER MAN IS IMMUTABLE...
GRIFFY
TIP O'TH'PIN TO: KERRY BRIX
4-30
Inside
80+ Cars
Memorabilia
& More
©2007 Bill Griffith. World rights reserved. Distributed by King Features Syndicate
ZIPPY IS ALWAYS ON THE MOVE... ZIPPY IS PERIPATETIC...
THERE ARE CERTAIN ADVANTAGES TO IMMUTABILITY..
HEY--YOU ALWAYS KNOW WHERE TO FIND ME...
I HAVE A CONSISTENT POLICY!
Inside
80+ Cars
Memorabilia
& More
BUT ZIPPY IS FIRMLY COMMITTED TO THE PERIPATETIC LIFESTYLE--
I SHIFT POSITIONS, THEREFORE I AM!
CATCH ME IF YOU CAN!

26

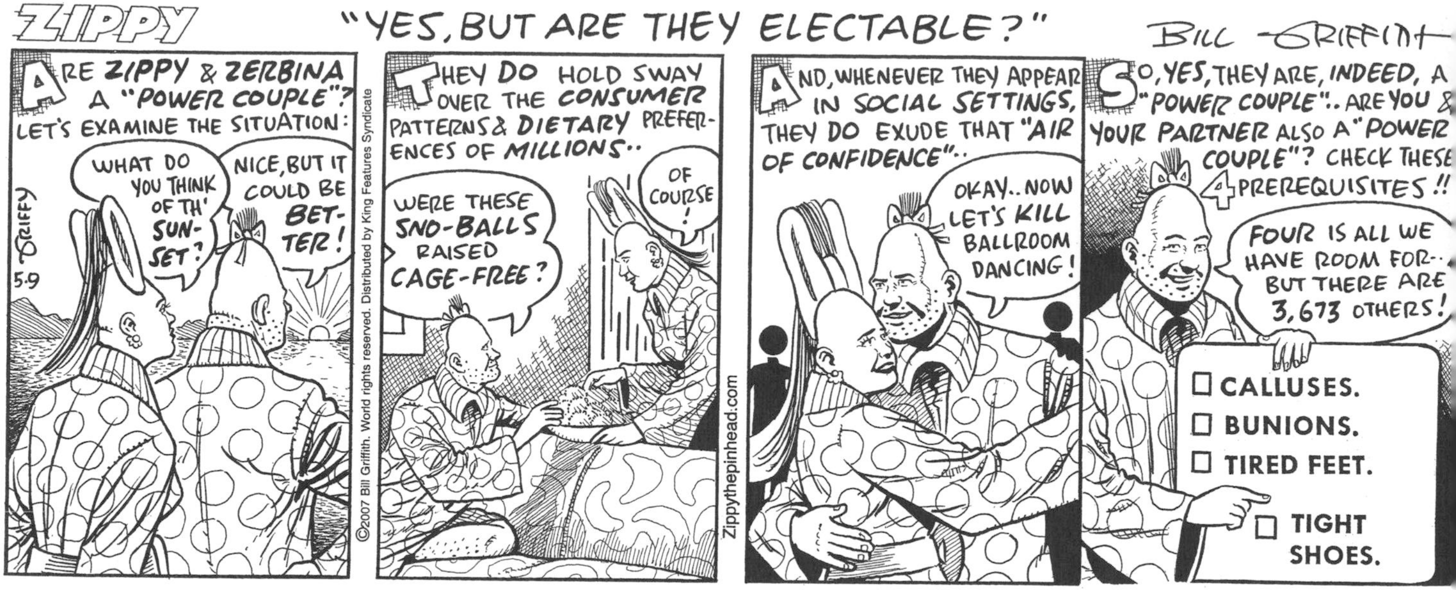
ZIPPY
"YES, BUT ARE THEY ELECTABLE?"
BILL GRIFFITH
ARE ZIPPY & ZERBINA A "POWER COUPLE"? LET'S EXAMINE THE SITUATION:
WHAT DO YOU THINK OF TH' SUNSET?
NICE, BUT IT COULD BE BETTER!
GRIFFY 5-9
©2007 Bill Griffith. World rights reserved. Distributed by King Features Syndicate
THEY DO HOLD SWAY OVER THE CONSUMER PATTERNS & DIETARY PREFERENCES OF MILLIONS..
WERE THESE SNO-BALLS RAISED CAGE-FREE?
OF COURSE!
Zippythepinhead.com
AND, WHENEVER THEY APPEAR IN SOCIAL SETTINGS, THEY DO EXUDE THAT "AIR OF CONFIDENCE"..
OKAY.. NOW LET'S KILL BALLROOM DANCING!
SO, YES, THEY ARE, INDEED, A "POWER COUPLE".. ARE YOU & YOUR PARTNER ALSO A "POWER COUPLE"? CHECK THESE 4 PREREQUISITES!!
FOUR IS ALL WE HAVE ROOM FOR.. BUT THERE ARE 3,673 OTHERS!
CALLUSES.
BUNIONS.
TIRED FEET.
TIGHT SHOES.

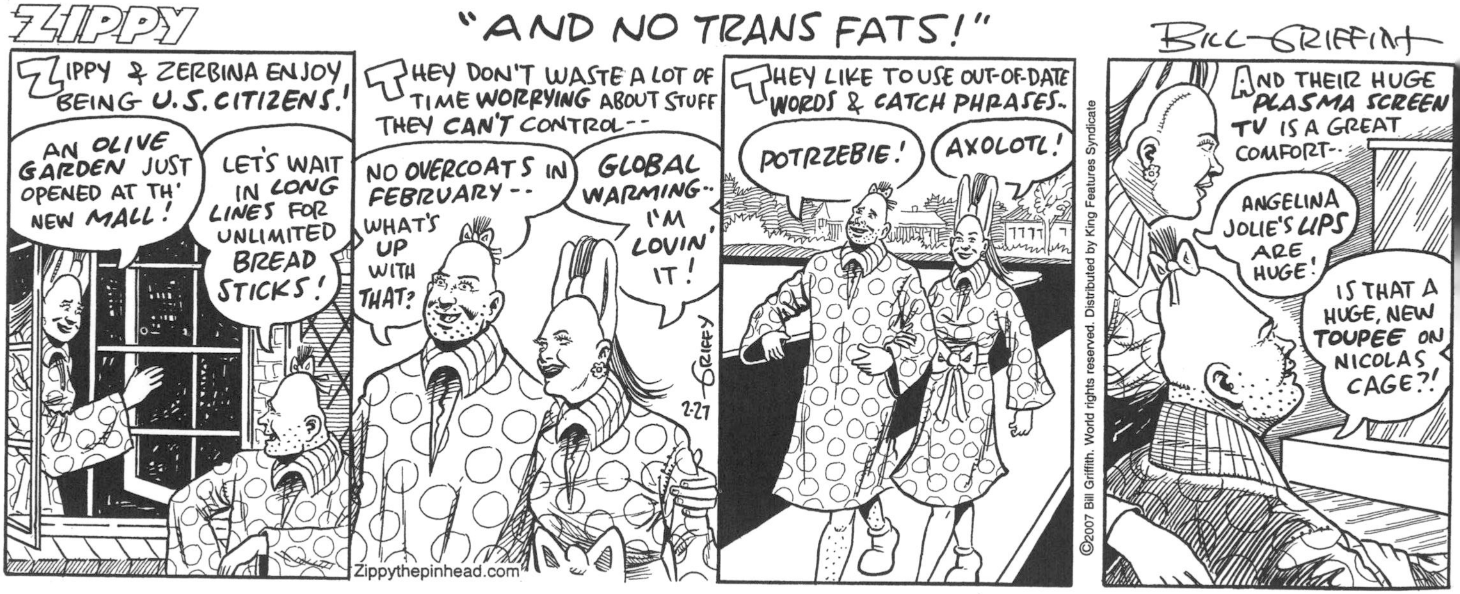
ZIPPY
"AND NO TRANS FATS!"
BILL GRIFFITH
ZIPPY & ZERBINA ENJOY BEING U.S. CITIZENS!
AN OLIVE GARDEN JUST OPENED AT TH' NEW MALL!
LET'S WAIT IN LONG LINES FOR UNLIMITED BREAD STICKS!
Zippythepinhead.com
THEY DON'T WASTE A LOT OF TIME WORRYING ABOUT STUFF THEY CAN'T CONTROL--
NO OVERCOATS IN FEBRUARY-- WHAT'S UP WITH THAT?
GLOBAL WARMING.. I'M LOVIN' IT!
GRIFFY 2-27
THEY LIKE TO USE OUT-OF-DATE WORDS & CATCH PHRASES..
POTRZEBIE!
AXOLOTL!
©2007 Bill Griffith. World rights reserved. Distributed by King Features Syndicate
AND THEIR HUGE PLASMA SCREEN TV IS A GREAT COMFORT--
ANGELINA JOLIE'S LIPS ARE HUGE!
IS THAT A HUGE, NEW TOUPEE ON NICOLAS CAGE?!

27

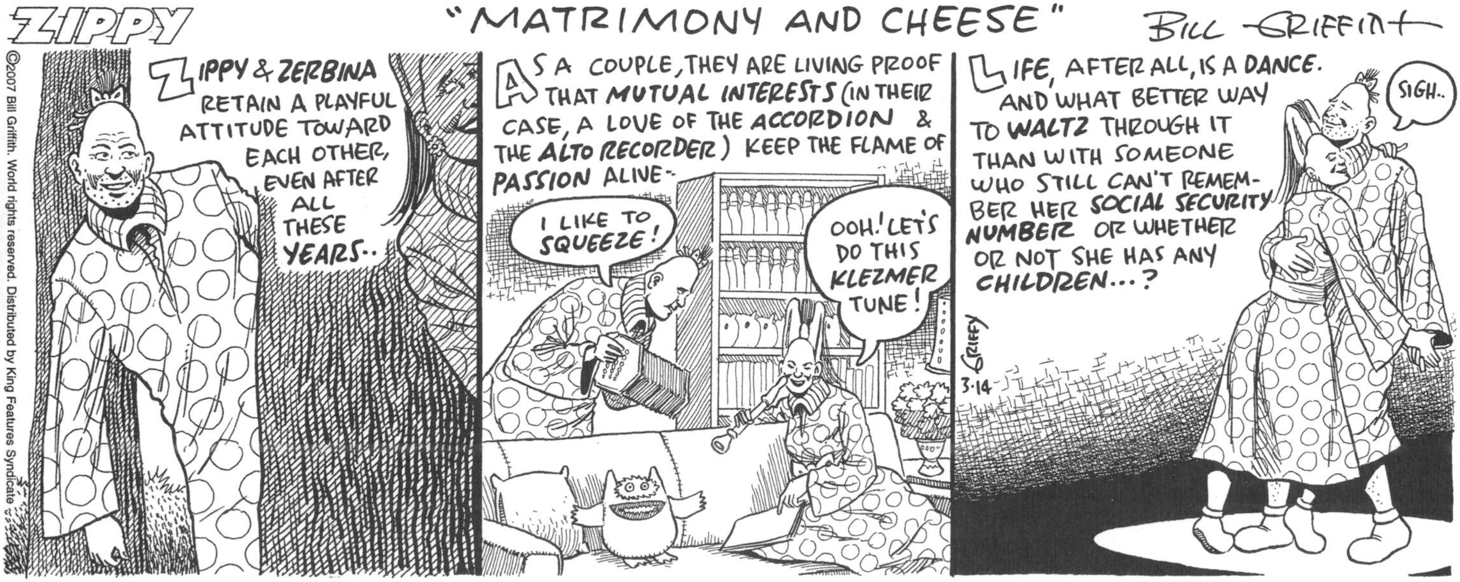
ZIPPY
"MATRIMONY AND CHEESE"
BILL GRIFFITH
©2007 Bill Griffith. World rights reserved. Distributed by King Features Syndicate
ZIPPY & ZERBINA RETAIN A PLAYFUL ATTITUDE TOWARD EACH OTHER, EVEN AFTER ALL THESE YEARS..
AS A COUPLE, THEY ARE LIVING PROOF THAT MUTUAL INTERESTS (IN THEIR CASE, A LOVE OF THE ACCORDION & THE ALTO RECORDER) KEEP THE FLAME OF PASSION ALIVE--
I LIKE TO SQUEEZE!
OOH! LET'S DO THIS KLEZMER TUNE!
LIFE, AFTER ALL, IS A DANCE. AND WHAT BETTER WAY TO WALTZ THROUGH IT THAN WITH SOMEONE WHO STILL CAN'T REMEMBER HER SOCIAL SECURITY NUMBER OR WHETHER OR NOT SHE HAS ANY CHILDREN...?
SIGH..
GRIFFY
3-14

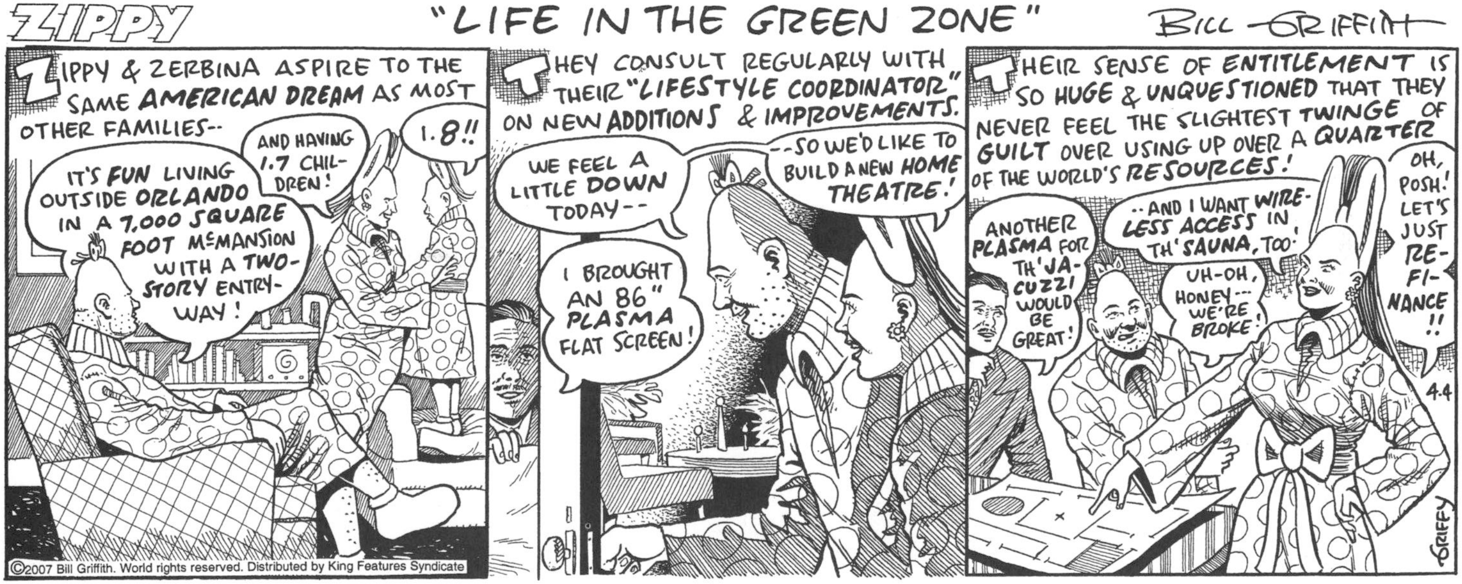
ZIPPY
"LIFE IN THE GREEN ZONE"
BILL GRIFFITH
ZIPPY & ZERBINA ASPIRE TO THE SAME AMERICAN DREAM AS MOST OTHER FAMILIES--
IT'S FUN LIVING OUTSIDE ORLANDO IN A 7,000 SQUARE FOOT McMANSION WITH A TWO-STORY ENTRYWAY!
AND HAVING 1.7 CHILDREN!
1.8!!
THEY CONSULT REGULARLY WITH THEIR "LIFESTYLE COORDINATOR" ON NEW ADDITIONS & IMPROVEMENTS.
WE FEEL A LITTLE DOWN TODAY--
--SO WE'D LIKE TO BUILD A NEW HOME THEATRE!
I BROUGHT AN 86" PLASMA FLAT SCREEN!
THEIR SENSE OF ENTITLEMENT IS SO HUGE & UNQUESTIONED THAT THEY NEVER FEEL THE SLIGHTEST TWINGE OF GUILT OVER USING UP OVER A QUARTER OF THE WORLD'S RESOURCES!
ANOTHER PLASMA FOR TH' JACUZZI WOULD BE GREAT!
..AND I WANT WIRELESS ACCESS IN TH' SAUNA, TOO!
UH-OH, HONEY--- WE'RE BROKE!
OH, POSH! LET'S JUST REFINANCE!!
4-4
GRIFFY
©2007 Bill Griffith. World rights reserved. Distributed by King Features Syndicate

ZIPPY
"THE COMICAL COUPLE"
BILL GRIFFITH
ZIPPY and ZERBINA ARE VERY MUCH IN LOVE... BUT IT'S NOT AN ORDINARY LOVE--
MAY I OFFER YOU A SMALL, PLASTIC SUBMARINE?
AS LONG AS IT'S NOT ALREADY IN MY SMALL PLASTIC SUBMARINE COLLECTION!
SMALL PLASTIC SUBMARINES
S.P.S.
THEY LIKE TO TAKE LONG, LEISURELY DRIVES INTO THE COUNTRY AND LISTEN TO "MR. NEOLITE" TELL THEM STORIES ABOUT THE SIXTIES--
HE WAS AT ALTAMONT!
HE KNEW NIXON!
ONE DAY, ZERBINA BOUGHT AN UNOPENED 24-PACK OF CLARK BARS FROM THE EARLY SEVENTIES. WHEN SHE TOLD ZIPPY, THEY LAUGHED & LAUGHED--
I GOT THEM ON EBAY!
TH' WORLD WIDE WEB SAVED OUR MARRIAGE-- --AGAIN!
CLARK
GRIFFY
3·13
©2007 Bill Griffith. World rights reserved. Distributed by King Features Syndicate

28

ZIPPY
"TWEAKING THE SCRIPT"
BILL GRIFFITH
HONEY, YOU DON'T SEEM AS INTERESTED IN DINER FOOD AS MUCH AS YOU USED TO.. IS IT MY COFFEE? OR A COURT-ORDERED ANTI-STALKING MANDATE?
UH-OH, ARE WE SUDDENLY CHARACTERS IN A RAUNCHY CABLE TV REALITY SHOW?
...BECAUSE I'M CONSIDERING HIRING A TEAM OF SITCOM WRITERS TO GIVE OUR LIVES MORE OF A DRAMATIC ARC... I THINK WE MIGHT BE MISSING AN ARC... OR, PERHAPS, A PAIR OF JET SKIS...
I'VE BEEN THINKING A LOT ABOUT REALITY, TOO, ZIPPY--.
©2007 Bill Griffith. World rights reserved. Distributed by King Features Syndicate.
GRIFFY
6·6
--AND I'VE DECIDED THAT RIGHT NOW WOULD BE TH' TIME FOR A COUPLE OF VERY FUNNY COMMERCIALS!
LUNESTA, OR GEICO?

29

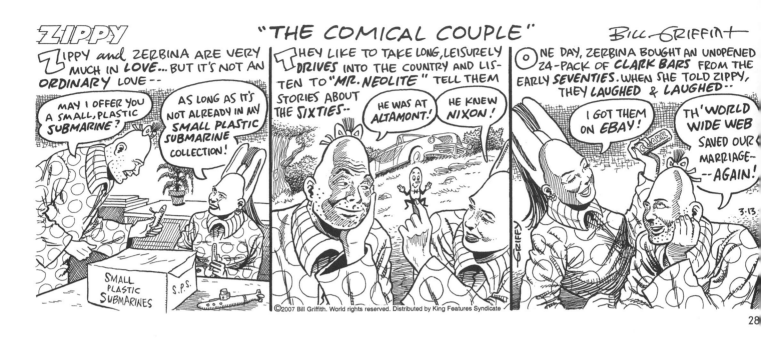

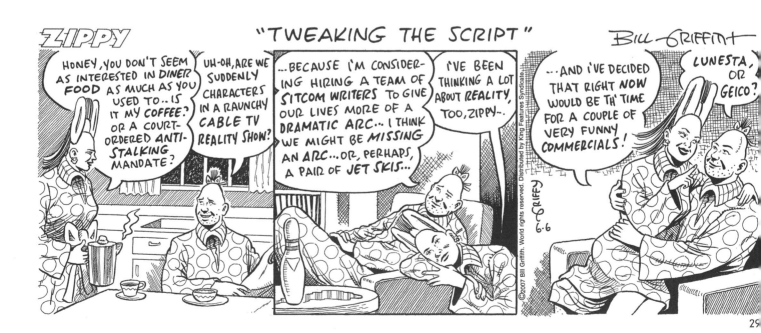

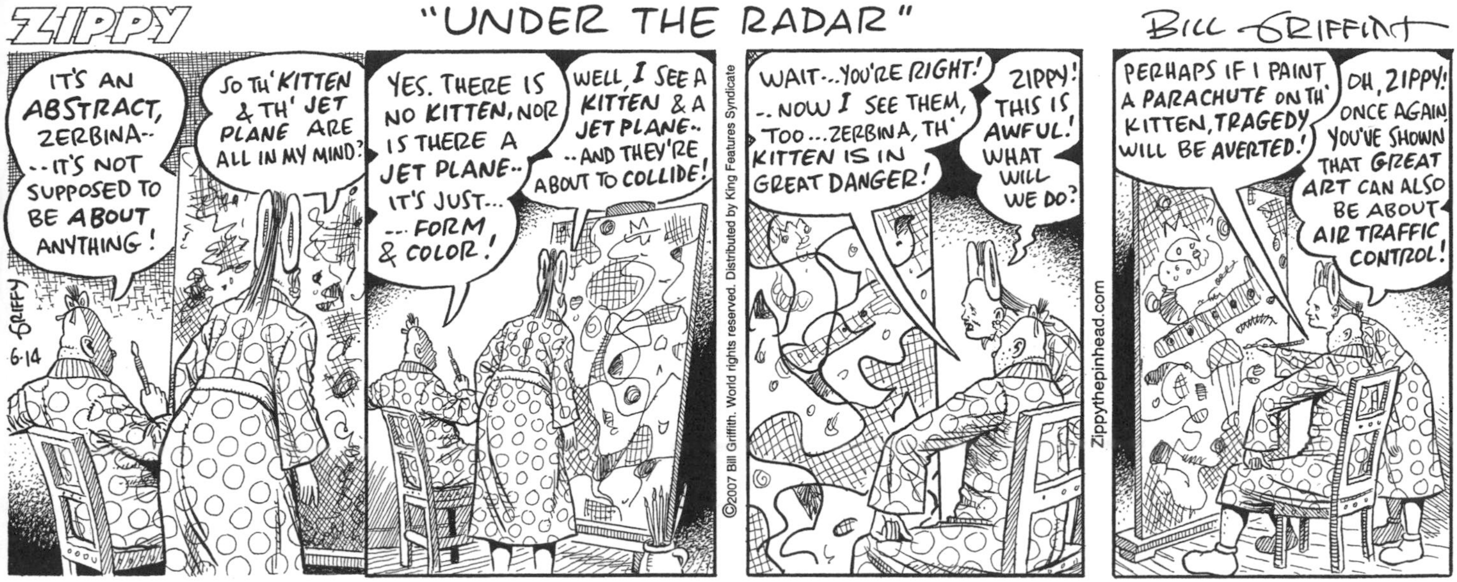
ZIPPY
"UNDER THE RADAR"
BILL GRIFFITH
IT'S AN ABSTRACT, ZERBINA-- --IT'S NOT SUPPOSED TO BE ABOUT ANYTHING!
SO TH' KITTEN & TH' JET PLANE ARE ALL IN MY MIND?
GRIFFY 6-14
YES. THERE IS NO KITTEN, NOR IS THERE A JET PLANE.. IT'S JUST... --FORM & COLOR!
WELL, I SEE A KITTEN & A JET PLANE.. ..AND THEY'RE ABOUT TO COLLIDE!
©2007 Bill Griffith. World rights reserved. Distributed by King Features Syndicate
WAIT...YOU'RE RIGHT! ..NOW I SEE THEM, TOO...ZERBINA, TH' KITTEN IS IN GREAT DANGER!
ZIPPY! THIS IS AWFUL! WHAT WILL WE DO?
Zippythepinhead.com
PERHAPS IF I PAINT A PARACHUTE ON TH' KITTEN, TRAGEDY WILL BE AVERTED!
OH, ZIPPY! ONCE AGAIN YOU'VE SHOWN THAT GREAT ART CAN ALSO BE ABOUT AIR TRAFFIC CONTROL!

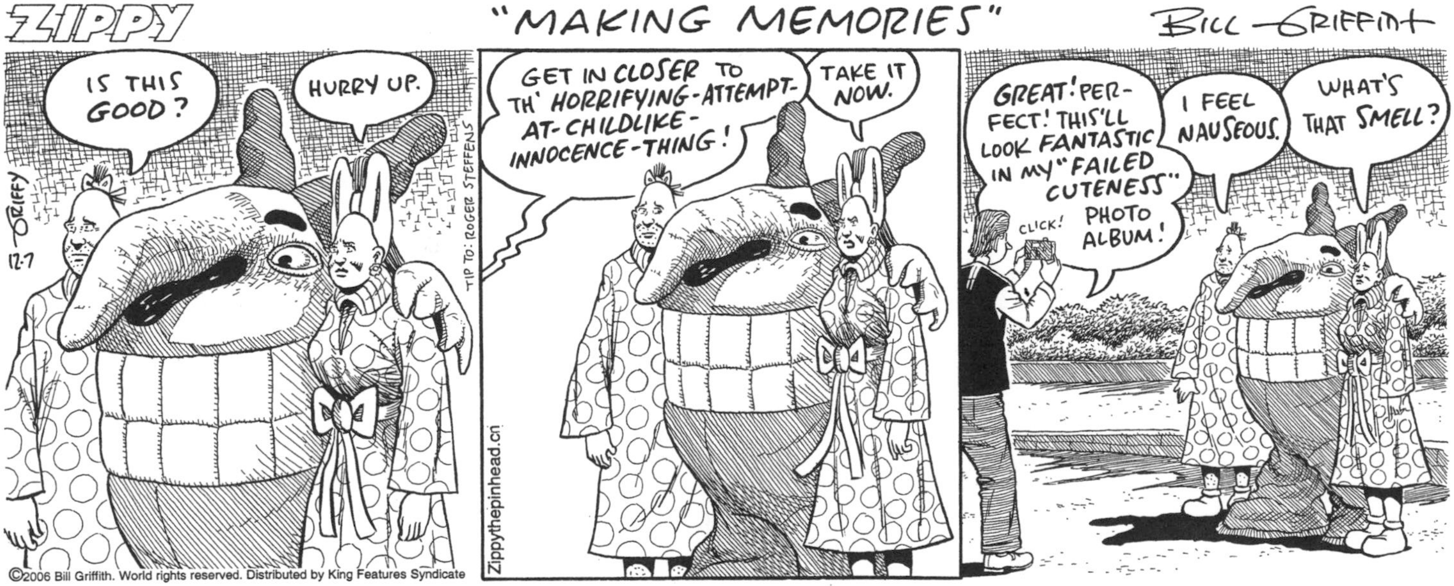
ZIPPY
"MAKING MEMORIES"
BILL GRIFFITH
IS THIS GOOD?
HURRY UP.
GRIFFY 12-7
TIP TO: ROGER STEFFENS
©2006 Bill Griffith. World rights reserved. Distributed by King Features Syndicate
GET IN CLOSER TO TH' HORRIFYING-ATTEMPT-AT-CHILDLIKE-INNOCENCE-THING!
TAKE IT NOW.
Zippythepinhead.cn
GREAT! PERFECT! THIS'LL LOOK FANTASTIC IN MY "FAILED CUTENESS" PHOTO ALBUM!
CLICK!
I FEEL NAUSEOUS.
WHAT'S THAT SMELL?

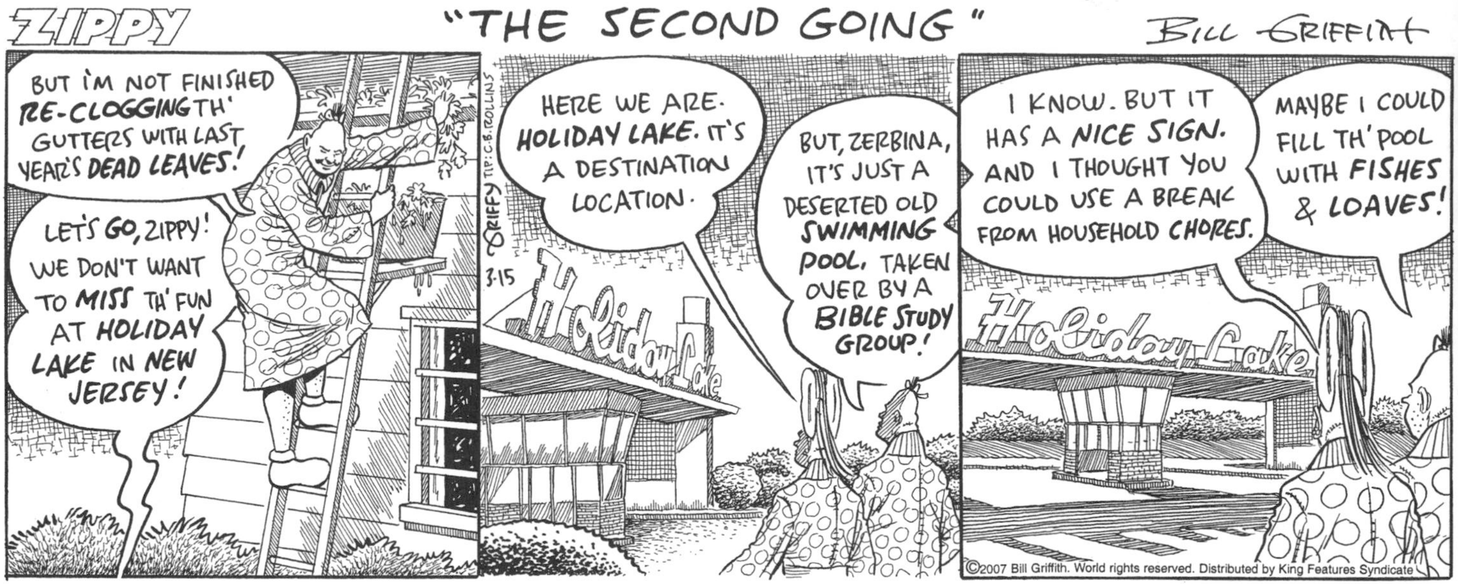
ZIPPY
"THE SECOND GOING"
BILL GRIFFITH
BUT I'M NOT FINISHED RE-CLOGGING TH' GUTTERS WITH LAST YEAR'S DEAD LEAVES!
LET'S GO, ZIPPY! WE DON'T WANT TO MISS TH' FUN AT HOLIDAY LAKE IN NEW JERSEY!
GRIFFY TIP: C.B. ROLLINS
3-15
HERE WE ARE. HOLIDAY LAKE. IT'S A DESTINATION LOCATION.
BUT, ZERBINA, IT'S JUST A DESERTED OLD SWIMMING POOL, TAKEN OVER BY A BIBLE STUDY GROUP!
Holiday Lake
I KNOW. BUT IT HAS A NICE SIGN. AND I THOUGHT YOU COULD USE A BREAK FROM HOUSEHOLD CHORES.
MAYBE I COULD FILL TH' POOL WITH FISHES & LOAVES!
Holiday Lake
©2007 Bill Griffith. World rights reserved. Distributed by King Features Syndicate

31

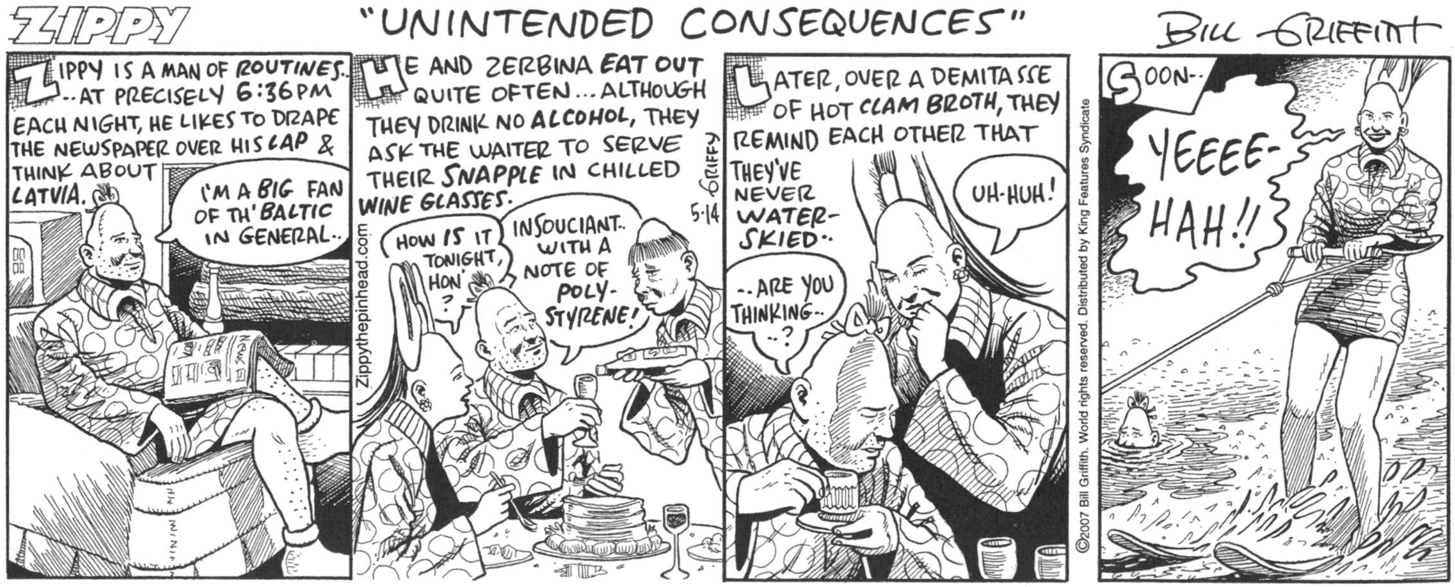
ZIPPY
"UNINTENDED CONSEQUENCES"
BILL GRIFFITH
ZIPPY IS A MAN OF ROUTINES.. ..AT PRECISELY 6:36 PM EACH NIGHT, HE LIKES TO DRAPE THE NEWSPAPER OVER HIS LAP & THINK ABOUT LATVIA.
I'M A BIG FAN OF TH' BALTIC IN GENERAL..
HE AND ZERBINA EAT OUT QUITE OFTEN... ALTHOUGH THEY DRINK NO ALCOHOL, THEY ASK THE WAITER TO SERVE THEIR SNAPPLE IN CHILLED WINE GLASSES.
GRIFFY
5-14
Zippythepinhead.com
HOW IS IT TONIGHT, HON'?
INSOUCIANT.. WITH A NOTE OF POLY-STYRENE!
LATER, OVER A DEMITASSE OF HOT CLAM BROTH, THEY REMIND EACH OTHER THAT THEY'VE NEVER WATER-SKIED..
UH-HUH!
..ARE YOU THINKING.. ..?
©2007 Bill Griffith. World rights reserved. Distributed by King Features Syndicate
SOON..
YEEEE-HAH!!

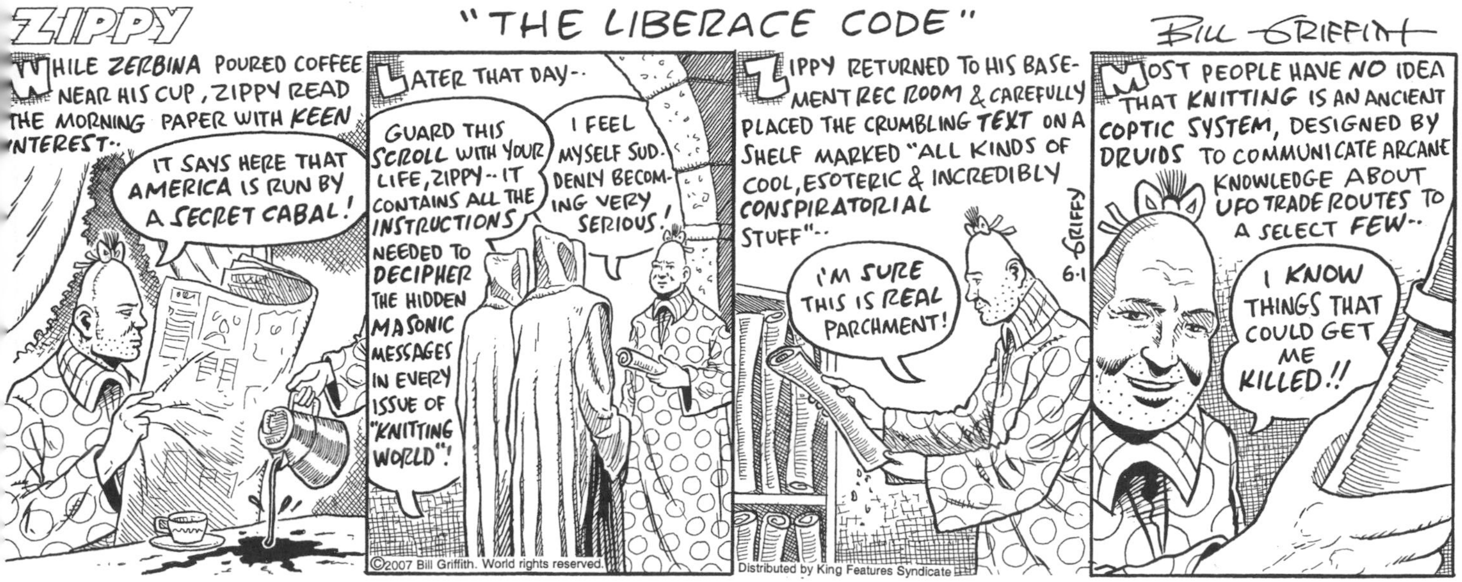
ZIPPY
"THE LIBERACE CODE"
BILL GRIFFITH
WHILE ZERBINA POURED COFFEE NEAR HIS CUP, ZIPPY READ THE MORNING PAPER WITH KEEN INTEREST..
IT SAYS HERE THAT AMERICA IS RUN BY A SECRET CABAL!
LATER THAT DAY..
GUARD THIS SCROLL WITH YOUR LIFE, ZIPPY.. IT CONTAINS ALL THE INSTRUCTIONS NEEDED TO DECIPHER THE HIDDEN MASONIC MESSAGES IN EVERY ISSUE OF "KNITTING WORLD"!
I FEEL MYSELF SUDDENLY BECOMING VERY SERIOUS!
©2007 Bill Griffith. World rights reserved.
ZIPPY RETURNED TO HIS BASEMENT REC ROOM & CAREFULLY PLACED THE CRUMBLING TEXT ON A SHELF MARKED "ALL KINDS OF COOL, ESOTERIC & INCREDIBLY CONSPIRATORIAL STUFF"..
GRIFFY 6·1
I'M SURE THIS IS REAL PARCHMENT!
Distributed by King Features Syndicate
MOST PEOPLE HAVE NO IDEA THAT KNITTING IS AN ANCIENT COPTIC SYSTEM, DESIGNED BY DRUIDS TO COMMUNICATE ARCANE KNOWLEDGE ABOUT UFO TRADE ROUTES TO A SELECT FEW..
I KNOW THINGS THAT COULD GET ME KILLED!!

32

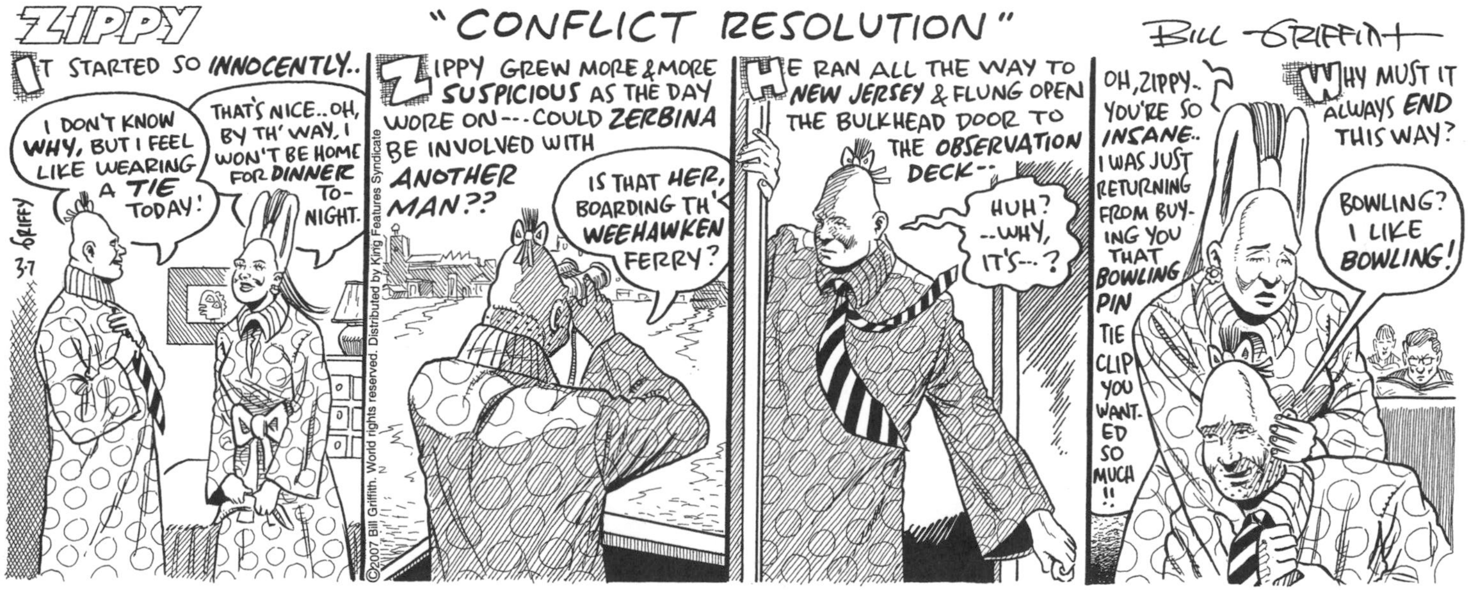
ZIPPY
"CONFLICT RESOLUTION"
BILL GRIFFITH
IT STARTED SO INNOCENTLY..
I DON'T KNOW WHY, BUT I FEEL LIKE WEARING A TIE TODAY!
THAT'S NICE.. OH, BY TH' WAY, I WON'T BE HOME FOR DINNER TONIGHT.
GRIFFY 3·7
ZIPPY GREW MORE & MORE SUSPICIOUS AS THE DAY WORE ON--- COULD ZERBINA BE INVOLVED WITH ANOTHER MAN??
IS THAT HER, BOARDING TH' WEEHAWKEN FERRY?
©2007 Bill Griffith. World rights reserved. Distributed by King Features Syndicate
HE RAN ALL THE WAY TO NEW JERSEY & FLUNG OPEN THE BULKHEAD DOOR TO THE OBSERVATION DECK--
HUH? --WHY, IT'S--?
OH, ZIPPY.. YOU'RE SO INSANE.. I WAS JUST RETURNING FROM BUYING YOU THAT BOWLING PIN TIE CLIP YOU WANTED SO MUCH!!
WHY MUST IT ALWAYS END THIS WAY?
BOWLING? I LIKE BOWLING!

33

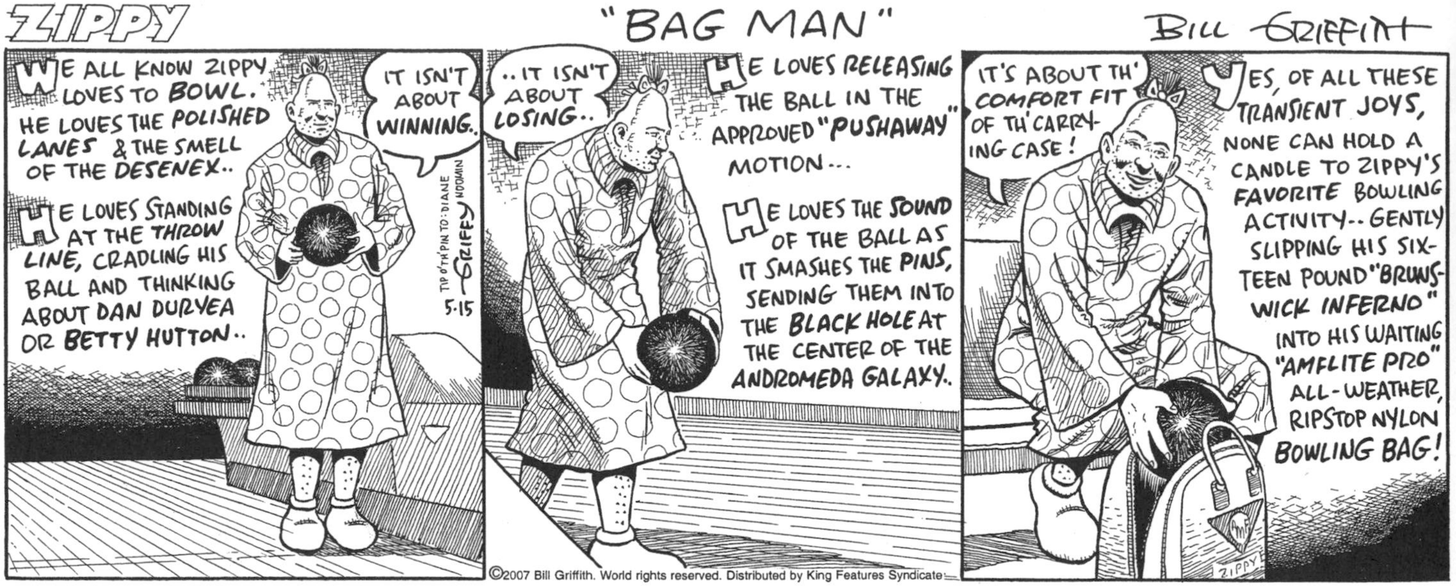
ZIPPY
"BAG MAN"
BILL GRIFFITH
WE ALL KNOW ZIPPY LOVES TO BOWL. HE LOVES THE POLISHED LANES & THE SMELL OF THE DESENEX..
HE LOVES STANDING AT THE THROW LINE, CRADLING HIS BALL AND THINKING ABOUT DAN DURYEA OR BETTY HUTTON..
IT ISN'T ABOUT WINNING..
TIP O'TH PIN TO: DIANE NOOMIN
GRIFFY
5.15
..IT ISN'T ABOUT LOSING..
HE LOVES RELEASING THE BALL IN THE APPROVED "PUSHAWAY" MOTION...
HE LOVES THE SOUND OF THE BALL AS IT SMASHES THE PINS, SENDING THEM INTO THE BLACK HOLE AT THE CENTER OF THE ANDROMEDA GALAXY..
IT'S ABOUT TH' COMFORT FIT OF TH' CARRYING CASE!
YES, OF ALL THESE TRANSIENT JOYS, NONE CAN HOLD A CANDLE TO ZIPPY'S FAVORITE BOWLING ACTIVITY.. GENTLY SLIPPING HIS SIXTEEN POUND "BRUNSWICK INFERNO" INTO HIS WAITING "AMFLITE PRO" ALL-WEATHER, RIPSTOP NYLON BOWLING BAG!
ZIPPY
©2007 Bill Griffith. World rights reserved. Distributed by King Features Syndicate

34

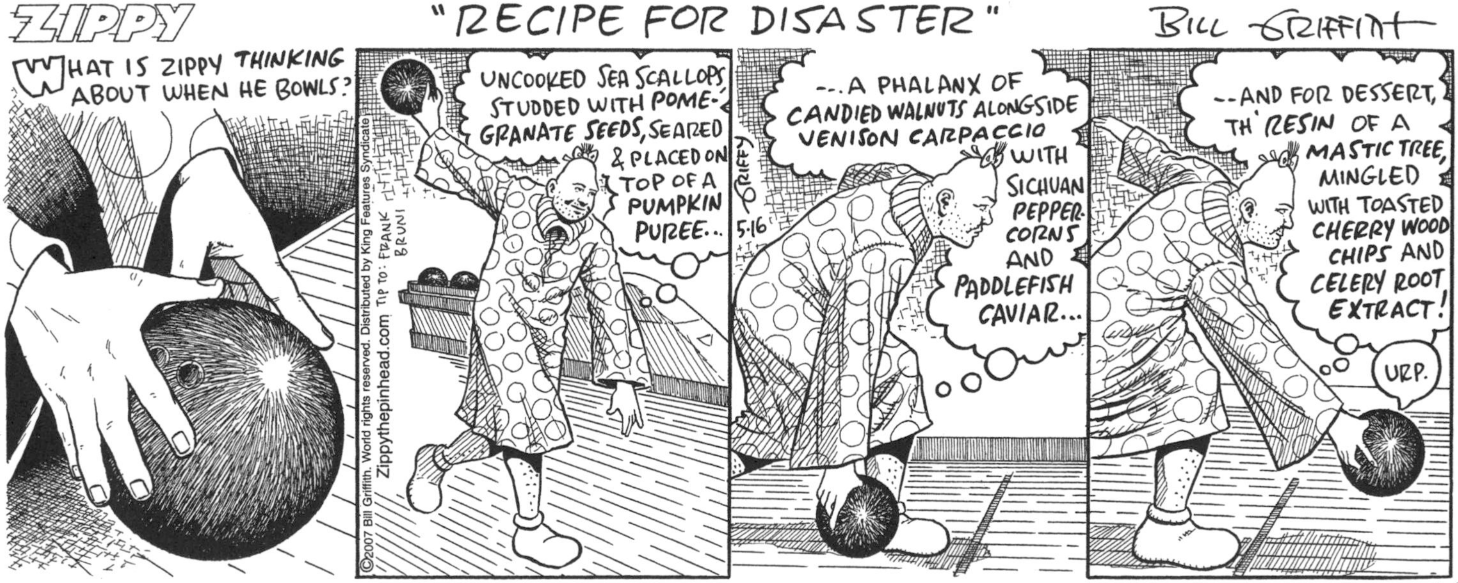
ZIPPY
"RECIPE FOR DISASTER"
BILL GRIFFITH
WHAT IS ZIPPY THINKING ABOUT WHEN HE BOWLS?
©2007 Bill Griffith. World rights reserved. Distributed by King Features Syndicate
Zippythepinhead.com
TIP TO: FRANK BRUNI
UNCOOKED SEA SCALLOPS STUDDED WITH POMEGRANATE SEEDS, SEARED & PLACED ON TOP OF A PUMPKIN PUREE...
GRIFFY
5.16
--.A PHALANX OF CANDIED WALNUTS ALONGSIDE VENISON CARPACCIO WITH SICHUAN PEPPERCORNS AND PADDLEFISH CAVIAR...
--AND FOR DESSERT, TH' RESIN OF A MASTIC TREE, MINGLED WITH TOASTED CHERRY WOOD CHIPS AND CELERY ROOT EXTRACT!
URP.

35

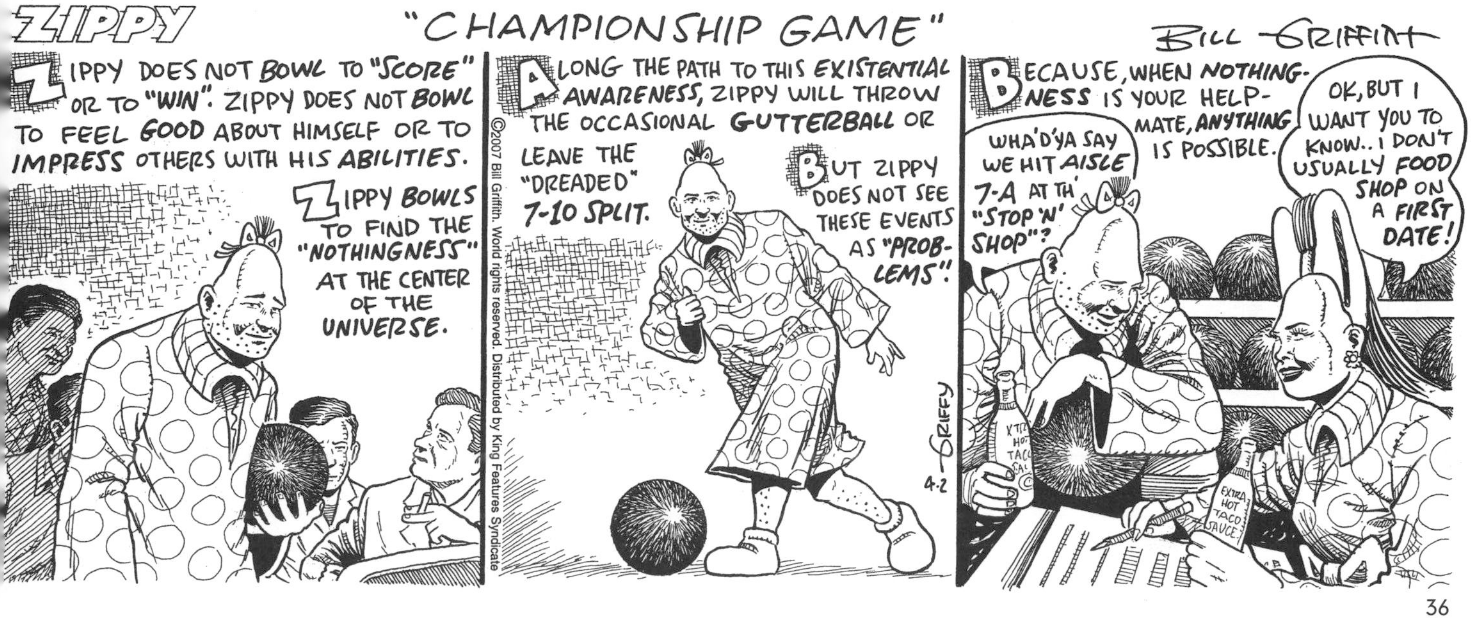
ZIPPY
"CHAMPIONSHIP GAME"
BILL GRIFFITH
ZIPPY DOES NOT BOWL TO "SCORE" OR TO "WIN". ZIPPY DOES NOT BOWL TO FEEL GOOD ABOUT HIMSELF OR TO IMPRESS OTHERS WITH HIS ABILITIES.
ZIPPY BOWLS TO FIND THE "NOTHINGNESS" AT THE CENTER OF THE UNIVERSE.
ALONG THE PATH TO THIS EXISTENTIAL AWARENESS, ZIPPY WILL THROW THE OCCASIONAL GUTTERBALL OR
LEAVE THE "DREADED" 7-10 SPLIT.
BUT ZIPPY DOES NOT SEE THESE EVENTS AS "PROBLEMS".
©2007 Bill Griffith. World rights reserved. Distributed by King Features Syndicate
GRIFFY 4-2
BECAUSE, WHEN NOTHINGNESS IS YOUR HELPMATE, ANYTHING IS POSSIBLE.
WHA'D'YA SAY WE HIT AISLE 7-A AT TH' "STOP 'N' SHOP"?
OK, BUT I WANT YOU TO KNOW.. I DON'T USUALLY FOOD SHOP ON A FIRST DATE!
EXTRA HOT TACO SAUCE!
36

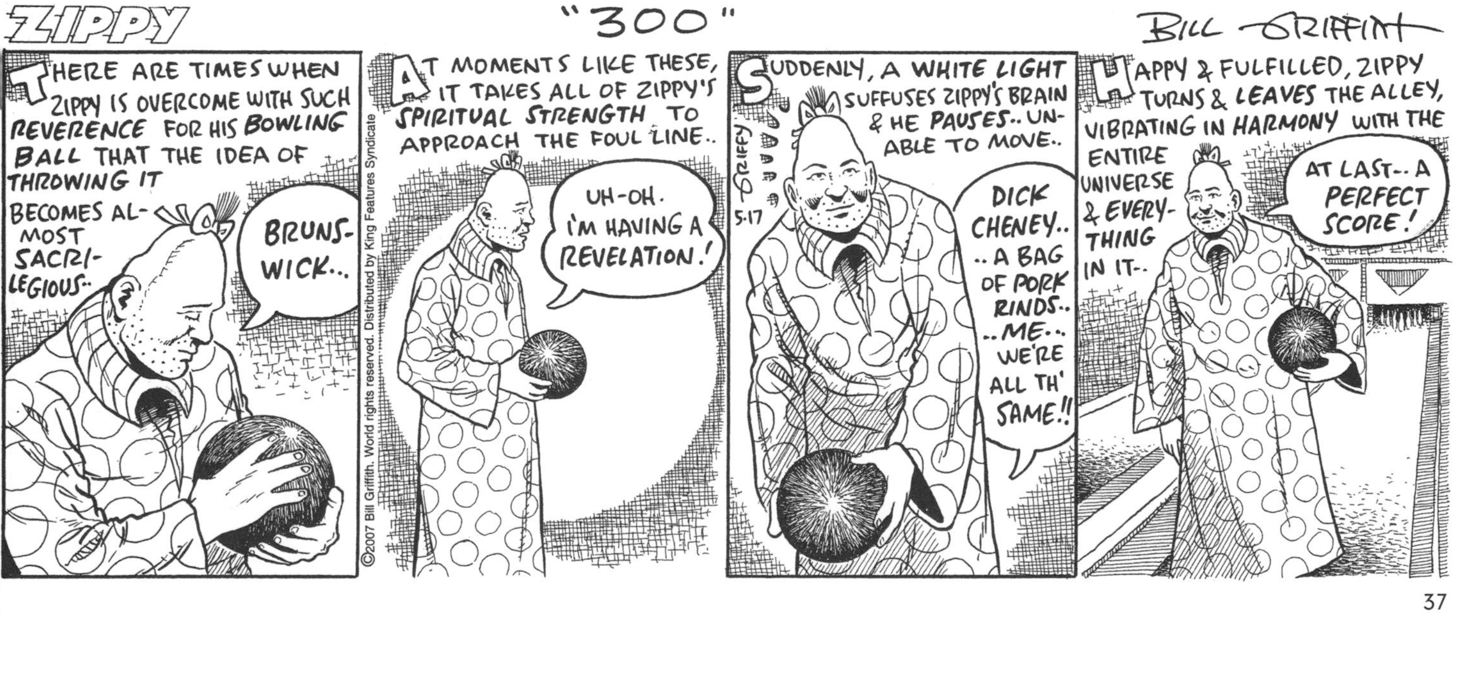
ZIPPY
"300"
BILL GRIFFITH
THERE ARE TIMES WHEN ZIPPY IS OVERCOME WITH SUCH REVERENCE FOR HIS BOWLING BALL THAT THE IDEA OF THROWING IT BECOMES ALMOST SACRILEGIOUS..
BRUNSWICK...
AT MOMENTS LIKE THESE, IT TAKES ALL OF ZIPPY'S SPIRITUAL STRENGTH TO APPROACH THE FOUL LINE..
UH-OH. I'M HAVING A REVELATION!
©2007 Bill Griffith. World rights reserved. Distributed by King Features Syndicate
SUDDENLY, A WHITE LIGHT SUFFUSES ZIPPY'S BRAIN & HE PAUSES.. UNABLE TO MOVE..
GRIFFY 5-17
DICK CHENEY.. ..A BAG OF PORK RINDS.. ..ME.. WE'RE ALL TH' SAME!!
HAPPY & FULFILLED, ZIPPY TURNS & LEAVES THE ALLEY, VIBRATING IN HARMONY WITH THE ENTIRE UNIVERSE & EVERYTHING IN IT..
AT LAST.. A PERFECT SCORE!
37

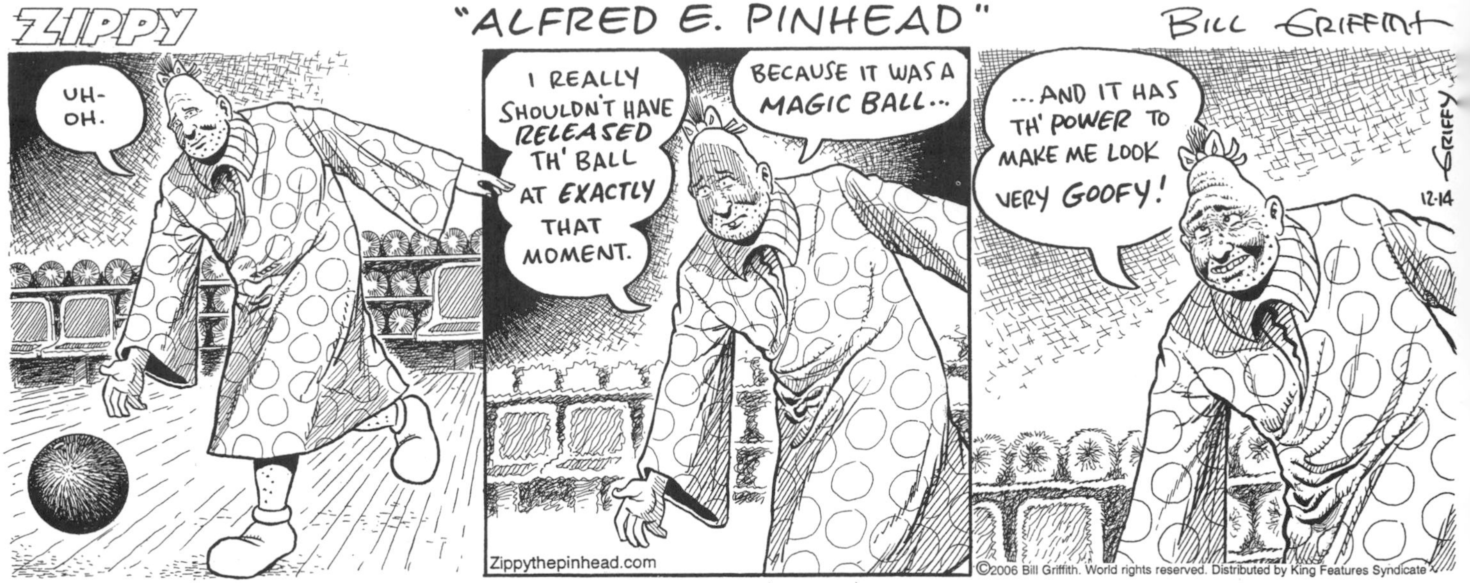
ZIPPY
"ALFRED E. PINHEAD"
BILL GRIFFITH
UH-OH.
I REALLY SHOULDN'T HAVE RELEASED TH' BALL AT EXACTLY THAT MOMENT.
BECAUSE IT WAS A MAGIC BALL...
...AND IT HAS TH' POWER TO MAKE ME LOOK VERY GOOFY!
GRIFFY
12-14
Zippythepinhead.com
©2006 Bill Griffith. World rights reserved. Distributed by King Features Syndicate

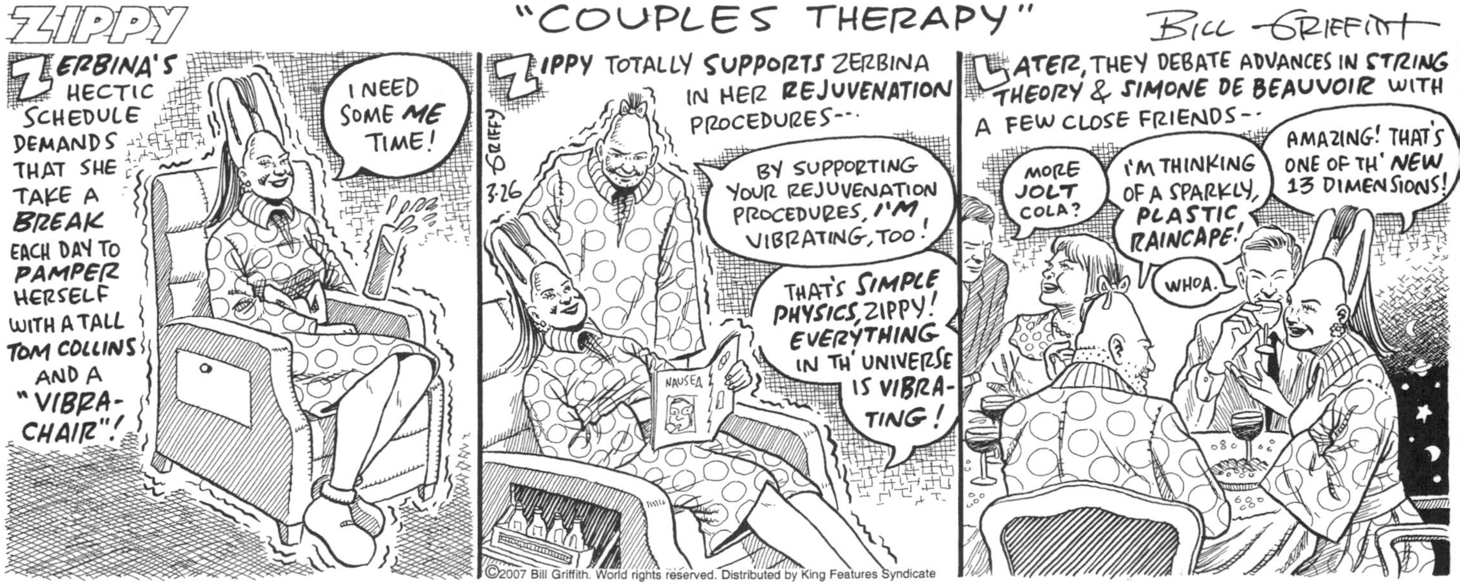
ZIPPY
"COUPLES THERAPY"
BILL GRIFFITH
ZERBINA'S HECTIC SCHEDULE DEMANDS THAT SHE TAKE A BREAK EACH DAY TO PAMPER HERSELF WITH A TALL TOM COLLINS AND A "VIBRA-CHAIR"!
I NEED SOME ME TIME!
ZIPPY TOTALLY SUPPORTS ZERBINA IN HER REJUVENATION PROCEDURES--
GRIFFY
3-26
BY SUPPORTING YOUR REJUVENATION PROCEDURES, I'M VIBRATING, TOO!
THAT'S SIMPLE PHYSICS, ZIPPY! EVERYTHING IN TH' UNIVERSE IS VIBRA-TING!
NAUSEA
LATER, THEY DEBATE ADVANCES IN STRING THEORY & SIMONE DE BEAUVOIR WITH A FEW CLOSE FRIENDS--
MORE JOLT COLA?
I'M THINKING OF A SPARKLY, PLASTIC RAINCAPE!
WHOA.
AMAZING! THAT'S ONE OF TH' NEW 13 DIMENSIONS!
©2007 Bill Griffith. World rights reserved. Distributed by King Features Syndicate

38

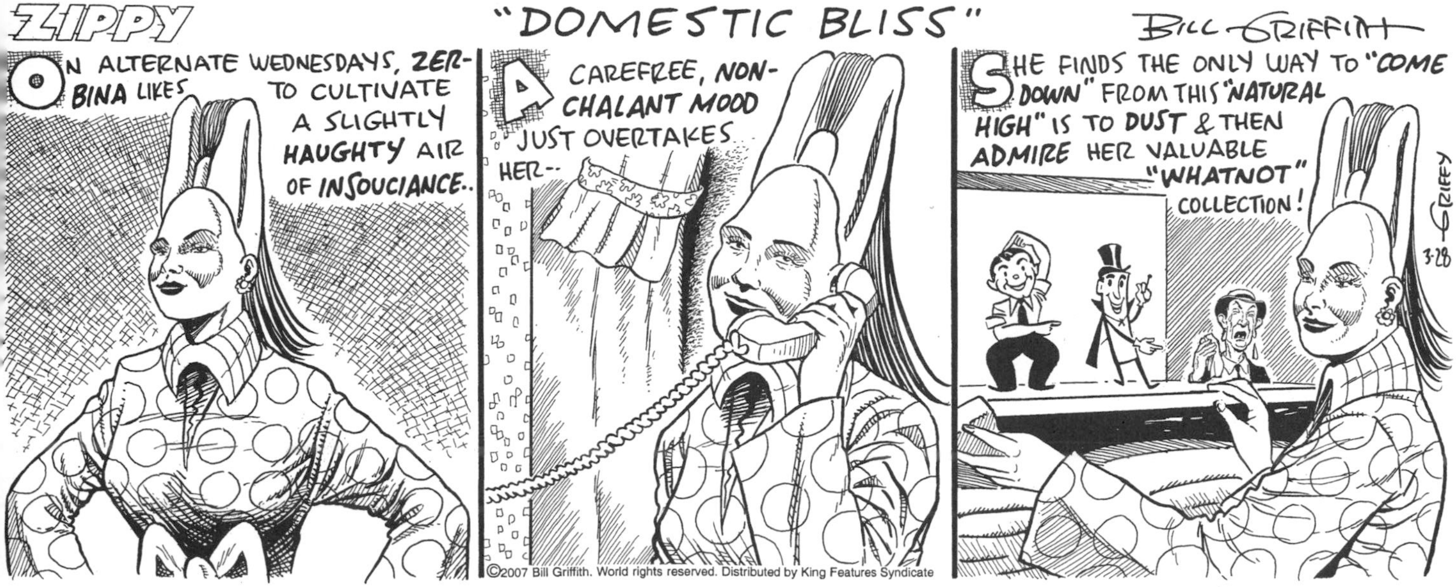
ZIPPY
"DOMESTIC BLISS"
BILL GRIFFITH
ON ALTERNATE WEDNESDAYS, ZERBINA LIKES TO CULTIVATE A SLIGHTLY HAUGHTY AIR OF INSOUCIANCE..
A CAREFREE, NON-CHALANT MOOD JUST OVERTAKES HER--
SHE FINDS THE ONLY WAY TO "COME DOWN" FROM THIS "NATURAL HIGH" IS TO DUST & THEN ADMIRE HER VALUABLE "WHATNOT" COLLECTION!
GRIFFY 3-28
©2007 Bill Griffith. World rights reserved. Distributed by King Features Syndicate

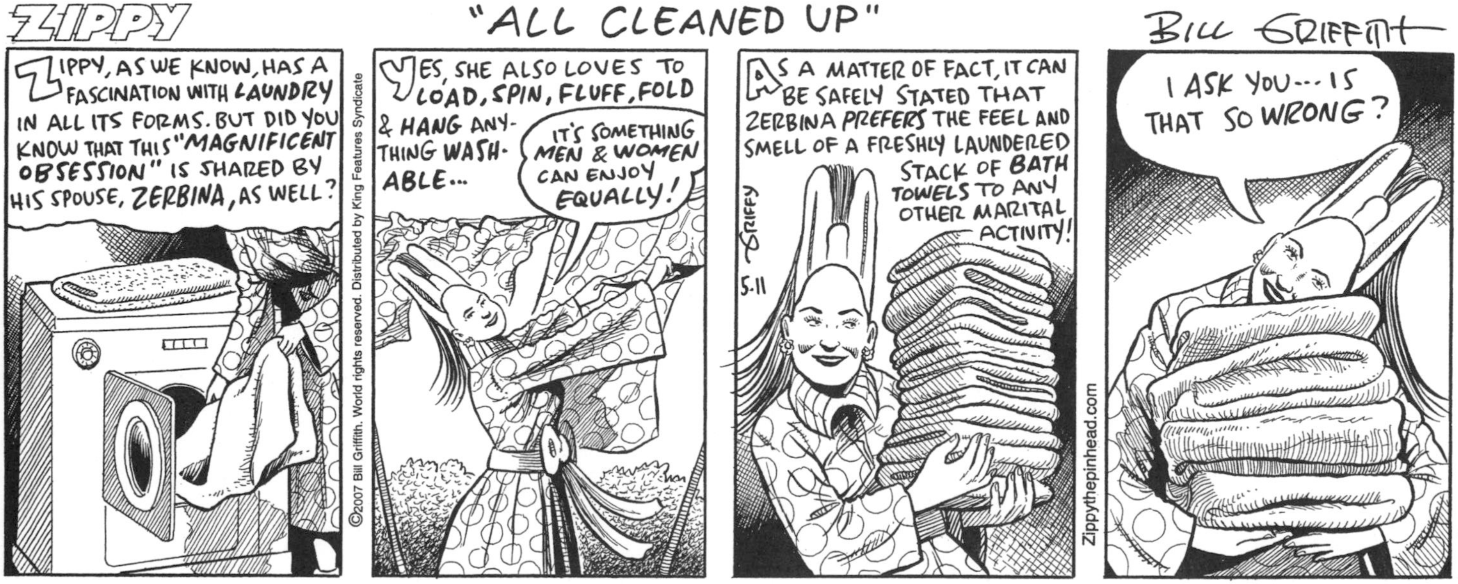
ZIPPY
"ALL CLEANED UP"
BILL GRIFFITH
ZIPPY, AS WE KNOW, HAS A FASCINATION WITH LAUNDRY IN ALL ITS FORMS. BUT DID YOU KNOW THAT THIS "MAGNIFICENT OBSESSION" IS SHARED BY HIS SPOUSE, ZERBINA, AS WELL?
©2007 Bill Griffith. World rights reserved. Distributed by King Features Syndicate
YES, SHE ALSO LOVES TO LOAD, SPIN, FLUFF, FOLD & HANG ANY-THING WASH-ABLE...
IT'S SOMETHING MEN & WOMEN CAN ENJOY EQUALLY!
AS A MATTER OF FACT, IT CAN BE SAFELY STATED THAT ZERBINA PREFERS THE FEEL AND SMELL OF A FRESHLY LAUNDERED STACK OF BATH TOWELS TO ANY OTHER MARITAL ACTIVITY!
GRIFFY 5.11
Zippythepinhead.com
I ASK YOU--- IS THAT SO WRONG?

39

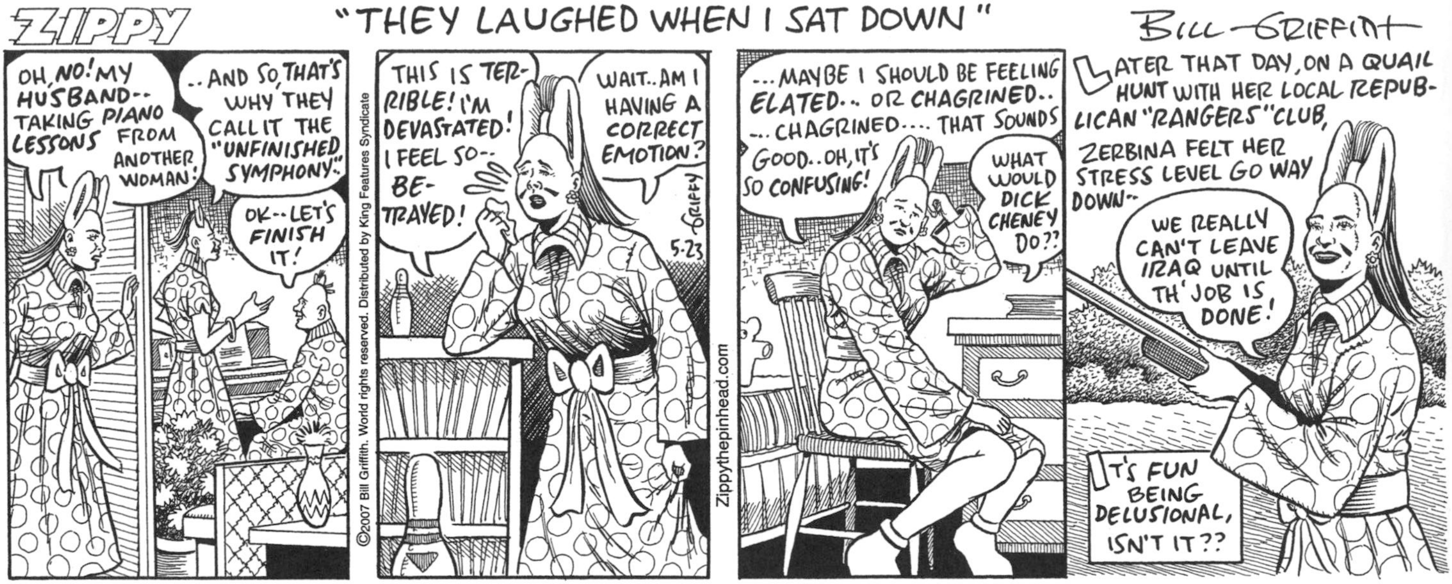
ZIPPY
"THEY LAUGHED WHEN I SAT DOWN"
BILL GRIFFITH
OH, NO! MY HUSBAND-- TAKING PIANO LESSONS FROM ANOTHER WOMAN!
..AND SO, THAT'S WHY THEY CALL IT THE "UNFINISHED SYMPHONY."
OK--LET'S FINISH IT!
©2007 Bill Griffith. World rights reserved. Distributed by King Features Syndicate
THIS IS TERRIBLE! I'M DEVASTATED! I FEEL SO-- BE-TRAYED!
WAIT.. AM I HAVING A CORRECT EMOTION?
GRIFFY 5-23
Zippythepinhead.com
...MAYBE I SHOULD BE FEELING ELATED.. OR CHAGRINED.. ...CHAGRINED.... THAT SOUNDS GOOD.. OH, IT'S SO CONFUSING!
WHAT WOULD DICK CHENEY DO??
LATER THAT DAY, ON A QUAIL HUNT WITH HER LOCAL REPUBLICAN "RANGERS" CLUB, ZERBINA FELT HER STRESS LEVEL GO WAY DOWN--
WE REALLY CAN'T LEAVE IRAQ UNTIL TH' JOB IS DONE!
IT'S FUN BEING DELUSIONAL, ISN'T IT??

40

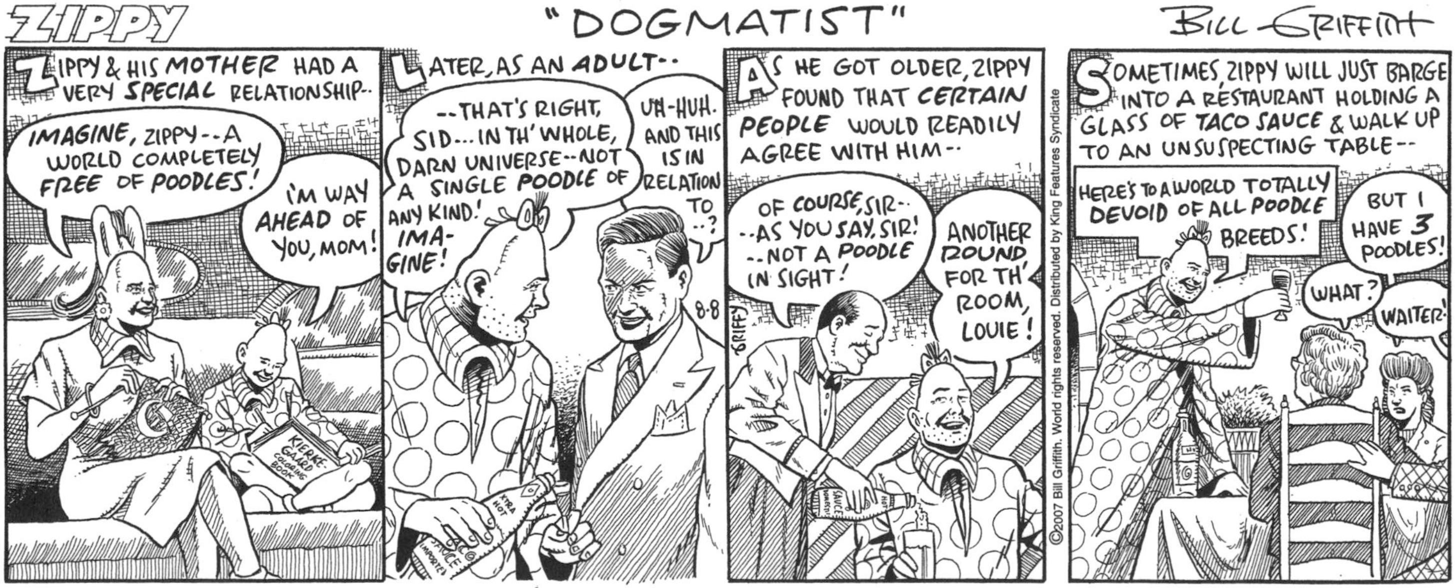
ZIPPY
"DOGMATIST"
BILL GRIFFITH
ZIPPY & HIS MOTHER HAD A VERY SPECIAL RELATIONSHIP..
IMAGINE, ZIPPY--A WORLD COMPLETELY FREE OF POODLES!
I'M WAY AHEAD OF YOU, MOM!
KIERKEGAARD COLORING BOOK
LATER, AS AN ADULT--
--THAT'S RIGHT, SID... IN TH' WHOLE, DARN UNIVERSE--NOT A SINGLE POODLE OF ANY KIND! IMA-GINE!
UH-HUH. AND THIS IS IN RELATION TO ..?
8-8
AS HE GOT OLDER, ZIPPY FOUND THAT CERTAIN PEOPLE WOULD READILY AGREE WITH HIM--
OF COURSE, SIR-- --AS YOU SAY, SIR! --NOT A POODLE IN SIGHT!
ANOTHER ROUND FOR TH' ROOM, LOUIE!
GRIFFY
©2007 Bill Griffith. World rights reserved. Distributed by King Features Syndicate
SOMETIMES, ZIPPY WILL JUST BARGE INTO A RESTAURANT HOLDING A GLASS OF TACO SAUCE & WALK UP TO AN UNSUSPECTING TABLE--
HERE'S TO A WORLD TOTALLY DEVOID OF ALL POODLE BREEDS!
BUT I HAVE 3 POODLES!
WHAT?
WAITER!

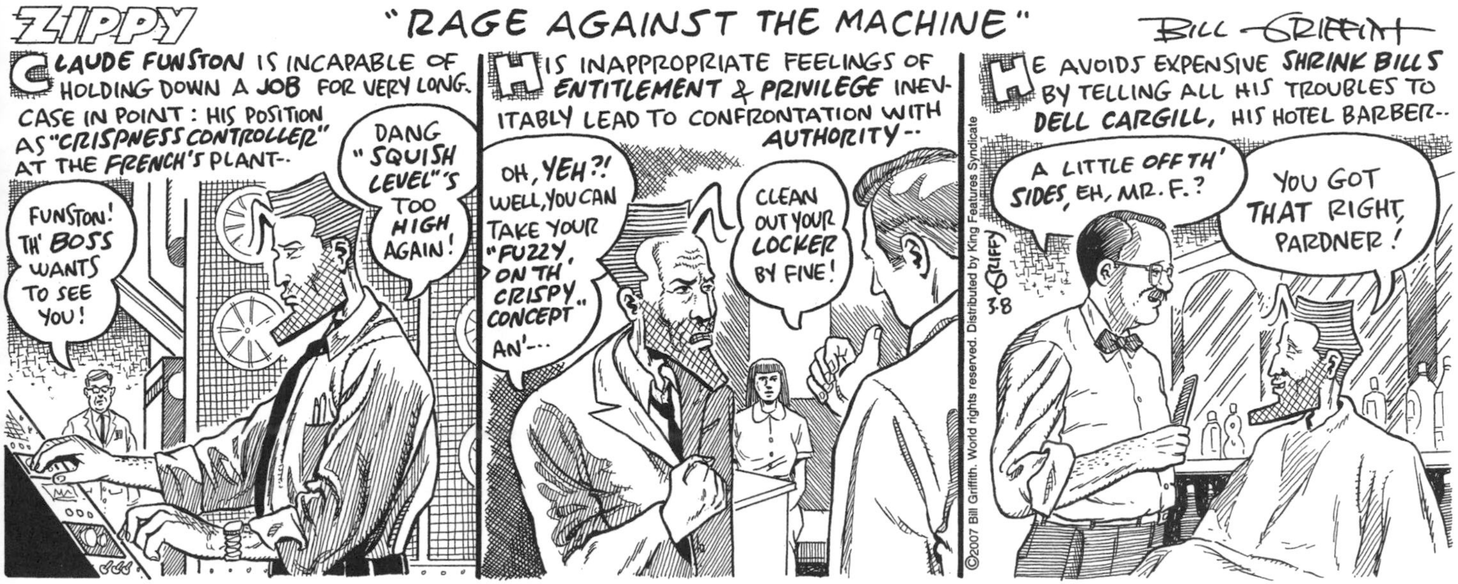
ZIPPY
"RAGE AGAINST THE MACHINE"
BILL GRIFFITH
CLAUDE FUNSTON IS INCAPABLE OF HOLDING DOWN A JOB FOR VERY LONG. CASE IN POINT: HIS POSITION AS "CRISPNESS CONTROLLER" AT THE FRENCH'S PLANT--
FUNSTON! TH' BOSS WANTS TO SEE YOU!
DANG "SQUISH LEVEL"'S TOO HIGH AGAIN!
HIS INAPPROPRIATE FEELINGS OF ENTITLEMENT & PRIVILEGE INEVITABLY LEAD TO CONFRONTATION WITH AUTHORITY--
OH, YEH?! WELL, YOU CAN TAKE YOUR "FUZZY, ON TH CRISPY CONCEPT" AN'--
CLEAN OUT YOUR LOCKER BY FIVE!
HE AVOIDS EXPENSIVE SHRINK BILLS BY TELLING ALL HIS TROUBLES TO DELL CARGILL, HIS HOTEL BARBER--
A LITTLE OFF TH' SIDES, EH, MR. F.?
YOU GOT THAT RIGHT, PARDNER!
GRIFFY 3-8

41

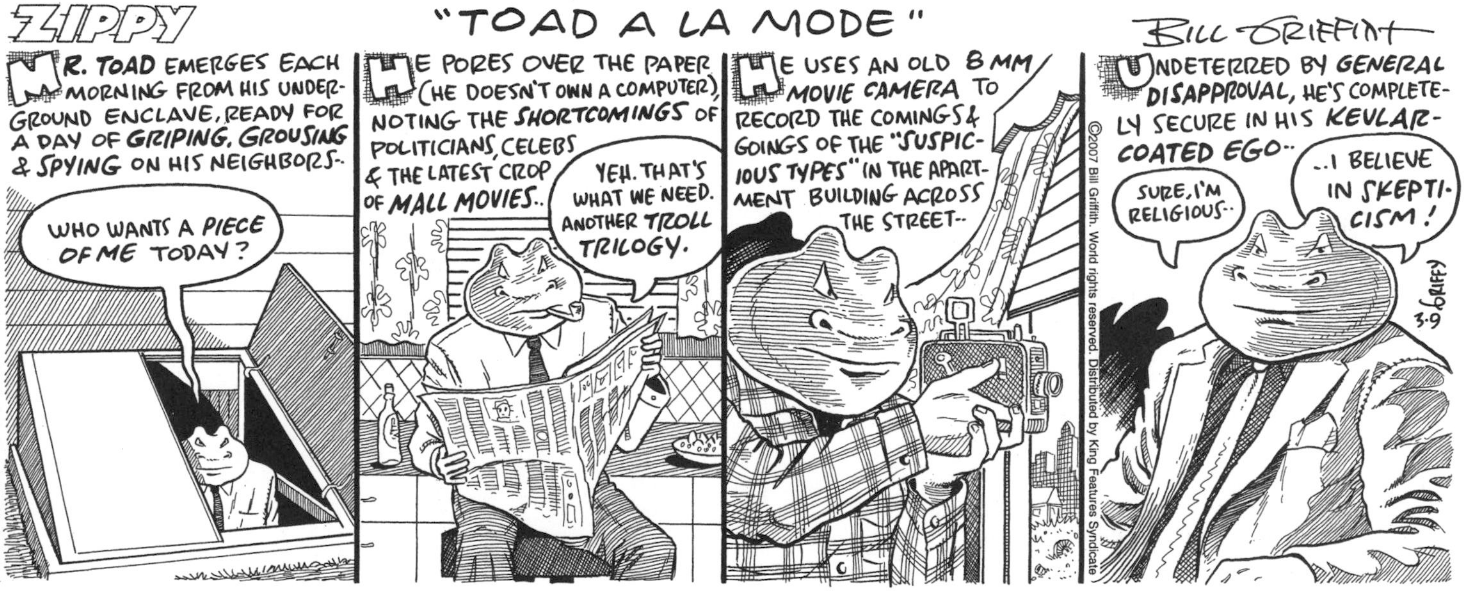
ZIPPY
"TOAD A LA MODE"
BILL GRIFFITH
MR. TOAD EMERGES EACH MORNING FROM HIS UNDERGROUND ENCLAVE, READY FOR A DAY OF GRIPING, GROUSING & SPYING ON HIS NEIGHBORS--
WHO WANTS A PIECE OF ME TODAY?
HE PORES OVER THE PAPER (HE DOESN'T OWN A COMPUTER), NOTING THE SHORTCOMINGS OF POLITICIANS, CELEBS & THE LATEST CROP OF MALL MOVIES..
YEH. THAT'S WHAT WE NEED. ANOTHER TROLL TRILOGY.
HE USES AN OLD 8 MM MOVIE CAMERA TO RECORD THE COMINGS & GOINGS OF THE "SUSPICIOUS TYPES" IN THE APARTMENT BUILDING ACROSS THE STREET--
UNDETERRED BY GENERAL DISAPPROVAL, HE'S COMPLETELY SECURE IN HIS KEVLAR-COATED EGO--
SURE, I'M RELIGIOUS--
--I BELIEVE IN SKEPTICISM!
GRIFFY 3-9

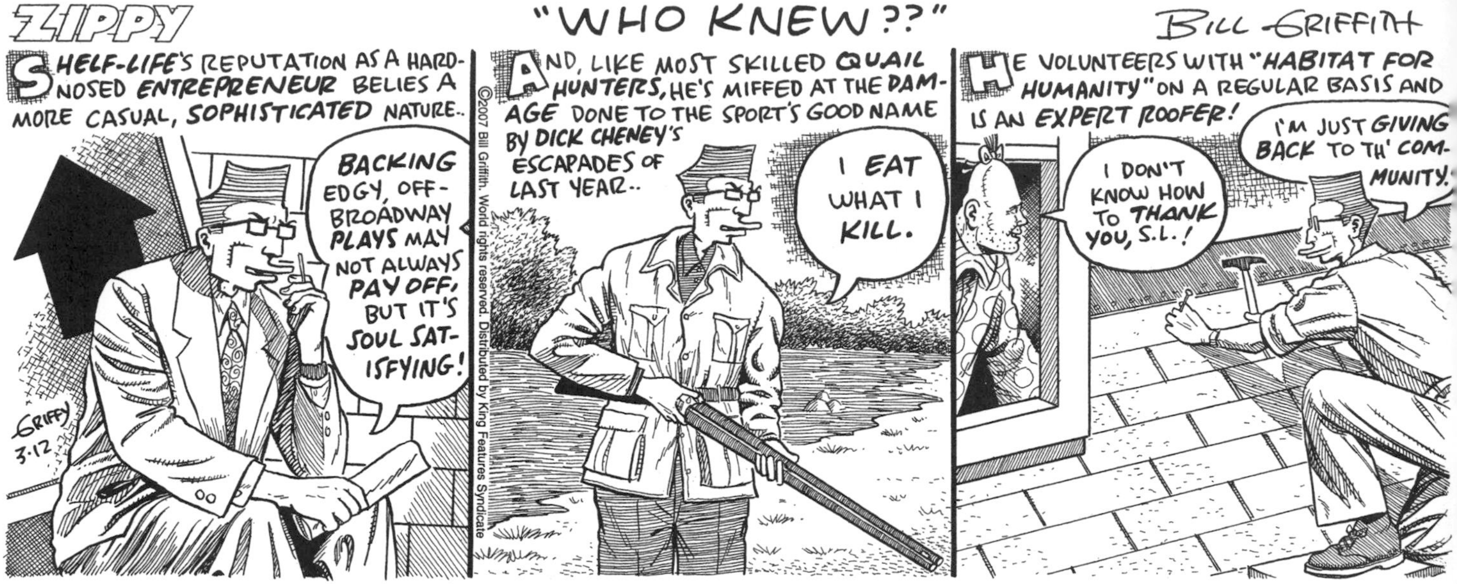
ZIPPY
"WHO KNEW??"
BILL GRIFFITH
SHELF-LIFE'S REPUTATION AS A HARD-NOSED ENTREPRENEUR BELIES A MORE CASUAL, SOPHISTICATED NATURE..
BACKING EDGY, OFF-BROADWAY PLAYS MAY NOT ALWAYS PAY OFF, BUT IT'S SOUL SATISFYING!
GRIFFY 3·12
AND, LIKE MOST SKILLED QUAIL HUNTERS, HE'S MIFFED AT THE DAMAGE DONE TO THE SPORT'S GOOD NAME BY DICK CHENEY'S ESCAPADES OF LAST YEAR..
I EAT WHAT I KILL.
©2007 Bill Griffith. World rights reserved. Distributed by King Features Syndicate
HE VOLUNTEERS WITH "HABITAT FOR HUMANITY" ON A REGULAR BASIS AND IS AN EXPERT ROOFER!
I DON'T KNOW HOW TO THANK YOU, S.L.!
I'M JUST GIVING BACK TO TH' COMMUNITY.

42

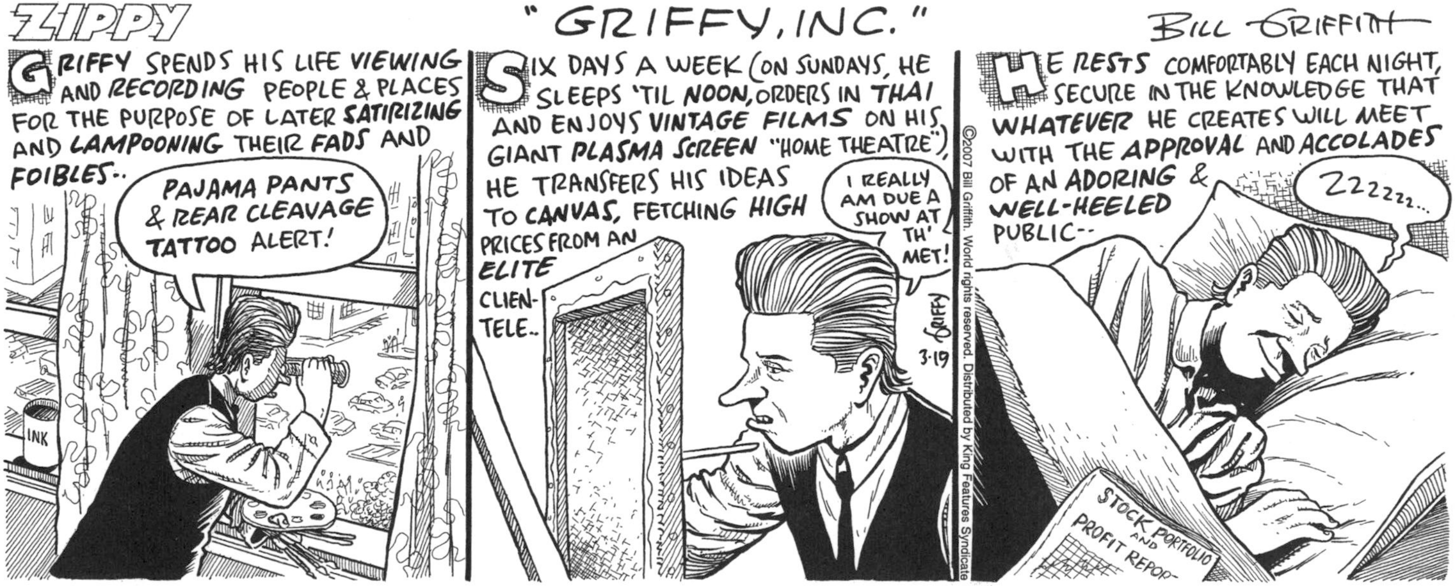
ZIPPY
"GRIFFY, INC."
BILL GRIFFITH
GRIFFY SPENDS HIS LIFE VIEWING AND RECORDING PEOPLE & PLACES FOR THE PURPOSE OF LATER SATIRIZING AND LAMPOONING THEIR FADS AND FOIBLES..
PAJAMA PANTS & REAR CLEAVAGE TATTOO ALERT!
INK
SIX DAYS A WEEK (ON SUNDAYS, HE SLEEPS 'TIL NOON, ORDERS IN THAI AND ENJOYS VINTAGE FILMS ON HIS GIANT PLASMA SCREEN "HOME THEATRE"), HE TRANSFERS HIS IDEAS TO CANVAS, FETCHING HIGH PRICES FROM AN ELITE CLIENTELE..
I REALLY AM DUE A SHOW AT TH' MET!
GRIFFY 3·19
©2007 Bill Griffith. World rights reserved. Distributed by King Features Syndicate
HE RESTS COMFORTABLY EACH NIGHT, SECURE IN THE KNOWLEDGE THAT WHATEVER HE CREATES WILL MEET WITH THE APPROVAL AND ACCOLADES OF AN ADORING & WELL-HEELED PUBLIC--
ZZZZZZ...
STOCK PORTFOLIO AND PROFIT REPOR-

43

TRANSCENDENTAL MEDICATION

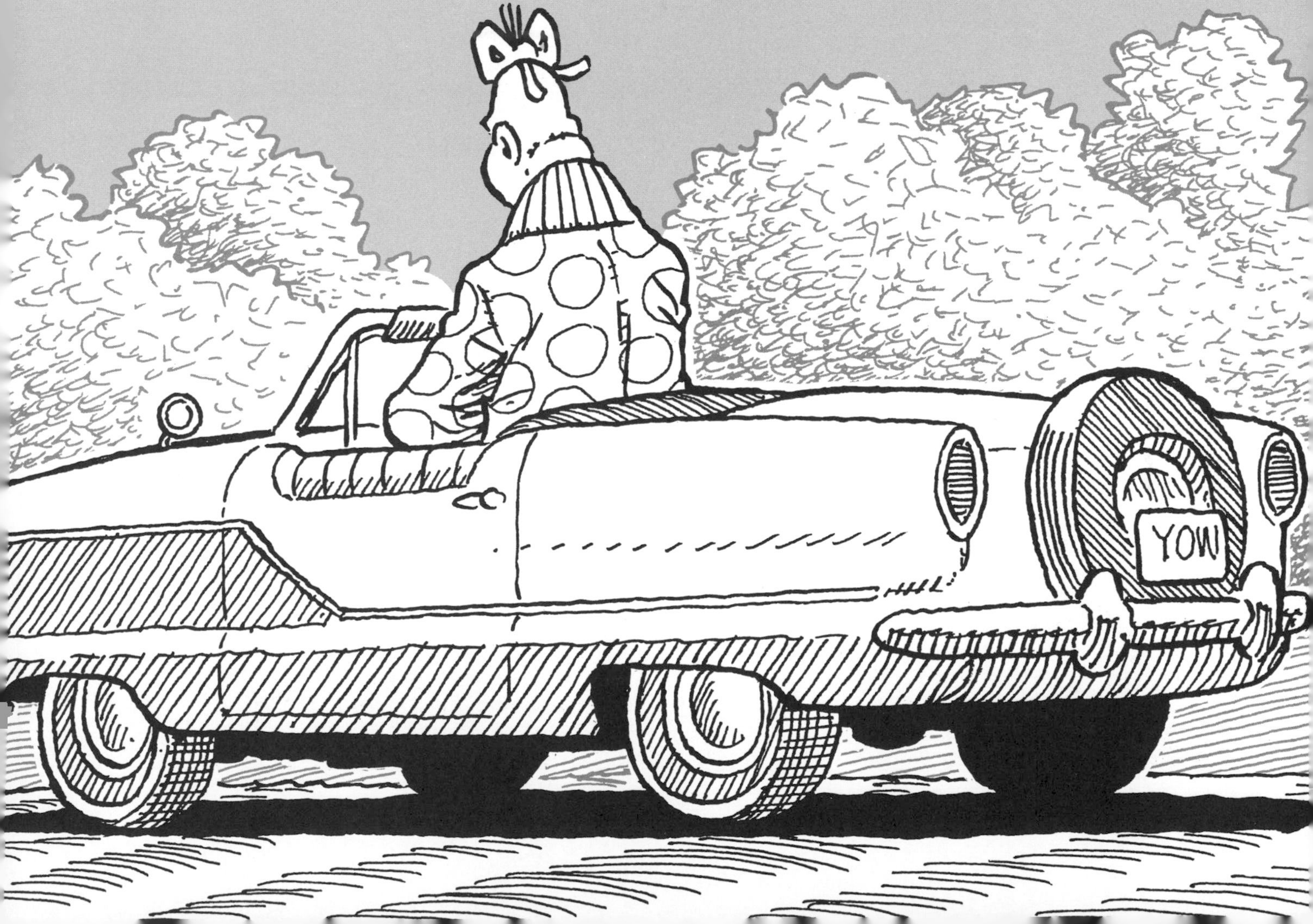
YOW

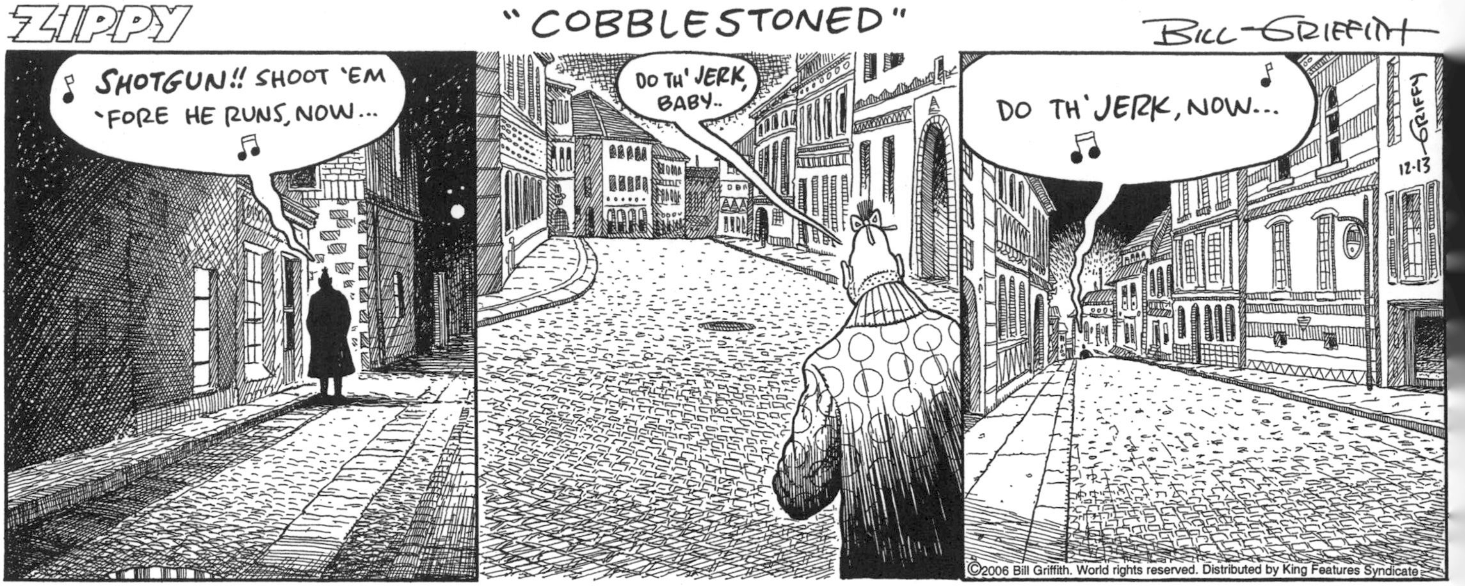
ZIPPY
"COBBLESTONED"
BILL GRIFFITH
SHOTGUN!! SHOOT 'EM 'FORE HE RUNS, NOW...
DO TH' JERK, BABY..
DO TH' JERK, NOW...
GRIFFY 12-13
©2006 Bill Griffith. World rights reserved. Distributed by King Features Syndicate

44

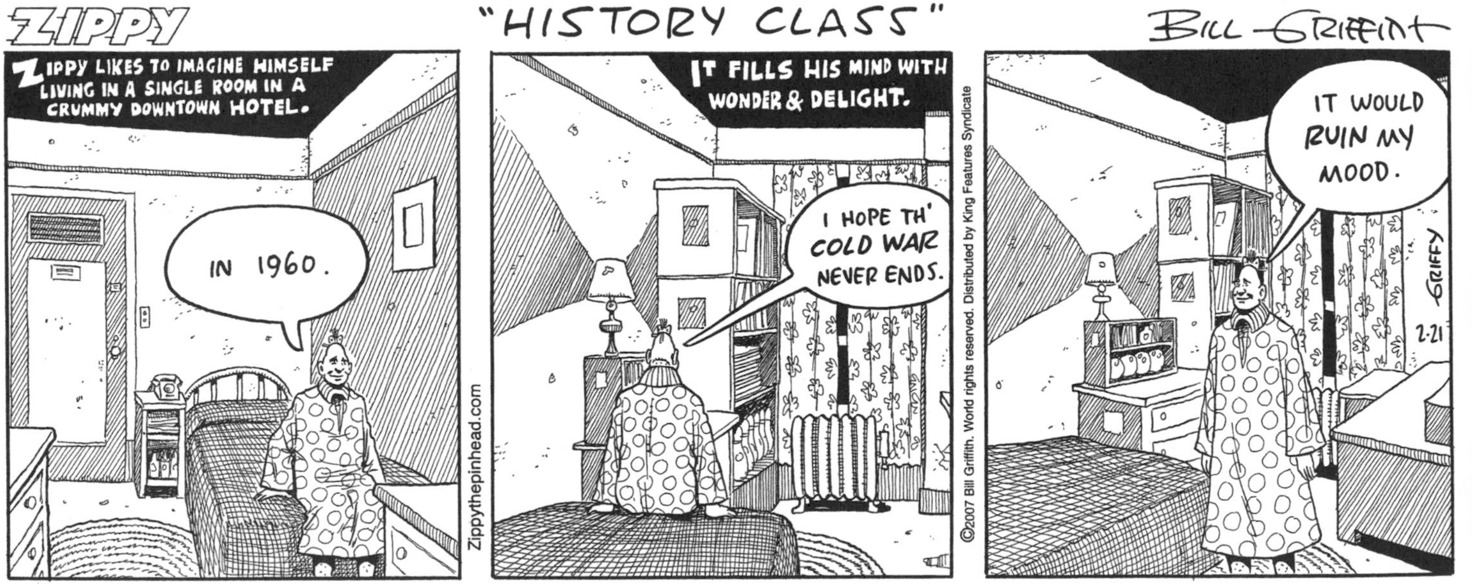
ZIPPY
"HISTORY CLASS"
BILL GRIFFITH
ZIPPY LIKES TO IMAGINE HIMSELF LIVING IN A SINGLE ROOM IN A CRUMMY DOWNTOWN HOTEL.
IN 1960.
Zippythepinhead.com
IT FILLS HIS MIND WITH WONDER & DELIGHT.
I HOPE TH' COLD WAR NEVER ENDS.
©2007 Bill Griffith. World rights reserved. Distributed by King Features Syndicate
IT WOULD RUIN MY MOOD.
GRIFFY 2-21

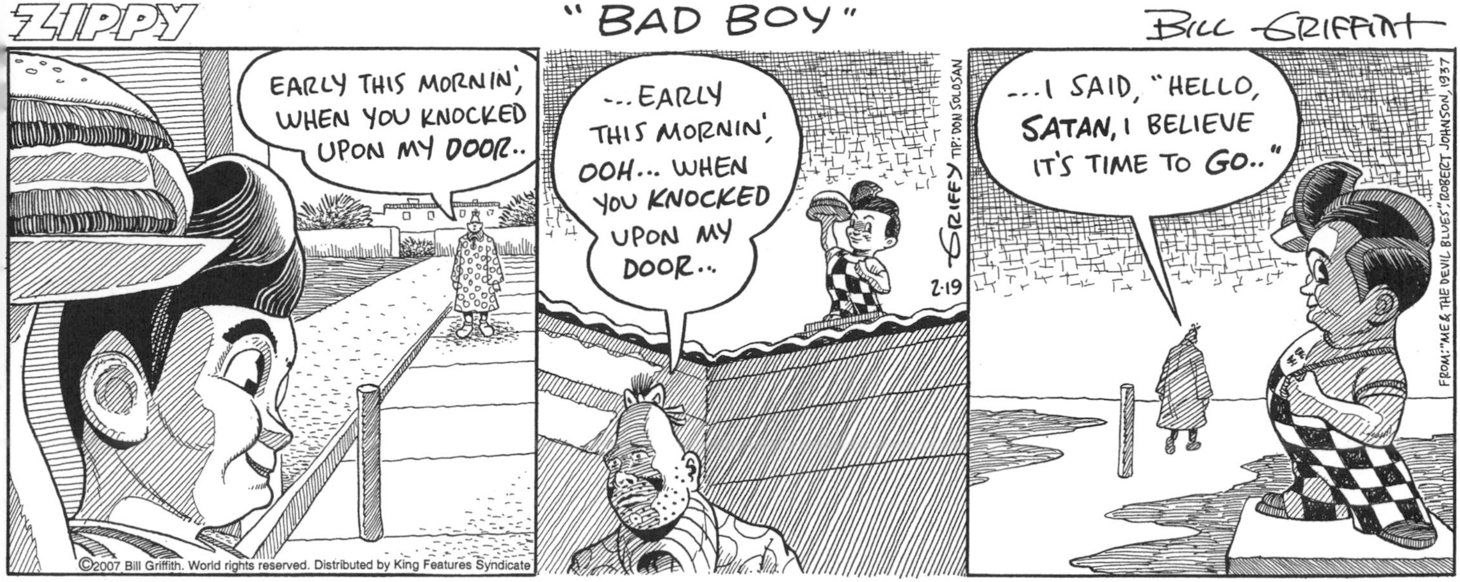
ZIPPY
"BAD BOY"
BILL GRIFFITH
EARLY THIS MORNIN', WHEN YOU KNOCKED UPON MY DOOR..
©2007 Bill Griffith. World rights reserved. Distributed by King Features Syndicate
...EARLY THIS MORNIN', OOH... WHEN YOU KNOCKED UPON MY DOOR..
GRIFFY 2·19
TIP: DON SOLOSAN
...I SAID, "HELLO, SATAN, I BELIEVE IT'S TIME TO GO.."
FROM: "ME & THE DEVIL BLUES", ROBERT JOHNSON, 1937

45

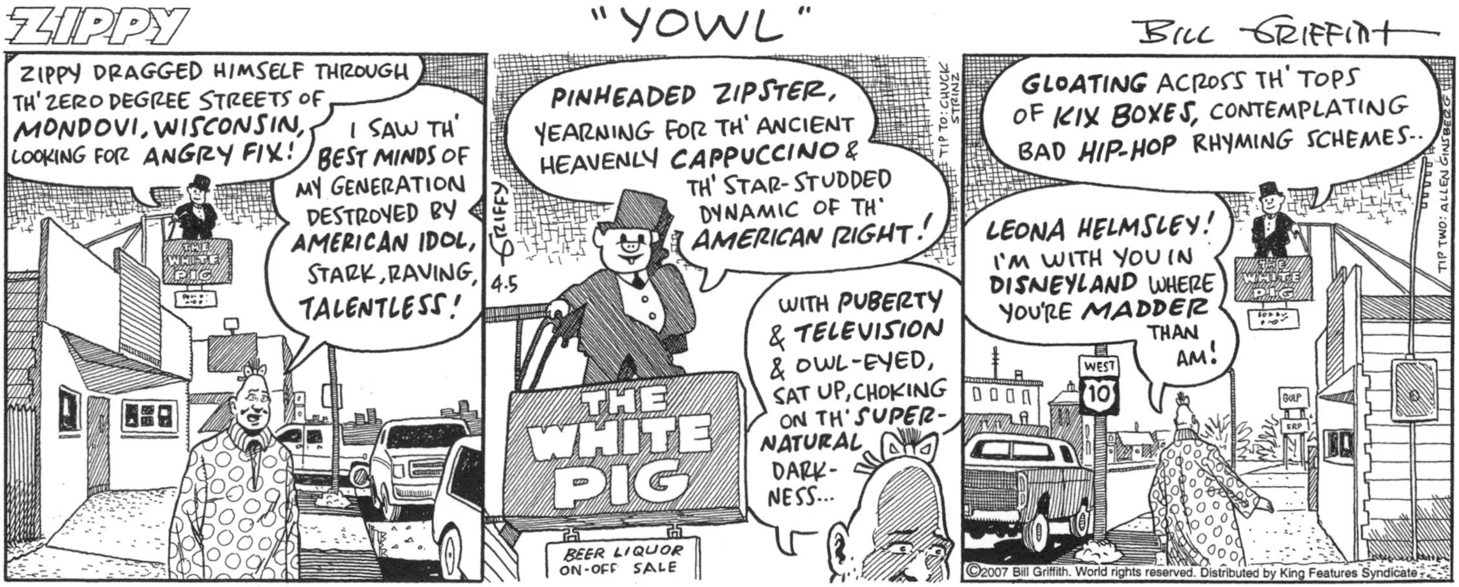
ZIPPY
"YOWL"
BILL GRIFFITH
ZIPPY DRAGGED HIMSELF THROUGH TH' ZERO DEGREE STREETS OF MONDOVI, WISCONSIN, LOOKING FOR ANGRY FIX!
I SAW TH' BEST MINDS OF MY GENERATION DESTROYED BY AMERICAN IDOL, STARK, RAVING, TALENTLESS!
THE WHITE PIG
GRIFFY 4·5
TIP TO: CHUCK STRINZ
PINHEADED ZIPSTER, YEARNING FOR TH' ANCIENT HEAVENLY CAPPUCCINO & TH' STAR-STUDDED DYNAMIC OF TH' AMERICAN RIGHT!
THE WHITE PIG
BEER LIQUOR ON-OFF SALE
WITH PUBERTY & TELEVISION & OWL-EYED, SAT UP, CHOKING ON TH' SUPER-NATURAL DARK-NESS...
GLOATING ACROSS TH' TOPS OF KIX BOXES, CONTEMPLATING BAD HIP-HOP RHYMING SCHEMES..
LEONA HELMSLEY! I'M WITH YOU IN DISNEYLAND WHERE YOU'RE MADDER THAN I AM!
TIP TWO: ALLEN GINSBERG
WEST 10
GULF
©2007 Bill Griffith. World rights reserved. Distributed by King Features Syndicate

46

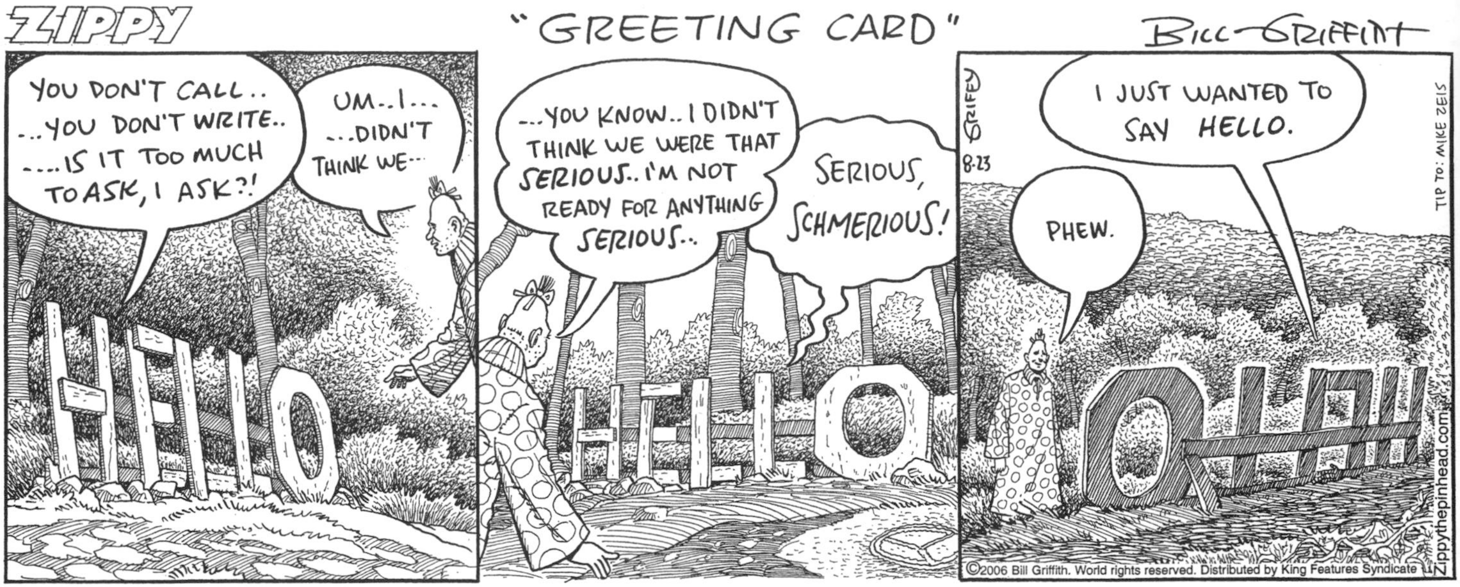
ZIPPY
"GREETING CARD"
BILL GRIFFITH
YOU DON'T CALL.. ...YOU DON'T WRITE.. ....IS IT TOO MUCH TO ASK, I ASK?!
UM..I... ...DIDN'T THINK WE--
...YOU KNOW.. I DIDN'T THINK WE WERE THAT SERIOUS.. I'M NOT READY FOR ANYTHING SERIOUS..
SERIOUS, SCHMERIOUS!
GRIFFY 8-23
I JUST WANTED TO SAY HELLO.
PHEW.
TIP TO: MIKE ZEIS
zippythepinhead.com
©2006 Bill Griffith. World rights reserved. Distributed by King Features Syndicate

47 A

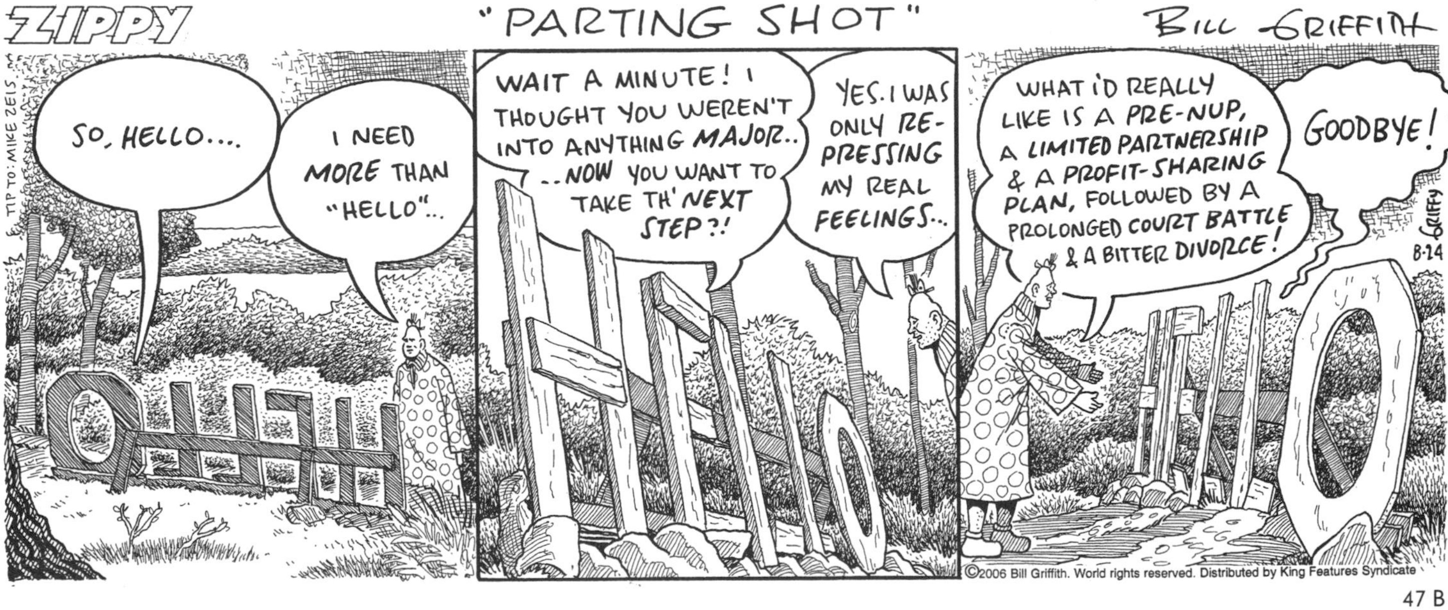
ZIPPY
"PARTING SHOT"
BILL GRIFFITH
TIP TO: MIKE ZEIS
SO, HELLO....
I NEED MORE THAN "HELLO"...
WAIT A MINUTE! I THOUGHT YOU WEREN'T INTO ANYTHING MAJOR.. ..NOW YOU WANT TO TAKE TH' NEXT STEP?!
YES. I WAS ONLY RE-PRESSING MY REAL FEELINGS..
WHAT I'D REALLY LIKE IS A PRE-NUP, A LIMITED PARTNERSHIP & A PROFIT-SHARING PLAN, FOLLOWED BY A PROLONGED COURT BATTLE & A BITTER DIVORCE!
GOODBYE!
GRIFFY 8-24
©2006 Bill Griffith. World rights reserved. Distributed by King Features Syndicate

47 B

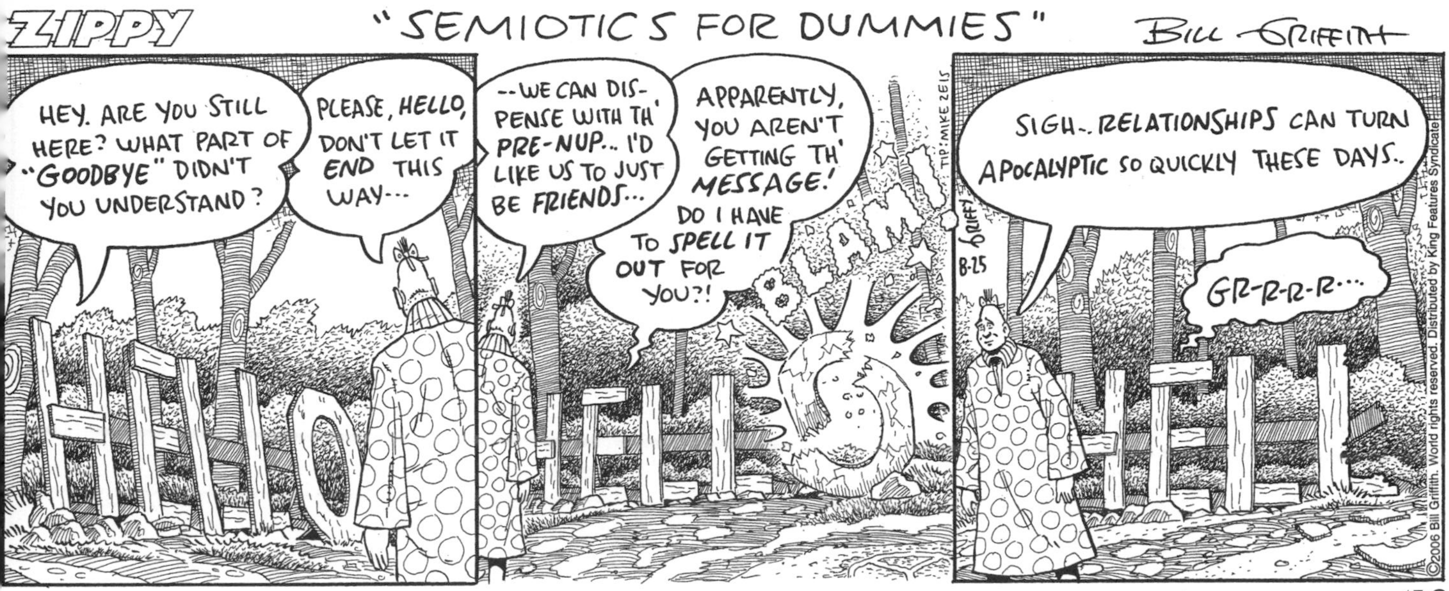
ZIPPY
"SEMIOTICS FOR DUMMIES"
BILL GRIFFITH
HEY. ARE YOU STILL HERE? WHAT PART OF "GOODBYE" DIDN'T YOU UNDERSTAND?
PLEASE, HELLO, DON'T LET IT END THIS WAY...
--WE CAN DISPENSE WITH TH' PRE-NUP.. I'D LIKE US TO JUST BE FRIENDS...
APPARENTLY, YOU AREN'T GETTING TH' MESSAGE!
DO I HAVE TO SPELL IT OUT FOR YOU?!
BLAM!!
TIP: MIKE ZEIS
GRIFFY 8-25
SIGH.. RELATIONSHIPS CAN TURN APOCALYPTIC SO QUICKLY THESE DAYS..
GR-R-R-R...
©2006 Bill Griffith. World rights reserved. Distributed by King Features Syndicate

47 C

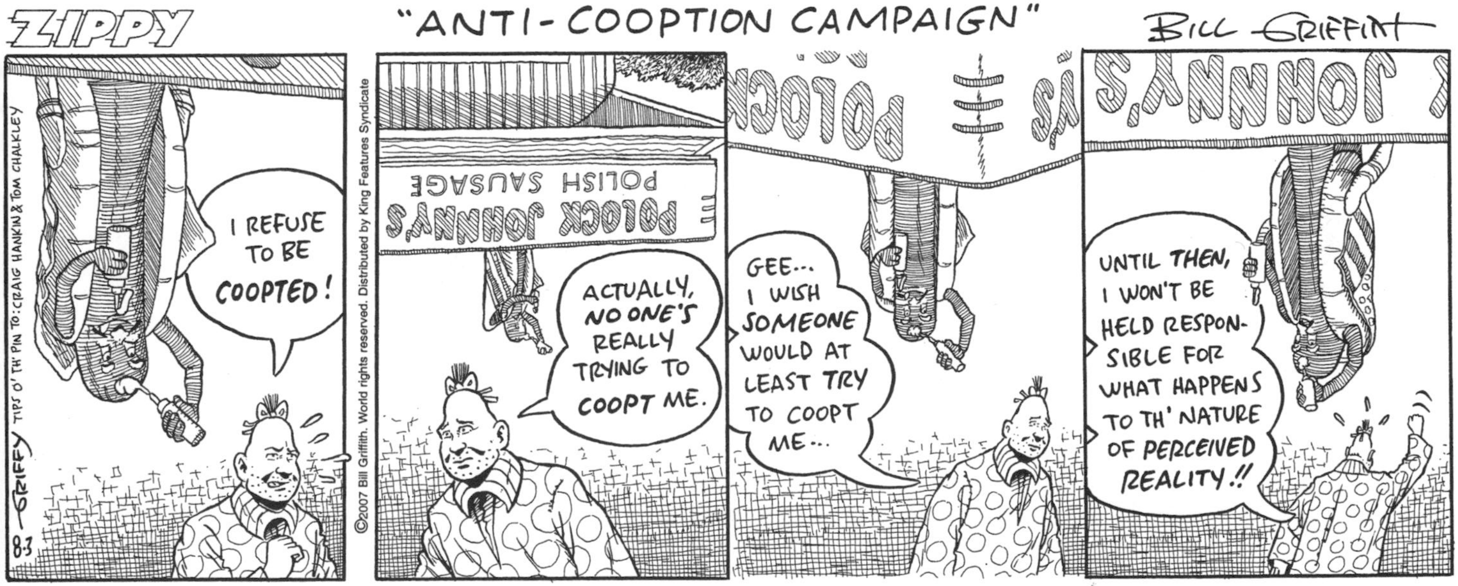
ZIPPY
"ANTI-COOPTION CAMPAIGN"
BILL GRIFFITH
GRIFFY 8-3
TIPS O' TH' PIN TO: CRAIG HANKIN & TOM CHALKLEY
I REFUSE TO BE COOPTED!
©2007 Bill Griffith. World rights reserved. Distributed by King Features Syndicate
POLOCK JOHNNY'S
POLISH SAUSAGE
ACTUALLY, NO ONE'S REALLY TRYING TO COOPT ME.
GEE... I WISH SOMEONE WOULD AT LEAST TRY TO COOPT ME...
JOHNNY'S
UNTIL THEN, I WON'T BE HELD RESPONSIBLE FOR WHAT HAPPENS TO TH' NATURE OF PERCEIVED REALITY!!

48

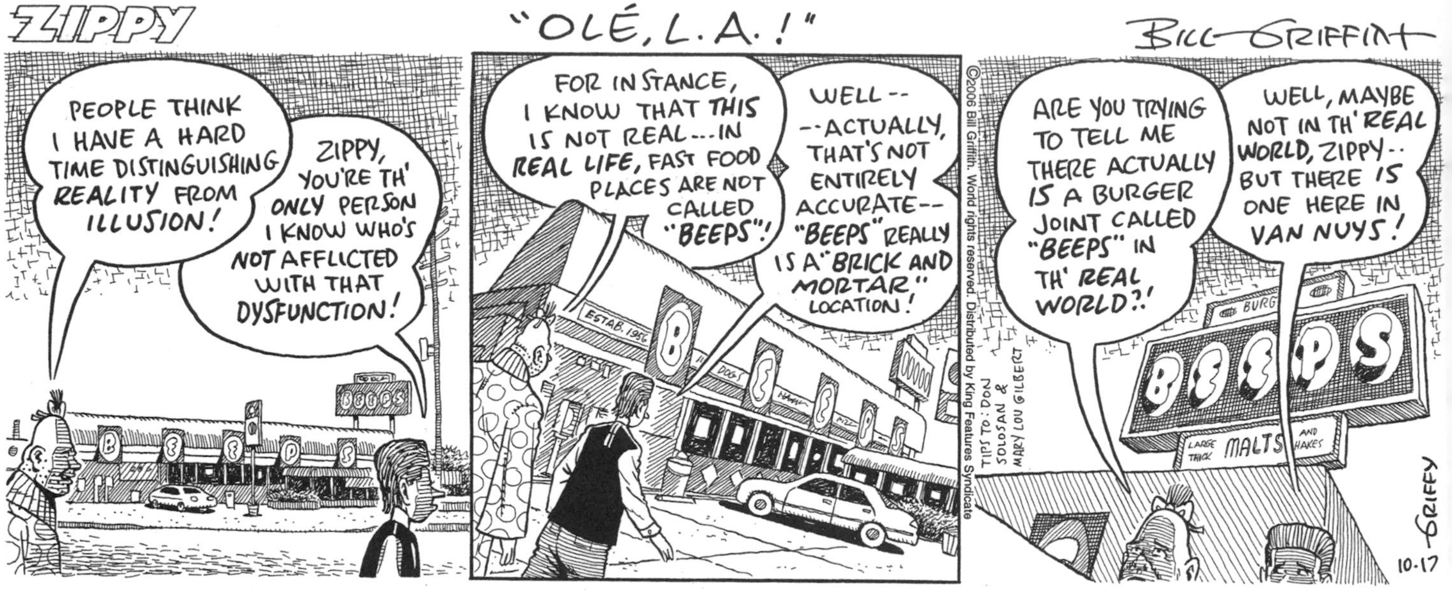
ZIPPY
"OLÉ, L.A.!"
BILL GRIFFITH
PEOPLE THINK I HAVE A HARD TIME DISTINGUISHING REALITY FROM ILLUSION!
ZIPPY, YOU'RE TH' ONLY PERSON I KNOW WHO'S NOT AFFLICTED WITH THAT DYSFUNCTION!
FOR INSTANCE, I KNOW THAT THIS IS NOT REAL---IN REAL LIFE, FAST FOOD PLACES ARE NOT CALLED "BEEPS"!
WELL--
--ACTUALLY, THAT'S NOT ENTIRELY ACCURATE-- "BEEPS" REALLY IS A "BRICK AND MORTAR" LOCATION!
ESTAB. 1956
©2006 Bill Griffith. World rights reserved. Distributed by King Features Syndicate
TIPS TO: DON SOLOSAN & MARY LOU GILBERT
ARE YOU TRYING TO TELL ME THERE ACTUALLY IS A BURGER JOINT CALLED "BEEPS" IN TH' REAL WORLD?!
WELL, MAYBE NOT IN TH' REAL WORLD, ZIPPY.. BUT THERE IS ONE HERE IN VAN NUYS!
BEEPS
LARGE THICK MALTS
GRIFFY
10.17

49

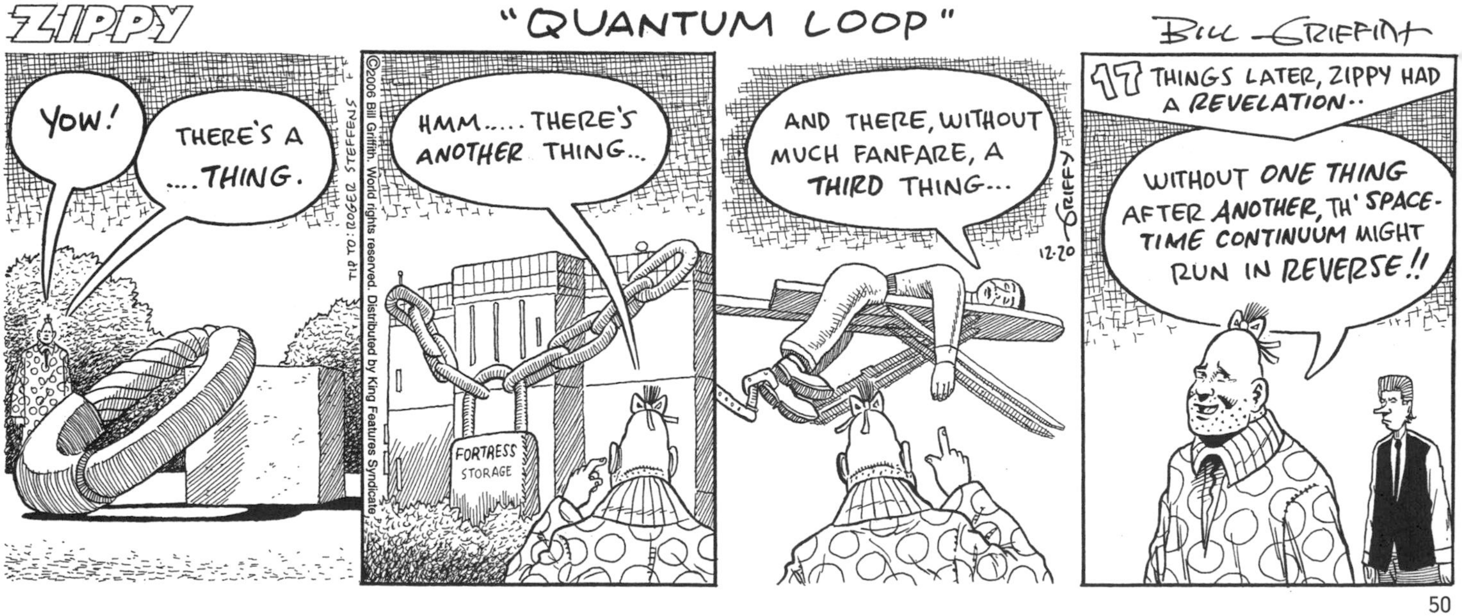
ZIPPY
"QUANTUM LOOP"
BILL GRIFFITH
YOW!
THERE'S A ....THING.
TIP TO: ROGER STEFFENS
©2006 Bill Griffith. World rights reserved. Distributed by King Features Syndicate
HMM..... THERE'S ANOTHER THING...
FORTRESS STORAGE
AND THERE, WITHOUT MUCH FANFARE, A THIRD THING...
GRIFFY
12.20
17 THINGS LATER, ZIPPY HAD A REVELATION..
WITHOUT ONE THING AFTER ANOTHER, TH' SPACE-TIME CONTINUUM MIGHT RUN IN REVERSE!!

50

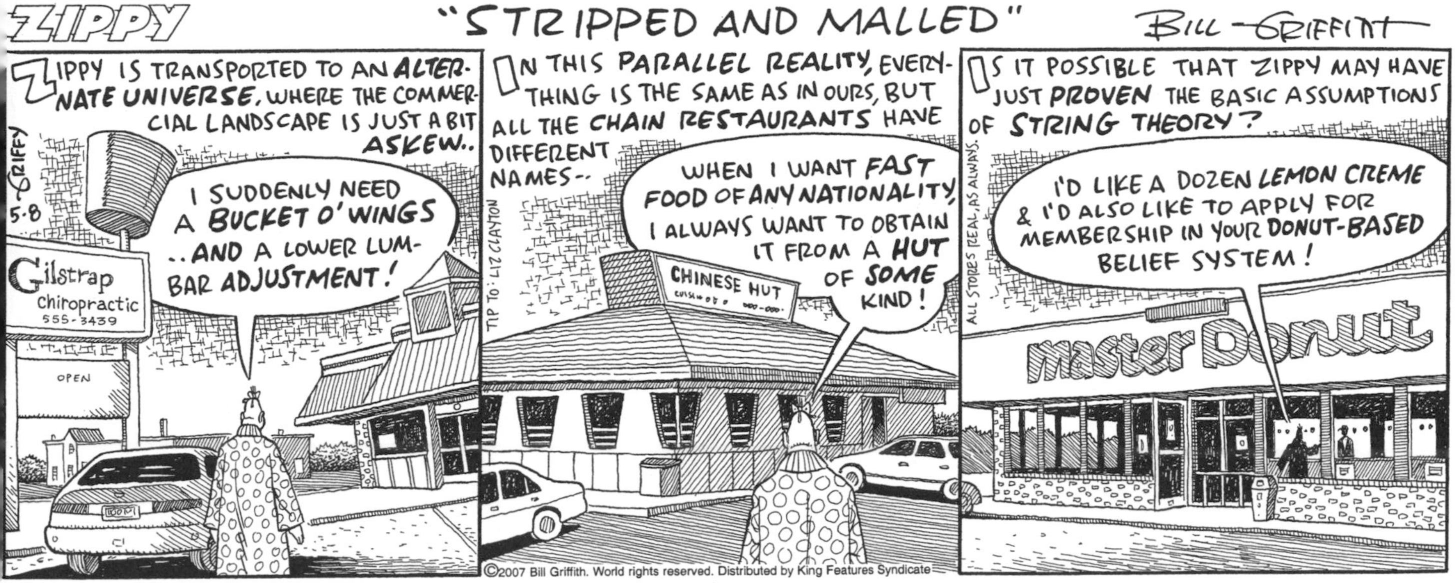
ZIPPY
"STRIPPED AND MALLED"
BILL GRIFFITH
ZIPPY IS TRANSPORTED TO AN ALTERNATE UNIVERSE, WHERE THE COMMERCIAL LANDSCAPE IS JUST A BIT ASKEW..
GRIFFY 5-8
Gilstrap Chiropractic 555-3439
OPEN
I SUDDENLY NEED A BUCKET O' WINGS ..AND A LOWER LUMBAR ADJUSTMENT!
IN THIS PARALLEL REALITY, EVERYTHING IS THE SAME AS IN OURS, BUT ALL THE CHAIN RESTAURANTS HAVE DIFFERENT NAMES--
TIP TO: LIZ CLAYTON
CHINESE HUT
WHEN I WANT FAST FOOD OF ANY NATIONALITY, I ALWAYS WANT TO OBTAIN IT FROM A HUT OF SOME KIND!
IS IT POSSIBLE THAT ZIPPY MAY HAVE JUST PROVEN THE BASIC ASSUMPTIONS OF STRING THEORY?
ALL STORES REAL, AS ALWAYS.
I'D LIKE A DOZEN LEMON CREME & I'D ALSO LIKE TO APPLY FOR MEMBERSHIP IN YOUR DONUT-BASED BELIEF SYSTEM!
master Donut
©2007 Bill Griffith. World rights reserved. Distributed by King Features Syndicate

51

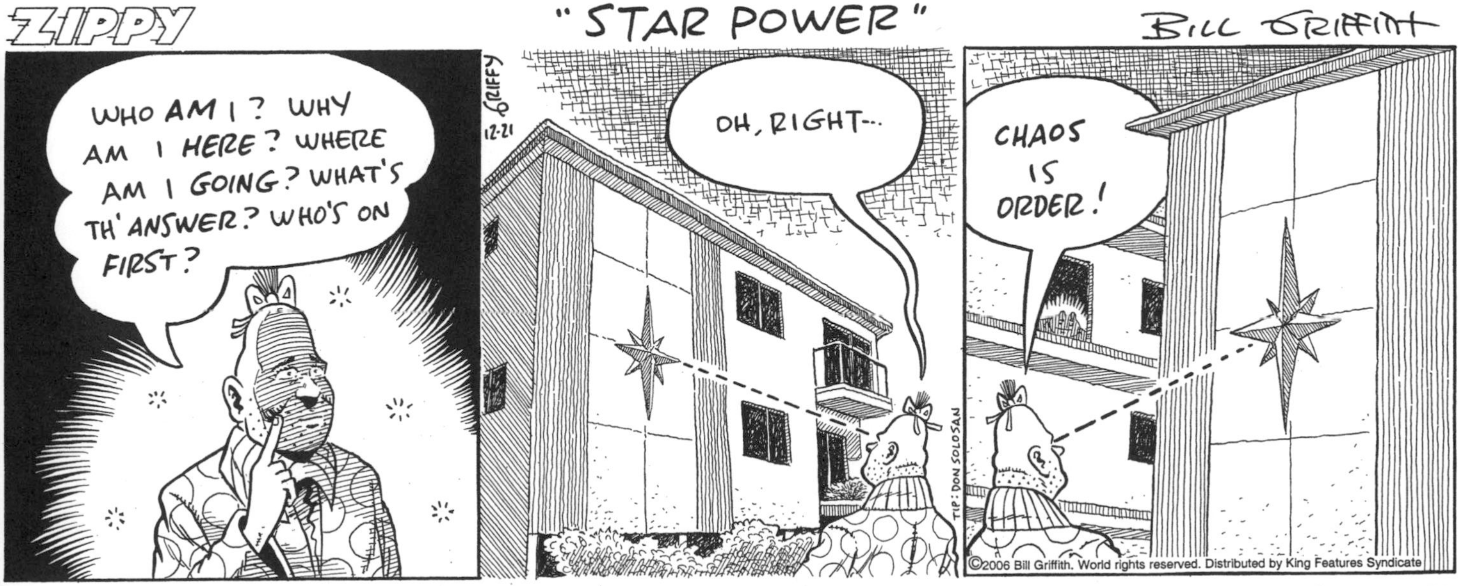
ZIPPY
"STAR POWER"
BILL GRIFFITH
WHO AM I? WHY AM I HERE? WHERE AM I GOING? WHAT'S TH' ANSWER? WHO'S ON FIRST?
GRIFFY 12-21
OH, RIGHT--
TIP: DON SOLOSAN
CHAOS IS ORDER!
©2006 Bill Griffith. World rights reserved. Distributed by King Features Syndicate

52

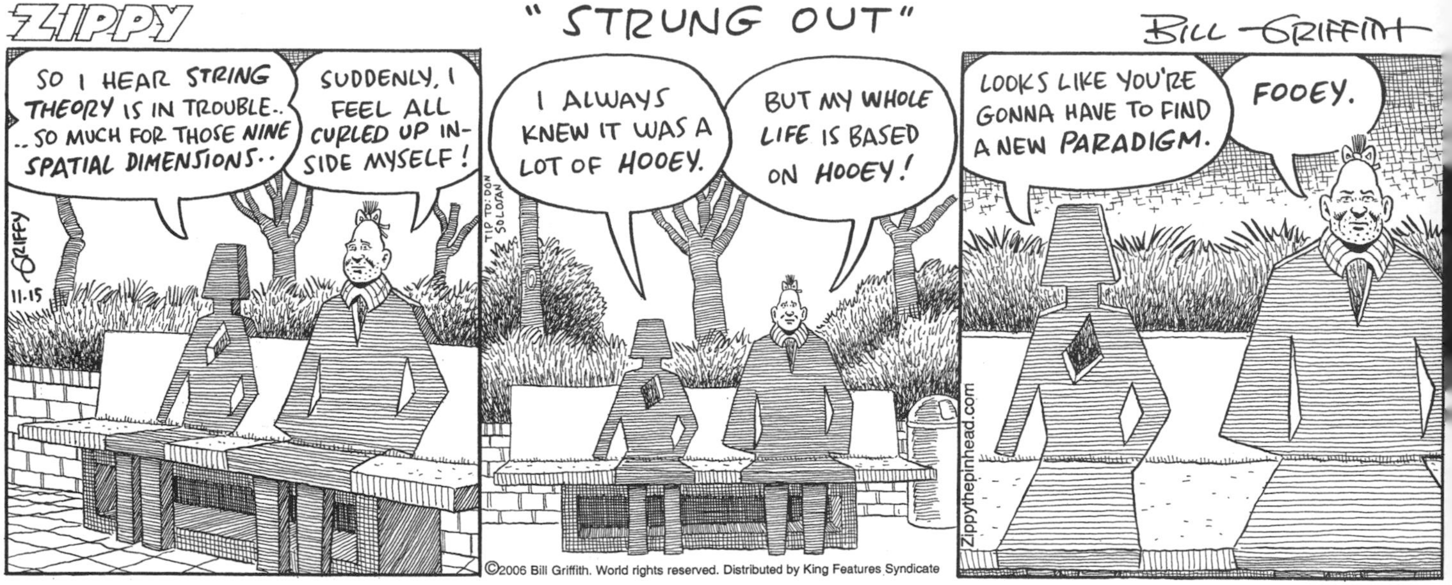
ZIPPY
"STRUNG OUT"
BILL GRIFFITH
SO I HEAR STRING THEORY IS IN TROUBLE.. ..SO MUCH FOR THOSE NINE SPATIAL DIMENSIONS..
SUDDENLY, I FEEL ALL CURLED UP INSIDE MYSELF!
GRIFFY 11-15
TIP TO: DON SOLOSAN
I ALWAYS KNEW IT WAS A LOT OF HOOEY.
BUT MY WHOLE LIFE IS BASED ON HOOEY!
©2006 Bill Griffith. World rights reserved. Distributed by King Features Syndicate
LOOKS LIKE YOU'RE GONNA HAVE TO FIND A NEW PARADIGM.
FOOEY.
Zippythepinhead.com

53

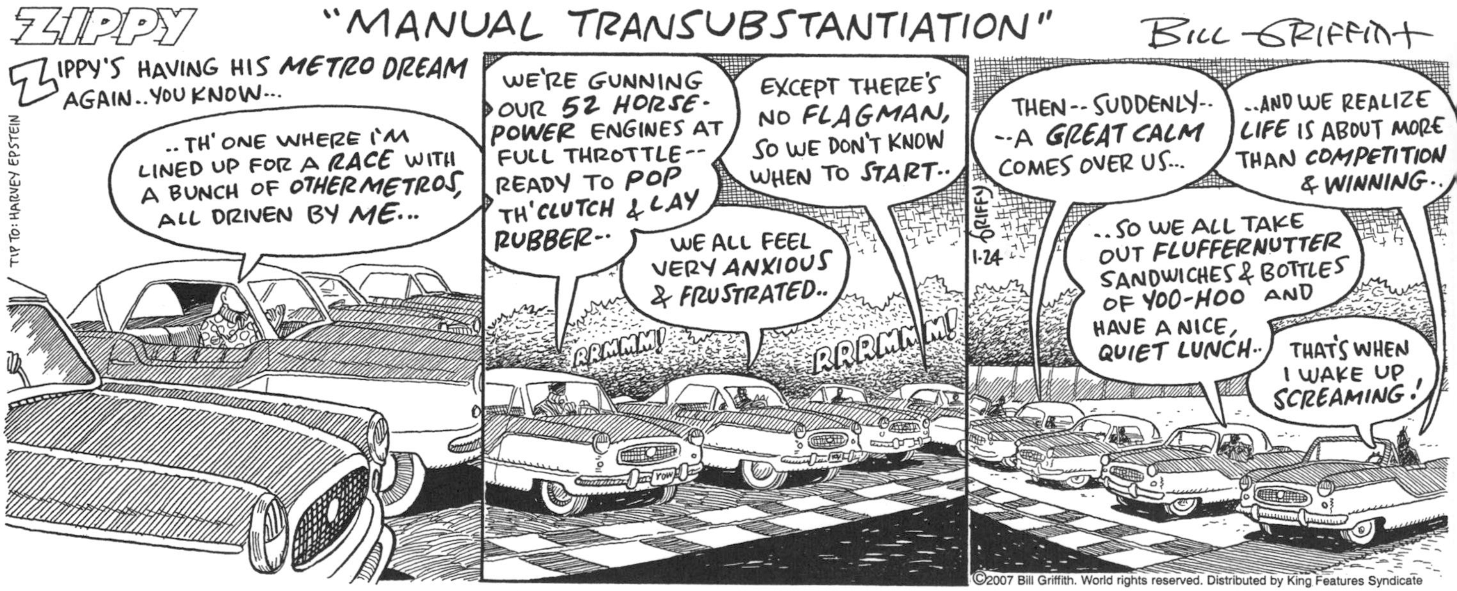
ZIPPY
"MANUAL TRANSUBSTANTIATION"
BILL GRIFFITH
ZIPPY'S HAVING HIS METRO DREAM AGAIN..YOU KNOW...
TIP TO: HARVEY EPSTEIN
..TH' ONE WHERE I'M LINED UP FOR A RACE WITH A BUNCH OF OTHER METROS, ALL DRIVEN BY ME...
WE'RE GUNNING OUR 52 HORSE-POWER ENGINES AT FULL THROTTLE--READY TO POP TH' CLUTCH & LAY RUBBER..
EXCEPT THERE'S NO FLAGMAN, SO WE DON'T KNOW WHEN TO START..
WE ALL FEEL VERY ANXIOUS & FRUSTRATED..
RRMMM!
RRRMMM!
GRIFFY 1-24
THEN--SUDDENLY-- --A GREAT CALM COMES OVER US...
..AND WE REALIZE LIFE IS ABOUT MORE THAN COMPETITION & WINNING..
..SO WE ALL TAKE OUT FLUFFERNUTTER SANDWICHES & BOTTLES OF YOO-HOO AND HAVE A NICE, QUIET LUNCH..
THAT'S WHEN I WAKE UP SCREAMING!
©2007 Bill Griffith. World rights reserved. Distributed by King Features Syndicate

54 A

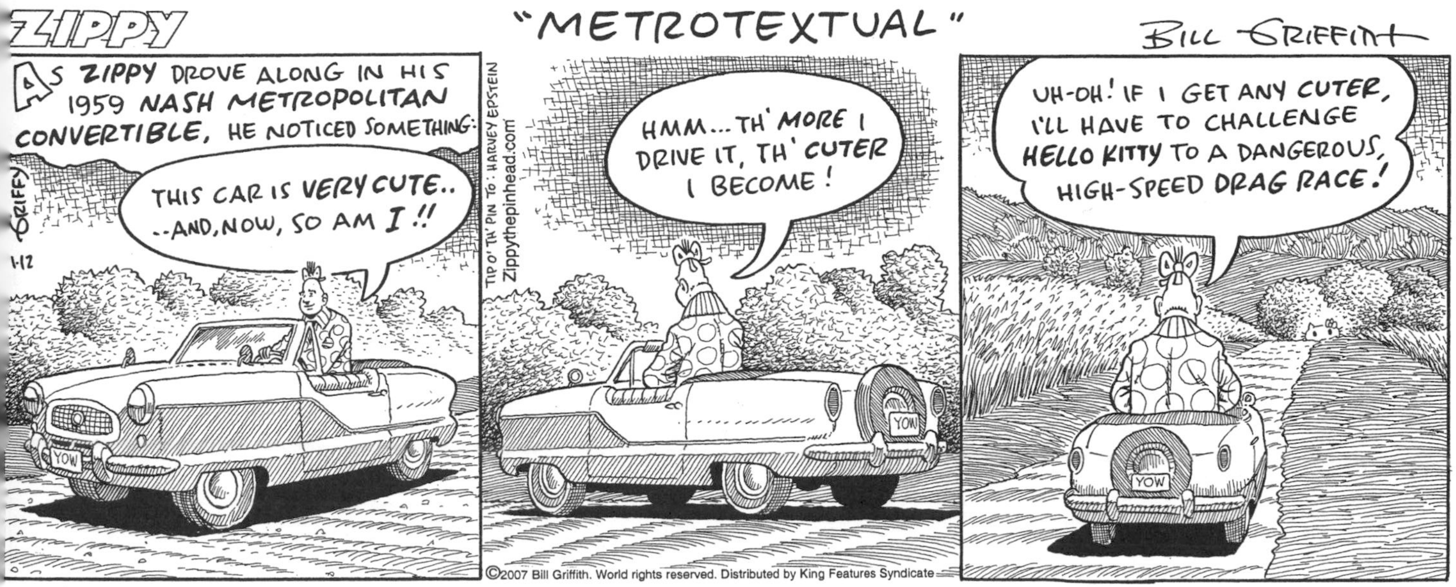
ZIPPY
"METROTEXTUAL"
BILL GRIFFITH
AS ZIPPY DROVE ALONG IN HIS 1959 NASH METROPOLITAN CONVERTIBLE, HE NOTICED SOMETHING:
THIS CAR IS VERY CUTE.. ..AND, NOW, SO AM I !!
GRIFFY 1-12
YOW
TIP O' TH' PIN TO: HARVEY EPSTEIN
Zippythepinhead.com
HMM... TH' MORE I DRIVE IT, TH' CUTER I BECOME!
YOW
UH-OH! IF I GET ANY CUTER, I'LL HAVE TO CHALLENGE HELLO KITTY TO A DANGEROUS, HIGH-SPEED DRAG RACE!
YOW
©2007 Bill Griffith. World rights reserved. Distributed by King Features Syndicate

54 B

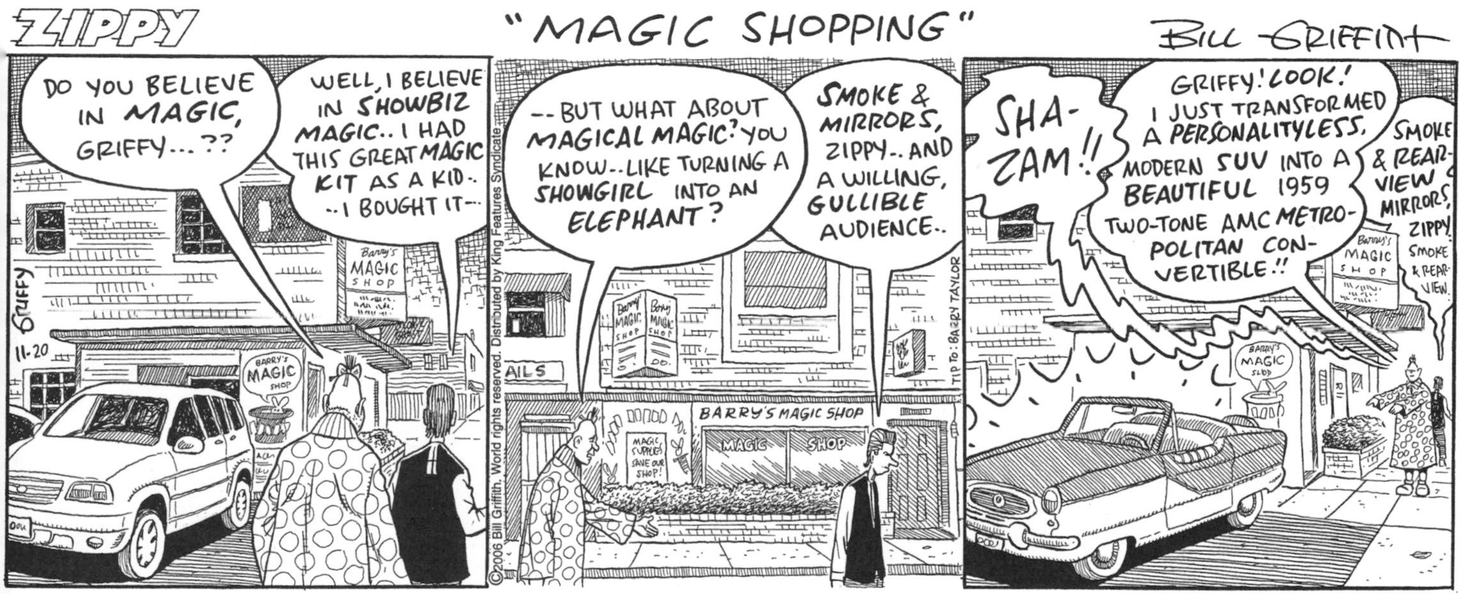
ZIPPY
"MAGIC SHOPPING"
BILL GRIFFITH
DO YOU BELIEVE IN MAGIC, GRIFFY...??
WELL, I BELIEVE IN SHOWBIZ MAGIC.. I HAD THIS GREAT MAGIC KIT AS A KID.. ..I BOUGHT IT..
Barry's MAGIC SHOP
BARRY'S MAGIC SHOP
GRIFFY 11-20
©2006 Bill Griffith. World rights reserved. Distributed by King Features Syndicate
--BUT WHAT ABOUT MAGICAL MAGIC? YOU KNOW..LIKE TURNING A SHOWGIRL INTO AN ELEPHANT?
SMOKE & MIRRORS, ZIPPY.. AND A WILLING, GULLIBLE AUDIENCE..
BARRY'S MAGIC SHOP
MAGIC SHOP
MAGIC SUPPLIES SAVE OUR SHOP!
TIP TO: BARRY TAYLOR
SHA-ZAM!!
GRIFFY! LOOK! I JUST TRANSFORMED A PERSONALITYLESS, MODERN SUV INTO A BEAUTIFUL 1959 TWO-TONE AMC METROPOLITAN CONVERTIBLE!!
SMOKE & REAR-VIEW MIRRORS, ZIPPY. SMOKE & REAR-VIEW.
Barry's MAGIC SHOP

55

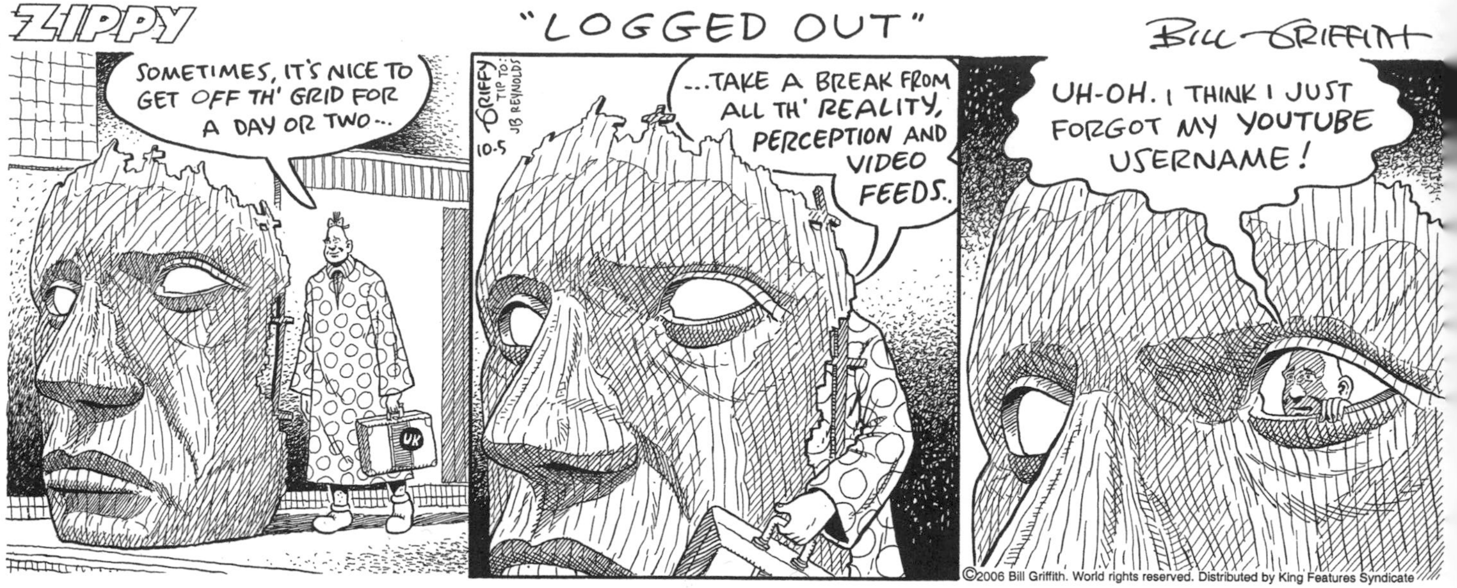
ZIPPY
"LOGGED OUT"
BILL GRIFFITH
SOMETIMES, IT'S NICE TO GET OFF TH' GRID FOR A DAY OR TWO...
GRIFFY TIP TO: JB REYNOLDS 10.5
...TAKE A BREAK FROM ALL TH' REALITY, PERCEPTION AND VIDEO FEEDS..
UH-OH. I THINK I JUST FORGOT MY YOUTUBE USERNAME!
©2006 Bill Griffith. World rights reserved. Distributed by King Features Syndicate

56

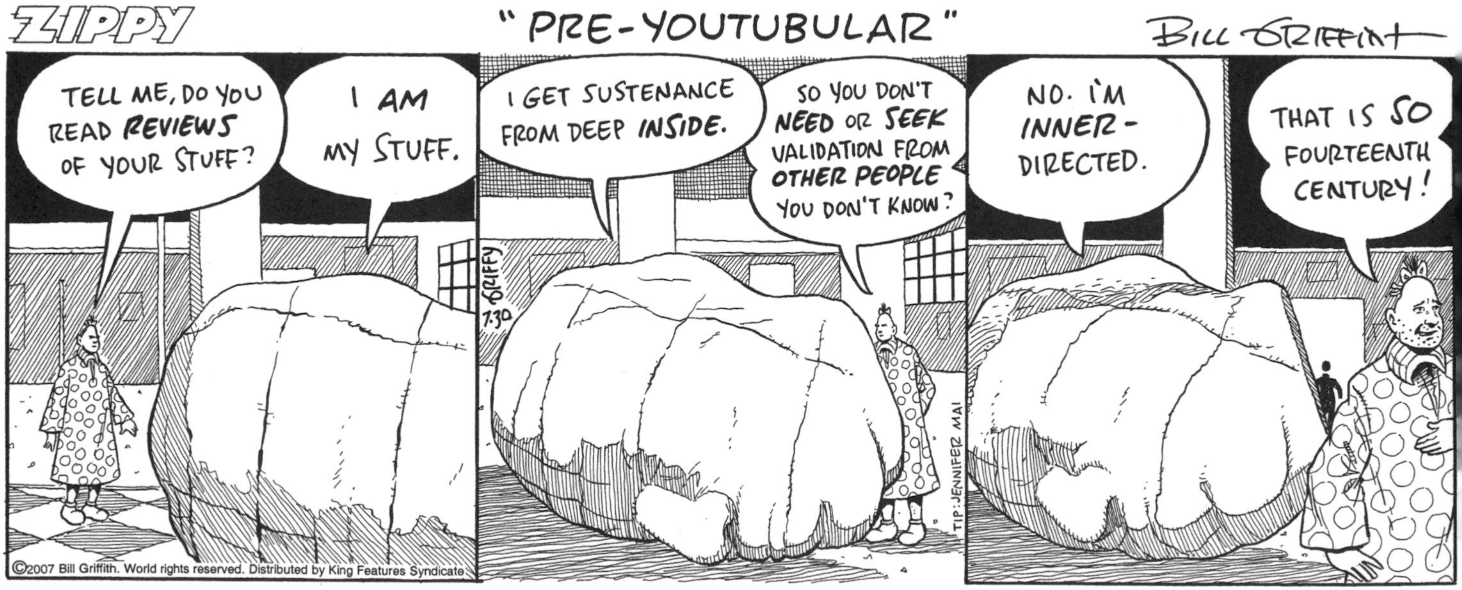
ZIPPY
"PRE-YOUTUBULAR"
BILL GRIFFITH
TELL ME, DO YOU READ REVIEWS OF YOUR STUFF?
I AM MY STUFF.
I GET SUSTENANCE FROM DEEP INSIDE.
SO YOU DON'T NEED OR SEEK VALIDATION FROM OTHER PEOPLE YOU DON'T KNOW?
GRIFFY 7.30
TIP: JENNIFER MAI
NO. I'M INNER-DIRECTED.
THAT IS SO FOURTEENTH CENTURY!
©2007 Bill Griffith. World rights reserved. Distributed by King Features Syndicate

57

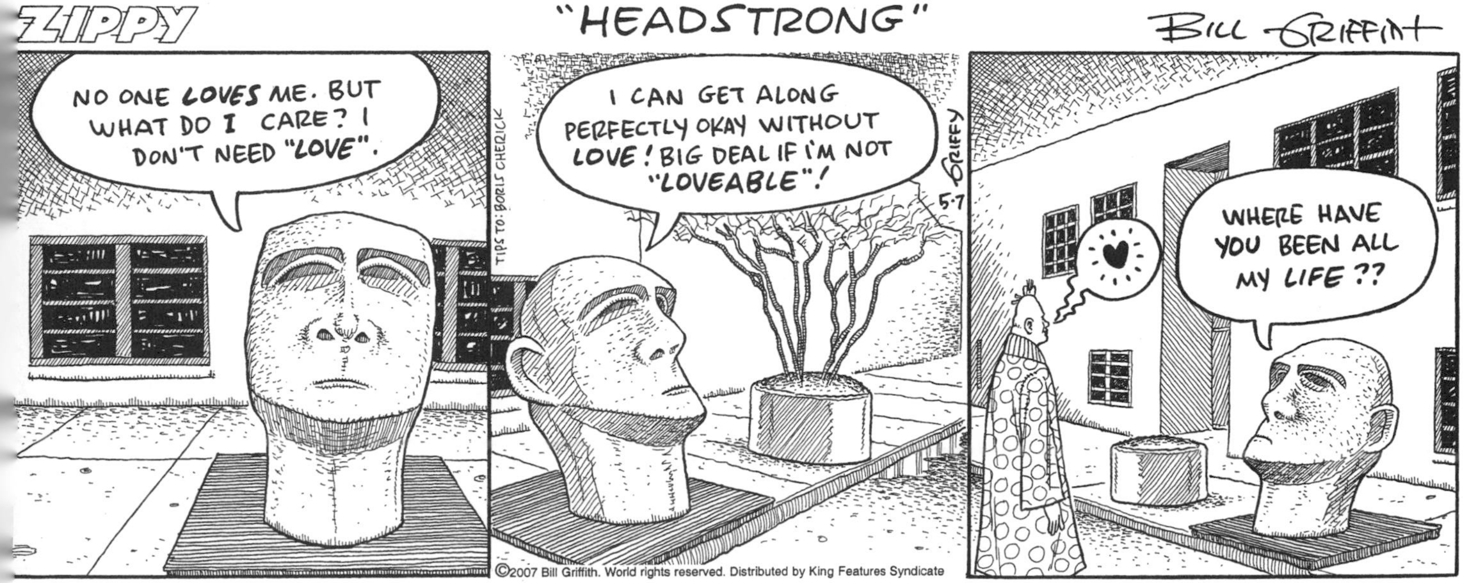
ZIPPY
"HEADSTRONG"
BILL GRIFFITH
NO ONE LOVES ME. BUT WHAT DO I CARE? I DON'T NEED "LOVE".
TIPS TO: BORIS CHERICK
I CAN GET ALONG PERFECTLY OKAY WITHOUT LOVE! BIG DEAL IF I'M NOT "LOVEABLE"!
GRIFFY
5·7
WHERE HAVE YOU BEEN ALL MY LIFE??
©2007 Bill Griffith. World rights reserved. Distributed by King Features Syndicate

58

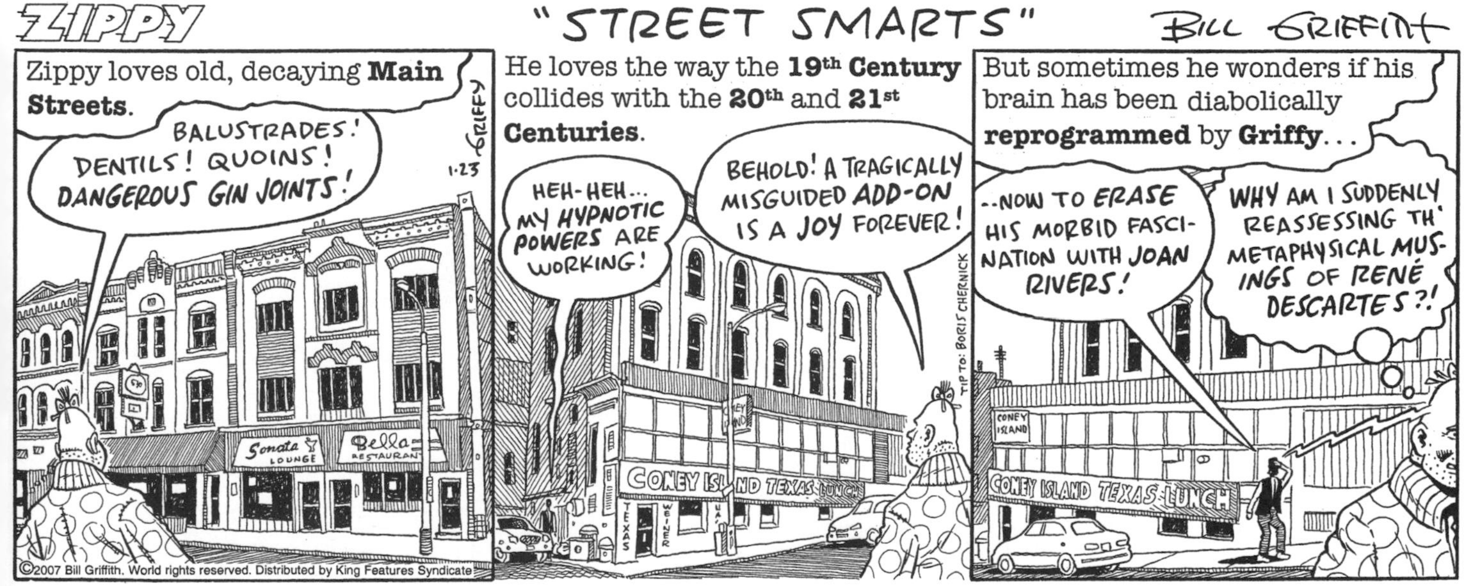
ZIPPY
"STREET SMARTS"
BILL GRIFFITH
Zippy loves old, decaying **Main Streets**.
BALUSTRADES! DENTILS! QUOINS! DANGEROUS GIN JOINTS!
GRIFFY
1·23
Sonata LOUNGE
Bella RESTAURANT
©2007 Bill Griffith. World rights reserved. Distributed by King Features Syndicate
He loves the way the **19th Century** collides with the **20th** and **21st Centuries**.
HEH-HEH... MY HYPNOTIC POWERS ARE WORKING!
BEHOLD! A TRAGICALLY MISGUIDED ADD-ON IS A JOY FOREVER!
TIP TO: BORIS CHERNICK
CONEY ISLAND TEXAS LUNCH
But sometimes he wonders if his brain has been diabolically **reprogrammed** by **Griffy**...
--NOW TO ERASE HIS MORBID FASCINATION WITH JOAN RIVERS!
WHY AM I SUDDENLY REASSESSING TH' METAPHYSICAL MUSINGS OF RENÉ DESCARTES?!
CONEY ISLAND
CONEY ISLAND TEXAS LUNCH

59

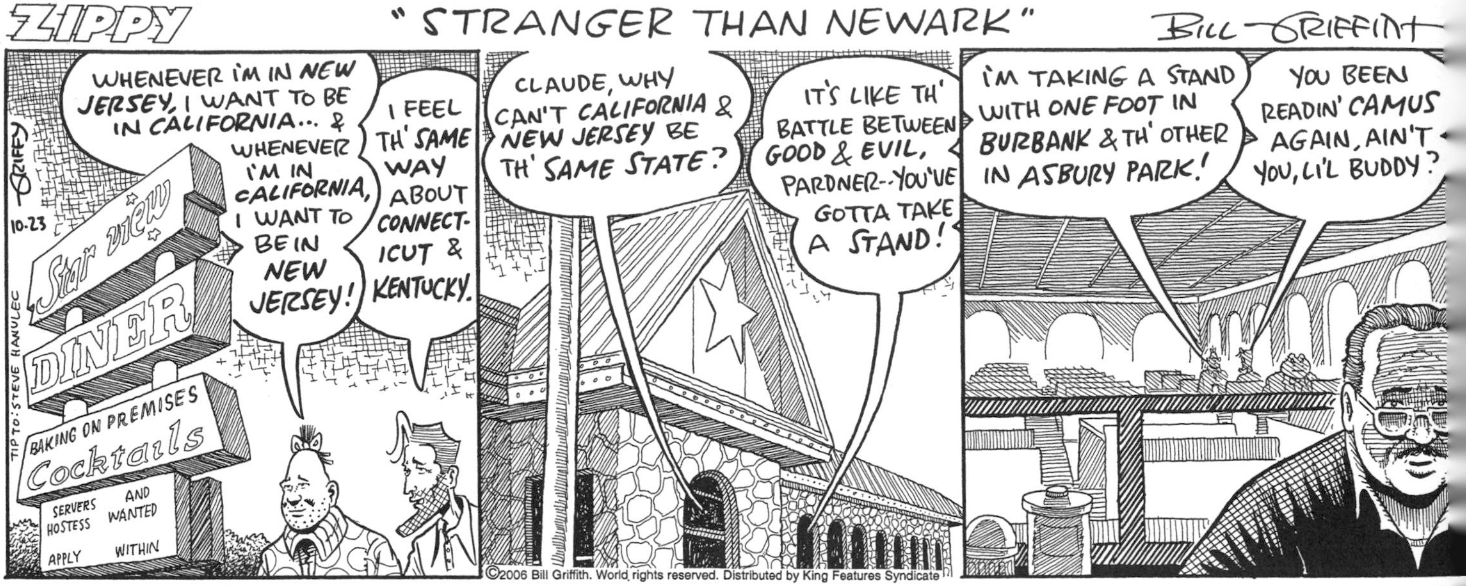
ZIPPY
"STRANGER THAN NEWARK"
BILL GRIFFITH
GRIFFY
10-23
TIP TO: STEVE HANULEC
WHENEVER I'M IN NEW JERSEY, I WANT TO BE IN CALIFORNIA... & WHENEVER I'M IN CALIFORNIA, I WANT TO BE IN NEW JERSEY!
I FEEL TH' SAME WAY ABOUT CONNECTICUT & KENTUCKY.
Star view
DINER
BAKING ON PREMISES
Cocktails
SERVERS AND HOSTESS WANTED
APPLY WITHIN
CLAUDE, WHY CAN'T CALIFORNIA & NEW JERSEY BE TH' SAME STATE?
IT'S LIKE TH' BATTLE BETWEEN GOOD & EVIL, PARDNER--YOU'VE GOTTA TAKE A STAND!
I'M TAKING A STAND WITH ONE FOOT IN BURBANK & TH' OTHER IN ASBURY PARK!
YOU BEEN READIN' CAMUS AGAIN, AIN'T YOU, LI'L BUDDY?
©2006 Bill Griffith. World rights reserved. Distributed by King Features Syndicate

60

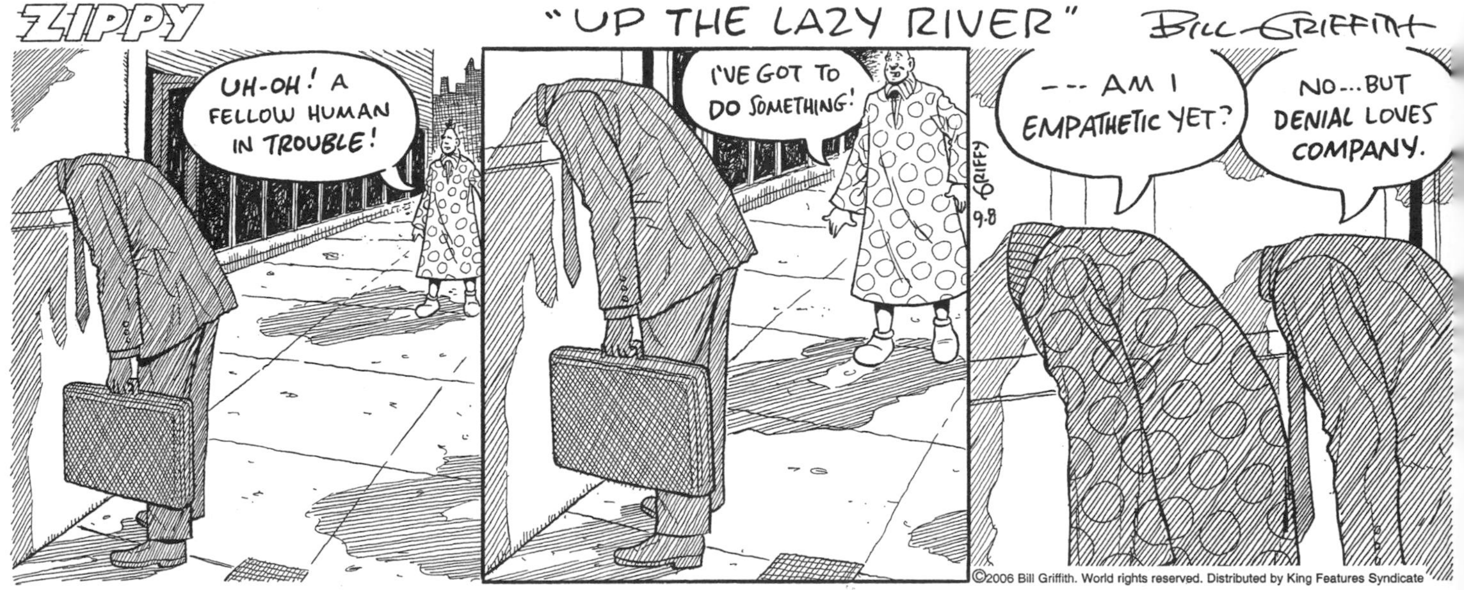
ZIPPY
"UP THE LAZY RIVER"
BILL GRIFFITH
UH-OH! A FELLOW HUMAN IN TROUBLE!
I'VE GOT TO DO SOMETHING!
GRIFFY
9-8
--- AM I EMPATHETIC YET?
NO... BUT DENIAL LOVES COMPANY.
©2006 Bill Griffith. World rights reserved. Distributed by King Features Syndicate

61

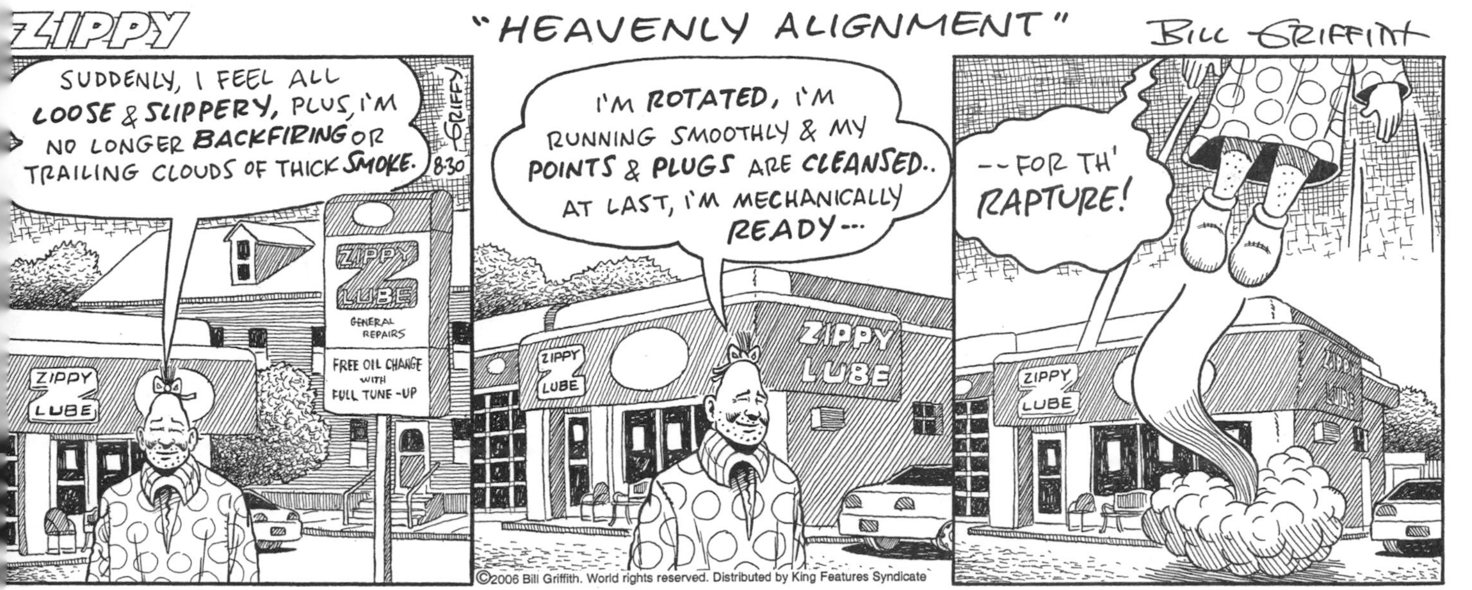
ZIPPY
"HEAVENLY ALIGNMENT"
BILL GRIFFITH
SUDDENLY, I FEEL ALL LOOSE & SLIPPERY, PLUS, I'M NO LONGER BACKFIRING OR TRAILING CLOUDS OF THICK SMOKE.
GRIFFY 8-30
ZIPPY Z LUBE
GENERAL REPAIRS
FREE OIL CHANGE WITH FULL TUNE-UP
ZIPPY LUBE
I'M ROTATED, I'M RUNNING SMOOTHLY & MY POINTS & PLUGS ARE CLEANSED.. AT LAST, I'M MECHANICALLY READY--
ZIPPY LUBE
--FOR TH' RAPTURE!
©2006 Bill Griffith. World rights reserved. Distributed by King Features Syndicate

62

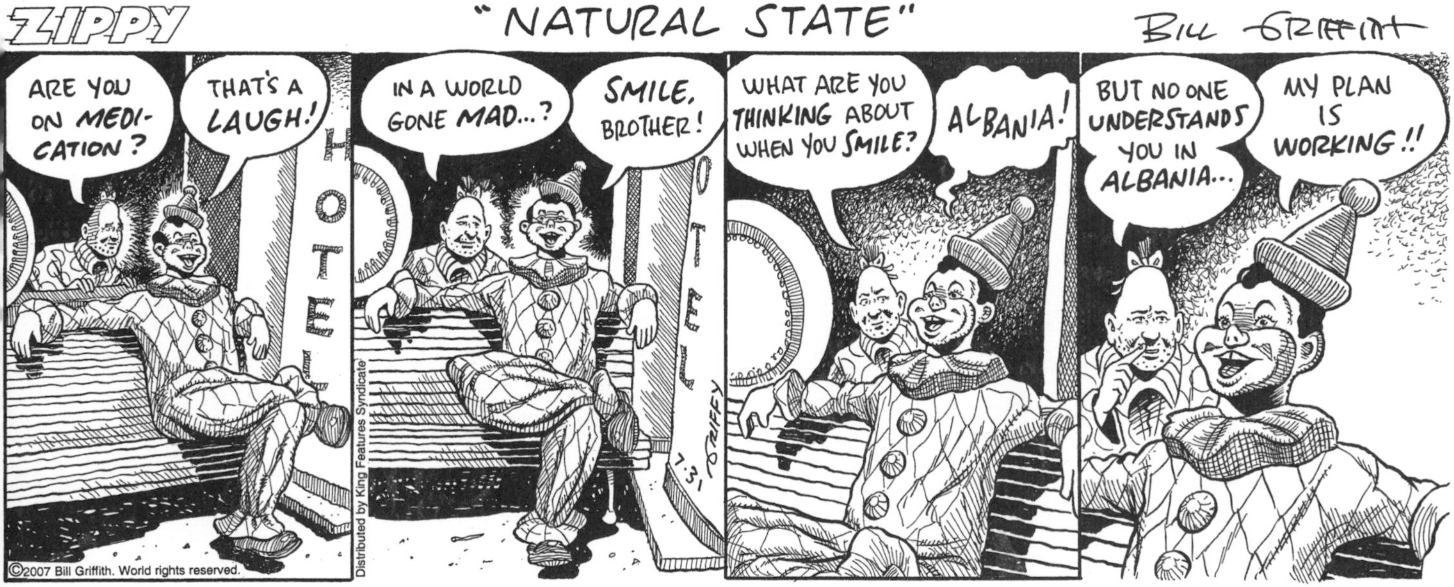
ZIPPY
"NATURAL STATE"
BILL GRIFFITH
ARE YOU ON MEDICATION?
THAT'S A LAUGH!
HOTEL
IN A WORLD GONE MAD...?
SMILE, BROTHER!
GRIFFY 7-31
WHAT ARE YOU THINKING ABOUT WHEN YOU SMILE?
ALBANIA!
BUT NO ONE UNDERSTANDS YOU IN ALBANIA...
MY PLAN IS WORKING!!
©2007 Bill Griffith. World rights reserved.
Distributed by King Features Syndicate

63

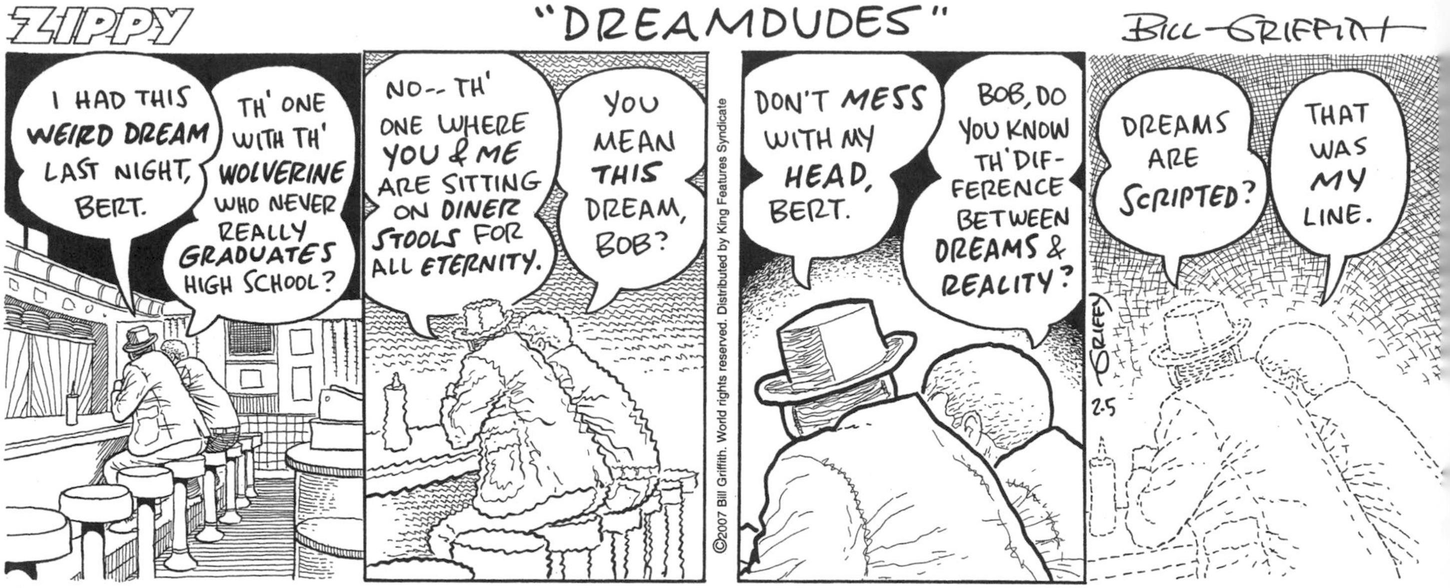

ZIPPY
"DREAMDUDES"
BILL GRIFFITH
I HAD THIS WEIRD DREAM LAST NIGHT, BERT.
TH' ONE WITH TH' WOLVERINE WHO NEVER REALLY GRADUATES HIGH SCHOOL?
NO-- TH' ONE WHERE YOU & ME ARE SITTING ON DINER STOOLS FOR ALL ETERNITY.
YOU MEAN THIS DREAM, BOB?
©2007 Bill Griffith. World rights reserved. Distributed by King Features Syndicate
DON'T MESS WITH MY HEAD, BERT.
BOB, DO YOU KNOW TH' DIF-FERENCE BETWEEN DREAMS & REALITY?
DREAMS ARE SCRIPTED?
THAT WAS MY LINE.
GRIFFY
2-5

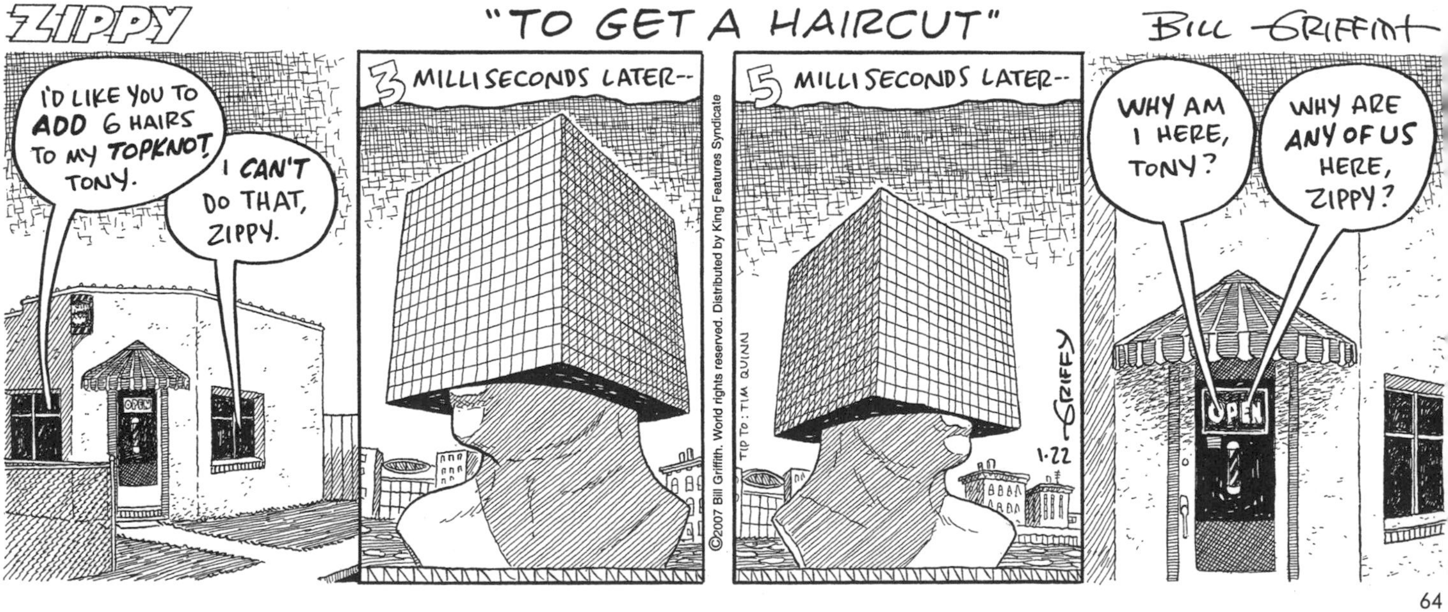

ZIPPY
"TO GET A HAIRCUT"
BILL GRIFFITH
I'D LIKE YOU TO ADD 6 HAIRS TO MY TOPKNOT, TONY.
I CAN'T DO THAT, ZIPPY.
OPEN
3 MILLISECONDS LATER--
©2007 Bill Griffith. World rights reserved. Distributed by King Features Syndicate
5 MILLISECONDS LATER--
TIP TO: TIM QUINN
GRIFFY
1-22
WHY AM I HERE, TONY?
WHY ARE ANY OF US HERE, ZIPPY?
OPEN

64

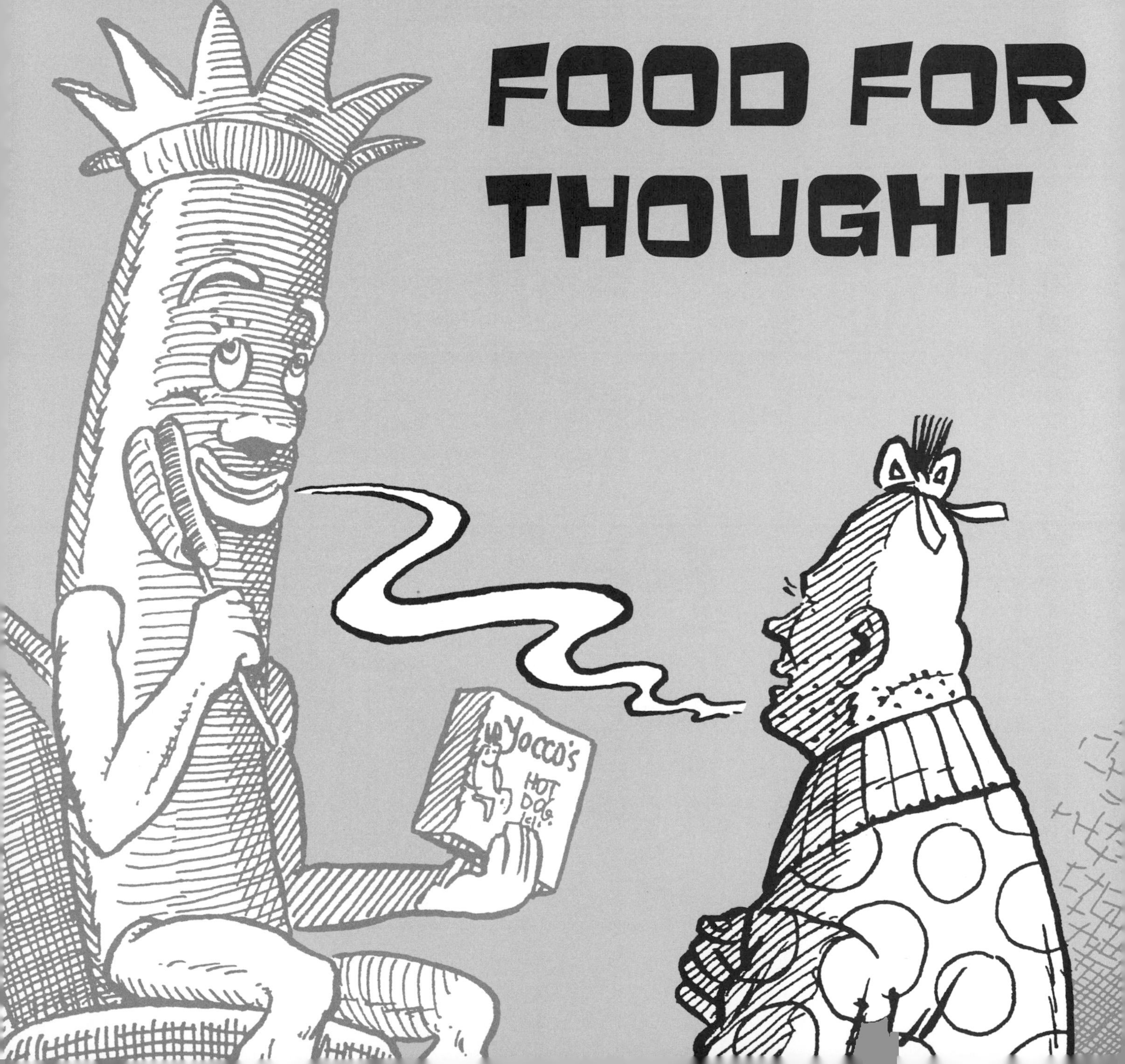
FOOD FOR THOUGHT
Yocco's
HOT DOG

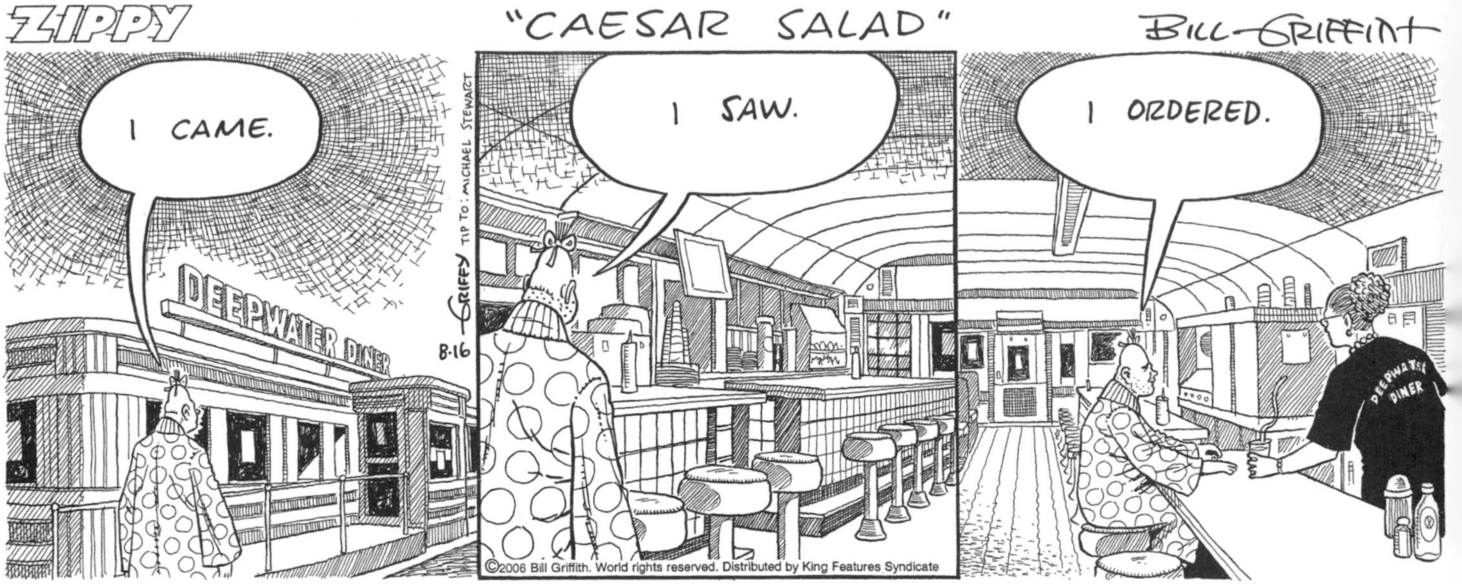
ZIPPY
"CAESAR SALAD"
BILL GRIFFITH
I CAME.
DEEPWATER DINER
GRIFFY 8-16
TIP TO: MICHAEL STEWART
I SAW.
I ORDERED.
DEEPWATER DINER
©2006 Bill Griffith. World rights reserved. Distributed by King Features Syndicate

65

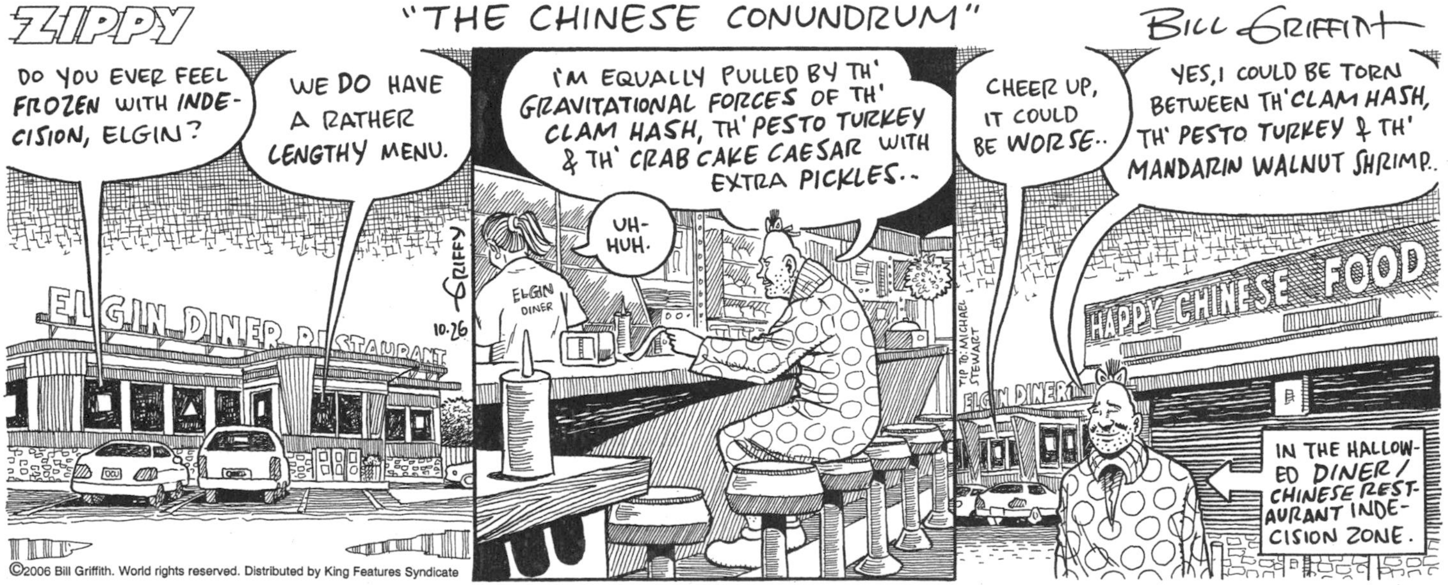
ZIPPY
"THE CHINESE CONUNDRUM"
BILL GRIFFITH
DO YOU EVER FEEL FROZEN WITH INDECISION, ELGIN?
WE DO HAVE A RATHER LENGTHY MENU.
ELGIN DINER RESTAURANT
GRIFFY 10-26
I'M EQUALLY PULLED BY TH' GRAVITATIONAL FORCES OF TH' CLAM HASH, TH' PESTO TURKEY & TH' CRAB CAKE CAESAR WITH EXTRA PICKLES..
UH-HUH.
ELGIN DINER
CHEER UP, IT COULD BE WORSE..
YES, I COULD BE TORN BETWEEN TH' CLAM HASH, TH' PESTO TURKEY & TH' MANDARIN WALNUT SHRIMP..
HAPPY CHINESE FOOD
TIP TO: MICHAEL STEWART
ELGIN DINER
IN THE HALLOWED DINER / CHINESE RESTAURANT INDECISION ZONE.
©2006 Bill Griffith. World rights reserved. Distributed by King Features Syndicate

66

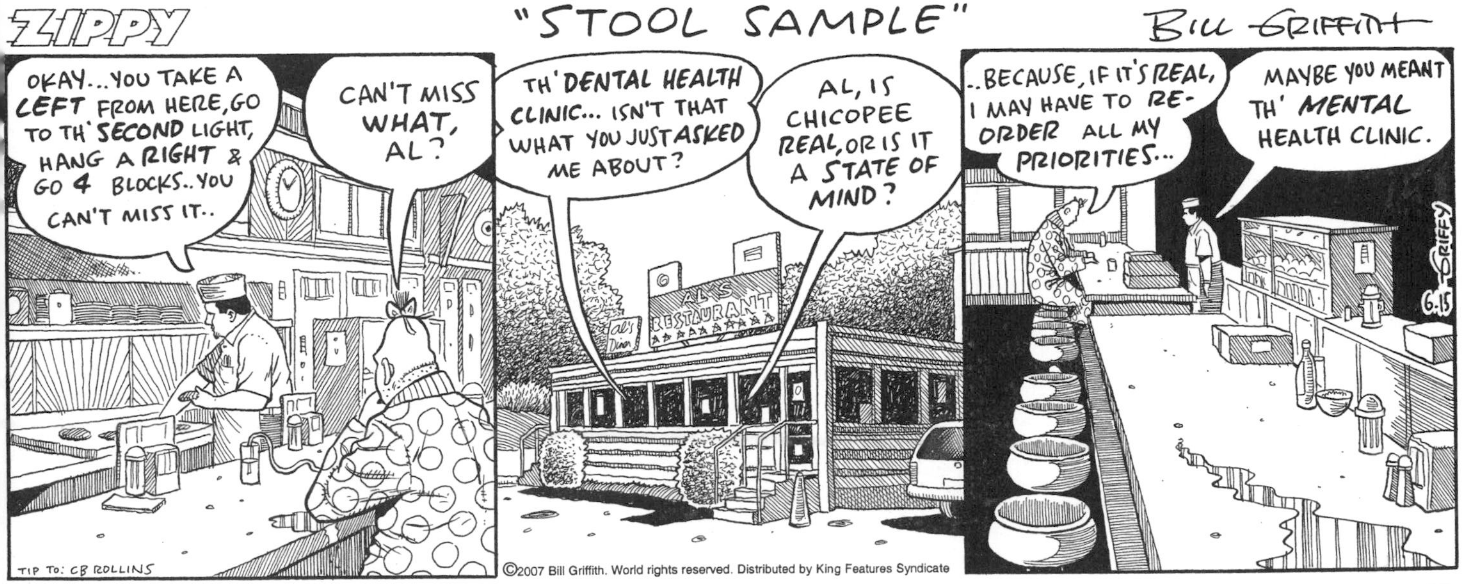
ZIPPY
"STOOL SAMPLE"
BILL GRIFFITH
OKAY... YOU TAKE A LEFT FROM HERE, GO TO TH' SECOND LIGHT, HANG A RIGHT & GO 4 BLOCKS.. YOU CAN'T MISS IT..
CAN'T MISS WHAT, AL?
TH' DENTAL HEALTH CLINIC... ISN'T THAT WHAT YOU JUST ASKED ME ABOUT?
AL, IS CHICOPEE REAL, OR IS IT A STATE OF MIND?
..BECAUSE, IF IT'S REAL, I MAY HAVE TO RE-ORDER ALL MY PRIORITIES...
MAYBE YOU MEANT TH' MENTAL HEALTH CLINIC.
AL'S RESTAURANT
GRIFFY 6.15
TIP TO: CB ROLLINS
©2007 Bill Griffith. World rights reserved. Distributed by King Features Syndicate

67

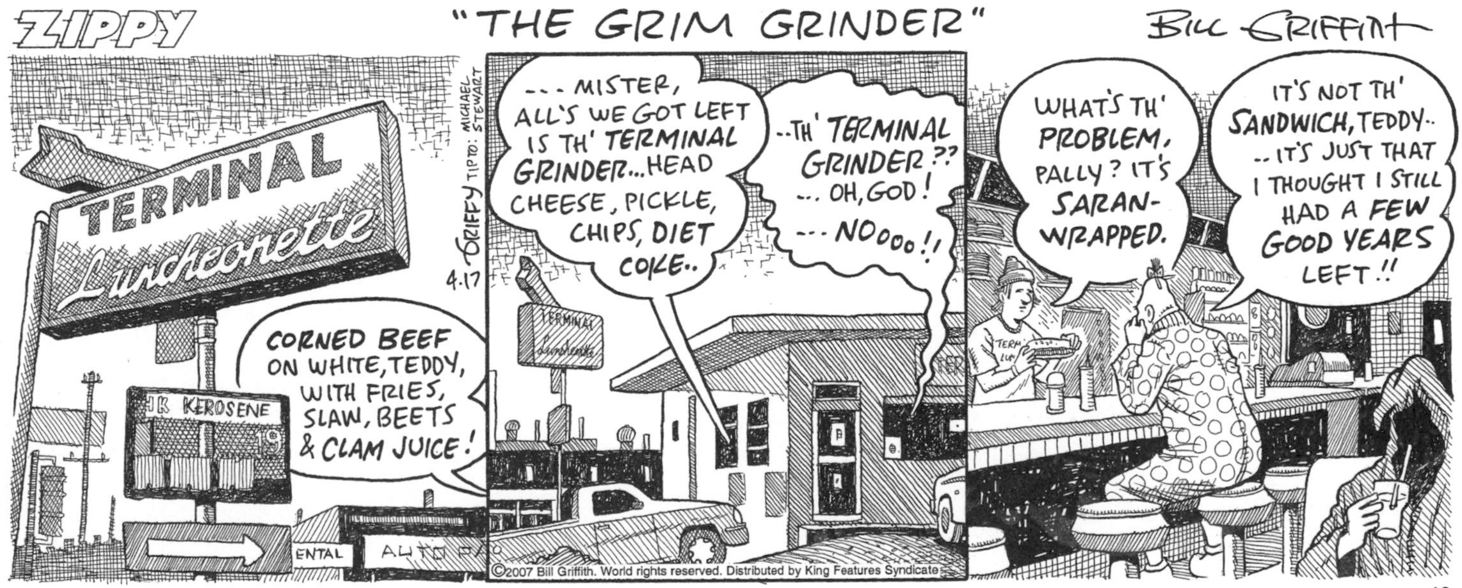
ZIPPY
"THE GRIM GRINDER"
BILL GRIFFITH
TERMINAL Luncheonette
CORNED BEEF ON WHITE, TEDDY, WITH FRIES, SLAW, BEETS & CLAM JUICE!
K KEROSENE
GRIFFY 4.17
TIP TO: MICHAEL STEWART
--- MISTER, ALL'S WE GOT LEFT IS TH' TERMINAL GRINDER... HEAD CHEESE, PICKLE, CHIPS, DIET COKE..
..TH' TERMINAL GRINDER?? ... OH, GOD! ... NOooo!!
WHAT'S TH' PROBLEM, PALLY? IT'S SARAN-WRAPPED.
IT'S NOT TH' SANDWICH, TEDDY.. ..IT'S JUST THAT I THOUGHT I STILL HAD A FEW GOOD YEARS LEFT!!
©2007 Bill Griffith. World rights reserved. Distributed by King Features Syndicate

68

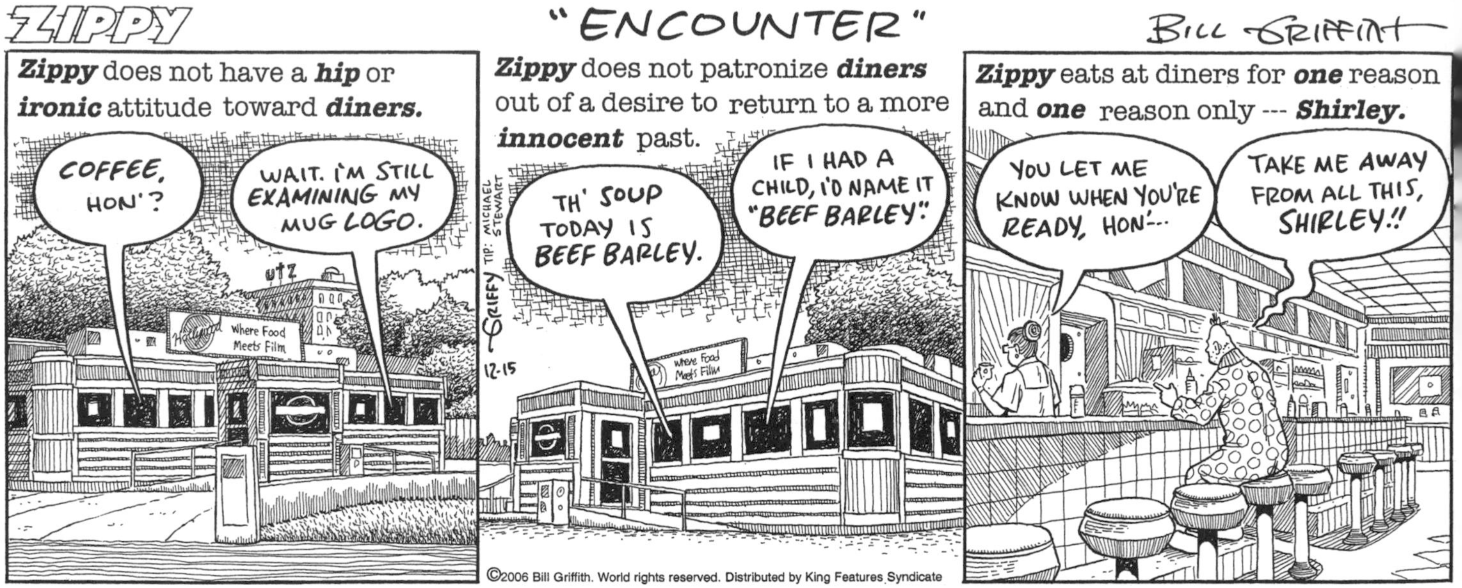
ZIPPY
"ENCOUNTER"
BILL GRIFFITH
Zippy does not have a hip or ironic attitude toward diners.
COFFEE, HON'?
WAIT. I'M STILL EXAMINING MY MUG LOGO.
Where Food Meets Film
UTZ
Zippy does not patronize diners out of a desire to return to a more innocent past.
TH' SOUP TODAY IS BEEF BARLEY.
IF I HAD A CHILD, I'D NAME IT "BEEF BARLEY."
TIP: MICHAEL STEWART
GRIFFY 12-15
Where Food Meets Film
Zippy eats at diners for one reason and one reason only --- Shirley.
YOU LET ME KNOW WHEN YOU'RE READY, HON'...
TAKE ME AWAY FROM ALL THIS, SHIRLEY!!
©2006 Bill Griffith. World rights reserved. Distributed by King Features Syndicate

69

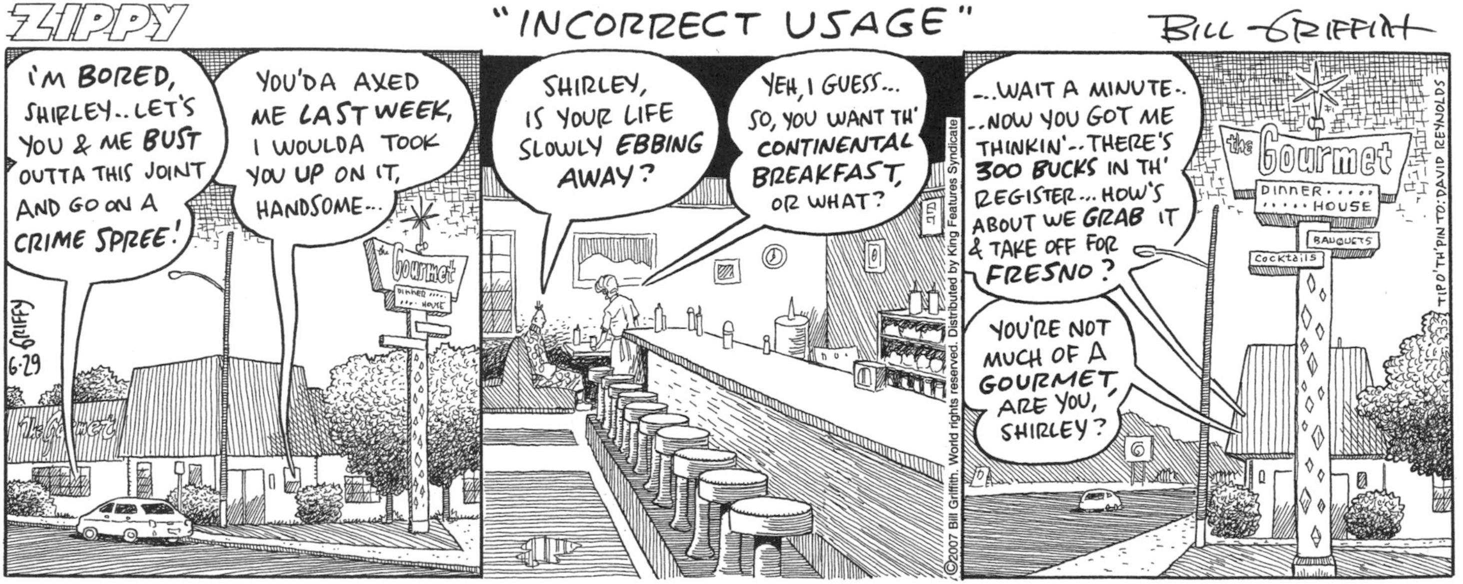
ZIPPY
"INCORRECT USAGE"
BILL GRIFFITH
I'M BORED, SHIRLEY.. LET'S YOU & ME BUST OUTTA THIS JOINT AND GO ON A CRIME SPREE!
YOU'DA AXED ME LAST WEEK, I WOULDA TOOK YOU UP ON IT, HANDSOME...
GRIFFY 6-29
the Gourmet
SHIRLEY, IS YOUR LIFE SLOWLY EBBING AWAY?
YEH, I GUESS... SO, YOU WANT TH' CONTINENTAL BREAKFAST, OR WHAT?
©2007 Bill Griffith. World rights reserved. Distributed by King Features Syndicate
-..WAIT A MINUTE.. ..NOW YOU GOT ME THINKIN'.. THERE'S 300 BUCKS IN TH' REGISTER... HOW'S ABOUT WE GRAB IT & TAKE OFF FOR FRESNO?
YOU'RE NOT MUCH OF A GOURMET, ARE YOU, SHIRLEY?
the Gourmet
DINNER ..... HOUSE
BANQUETS
COCKTAILS
TIP O' TH' PIN TO: DAVID REYNOLDS

70

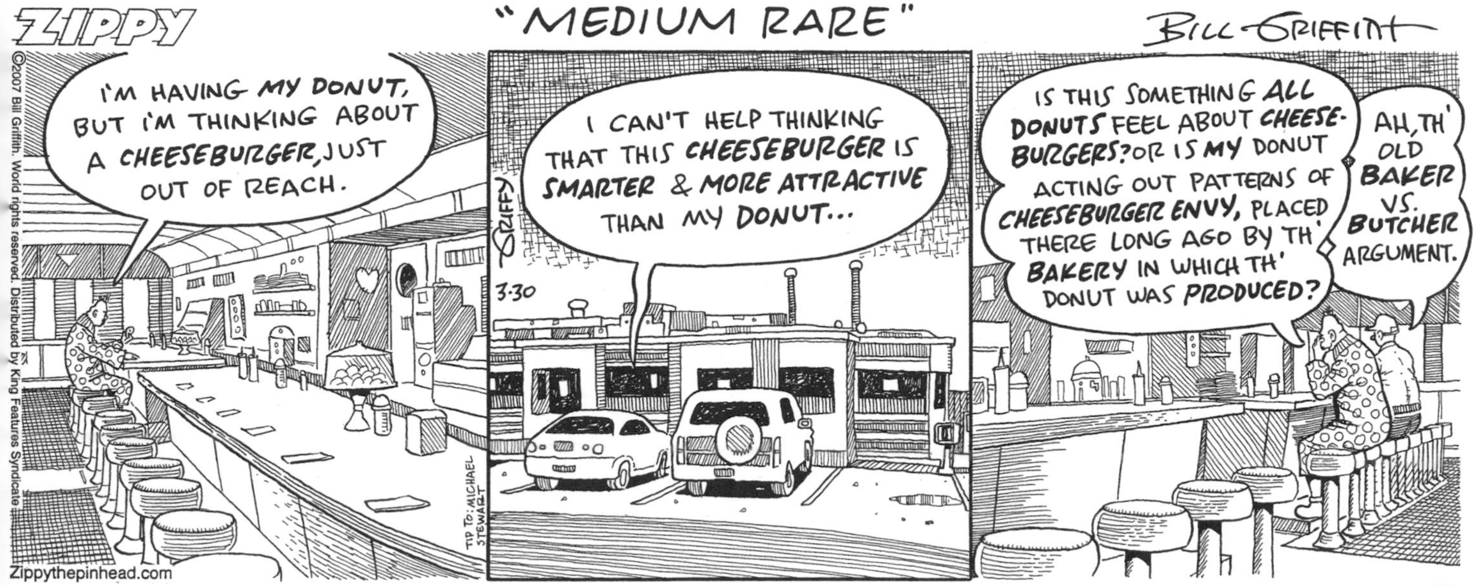
ZIPPY
"MEDIUM RARE"
BILL GRIFFITH
©2007 Bill Griffith. World rights reserved. Distributed by King Features Syndicate
I'M HAVING MY DONUT, BUT I'M THINKING ABOUT A CHEESEBURGER, JUST OUT OF REACH.
Zippythepinhead.com
TIP TO: MICHAEL STEWART
GRIFFY
3-30
I CAN'T HELP THINKING THAT THIS CHEESEBURGER IS SMARTER & MORE ATTRACTIVE THAN MY DONUT...
IS THIS SOMETHING ALL DONUTS FEEL ABOUT CHEESE-BURGERS? OR IS MY DONUT ACTING OUT PATTERNS OF CHEESEBURGER ENVY, PLACED THERE LONG AGO BY TH' BAKERY IN WHICH TH' DONUT WAS PRODUCED?
AH, TH' OLD BAKER VS. BUTCHER ARGUMENT.

71

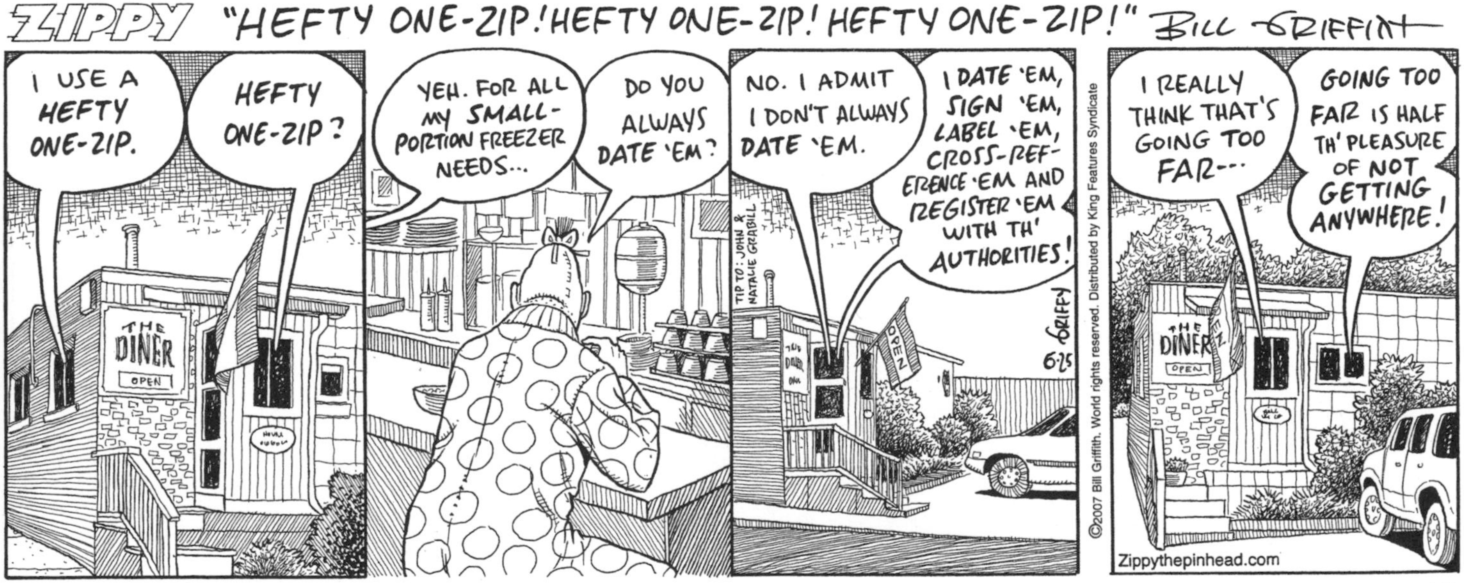
ZIPPY
"HEFTY ONE-ZIP! HEFTY ONE-ZIP! HEFTY ONE-ZIP!"
BILL GRIFFITH
I USE A HEFTY ONE-ZIP.
HEFTY ONE-ZIP?
THE DINER
OPEN
YEH. FOR ALL MY SMALL-PORTION FREEZER NEEDS...
DO YOU ALWAYS DATE 'EM?
NO. I ADMIT I DON'T ALWAYS DATE 'EM.
I DATE 'EM, SIGN 'EM, LABEL 'EM, CROSS-REF-ERENCE 'EM AND REGISTER 'EM WITH TH' AUTHORITIES!
TIP TO: JOHN & NATALIE GRABILL
OPEN
GRIFFY
6-25
©2007 Bill Griffith. World rights reserved. Distributed by King Features Syndicate
I REALLY THINK THAT'S GOING TOO FAR---
GOING TOO FAR IS HALF TH' PLEASURE OF NOT GETTING ANYWHERE!
THE DINER
OPEN
Zippythepinhead.com

72

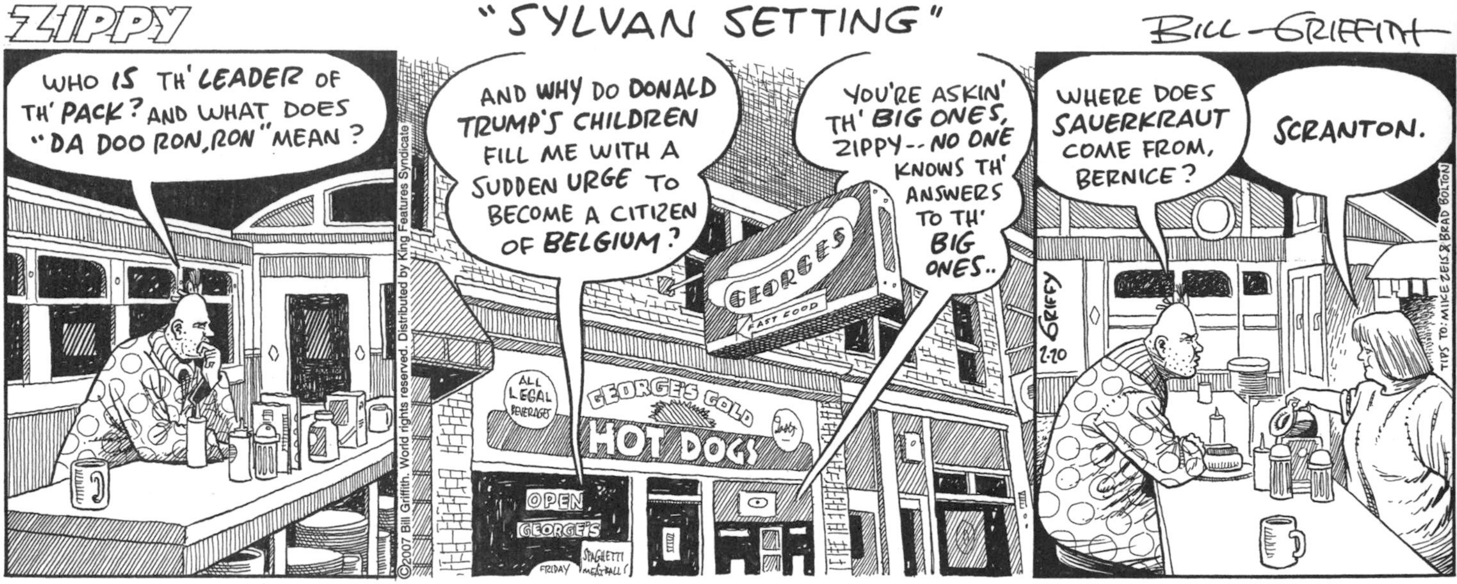
ZIPPY
"SYLVAN SETTING"
BILL GRIFFITH
WHO IS TH' LEADER OF TH' PACK? AND WHAT DOES "DA DOO RON, RON" MEAN?
©2007 Bill Griffith. World rights reserved. Distributed by King Features Syndicate
AND WHY DO DONALD TRUMP'S CHILDREN FILL ME WITH A SUDDEN URGE TO BECOME A CITIZEN OF BELGIUM?
YOU'RE ASKIN' TH' BIG ONES, ZIPPY-- NO ONE KNOWS TH' ANSWERS TO TH' BIG ONES..
GEORGE'S
FAST FOOD
ALL LEGAL BEVERAGES
GEORGE'S COLD HOT DOGS
OPEN
GEORGE'S
FRIDAY
SPAGHETTI MEATBALLS
GRIFFY 2-20
WHERE DOES SAUERKRAUT COME FROM, BERNICE?
SCRANTON.
TIPS TO: MIKE ZEIS & BRAD BOLTON

73

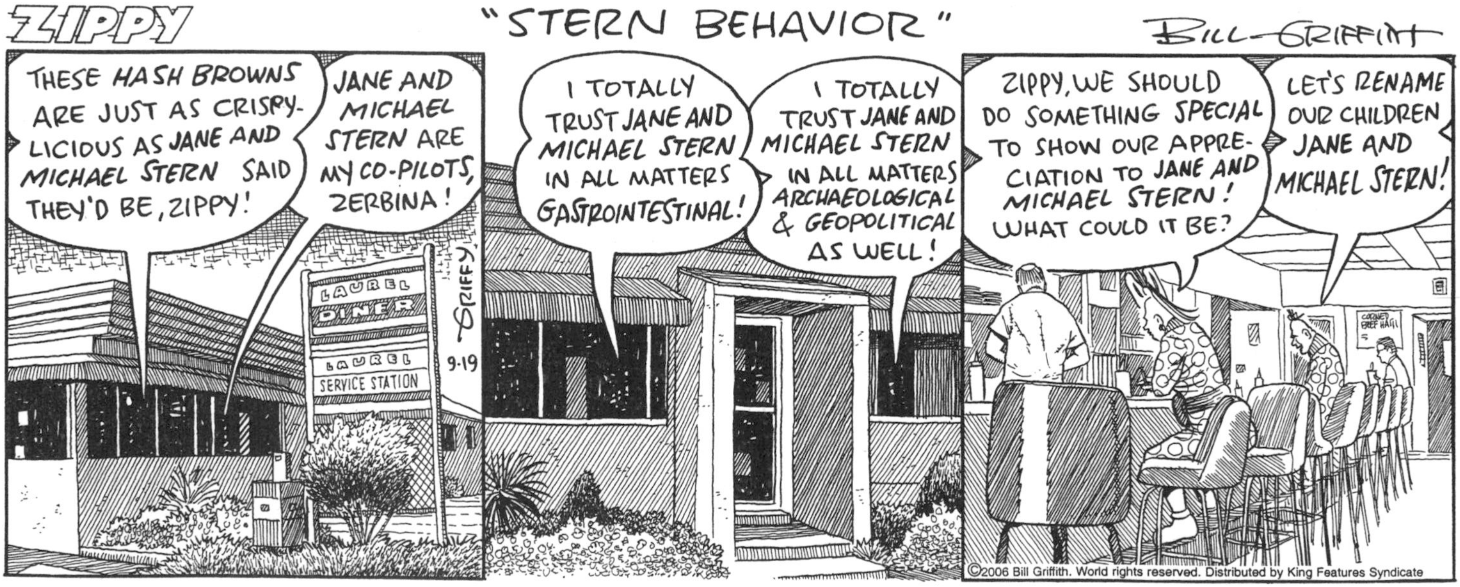
ZIPPY
"STERN BEHAVIOR"
BILL GRIFFITH
THESE HASH BROWNS ARE JUST AS CRISPY-LICIOUS AS JANE AND MICHAEL STERN SAID THEY'D BE, ZIPPY!
JANE AND MICHAEL STERN ARE MY CO-PILOTS, ZERBINA!
LAUREL DINER
LAUREL SERVICE STATION
GRIFFY 9-19
I TOTALLY TRUST JANE AND MICHAEL STERN IN ALL MATTERS GASTROINTESTINAL!
I TOTALLY TRUST JANE AND MICHAEL STERN IN ALL MATTERS ARCHAEOLOGICAL & GEOPOLITICAL AS WELL!
ZIPPY, WE SHOULD DO SOMETHING SPECIAL TO SHOW OUR APPRECIATION TO JANE AND MICHAEL STERN! WHAT COULD IT BE?
LET'S RENAME OUR CHILDREN JANE AND MICHAEL STERN!
©2006 Bill Griffith. World rights reserved. Distributed by King Features Syndicate

74

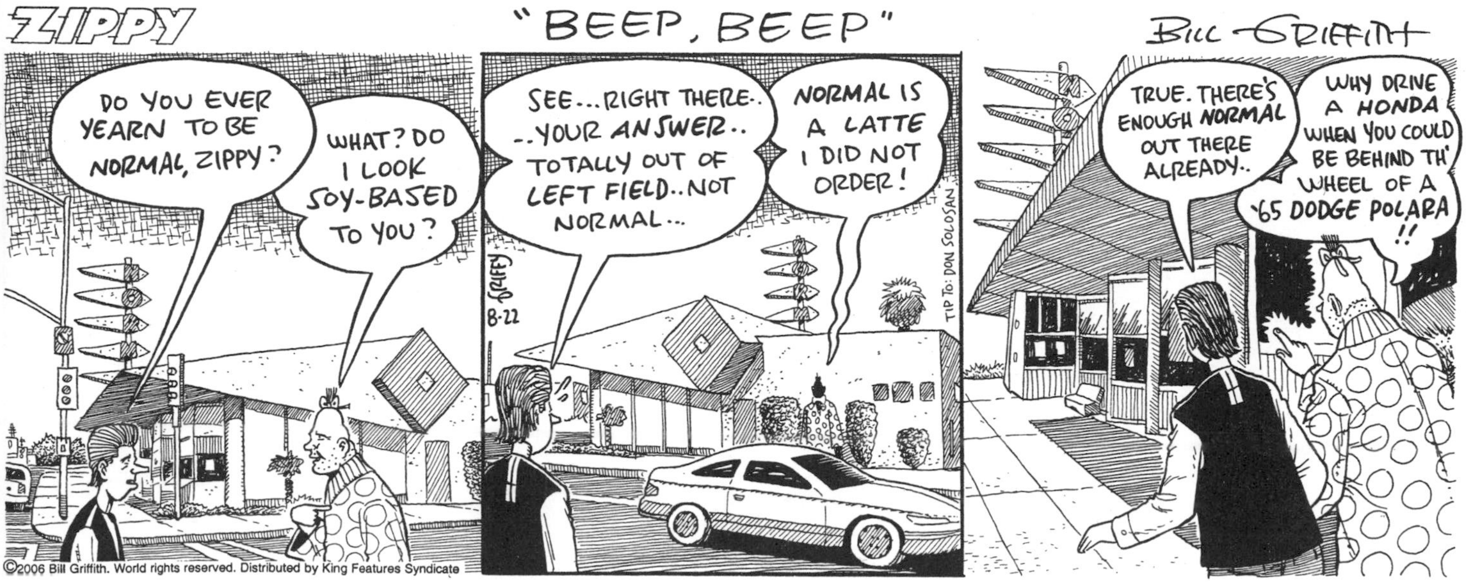
ZIPPY
"BEEP, BEEP"
BILL GRIFFITH
DO YOU EVER YEARN TO BE NORMAL, ZIPPY?
WHAT? DO I LOOK SOY-BASED TO YOU?
©2006 Bill Griffith. World rights reserved. Distributed by King Features Syndicate
SEE... RIGHT THERE.. ..YOUR ANSWER.. TOTALLY OUT OF LEFT FIELD.. NOT NORMAL...
NORMAL IS A LATTE I DID NOT ORDER!
GRIFFY 8-22
TIP TO: DON SOLOSAN
TRUE. THERE'S ENOUGH NORMAL OUT THERE ALREADY..
WHY DRIVE A HONDA WHEN YOU COULD BE BEHIND TH' WHEEL OF A '65 DODGE POLARA!!

75

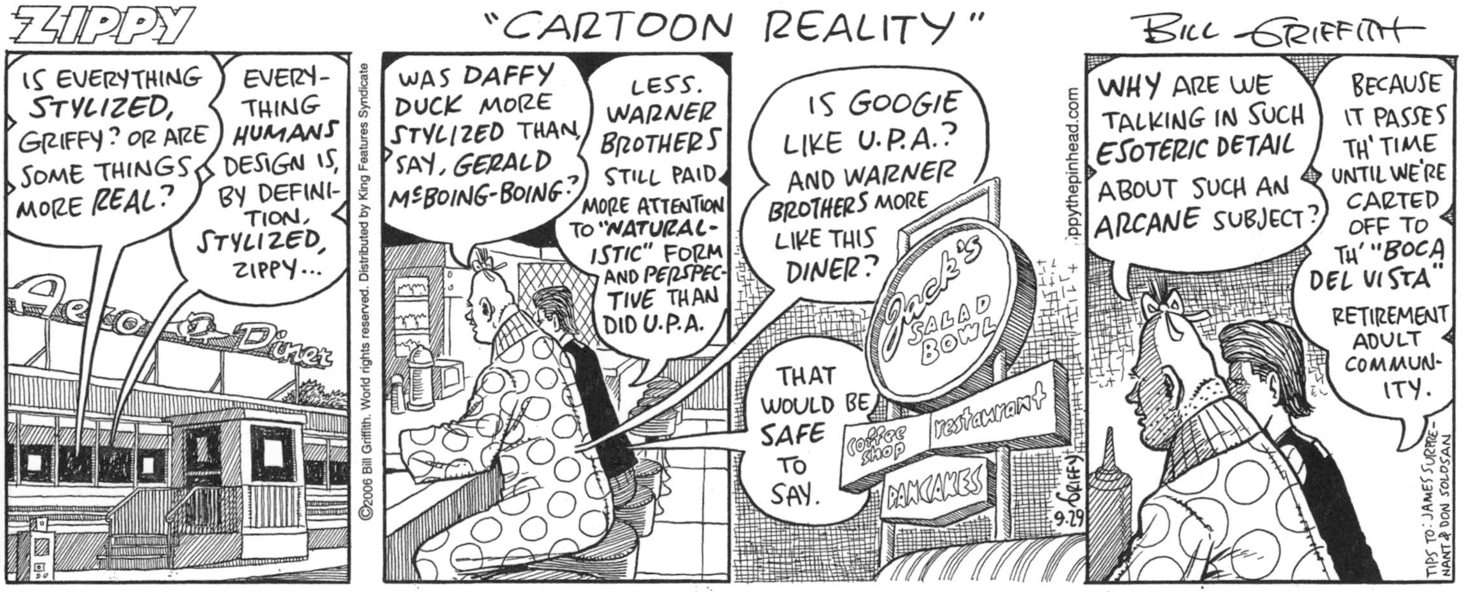
ZIPPY
"CARTOON REALITY"
BILL GRIFFITH
IS EVERYTHING STYLIZED, GRIFFY? OR ARE SOME THINGS MORE REAL?
EVERYTHING HUMANS DESIGN IS, BY DEFINITION, STYLIZED, ZIPPY...
Aero Diner
©2006 Bill Griffith. World rights reserved. Distributed by King Features Syndicate
WAS DAFFY DUCK MORE STYLIZED THAN, SAY, GERALD McBOING-BOING?
LESS. WARNER BROTHERS STILL PAID MORE ATTENTION TO "NATURALISTIC" FORM AND PERSPECTIVE THAN DID U.P.A.
IS GOOGIE LIKE U.P.A.? AND WARNER BROTHERS MORE LIKE THIS DINER?
THAT WOULD BE SAFE TO SAY.
Jack's SALAD BOWL
coffee shop
restaurant
PANCAKES
zippythepinhead.com
GRIFFY 9-29
WHY ARE WE TALKING IN SUCH ESOTERIC DETAIL ABOUT SUCH AN ARCANE SUBJECT?
BECAUSE IT PASSES TH' TIME UNTIL WE'RE CARTED OFF TO TH' "BOCA DEL VISTA" RETIREMENT ADULT COMMUNITY.
TIPS TO: JAMES SURRE-NANT & DON SOLOSAN

76

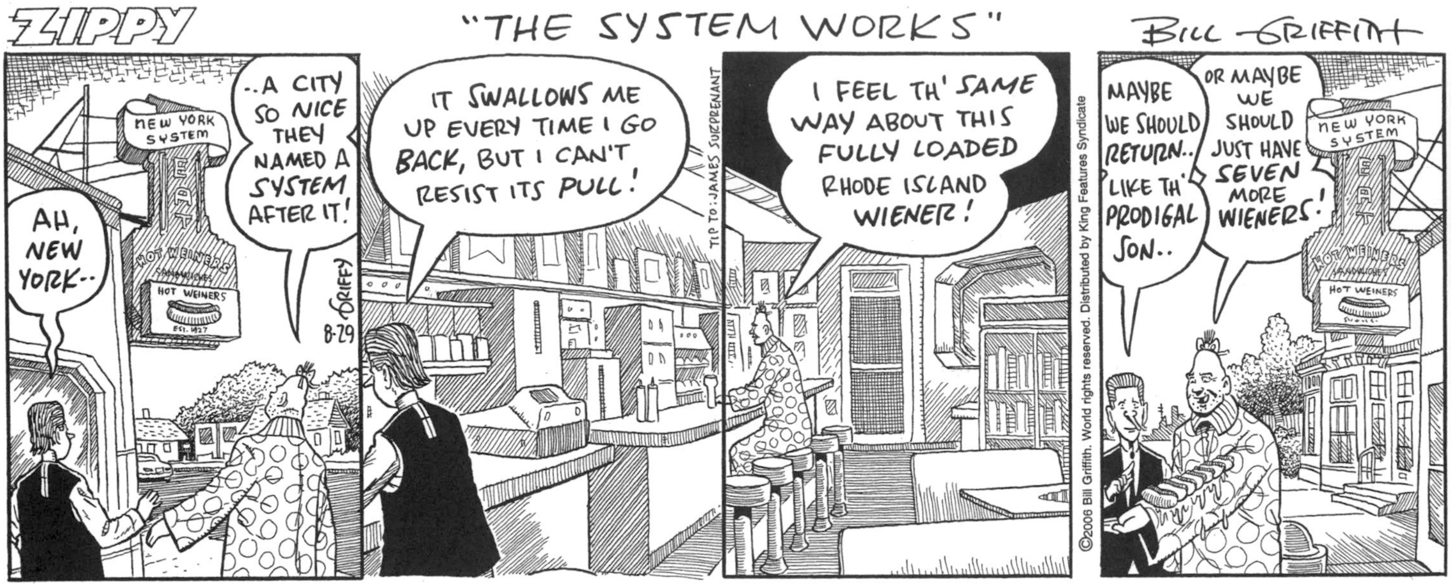
ZIPPY
"THE SYSTEM WORKS"
BILL GRIFFITH
AH, NEW YORK..
..A CITY SO NICE THEY NAMED A SYSTEM AFTER IT!
NEW YORK SYSTEM
HOT WEINERS
EST. 1927
GRIFFY 8·29
IT SWALLOWS ME UP EVERY TIME I GO BACK, BUT I CAN'T RESIST ITS PULL!
TIP TO: JAMES SURPRENANT
I FEEL TH' SAME WAY ABOUT THIS FULLY LOADED RHODE ISLAND WIENER!
©2006 Bill Griffith. World rights reserved. Distributed by King Features Syndicate
MAYBE WE SHOULD RETURN.. LIKE TH' PRODIGAL SON..
OR MAYBE WE SHOULD JUST HAVE SEVEN MORE WIENERS!
NEW YORK SYSTEM
HOT WEINERS

77

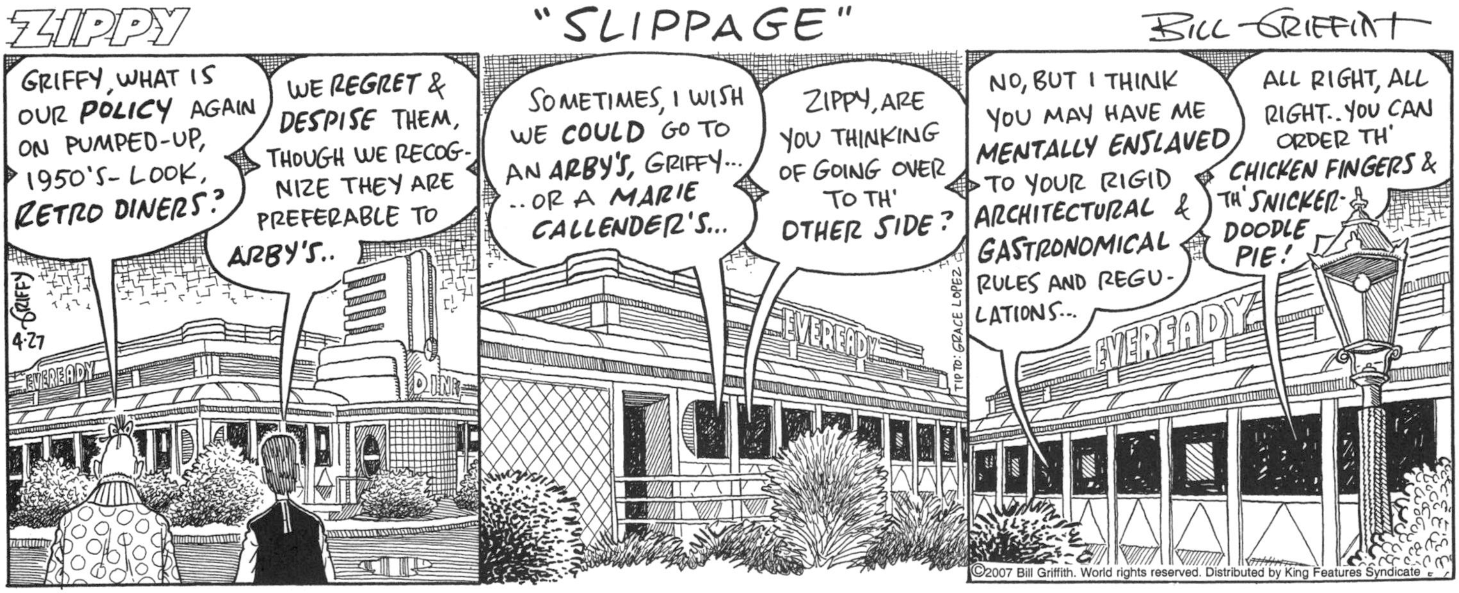
ZIPPY
"SLIPPAGE"
BILL GRIFFITH
GRIFFY, WHAT IS OUR POLICY AGAIN ON PUMPED-UP, 1950'S-LOOK, RETRO DINERS?
WE REGRET & DESPISE THEM, THOUGH WE RECOGNIZE THEY ARE PREFERABLE TO ARBY'S..
GRIFFY 4·27
EVEREADY
SOMETIMES, I WISH WE COULD GO TO AN ARBY'S, GRIFFY... ..OR A MARIE CALLENDER'S...
ZIPPY, ARE YOU THINKING OF GOING OVER TO TH' OTHER SIDE?
EVEREADY
TIP TO: GRACE LOPEZ
NO, BUT I THINK YOU MAY HAVE ME MENTALLY ENSLAVED TO YOUR RIGID ARCHITECTURAL & GASTRONOMICAL RULES AND REGULATIONS...
ALL RIGHT, ALL RIGHT.. YOU CAN ORDER TH' CHICKEN FINGERS & TH' SNICKERDOODLE PIE!
EVEREADY
©2007 Bill Griffith. World rights reserved. Distributed by King Features Syndicate

78

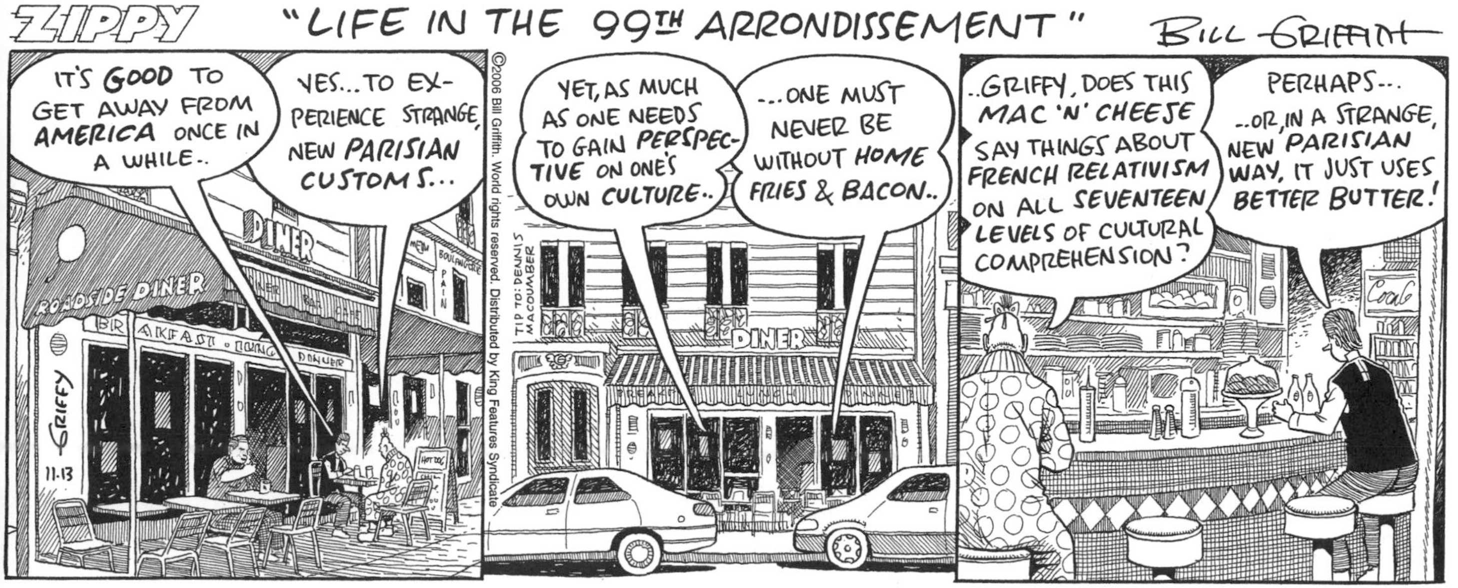

ZIPPY
"LIFE IN THE 99TH ARRONDISSEMENT"
BILL GRIFFITH
IT'S GOOD TO GET AWAY FROM AMERICA ONCE IN A WHILE..
YES... TO EXPERIENCE STRANGE, NEW PARISIAN CUSTOMS...
ROADSIDE DINER
DINER
GRIFFY 11-13
©2006 Bill Griffith. World rights reserved. Distributed by King Features Syndicate
TIP TO: DENNIS MACOUMBER
YET, AS MUCH AS ONE NEEDS TO GAIN PERSPECTIVE ON ONE'S OWN CULTURE..
...ONE MUST NEVER BE WITHOUT HOME FRIES & BACON..
DINER
..GRIFFY, DOES THIS MAC 'N' CHEESE SAY THINGS ABOUT FRENCH RELATIVISM ON ALL SEVENTEEN LEVELS OF CULTURAL COMPREHENSION?
PERHAPS... ..OR, IN A STRANGE, NEW PARISIAN WAY, IT JUST USES BETTER BUTTER!

79

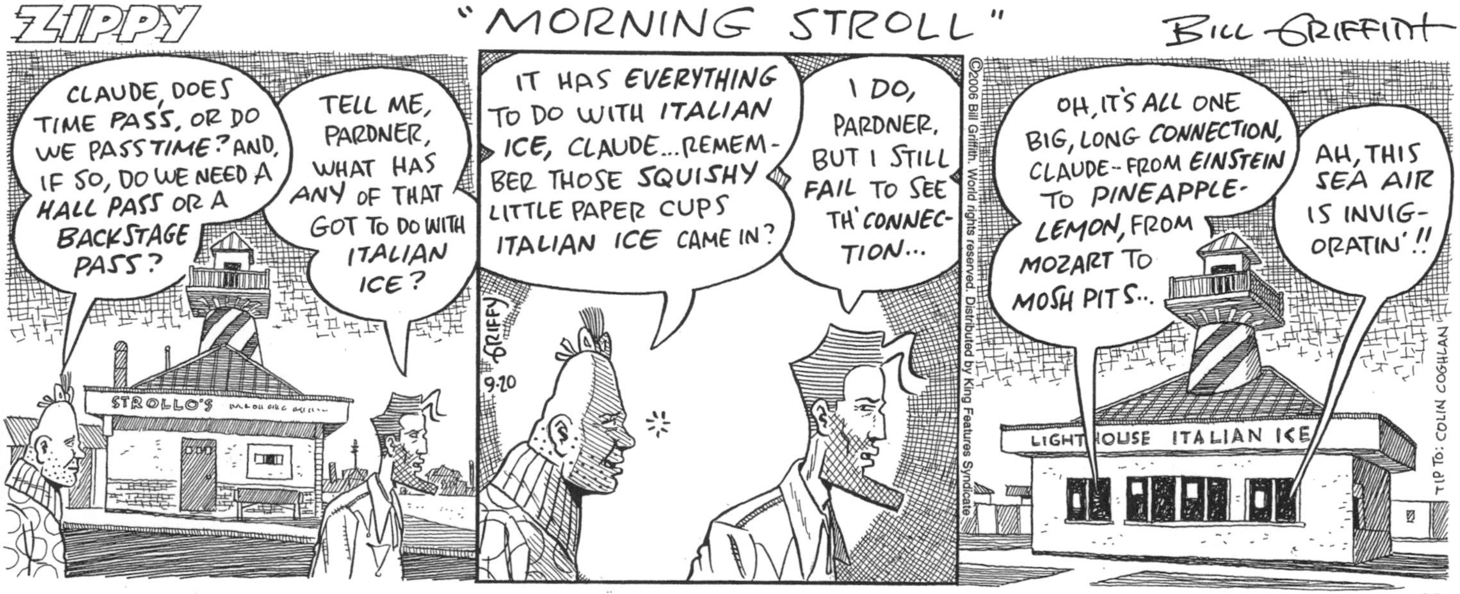

ZIPPY
"MORNING STROLL"
BILL GRIFFITH
CLAUDE, DOES TIME PASS, OR DO WE PASS TIME? AND, IF SO, DO WE NEED A HALL PASS OR A BACKSTAGE PASS?
TELL ME, PARDNER, WHAT HAS ANY OF THAT GOT TO DO WITH ITALIAN ICE?
STROLLO'S
IT HAS EVERYTHING TO DO WITH ITALIAN ICE, CLAUDE... REMEMBER THOSE SQUISHY LITTLE PAPER CUPS ITALIAN ICE CAME IN?
I DO, PARDNER, BUT I STILL FAIL TO SEE TH' CONNECTION...
GRIFFY 9-20
©2006 Bill Griffith. World rights reserved. Distributed by King Features Syndicate
OH, IT'S ALL ONE BIG, LONG CONNECTION, CLAUDE-- FROM EINSTEIN TO PINEAPPLE-LEMON, FROM MOZART TO MOSH PITS...
AH, THIS SEA AIR IS INVIGORATIN'!!
LIGHTHOUSE ITALIAN ICE
TIP TO: COLIN COGHLAN

80

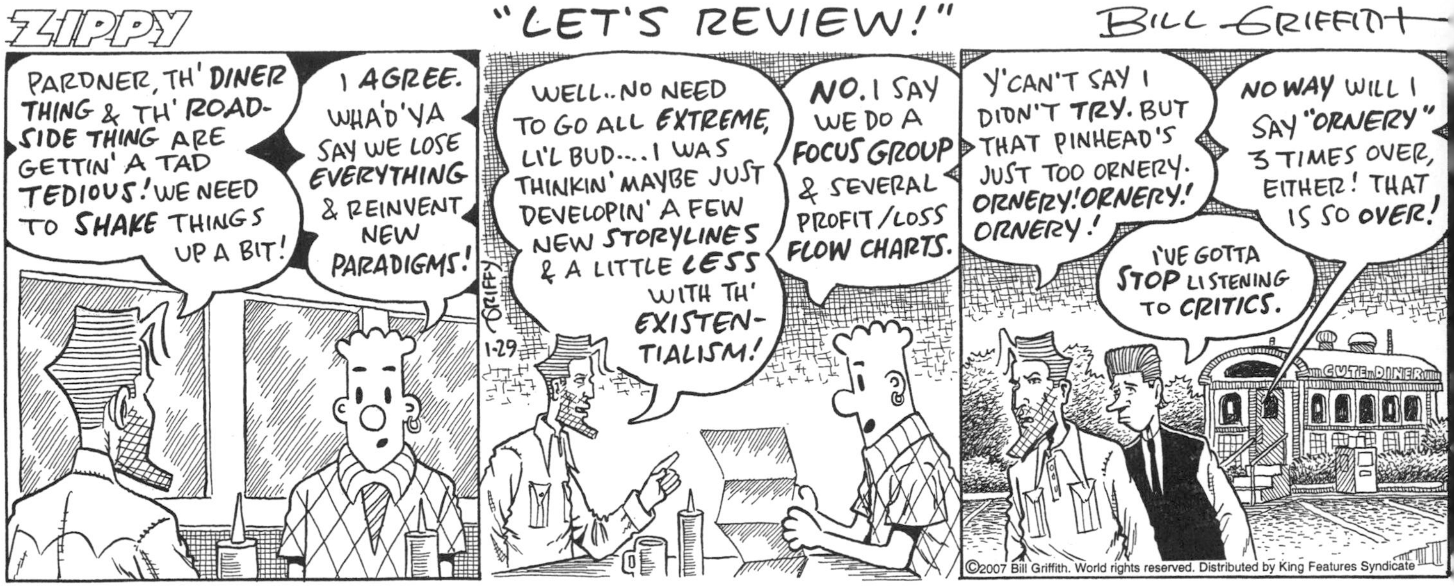
ZIPPY
"LET'S REVIEW!"
BILL GRIFFITH
PARDNER, TH' DINER THING & TH' ROAD-SIDE THING ARE GETTIN' A TAD TEDIOUS! WE NEED TO SHAKE THINGS UP A BIT!
I AGREE. WHA'D'YA SAY WE LOSE EVERYTHING & REINVENT NEW PARADIGMS!
WELL.. NO NEED TO GO ALL EXTREME, LI'L BUD.... I WAS THINKIN' MAYBE JUST DEVELOPIN' A FEW NEW STORYLINES & A LITTLE LESS WITH TH' EXISTEN-TIALISM!
NO. I SAY WE DO A FOCUS GROUP & SEVERAL PROFIT/LOSS FLOW CHARTS.
GRIFFY
1-29
Y'CAN'T SAY I DIDN'T TRY. BUT THAT PINHEAD'S JUST TOO ORNERY. ORNERY! ORNERY! ORNERY!
NO WAY WILL I SAY "ORNERY" 3 TIMES OVER, EITHER! THAT IS SO OVER!
I'VE GOTTA STOP LISTENING TO CRITICS.
CUTE DINER
©2007 Bill Griffith. World rights reserved. Distributed by King Features Syndicate

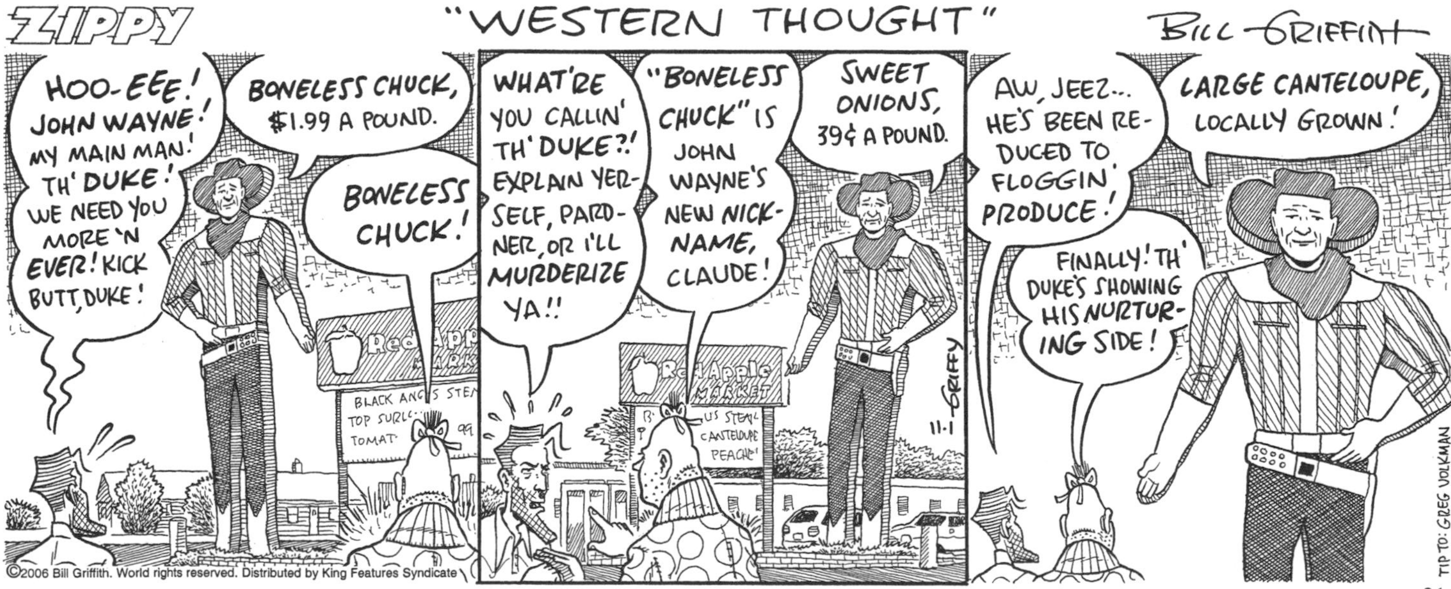
ZIPPY
"WESTERN THOUGHT"
BILL GRIFFITH
HOO-EEE! JOHN WAYNE! MY MAIN MAN! TH' DUKE! WE NEED YOU MORE 'N EVER! KICK BUTT, DUKE!
BONELESS CHUCK, $1.99 A POUND.
BONELESS CHUCK!
WHAT'RE YOU CALLIN' TH' DUKE?! EXPLAIN YER-SELF, PARD-NER, OR I'LL MURDERIZE YA!!
"BONELESS CHUCK" IS JOHN WAYNE'S NEW NICK-NAME, CLAUDE!
SWEET ONIONS, 39¢ A POUND.
Red Apple MARKET
GRIFFY
11-1
AW, JEEZ... HE'S BEEN RE-DUCED TO FLOGGIN' PRODUCE!
LARGE CANTELOUPE, LOCALLY GROWN!
FINALLY! TH' DUKE'S SHOWING HIS NURTUR-ING SIDE!
TIP TO: GREG VOLKMAN
©2006 Bill Griffith. World rights reserved. Distributed by King Features Syndicate

81

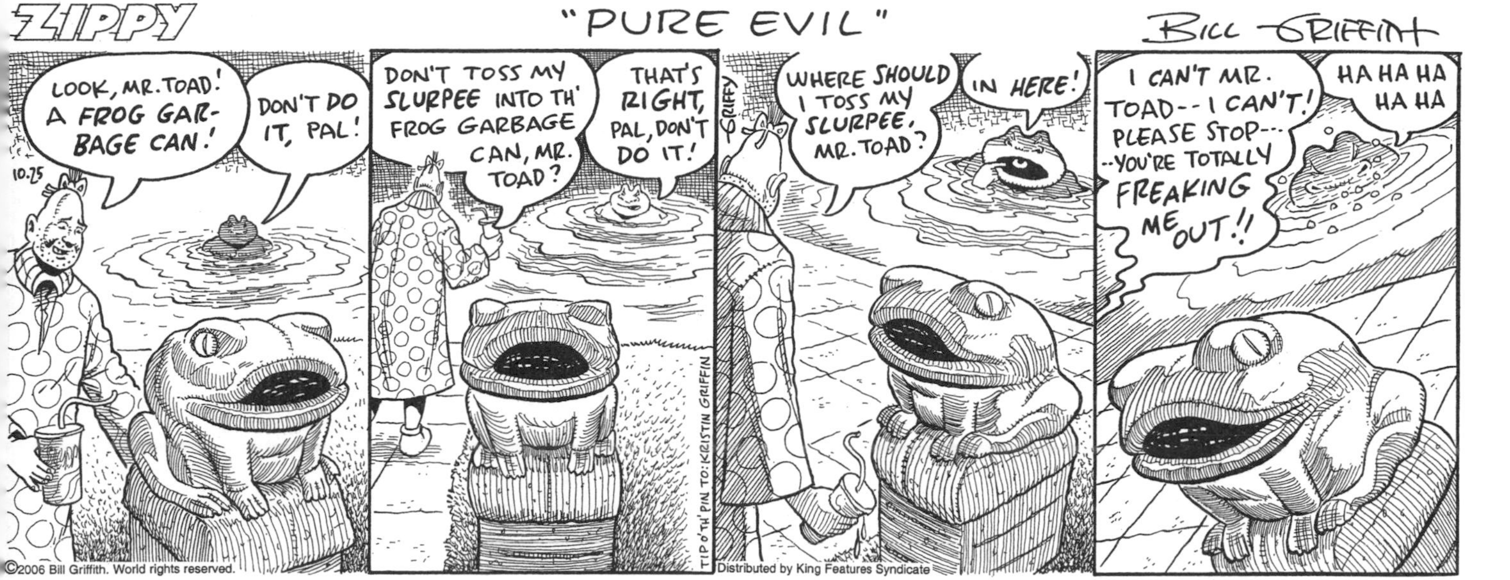
ZIPPY
"PURE EVIL"
BILL GRIFFITH
LOOK, MR. TOAD! A FROG GARBAGE CAN!
DON'T DO IT, PAL!
DON'T TOSS MY SLURPEE INTO TH' FROG GARBAGE CAN, MR. TOAD?
THAT'S RIGHT, PAL, DON'T DO IT!
TIP O'TH' PIN TO: KRISTIN GRIFFIN
WHERE SHOULD I TOSS MY SLURPEE, MR. TOAD?
IN HERE!
I CAN'T MR. TOAD-- I CAN'T! PLEASE STOP-- --YOU'RE TOTALLY FREAKING ME OUT!!
HA HA HA HA HA HA
©2006 Bill Griffith. World rights reserved.
Distributed by King Features Syndicate

82

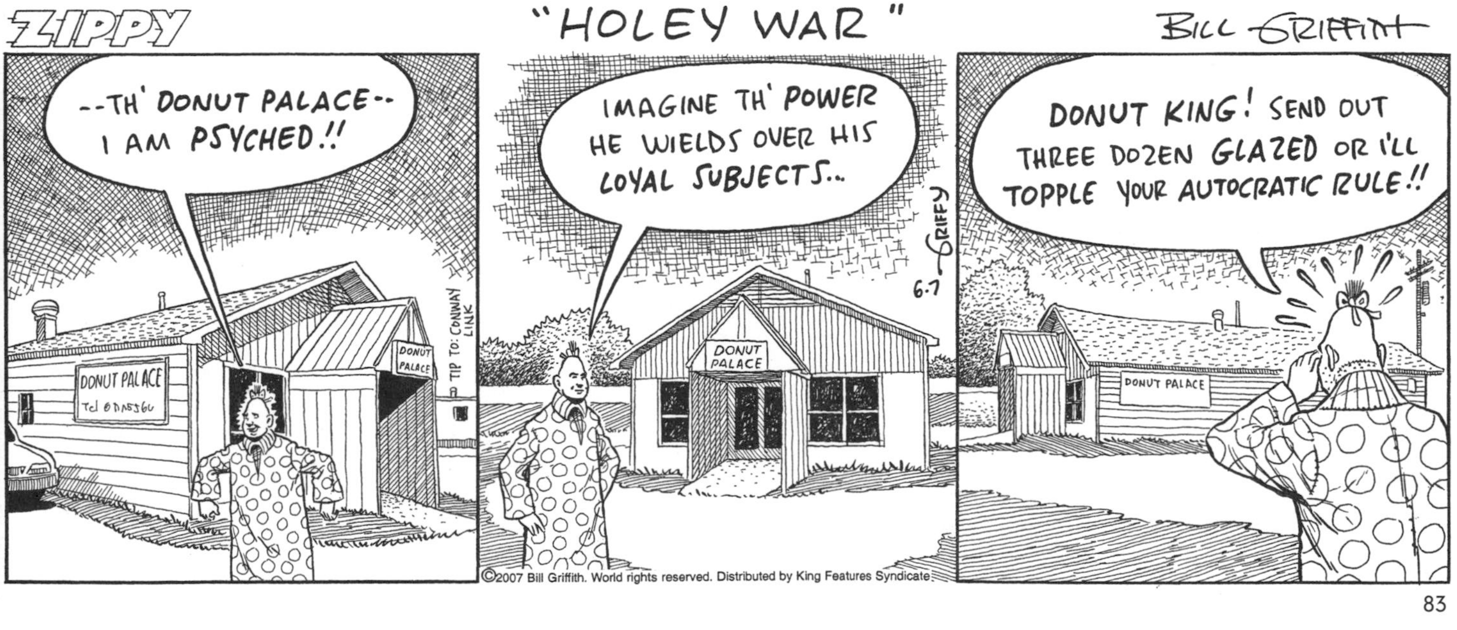
ZIPPY
"HOLEY WAR"
BILL GRIFFITH
--TH' DONUT PALACE-- I AM PSYCHED!!
DONUT PALACE
TIP TO: CONWAY LINK
IMAGINE TH' POWER HE WIELDS OVER HIS LOYAL SUBJECTS..
DONUT PALACE
DONUT KING! SEND OUT THREE DOZEN GLAZED OR I'LL TOPPLE YOUR AUTOCRATIC RULE!!
©2007 Bill Griffith. World rights reserved. Distributed by King Features Syndicate

83

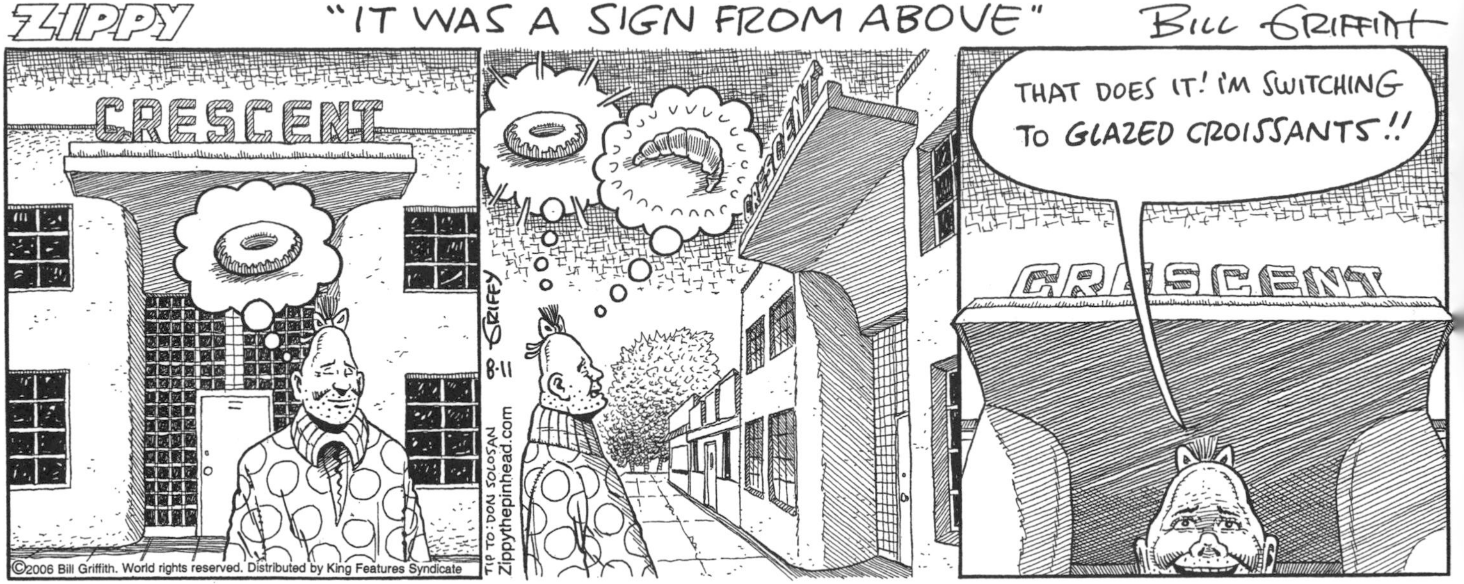
ZIPPY
"IT WAS A SIGN FROM ABOVE"
BILL GRIFFITH
CRESCENT
©2006 Bill Griffith. World rights reserved. Distributed by King Features Syndicate
TIP TO: DON SOLOSAN
Zippythepinhead.com
8-11
GRIFFY
CRESCENT
THAT DOES IT! I'M SWITCHING TO GLAZED CROISSANTS!!
CRESCENT

84

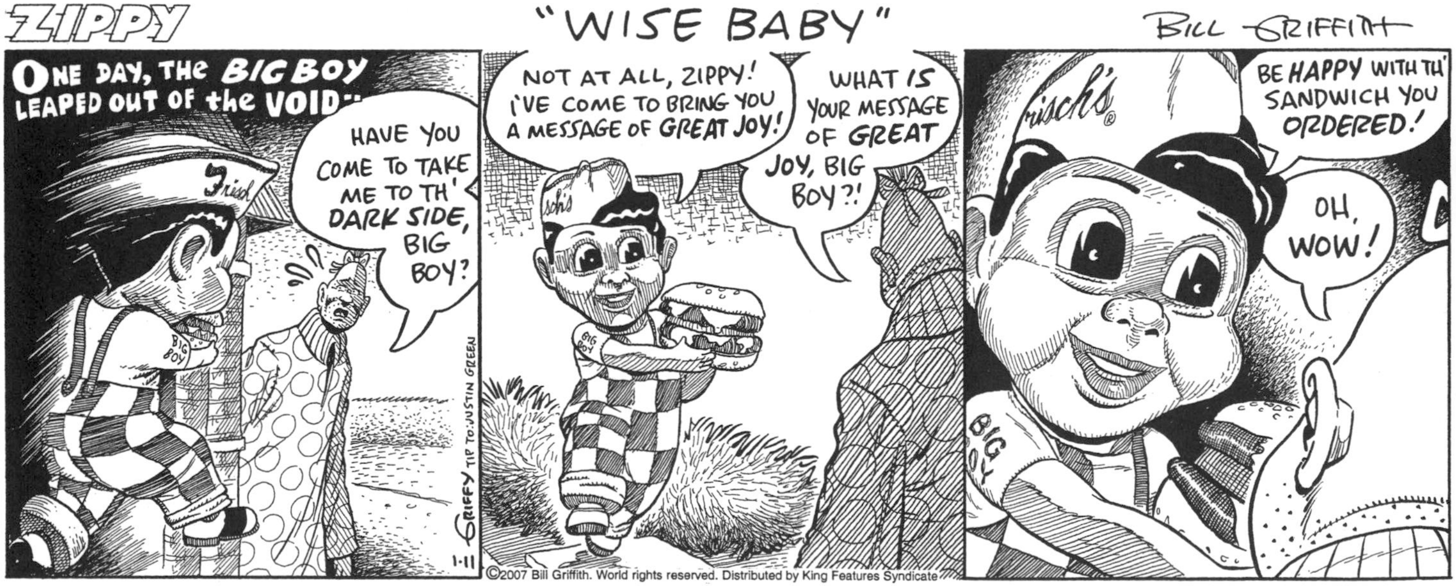
ZIPPY
"WISE BABY"
BILL GRIFFITH
ONE DAY, THE BIG BOY LEAPED OUT OF THE VOID--
HAVE YOU COME TO TAKE ME TO TH' DARK SIDE, BIG BOY?
GRIFFY TIP TO: JUSTIN GREEN
1-11
NOT AT ALL, ZIPPY! I'VE COME TO BRING YOU A MESSAGE OF GREAT JOY!
WHAT IS YOUR MESSAGE OF GREAT JOY, BIG BOY?!
©2007 Bill Griffith. World rights reserved. Distributed by King Features Syndicate
BE HAPPY WITH TH' SANDWICH YOU ORDERED!
OH, WOW!

85

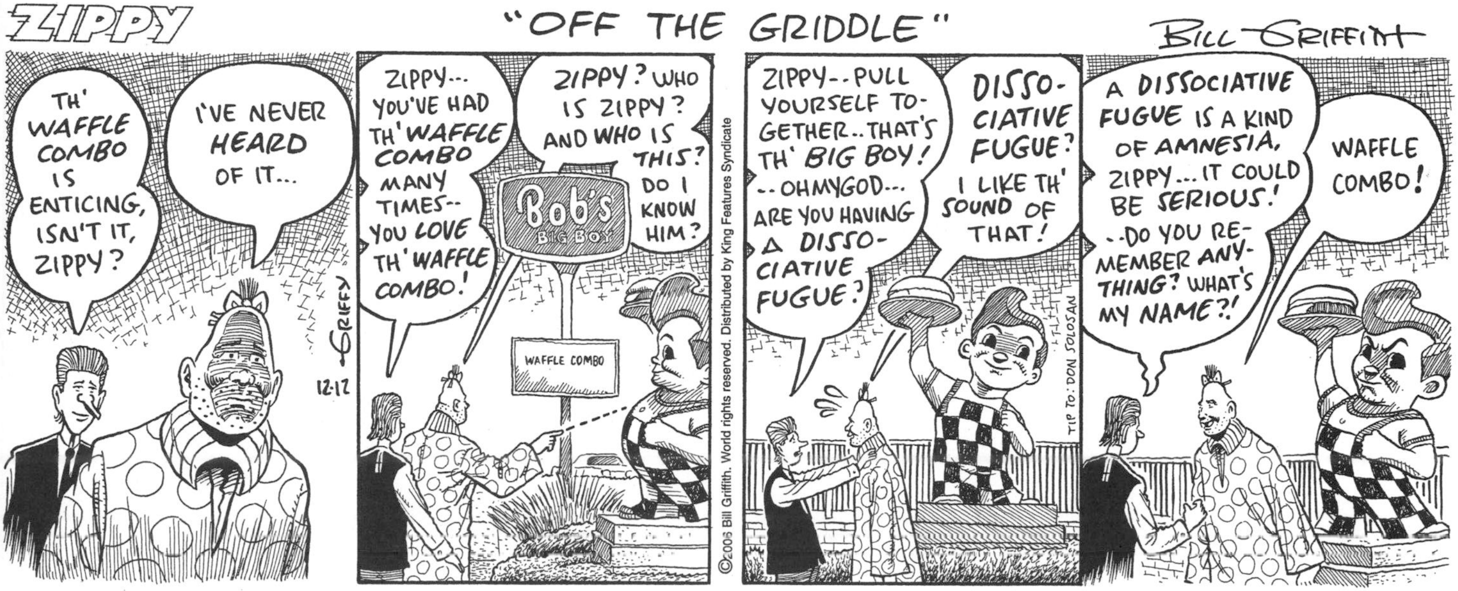
ZIPPY
"OFF THE GRIDDLE"
BILL GRIFFITH
TH' WAFFLE COMBO IS ENTICING, ISN'T IT, ZIPPY?
I'VE NEVER HEARD OF IT...
GRIFFY 12.12
ZIPPY... YOU'VE HAD TH' WAFFLE COMBO MANY TIMES-- YOU LOVE TH' WAFFLE COMBO!
ZIPPY? WHO IS ZIPPY? AND WHO IS THIS? DO I KNOW HIM?
Bob's BIG BOY
WAFFLE COMBO
©2006 Bill Griffith. World rights reserved. Distributed by King Features Syndicate
ZIPPY--PULL YOURSELF TOGETHER.. THAT'S TH' BIG BOY! --OHMYGOD--. ARE YOU HAVING A DISSOCIATIVE FUGUE?
DISSOCIATIVE FUGUE? I LIKE TH' SOUND OF THAT!
TIP TO: DON SOLOSAN
A DISSOCIATIVE FUGUE IS A KIND OF AMNESIA, ZIPPY... IT COULD BE SERIOUS! --DO YOU REMEMBER ANYTHING? WHAT'S MY NAME?!
WAFFLE COMBO!

86

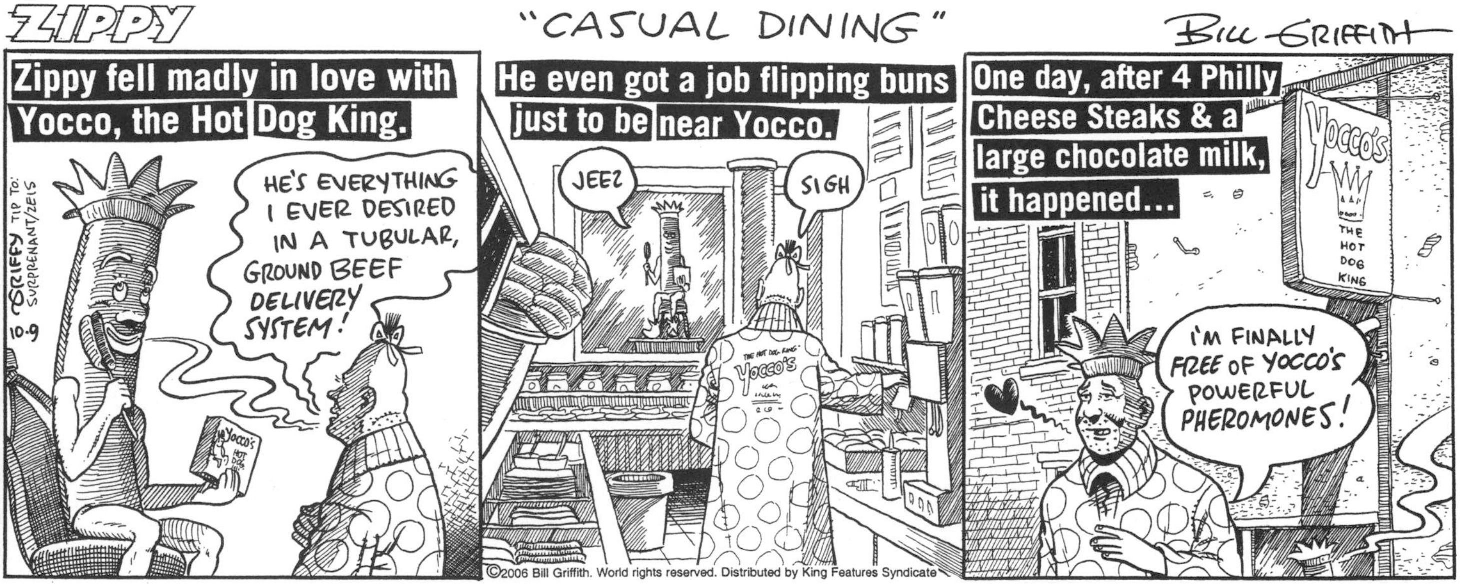
ZIPPY
"CASUAL DINING"
BILL GRIFFITH
Zippy fell madly in love with Yocco, the Hot Dog King.
TIP TO: SURPRENANT/ZEIS
GRIFFY 10.9
HE'S EVERYTHING I EVER DESIRED IN A TUBULAR, GROUND BEEF DELIVERY SYSTEM!
He even got a job flipping buns just to be near Yocco.
JEEZ
SIGH
Yocco's
©2006 Bill Griffith. World rights reserved. Distributed by King Features Syndicate
One day, after 4 Philly Cheese Steaks & a large chocolate milk, it happened...
Yocco's THE HOT DOG KING
I'M FINALLY FREE OF YOCCO'S POWERFUL PHEROMONES!

87

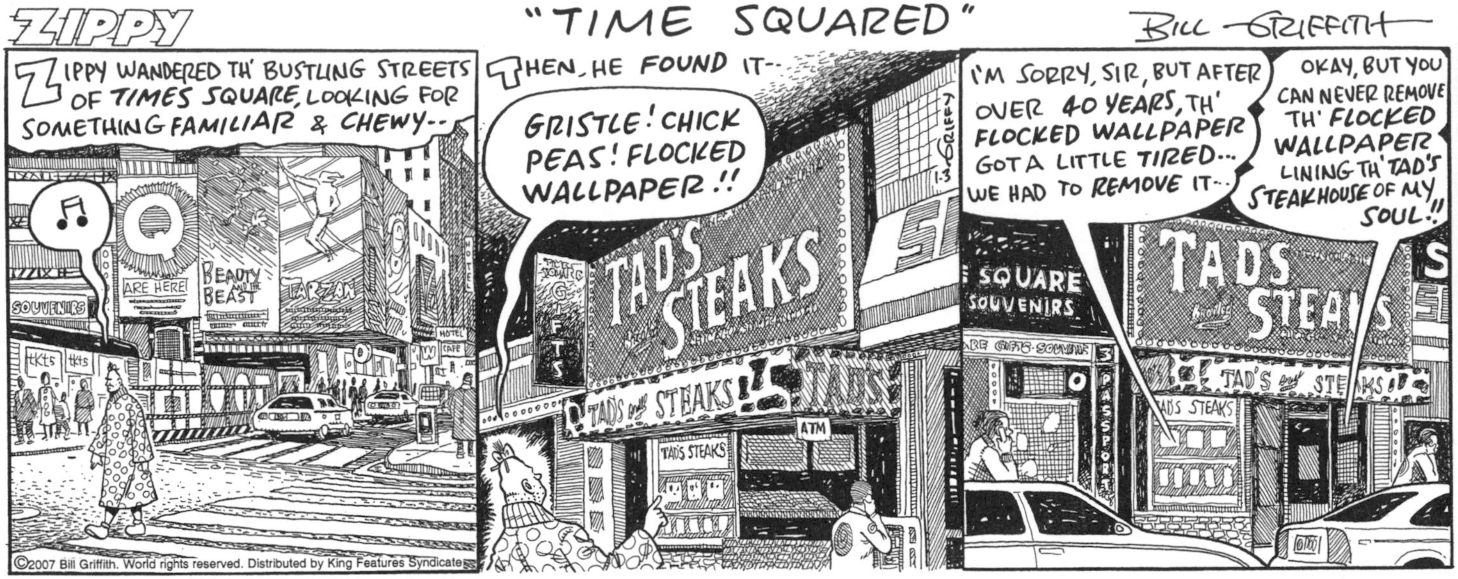
ZIPPY
"TIME SQUARED"
BILL GRIFFITH
ZIPPY WANDERED TH' BUSTLING STREETS OF TIMES SQUARE, LOOKING FOR SOMETHING FAMILIAR & CHEWY--
THEN, HE FOUND IT--
GRISTLE! CHICK PEAS! FLOCKED WALLPAPER!!
I'M SORRY, SIR, BUT AFTER OVER 40 YEARS, TH' FLOCKED WALLPAPER GOT A LITTLE TIRED... WE HAD TO REMOVE IT--
OKAY, BUT YOU CAN NEVER REMOVE TH' FLOCKED WALLPAPER LINING TH' TAD'S STEAKHOUSE OF MY SOUL!!
TAD'S STEAKS
SQUARE SOUVENIRS
©2007 Bill Griffith. World rights reserved. Distributed by King Features Syndicate

88

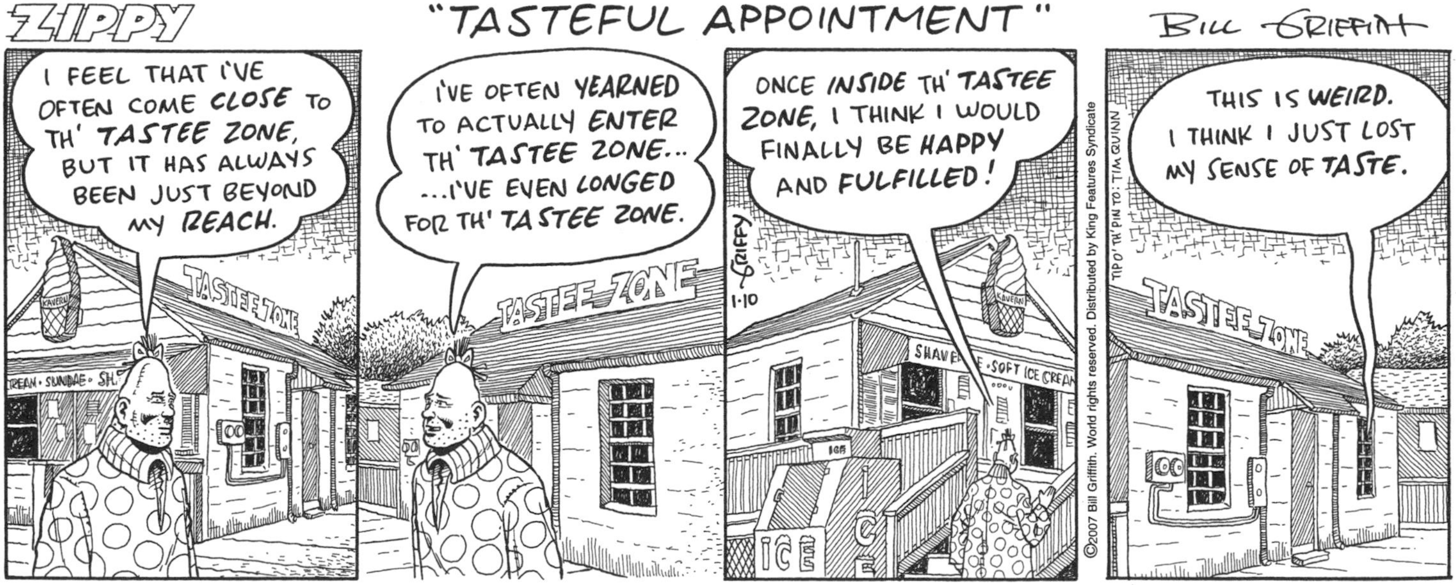
ZIPPY
"TASTEFUL APPOINTMENT"
BILL GRIFFITH
I FEEL THAT I'VE OFTEN COME CLOSE TO TH' TASTEE ZONE, BUT IT HAS ALWAYS BEEN JUST BEYOND MY REACH.
I'VE OFTEN YEARNED TO ACTUALLY ENTER TH' TASTEE ZONE... ...I'VE EVEN LONGED FOR TH' TASTEE ZONE.
ONCE INSIDE TH' TASTEE ZONE, I THINK I WOULD FINALLY BE HAPPY AND FULFILLED!
THIS IS WEIRD. I THINK I JUST LOST MY SENSE OF TASTE.
TASTEE ZONE
©2007 Bill Griffith. World rights reserved. Distributed by King Features Syndicate
TIP O' TH' PIN TO: TIM QUINN

89

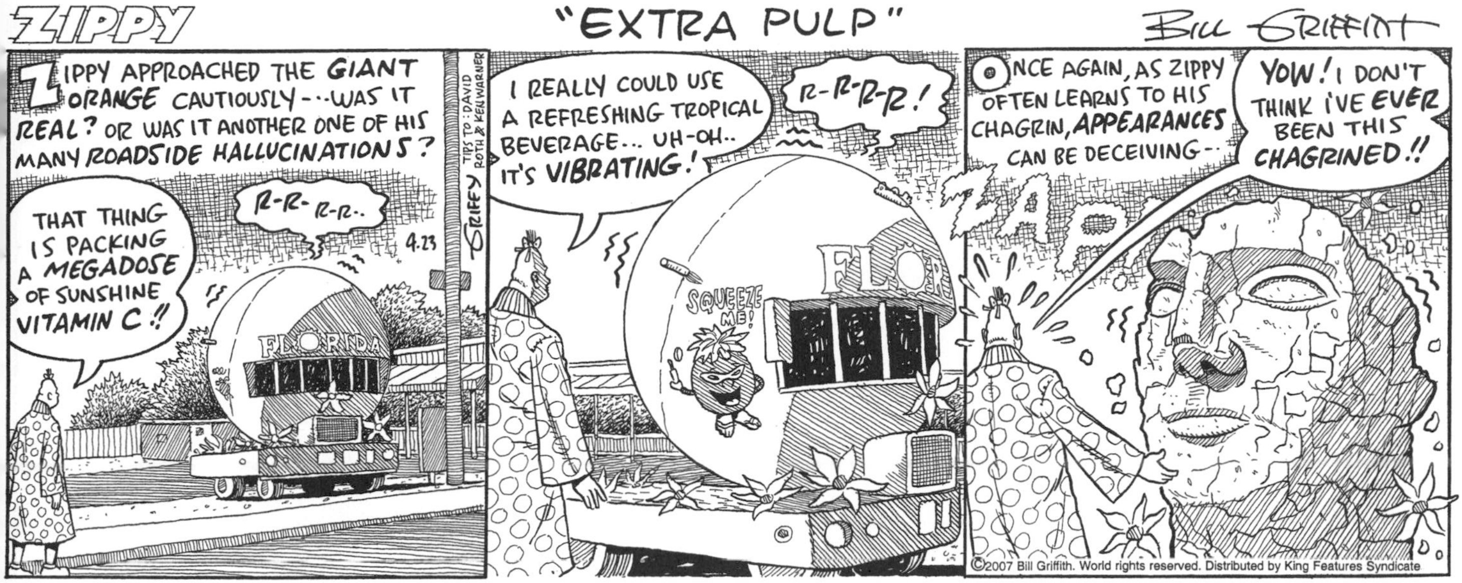
ZIPPY
"EXTRA PULP"
BILL GRIFFITH
ZIPPY APPROACHED THE GIANT ORANGE CAUTIOUSLY--..WAS IT REAL? OR WAS IT ANOTHER ONE OF HIS MANY ROADSIDE HALLUCINATIONS?
THAT THING IS PACKING A MEGADOSE OF SUNSHINE VITAMIN C!!
R-R- R-R..
FLORIDA
TIPS TO: DAVID ROTH & KEN WARNER
GRIFFY 4.23
I REALLY COULD USE A REFRESHING TROPICAL BEVERAGE... UH-OH.. IT'S VIBRATING!
R-R-R-R!
SQUEEZE ME!
FLOR
ONCE AGAIN, AS ZIPPY OFTEN LEARNS TO HIS CHAGRIN, APPEARANCES CAN BE DECEIVING--
YOW! I DON'T THINK I'VE EVER BEEN THIS CHAGRINED!!
ZAP!
©2007 Bill Griffith. World rights reserved. Distributed by King Features Syndicate

90

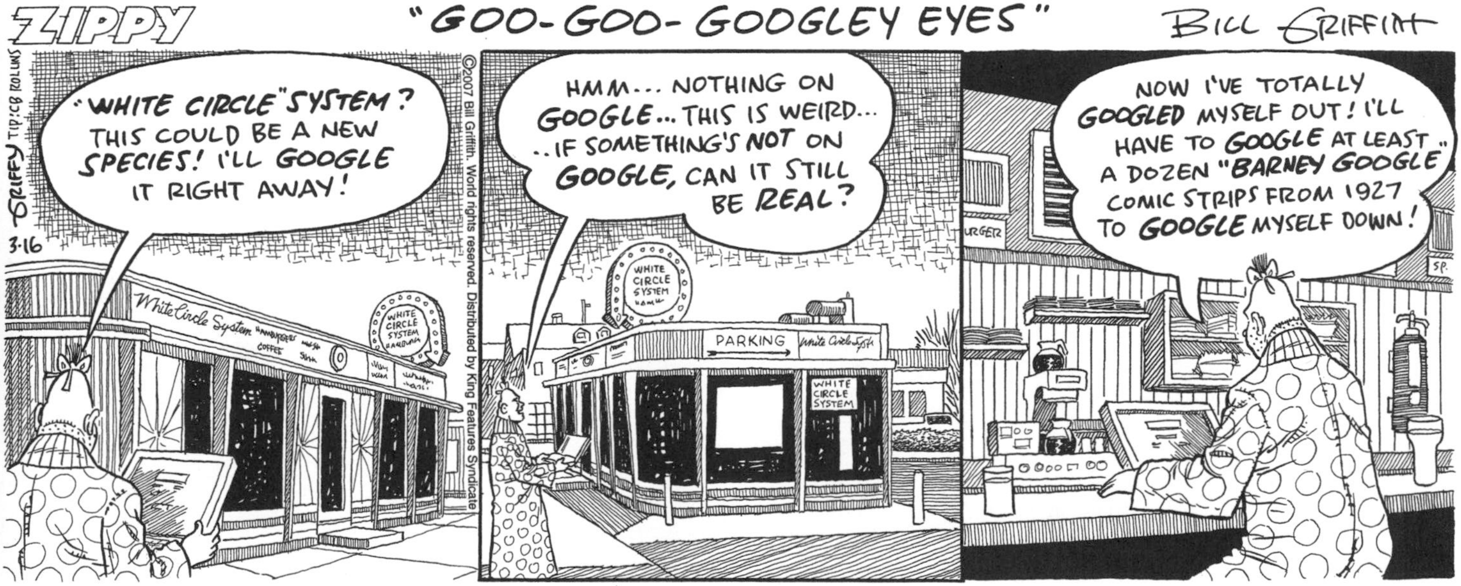
ZIPPY
"GOO-GOO-GOOGLEY EYES"
BILL GRIFFITH
GRIFFY TIP: CB ROLLINS
3.16
"WHITE CIRCLE" SYSTEM? THIS COULD BE A NEW SPECIES! I'LL GOOGLE IT RIGHT AWAY!
White Circle System
WHITE CIRCLE SYSTEM
©2007 Bill Griffith. World rights reserved. Distributed by King Features Syndicate
HMM... NOTHING ON GOOGLE... THIS IS WEIRD... ..IF SOMETHING'S NOT ON GOOGLE, CAN IT STILL BE REAL?
WHITE CIRCLE SYSTEM
PARKING
WHITE CIRCLE SYSTEM
NOW I'VE TOTALLY GOOGLED MYSELF OUT! I'LL HAVE TO GOOGLE AT LEAST A DOZEN "BARNEY GOOGLE" COMIC STRIPS FROM 1927 TO GOOGLE MYSELF DOWN!

91

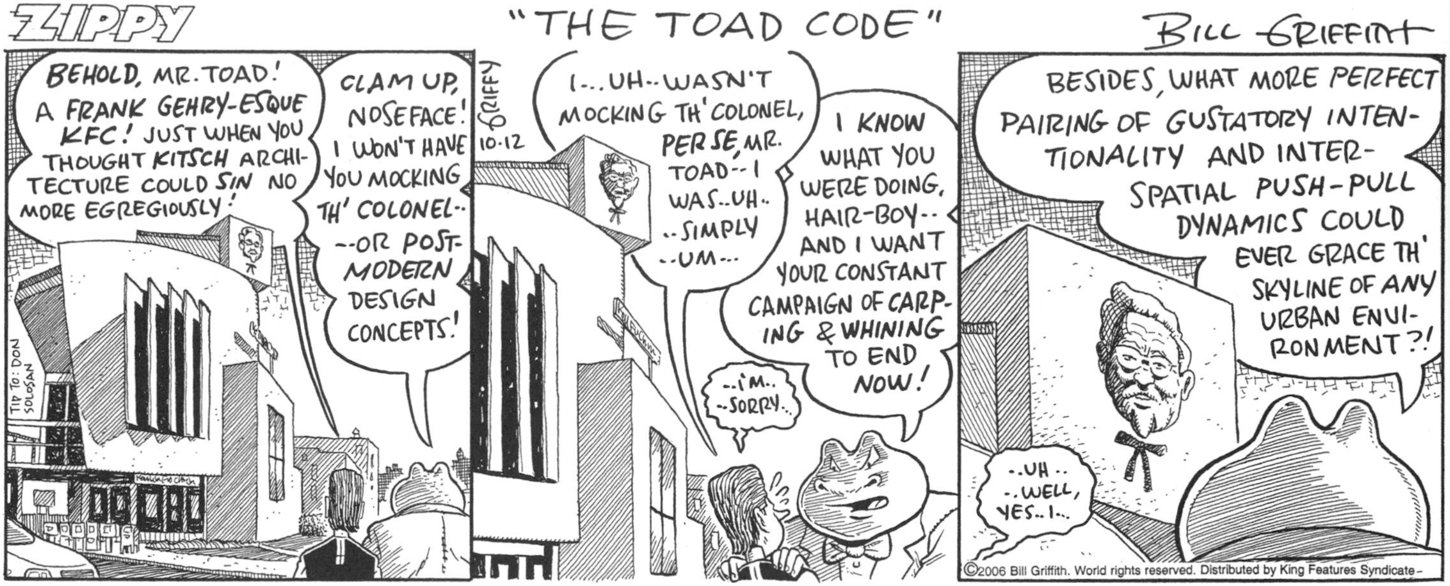
ZIPPY
"THE TOAD CODE"
BILL GRIFFITH
BEHOLD, MR. TOAD! A FRANK GEHRY-ESQUE KFC! JUST WHEN YOU THOUGHT KITSCH ARCHITECTURE COULD SIN NO MORE EGREGIOUSLY!
CLAM UP, NOSEFACE! I WON'T HAVE YOU MOCKING TH' COLONEL-- --OR POST-MODERN DESIGN CONCEPTS!
TIP TO: DON SOLOSAN
GRIFFY 10-12
I-.. UH-- WASN'T MOCKING TH' COLONEL, PER SE, MR. TOAD--I WAS..UH.. ..SIMPLY --UM--
I KNOW WHAT YOU WERE DOING, HAIR-BOY-- AND I WANT YOUR CONSTANT CAMPAIGN OF CARPING & WHINING TO END NOW!
--I'M.. --SORRY..
BESIDES, WHAT MORE PERFECT PAIRING OF GUSTATORY INTENTIONALITY AND INTER-SPATIAL PUSH-PULL DYNAMICS COULD EVER GRACE TH' SKYLINE OF ANY URBAN ENVIRONMENT?!
--UH.. --WELL, YES.. I..
©2006 Bill Griffith. World rights reserved. Distributed by King Features Syndicate

92

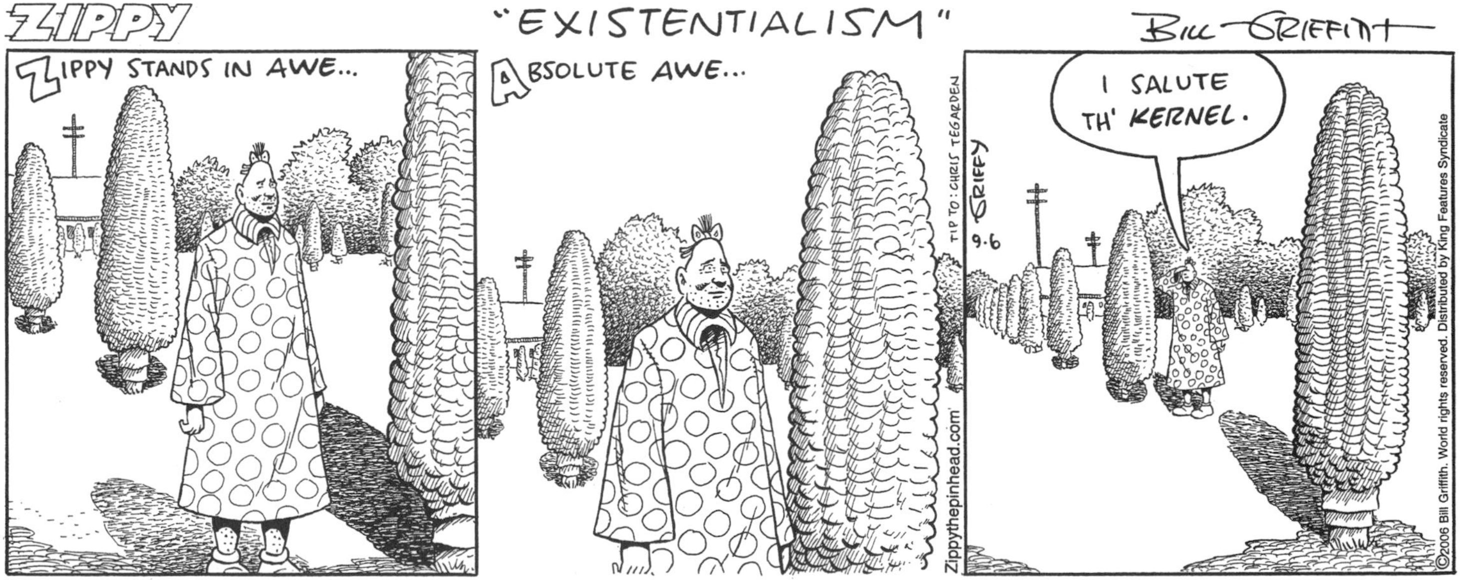
ZIPPY
"EXISTENTIALISM"
BILL GRIFFITH
ZIPPY STANDS IN AWE...
ABSOLUTE AWE...
TIP TO: CHRIS TEGARDEN
GRIFFY 9-6
Zippythepinhead.com
I SALUTE TH' KERNEL.
©2006 Bill Griffith. World rights reserved. Distributed by King Features Syndicate

93

DEEP DISH

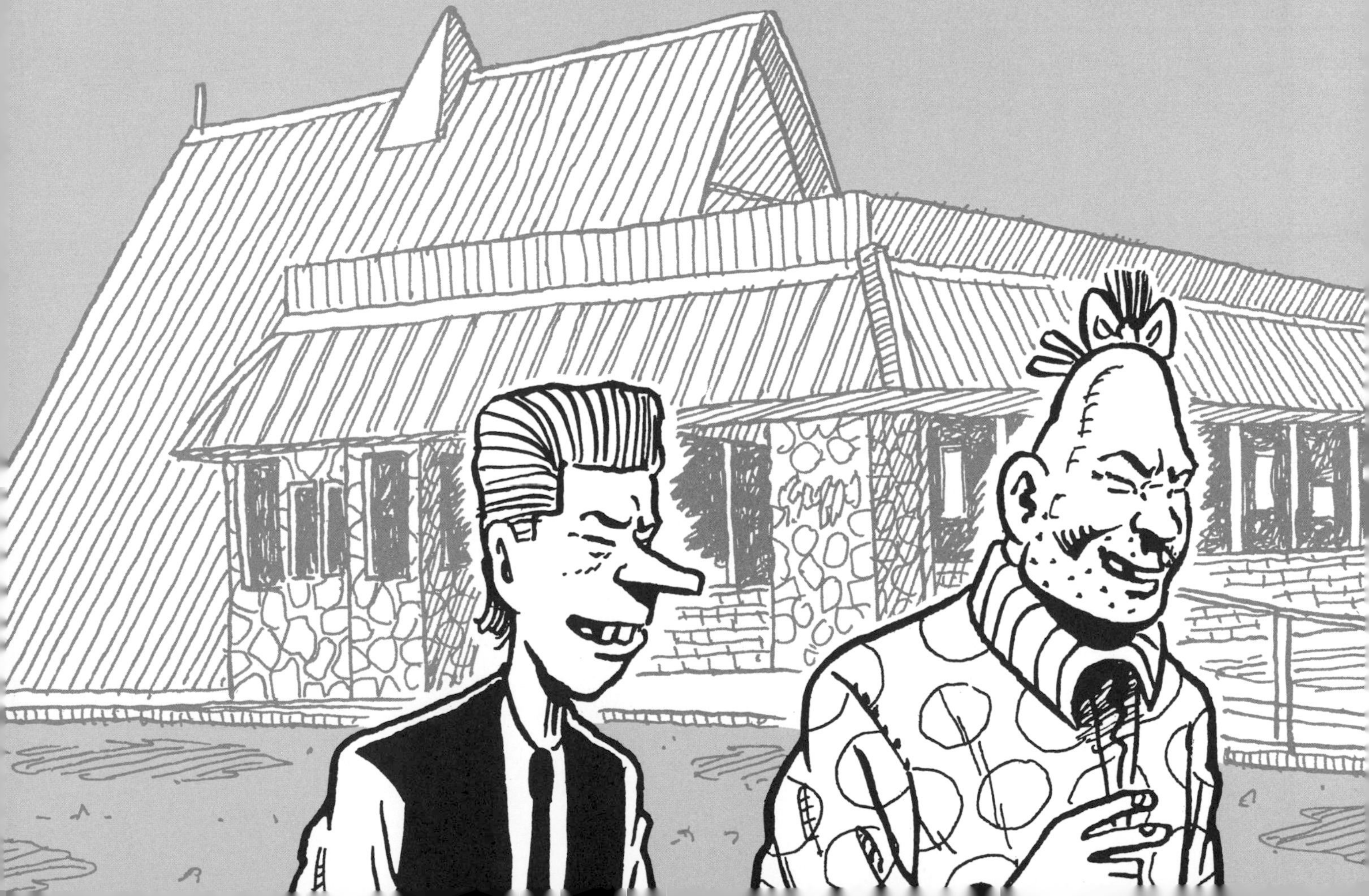

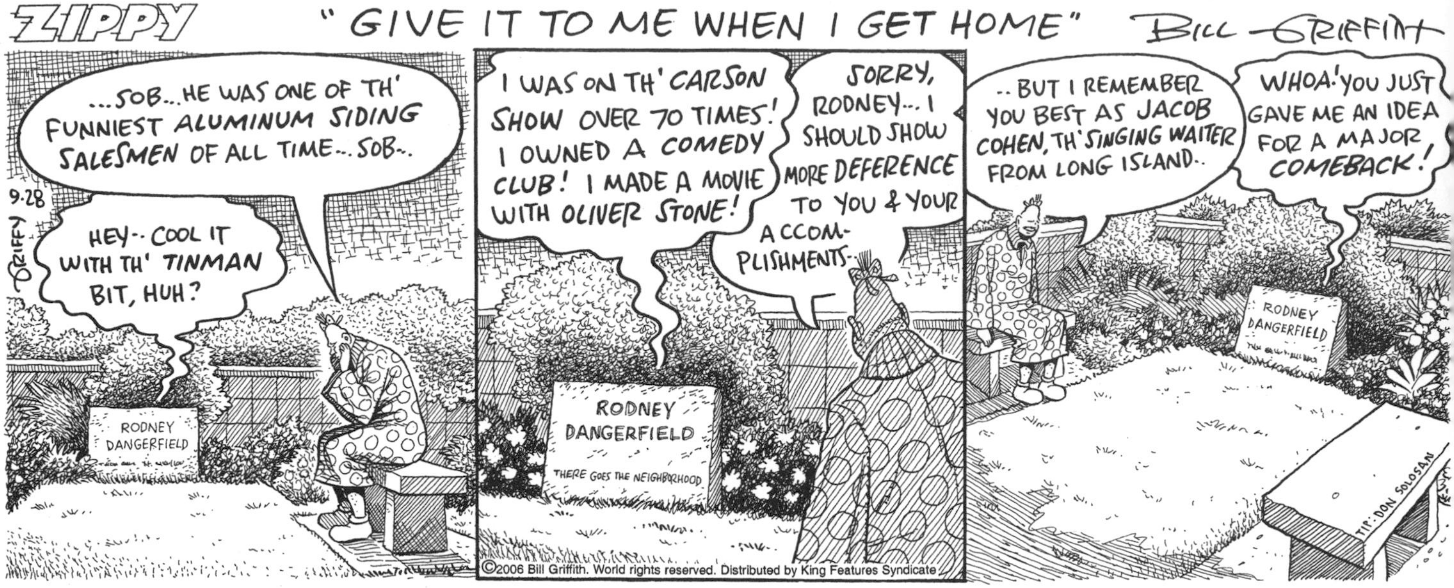
ZIPPY
"GIVE IT TO ME WHEN I GET HOME"
BILL GRIFFITH
...SOB...HE WAS ONE OF TH' FUNNIEST ALUMINUM SIDING SALESMEN OF ALL TIME...SOB..
9-28
GRIFFY
HEY.. COOL IT WITH TH' TINMAN BIT, HUH?
RODNEY DANGERFIELD
I WAS ON TH' CARSON SHOW OVER 70 TIMES! I OWNED A COMEDY CLUB! I MADE A MOVIE WITH OLIVER STONE!
SORRY, RODNEY... I SHOULD SHOW MORE DEFERENCE TO YOU & YOUR ACCOMPLISHMENTS..
RODNEY DANGERFIELD
THERE GOES THE NEIGHBORHOOD
©2006 Bill Griffith. World rights reserved. Distributed by King Features Syndicate
..BUT I REMEMBER YOU BEST AS JACOB COHEN, TH' SINGING WAITER FROM LONG ISLAND..
WHOA! YOU JUST GAVE ME AN IDEA FOR A MAJOR COMEBACK!
RODNEY DANGERFIELD
TIP: DON SOLOSAN

94

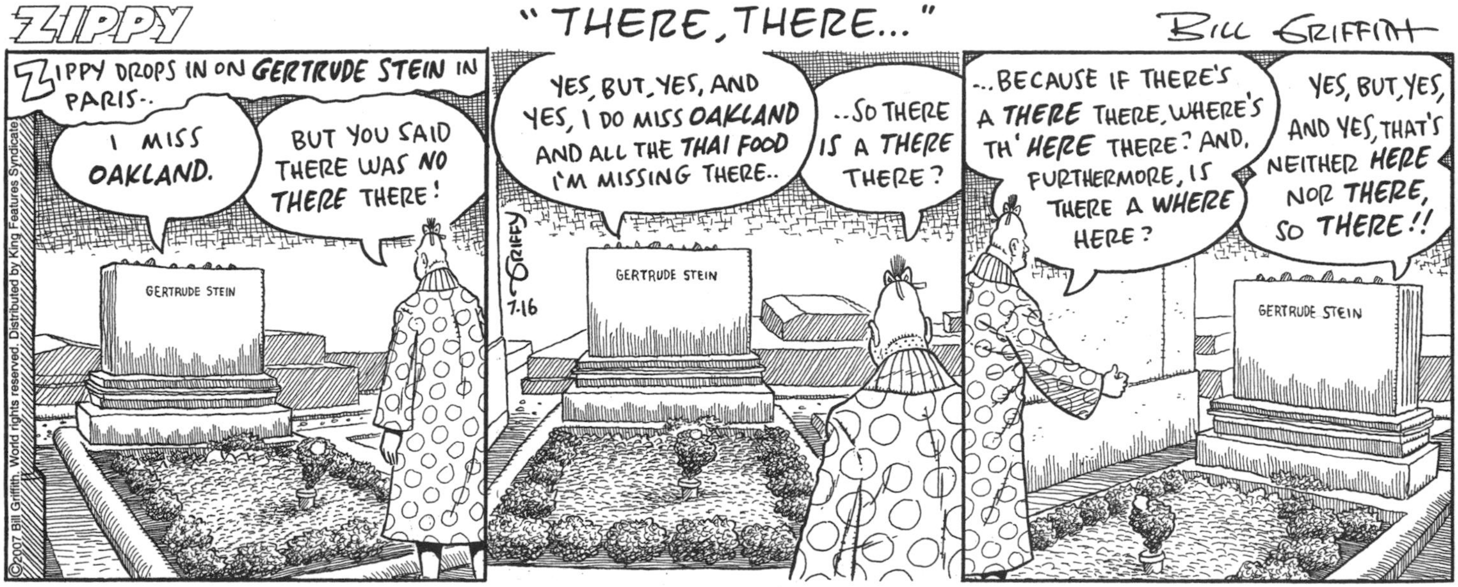
ZIPPY
"THERE, THERE..."
BILL GRIFFITH
ZIPPY DROPS IN ON GERTRUDE STEIN IN PARIS..
I MISS OAKLAND.
BUT YOU SAID THERE WAS NO THERE THERE!
GERTRUDE STEIN
©2007 Bill Griffith. World rights reserved. Distributed by King Features Syndicate
YES, BUT, YES, AND YES, I DO MISS OAKLAND AND ALL THE THAI FOOD I'M MISSING THERE..
..SO THERE IS A THERE THERE?
GRIFFY
7-16
GERTRUDE STEIN
...BECAUSE IF THERE'S A THERE THERE, WHERE'S TH' HERE THERE? AND, FURTHERMORE, IS THERE A WHERE HERE?
YES, BUT, YES, AND YES, THAT'S NEITHER HERE NOR THERE, SO THERE!!
GERTRUDE STEIN

95 A

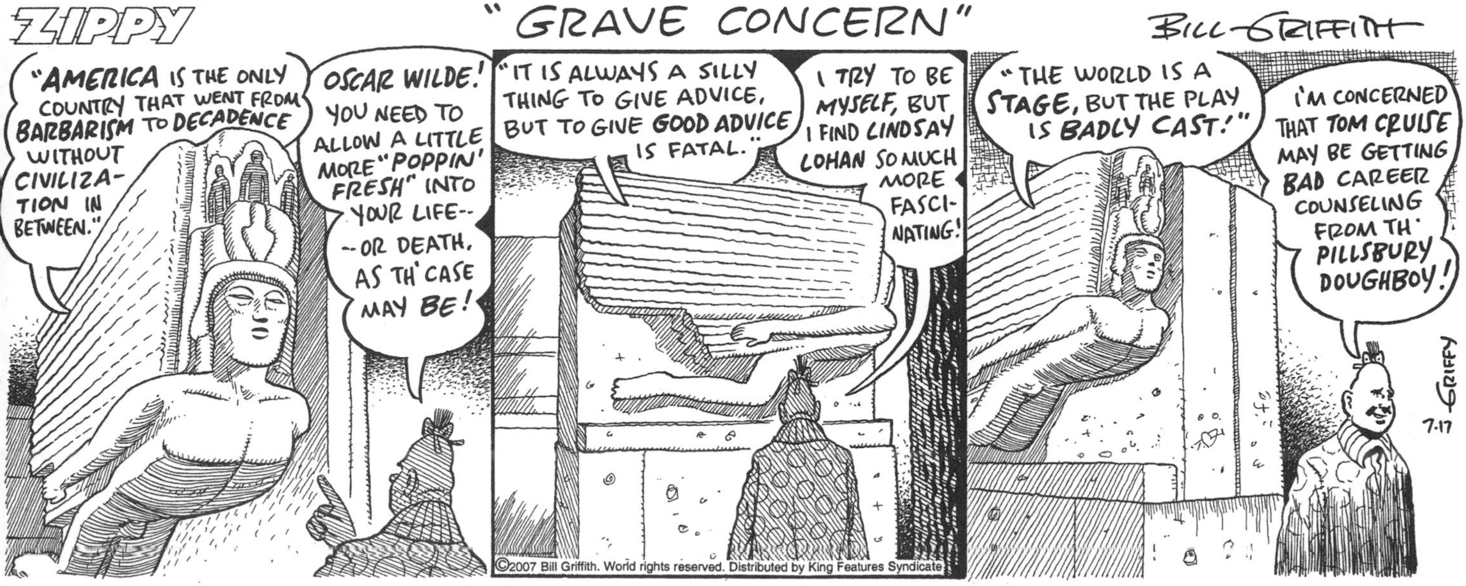
ZIPPY
"GRAVE CONCERN"
BILL GRIFFITH
"AMERICA IS THE ONLY COUNTRY THAT WENT FROM BARBARISM TO DECADENCE WITHOUT CIVILIZA-TION IN BETWEEN."
OSCAR WILDE! YOU NEED TO ALLOW A LITTLE MORE "POPPIN' FRESH" INTO YOUR LIFE-- --OR DEATH, AS TH' CASE MAY BE!
"IT IS ALWAYS A SILLY THING TO GIVE ADVICE, BUT TO GIVE GOOD ADVICE IS FATAL."
I TRY TO BE MYSELF, BUT I FIND LINDSAY LOHAN SO MUCH MORE FASCI-NATING!
"THE WORLD IS A STAGE, BUT THE PLAY IS BADLY CAST!"
I'M CONCERNED THAT TOM CRUISE MAY BE GETTING BAD CAREER COUNSELING FROM TH' PILLSBURY DOUGHBOY!
GRIFFY
7-17
©2007 Bill Griffith. World rights reserved. Distributed by King Features Syndicate

95 B

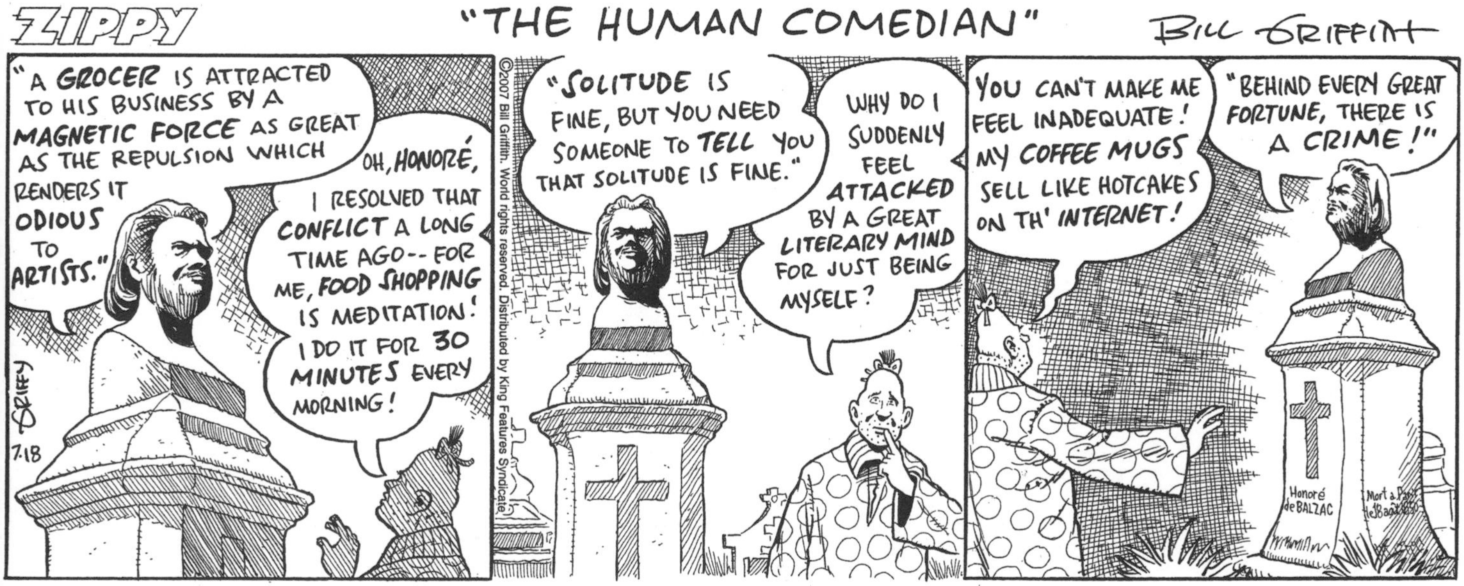
ZIPPY
"THE HUMAN COMEDIAN"
BILL GRIFFITH
"A GROCER IS ATTRACTED TO HIS BUSINESS BY A MAGNETIC FORCE AS GREAT AS THE REPULSION WHICH RENDERS IT ODIOUS TO ARTISTS."
OH, HONORÉ, I RESOLVED THAT CONFLICT A LONG TIME AGO-- FOR ME, FOOD SHOPPING IS MEDITATION! I DO IT FOR 30 MINUTES EVERY MORNING!
GRIFFY
7-18
©2007 Bill Griffith. World rights reserved. Distributed by King Features Syndicate
"SOLITUDE IS FINE, BUT YOU NEED SOMEONE TO TELL YOU THAT SOLITUDE IS FINE."
WHY DO I SUDDENLY FEEL ATTACKED BY A GREAT LITERARY MIND FOR JUST BEING MYSELF?
YOU CAN'T MAKE ME FEEL INADEQUATE! MY COFFEE MUGS SELL LIKE HOTCAKES ON TH' INTERNET!
"BEHIND EVERY GREAT FORTUNE, THERE IS A CRIME!"
Honoré de BALZAC

95 C

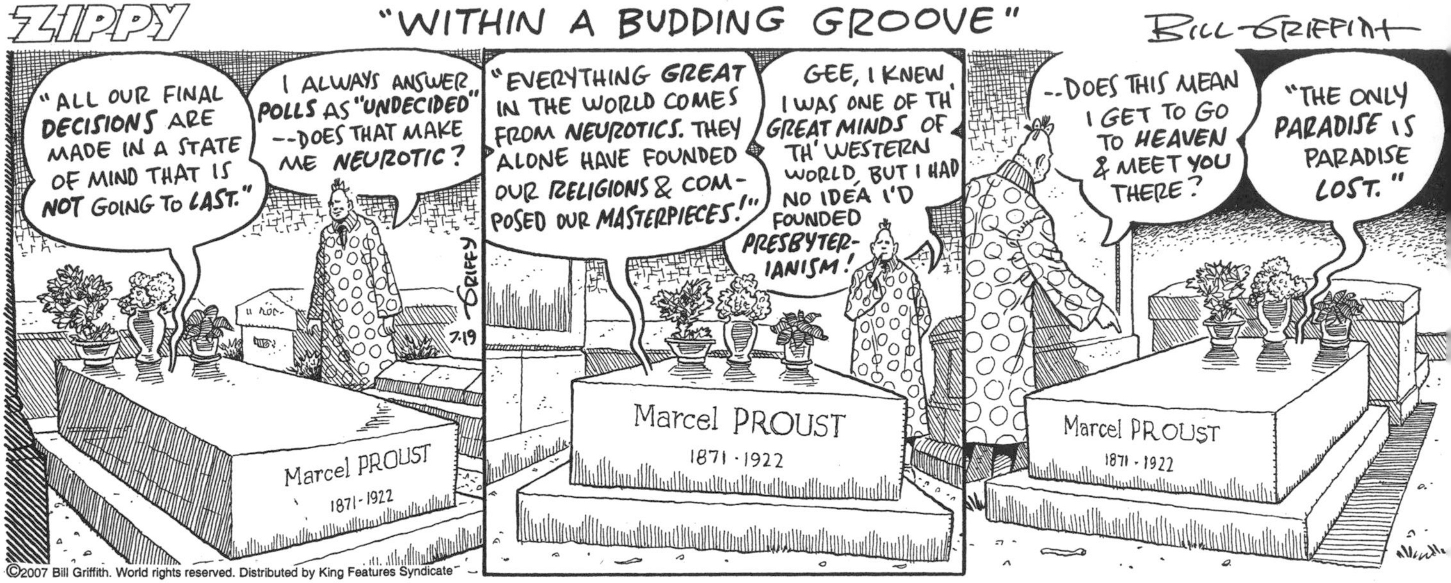

ZIPPY
"WITHIN A BUDDING GROOVE"
BILL GRIFFITH
"ALL OUR FINAL DECISIONS ARE MADE IN A STATE OF MIND THAT IS NOT GOING TO LAST."
I ALWAYS ANSWER POLLS AS "UNDECIDED" --DOES THAT MAKE ME NEUROTIC?
GRIFFY 7-19
Marcel PROUST 1871-1922
"EVERYTHING GREAT IN THE WORLD COMES FROM NEUROTICS. THEY ALONE HAVE FOUNDED OUR RELIGIONS & COMPOSED OUR MASTERPIECES!"
GEE, I KNEW I WAS ONE OF TH' GREAT MINDS OF TH' WESTERN WORLD, BUT I HAD NO IDEA I'D FOUNDED PRESBYTERIANISM!
Marcel PROUST 1871-1922
--DOES THIS MEAN I GET TO GO TO HEAVEN & MEET YOU THERE?
"THE ONLY PARADISE IS PARADISE LOST."
Marcel PROUST 1871-1922
©2007 Bill Griffith. World rights reserved. Distributed by King Features Syndicate

95 D

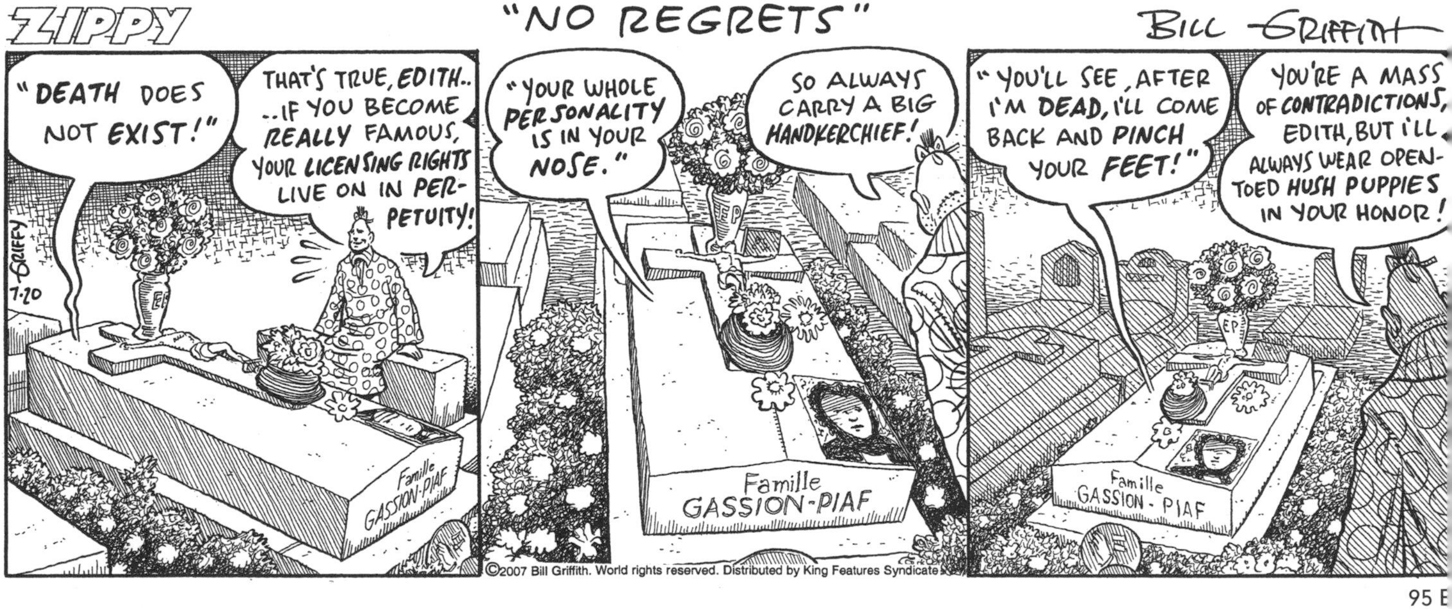

ZIPPY
"NO REGRETS"
BILL GRIFFITH
"DEATH DOES NOT EXIST!"
THAT'S TRUE, EDITH.. ..IF YOU BECOME REALLY FAMOUS, YOUR LICENSING RIGHTS LIVE ON IN PERPETUITY!
GRIFFY 7-20
Famille GASSION-PIAF
"YOUR WHOLE PERSONALITY IS IN YOUR NOSE."
SO ALWAYS CARRY A BIG HANDKERCHIEF!
Famille GASSION-PIAF
"YOU'LL SEE, AFTER I'M DEAD, I'LL COME BACK AND PINCH YOUR FEET!"
YOU'RE A MASS OF CONTRADICTIONS, EDITH, BUT I'LL ALWAYS WEAR OPEN-TOED HUSH PUPPIES IN YOUR HONOR!
Famille GASSION-PIAF
©2007 Bill Griffith. World rights reserved. Distributed by King Features Syndicate

95 E

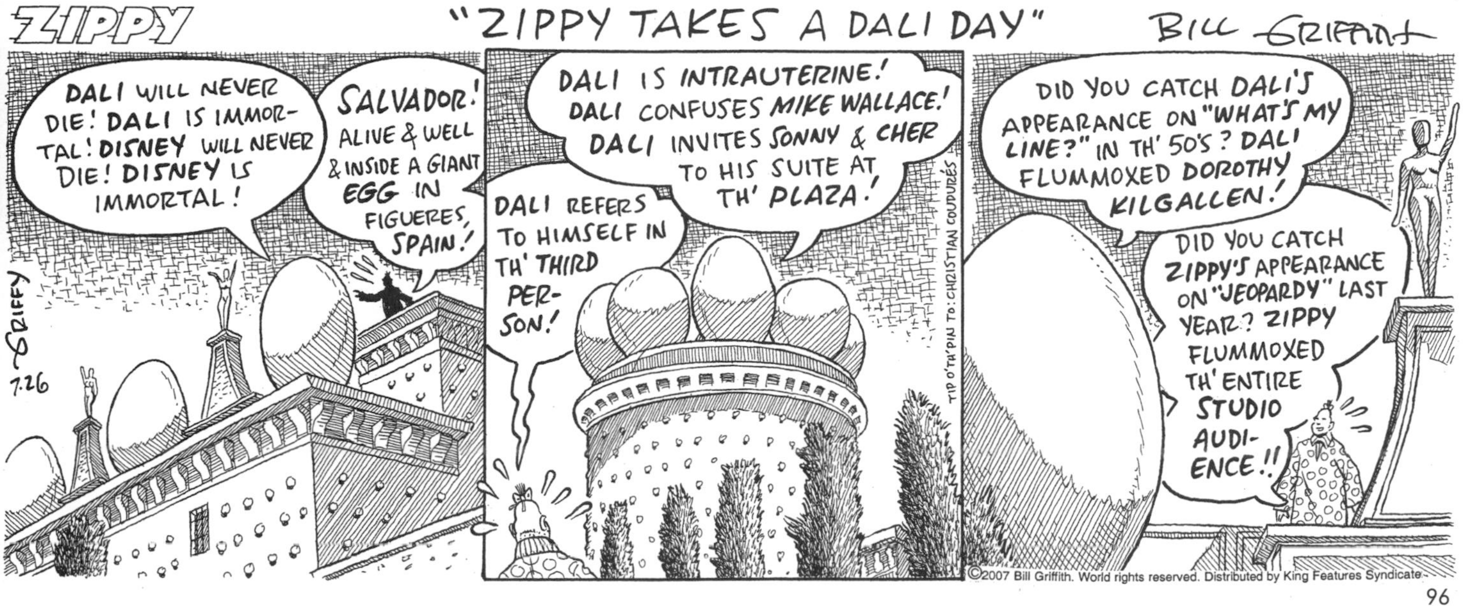
ZIPPY
"ZIPPY TAKES A DALI DAY"
BILL GRIFFITH
DALI WILL NEVER DIE! DALI IS IMMORTAL! DISNEY WILL NEVER DIE! DISNEY IS IMMORTAL!
SALVADOR! ALIVE & WELL & INSIDE A GIANT EGG IN FIGUERES, SPAIN!
GRIFFY 7.26
DALI IS INTRAUTERINE! DALI CONFUSES MIKE WALLACE! DALI INVITES SONNY & CHER TO HIS SUITE AT TH' PLAZA!
DALI REFERS TO HIMSELF IN TH' THIRD PERSON!
TIP O'TH'PIN TO: CHRISTIAN COUDURÉS
DID YOU CATCH DALI'S APPEARANCE ON "WHAT'S MY LINE?" IN TH' 50'S? DALI FLUMMOXED DOROTHY KILGALLEN!
DID YOU CATCH ZIPPY'S APPEARANCE ON "JEOPARDY" LAST YEAR? ZIPPY FLUMMOXED TH' ENTIRE STUDIO AUDIENCE!!
©2007 Bill Griffith. World rights reserved. Distributed by King Features Syndicate

96

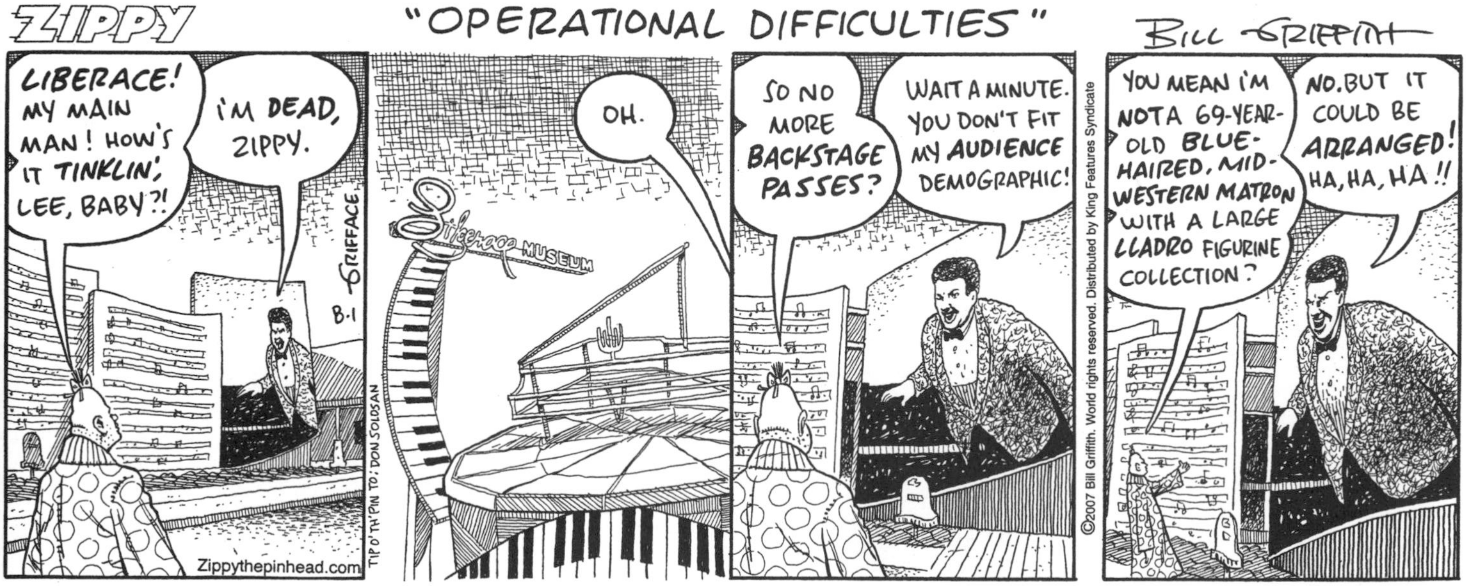
ZIPPY
"OPERATIONAL DIFFICULTIES"
BILL GRIFFITH
LIBERACE! MY MAIN MAN! HOW'S IT TINKLIN', LEE, BABY?!
I'M DEAD, ZIPPY.
GRIFFACE. 8.1
Zippythepinhead.com
TIP O'TH'PIN TO: DON SOLOSAN
Liberace MUSEUM
OH.
SO NO MORE BACKSTAGE PASSES?
WAIT A MINUTE. YOU DON'T FIT MY AUDIENCE DEMOGRAPHIC!
©2007 Bill Griffith. World rights reserved. Distributed by King Features Syndicate
YOU MEAN I'M NOT A 69-YEAR-OLD BLUE-HAIRED, MID-WESTERN MATRON WITH A LARGE LLADRO FIGURINE COLLECTION?
NO. BUT IT COULD BE ARRANGED! HA, HA, HA!!

97

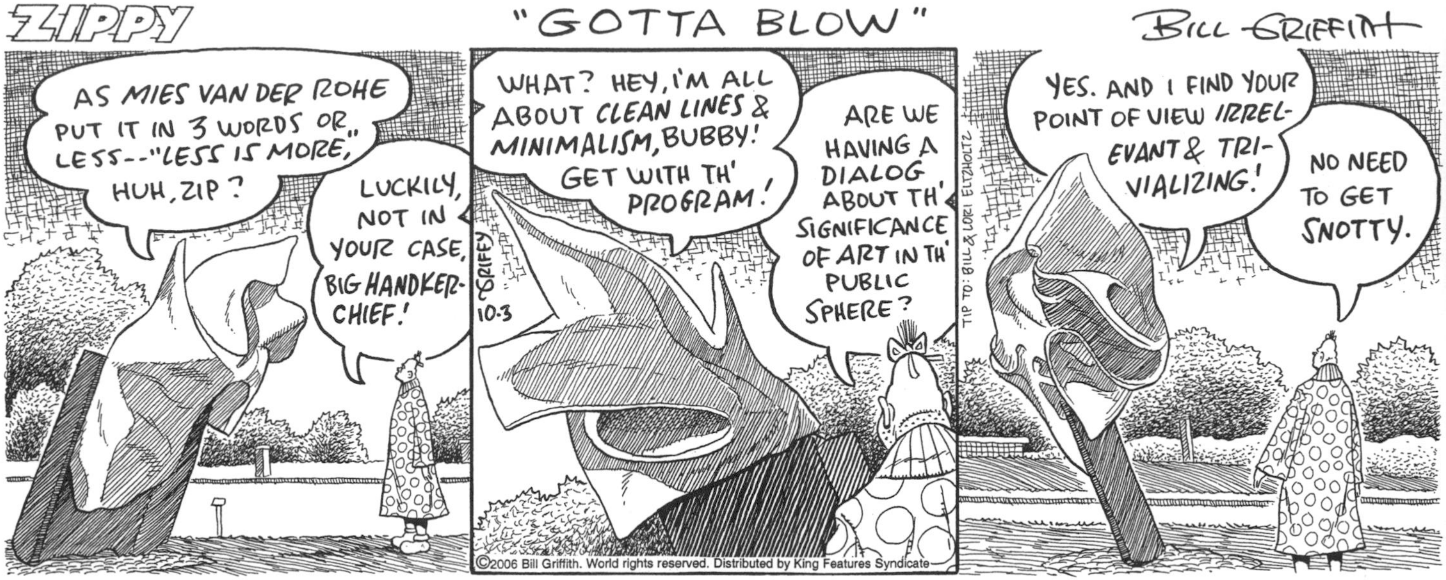
ZIPPY
"GOTTA BLOW"
BILL GRIFFITH
AS MIES VAN DER ROHE PUT IT IN 3 WORDS OR LESS--"LESS IS MORE," HUH, ZIP?
LUCKILY, NOT IN YOUR CASE, BIG HANDKERCHIEF!
GRIFFY 10.3
WHAT? HEY, I'M ALL ABOUT CLEAN LINES & MINIMALISM, BUBBY! GET WITH TH' PROGRAM!
ARE WE HAVING A DIALOG ABOUT TH' SIGNIFICANCE OF ART IN TH' PUBLIC SPHERE?
©2006 Bill Griffith. World rights reserved. Distributed by King Features Syndicate
TIP TO: BILL & LORI ELTZHOLTZ
YES. AND I FIND YOUR POINT OF VIEW IRRELEVANT & TRIVIALIZING!
NO NEED TO GET SNOTTY.

98

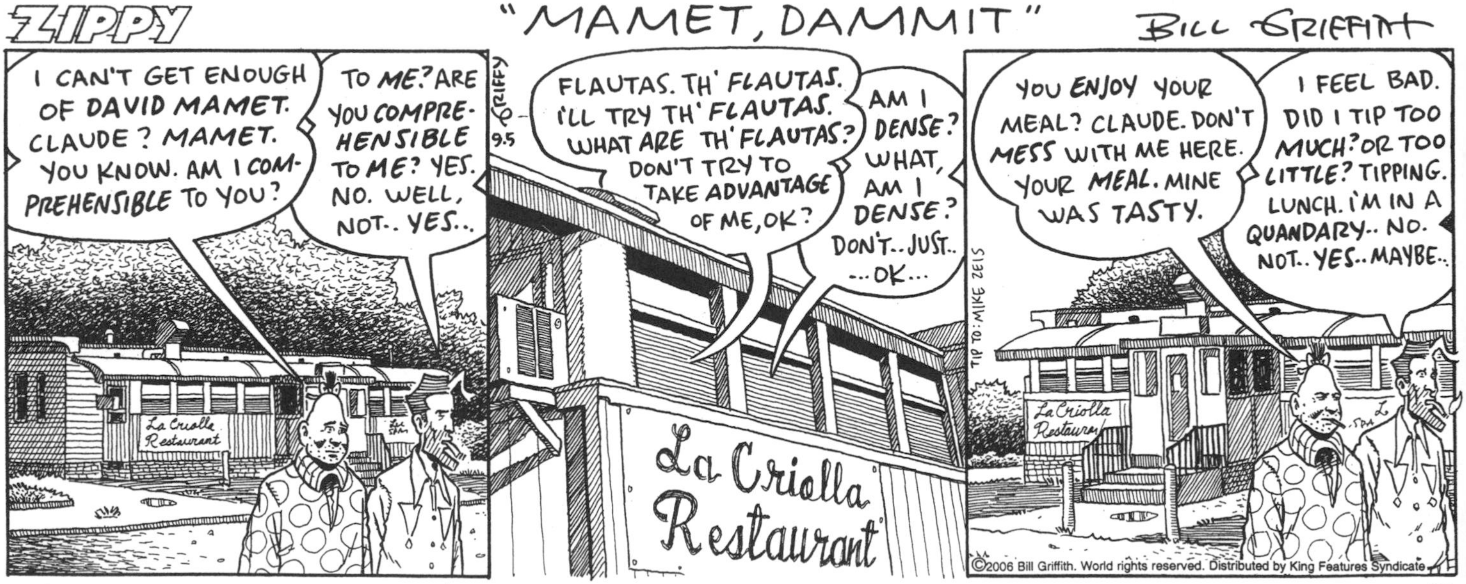
ZIPPY
"MAMET, DAMMIT"
BILL GRIFFITH
I CAN'T GET ENOUGH OF DAVID MAMET. CLAUDE? MAMET. YOU KNOW. AM I COMPREHENSIBLE TO YOU?
TO ME? ARE YOU COMPREHENSIBLE TO ME? YES. NO. WELL, NOT.. YES..
La Criolla Restaurant
GRIFFY 9.5
FLAUTAS. TH' FLAUTAS. I'LL TRY TH' FLAUTAS. WHAT ARE TH' FLAUTAS? DON'T TRY TO TAKE ADVANTAGE OF ME, OK?
AM I DENSE? WHAT, AM I DENSE? DON'T.. JUST.. ...OK...
La Criolla Restaurant
TIP TO: MIKE ZEIS
YOU ENJOY YOUR MEAL? CLAUDE. DON'T MESS WITH ME HERE. YOUR MEAL. MINE WAS TASTY.
I FEEL BAD. DID I TIP TOO MUCH? OR TOO LITTLE? TIPPING. LUNCH. I'M IN A QUANDARY.. NO. NOT.. YES.. MAYBE..
©2006 Bill Griffith. World rights reserved. Distributed by King Features Syndicate

99

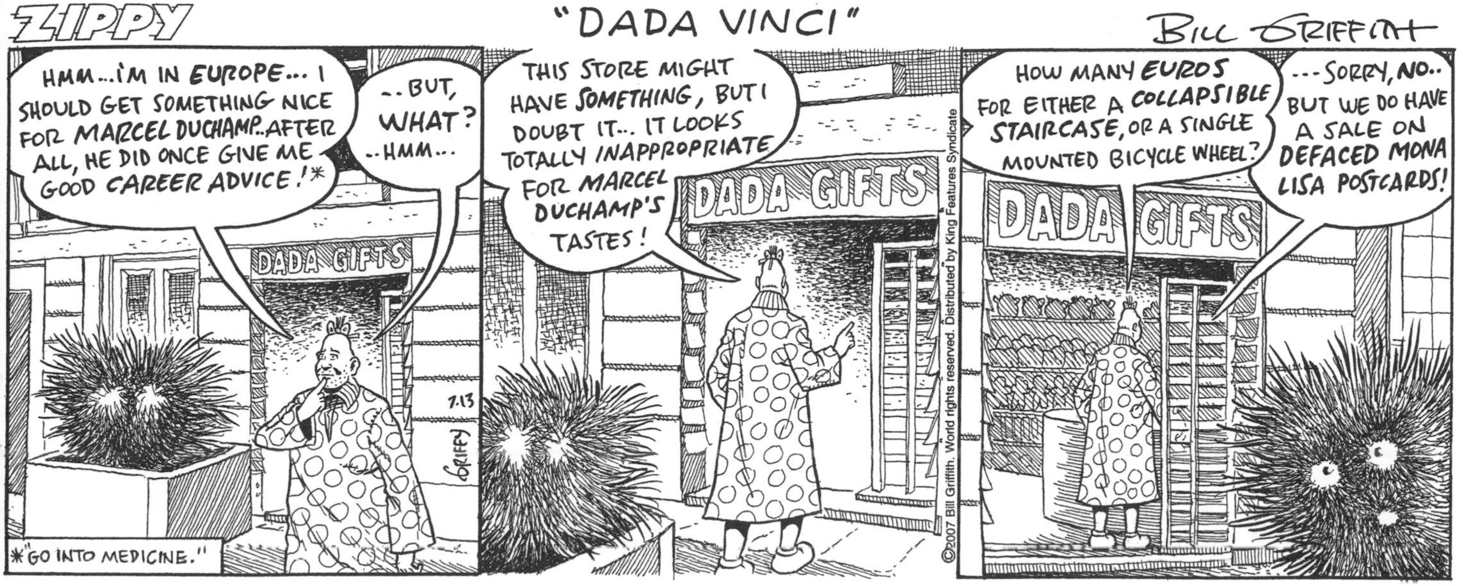

ZIPPY
"DADA VINCI"
BILL GRIFFITH
HMM...I'M IN EUROPE... I SHOULD GET SOMETHING NICE FOR MARCEL DUCHAMP..AFTER ALL, HE DID ONCE GIVE ME GOOD CAREER ADVICE!*
--BUT, WHAT? ..HMM...
DADA GIFTS
7.13
GRIFFY
*"GO INTO MEDICINE."
THIS STORE MIGHT HAVE SOMETHING, BUT I DOUBT IT... IT LOOKS TOTALLY INAPPROPRIATE FOR MARCEL DUCHAMP'S TASTES!
DADA GIFTS
©2007 Bill Griffith. World rights reserved. Distributed by King Features Syndicate
HOW MANY EUROS FOR EITHER A COLLAPSIBLE STAIRCASE, OR A SINGLE MOUNTED BICYCLE WHEEL?
---SORRY, NO.. BUT WE DO HAVE A SALE ON DEFACED MONA LISA POSTCARDS!
DADA GIFTS

100

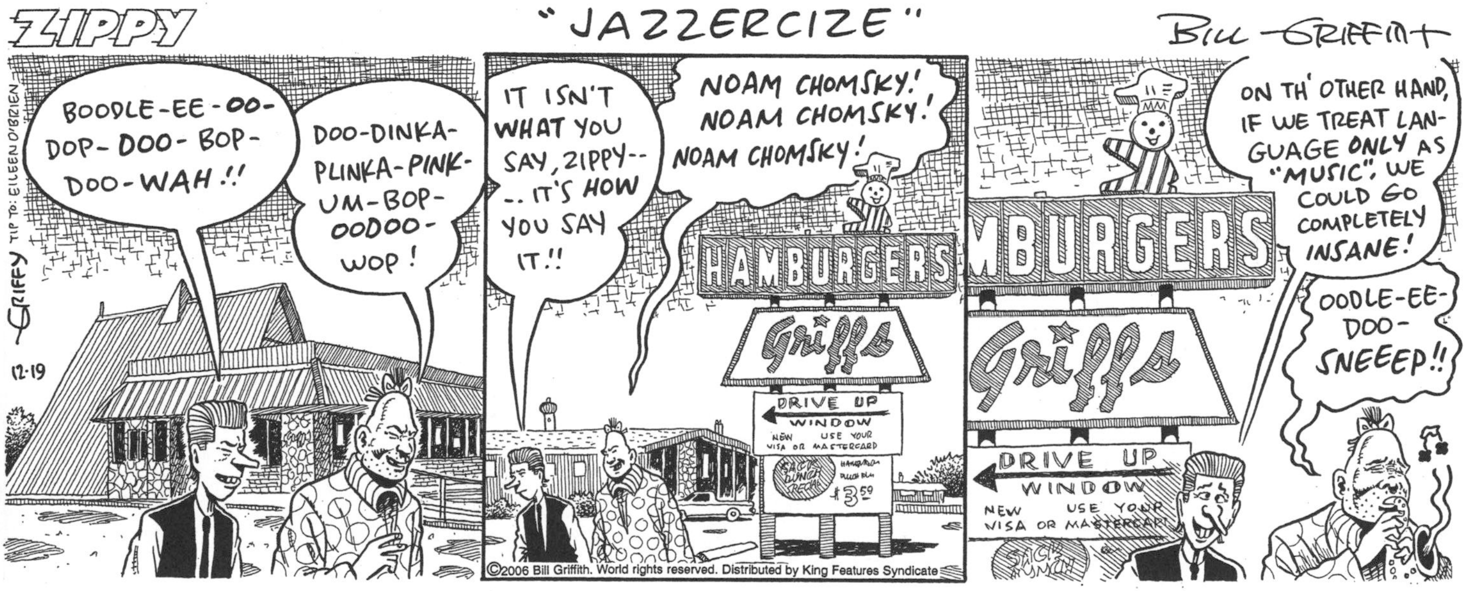

ZIPPY
"JAZZERCIZE"
BILL GRIFFITH
GRIFFY TIP TO: EILEEN O'BRIEN
12.19
BOODLE-EE-OO-DOP-DOO-BOP-DOO-WAH!!
DOO-DINKA-PLINKA-PINK-UM-BOP-OODOO-WOP!
IT ISN'T WHAT YOU SAY, ZIPPY-- -- IT'S HOW YOU SAY IT!!
NOAM CHOMSKY! NOAM CHOMSKY! NOAM CHOMSKY!
HAMBURGERS
Griffs
DRIVE UP WINDOW
NEW USE YOUR VISA OR MASTERCARD
$3.59
©2006 Bill Griffith. World rights reserved. Distributed by King Features Syndicate
ON TH' OTHER HAND, IF WE TREAT LANGUAGE ONLY AS "MUSIC", WE COULD GO COMPLETELY INSANE!
OODLE-EE-DOO-SNEEEP!!
MBURGERS
Griffs
DRIVE UP WINDOW
NEW USE YOUR VISA OR MASTERCARD

101

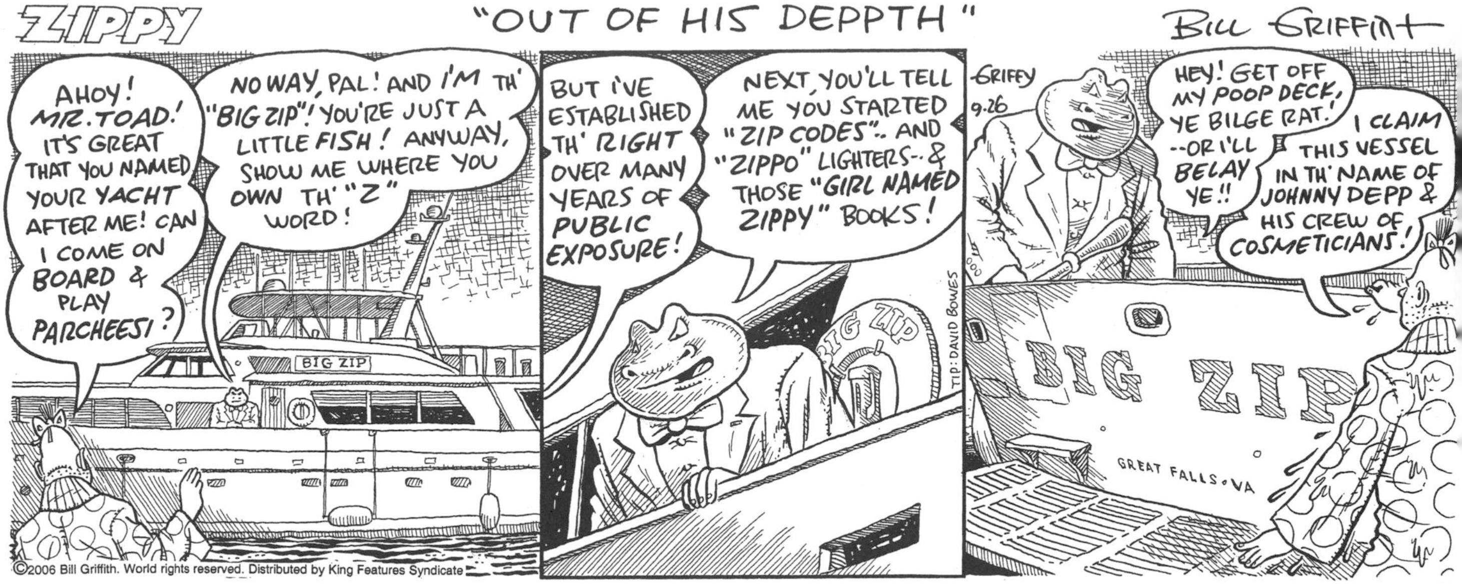
ZIPPY
"OUT OF HIS DEPPTH"
BILL GRIFFITH
AHOY! MR. TOAD! IT'S GREAT THAT YOU NAMED YOUR YACHT AFTER ME! CAN I COME ON BOARD & PLAY PARCHEESI?
NO WAY, PAL! AND I'M TH' "BIG ZIP"! YOU'RE JUST A LITTLE FISH! ANYWAY, SHOW ME WHERE YOU OWN TH' "Z" WORD!
BIG ZIP
BUT I'VE ESTABLISHED TH' RIGHT OVER MANY YEARS OF PUBLIC EXPOSURE!
NEXT, YOU'LL TELL ME YOU STARTED "ZIP CODES".. AND "ZIPPO" LIGHTERS.. & THOSE "GIRL NAMED ZIPPY" BOOKS!
BIG ZIP
TIP: DAVID BOWES
GRIFFY 9-26
HEY! GET OFF MY POOP DECK, YE BILGE RAT! --OR I'LL BELAY YE!!
I CLAIM THIS VESSEL IN TH' NAME OF JOHNNY DEPP & HIS CREW OF COSMETICIANS!
BIG ZIP
GREAT FALLS, VA
©2006 Bill Griffith. World rights reserved. Distributed by King Features Syndicate

102

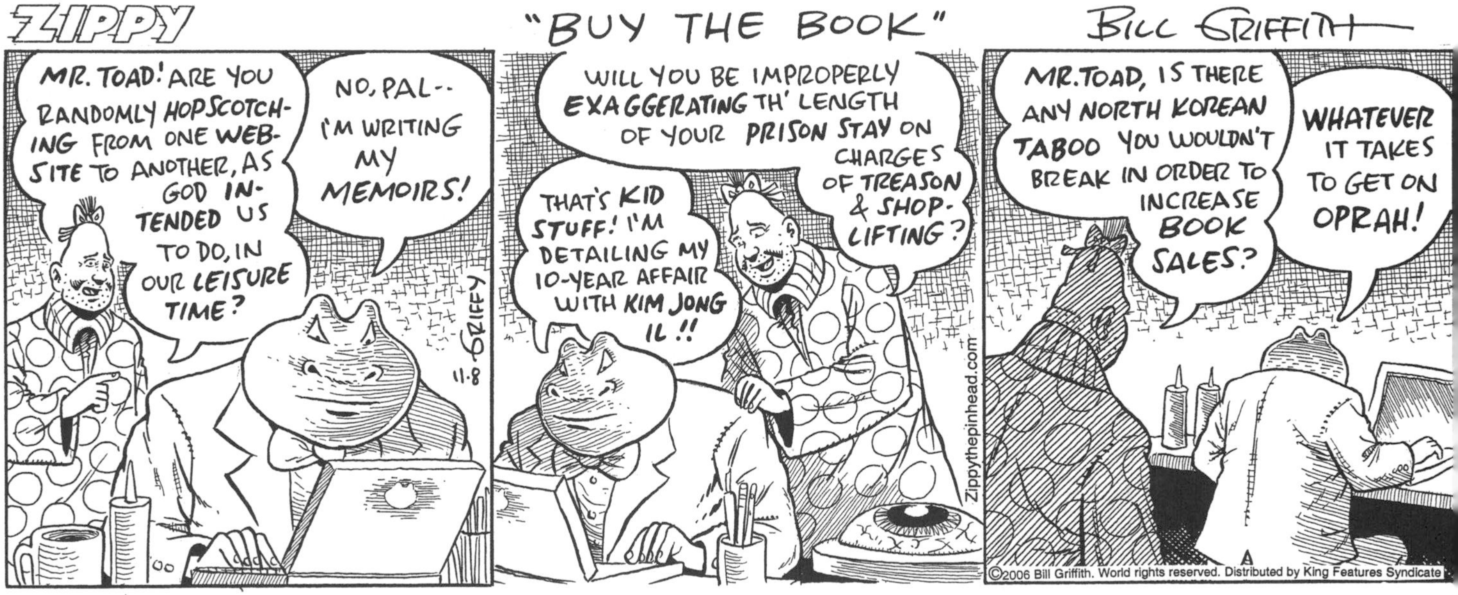
ZIPPY
"BUY THE BOOK"
BILL GRIFFITH
MR. TOAD! ARE YOU RANDOMLY HOPSCOTCHING FROM ONE WEB-SITE TO ANOTHER, AS GOD INTENDED US TO DO, IN OUR LEISURE TIME?
NO, PAL-- I'M WRITING MY MEMOIRS!
GRIFFY 11-8
WILL YOU BE IMPROPERLY EXAGGERATING TH' LENGTH OF YOUR PRISON STAY ON CHARGES OF TREASON & SHOP-LIFTING?
THAT'S KID STUFF! I'M DETAILING MY 10-YEAR AFFAIR WITH KIM JONG IL!!
Zippythepinhead.com
MR. TOAD, IS THERE ANY NORTH KOREAN TABOO YOU WOULDN'T BREAK IN ORDER TO INCREASE BOOK SALES?
WHATEVER IT TAKES TO GET ON OPRAH!
©2006 Bill Griffith. World rights reserved. Distributed by King Features Syndicate

103

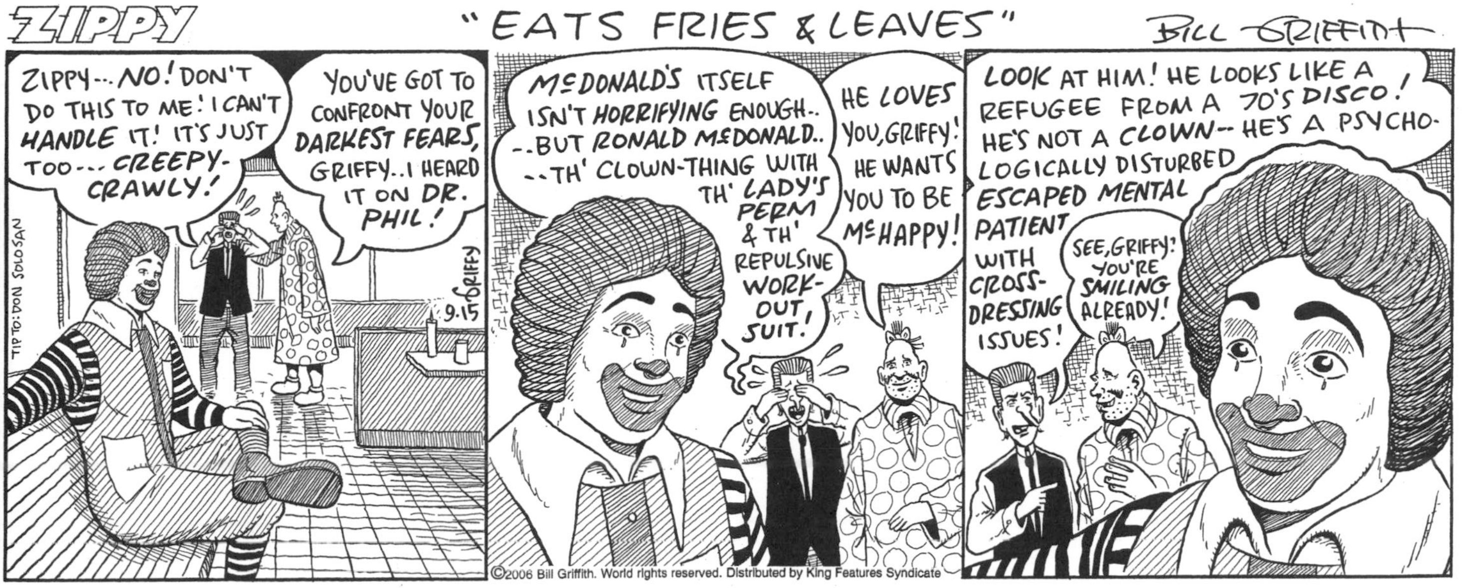
ZIPPY
"EATS FRIES & LEAVES"
BILL GRIFFITH
ZIPPY-- NO! DON'T DO THIS TO ME! I CAN'T HANDLE IT! IT'S JUST TOO-- CREEPY-CRAWLY!
YOU'VE GOT TO CONFRONT YOUR DARKEST FEARS, GRIFFY.. I HEARD IT ON DR. PHIL!
TIP TO: DON SOLOSAN
GRIFFY 9.15
McDONALD'S ITSELF ISN'T HORRIFYING ENOUGH.. --BUT RONALD McDONALD.. --TH' CLOWN-THING WITH TH' LADY'S PERM & TH' REPULSIVE WORK-OUT SUIT!
HE LOVES YOU, GRIFFY! HE WANTS YOU TO BE McHAPPY!
LOOK AT HIM! HE LOOKS LIKE A REFUGEE FROM A 70'S DISCO! HE'S NOT A CLOWN-- HE'S A PSYCHO-LOGICALLY DISTURBED ESCAPED MENTAL PATIENT WITH CROSS-DRESSING ISSUES!
SEE, GRIFFY! YOU'RE SMILING ALREADY!
©2006 Bill Griffith. World rights reserved. Distributed by King Features Syndicate

104

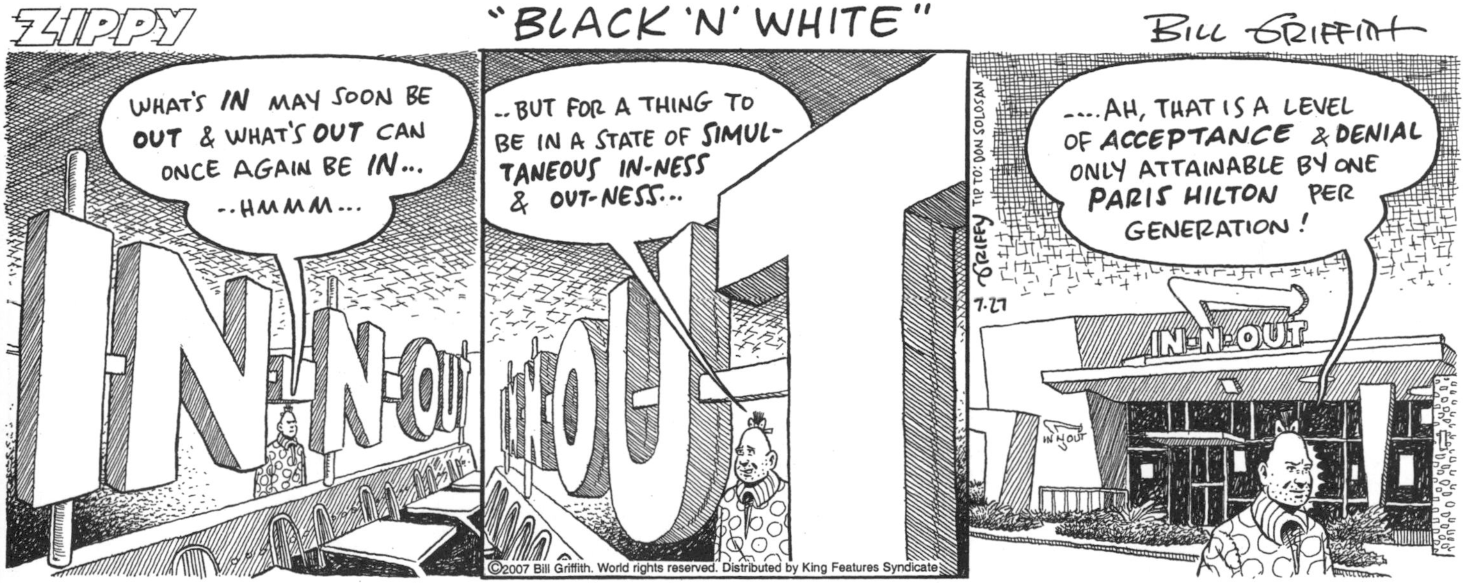
ZIPPY
"BLACK 'N' WHITE"
BILL GRIFFITH
WHAT'S IN MAY SOON BE OUT & WHAT'S OUT CAN ONCE AGAIN BE IN... --HMMM...
IN-N-OUT
--BUT FOR A THING TO BE IN A STATE OF SIMUL-TANEOUS IN-NESS & OUT-NESS...
TIP TO: DON SOLOSAN
GRIFFY 7.27
----AH, THAT IS A LEVEL OF ACCEPTANCE & DENIAL ONLY ATTAINABLE BY ONE PARIS HILTON PER GENERATION!
IN-N-OUT
IN-N-OUT
©2007 Bill Griffith. World rights reserved. Distributed by King Features Syndicate

105

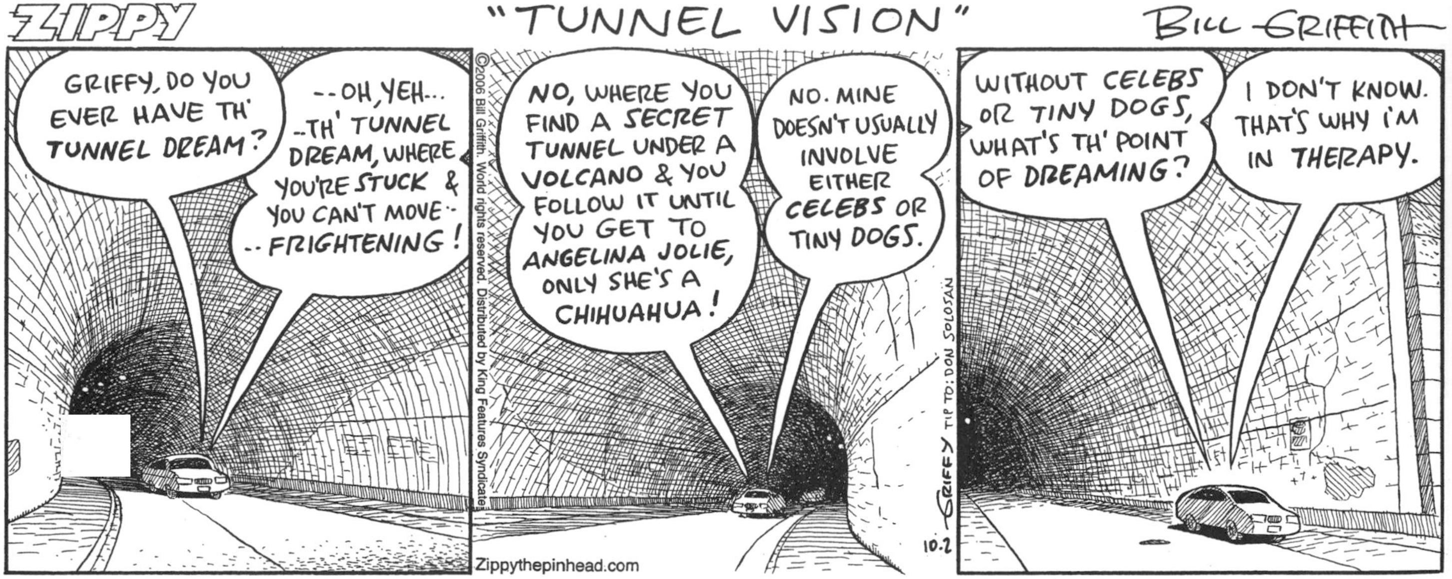
ZIPPY
"TUNNEL VISION"
BILL GRIFFITH
GRIFFY, DO YOU EVER HAVE TH' TUNNEL DREAM?
--OH, YEH... --TH' TUNNEL DREAM, WHERE YOU'RE STUCK & YOU CAN'T MOVE-- --FRIGHTENING!
©2006 Bill Griffith. World rights reserved. Distributed by King Features Syndicate
NO, WHERE YOU FIND A SECRET TUNNEL UNDER A VOLCANO & YOU FOLLOW IT UNTIL YOU GET TO ANGELINA JOLIE, ONLY SHE'S A CHIHUAHUA!
NO. MINE DOESN'T USUALLY INVOLVE EITHER CELEBS OR TINY DOGS.
TIP TO: DON SOLOSAN
GRIFFY
10.2
Zippythepinhead.com
WITHOUT CELEBS OR TINY DOGS, WHAT'S TH' POINT OF DREAMING?
I DON'T KNOW. THAT'S WHY I'M IN THERAPY.

106

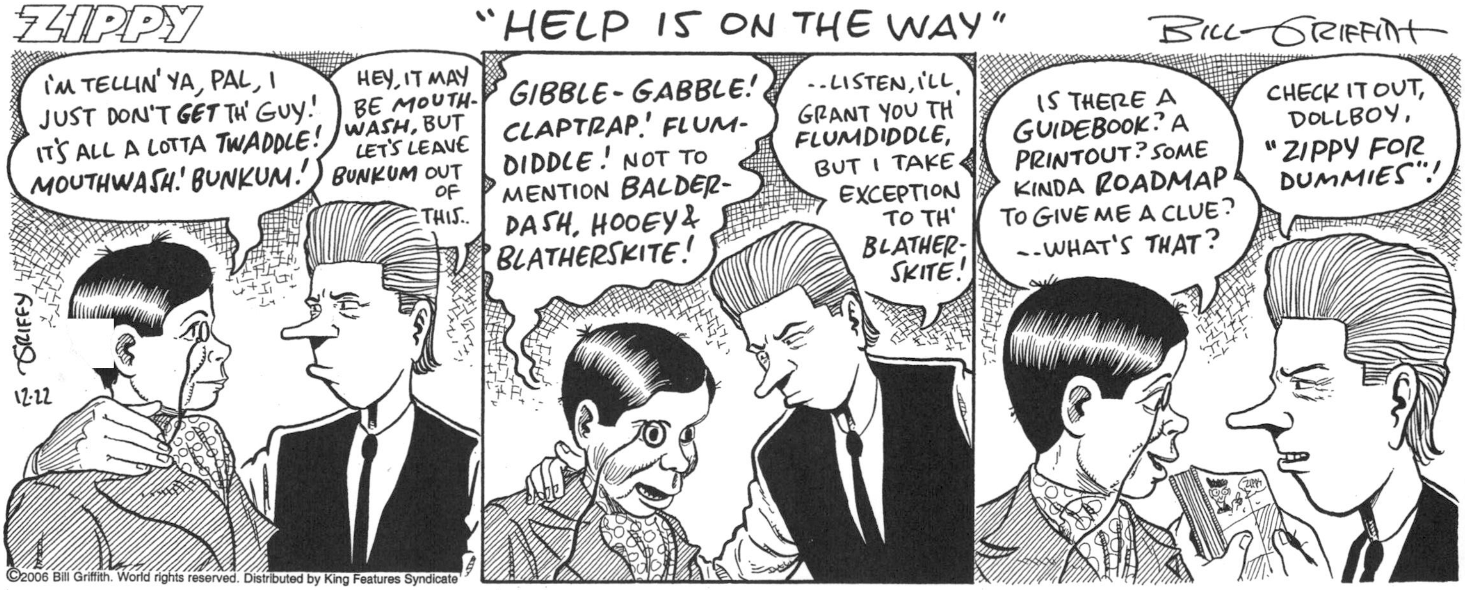
ZIPPY
"HELP IS ON THE WAY"
BILL GRIFFITH
I'M TELLIN' YA, PAL, I JUST DON'T GET TH' GUY! IT'S ALL A LOTTA TWADDLE! MOUTHWASH! BUNKUM!
HEY, IT MAY BE MOUTHWASH, BUT LET'S LEAVE BUNKUM OUT OF THIS..
GRIFFY
12.22
GIBBLE-GABBLE! CLAPTRAP! FLUMDIDDLE! NOT TO MENTION BALDERDASH, HOOEY & BLATHERSKITE!
--LISTEN, I'LL GRANT YOU TH' FLUMDIDDLE, BUT I TAKE EXCEPTION TO TH' BLATHERSKITE!
IS THERE A GUIDEBOOK? A PRINTOUT? SOME KINDA ROADMAP TO GIVE ME A CLUE? --WHAT'S THAT?
CHECK IT OUT, DOLLBOY, "ZIPPY FOR DUMMIES"!
©2006 Bill Griffith. World rights reserved. Distributed by King Features Syndicate

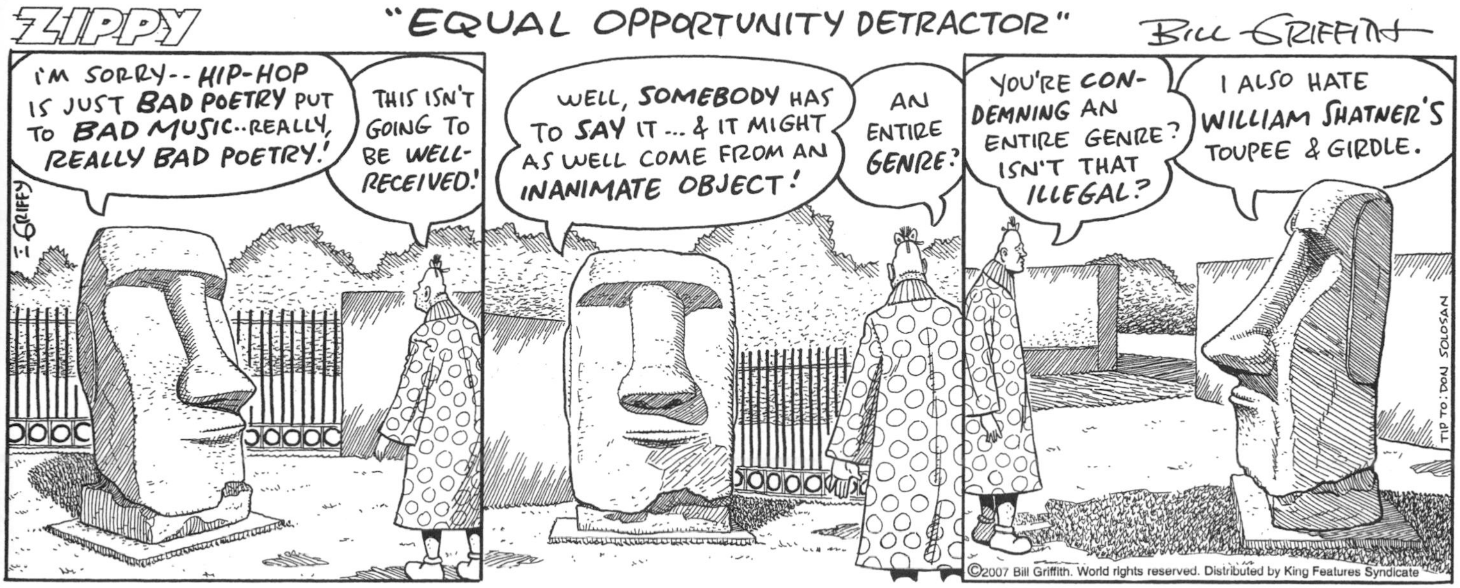
ZIPPY
"EQUAL OPPORTUNITY DETRACTOR"
BILL GRIFFITH
I'M SORRY-- HIP-HOP IS JUST BAD POETRY PUT TO BAD MUSIC..REALLY, REALLY BAD POETRY!
THIS ISN'T GOING TO BE WELL-RECEIVED!
GRIFFY
WELL, SOMEBODY HAS TO SAY IT ... & IT MIGHT AS WELL COME FROM AN INANIMATE OBJECT!
AN ENTIRE GENRE?
YOU'RE CON-DEMNING AN ENTIRE GENRE? ISN'T THAT ILLEGAL?
I ALSO HATE WILLIAM SHATNER'S TOUPEE & GIRDLE.
TIP TO: DON SOLOSAN
©2007 Bill Griffith. World rights reserved. Distributed by King Features Syndicate

107

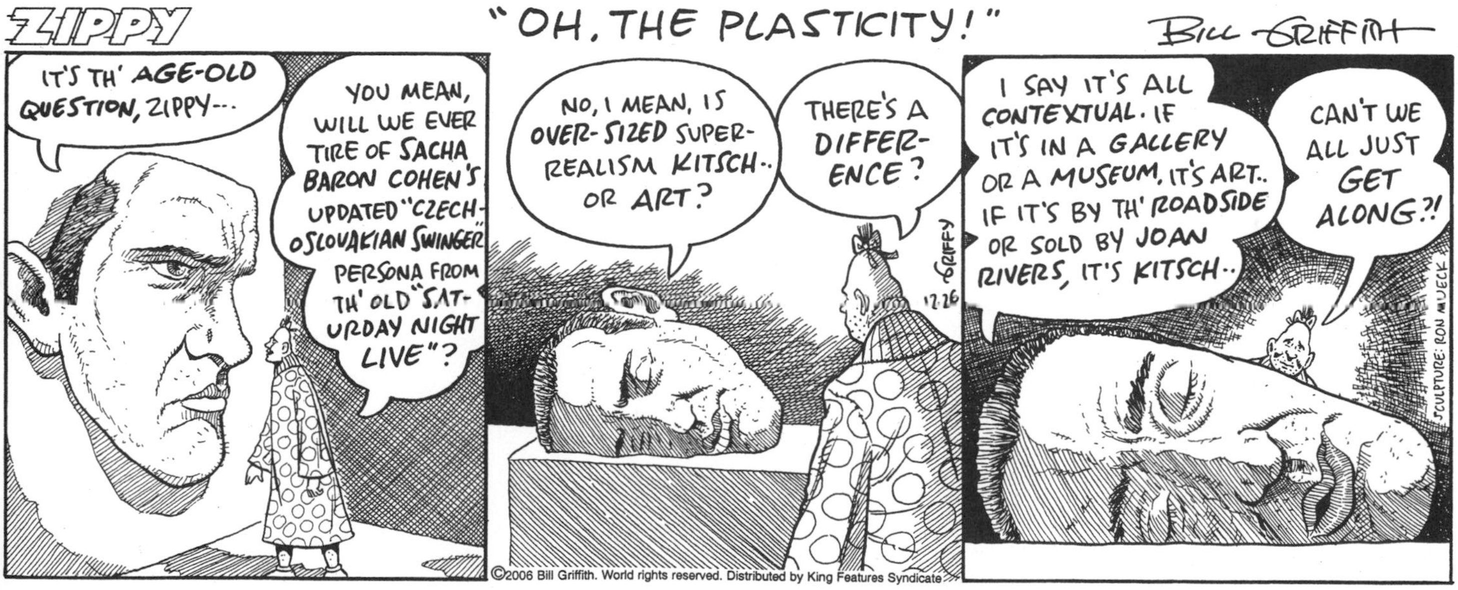
ZIPPY
"OH, THE PLASTICITY!"
BILL GRIFFITH
IT'S TH' AGE-OLD QUESTION, ZIPPY...
YOU MEAN, WILL WE EVER TIRE OF SACHA BARON COHEN'S UPDATED "CZECH-OSLOVAKIAN SWINGER" PERSONA FROM TH' OLD "SATURDAY NIGHT LIVE"?
NO, I MEAN, IS OVER-SIZED SUPER-REALISM KITSCH.. OR ART?
THERE'S A DIFFER-ENCE?
GRIFFY
12-26
I SAY IT'S ALL CONTEXTUAL. IF IT'S IN A GALLERY OR A MUSEUM, IT'S ART.. IF IT'S BY TH' ROADSIDE OR SOLD BY JOAN RIVERS, IT'S KITSCH..
CAN'T WE ALL JUST GET ALONG?!
SCULPTURE: RON MUECK
©2006 Bill Griffith. World rights reserved. Distributed by King Features Syndicate

108

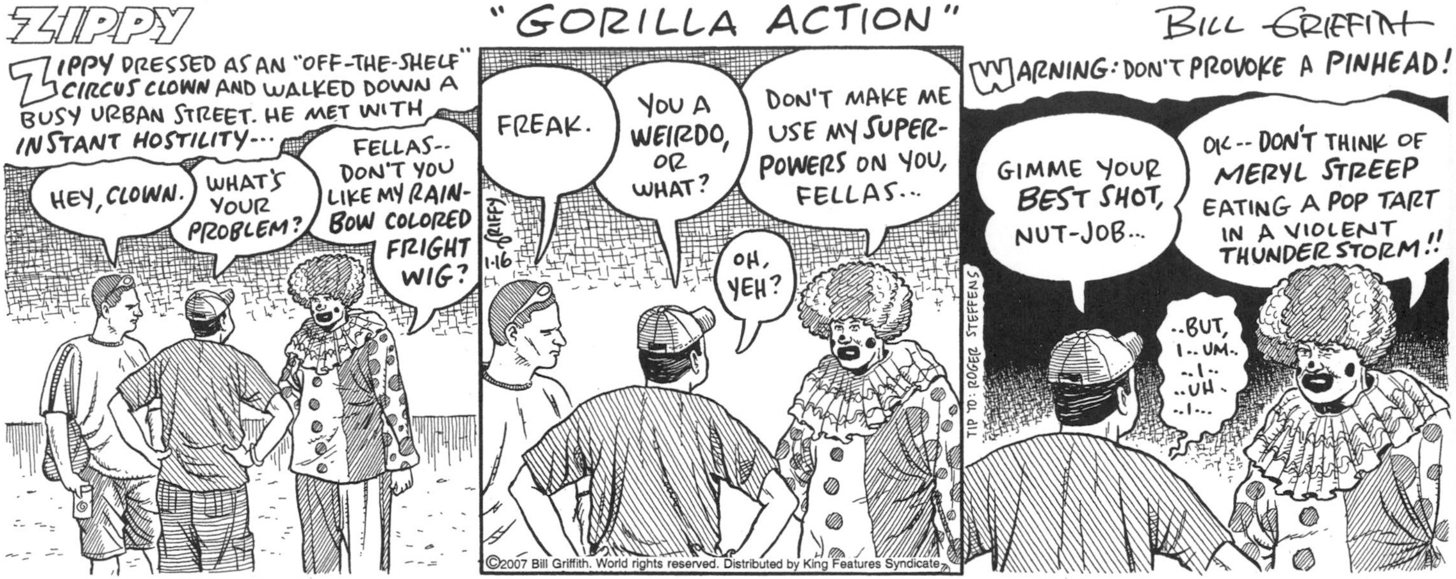
ZIPPY
"GORILLA ACTION"
BILL GRIFFITH
ZIPPY DRESSED AS AN "OFF-THE-SHELF" CIRCUS CLOWN AND WALKED DOWN A BUSY URBAN STREET. HE MET WITH INSTANT HOSTILITY...
HEY, CLOWN.
WHAT'S YOUR PROBLEM?
FELLAS-- DON'T YOU LIKE MY RAIN-BOW COLORED FRIGHT WIG?
GRIFFY 1-16
FREAK.
YOU A WEIRDO, OR WHAT?
DON'T MAKE ME USE MY SUPER-POWERS ON YOU, FELLAS...
OH, YEH?
©2007 Bill Griffith. World rights reserved. Distributed by King Features Syndicate
WARNING: DON'T PROVOKE A PINHEAD!
TIP TO: ROGER STEFFENS
GIMME YOUR BEST SHOT, NUT-JOB...
OK-- DON'T THINK OF MERYL STREEP EATING A POP TART IN A VIOLENT THUNDERSTORM!!
..BUT, I.. UM.. ..I.. ..UH.. ..I...

109

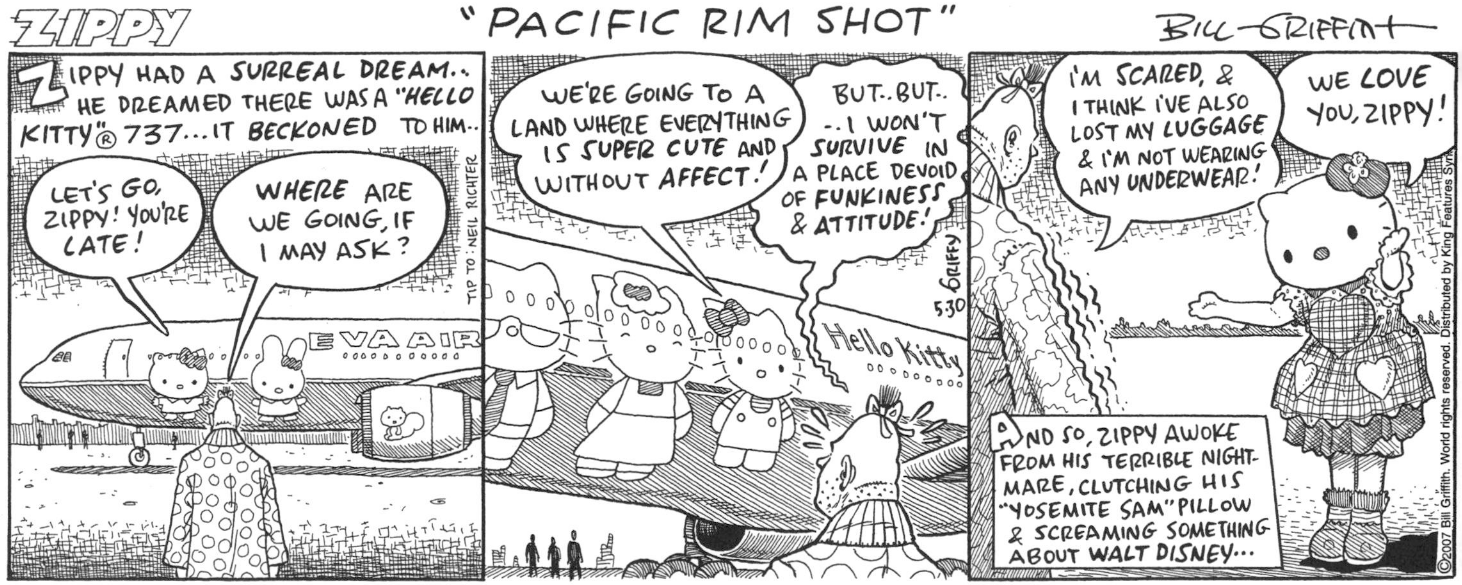
ZIPPY
"PACIFIC RIM SHOT"
BILL GRIFFITH
ZIPPY HAD A SURREAL DREAM.. HE DREAMED THERE WAS A "HELLO KITTY"® 737... IT BECKONED TO HIM..
LET'S GO, ZIPPY! YOU'RE LATE!
WHERE ARE WE GOING, IF I MAY ASK?
TIP TO: NEIL RICHTER
EVA AIR
WE'RE GOING TO A LAND WHERE EVERYTHING IS SUPER CUTE AND WITHOUT AFFECT!
BUT..BUT.. ..I WON'T SURVIVE IN A PLACE DEVOID OF FUNKINESS & ATTITUDE!
GRIFFY 5.30
Hello Kitty
I'M SCARED, & I THINK I'VE ALSO LOST MY LUGGAGE & I'M NOT WEARING ANY UNDERWEAR!
WE LOVE YOU, ZIPPY!
AND SO, ZIPPY AWOKE FROM HIS TERRIBLE NIGHT-MARE, CLUTCHING HIS "YOSEMITE SAM" PILLOW & SCREAMING SOMETHING ABOUT WALT DISNEY...
©2007 Bill Griffith. World rights reserved. Distributed by King Features Syn.

110

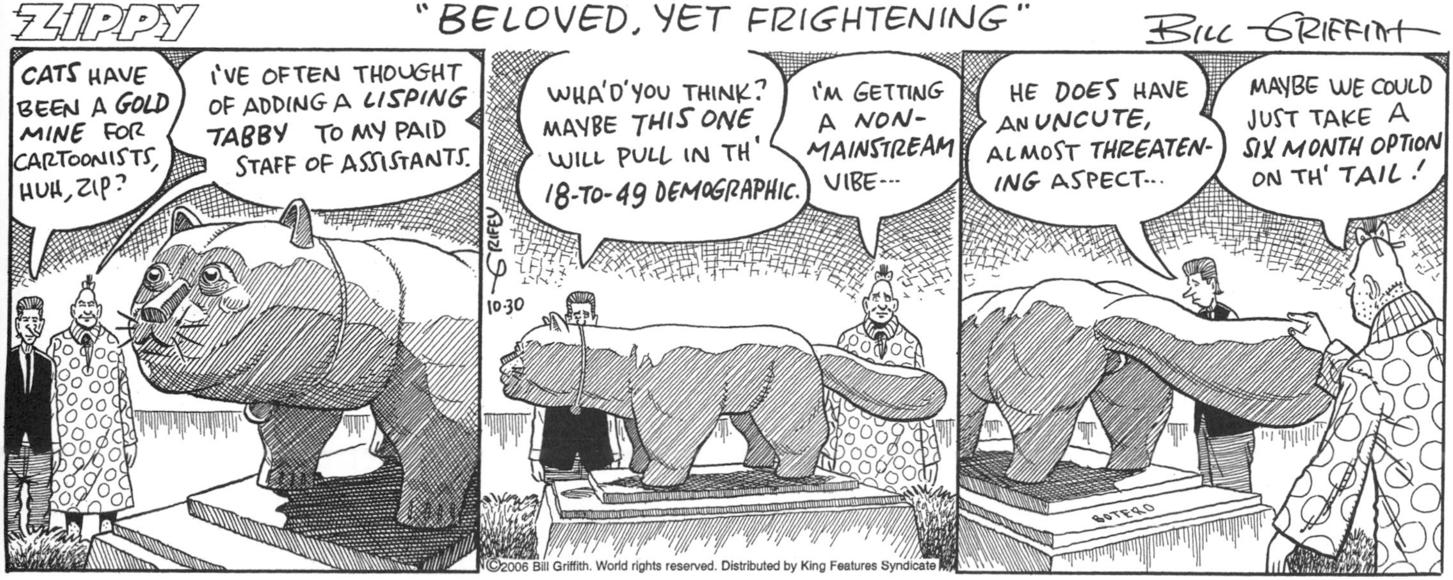
ZIPPY
"BELOVED, YET FRIGHTENING"
BILL GRIFFITH
CATS HAVE BEEN A GOLD MINE FOR CARTOONISTS, HUH, ZIP?
I'VE OFTEN THOUGHT OF ADDING A LISPING TABBY TO MY PAID STAFF OF ASSISTANTS.
WHA'D'YOU THINK? MAYBE THIS ONE WILL PULL IN TH' 18-TO-49 DEMOGRAPHIC.
I'M GETTING A NON-MAINSTREAM VIBE---
GRIFFY
10-30
HE DOES HAVE AN UNCUTE, ALMOST THREATENING ASPECT...
MAYBE WE COULD JUST TAKE A SIX MONTH OPTION ON TH' TAIL!
BOTERO
©2006 Bill Griffith. World rights reserved. Distributed by King Features Syndicate

111

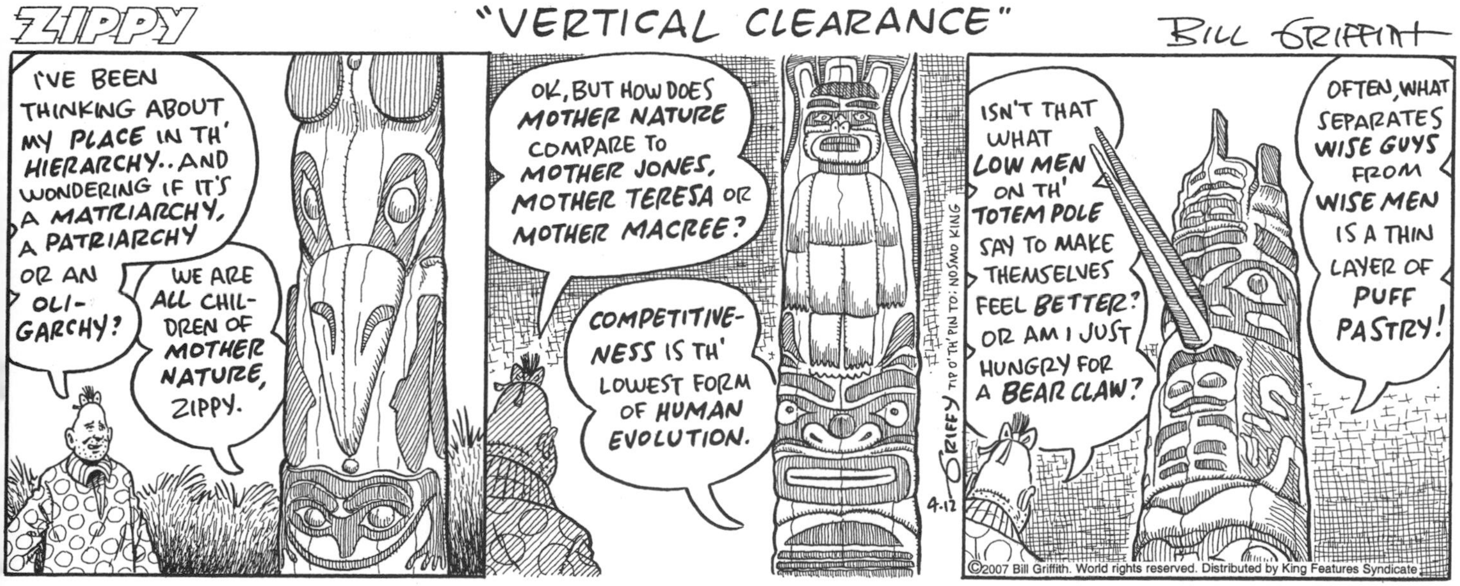
ZIPPY
"VERTICAL CLEARANCE"
BILL GRIFFITH
I'VE BEEN THINKING ABOUT MY PLACE IN TH' HIERARCHY.. AND WONDERING IF IT'S A MATRIARCHY, A PATRIARCHY OR AN OLIGARCHY?
WE ARE ALL CHILDREN OF MOTHER NATURE, ZIPPY.
OK, BUT HOW DOES MOTHER NATURE COMPARE TO MOTHER JONES, MOTHER TERESA OR MOTHER MACREE?
COMPETITIVENESS IS TH' LOWEST FORM OF HUMAN EVOLUTION.
GRIFFY TIP O'TH' PIN TO: NOSMO KING
4-12
ISN'T THAT WHAT LOW MEN ON TH' TOTEM POLE SAY TO MAKE THEMSELVES FEEL BETTER? OR AM I JUST HUNGRY FOR A BEAR CLAW?
OFTEN, WHAT SEPARATES WISE GUYS FROM WISE MEN IS A THIN LAYER OF PUFF PASTRY!
©2007 Bill Griffith. World rights reserved. Distributed by King Features Syndicate

112

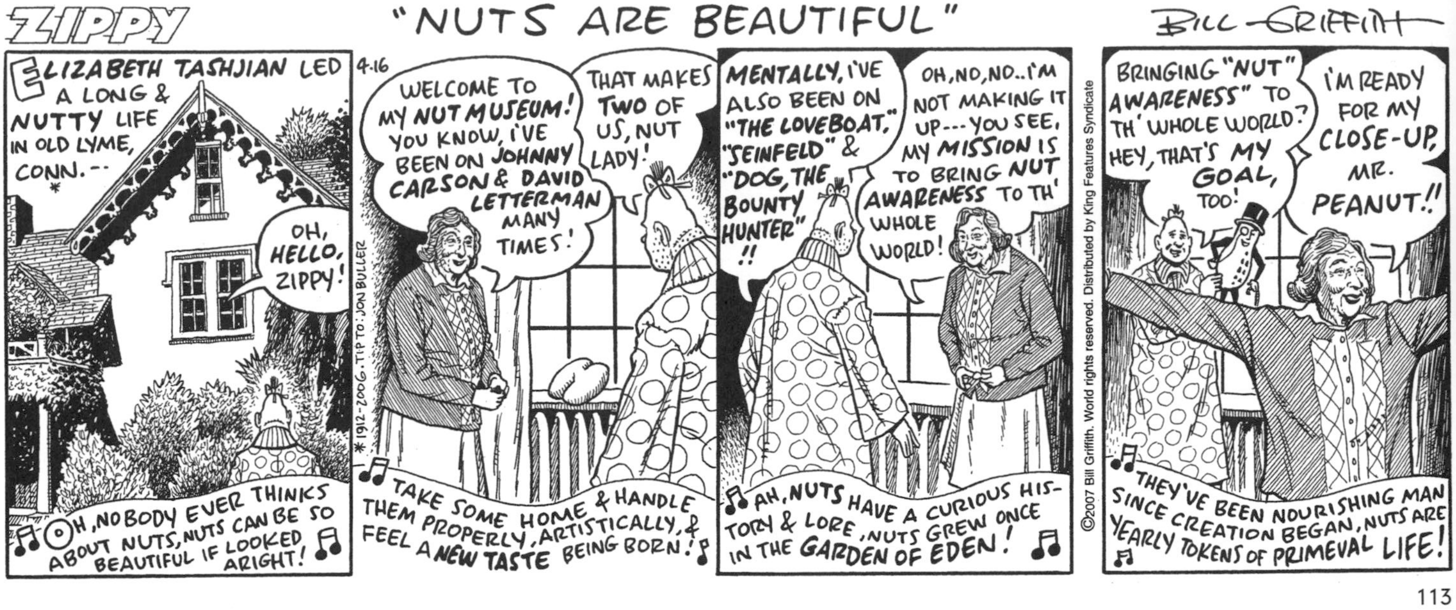
ZIPPY
"NUTS ARE BEAUTIFUL"
BILL GRIFFITH
ELIZABETH TASHJIAN LED A LONG & NUTTY LIFE IN OLD LYME, CONN.-- *
OH, HELLO, ZIPPY!
OH, NOBODY EVER THINKS ABOUT NUTS, NUTS CAN BE SO BEAUTIFUL IF LOOKED ARIGHT!
4-16
WELCOME TO MY NUT MUSEUM! YOU KNOW, I'VE BEEN ON JOHNNY CARSON & DAVID LETTERMAN MANY TIMES!
THAT MAKES TWO OF US, NUT LADY!
* 1912-2006. TIP TO: JON BULLER
TAKE SOME HOME & HANDLE THEM PROPERLY, ARTISTICALLY, & FEEL A NEW TASTE BEING BORN!
MENTALLY, I'VE ALSO BEEN ON "THE LOVEBOAT," "SEINFELD" & "DOG, THE BOUNTY HUNTER"!!
OH, NO, NO.. I'M NOT MAKING IT UP--- YOU SEE, MY MISSION IS TO BRING NUT AWARENESS TO TH' WHOLE WORLD!
AH, NUTS HAVE A CURIOUS HISTORY & LORE, NUTS GREW ONCE IN THE GARDEN OF EDEN!
BRINGING "NUT" AWARENESS" TO TH' WHOLE WORLD? HEY, THAT'S MY GOAL, TOO!
I'M READY FOR MY CLOSE-UP, MR. PEANUT!!
THEY'VE BEEN NOURISHING MAN SINCE CREATION BEGAN, NUTS ARE YEARLY TOKENS OF PRIMEVAL LIFE!
©2007 Bill Griffith. World rights reserved. Distributed by King Features Syndicate
113

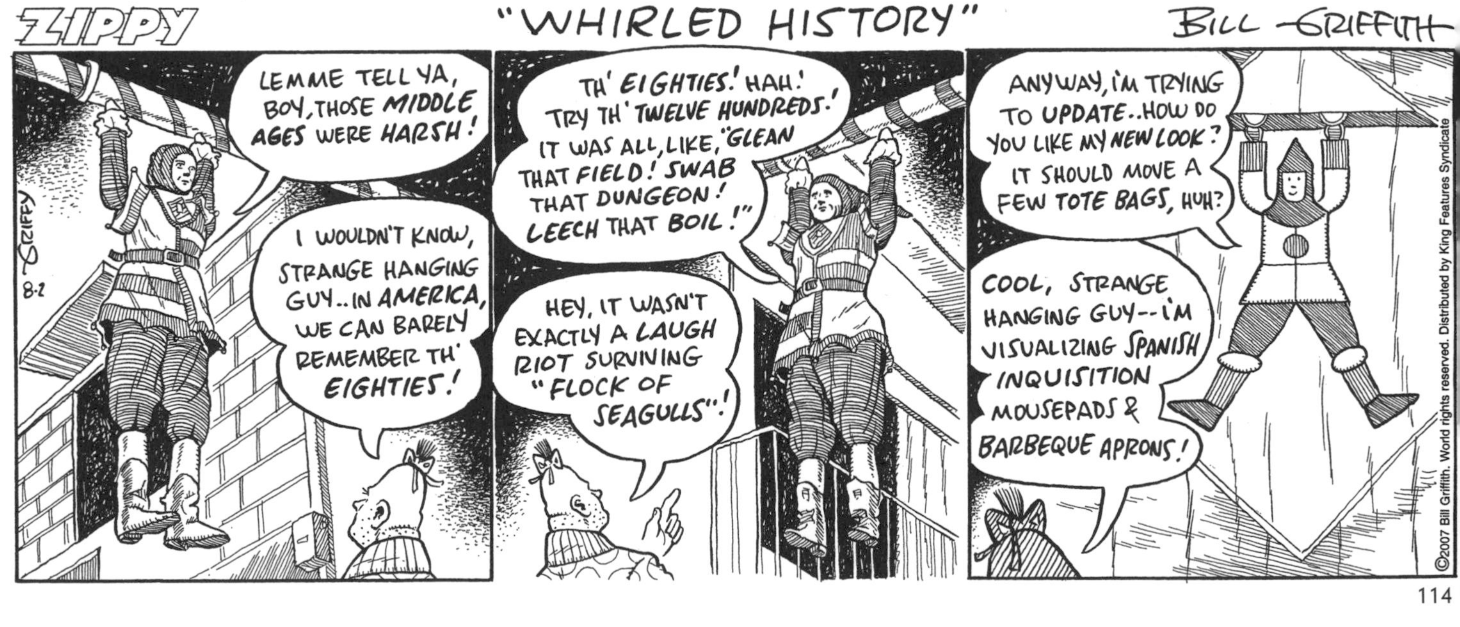
ZIPPY
"WHIRLED HISTORY"
BILL GRIFFITH
LEMME TELL YA, BOY, THOSE MIDDLE AGES WERE HARSH!
GRIFFY 8-2
I WOULDN'T KNOW, STRANGE HANGING GUY.. IN AMERICA, WE CAN BARELY REMEMBER TH' EIGHTIES!
TH' EIGHTIES! HAH! TRY TH' TWELVE HUNDREDS! IT WAS ALL, LIKE, "GLEAN THAT FIELD! SWAB THAT DUNGEON! LEECH THAT BOIL!"
HEY, IT WASN'T EXACTLY A LAUGH RIOT SURVIVING "FLOCK OF SEAGULLS"!
ANYWAY, I'M TRYING TO UPDATE.. HOW DO YOU LIKE MY NEW LOOK? IT SHOULD MOVE A FEW TOTE BAGS, HUH?
COOL, STRANGE HANGING GUY-- I'M VISUALIZING SPANISH INQUISITION MOUSEPADS & BARBEQUE APRONS!
©2007 Bill Griffith. World rights reserved. Distributed by King Features Syndicate
114

Sunday Color

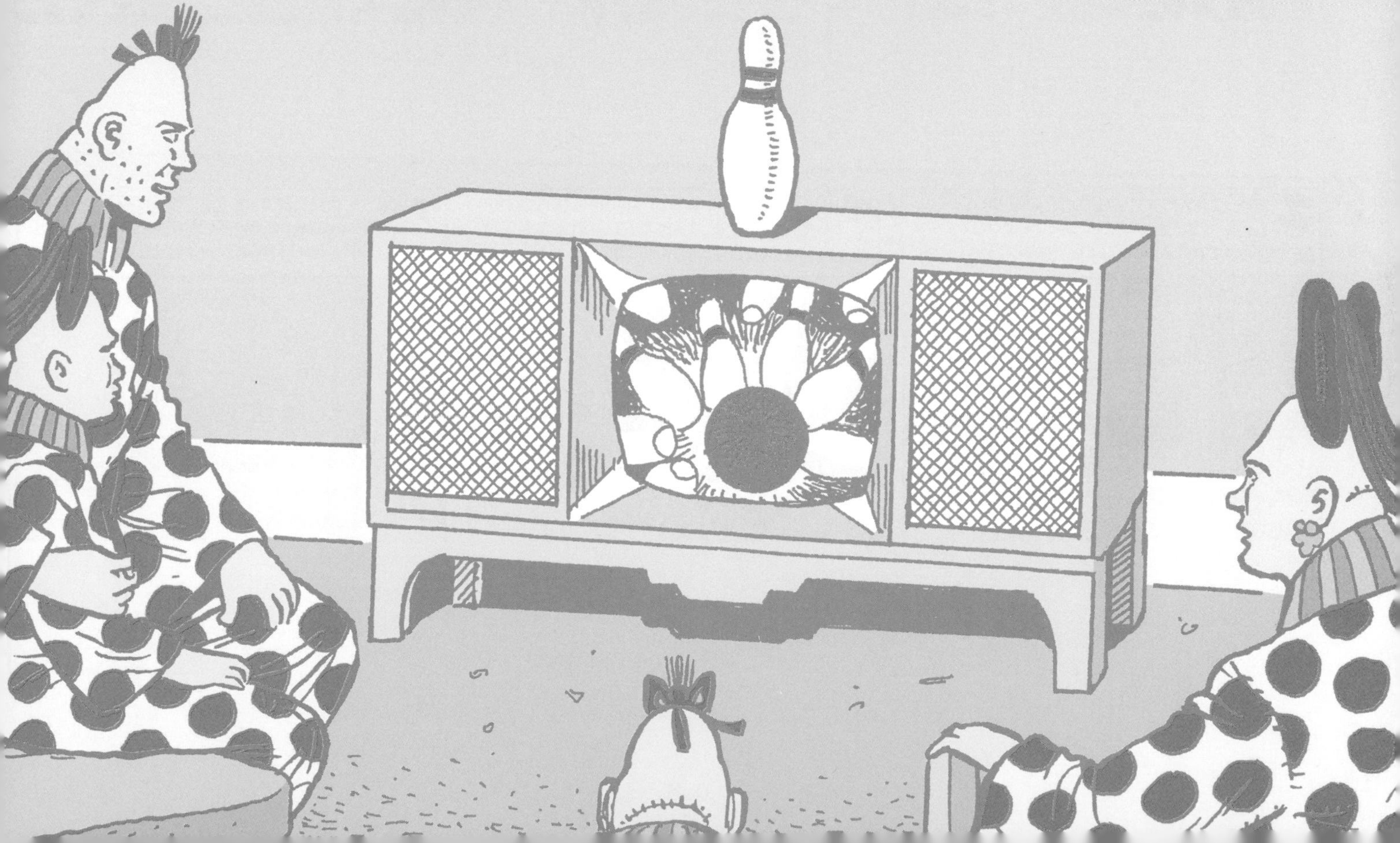

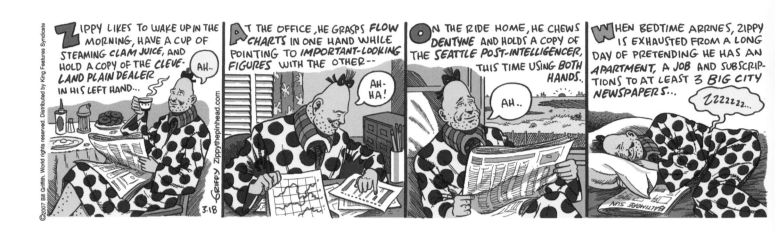

©2007 Bill Griffith. World rights reserved. Distributed by King Features Syndicate
ZIPPY LIKES TO WAKE UP IN THE MORNING, HAVE A CUP OF STEAMING CLAM JUICE, AND HOLD A COPY OF THE CLEVELAND PLAIN DEALER IN HIS LEFT HAND...
AH..
GRIFFY
3·18
Zippythepinhead.com
AT THE OFFICE, HE GRASPS FLOW CHARTS IN ONE HAND WHILE POINTING TO IMPORTANT-LOOKING FIGURES WITH THE OTHER--
AH-HA!
ON THE RIDE HOME, HE CHEWS DENTYNE AND HOLDS A COPY OF THE SEATTLE POST-INTELLIGENCER, THIS TIME USING BOTH HANDS..
AH..
WHEN BEDTIME ARRIVES, ZIPPY IS EXHAUSTED FROM A LONG DAY OF PRETENDING HE HAS AN APARTMENT, A JOB AND SUBSCRIPTIONS TO AT LEAST 3 BIG CITY NEWSPAPERS...
ZZZZZZZ...
BALTIMORE SUN

ZIPPY THOUGHT ABOUT CREME SODA. THEN HE THOUGHT ABOUT BEETS. THEN HE THOUGHT ABOUT DONALD TRUMP'S CHILDREN.
Piccadilly Grill
UTY SCHOO
Cigars
©2007 Bill Griffith. World rights reserved. Distributed by King Features Syndicate
THEN HE THOUGHT ABOUT FIXING THE SCREEN DOOR. THEN HE THOUGHT ABOUT RISING HEALTH CARE COSTS. THEN HE THOUGHT ABOUT BINGO.
GRIFFY
7·8
Zippythepinhead.com
TIP O' TH' PIN TO: MICHAEL STEWART
THEN HE REALIZED HE WAS STARTING TO THINK THE THOUGHTS OF THE GUY ACROSS THE ROOM, SO HE THOUGHT ABOUT LAVA & EVERYTHING WAS OK AGAIN.

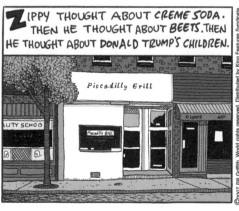

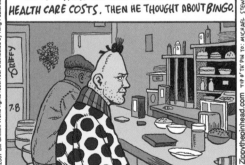

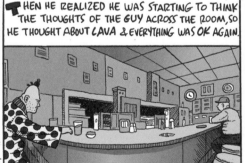

115

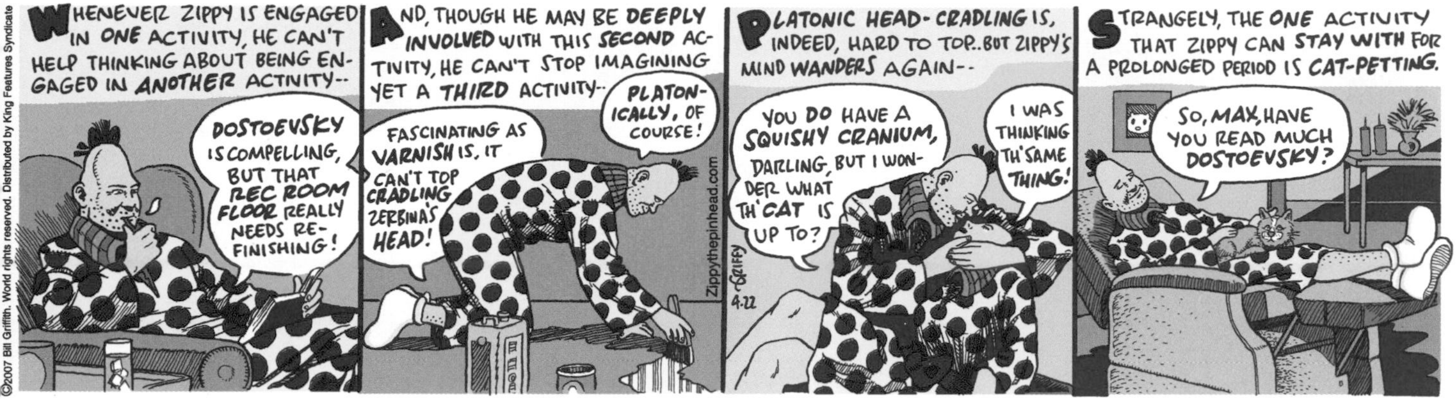
WHENEVER ZIPPY IS ENGAGED IN ONE ACTIVITY, HE CAN'T HELP THINKING ABOUT BEING ENGAGED IN ANOTHER ACTIVITY--
DOSTOEVSKY IS COMPELLING, BUT THAT REC ROOM FLOOR REALLY NEEDS REFINISHING!
AND, THOUGH HE MAY BE DEEPLY INVOLVED WITH THIS SECOND ACTIVITY, HE CAN'T STOP IMAGINING YET A THIRD ACTIVITY..
FASCINATING AS VARNISH IS, IT CAN'T TOP CRADLING ZERBINA'S HEAD!
PLATONICALLY, OF COURSE!
Zippythepinhead.com
GRIFFY 4-22
PLATONIC HEAD-CRADLING IS, INDEED, HARD TO TOP.. BUT ZIPPY'S MIND WANDERS AGAIN--
YOU DO HAVE A SQUISHY CRANIUM, DARLING, BUT I WONDER WHAT TH' CAT IS UP TO?
I WAS THINKING TH' SAME THING!
STRANGELY, THE ONE ACTIVITY THAT ZIPPY CAN STAY WITH FOR A PROLONGED PERIOD IS CAT-PETTING.
SO, MAX, HAVE YOU READ MUCH DOSTOEVSKY?
©2007 Bill Griffith. World rights reserved. Distributed by King Features Syndicate

116

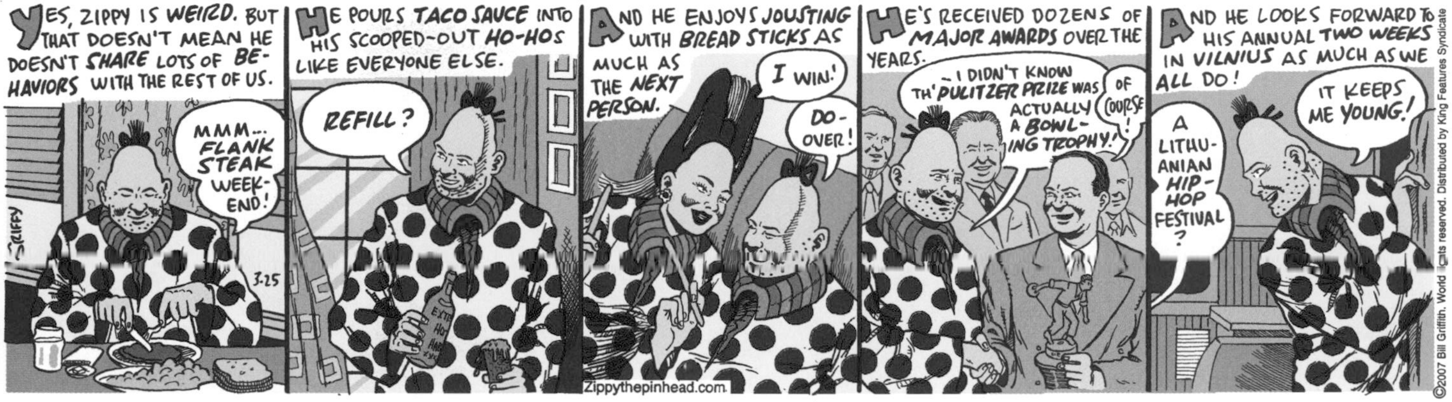
YES, ZIPPY IS WEIRD. BUT THAT DOESN'T MEAN HE DOESN'T SHARE LOTS OF BEHAVIORS WITH THE REST OF US.
MMM... FLANK STEAK WEEKEND!
GRIFFY 3-25
HE POURS TACO SAUCE INTO HIS SCOOPED-OUT HO-HOS LIKE EVERYONE ELSE.
REFILL?
AND HE ENJOYS JOUSTING WITH BREAD STICKS AS MUCH AS THE NEXT PERSON.
I WIN!
DO-OVER!
Zippythepinhead.com
HE'S RECEIVED DOZENS OF MAJOR AWARDS OVER THE YEARS.
--I DIDN'T KNOW TH' PULITZER PRIZE WAS ACTUALLY A BOWLING TROPHY!
OF COURSE!
AND HE LOOKS FORWARD TO HIS ANNUAL TWO WEEKS IN VILNIUS AS MUCH AS WE ALL DO!
IT KEEPS ME YOUNG!
A LITHUANIAN HIP-HOP FESTIVAL?
©2007 Bill Griffith. World rights reserved. Distributed by King Features Syndicate

117

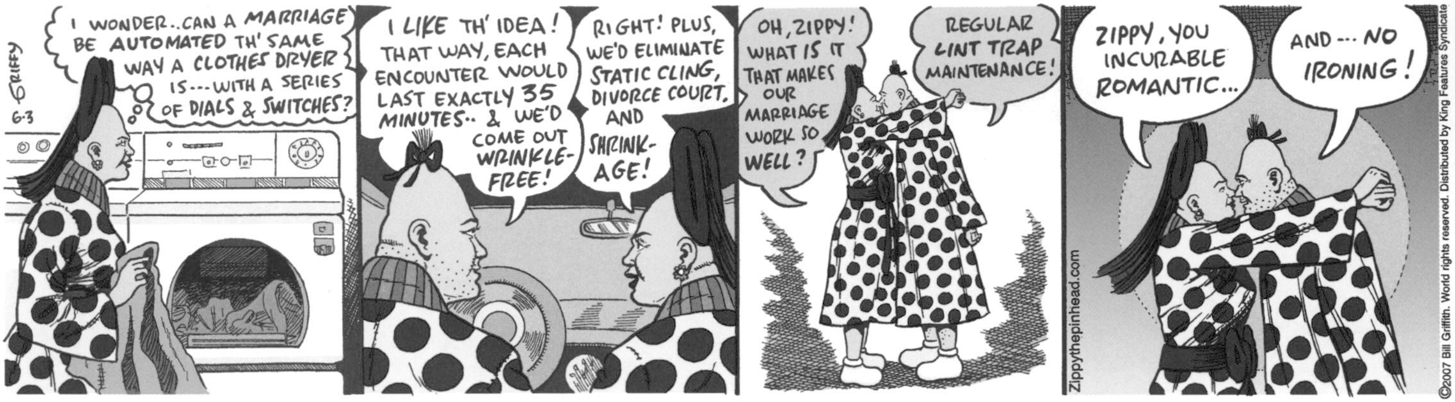
I WONDER..CAN A MARRIAGE BE AUTOMATED TH' SAME WAY A CLOTHES DRYER IS---WITH A SERIES OF DIALS & SWITCHES?
GRIFFY
6-3
I LIKE TH' IDEA! THAT WAY, EACH ENCOUNTER WOULD LAST EXACTLY 35 MINUTES.. & WE'D COME OUT WRINKLE-FREE!
RIGHT! PLUS, WE'D ELIMINATE STATIC CLING, DIVORCE COURT, AND SHRINK-AGE!
OH, ZIPPY! WHAT IS IT THAT MAKES OUR MARRIAGE WORK SO WELL?
REGULAR LINT TRAP MAINTENANCE!
ZIPPY, YOU INCURABLE ROMANTIC...
AND --- NO IRONING!
Zippythepinhead.com
©2007 Bill Griffith. World rights reserved. Distributed by King Features Syndicate

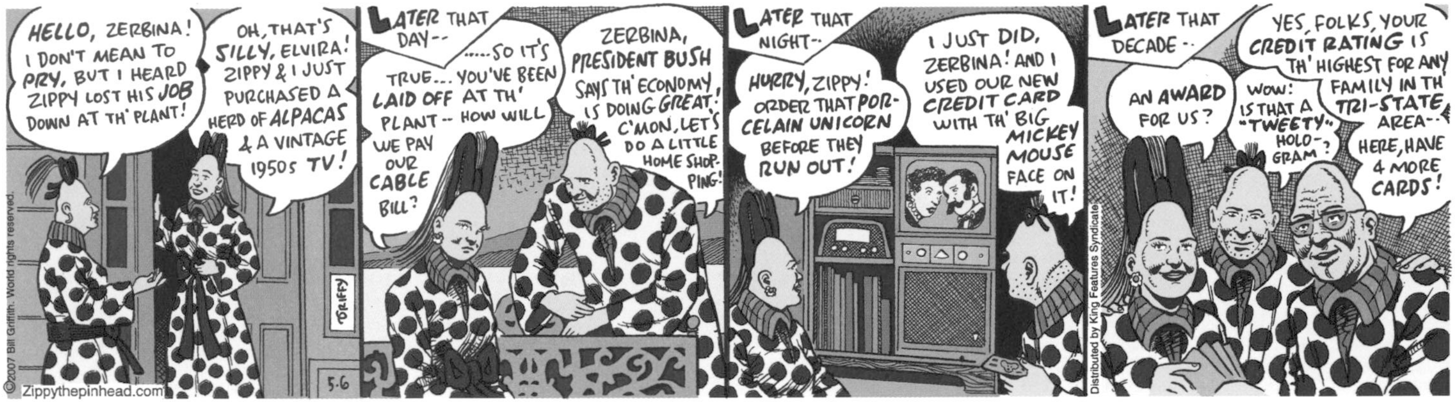
HELLO, ZERBINA! I DON'T MEAN TO PRY, BUT I HEARD ZIPPY LOST HIS JOB DOWN AT TH' PLANT!
OH, THAT'S SILLY, ELVIRA! ZIPPY & I JUST PURCHASED A HERD OF ALPACAS & A VINTAGE 1950s TV!
©2007 Bill Griffith. World rights reserved.
Zippythepinhead.com
5-6
LATER THAT DAY--
.....SO IT'S TRUE... YOU'VE BEEN LAID OFF AT TH' PLANT-- HOW WILL WE PAY OUR CABLE BILL?
ZERBINA, PRESIDENT BUSH SAYS TH' ECONOMY IS DOING GREAT! C'MON, LET'S DO A LITTLE HOME SHOP-PING!
GRIFFY
LATER THAT NIGHT--
HURRY, ZIPPY! ORDER THAT POR-CELAIN UNICORN BEFORE THEY RUN OUT!
I JUST DID, ZERBINA! AND I USED OUR NEW CREDIT CARD WITH TH' BIG MICKEY MOUSE FACE ON IT!
LATER THAT DECADE--
AN AWARD FOR US?
YES, FOLKS, YOUR CREDIT RATING IS TH' HIGHEST FOR ANY FAMILY IN TH' TRI-STATE AREA-- HERE, HAVE 4 MORE CARDS!
WOW! IS THAT A "TWEETY" HOLO-GRAM?
Distributed by King Features Syndicate

ZIPPY & ZERBINA HAVE GIVEN UP TV VIEWING... "WE HAD ALL TH' 'RAYMONDS' MEMORIZED," ZIPPY SAID, "SO WHAT'S TH' POINT?"
C'MON, HONEY! LET'S BOOGIE!
I'M GAME!
©2007 Bill Griffith. World rights reserved. Distributed by King Features Syndicate
ARE WE BOOGIE-ING CORRECTLY?
I THINK SO!
GRIFFY
8·19
OH, ZIPPY! THIS IS SO MUCH FUN! I NEVER WANT TO WATCH TV AGAIN!
OKAY, I AGREE!
...BUT THIS DOESN'T INCLUDE TH' WEATHER CHANNEL, RIGHT?
Zippythepinhead.com

118

ZIPPY WONDERED WHAT THE WORLD WOULD BE LIKE IF THE PINHEADS TOOK CONTROL--
--FROM TH' KID BEHIND TH' DONUT COUNTER, ALL TH' WAY TO TH' WHITE HOUSE!
©2007 Bill Griffith. World rights reserved. Distributed by King Features Syndicate
Zippythepinhead.com
AFTER ALL, HE FIGURED, "NORMAL" PEOPLE HAVE HAD A GOOD RUN.. WASN'T IT TIME TO TRY SOMETHING TOTALLY DIFFERENT?
FOR ONE THING, WE'D ALL WEAR LOOSE-FITTING MUU-MUUS.. ..IMAGINE TH' FASHION SAVINGS!
THE MORE HE THOUGHT ABOUT IT, THE MORE CONVINCED HE BECAME THAT IT WAS A "FANTASTIC IDEA"-- --HOWEVER, THERE WAS A CATCH--
GRIFFY
4·15
IT'S A GOOD THEORY, BUT HOW PRACTICAL IS IT? FOR INSTANCE, HOW WOULD IT AFFECT TH' LANDSCAPING BUSINESS??
SORRY, FOLKS! I JUST THOUGHT IT'D BE FUN TO DIG A BIG HOLE IN YOUR YARD!
TODD, DID YOU HIRE THIS PINHEAD?
GEE, ELVIRA, I CAN'T REMEMBER!
OH, WELL!!

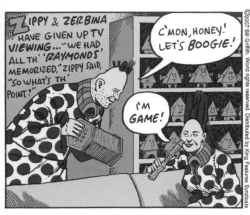

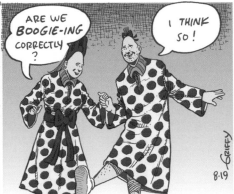

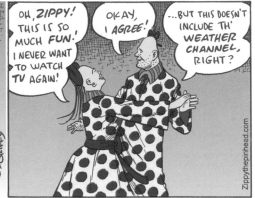

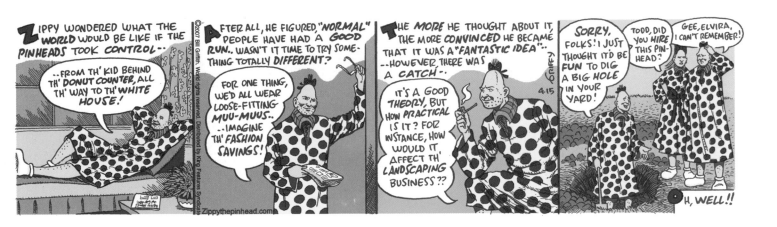

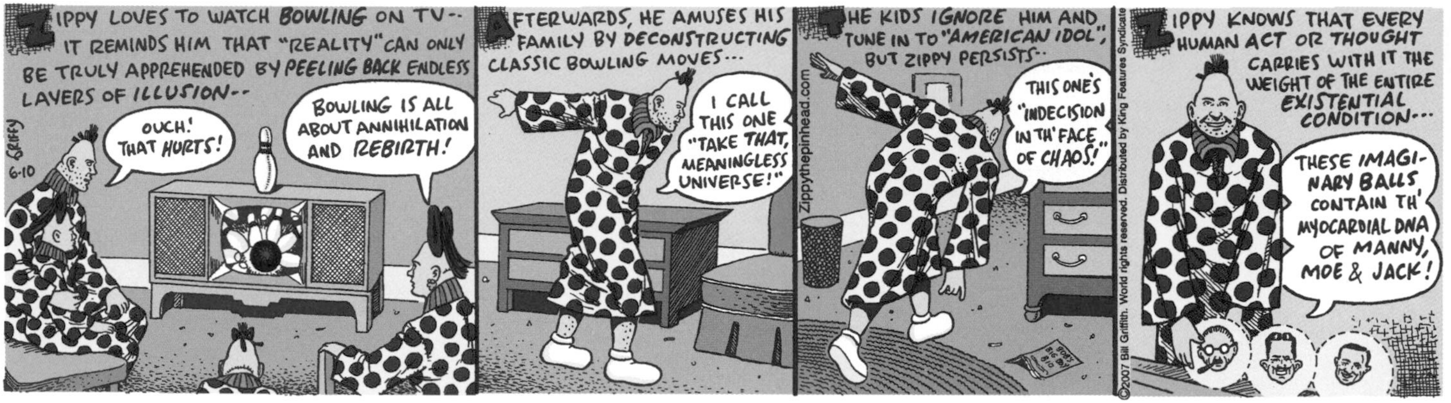
ZIPPY LOVES TO WATCH BOWLING ON TV-- IT REMINDS HIM THAT "REALITY" CAN ONLY BE TRULY APPREHENDED BY PEELING BACK ENDLESS LAYERS OF ILLUSION--
GRIFFY 6-10
OUCH! THAT HURTS!
BOWLING IS ALL ABOUT ANNIHILATION AND REBIRTH!
AFTERWARDS, HE AMUSES HIS FAMILY BY DECONSTRUCTING CLASSIC BOWLING MOVES...
I CALL THIS ONE "TAKE THAT, MEANINGLESS UNIVERSE!"
THE KIDS IGNORE HIM AND TUNE IN TO "AMERICAN IDOL", BUT ZIPPY PERSISTS--
Zippythepinhead.com
THIS ONE'S "INDECISION IN TH' FACE OF CHAOS!"
ZIPPY KNOWS THAT EVERY HUMAN ACT OR THOUGHT CARRIES WITH IT THE WEIGHT OF THE ENTIRE EXISTENTIAL CONDITION...
THESE IMAGINARY BALLS CONTAIN TH' MYOCARDIAL DNA OF MANNY, MOE & JACK!
©2007 Bill Griffith. World rights reserved. Distributed by King Features Syndicate

119

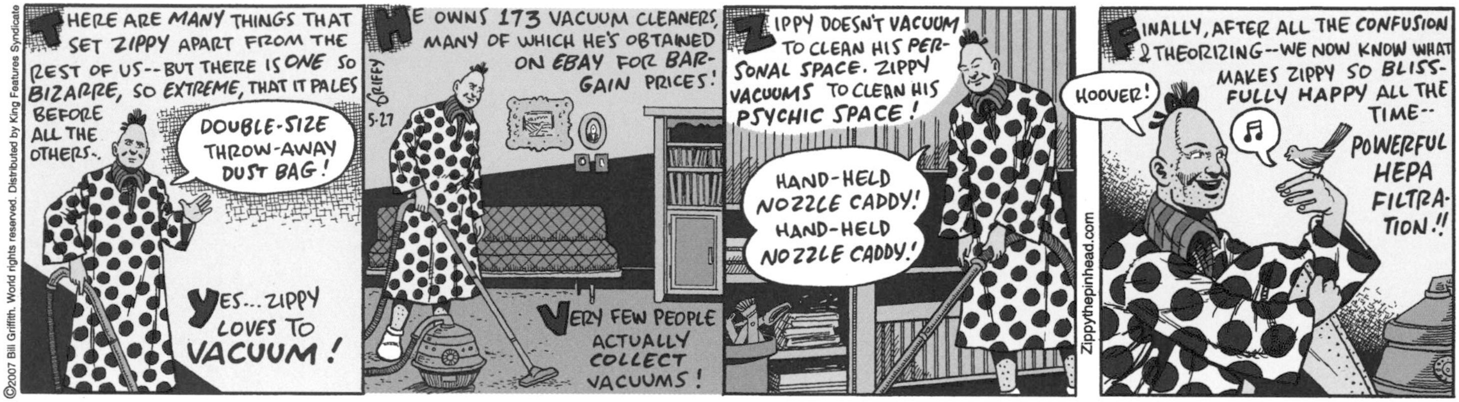
THERE ARE MANY THINGS THAT SET ZIPPY APART FROM THE REST OF US--BUT THERE IS ONE SO BIZARRE, SO EXTREME, THAT IT PALES BEFORE ALL THE OTHERS--
DOUBLE-SIZE THROW-AWAY DUST BAG!
YES... ZIPPY LOVES TO VACUUM!
©2007 Bill Griffith. World rights reserved. Distributed by King Features Syndicate
HE OWNS 173 VACUUM CLEANERS, MANY OF WHICH HE'S OBTAINED ON EBAY FOR BARGAIN PRICES!
GRIFFY 5-27
VERY FEW PEOPLE ACTUALLY COLLECT VACUUMS!
ZIPPY DOESN'T VACUUM TO CLEAN HIS PERSONAL SPACE. ZIPPY VACUUMS TO CLEAN HIS PSYCHIC SPACE!
HAND-HELD NOZZLE CADDY! HAND-HELD NOZZLE CADDY!
Zippythepinhead.com
FINALLY, AFTER ALL THE CONFUSION & THEORIZING--WE NOW KNOW WHAT MAKES ZIPPY SO BLISSFULLY HAPPY ALL THE TIME--
HOOVER!
POWERFUL HEPA FILTRATION!!

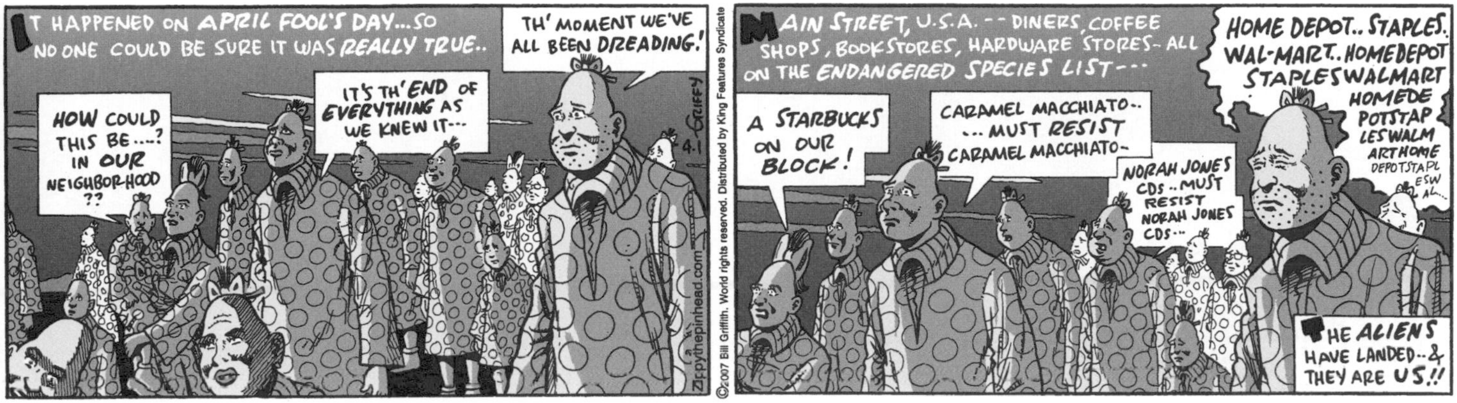
IT HAPPENED ON APRIL FOOL'S DAY... SO NO ONE COULD BE SURE IT WAS REALLY TRUE..
TH' MOMENT WE'VE ALL BEEN DREADING!
IT'S TH' END OF EVERYTHING AS WE KNEW IT---
HOW COULD THIS BE....? IN OUR NEIGHBOR-HOOD ??
GRIFFY 4.1
zippythepinhead.com
©2007 Bill Griffith. World rights reserved. Distributed by King Features Syndicate
MAIN STREET, U.S.A. -- DINERS, COFFEE SHOPS, BOOKSTORES, HARDWARE STORES - ALL ON THE ENDANGERED SPECIES LIST---
HOME DEPOT.. STAPLES. WAL-MART.. HOMEDEPOT STAPLESWALMART HOMEDE POTSTAP LESWALM ARTHOME DEPOTSTAPL ESW AL..
A STARBUCKS ON OUR BLOCK!
CARAMEL MACCHIATO.. ...MUST RESIST CARAMEL MACCHIATO-
NORAH JONES CDS .. MUST RESIST NORAH JONES CDS...
THE ALIENS HAVE LANDED.. & THEY ARE US!!

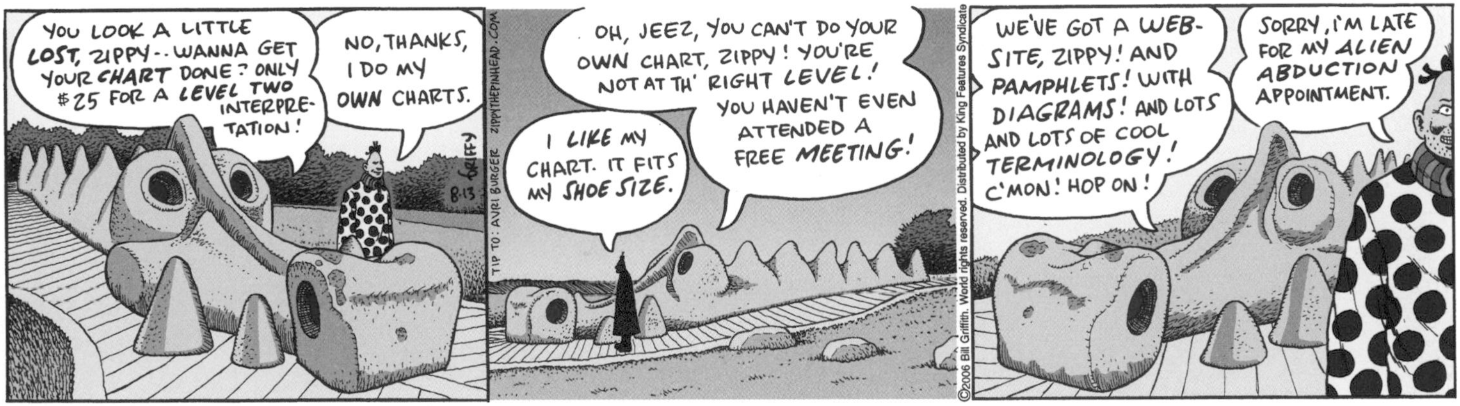
YOU LOOK A LITTLE LOST, ZIPPY.. WANNA GET YOUR CHART DONE? ONLY $25 FOR A LEVEL TWO INTERPRE-TATION!
NO, THANKS, I DO MY OWN CHARTS.
GRIFFY 8.13
TIP TO: AVRI BURGER ZIPPYTHEPINHEAD.COM
OH, JEEZ, YOU CAN'T DO YOUR OWN CHART, ZIPPY! YOU'RE NOT AT TH' RIGHT LEVEL! YOU HAVEN'T EVEN ATTENDED A FREE MEETING!
I LIKE MY CHART. IT FITS MY SHOE SIZE.
©2006 Bill Griffith. World rights reserved. Distributed by King Features Syndicate
WE'VE GOT A WEB-SITE, ZIPPY! AND PAMPHLETS! WITH DIAGRAMS! AND LOTS AND LOTS OF COOL TERMINOLOGY! C'MON! HOP ON!
SORRY, I'M LATE FOR MY ALIEN ABDUCTION APPOINTMENT.

120

ZIPPY, DOES TH' CLASSIC "PAUL BUNYAN" STYLE MUFFLER MAN REMIND YOU OF ANYONE?
SORRY, GRIFFY, I DON'T DO "ROADSIDE PROFILING."
& SONS TIRE CO.
USED TIRES
TIRE SERVICE
SPEED BALANCING
BUDGET TERMS
©2006 Bill Griffith. World rights reserved. Distributed by King Features Syndicate
GRIFFY 10.15
MY POINT EXACTLY! ...HIS RESEMBLANCE TO TH' STEREOTYPICAL "MIDEAST TERRORIST" IS UNAVOIDABLE!
..BUT MUFFY IS KIND AND GENTLE! HE LOVES KITTENS, SNAPPLE & ALL LIVING THINGS!
Zippythepinhead.com
BUY MY STUDDED SNOW TIRES, INFIDELS, OR I'LL DESTROY YOUR INFRASTRUCTURE!!
UH-OH, ZIPPY, I THINK HE'S BEEN RADICALIZED!
WE REALLY DO NEED TO END OUR DEPENDENCE ON FOREIGN OIL!
TIP O' TH' PIN TO: CHRIS QUINN

121

TH' FIFTIES ARE TO TH' 21ST CENTURY WHAT TH' 1890S WERE TO TH' 20TH!
I DON'T KNOW WHAT YOU'RE SAYING, BUT I LOVE IT WHEN YOU SOUND SO CERTAIN!
50's DINER
BREAKFAST LUNCH
FOOD TO TAKE OUT
©2006 Bill Griffith. World rights reserved. Distributed by King Features Syndicate
..SAFELY REMOVED, IDEALIZED, REDUCED TO A FEW COMFORTING IMAGES..
THEY DID HAVE COOLER SPORT SHIRTS!
I WAS THERE! IT WAS MOSTLY ANTISEPTIC. AND MORE THAN A BIT BLAND & VAGUELY PARANOIAC..
"BLAND & PARANOIAC"! MY FAVORITE FIFTIES SATURDAY MORNING TV SHOW!
Zippythepinhead.com
GRIFFY 11.19
TIP O' TH' PIN TO: SPENCER STEWART
DON'T LISTEN TO THAT CITY SLICKER, BUCKAROO! HE'S A REVISIONIST, ANARCHO-SYNDICALIST, SIDE-WINDIN' PANTYWAIST!
I LIKED IT WHEN PARANOIAC RAN OFF A CLIFF.

122

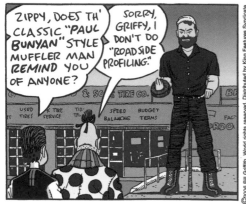

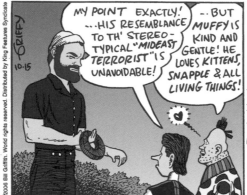

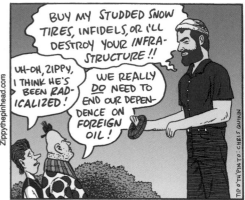

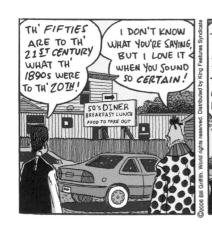

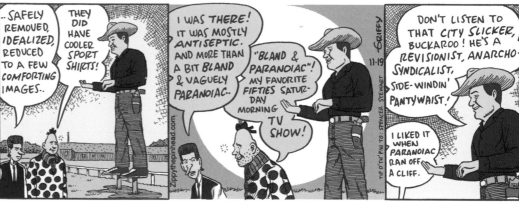

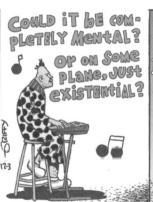

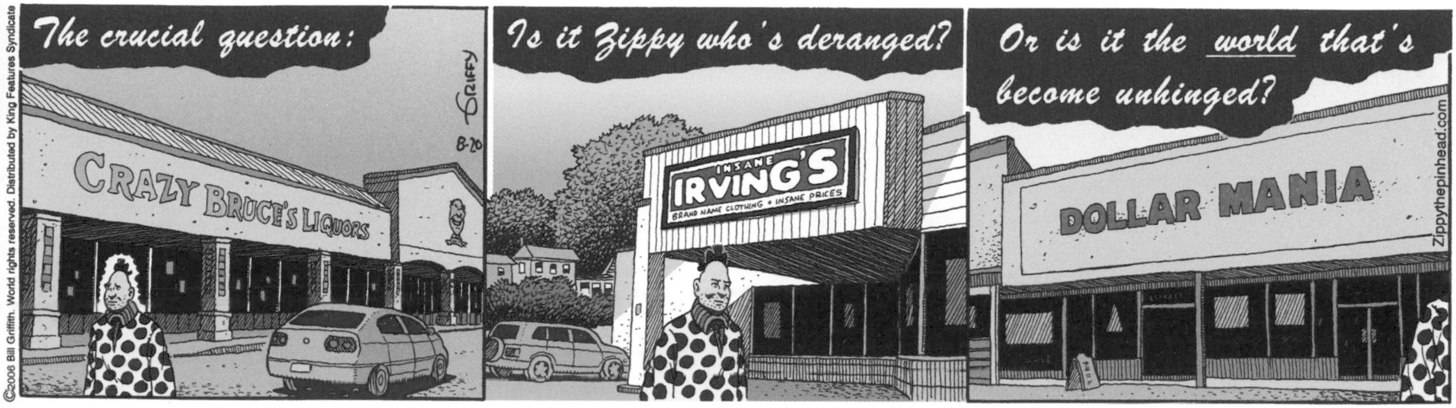

The crucial question:
Is it Zippy who's deranged?
Or is it the world that's become unhinged?
CRAZY BRUCE'S LIQUORS
INSANE IRVING'S
BRAND NAME CLOTHING • INSANE PRICES
DOLLAR MANIA
©2006 Bill Griffith. World rights reserved. Distributed by King Features Syndicate
Zippythepinhead.com

123

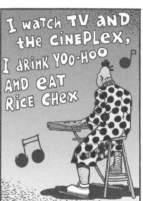

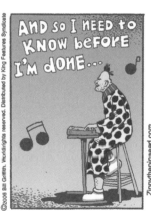

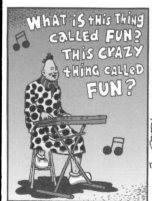

WHAT IS THIS THING CALLED FUN? THIS CRAZY THING CALLED FUN?
COULD IT BE COMPLETELY MENTAL?
OR ON SOME PLANE, JUST EXISTENTIAL?
I WATCH TV AND THE CINEPLEX,
I DRINK YOO-HOO AND EAT RICE CHEX
AND SO I NEED TO KNOW BEFORE I'M DONE...
WHAT IS THIS THING CALLED FUN?
©2006 Bill Griffith. World rights reserved. Distributed by King Features Syndicate
Zippythepinhead.com
TIP O' TH' PIN T' COLE PORTER

124

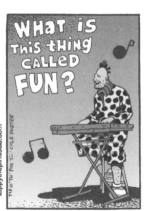

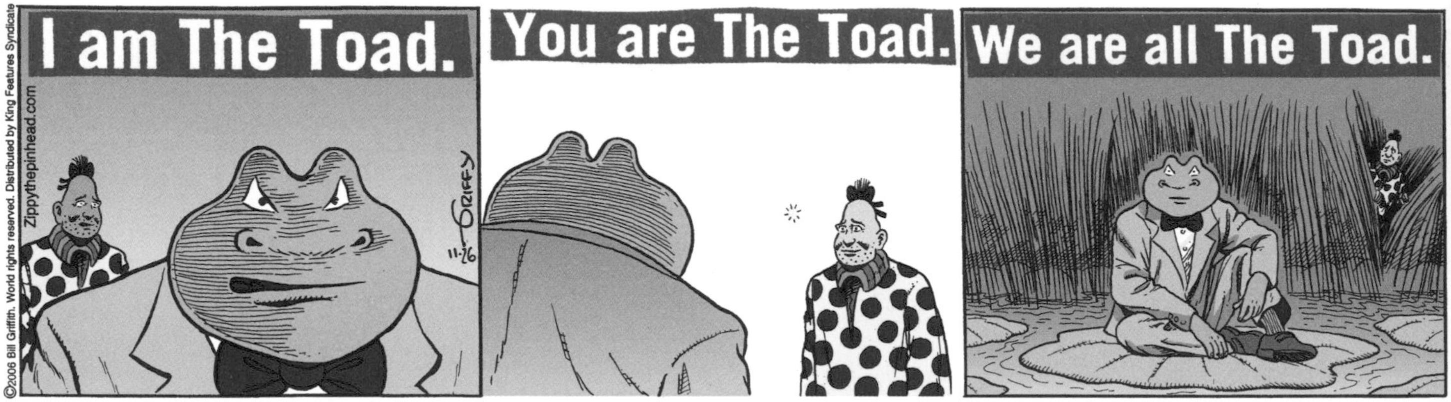
©2006 Bill Griffith. World rights reserved. Distributed by King Features Syndicate
Zippythepinhead.com
I am The Toad.
GRIFFY 11-26
You are The Toad.
We are all The Toad.

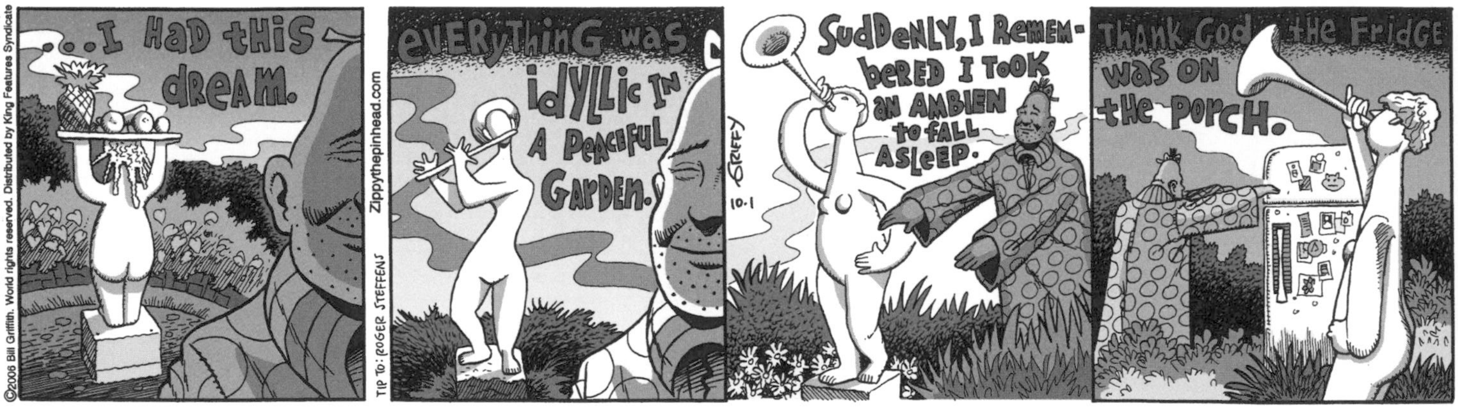
©2006 Bill Griffith. World rights reserved. Distributed by King Features Syndicate
...I HAD THIS DREAM.
Zippythepinhead.com
TIP TO: ROGER STEFFENS
EVERYTHING WAS IDYLLIC IN A PEACEFUL GARDEN.
GRIFFY 10-1
SUDDENLY, I REMEMBERED I TOOK AN AMBIEN TO FALL ASLEEP.
THANK GOD THE FRIDGE WAS ON THE PORCH.

©2006 Bill Griffith. World rights reserved. Distributed by King Features Syndicate
IT'S NANCY & SLUGGO'S WORLD-- WE JUST QUESTION REALITY IN IT!!
1.
2.
3.
10.29 GRIFFY Zippythepinhead.com

125

HUH? ZIPPY'S LIVING INSIDE UNCLE SCROOGE'S MONEY BIN?!
IT'LL BE LIKE TAKING POP-TARTS FROM A PINHEAD!
176-167
BEAGLE BOYS INC.
©2007 Bill Griffith. W rights reserved. Distributed by King Features Syndicate
BEAGLE BOYS! WAIT! I'M SURE THERE'S NO MONEY IN THERE! IT'S PROBABLY FILLED WITH TACO SAUCE!
YOU CAN'T FOOL US, WISE GUY!
WE CAN SMELL MONEY!
Zippythepinhead.com
INSIDE--
GRIFFY 2·4
MMM! MY MORNING SWIM IN INVIGORATING, DELICIOUS, EXTRA HOT TACO SAUCE!!
HOW I LOVE IT!
TACO SAUCE
POP!
NOOOOOOOO!!
I HAD THAT DREAM AGAIN WHERE THE MILLIONS IN COINS ARE REPLACED BY TACO SAUCE-- WANNNHH!
CAN'T WE EVER CATCH A BREAK?
WILL THIS NIGHTMARE NEVER END?
176-167
176-716
176-617 BEAGLE
176-671 BEAGLE
the End

126

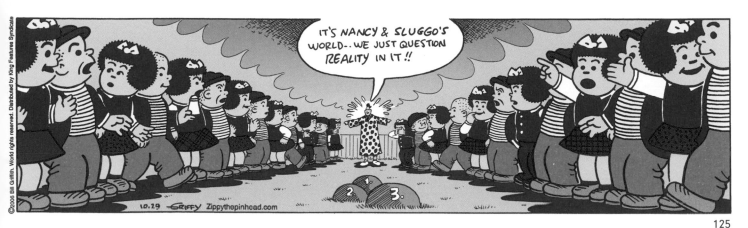

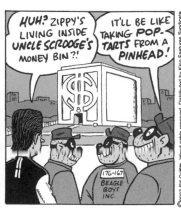

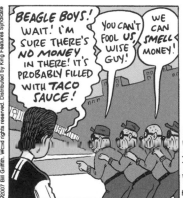

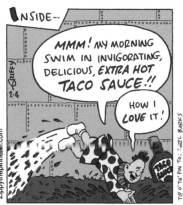

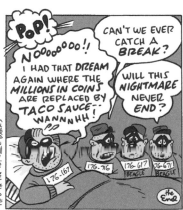

Suddenly, the **dialogue balloons** in this week's **Zippy strip** were **hijacked** by forces from beyond **the known universe**!!

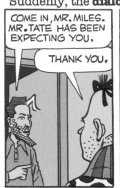

COME IN, MR. MILES. MR. TATE HAS BEEN EXPECTING YOU.
THANK YOU.
GLAD TO SEE YOU, QUENTIN! WHAT'RE YOU DOING OUT ON THE COAST?
I HAD SOME BUSINESS IN LOS ANGELES, SO I THOUGHT I'D JUST SAY HELLO. I'M ON MY WAY TO A DUDE RANCH IN CACTUS KNOB.
©2007 Bill Griffith. World rights reserved. Distributed by King Features
DID YOU SAY CACTUS KNOB? BY GEORGE! THAT'S WHERE I'M THINKING OF BUILDING A BIG SOUND STUDIO JUST TO MAKE WESTERNS!
IT SURELY HAS THE LANDSCAPE FOR IT. HAVE YOU BOUGHT SOME LAND THERE?
GRIFFY
NOT YET. BUT IF YOU'RE GOING TO BE THERE, I THINK I'LL GO MYSELF!
FINE! WE'LL GET IN A LITTLE TROUT FISHING!
2-25
Zippythepinhead.com

127

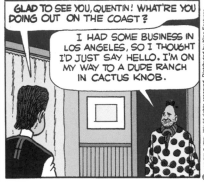

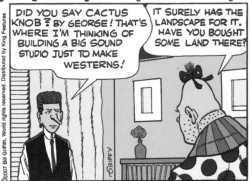

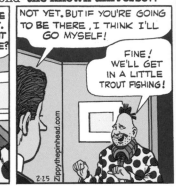

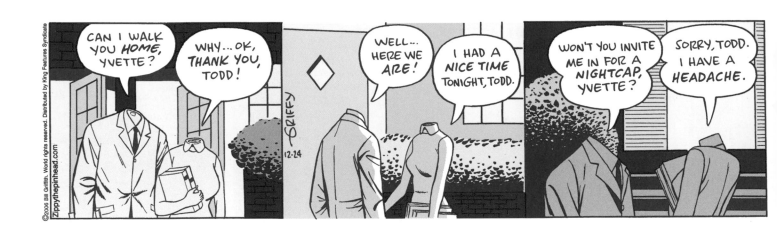

©2006 Bill Griffith. World rights reserved. Distributed by King Features Syndicate
Zippythepinhead.com
CAN I WALK YOU *HOME*, YVETTE?
WHY... OK, THANK YOU, TODD!
GRIFFY
12-24
WELL... HERE WE ARE!
I HAD A NICE TIME TONIGHT, TODD.
WON'T YOU INVITE ME IN FOR A NIGHTCAP, YVETTE?
SORRY, TODD. I HAVE A HEADACHE.

THE OFFICIAL, AUTHORIZED, SANCTIONED AND EDUCATIONAL ZIPPY THE PINHEAD ALPHABET of the ENGLISH LANGUAGE
©2007 Bill Griffith. World rights reserved. Distributed by King Features Syndicate
A IS FOR ANTHROPOMORPHISM
B IS FOR BAROTHERMOHYGROGRAPH
C IS FOR CRYPTOCLIMATOLOGY
D IS FOR DIHYDROXYPHENYLALANINE
E IS FOR EQUIPROBABILISM
OK!
F IS FOR FUNGITOXIC
AARGH.
G IS FOR GLOSSOPHARYNGEAL
H IS FOR HOUPPELANDE
I IS FOR ISOAGGLUTINATION
J IS FOR JUXTAPOSITION
K IS FOR KINNIKINNICK
L IS FOR LEPIDOPTEROLOGY
M IS FOR MEGAKARYOBLAST
BOOM!
N IS FOR NOVEMDECILLION
O IS FOR ORTHOMOLECULAR
YUM!
P IS FOR PECCATOPHOBIA
Q IS FOR QUINQUEVALENT
R IS FOR RHABDOMANCY
S IS FOR SEQUESTRECTOMY
T IS FOR TETRAGRAMMATON
U IS FOR USUFRUCTORY
V IS FOR VALVULOTOMY
W IS FOR WHIGMALEERIE
X IS FOR XANTHOSIDERITE
Y IS FOR YIDDISHISM
OY.
Z IS FOR ZUGZWANG
4-29
FOR WORD DEFINITIONS, GO TO ZIPPYTHEPINHEAD.COM HOME PAGE.

128

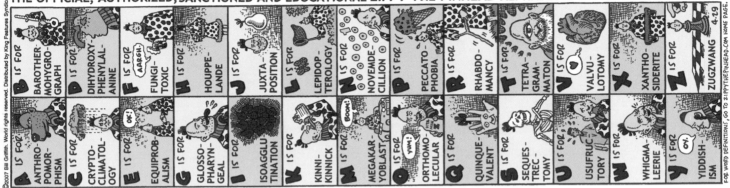

HOW TO DRAW ZIPPY the PINHEAD USING DIFFERENT STYLES and METHODS SUITABLE for HUMOROUS EXPRESSIONS
GRIFFY
2-11
1. ZIPPY the PINHEAD, Heads, Caricatured
©2007 Bill Griffith. World rights reserved.
2. ZIPPY the PINHEAD, Heads, Illustrative
Distributed by King Features Syndicate Zippythepinhead.com
YOW COMICS
3. ZIPPY the PINHEAD, Arms and Hands, Illustrative

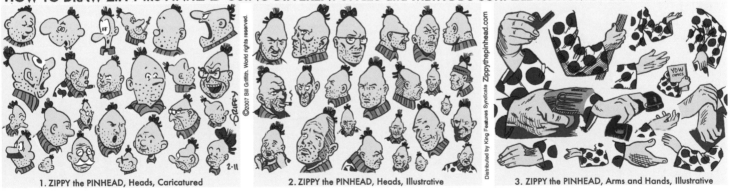

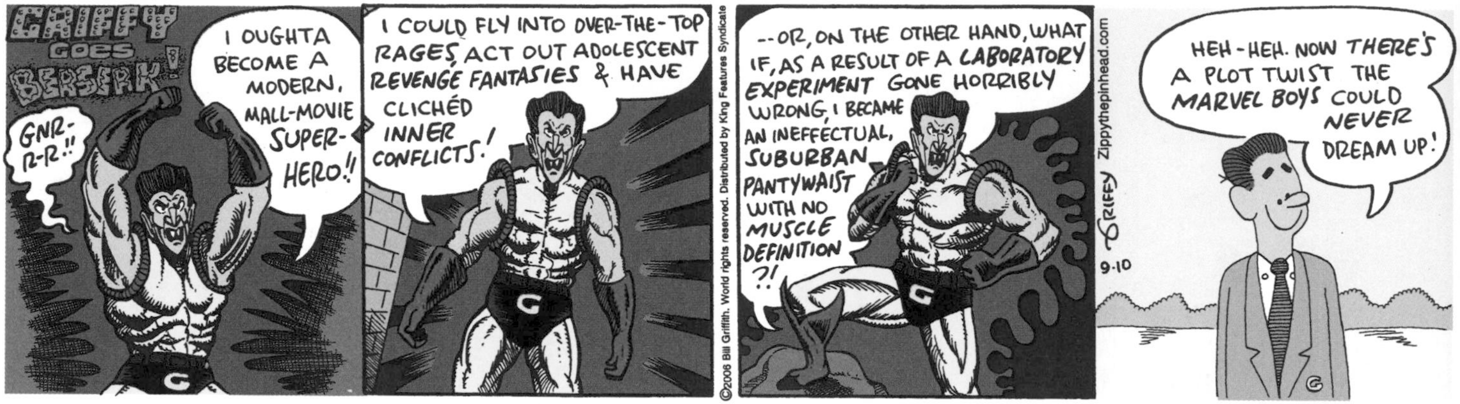
GRIFFY GOES BERSERK!
GNR-R-R!!
I OUGHTA BECOME A MODERN, MALL-MOVIE SUPER-HERO!!
I COULD FLY INTO OVER-THE-TOP RAGES, ACT OUT ADOLESCENT REVENGE FANTASIES & HAVE CLICHÉD INNER CONFLICTS!
©2006 Bill Griffith. World rights reserved. Distributed by King Features Syndicate
--OR, ON THE OTHER HAND, WHAT IF, AS A RESULT OF A LABORATORY EXPERIMENT GONE HORRIBLY WRONG, I BECAME AN INEFFECTUAL, SUBURBAN PANTYWAIST WITH NO MUSCLE DEFINITION ?!
Zippythepinhead.com
GRIFFY
9.10
HEH-HEH. NOW THERE'S A PLOT TWIST THE MARVEL BOYS COULD NEVER DREAM UP!

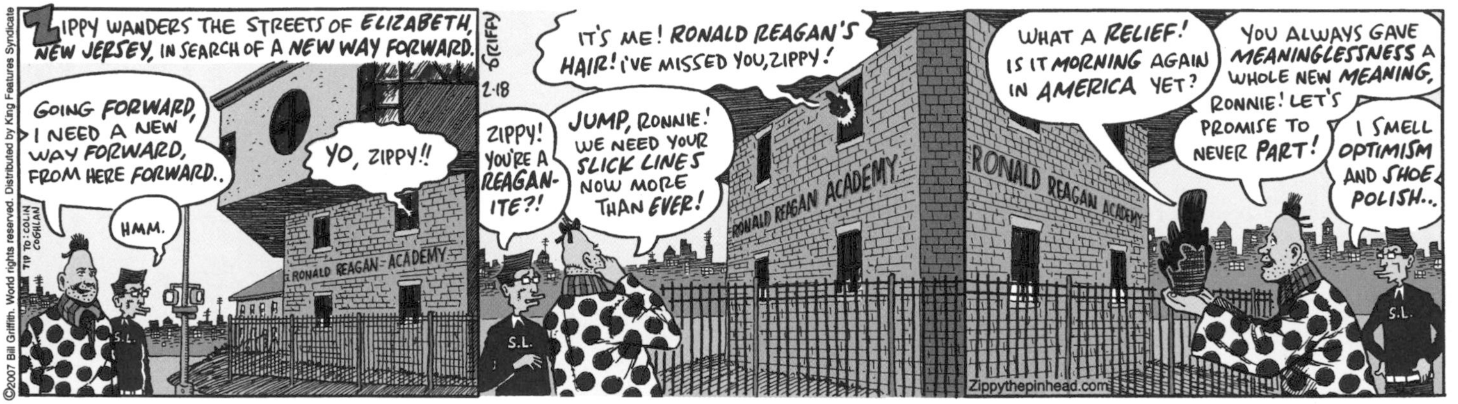
©2007 Bill Griffith. World rights reserved. Distributed by King Features Syndicate
ZIPPY WANDERS THE STREETS OF ELIZABETH, NEW JERSEY, IN SEARCH OF A NEW WAY FORWARD.
GOING FORWARD, I NEED A NEW WAY FORWARD, FROM HERE FORWARD..
YO, ZIPPY!!
HMM.
TIP TO: COLIN COGHLAN
RONALD REAGAN-ACADEMY
GRIFFY
2.18
IT'S ME! RONALD REAGAN'S HAIR! I'VE MISSED YOU, ZIPPY!
ZIPPY! YOU'RE A REAGAN-ITE?!
JUMP, RONNIE! WE NEED YOUR SLICK LINES NOW MORE THAN EVER!
RONALD REAGAN ACADEMY
WHAT A RELIEF! IS IT MORNING AGAIN IN AMERICA YET?
YOU ALWAYS GAVE MEANINGLESSNESS A WHOLE NEW MEANING, RONNIE! LET'S PROMISE TO NEVER PART!
I SMELL OPTIMISM AND SHOE POLISH...
Zippythepinhead.com

HEE-HEE, ZIPPY!

YOU'RE SCARING ME AGAIN, BIG BOY!

BUT I'M JOYFUL, ZIPPY! I'M TH' JOY BRINGER!

YOU LOOK LIKE A LITTLE DEMON, BIG BOY!

THAT'S SILLY! I'M FUN-LOVING! AND FRISKY! C'MON, LET'S PLAY! HA, HA, HA!

THAT LAUGH! THAT DEVILISH CHORTLE!

BUT THEY LOVE ME IN JAPAN, ZIPPY! AND CINCINNATI! I'M TH' JOY BRINGER! HEE-HEE!

HELLLLLPP!! I DON'T UNDERSTAND TH' SUBTLE DIFFERENCE BETWEEN SINCERITY & SARCASM!!

©2007 Bill Griffith. World rights reserved. Distributed by King Features Syndicate

Zippythepinhead.com TIP TO: JUSTIN GREEN

GRIFFY 1-28

129

I LIKE TH' DIFFERENT WACKY BELIEFS OF OTHER RELIGIONS.

GNOMISM IS TEMPTING.

AND BOBISM HAS ITS APPEAL.

BUT IN TH' END, I THINK I'LL STAY ON TH' ONE TRUE SPIRITUAL PATH.

©2006 Bill Griffith. World rights reserved. Distributed by King Features Syndicate

Zippythepinhead.com TIPS TO: DON SOLOSAN & PATRICE MILLER

GRIFFY 12-10

130

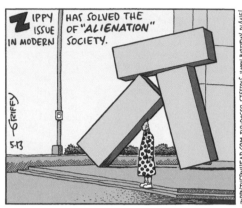

ZIPPY HAS SOLVED THE ISSUE OF "ALIENATION" IN MODERN SOCIETY.
GRIFFY
5-13
ZIPPYTHEPINHEAD.COM TIP: ROGER STEFFENS HAPPY BIRTHDAY DIANE!
IT'S QUITE SIMPLE.
JUST NEVER POP OUT YOUR EARBUDS!
©2007 Bill Griffith. World rights reserved. Distributed by King Features Syndicate

131

©2006 Bill Griffith. World rights reserved. Distributed by King Features Syndicate
IF PLUTO IS NO LONGER A PLANET, IS WALT DISNEY STILL FROZEN, SOMEWHERE OUTSIDE ALBUQUERQUE?
EVERYTHING IS IN FLUX, ZIPPY.. WHO KNOWS.. OPRAH MAY BE OUR NEXT PRESIDENT!
GRIFFY
10-22
THAT WOULD FREAK ME OUT. MORE THAN PLUTO.
"GYRO GEARLOOSE" WAS ALWAYS MY FAVORITE UNFROZEN DISNEY CHARACTER..
I CAN'T STOP WORRYING ABOUT TOM CRUISE'S CAREER DOWNTURN!
STARS FADE. OPRAH RULES TH' SOLAR SYSTEM.
Zippythepinhead.com

132

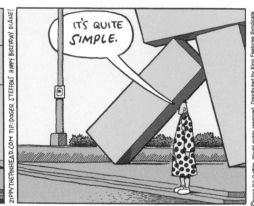

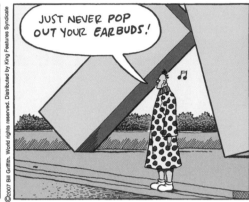

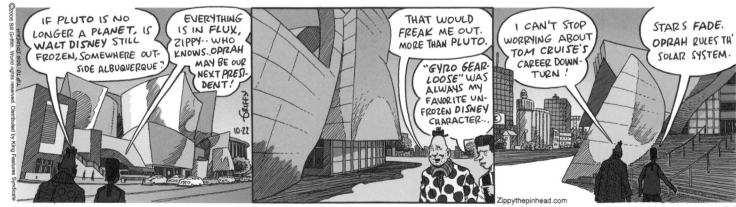

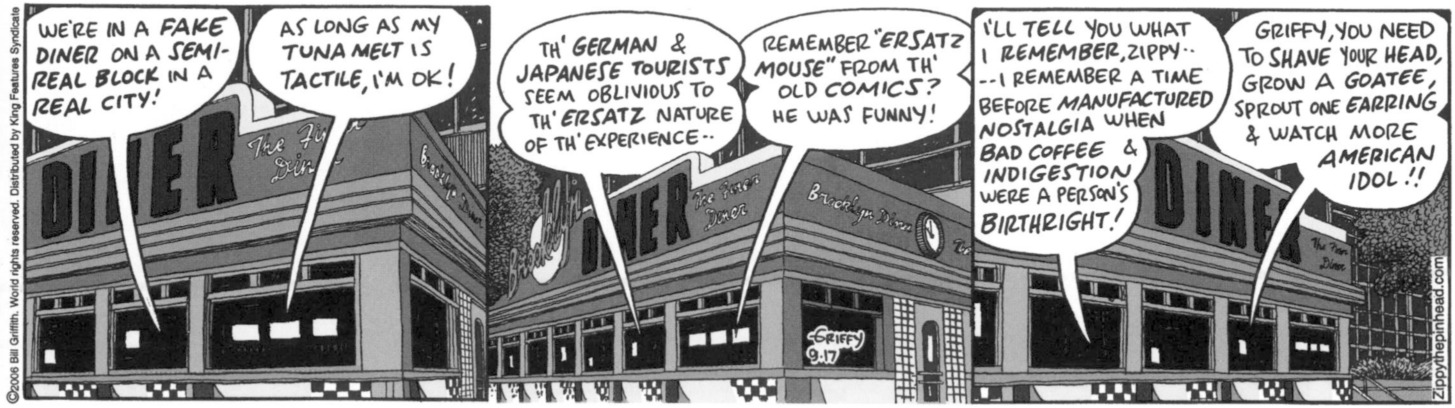
©2006 Bill Griffith. World rights reserved. Distributed by King Features Syndicate
WE'RE IN A FAKE DINER ON A SEMI-REAL BLOCK IN A REAL CITY!
AS LONG AS MY TUNA MELT IS TACTILE, I'M OK!
DINER
TH' GERMAN & JAPANESE TOURISTS SEEM OBLIVIOUS TO TH' ERSATZ NATURE OF TH' EXPERIENCE..
REMEMBER "ERSATZ MOUSE" FROM TH' OLD COMICS? HE WAS FUNNY!
DINER
GRIFFY 9.17
I'LL TELL YOU WHAT I REMEMBER, ZIPPY.. --I REMEMBER A TIME BEFORE MANUFACTURED NOSTALGIA WHEN BAD COFFEE & INDIGESTION WERE A PERSON'S BIRTHRIGHT!
GRIFFY, YOU NEED TO SHAVE YOUR HEAD, GROW A GOATEE, SPROUT ONE EARRING & WATCH MORE AMERICAN IDOL!!
DINER
Zippythepinhead.com

133

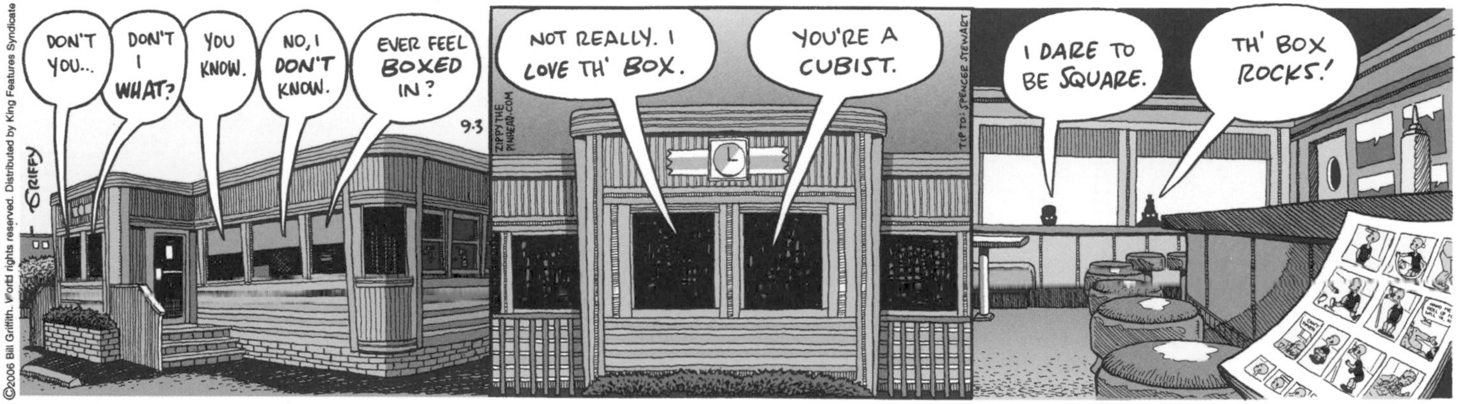
©2006 Bill Griffith. World rights reserved. Distributed by King Features Syndicate
DON'T YOU...
DON'T I WHAT?
YOU KNOW.
NO, I DON'T KNOW.
EVER FEEL BOXED IN?
GRIFFY
9.3
NOT REALLY. I LOVE TH' BOX.
YOU'RE A CUBIST.
ZIPPYTHEPINHEAD.COM
TIP TO: SPENCER STEWART
I DARE TO BE SQUARE.
TH' BOX ROCKS!

134

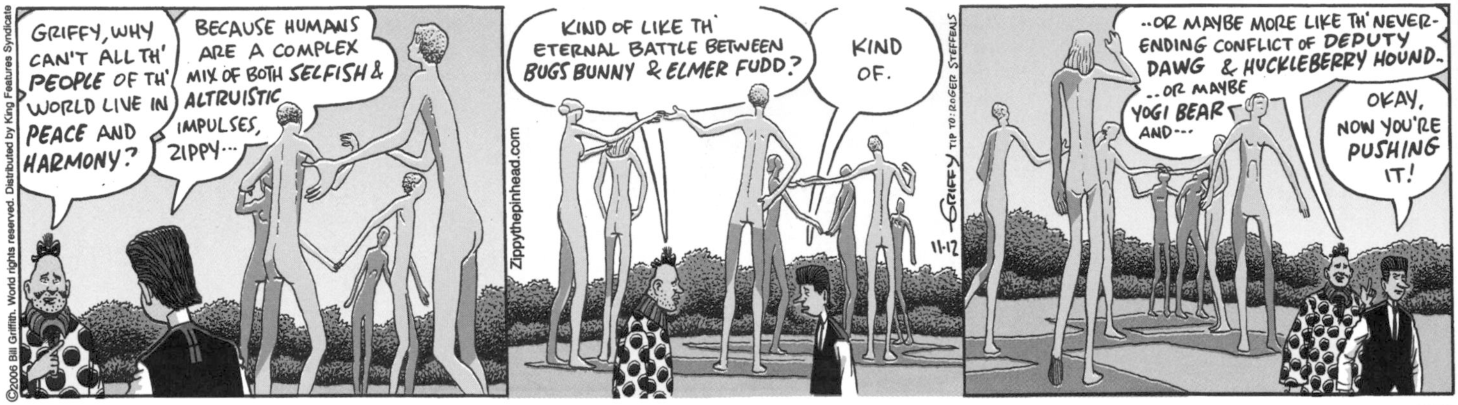
©2006 Bill Griffith. World rights reserved. Distributed by King Features Syndicate
GRIFFY, WHY CAN'T ALL TH' PEOPLE OF TH' WORLD LIVE IN PEACE AND HARMONY?
BECAUSE HUMANS ARE A COMPLEX MIX OF BOTH SELFISH & ALTRUISTIC IMPULSES, ZIPPY...
Zippythepinhead.com
KIND OF LIKE TH' ETERNAL BATTLE BETWEEN BUGS BUNNY & ELMER FUDD?
KIND OF.
GRIFFY
11-12
TIP TO: ROGER STEFFENS
..OR MAYBE MORE LIKE TH' NEVER-ENDING CONFLICT OF DEPUTY DAWG & HUCKLEBERRY HOUND..
..OR MAYBE YOGI BEAR AND---
OKAY, NOW YOU'RE PUSHING IT!

135

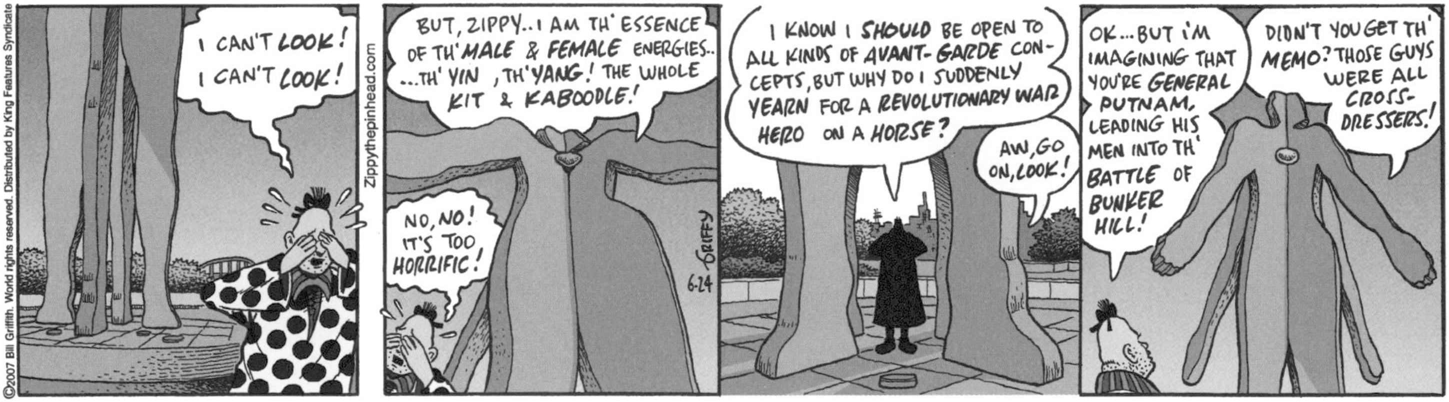
©2007 Bill Griffith. World rights reserved. Distributed by King Features Syndicate
I CAN'T LOOK! I CAN'T LOOK!
Zippythepinhead.com
BUT, ZIPPY.. I AM TH' ESSENCE OF TH' MALE & FEMALE ENERGIES.. ...TH' YIN, TH' YANG! THE WHOLE KIT & KABOODLE!
NO, NO! IT'S TOO HORRIFIC!
GRIFFY
6-24
I KNOW I SHOULD BE OPEN TO ALL KINDS OF AVANT-GARDE CONCEPTS, BUT WHY DO I SUDDENLY YEARN FOR A REVOLUTIONARY WAR HERO ON A HORSE?
AW, GO ON, LOOK!
OK... BUT I'M IMAGINING THAT YOU'RE GENERAL PUTNAM, LEADING HIS MEN INTO TH' BATTLE OF BUNKER HILL!
DIDN'T YOU GET TH' MEMO? THOSE GUYS WERE ALL CROSS-DRESSERS!

136

©2007 Bill Griffith. World rights reserved. Distributed by King Features Syndicate
ZIPPY ALWAYS WANTED TO MEET ANTONI GAUDÍ..THEN, ONE DAY IN BARCELONA--
YOU'RE A WEIRD OLD ARCHITECT, AREN'T YOU, ANTONI?
WEIRD? WHO IS TO SAY WHAT IS WEIRD?
AM I WEIRD BECAUSE MY BUILDINGS ESCHEW THE BOX & THE STRAIGHT LINE?
OR ARE YOU WEIRD BECAUSE YOU NEVER USED BLUEPRINTS & YOUR PARABOLIC ARCHES SEEM TO DEFY TH' FORCES OF GRAVITY?
WEIRD? WHO IS TO SAY WHAT WEIRD IS?
YES...YES.. ..WHO IS TO SAY...?
Zippythepinhead.com
YOU KNOW WHO WAS WEIRD? ARNOLD STANG! ARNOLD STANG WAS WEIRD!
YES...TO BE ARNOLD STANG.. THAT IS MY GOAL!
7-22
GRIFFY

137

THIS IS MY LAST FISHWICH HERE, LEONA.. --I'M LEAVING TOWN TOMORROW--
NO PROBLEM, MISTER..& MY NAME IS TINA, NOT LEONA..
©2006 Bill Griffith. World rights reserved. Distributed by King Features Syndicate
YOU'LL FORGET ALL ABOUT ME, EMILY-- YOU'VE GOT TO--BUT NEITHER OF US CAN EVER FORGET-- TH' BIG THUMB...
GRIFFY
9-24
Zippythepinhead.com
TH' BIG WHAT? DIDN'T YOU JUST SAY THAT THING WAS IN FRANCE SOMEWHERE?
YES, HELEN, I MUST LEAVE..BUT WE'LL ALWAYS HAVE PARIS.!!
TIP TO: MICHAEL STEWART

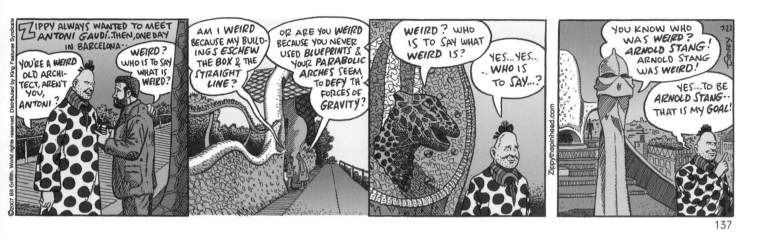

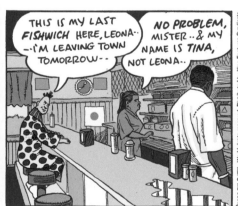

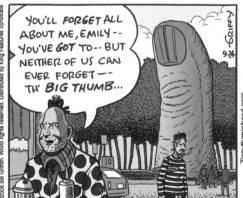

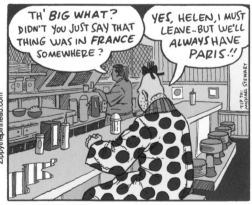

138

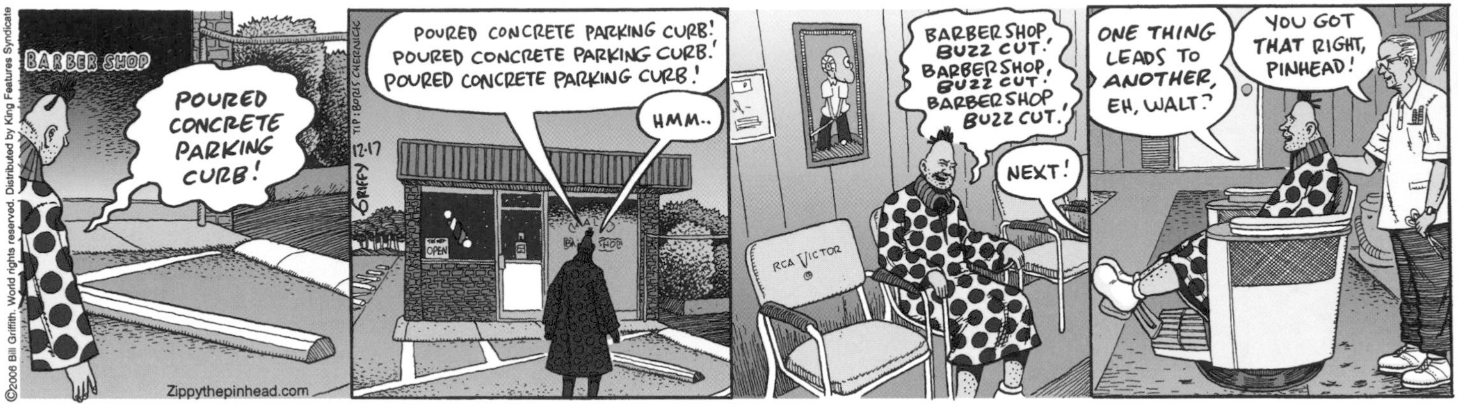
©2006 Bill Griffith. World rights reserved. Distributed by King Features Syndicate
BARBER SHOP
POURED CONCRETE PARKING CURB!
Zippythepinhead.com
TIP: BORIS CHERNICK
12-17
GRIFFY
POURED CONCRETE PARKING CURB! POURED CONCRETE PARKING CURB! POURED CONCRETE PARKING CURB!
HMM..
OPEN
BARBERSHOP, BUZZ CUT! BARBERSHOP, BUZZ CUT! BARBERSHOP BUZZ CUT!
NEXT!
RCA VICTOR
ONE THING LEADS TO ANOTHER, EH, WALT?
YOU GOT THAT RIGHT, PINHEAD!

139

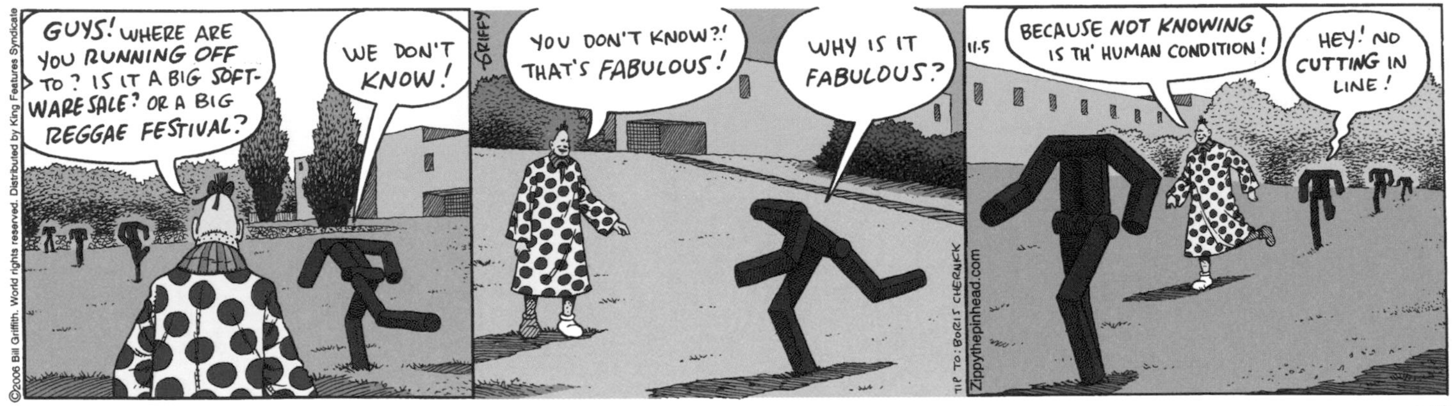
©2006 Bill Griffith. World rights reserved. Distributed by King Features Syndicate
GUYS! WHERE ARE YOU RUNNING OFF TO? IS IT A BIG SOFT-WARE SALE? OR A BIG REGGAE FESTIVAL?
WE DON'T KNOW!
GRIFFY
YOU DON'T KNOW?! THAT'S FABULOUS!
WHY IS IT FABULOUS?
TIP TO: BORIS CHERNICK
Zippythepinhead.com
11-5
BECAUSE NOT KNOWING IS TH' HUMAN CONDITION!
HEY! NO CUTTING IN LINE!

140

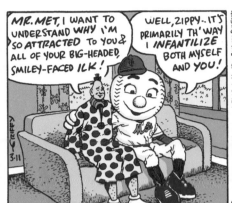

MR. MET, I WANT TO UNDERSTAND WHY I'M SO ATTRACTED TO YOU & ALL OF YOUR BIG-HEADED, SMILEY-FACED ILK!
WELL, ZIPPY.. IT'S PRIMARILY TH' WAY I INFANTILIZE BOTH MYSELF AND YOU!
GRIFFY
3-11
©2007 Bill Griffith. World rights reserved. Distributed by King Features Syndicate
MY ENORMOUS HEAD & DISPROPORTIONATELY SMALLER BODY NOT ONLY SIGNAL MY "BABY-ISHNESS".. BUT, CONVERSELY, I MAKE YOU FEEL SMALLER & CUTER!
I DON'T THINK THAT'S TH' REASON AT ALL, MR. MET!
Zippythepinhead.com
TIP O' TH' PIN TO: COLIN COGHLAN
I THINK IT'S BECAUSE YOU MAKE ME REALIZE THAT BEING REALLY WEIRD, AND NOT FITTING IN, IS OK & THAT I SHOULDN'T FEEL BAD ABOUT MY UNUSUALLY LOW BATTING AVERAGE..
JEEZ, IF I HAVE TO HEAR THAT TOUCHY-FEELY, "I'M OK, YOU'RE OK" GARBAGE ONE MORE TIME, I'M GONNA POP A STEROID!

141

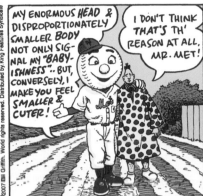

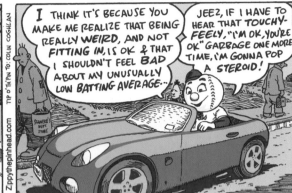

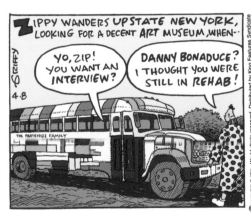

ZIPPY WANDERS UPSTATE NEW YORK, LOOKING FOR A DECENT ART MUSEUM, WHEN--
GRIFFY
4-8
YO, ZIP! YOU WANT AN INTERVIEW?
DANNY BONADUCE? I THOUGHT YOU WERE STILL IN REHAB!
THE PARTRIDGE FAMILY
©2007 Bill Griffith. World rights reserved. Distributed by King Features Syndicate
JUST ONE THING-- I DON'T WANT TO HEAR ANYTHING ABOUT "THE COWSILLS"!
BUT, DANNY! "THE PARTRIDGE FAMILY" WAS LOOSELY BASED ON "THE COWSILLS"!
Zippythepinhead.com
TIP O' TH' PIN TO: PATRICE MILLER
HEY, WE HAD OUR OWN SOUND, MAN! "C'MON, GET HAPPY" BROKE MAJOR MUSICAL GROUND!
ASIDE FROM "THE COWSILLS" FLAP, DID YOU EVER HEAR FROM MONDRIAN'S ATTORNEYS?

142

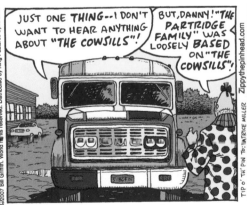

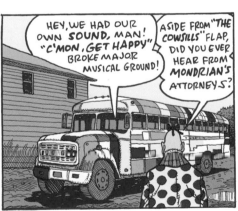

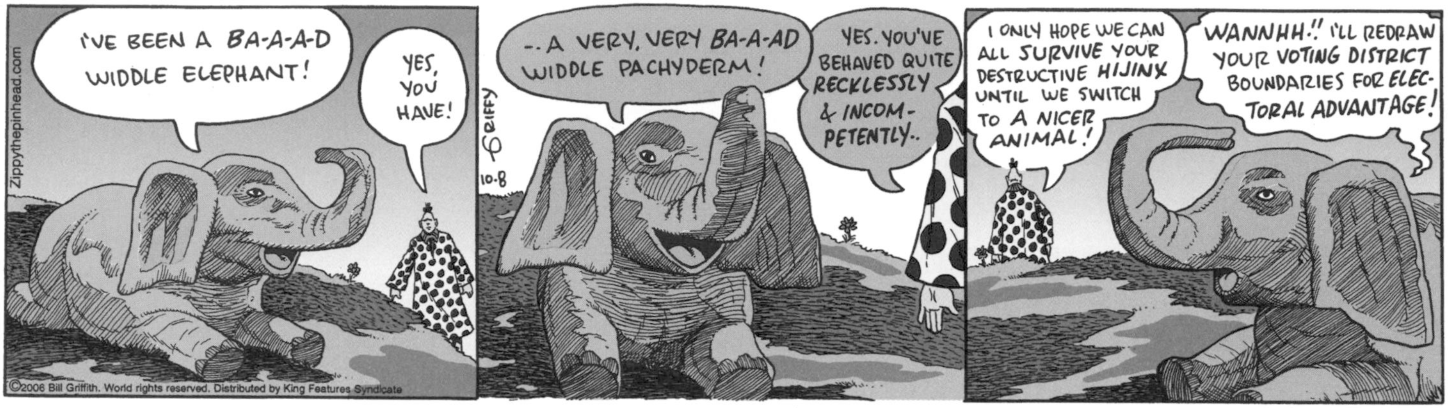
Zippythepinhead.com
I'VE BEEN A BA-A-A-D WIDDLE ELEPHANT!
YES, YOU HAVE!
GRIFFY 10-8
--A VERY, VERY BA-A-AD WIDDLE PACHYDERM!
YES. YOU'VE BEHAVED QUITE RECKLESSLY & INCOMPETENTLY..
I ONLY HOPE WE CAN ALL SURVIVE YOUR DESTRUCTIVE HIJINX UNTIL WE SWITCH TO A NICER ANIMAL!
WANNHH!! I'LL REDRAW YOUR VOTING DISTRICT BOUNDARIES FOR ELECTORAL ADVANTAGE!
©2006 Bill Griffith. World rights reserved. Distributed by King Features Syndicate

143

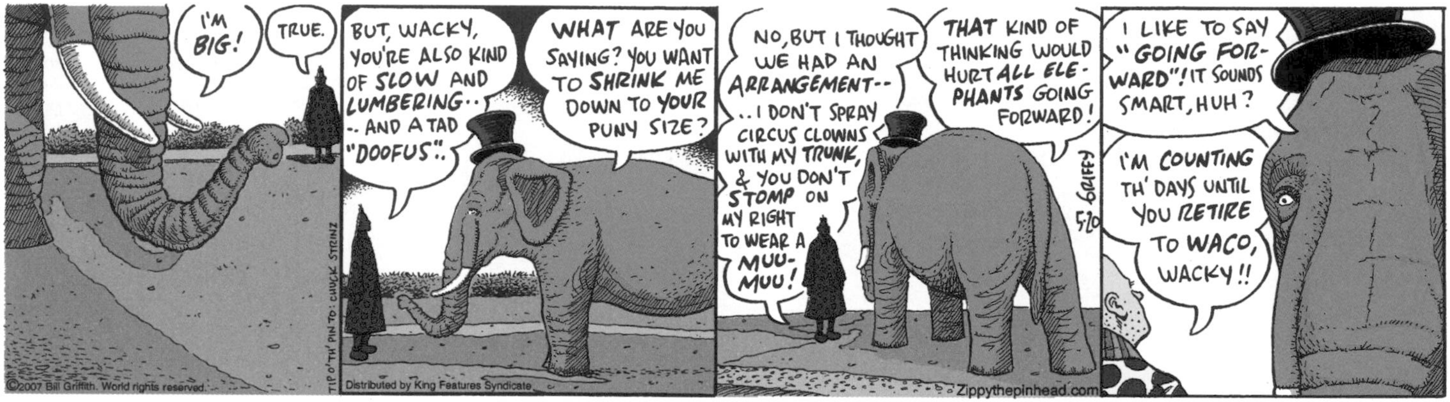
I'M BIG!
TRUE.
TIP O' TH' PIN TO: CHUCK STRINZ
BUT, WACKY, YOU'RE ALSO KIND OF SLOW AND LUMBERING.. -- AND A TAD "DOOFUS"..
WHAT ARE YOU SAYING? YOU WANT TO SHRINK ME DOWN TO YOUR PUNY SIZE?
NO, BUT I THOUGHT WE HAD AN ARRANGEMENT-- ..I DON'T SPRAY CIRCUS CLOWNS WITH MY TRUNK, & YOU DON'T STOMP ON MY RIGHT TO WEAR A MUU-MUU!
THAT KIND OF THINKING WOULD HURT ALL ELEPHANTS GOING FORWARD!
GRIFFY 5-20
I LIKE TO SAY "GOING FORWARD"! IT SOUNDS SMART, HUH?
I'M COUNTING TH' DAYS UNTIL YOU RETIRE TO WACO, WACKY!!
©2007 Bill Griffith. World rights reserved.
Distributed by King Features Syndicate
Zippythepinhead.com

144

HEY, WHAT IS THAT THING OUTLINED IN TH' AIR?!
IT'S SOME KIND OF AN INVISIBLE FORCE FIELD!
GEE...
GRIFFY 6-17
©2007 Bill Griffith. World rights reserved. Distributed by King Features Syndicate
EVER SINCE THAT INVISIBLE FORCE FIELD ARRIVED, WE'VE JUST BEEN SO HAPPY & CAREFREE!
THIS IS TH' SHAPE IT HAD-- I MADE A SKETCH OF TH' DOTTED LINES AROUND IT!
CAN I GET A COPY?
Zippythepinhead.com
IF WE ALL CONCENTRATE REALLY HARD, KIDS, MAYBE WE CAN BRING BACK TH' INVISIBLE FORCE FIELD!
YOU MEAN IT MIGHT REMATERIALIZE?
EAT ALL YOUR FROOT LOOPS, ARLINE, IT'S WHAT TH' INVISIBLE FORCE FIELD WOULD WANT YOU TO DO!

I ENJOYED TH' PLUSH CARPETING. AND TH' TWINKLING LIGHTS. AND TH' NON-STOP BEVERAGES!
YEH. WELL. ALL THAT DON'T COME FREE, PARDNER-- IT COST US $743.00!
Safari
Zippythepinhead.com
IS IT BAD TO LOSE, CLAUDE?
IT'S TH' WORST THING THERE IS, PARDNER.
"Lucky Cuss"
MOTEL
©2007 Bill Griffith. World rights reserved. Distributed by King Features Syndicate
WHAT DID YOU COME HERE FOR, CLAUDE?
I CAME TO WIN, PARDNER!
MOTEL
Holiday MOTEL
TO: DON SOLOSAN
I CAME FOR TH' COMPLIMENTARY HAND SANITIZER.
EGAS
TEL
HOURLY DAILY RATES
GRIFFY 7-4

145

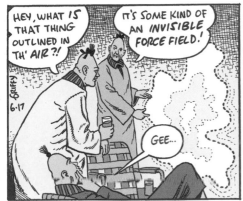

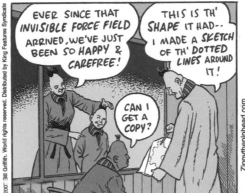

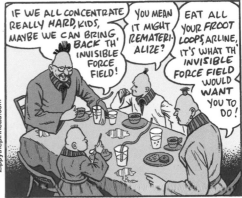

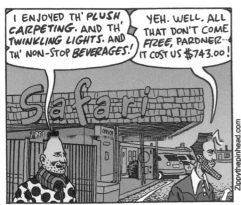

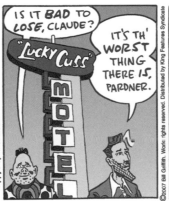

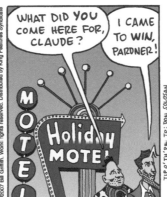

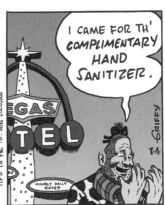

SO?
YES?
GRIFFY
B-6
TIPS O' TH' PIN TO: SPENCER STEWART & BRYAN LEE
...YOU'RE WEARING A SHORT-SLEEVE MUU-MUU...
IT'S MY SUMMER LOOK.
©2006 Bill Griffith. World rights reserved. Distributed by King Features Syndicate
OHMY GOD.
HEY. IT'S 93° OUT-- & HUMID!
ARE YOU SAYING YOU REALLY LIKE THIS OUTFIT?
I'VE NEVER FELT SO ALIVE!
Zippythepinhead.com
WELL, I GUESS MESSING WITH YOUR IDENTITY IS ONE WAY TO STAY HIP & RELEVANT..
I'M SO EXCITED, I CAN'T TELL MY ID FROM MY EGO!!

©2007 Bill Griffith. World rights reserved. Distributed by King Features Syndicate
GRIFFY STOOD ALONE IN TIMES SQUARE AND COMPLAINED--
DOES ANYONE EVER WAKE UP IN TH' MORNING & ASK, WHY DO I ALWAYS WEAR JEANS? OR, WHY DON'T I APPRECIATE OTTO DIX?
HERSHEY
GREY GARDENS
MAYBE I'M NOT GETTING ENOUGH CHOCOLATE.
RUBY FOO
1-21
GRIFFY
Zippythepinhead.com

146

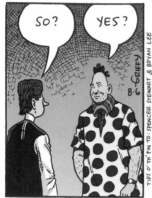

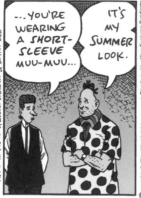

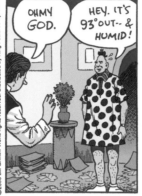

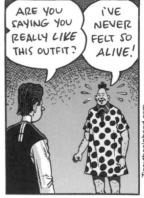

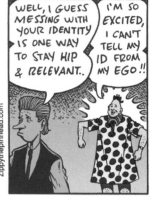

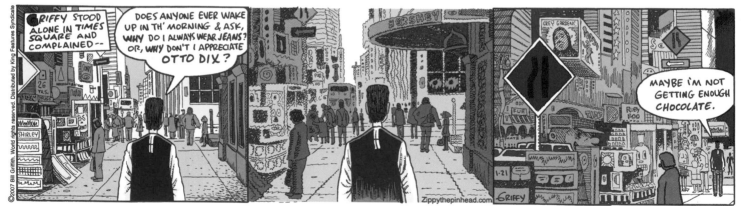

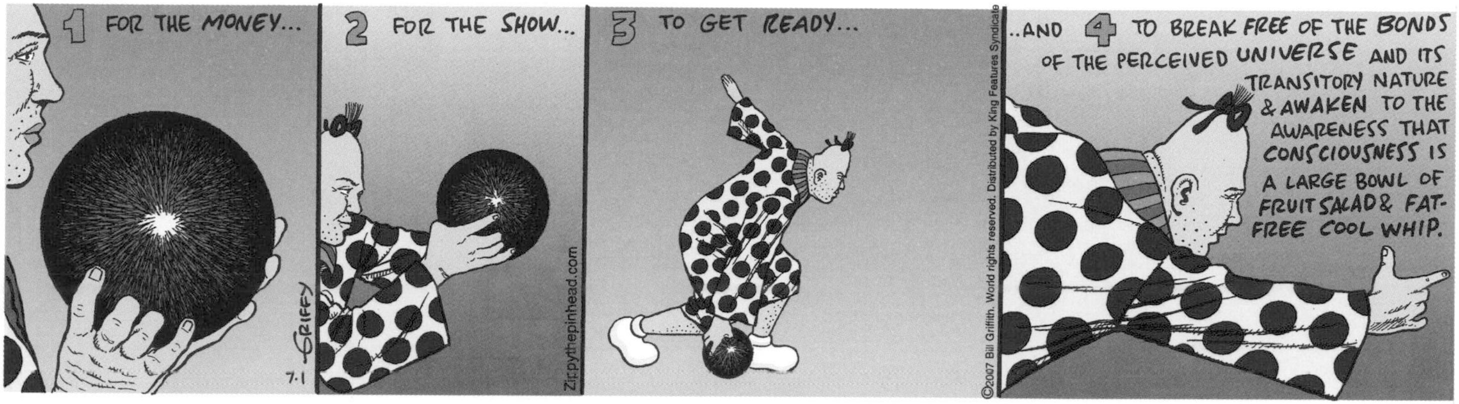
1 FOR THE MONEY...
GRIFFY
7-1
2 FOR THE SHOW...
Zippythepinhead.com
3 TO GET READY...
©2007 Bill Griffith. World rights reserved. Distributed by King Features Syndicate
..AND 4 TO BREAK FREE OF THE BONDS OF THE PERCEIVED UNIVERSE AND ITS TRANSITORY NATURE & AWAKEN TO THE AWARENESS THAT CONSCIOUSNESS IS A LARGE BOWL OF FRUIT SALAD & FAT-FREE COOL WHIP.

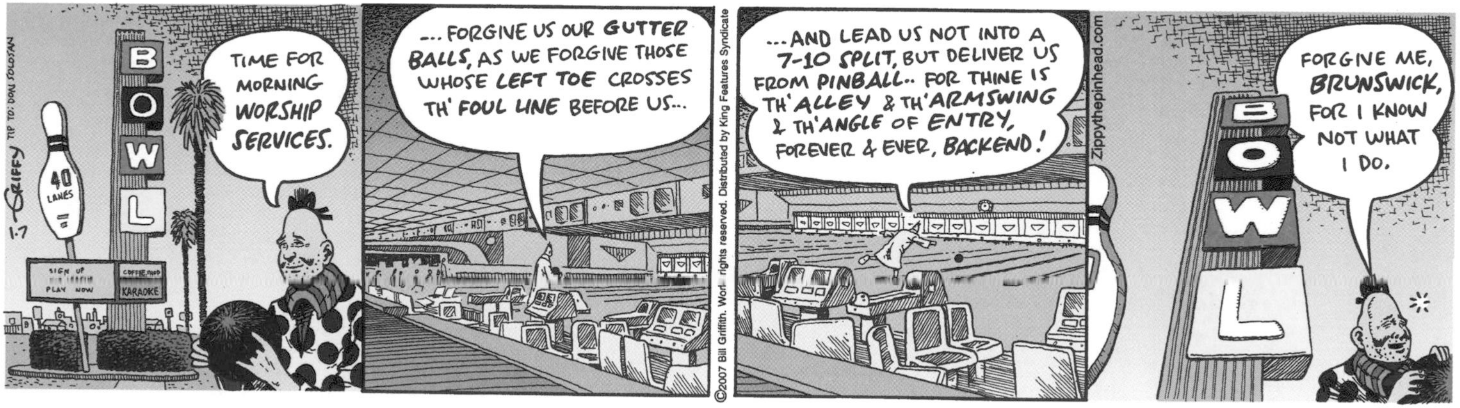
GRIFFY
1-7
BOWL
40 LANES
KARAOKE
TIME FOR MORNING WORSHIP SERVICES.
...FORGIVE US OUR GUTTER BALLS, AS WE FORGIVE THOSE WHOSE LEFT TOE CROSSES TH' FOUL LINE BEFORE US...
©2007 Bill Griffith. World rights reserved. Distributed by King Features Syndicate
...AND LEAD US NOT INTO A 7-10 SPLIT, BUT DELIVER US FROM PINBALL.. FOR THINE IS TH' ALLEY & TH' ARMSWING & TH' ANGLE OF ENTRY, FOREVER & EVER, BACKEND!
Zippythepinhead.com
BOWL
FORGIVE ME, BRUNSWICK, FOR I KNOW NOT WHAT I DO.

147

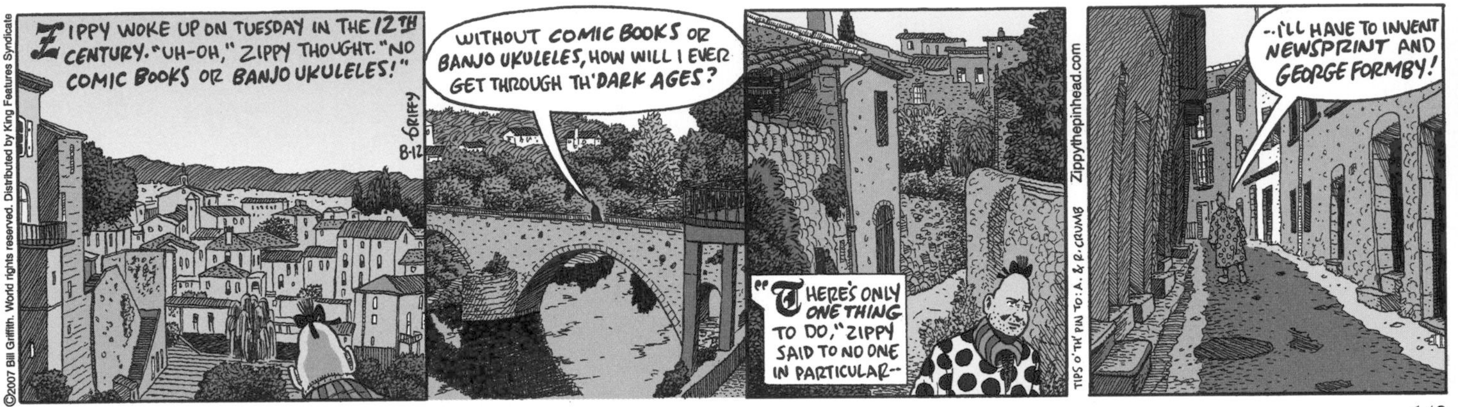
©2007 Bill Griffith. World rights reserved. Distributed by King Features Syndicate
ZIPPY WOKE UP ON TUESDAY IN THE 12TH CENTURY. "UH-OH," ZIPPY THOUGHT. "NO COMIC BOOKS OR BANJO UKULELES!"
GRIFFY 8-12
WITHOUT COMIC BOOKS OR BANJO UKULELES, HOW WILL I EVER GET THROUGH TH' DARK AGES?
"THERE'S ONLY ONE THING TO DO," ZIPPY SAID TO NO ONE IN PARTICULAR--
TIPS O' TH' PIN TO: A. & R. CRUMB
Zippythepinhead.com
--I'LL HAVE TO INVENT NEWSPRINT AND GEORGE FORMBY!

148

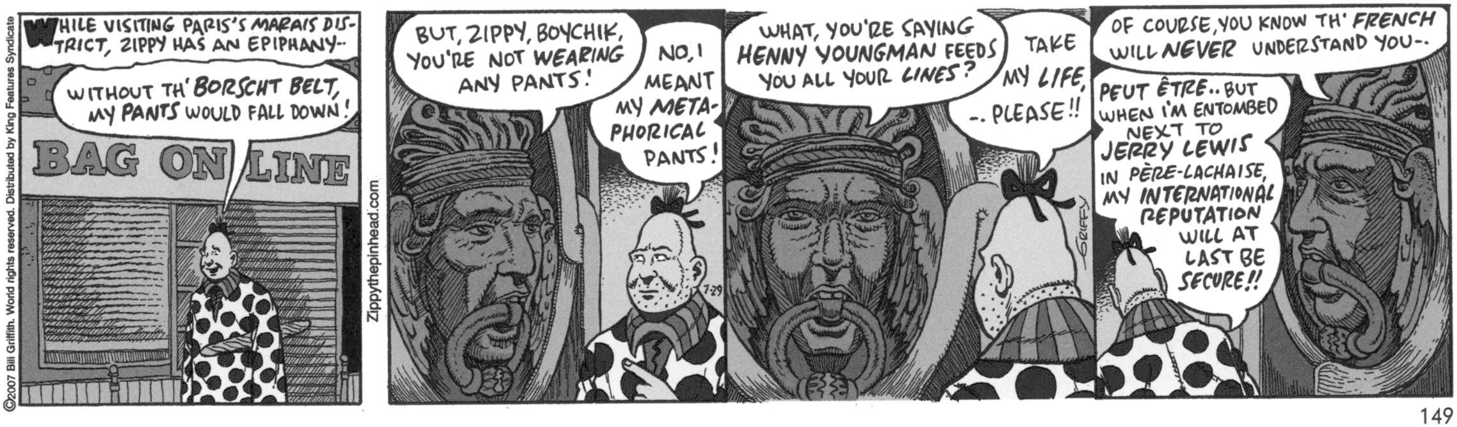
©2007 Bill Griffith. World rights reserved. Distributed by King Features Syndicate
WHILE VISITING PARIS'S MARAIS DISTRICT, ZIPPY HAS AN EPIPHANY--
WITHOUT TH' BORSCHT BELT, MY PANTS WOULD FALL DOWN!
BAG ON LINE
Zippythepinhead.com
BUT, ZIPPY, BOYCHIK, YOU'RE NOT WEARING ANY PANTS!
NO, I MEANT MY METAPHORICAL PANTS!
7-29
WHAT, YOU'RE SAYING HENNY YOUNGMAN FEEDS YOU ALL YOUR LINES?
TAKE MY LIFE, --. PLEASE!!
GRIFFY
OF COURSE, YOU KNOW TH' FRENCH WILL NEVER UNDERSTAND YOU--.
PEUT ÊTRE.. BUT WHEN I'M ENTOMBED NEXT TO JERRY LEWIS IN PÈRE-LACHAISE, MY INTERNATIONAL REPUTATION WILL AT LAST BE SECURE!!

149

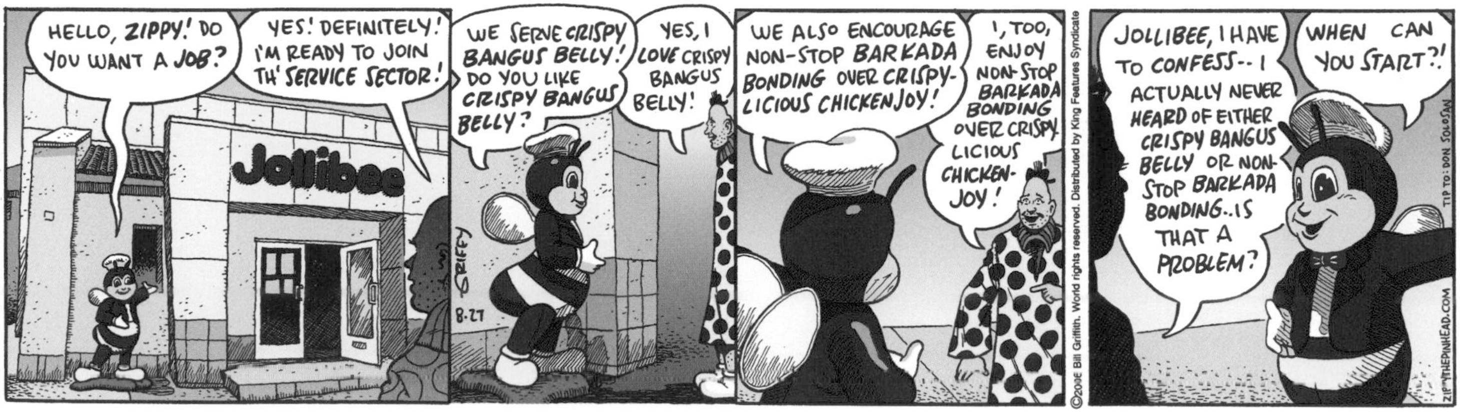
HELLO, ZIPPY! DO YOU WANT A JOB?
YES! DEFINITELY! I'M READY TO JOIN TH' SERVICE SECTOR!
Jollibee
WE SERVE CRISPY BANGUS BELLY! DO YOU LIKE CRISPY BANGUS BELLY?
YES, I LOVE CRISPY BANGUS BELLY!
GRIFFY
8-27
WE ALSO ENCOURAGE NON-STOP BARKADA BONDING OVER CRISPY-LICIOUS CHICKENJOY!
I, TOO, ENJOY NON-STOP BARKADA BONDING OVER CRISPY-LICIOUS CHICKEN-JOY!
©2008 Bill Griffith. World rights reserved. Distributed by King Features Syndicate
JOLLIBEE, I HAVE TO CONFESS-- I ACTUALLY NEVER HEARD OF EITHER CRISPY BANGUS BELLY OR NON-STOP BARKADA BONDING..IS THAT A PROBLEM?
WHEN CAN YOU START?!
TIP TO: DON SOLOSAN
ZIPPYTHEPINHEAD.COM

150

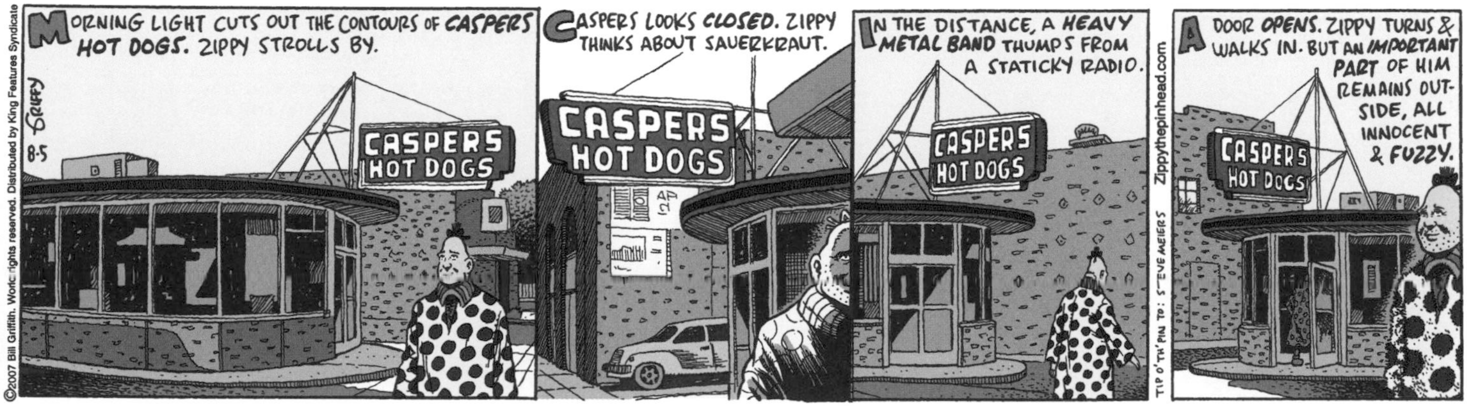
©2007 Bill Griffith. World rights reserved. Distributed by King Features Syndicate
MORNING LIGHT CUTS OUT THE CONTOURS OF CASPERS HOT DOGS. ZIPPY STROLLS BY.
GRIFFY
8-5
CASPERS HOT DOGS
CASPERS LOOKS CLOSED. ZIPPY THINKS ABOUT SAUERKRAUT.
CASPERS HOT DOGS
IN THE DISTANCE, A HEAVY METAL BAND THUMPS FROM A STATICKY RADIO.
CASPERS HOT DOGS
Zippythepinhead.com
TIP O' TH' PIN TO: STEVE MEIERS
A DOOR OPENS. ZIPPY TURNS & WALKS IN. BUT AN IMPORTANT PART OF HIM REMAINS OUTSIDE, ALL INNOCENT & FUZZY.
CASPERS HOT DOGS

151

POLITICS AS USUAL

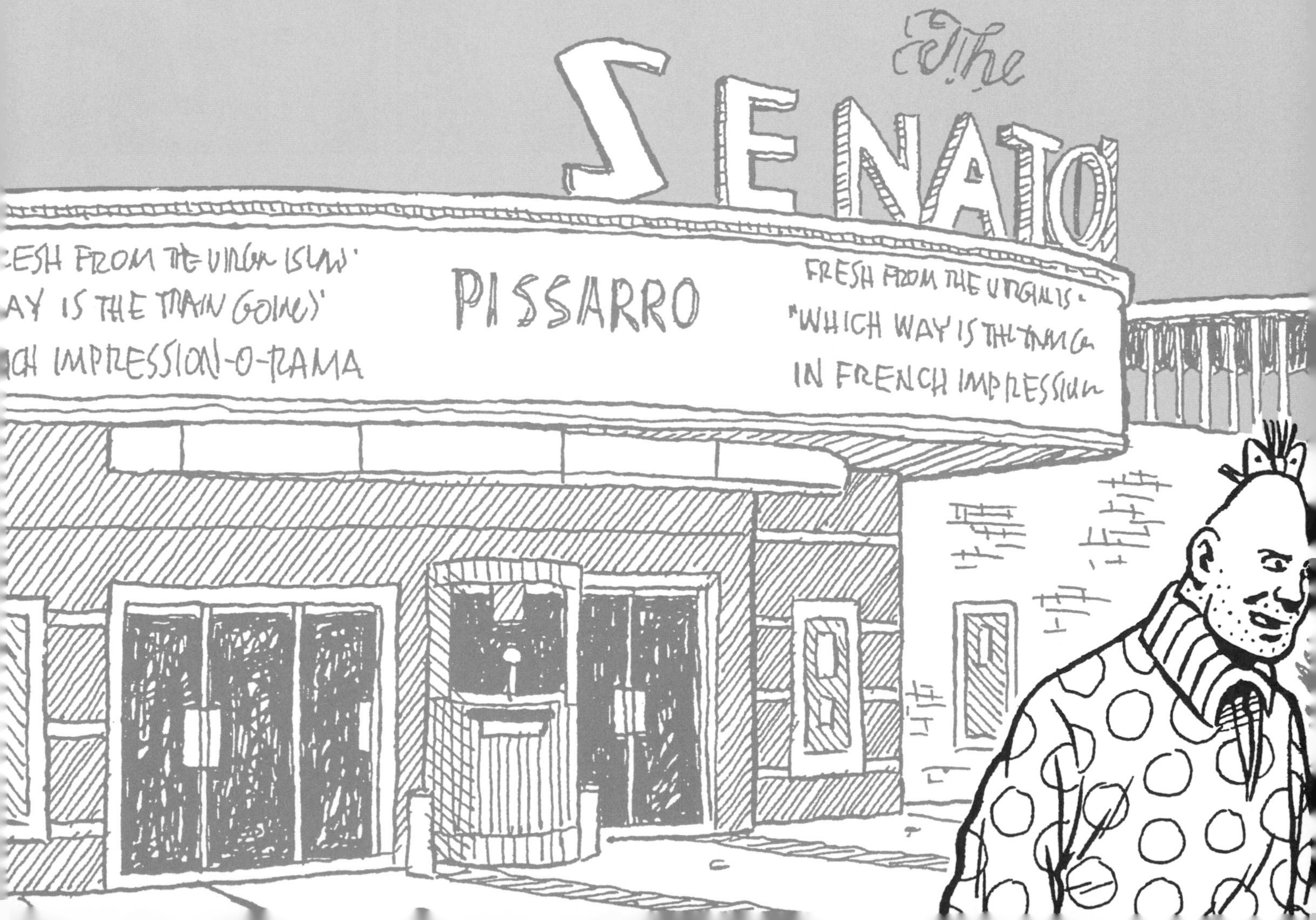
The
SENATO
ESH FROM THE VIRGIN ISLAN'
AY IS THE TRAIN GOING'
CH IMPRESSION-O-RAMA
PISSARRO
FRESH FROM THE VIRGIN IS
"WHICH WAY IS THE TRAIN G
IN FRENCH IMPRESSION

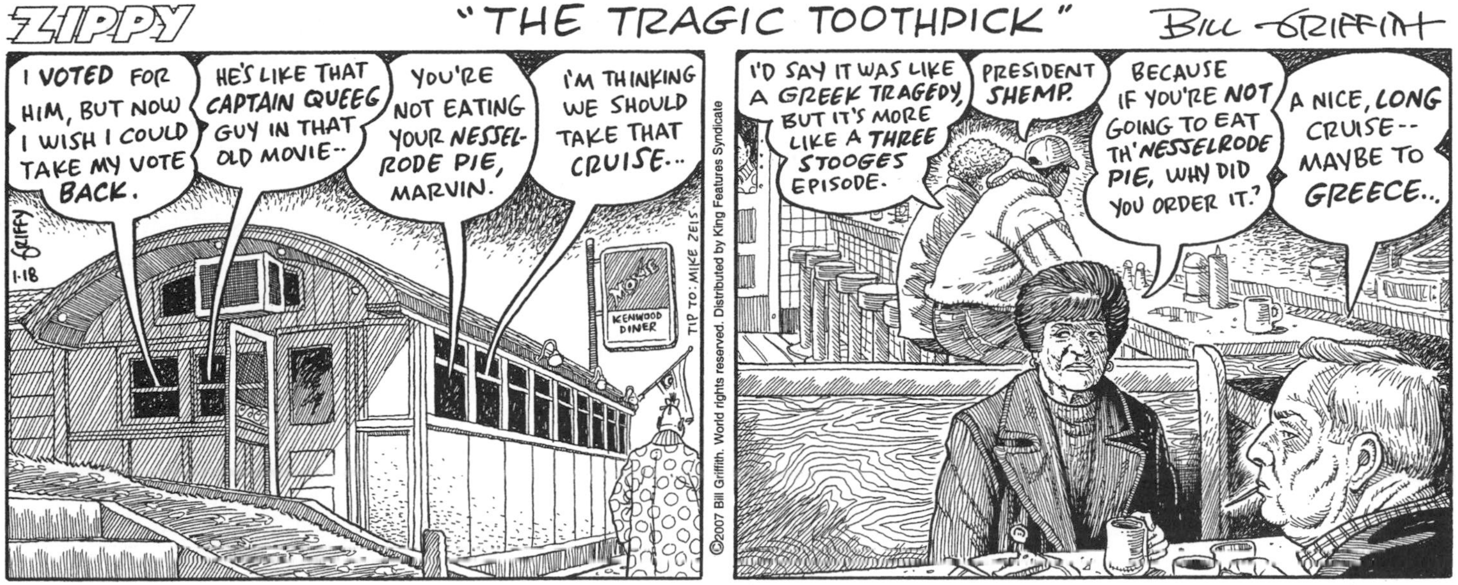
ZIPPY
"THE TRAGIC TOOTHPICK"
BILL GRIFFITH
I VOTED FOR HIM, BUT NOW I WISH I COULD TAKE MY VOTE BACK.
HE'S LIKE THAT CAPTAIN QUEEG GUY IN THAT OLD MOVIE..
YOU'RE NOT EATING YOUR NESSELRODE PIE, MARVIN.
I'M THINKING WE SHOULD TAKE THAT CRUISE...
KENWOOD DINER
TIP TO: MIKE ZEIS
GRIFFY 1-18
©2007 Bill Griffith. World rights reserved. Distributed by King Features Syndicate
I'D SAY IT WAS LIKE A GREEK TRAGEDY, BUT IT'S MORE LIKE A THREE STOOGES EPISODE.
PRESIDENT SHEMP.
BECAUSE IF YOU'RE NOT GOING TO EAT TH' NESSELRODE PIE, WHY DID YOU ORDER IT?
A NICE, LONG CRUISE-- MAYBE TO GREECE...

152 A

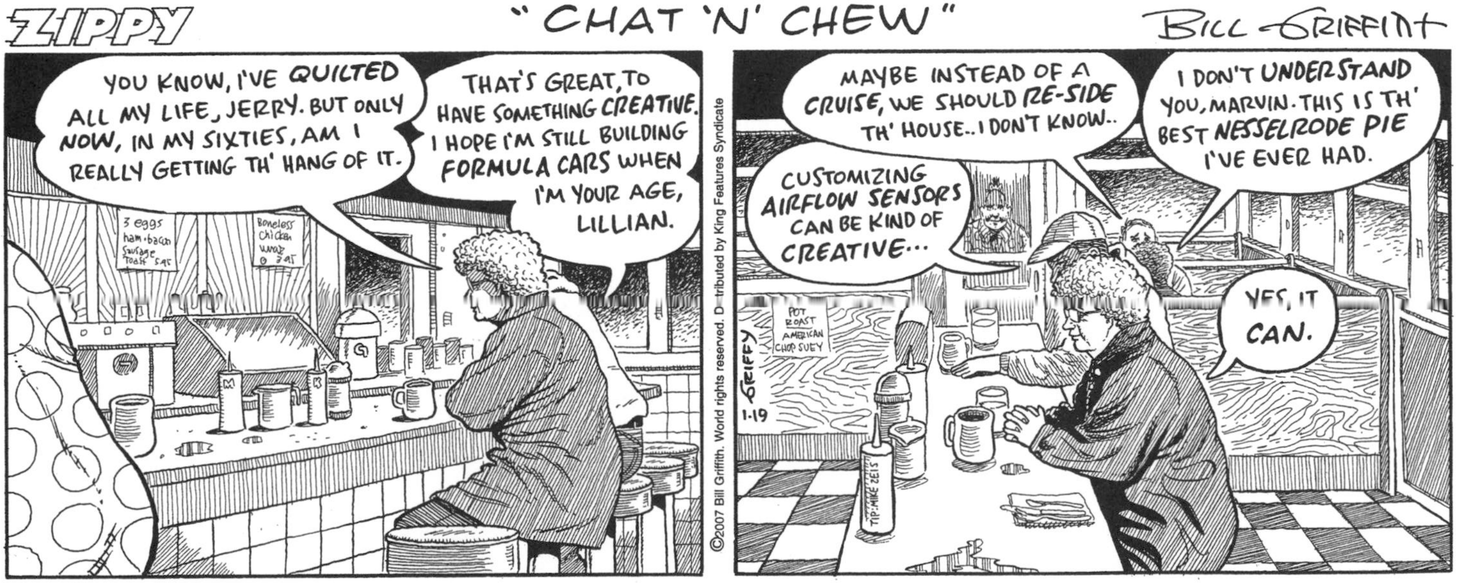
ZIPPY
"CHAT 'N' CHEW"
BILL GRIFFITH
YOU KNOW, I'VE QUILTED ALL MY LIFE, JERRY. BUT ONLY NOW, IN MY SIXTIES, AM I REALLY GETTING TH' HANG OF IT.
THAT'S GREAT, TO HAVE SOMETHING CREATIVE. I HOPE I'M STILL BUILDING FORMULA CARS WHEN I'M YOUR AGE, LILLIAN.
3 eggs ham-bacon sausage toast
Boneless Chicken wrap
©2007 Bill Griffith. World rights reserved. Distributed by King Features Syndicate
MAYBE INSTEAD OF A CRUISE, WE SHOULD RE-SIDE TH' HOUSE.. I DON'T KNOW..
I DON'T UNDERSTAND YOU, MARVIN. THIS IS TH' BEST NESSELRODE PIE I'VE EVER HAD.
CUSTOMIZING AIRFLOW SENSORS CAN BE KIND OF CREATIVE...
POT ROAST AMERICAN CHOP SUEY
YES, IT CAN.
GRIFFY 1-19
TIP: MIKE ZEIS

152 B

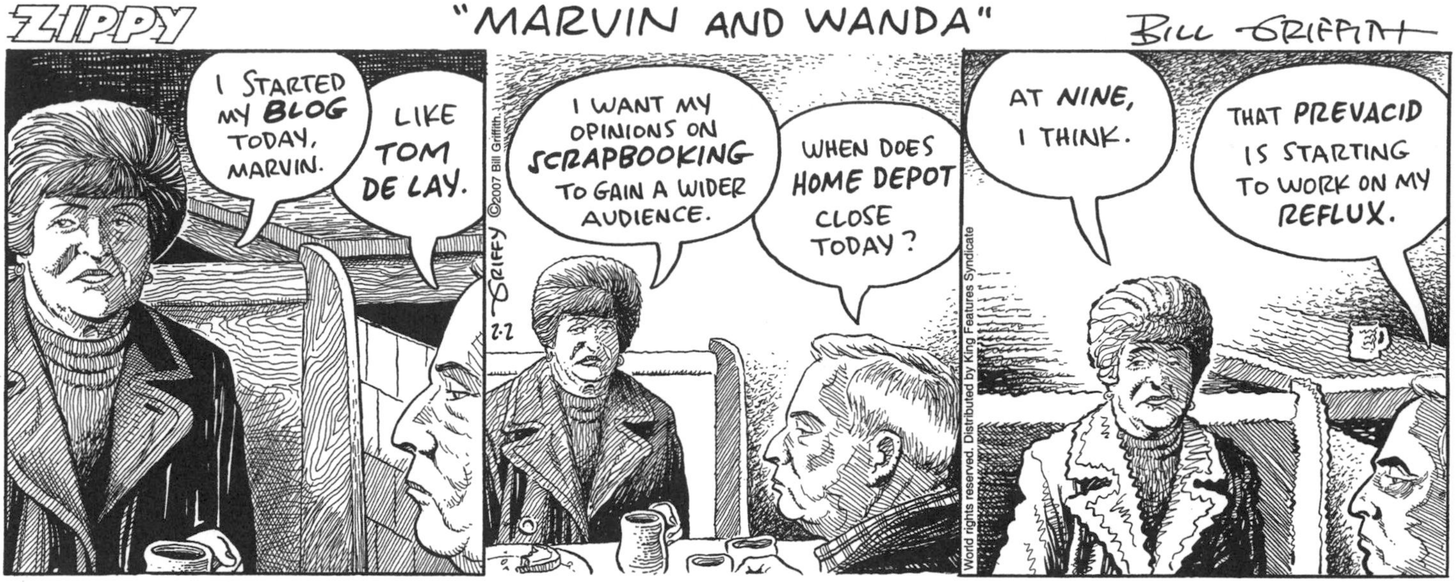
ZIPPY
"MARVIN AND WANDA"
BILL GRIFFITH
I STARTED MY BLOG TODAY, MARVIN.
LIKE TOM DE LAY.
GRIFFY 2-2
©2007 Bill Griffith.
I WANT MY OPINIONS ON SCRAPBOOKING TO GAIN A WIDER AUDIENCE.
WHEN DOES HOME DEPOT CLOSE TODAY?
World rights reserved. Distributed by King Features Syndicate
AT NINE, I THINK.
THAT PREVACID IS STARTING TO WORK ON MY REFLUX.

152 C

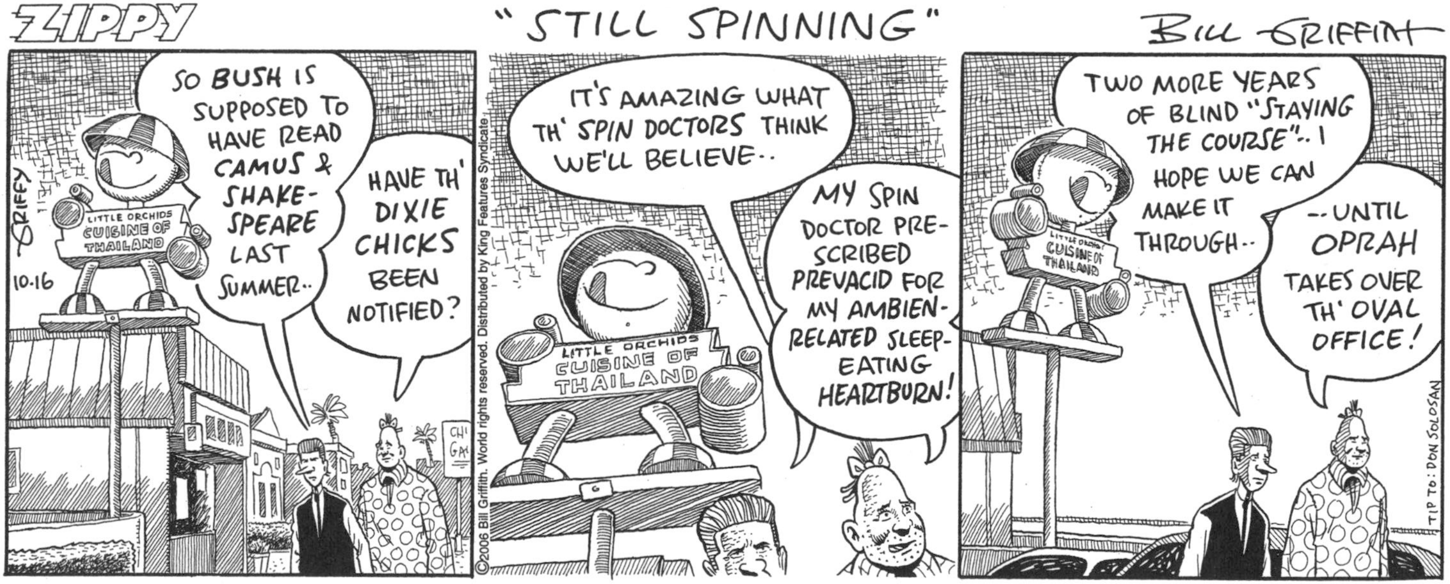
ZIPPY
"STILL SPINNING"
BILL GRIFFITH
GRIFFY 10-16
LITTLE ORCHIDS CUISINE OF THAILAND
SO BUSH IS SUPPOSED TO HAVE READ CAMUS & SHAKE-SPEARE LAST SUMMER..
HAVE TH' DIXIE CHICKS BEEN NOTIFIED?
©2006 Bill Griffith. World rights reserved. Distributed by King Features Syndicate.
IT'S AMAZING WHAT TH' SPIN DOCTORS THINK WE'LL BELIEVE..
MY SPIN DOCTOR PRE-SCRIBED PREVACID FOR MY AMBIEN-RELATED SLEEP-EATING HEARTBURN!
TWO MORE YEARS OF BLIND "STAYING THE COURSE".. I HOPE WE CAN MAKE IT THROUGH..
--UNTIL OPRAH TAKES OVER TH' OVAL OFFICE!
TIP TO: DON SOLOSAN

153

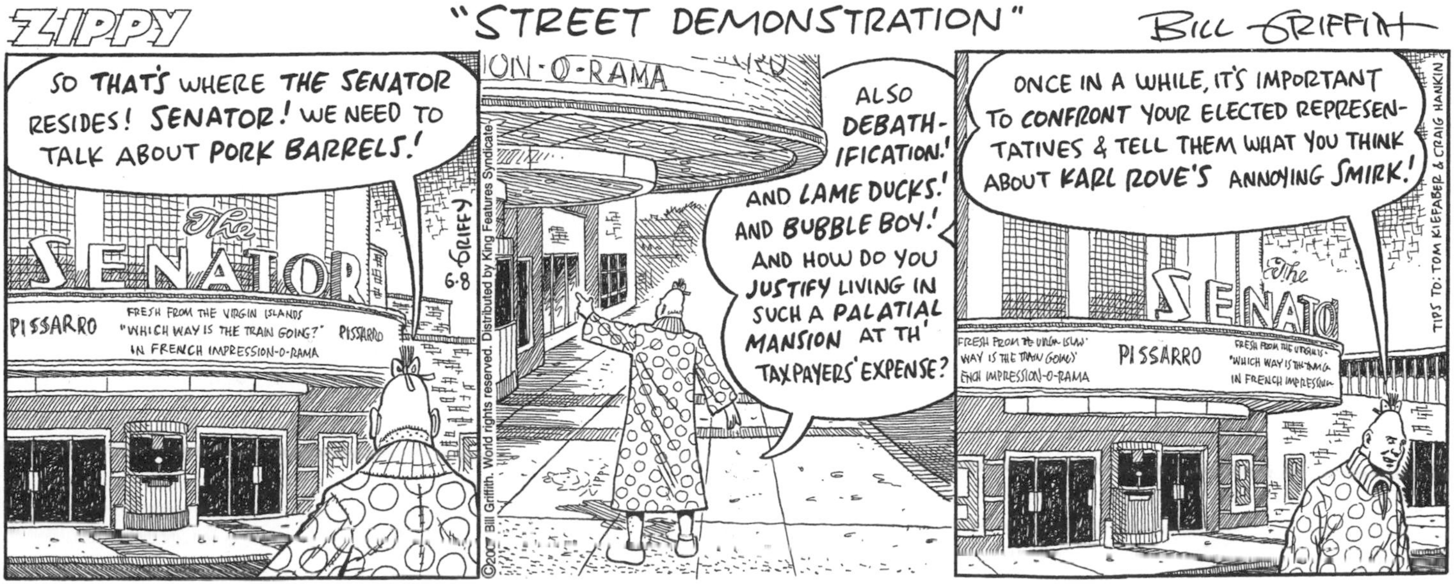
ZIPPY
"STREET DEMONSTRATION"
BILL GRIFFITH
SO THAT'S WHERE THE SENATOR RESIDES! SENATOR! WE NEED TO TALK ABOUT PORK BARRELS!
The SENATOR
PISSARRO
FRESH FROM THE VIRGIN ISLANDS "WHICH WAY IS THE TRAIN GOING?" IN FRENCH IMPRESSION-O-RAMA
GRIFFY 6-8
©2007 Bill Griffith. World rights reserved. Distributed by King Features Syndicate
ALSO DEBATH-IFICATION! AND LAME DUCKS! AND BUBBLE BOY! AND HOW DO YOU JUSTIFY LIVING IN SUCH A PALATIAL MANSION AT TH' TAXPAYERS' EXPENSE?
ONCE IN A WHILE, IT'S IMPORTANT TO CONFRONT YOUR ELECTED REPRESENTATIVES & TELL THEM WHAT YOU THINK ABOUT KARL ROVE'S ANNOYING SMIRK!
TIPS TO: TOM KIEFABER & CRAIG HANKIN

154

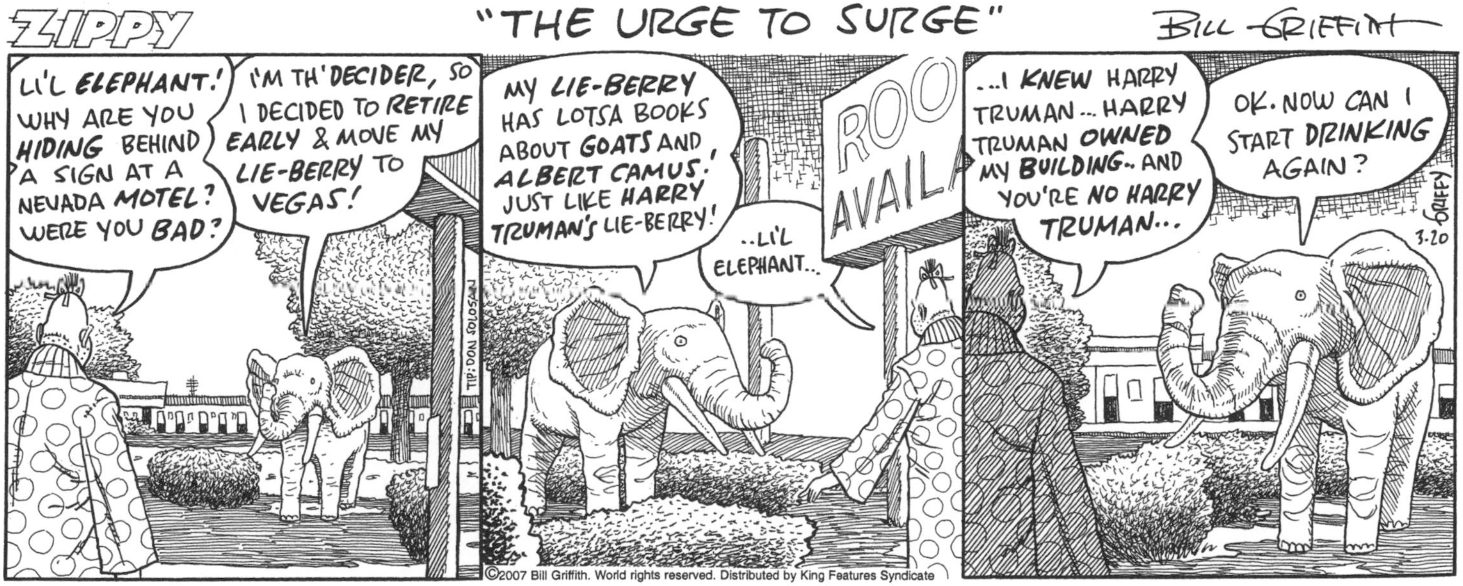
ZIPPY
"THE URGE TO SURGE"
BILL GRIFFITH
LI'L ELEPHANT! WHY ARE YOU HIDING BEHIND A SIGN AT A NEVADA MOTEL? WERE YOU BAD?
I'M TH' DECIDER, SO I DECIDED TO RETIRE EARLY & MOVE MY LIE-BERRY TO VEGAS!
TIP: DON SOLOSAN
MY LIE-BERRY HAS LOTSA BOOKS ABOUT GOATS AND ALBERT CAMUS! JUST LIKE HARRY TRUMAN'S LIE-BERRY!
..LI'L ELEPHANT...
ROO AVAILA
...I KNEW HARRY TRUMAN... HARRY TRUMAN OWNED MY BUILDING.. AND YOU'RE NO HARRY TRUMAN...
OK. NOW CAN I START DRINKING AGAIN?
GRIFFY 3-20
©2007 Bill Griffith. World rights reserved. Distributed by King Features Syndicate

155

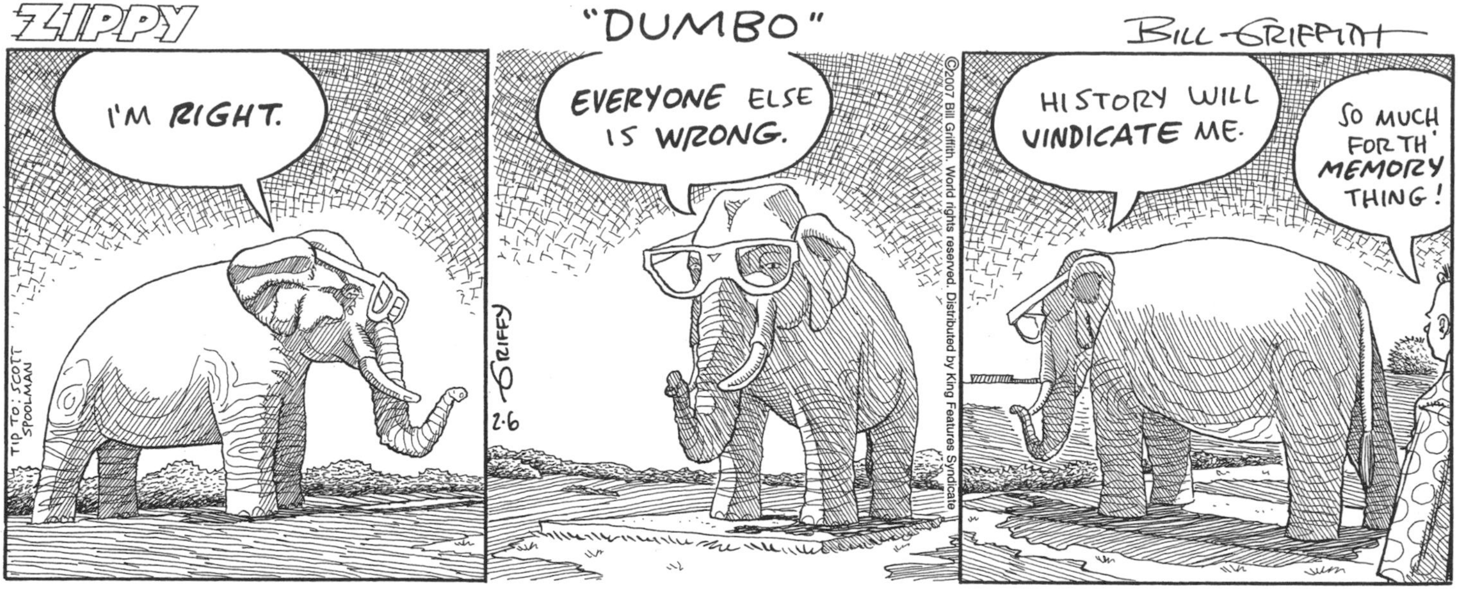
ZIPPY
"DUMBO"
BILL GRIFFITH
I'M RIGHT.
TIP TO: SCOTT SPOOLMAN
EVERYONE ELSE IS WRONG.
GRIFFY 2·6
©2007 Bill Griffith. World rights reserved. Distributed by King Features Syndicate
HISTORY WILL VINDICATE ME.
SO MUCH FOR TH' MEMORY THING!

156

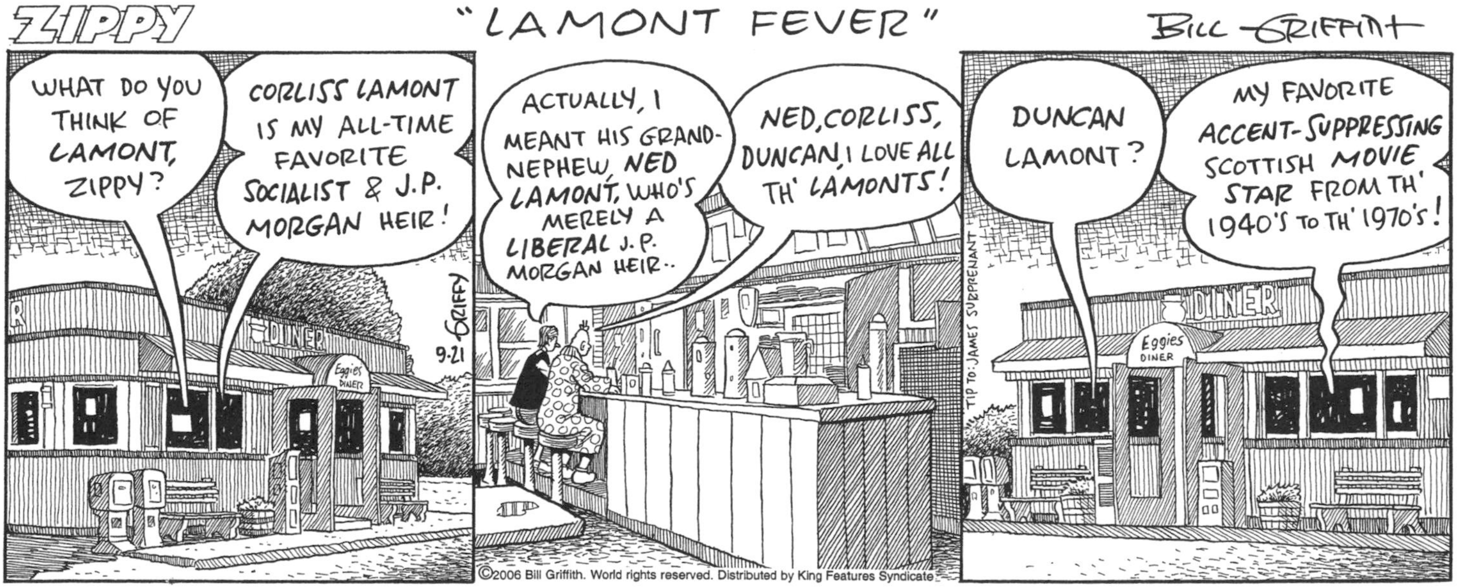
ZIPPY
"LAMONT FEVER"
BILL GRIFFITH
WHAT DO YOU THINK OF LAMONT, ZIPPY?
CORLISS LAMONT IS MY ALL-TIME FAVORITE SOCIALIST & J.P. MORGAN HEIR!
GRIFFY 9·21
DINER
Eggies DINER
ACTUALLY, I MEANT HIS GRAND-NEPHEW, NED LAMONT, WHO'S MERELY A LIBERAL J.P. MORGAN HEIR..
NED, CORLISS, DUNCAN, I LOVE ALL TH' LAMONTS!
©2006 Bill Griffith. World rights reserved. Distributed by King Features Syndicate
DUNCAN LAMONT?
MY FAVORITE ACCENT-SUPPRESSING SCOTTISH MOVIE STAR FROM TH' 1940'S TO TH' 1970'S!
TIP TO: JAMES SURPRENANT
DINER
Eggies DINER

157

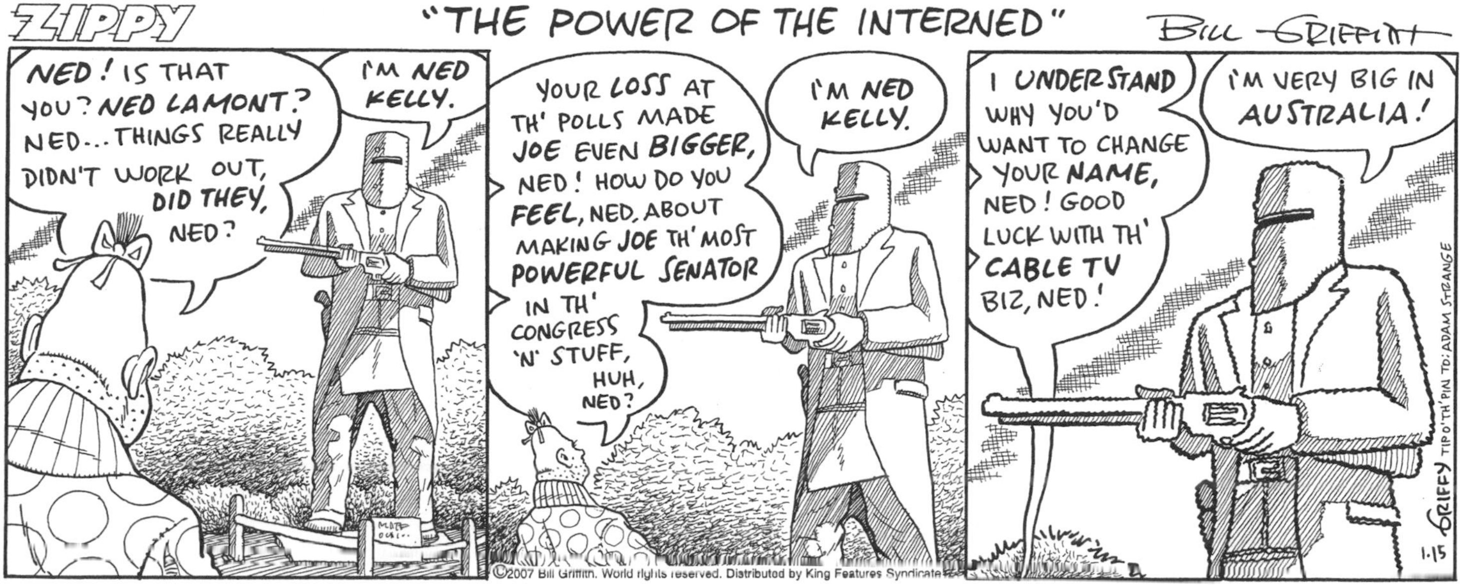
ZIPPY
"THE POWER OF THE INTERNED"
BILL GRIFFITH
NED! IS THAT YOU? NED LAMONT? NED... THINGS REALLY DIDN'T WORK OUT, DID THEY, NED?
I'M NED KELLY.
YOUR LOSS AT TH' POLLS MADE JOE EVEN BIGGER, NED! HOW DO YOU FEEL, NED, ABOUT MAKING JOE TH' MOST POWERFUL SENATOR IN TH' CONGRESS 'N' STUFF, HUH, NED?
I'M NED KELLY.
I UNDERSTAND WHY YOU'D WANT TO CHANGE YOUR NAME, NED! GOOD LUCK WITH TH' CABLE TV BIZ, NED!
I'M VERY BIG IN AUSTRALIA!
TIP O'TH' PIN TO: ADAM STRANGE
GRIFFY 1-15
©2007 Bill Griffith. World rights reserved. Distributed by King Features Syndicate

158

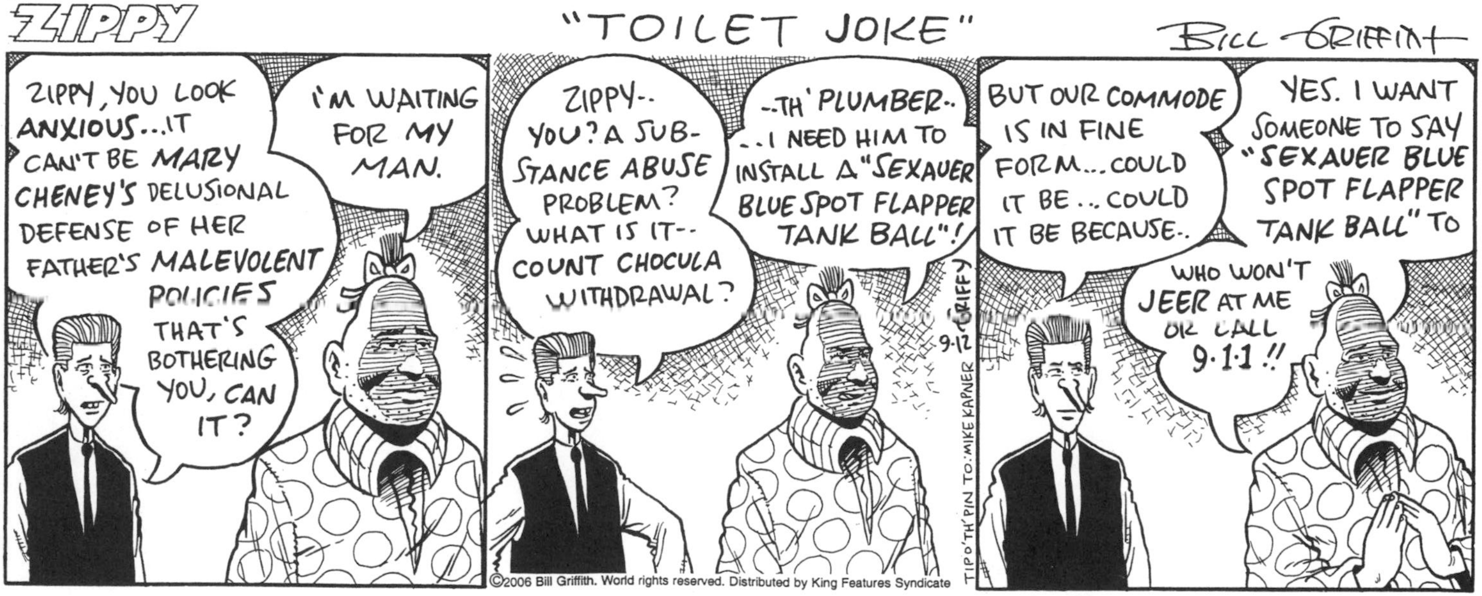
ZIPPY
"TOILET JOKE"
BILL GRIFFITH
ZIPPY, YOU LOOK ANXIOUS...IT CAN'T BE MARY CHENEY'S DELUSIONAL DEFENSE OF HER FATHER'S MALEVOLENT POLICIES THAT'S BOTHERING YOU, CAN IT?
I'M WAITING FOR MY MAN.
ZIPPY-- YOU? A SUB-STANCE ABUSE PROBLEM? WHAT IS IT-- COUNT CHOCULA WITHDRAWAL?
--TH' PLUMBER-- --I NEED HIM TO INSTALL A "SEXAUER BLUE SPOT FLAPPER TANK BALL"!
BUT OUR COMMODE IS IN FINE FORM... COULD IT BE... COULD IT BE BECAUSE--
YES. I WANT SOMEONE TO SAY "SEXAUER BLUE SPOT FLAPPER TANK BALL" TO
WHO WON'T JEER AT ME OR CALL 9-1-1!!
TIP O'TH' PIN TO: MIKE KAPNER
GRIFFY 9-12
©2006 Bill Griffith. World rights reserved. Distributed by King Features Syndicate

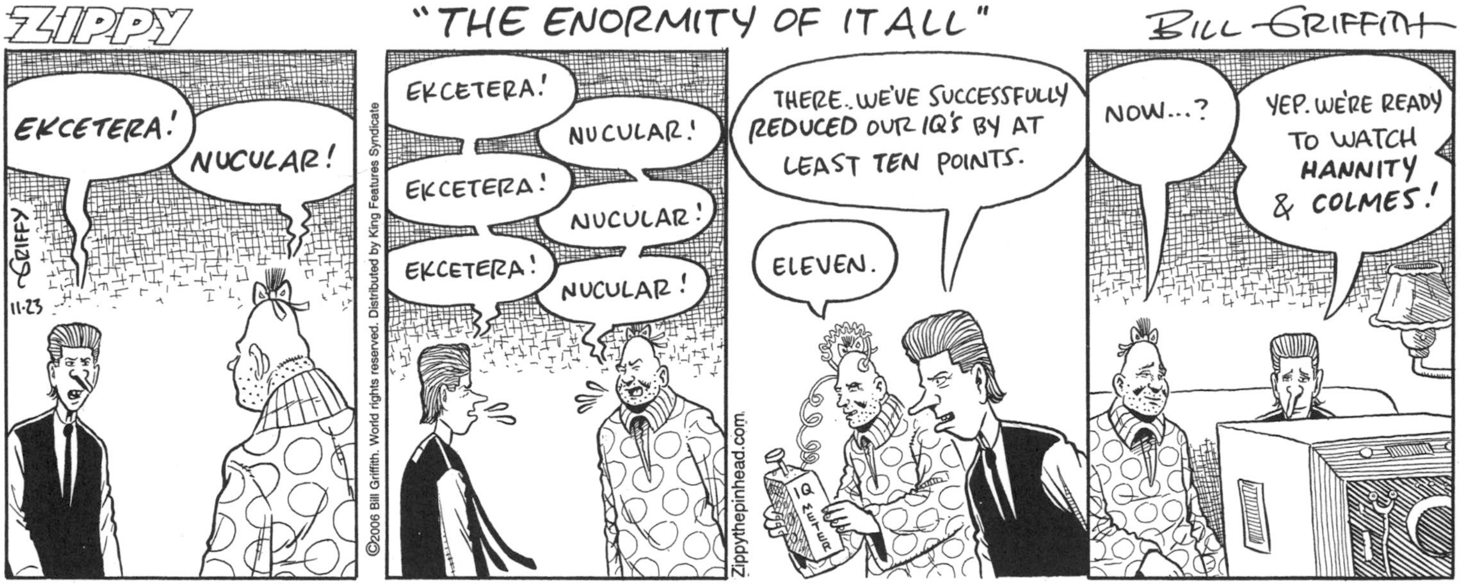
ZIPPY
"THE ENORMITY OF IT ALL"
BILL GRIFFITH
EKCETERA!
NUCULAR!
GRIFFY 11-23
EKCETERA!
NUCULAR!
EKCETERA!
NUCULAR!
EKCETERA!
NUCULAR!
©2006 Bill Griffith. World rights reserved. Distributed by King Features Syndicate
THERE.. WE'VE SUCCESSFULLY REDUCED OUR IQ'S BY AT LEAST TEN POINTS.
ELEVEN.
IQ METER
Zippythepinhead.com
NOW...?
YEP. WE'RE READY TO WATCH HANNITY & COLMES!

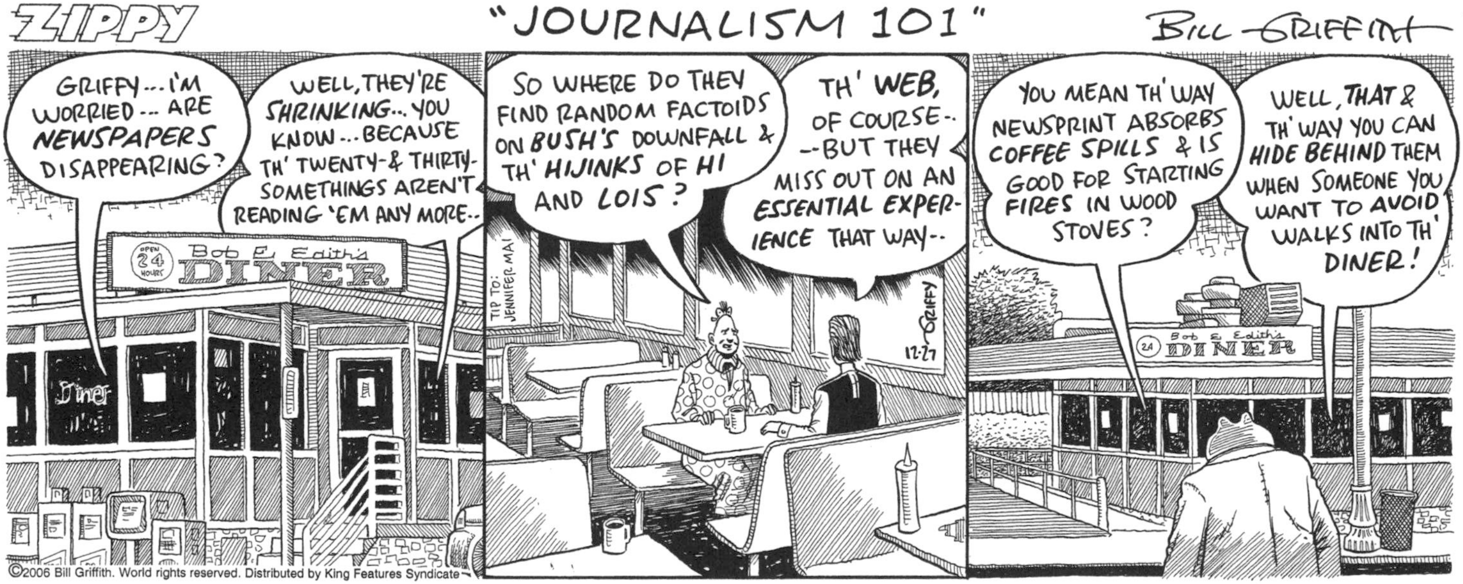
ZIPPY
"JOURNALISM 101"
BILL GRIFFITH
GRIFFY... I'M WORRIED... ARE NEWSPAPERS DISAPPEARING?
WELL, THEY'RE SHRINKING... YOU KNOW... BECAUSE TH' TWENTY-& THIRTY-SOMETHINGS AREN'T READING 'EM ANY MORE..
OPEN 24 HOURS Bob & Edith's DINER
Diner
©2006 Bill Griffith. World rights reserved. Distributed by King Features Syndicate
SO WHERE DO THEY FIND RANDOM FACTOIDS ON BUSH'S DOWNFALL & TH' HIJINKS OF HI AND LOIS?
TH' WEB, OF COURSE.. --BUT THEY MISS OUT ON AN ESSENTIAL EXPERIENCE THAT WAY--
TIP TO: JENNIFER MA!
GRIFFY 12-27
YOU MEAN TH' WAY NEWSPRINT ABSORBS COFFEE SPILLS & IS GOOD FOR STARTING FIRES IN WOOD STOVES?
WELL, THAT & TH' WAY YOU CAN HIDE BEHIND THEM WHEN SOMEONE YOU WANT TO AVOID WALKS INTO TH' DINER!
24 Bob & Edith's DINER

159

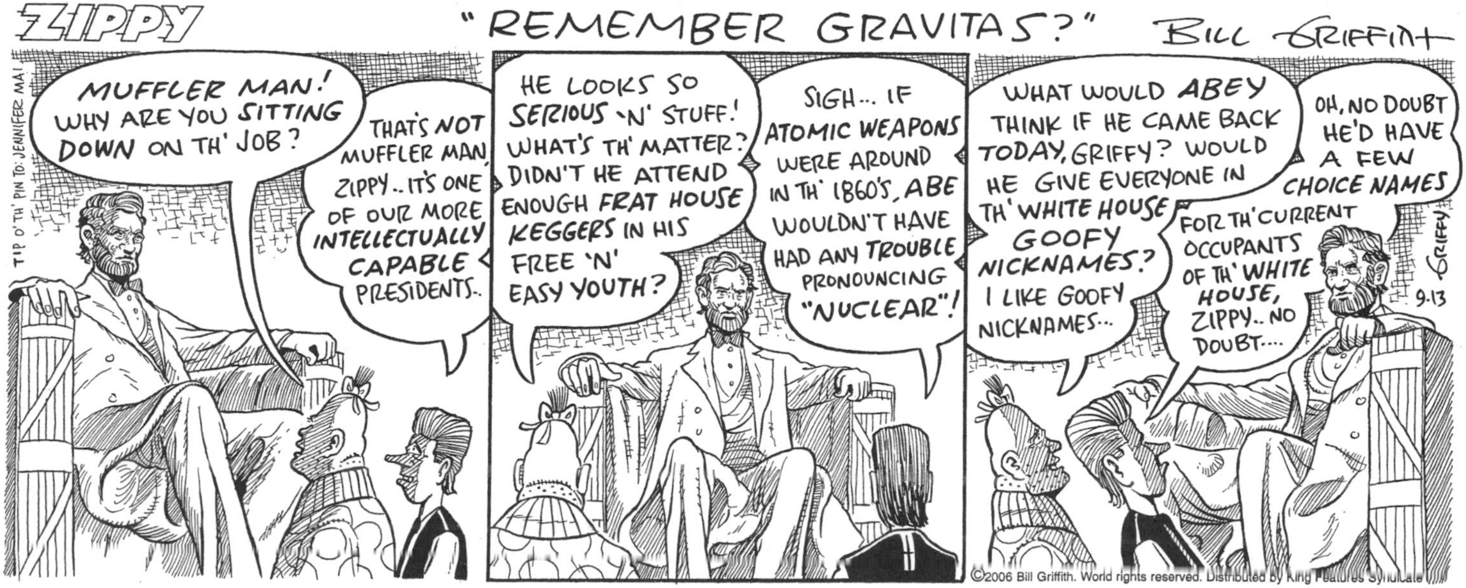
ZIPPY
"REMEMBER GRAVITAS?"
BILL GRIFFITH
TIP O' TH' PIN TO: JENNIFER MA!
MUFFLER MAN! WHY ARE YOU SITTING DOWN ON TH' JOB?
THAT'S NOT MUFFLER MAN, ZIPPY.. IT'S ONE OF OUR MORE INTELLECTUALLY CAPABLE PRESIDENTS..
HE LOOKS SO SERIOUS 'N' STUFF! WHAT'S TH' MATTER? DIDN'T HE ATTEND ENOUGH FRAT HOUSE KEGGERS IN HIS FREE 'N' EASY YOUTH?
SIGH... IF ATOMIC WEAPONS WERE AROUND IN TH' 1860'S, ABE WOULDN'T HAVE HAD ANY TROUBLE PRONOUNCING "NUCLEAR"!
WHAT WOULD ABEY THINK IF HE CAME BACK TODAY, GRIFFY? WOULD HE GIVE EVERYONE IN TH' WHITE HOUSE GOOFY NICKNAMES? I LIKE GOOFY NICKNAMES...
OH, NO DOUBT HE'D HAVE A FEW CHOICE NAMES FOR TH' CURRENT OCCUPANTS OF TH' WHITE HOUSE, ZIPPY.. NO DOUBT....
GRIFFY
9·13
©2006 Bill Griffith. World rights reserved. Distributed by King Features Syndicate

160

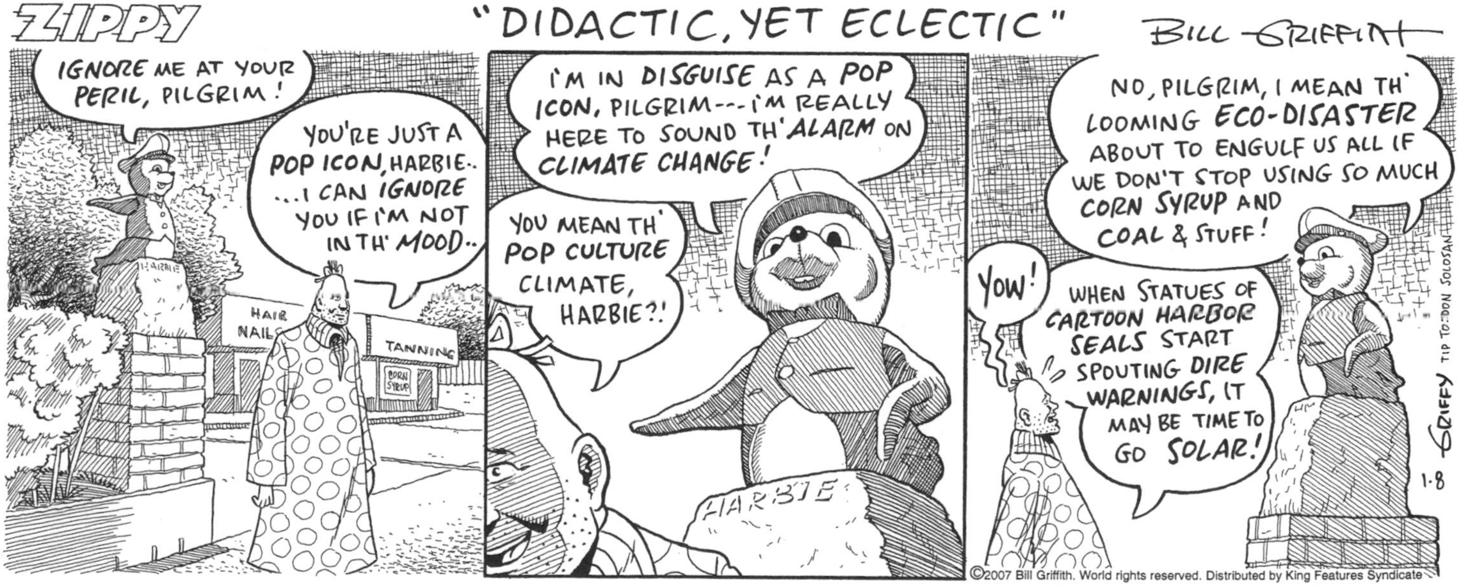
ZIPPY
"DIDACTIC, YET ECLECTIC"
BILL GRIFFITH
IGNORE ME AT YOUR PERIL, PILGRIM!
HARBIE
YOU'RE JUST A POP ICON, HARBIE.. ...I CAN IGNORE YOU IF I'M NOT IN TH' MOOD..
HAIR NAILS
TANNING
CORN SYRUP
I'M IN DISGUISE AS A POP ICON, PILGRIM--- I'M REALLY HERE TO SOUND TH' ALARM ON CLIMATE CHANGE!
YOU MEAN TH' POP CULTURE CLIMATE, HARBIE?!
HARBIE
NO, PILGRIM, I MEAN TH' LOOMING ECO-DISASTER ABOUT TO ENGULF US ALL IF WE DON'T STOP USING SO MUCH CORN SYRUP AND COAL & STUFF!
YOW!
WHEN STATUES OF CARTOON HARBOR SEALS START SPOUTING DIRE WARNINGS, IT MAY BE TIME TO GO SOLAR!
GRIFFY
TIP TO: DON SOLOSAN
1·8
©2007 Bill Griffith. World rights reserved. Distributed by King Features Syndicate

161

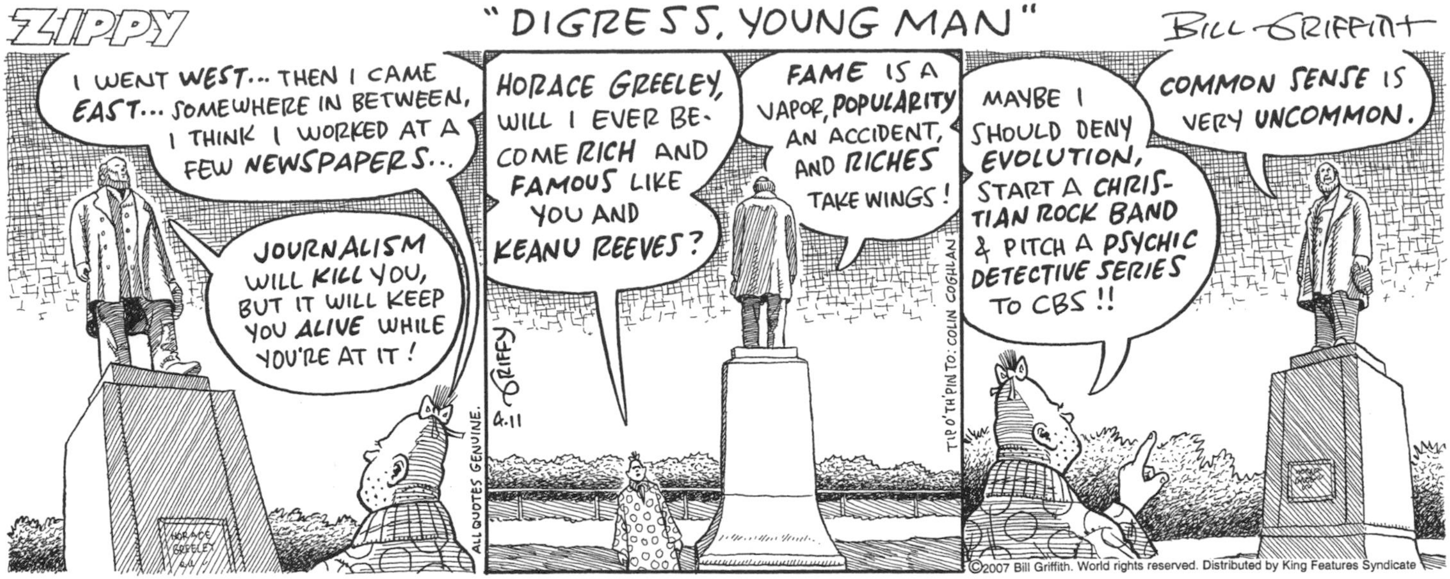
ZIPPY
"DIGRESS, YOUNG MAN"
BILL GRIFFITH
I WENT WEST... THEN I CAME EAST... SOMEWHERE IN BETWEEN, I THINK I WORKED AT A FEW NEWSPAPERS...
JOURNALISM WILL KILL YOU, BUT IT WILL KEEP YOU ALIVE WHILE YOU'RE AT IT!
HORACE GREELEY
ALL QUOTES GENUINE.
GRIFFY 4.11
HORACE GREELEY, WILL I EVER BECOME RICH AND FAMOUS LIKE YOU AND KEANU REEVES?
FAME IS A VAPOR, POPULARITY AN ACCIDENT, AND RICHES TAKE WINGS!
TIP O'TH' PIN TO: COLIN COGHLAN
MAYBE I SHOULD DENY EVOLUTION, START A CHRISTIAN ROCK BAND & PITCH A PSYCHIC DETECTIVE SERIES TO CBS!!
COMMON SENSE IS VERY UNCOMMON.
©2007 Bill Griffith. World rights reserved. Distributed by King Features Syndicate

162

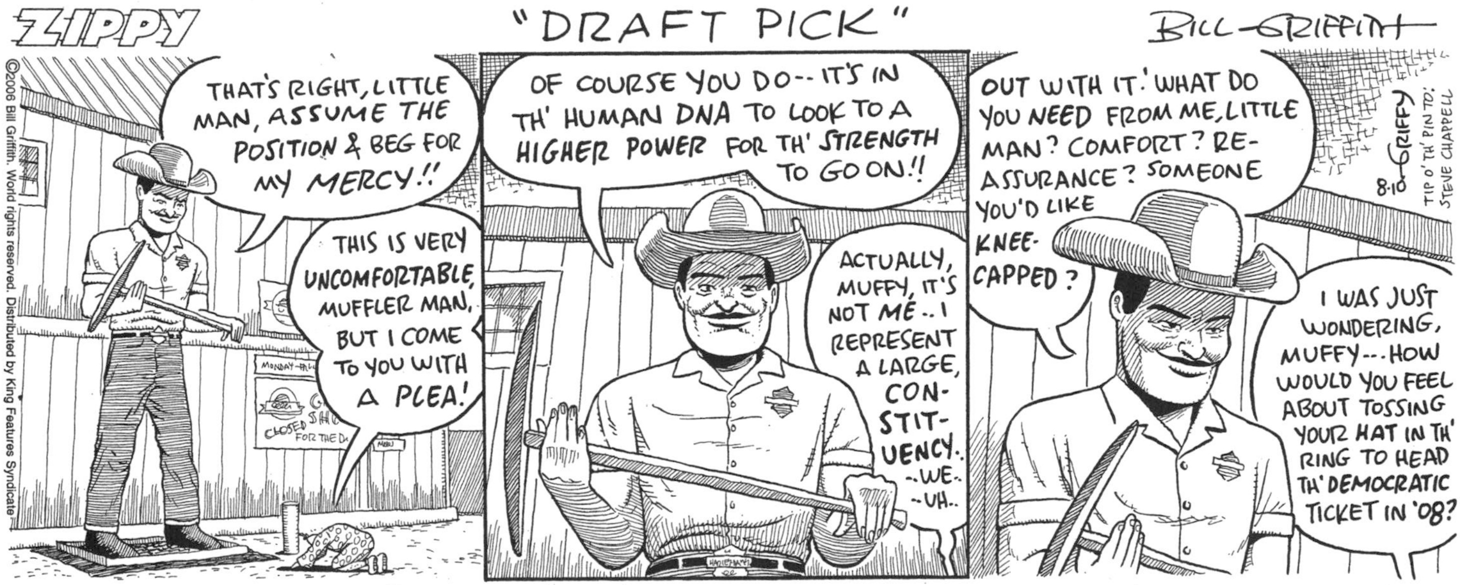
ZIPPY
"DRAFT PICK"
BILL GRIFFITH
©2006 Bill Griffith. World rights reserved. Distributed by King Features Syndicate
THAT'S RIGHT, LITTLE MAN, ASSUME THE POSITION & BEG FOR MY MERCY!!
THIS IS VERY UNCOMFORTABLE, MUFFLER MAN, BUT I COME TO YOU WITH A PLEA!
CLOSED
OF COURSE YOU DO-- IT'S IN TH' HUMAN DNA TO LOOK TO A HIGHER POWER FOR TH' STRENGTH TO GO ON!!
ACTUALLY, MUFFY, IT'S NOT ME.. I REPRESENT A LARGE, CONSTITUENCY.. --WE.. --UH..
OUT WITH IT! WHAT DO YOU NEED FROM ME, LITTLE MAN? COMFORT? REASSURANCE? SOMEONE YOU'D LIKE KNEECAPPED?
GRIFFY 8.10
TIP O' TH' PIN TO: STEVE CHAPPELL
I WAS JUST WONDERING, MUFFY--- HOW WOULD YOU FEEL ABOUT TOSSING YOUR HAT IN TH' RING TO HEAD TH' DEMOCRATIC TICKET IN '08?

163

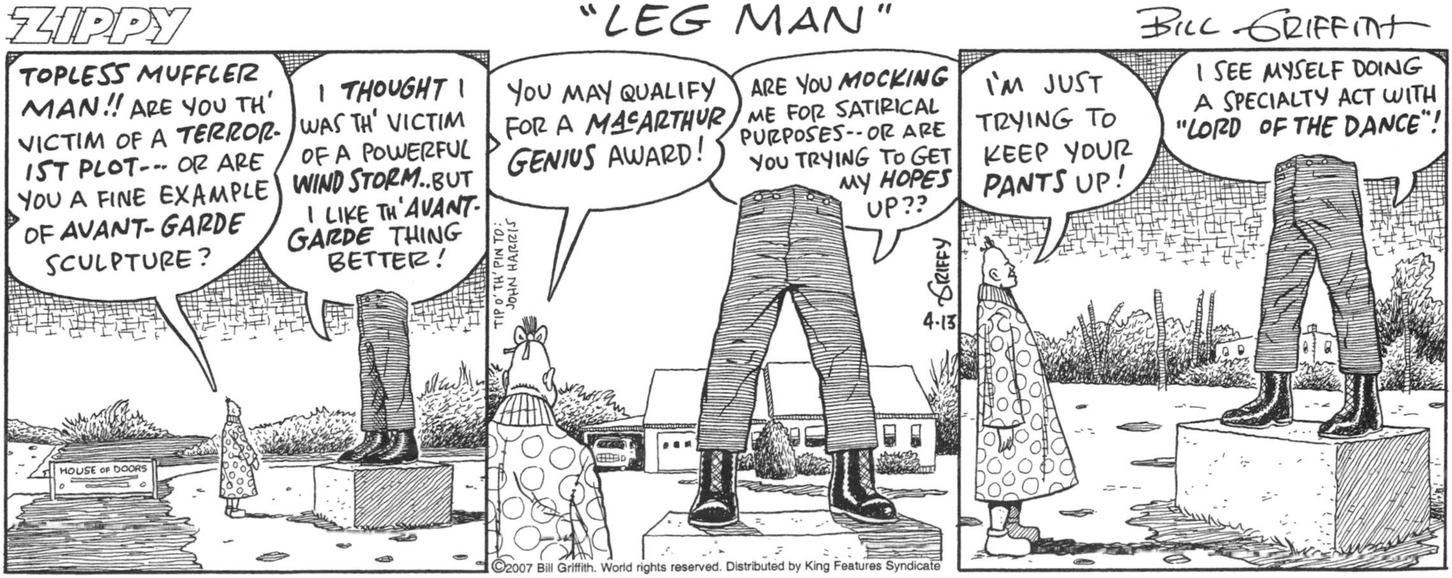
ZIPPY
"LEG MAN"
BILL GRIFFITH
TOPLESS MUFFLER MAN!! ARE YOU TH' VICTIM OF A TERRORIST PLOT-- OR ARE YOU A FINE EXAMPLE OF AVANT-GARDE SCULPTURE?
I THOUGHT I WAS TH' VICTIM OF A POWERFUL WIND STORM..BUT I LIKE TH' AVANT-GARDE THING BETTER!
HOUSE OF DOORS
YOU MAY QUALIFY FOR A MACARTHUR GENIUS AWARD!
ARE YOU MOCKING ME FOR SATIRICAL PURPOSES-- OR ARE YOU TRYING TO GET MY HOPES UP??
TIP O' TH' PIN TO: JOHN HARRIS
GRIFFY
4·13
I'M JUST TRYING TO KEEP YOUR PANTS UP!
I SEE MYSELF DOING A SPECIALTY ACT WITH "LORD OF THE DANCE"!

164

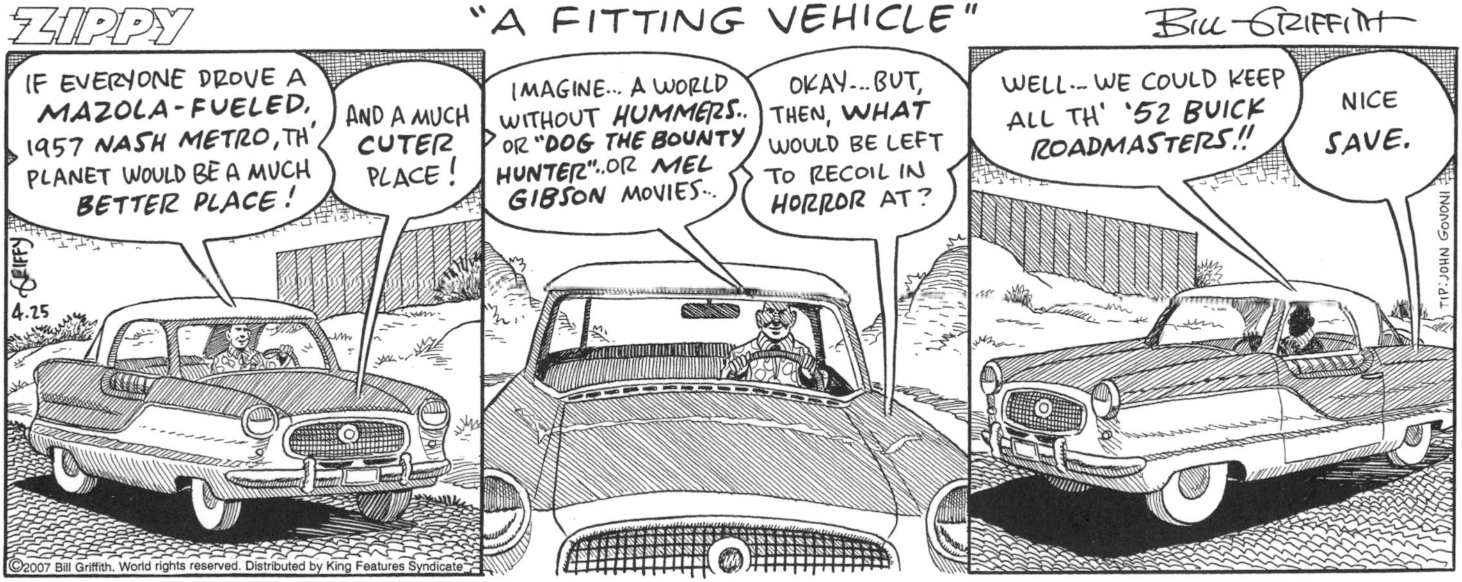
ZIPPY
"A FITTING VEHICLE"
BILL GRIFFITH
IF EVERYONE DROVE A MAZOLA-FUELED, 1957 NASH METRO, TH' PLANET WOULD BE A MUCH BETTER PLACE!
AND A MUCH CUTER PLACE!
GRIFFY
4.25
IMAGINE... A WORLD WITHOUT HUMMERS.. OR "DOG THE BOUNTY HUNTER"..OR MEL GIBSON MOVIES..
OKAY...BUT, THEN, WHAT WOULD BE LEFT TO RECOIL IN HORROR AT?
WELL... WE COULD KEEP ALL TH' '52 BUICK ROADMASTERS!!
NICE SAVE.
TIP: JOHN GOVONI

165

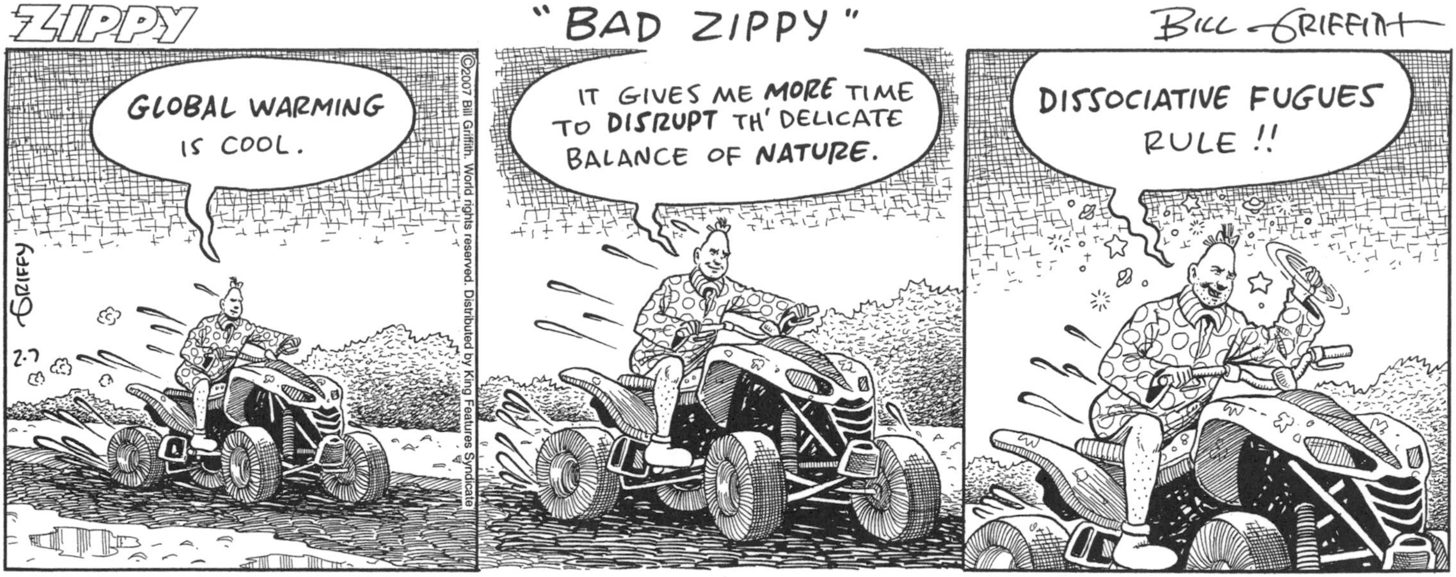
ZIPPY
"BAD ZIPPY"
BILL GRIFFITH
GLOBAL WARMING IS COOL.
IT GIVES ME MORE TIME TO DISRUPT TH' DELICATE BALANCE OF NATURE.
DISSOCIATIVE FUGUES RULE !!
GRIFFY
2-7
©2007 Bill Griffith. World rights reserved. Distributed by King Features Syndicate

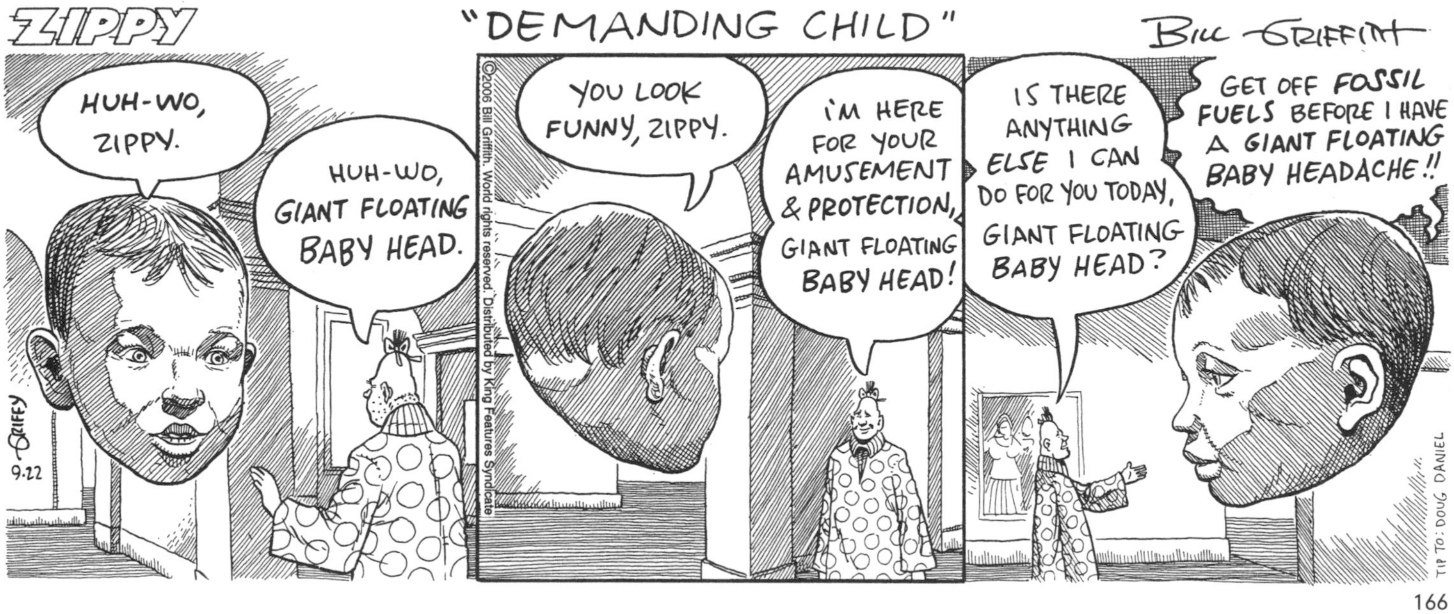
ZIPPY
"DEMANDING CHILD"
BILL GRIFFITH
HUH-WO, ZIPPY.
HUH-WO, GIANT FLOATING BABY HEAD.
YOU LOOK FUNNY, ZIPPY.
I'M HERE FOR YOUR AMUSEMENT & PROTECTION, GIANT FLOATING BABY HEAD!
IS THERE ANYTHING ELSE I CAN DO FOR YOU TODAY, GIANT FLOATING BABY HEAD?
GET OFF FOSSIL FUELS BEFORE I HAVE A GIANT FLOATING BABY HEADACHE!!
GRIFFY
9-22
©2006 Bill Griffith. World rights reserved. Distributed by King Features Syndicate
TIP TO: DOUG DANIEL
166

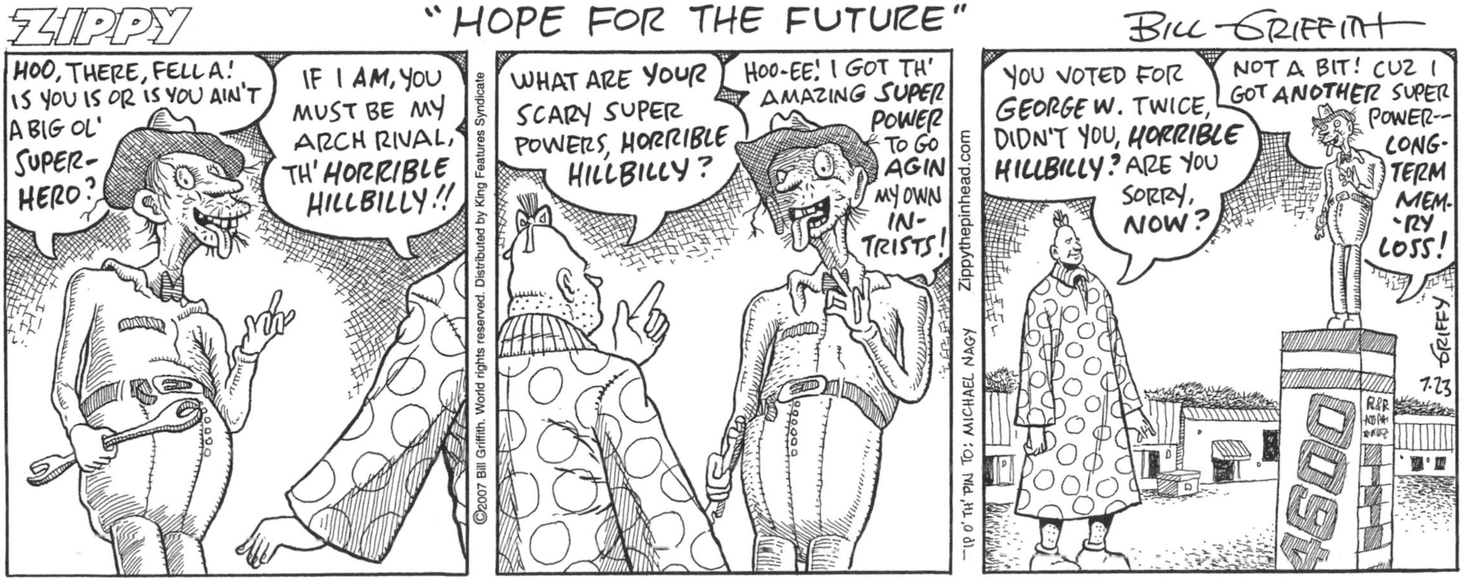
ZIPPY
"HOPE FOR THE FUTURE"
BILL GRIFFITH
HOO, THERE, FELLA! IS YOU IS OR IS YOU AIN'T A BIG OL' SUPER-HERO?
IF I AM, YOU MUST BE MY ARCH RIVAL, TH' HORRIBLE HILLBILLY!!
©2007 Bill Griffith. World rights reserved. Distributed by King Features Syndicate
WHAT ARE YOUR SCARY SUPER POWERS, HORRIBLE HILLBILLY?
HOO-EE! I GOT TH' AMAZING SUPER POWER TO GO AGIN MY OWN IN-TRISTS!
Zippythepinhead.com
TIP O' TH' PIN TO: MICHAEL NAGY
YOU VOTED FOR GEORGE W. TWICE, DIDN'T YOU, HORRIBLE HILLBILLY? ARE YOU SORRY, NOW?
NOT A BIT! CUZ I GOT ANOTHER SUPER POWER-- LONG-TERM MEM-'RY LOSS!
GRIFFY
7·23
4600

167

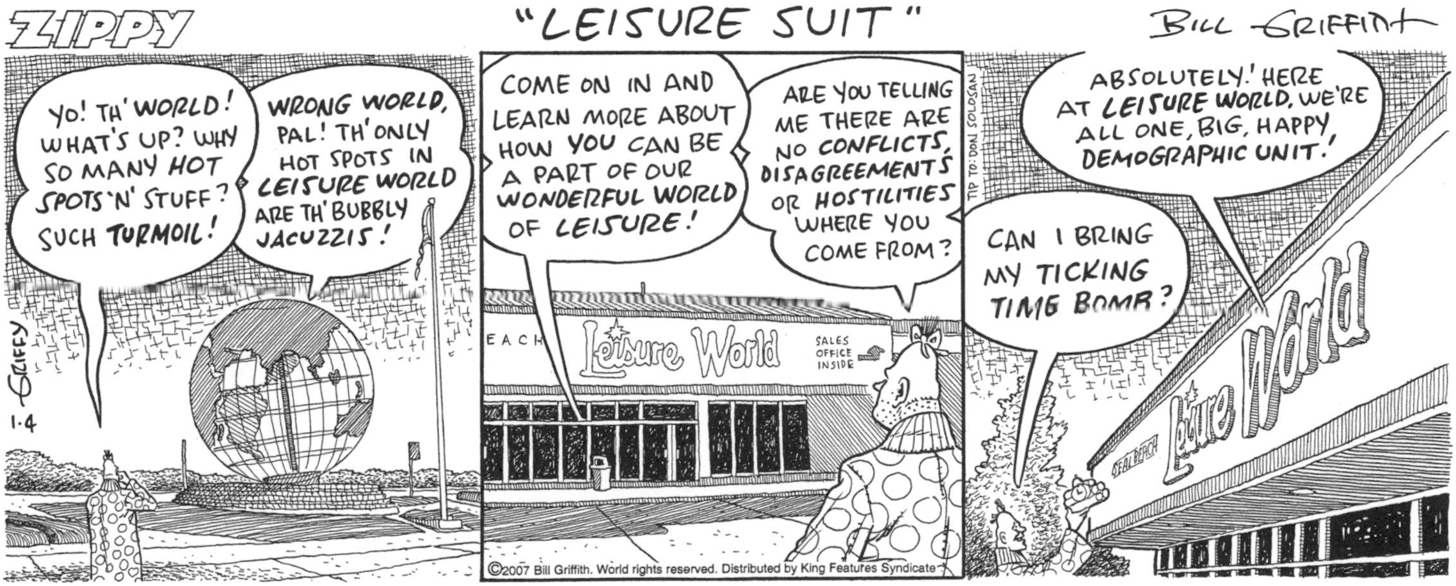
ZIPPY
"LEISURE SUIT"
BILL GRIFFITH
YO! TH' WORLD! WHAT'S UP? WHY SO MANY HOT SPOTS 'N' STUFF? SUCH TURMOIL!
WRONG WORLD, PAL! TH' ONLY HOT SPOTS IN LEISURE WORLD ARE TH' BUBBLY JACUZZIS!
GRIFFY
1·4
COME ON IN AND LEARN MORE ABOUT HOW YOU CAN BE A PART OF OUR WONDERFUL WORLD OF LEISURE!
ARE YOU TELLING ME THERE ARE NO CONFLICTS, DISAGREEMENTS OR HOSTILITIES WHERE YOU COME FROM?
EACH
Leisure World
SALES OFFICE INSIDE
©2007 Bill Griffith. World rights reserved. Distributed by King Features Syndicate
TIP TO: DON SOLDSAN
ABSOLUTELY! HERE AT LEISURE WORLD, WE'RE ALL ONE, BIG, HAPPY, DEMOGRAPHIC UNIT!
CAN I BRING MY TICKING TIME BOMB?
SEAL BEACH
Leisure World

168

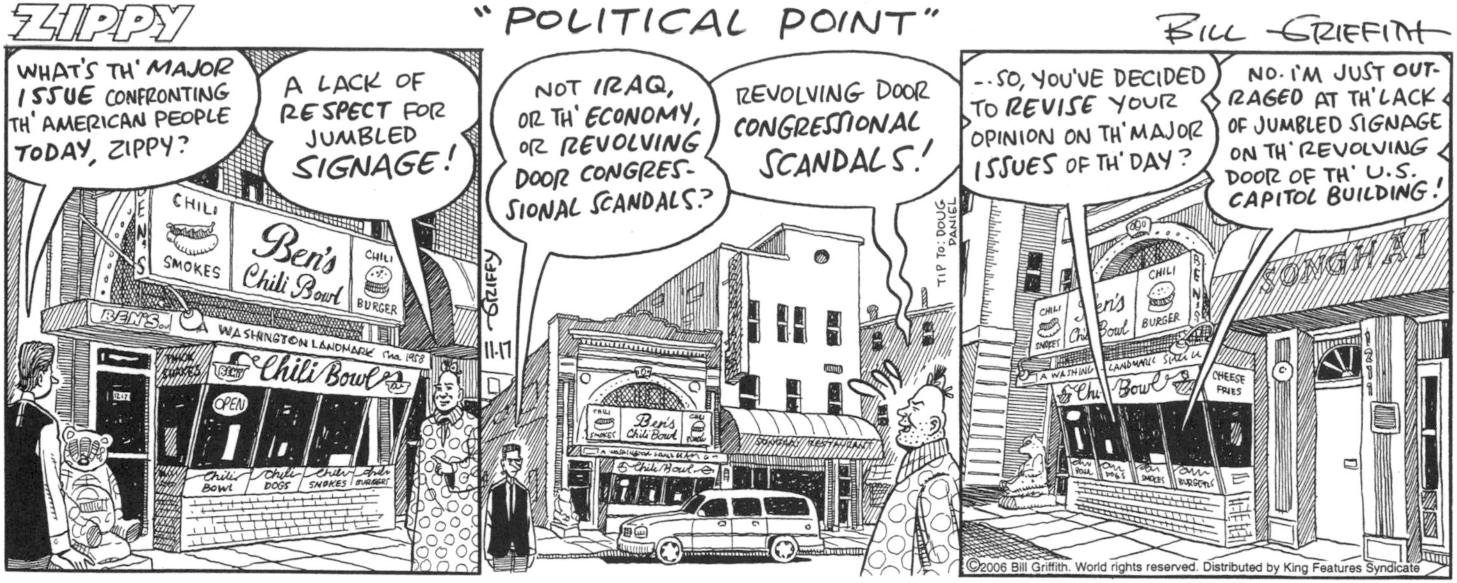
ZIPPY
"POLITICAL POINT"
BILL GRIFFITH
WHAT'S TH' MAJOR ISSUE CONFRONTING TH' AMERICAN PEOPLE TODAY, ZIPPY?
A LACK OF RESPECT FOR JUMBLED SIGNAGE!
CHILI SMOKES
Ben's Chili Bowl
CHILI BURGER
A WASHINGTON LANDMARK
Chili Bowl
OPEN
NOT IRAQ, OR TH' ECONOMY, OR REVOLVING DOOR CONGRESSIONAL SCANDALS?
REVOLVING DOOR CONGRESSIONAL SCANDALS!
TIP TO: DOUG DANIEL
GRIFFY 11-17
..SO, YOU'VE DECIDED TO REVISE YOUR OPINION ON TH' MAJOR ISSUES OF TH' DAY?
NO. I'M JUST OUTRAGED AT TH' LACK OF JUMBLED SIGNAGE ON TH' REVOLVING DOOR OF TH' U.S. CAPITOL BUILDING!
SONGHAI
CHEESE FRIES
©2006 Bill Griffith. World rights reserved. Distributed by King Features Syndicate

169

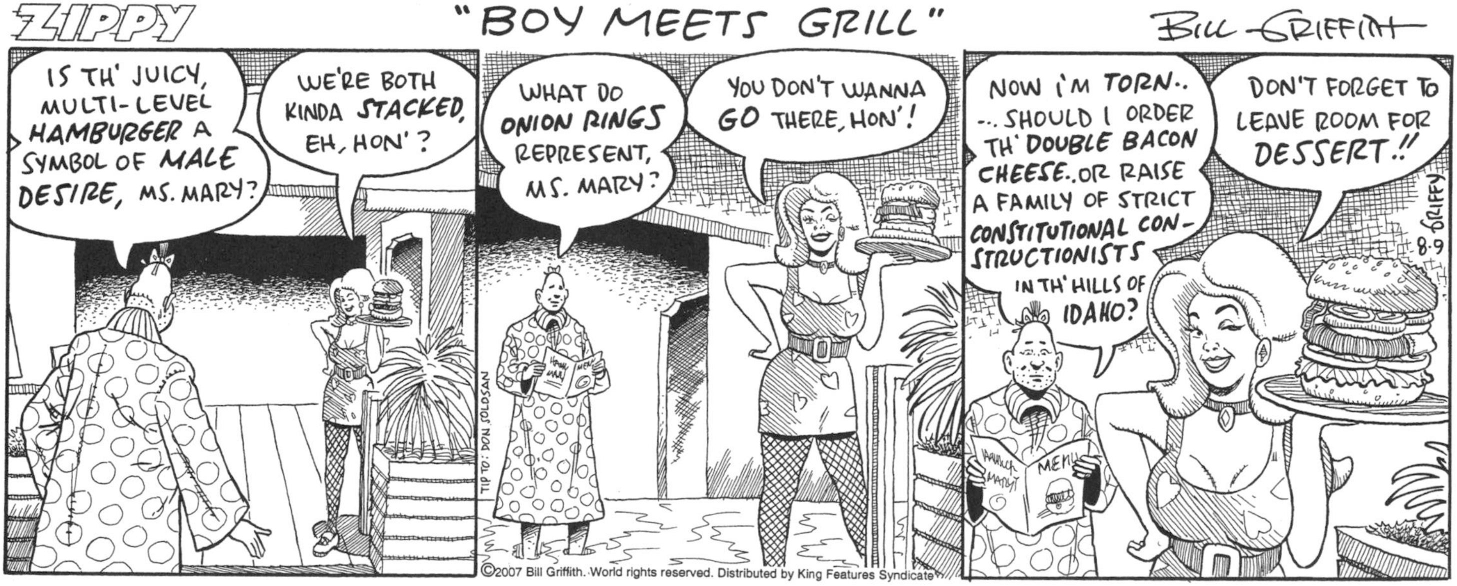
ZIPPY
"BOY MEETS GRILL"
BILL GRIFFITH
IS TH' JUICY, MULTI-LEVEL HAMBURGER A SYMBOL OF MALE DESIRE, MS. MARY?
WE'RE BOTH KINDA STACKED, EH, HON'?
WHAT DO ONION RINGS REPRESENT, MS. MARY?
YOU DON'T WANNA GO THERE, HON'!
TIP TO: DON SOLDSAN
NOW I'M TORN.. ..SHOULD I ORDER TH' DOUBLE BACON CHEESE..OR RAISE A FAMILY OF STRICT CONSTITUTIONAL CONSTRUCTIONISTS IN TH' HILLS OF IDAHO?
DON'T FORGET TO LEAVE ROOM FOR DESSERT!!
GRIFFY 8-9
MENU
©2007 Bill Griffith. World rights reserved. Distributed by King Features Syndicate

170

AMERICA THE BEAUTIFUL

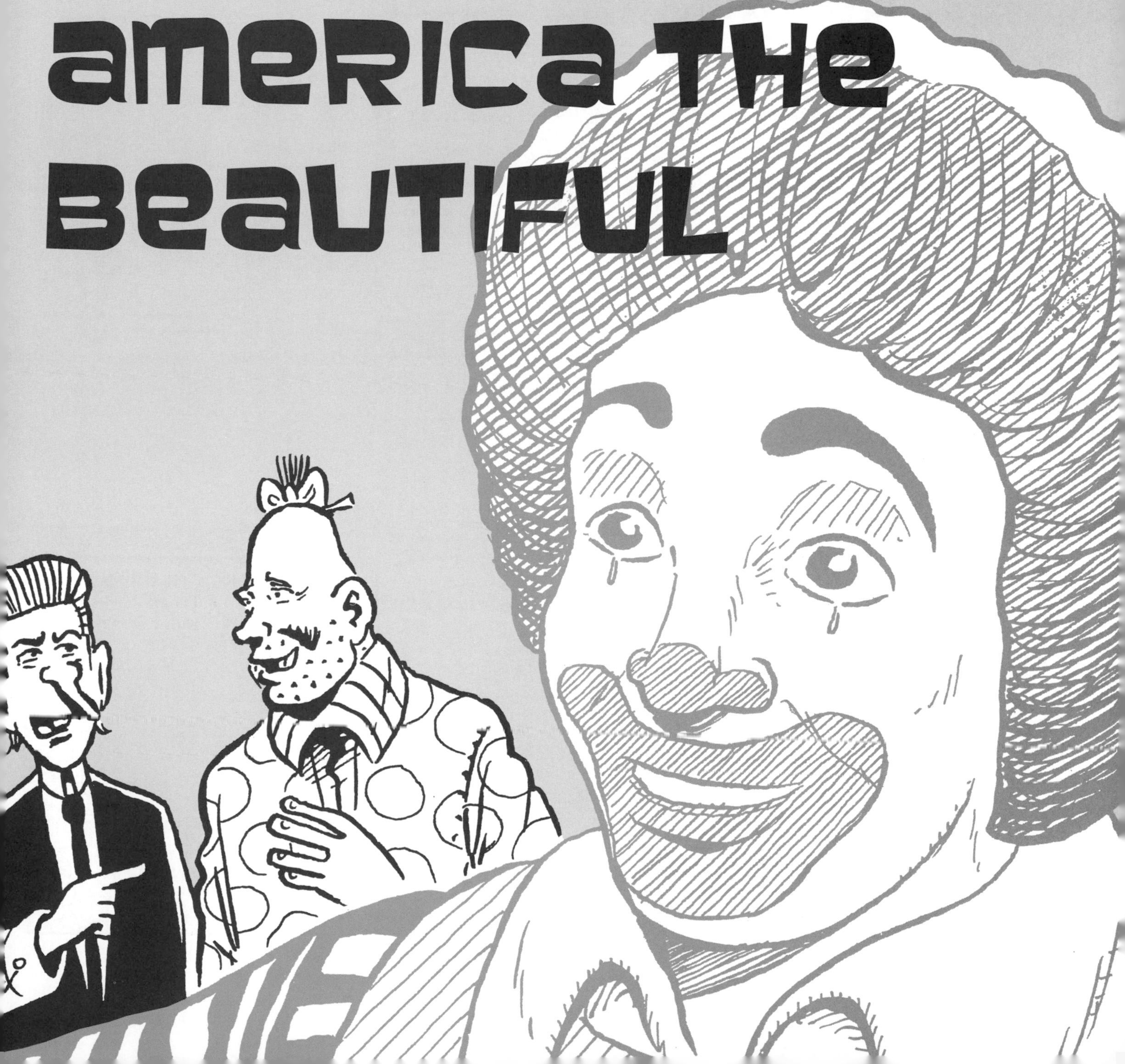

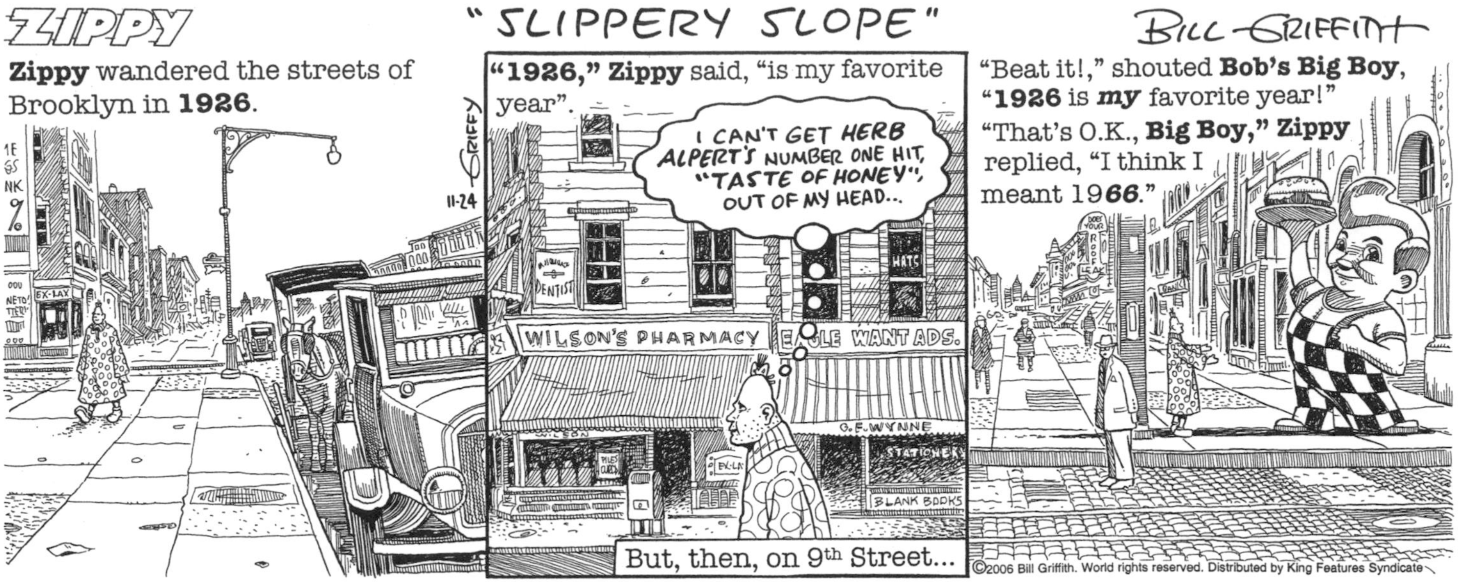
ZIPPY
"SLIPPERY SLOPE"
BILL GRIFFITH
Zippy wandered the streets of Brooklyn in **1926**.
GRIFFY 11-24
EX-LAX
"**1926,**" **Zippy** said, "is my favorite year".
I CAN'T GET *HERB ALPERT'S* NUMBER ONE HIT, *"TASTE OF HONEY"*, OUT OF MY HEAD...
DENTIST
HATS
WILSON'S PHARMACY
WANT ADS.
G.E. WYNNE
STATIONERY
BLANK BOOKS
But, then, on 9th Street...
"Beat it!," shouted **Bob's Big Boy**, "**1926** is ***my*** favorite year!"
"That's O.K., **Big Boy,**" **Zippy** replied, "I think I meant 19**66**."
©2006 Bill Griffith. World rights reserved. Distributed by King Features Syndicate

171

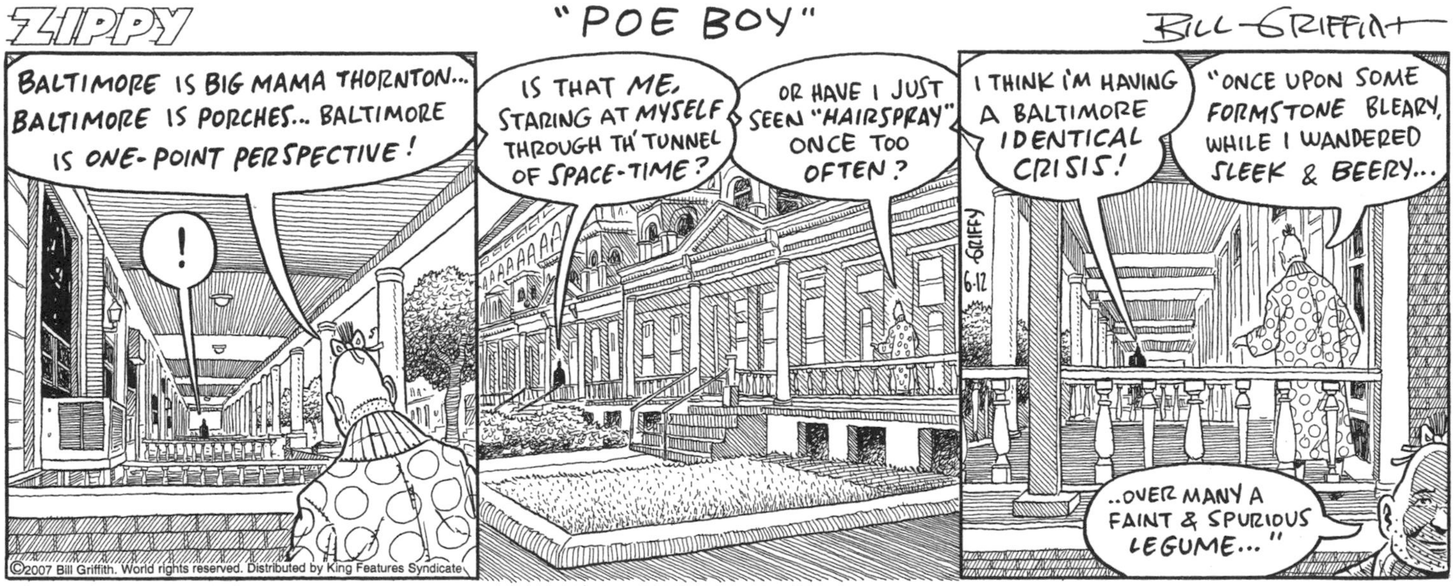
ZIPPY
"POE BOY"
BILL GRIFFITH
BALTIMORE IS BIG MAMA THORNTON... BALTIMORE IS PORCHES... BALTIMORE IS *ONE-POINT PERSPECTIVE!*
!
IS THAT *ME,* STARING AT *MYSELF* THROUGH TH' TUNNEL OF *SPACE-TIME?*
OR HAVE I JUST SEEN *"HAIRSPRAY"* ONCE TOO OFTEN?
GRIFFY 6-12
I THINK I'M HAVING A BALTIMORE *IDENTICAL CRISIS!*
"ONCE UPON SOME FORMSTONE BLEARY, WHILE I WANDERED SLEEK & BEERY...
..OVER MANY A FAINT & SPURIOUS LEGUME..."
©2007 Bill Griffith. World rights reserved. Distributed by King Features Syndicate

172

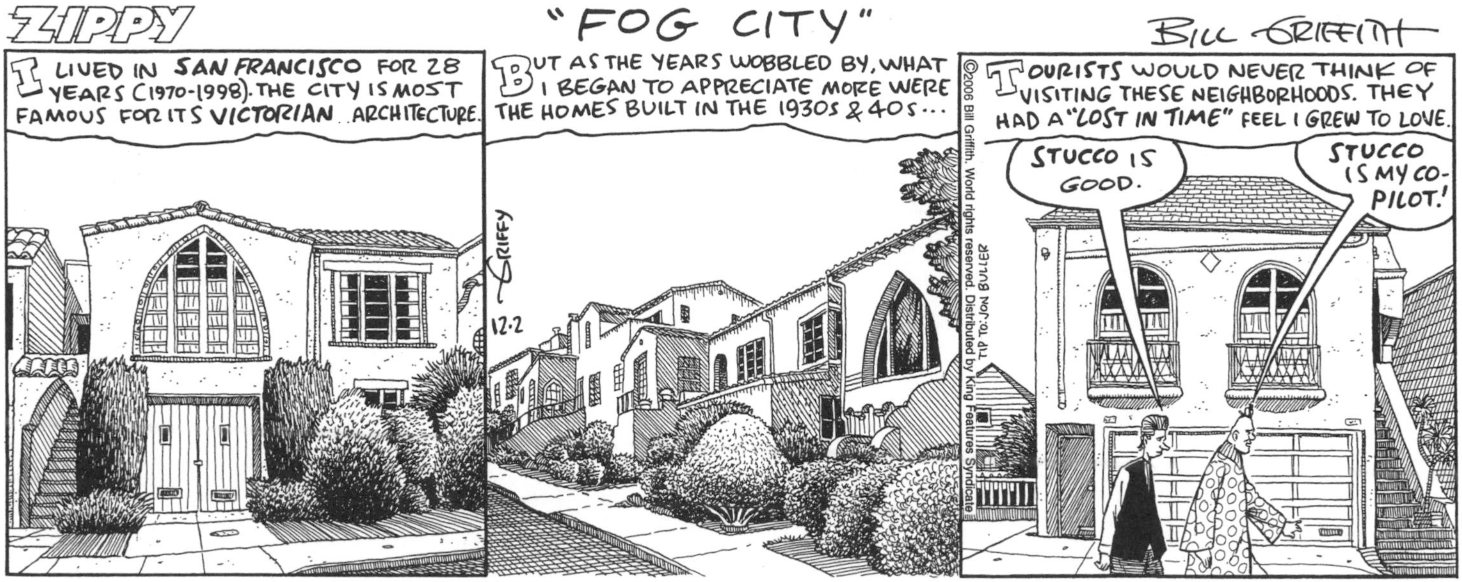
ZIPPY
"FOG CITY"
BILL GRIFFITH
I LIVED IN SAN FRANCISCO FOR 28 YEARS (1970-1998). THE CITY IS MOST FAMOUS FOR ITS VICTORIAN ..ARCHITECTURE.
BUT AS THE YEARS WOBBLED BY, WHAT I BEGAN TO APPRECIATE MORE WERE THE HOMES BUILT IN THE 1930s & 40s...
GRIFFY
12·2
©2006 Bill Griffith. World rights reserved. Distributed by King Features Syndicate
TOURISTS WOULD NEVER THINK OF VISITING THESE NEIGHBORHOODS. THEY HAD A "LOST IN TIME" FEEL I GREW TO LOVE.
STUCCO IS GOOD.
STUCCO IS MY CO-PILOT.!

173

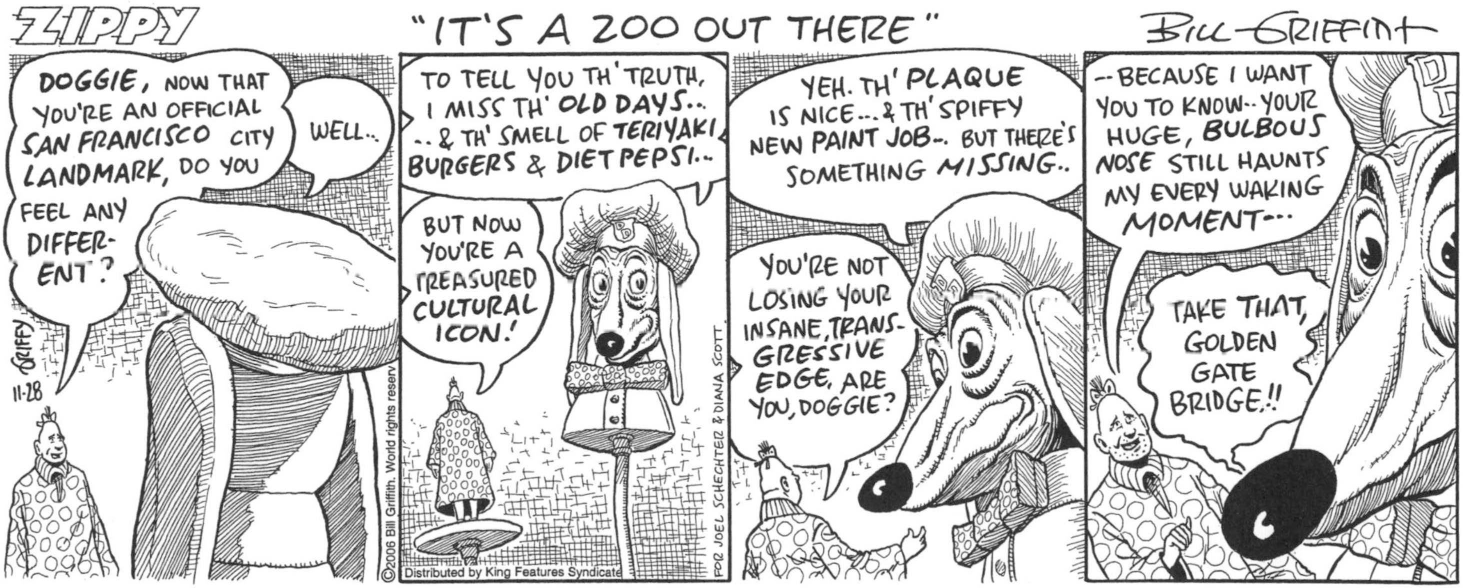
ZIPPY
"IT'S A ZOO OUT THERE"
BILL GRIFFITH
DOGGIE, NOW THAT YOU'RE AN OFFICIAL SAN FRANCISCO CITY LANDMARK, DO YOU FEEL ANY DIFFER-ENT?
WELL..
GRIFFY
11-28
©2006 Bill Griffith. World rights reserv
TO TELL YOU TH' TRUTH, I MISS TH' OLD DAYS.. ..& TH' SMELL OF TERIYAKI BURGERS & DIET PEPSI..
BUT NOW YOU'RE A TREASURED CULTURAL ICON.!
Distributed by King Features Syndicate
FOR JOEL SCHECHTER & DIANA SCOTT
YEH. TH' PLAQUE IS NICE...& TH' SPIFFY NEW PAINT JOB.. BUT THERE'S SOMETHING MISSING..
YOU'RE NOT LOSING YOUR INSANE, TRANS-GRESSIVE EDGE, ARE YOU, DOGGIE?
--BECAUSE I WANT YOU TO KNOW.. YOUR HUGE, BULBOUS NOSE STILL HAUNTS MY EVERY WAKING MOMENT---
TAKE THAT, GOLDEN GATE BRIDGE.!!

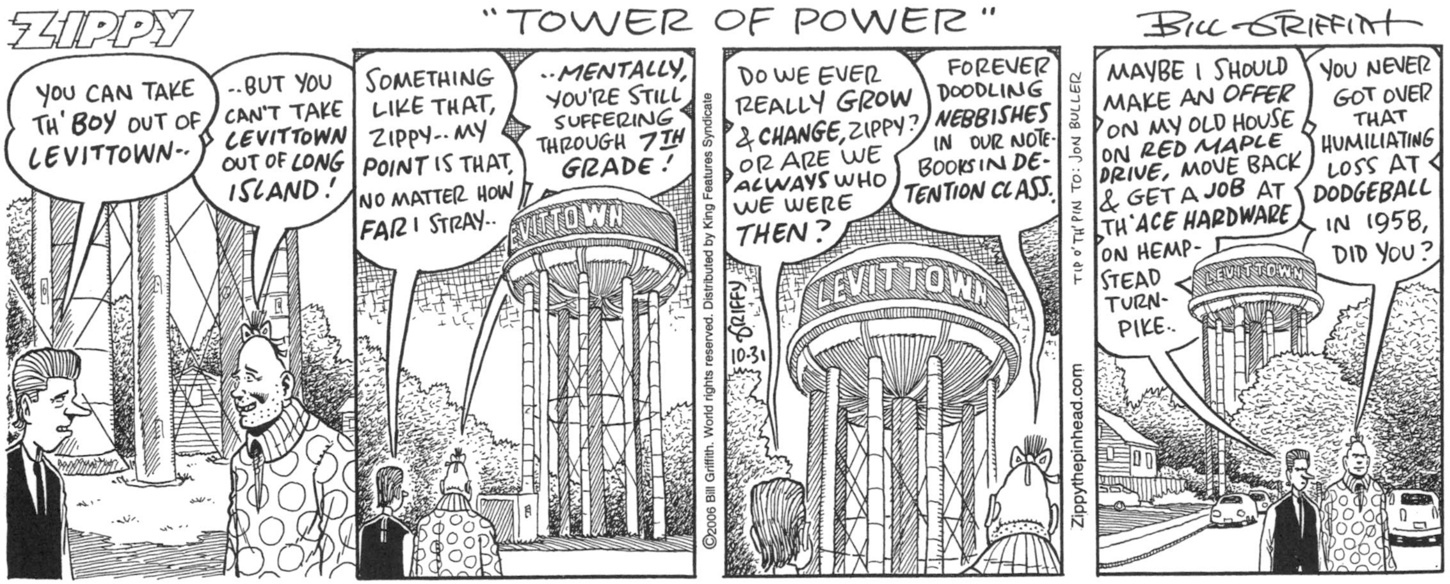
ZIPPY
"TOWER OF POWER"
BILL GRIFFITH
YOU CAN TAKE TH' BOY OUT OF LEVITTOWN--
--BUT YOU CAN'T TAKE LEVITTOWN OUT OF LONG ISLAND!
SOMETHING LIKE THAT, ZIPPY-- MY POINT IS THAT, NO MATTER HOW FAR I STRAY--
--MENTALLY, YOU'RE STILL SUFFERING THROUGH 7TH GRADE!
LEVITTOWN
©2006 Bill Griffith. World rights reserved. Distributed by King Features Syndicate
GRIFFY 10-31
DO WE EVER REALLY GROW & CHANGE, ZIPPY? OR ARE WE ALWAYS WHO WE WERE THEN?
FOREVER DOODLING NEBBISHES IN OUR NOTEBOOKS IN DETENTION CLASS.
LEVITTOWN
Zippythepinhead.com
TIP O' TH' PIN TO: JON BULLER
MAYBE I SHOULD MAKE AN OFFER ON MY OLD HOUSE ON RED MAPLE DRIVE, MOVE BACK & GET A JOB AT TH' ACE HARDWARE ON HEMPSTEAD TURNPIKE--
YOU NEVER GOT OVER THAT HUMILIATING LOSS AT DODGEBALL IN 1958, DID YOU?
LEVITTOWN

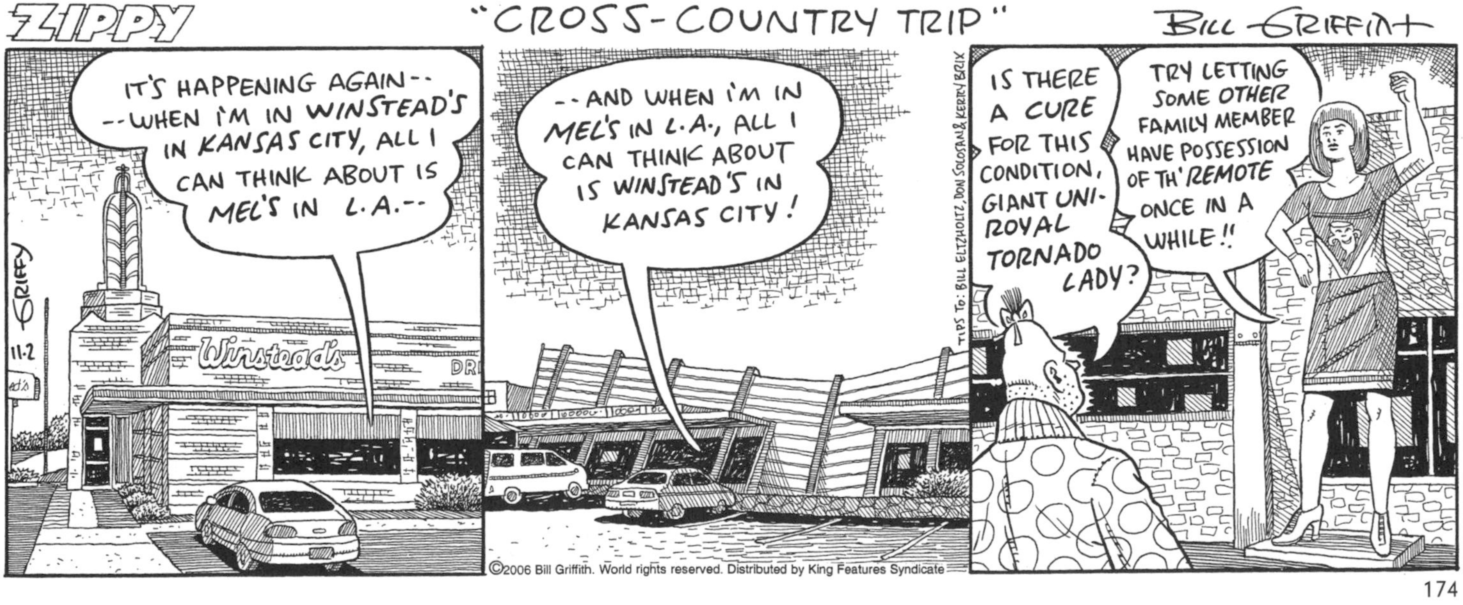
ZIPPY
"CROSS-COUNTRY TRIP"
BILL GRIFFITH
IT'S HAPPENING AGAIN-- --WHEN I'M IN WINSTEAD'S IN KANSAS CITY, ALL I CAN THINK ABOUT IS MEL'S IN L.A.--
GRIFFY 11-2
Winstead's
--AND WHEN I'M IN MEL'S IN L.A., ALL I CAN THINK ABOUT IS WINSTEAD'S IN KANSAS CITY!
©2006 Bill Griffith. World rights reserved. Distributed by King Features Syndicate
TIPS TO: BILL ELTZHOLTZ, DON SOLOSAN & KERRY BRIX
IS THERE A CURE FOR THIS CONDITION, GIANT UNI-ROYAL TORNADO LADY?
TRY LETTING SOME OTHER FAMILY MEMBER HAVE POSSESSION OF TH' REMOTE ONCE IN A WHILE!!

174

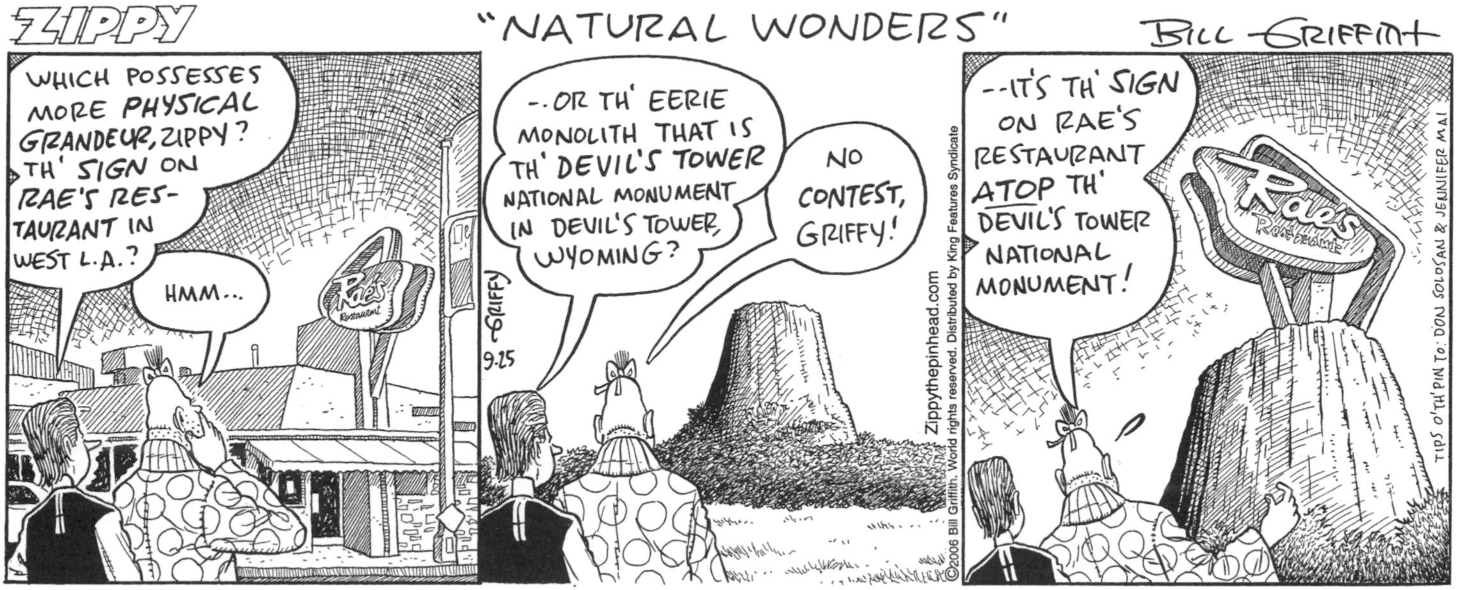
ZIPPY
"NATURAL WONDERS"
BILL GRIFFITH
WHICH POSSESSES MORE PHYSICAL GRANDEUR, ZIPPY? TH' SIGN ON RAE'S RESTAURANT IN WEST L.A.?
HMM...
-.OR TH' EERIE MONOLITH THAT IS TH' DEVIL'S TOWER NATIONAL MONUMENT IN DEVIL'S TOWER, WYOMING?
NO CONTEST, GRIFFY!
GRIFFY 9-25
©2006 Bill Griffith. World rights reserved. Distributed by King Features Syndicate
Zippythepinhead.com
--IT'S TH' SIGN ON RAE'S RESTAURANT ATOP TH' DEVIL'S TOWER NATIONAL MONUMENT!
TIPS O'TH' PIN TO: DON SOLOSAN & JENNIFER MAI

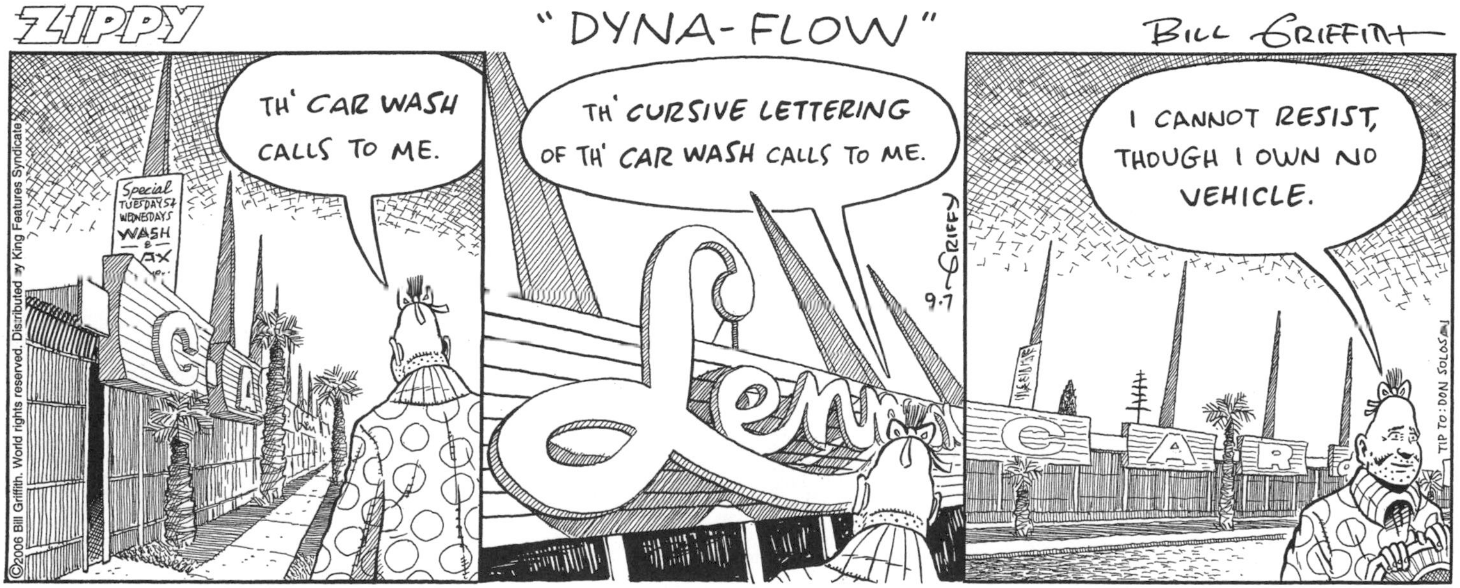
ZIPPY
"DYNA-FLOW"
BILL GRIFFITH
TH' CAR WASH CALLS TO ME.
©2006 Bill Griffith. World rights reserved. Distributed by King Features Syndicate
Special TUESDAYS & WEDNESDAYS WASH
TH' CURSIVE LETTERING OF TH' CAR WASH CALLS TO ME.
GRIFFY 9-7
I CANNOT RESIST, THOUGH I OWN NO VEHICLE.
TIP TO: DON SOLOSAN

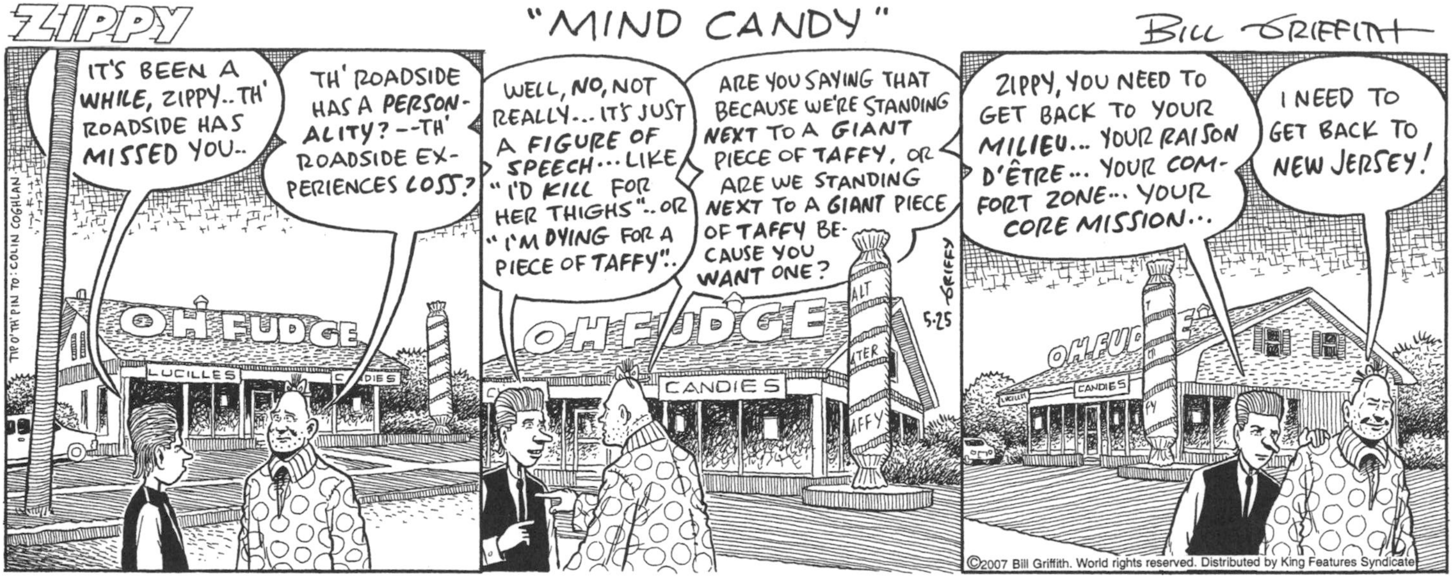
ZIPPY
"MIND CANDY"
BILL GRIFFITH
IT'S BEEN A WHILE, ZIPPY.. TH' ROADSIDE HAS MISSED YOU..
TH' ROADSIDE HAS A PERSONALITY? --TH' ROADSIDE EXPERIENCES LOSS?
TIP O' TH' PIN TO: COLIN COGHLAN
OH FUDGE
LUCILLES
CANDIES
WELL, NO, NOT REALLY... IT'S JUST A FIGURE OF SPEECH... LIKE "I'D KILL FOR HER THIGHS".. OR "I'M DYING FOR A PIECE OF TAFFY"..
ARE YOU SAYING THAT BECAUSE WE'RE STANDING NEXT TO A GIANT PIECE OF TAFFY, OR ARE WE STANDING NEXT TO A GIANT PIECE OF TAFFY BECAUSE YOU WANT ONE?
GRIFFY
5·25
ZIPPY, YOU NEED TO GET BACK TO YOUR MILIEU... YOUR RAISON D'ÊTRE... YOUR COMFORT ZONE... YOUR CORE MISSION...
I NEED TO GET BACK TO NEW JERSEY!
©2007 Bill Griffith. World rights reserved. Distributed by King Features Syndicate

176

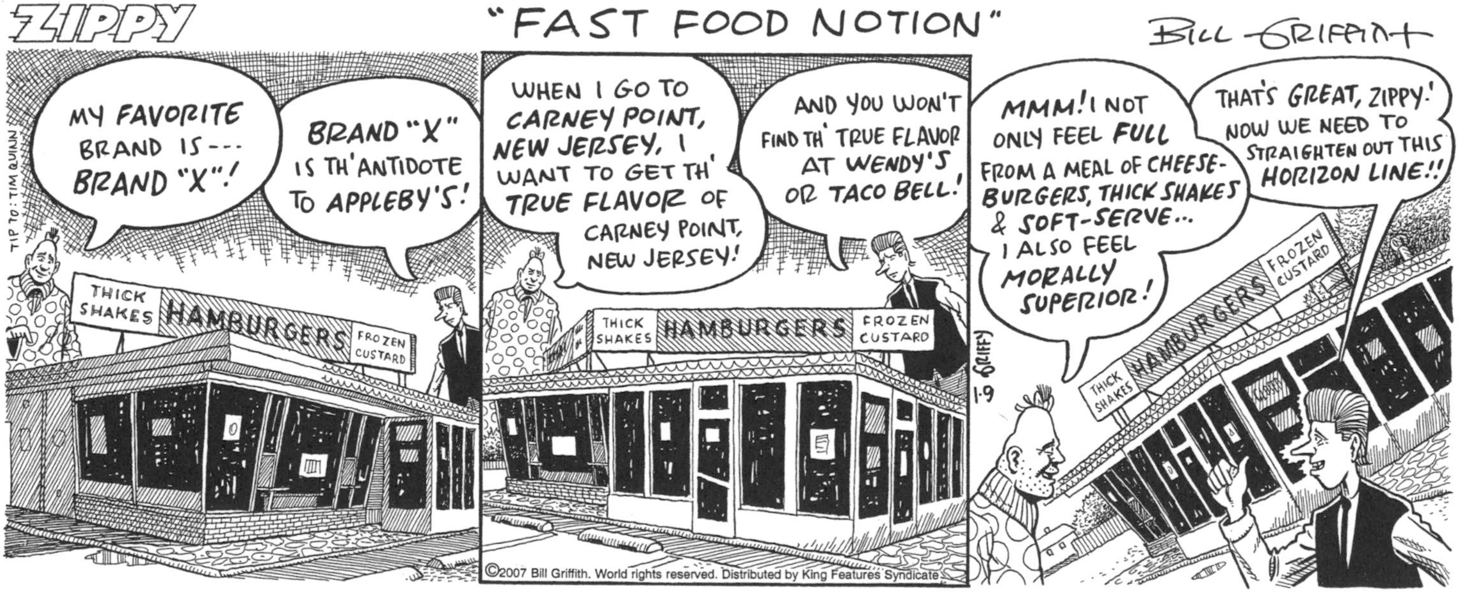
ZIPPY
"FAST FOOD NOTION"
BILL GRIFFITH
MY FAVORITE BRAND IS --- BRAND "X"!
BRAND "X" IS TH' ANTIDOTE TO APPLEBY'S!
TIP TO: TIM QUINN
THICK SHAKES
HAMBURGERS
FROZEN CUSTARD
WHEN I GO TO CARNEY POINT, NEW JERSEY, I WANT TO GET TH' TRUE FLAVOR OF CARNEY POINT, NEW JERSEY!
AND YOU WON'T FIND TH' TRUE FLAVOR AT WENDY'S OR TACO BELL!
GRIFFY
1·9
MMM! I NOT ONLY FEEL FULL FROM A MEAL OF CHEESEBURGERS, THICK SHAKES & SOFT-SERVE... I ALSO FEEL MORALLY SUPERIOR!
THAT'S GREAT, ZIPPY! NOW WE NEED TO STRAIGHTEN OUT THIS HORIZON LINE!!
©2007 Bill Griffith. World rights reserved. Distributed by King Features Syndicate

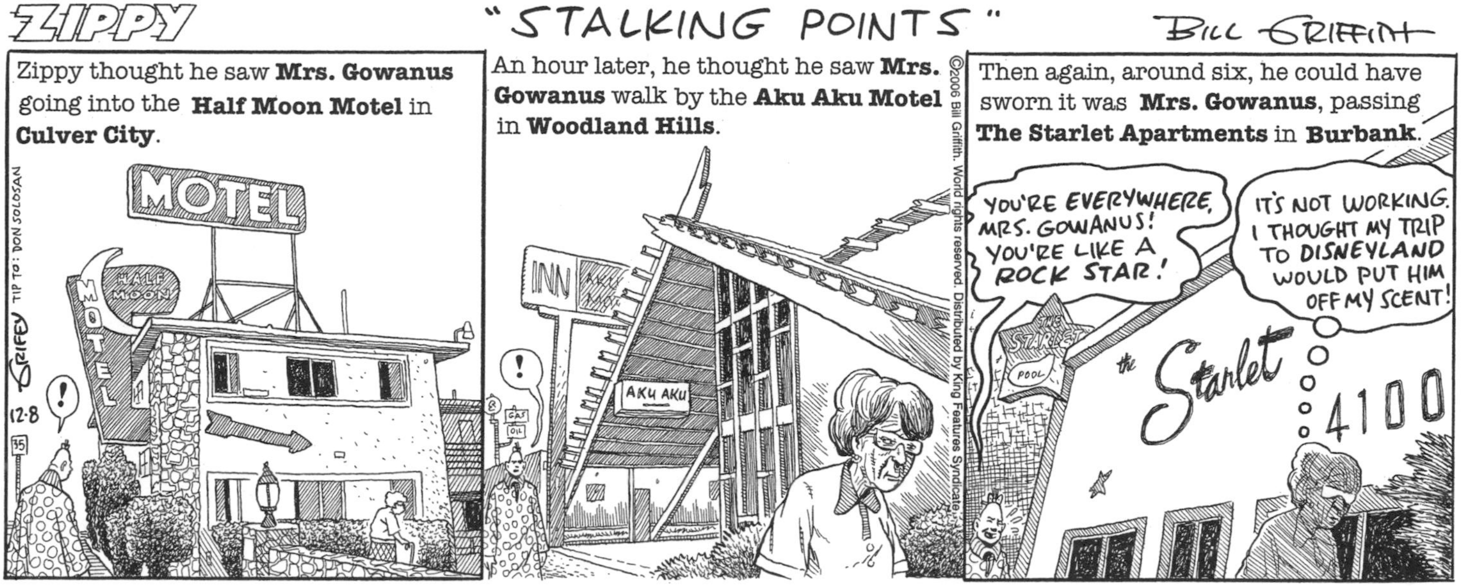
ZIPPY
"STALKING POINTS"
BILL GRIFFITH
Zippy thought he saw **Mrs. Gowanus** going into the **Half Moon Motel** in **Culver City**.
MOTEL
HALF MOON
MOTEL
TIP TO: DON SOLOSAN
GRIFFY 12-8
!
An hour later, he thought he saw **Mrs. Gowanus** walk by the **Aku Aku Motel** in **Woodland Hills**.
©2006 Bill Griffith. World rights reserved. Distributed by King Features Syndicate.
INN
AKU AKU
!
Then again, around six, he could have sworn it was **Mrs. Gowanus**, passing **The Starlet Apartments** in **Burbank**.
YOU'RE EVERYWHERE, MRS. GOWANUS! YOU'RE LIKE A ROCK STAR!
IT'S NOT WORKING. I THOUGHT MY TRIP TO DISNEYLAND WOULD PUT HIM OFF MY SCENT!
THE STARLET POOL
the Starlet
4100

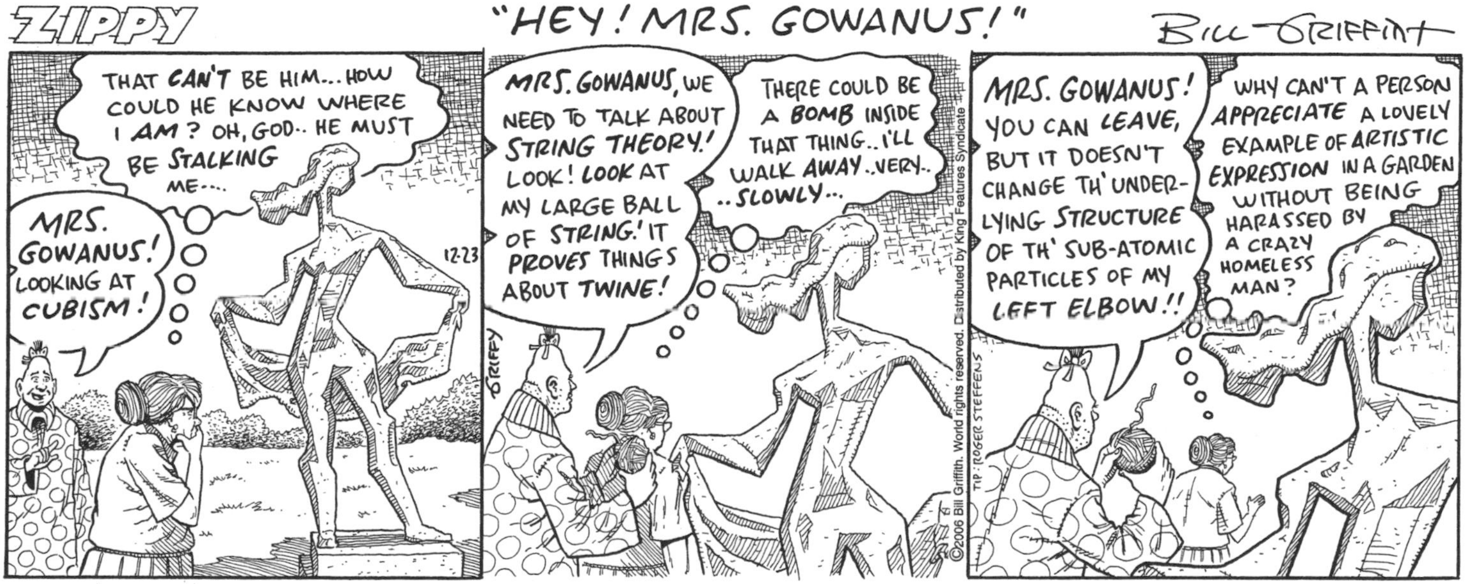
ZIPPY
"HEY! MRS. GOWANUS!"
BILL GRIFFITH
THAT CAN'T BE HIM... HOW COULD HE KNOW WHERE I AM? OH, GOD.. HE MUST BE STALKING ME....
MRS. GOWANUS! LOOKING AT CUBISM!
12-23
MRS. GOWANUS, WE NEED TO TALK ABOUT STRING THEORY! LOOK! LOOK AT MY LARGE BALL OF STRING! IT PROVES THINGS ABOUT TWINE!
THERE COULD BE A BOMB INSIDE THAT THING.. I'LL WALK AWAY.. VERY.. ..SLOWLY...
GRIFFY
©2006 Bill Griffith. World rights reserved. Distributed by King Features Syndicate
TIP: ROGER STEFFENS
MRS. GOWANUS! YOU CAN LEAVE, BUT IT DOESN'T CHANGE TH' UNDER-LYING STRUCTURE OF TH' SUB-ATOMIC PARTICLES OF MY LEFT ELBOW!!
WHY CAN'T A PERSON APPRECIATE A LOVELY EXAMPLE OF ARTISTIC EXPRESSION IN A GARDEN WITHOUT BEING HARASSED BY A CRAZY HOMELESS MAN?

177

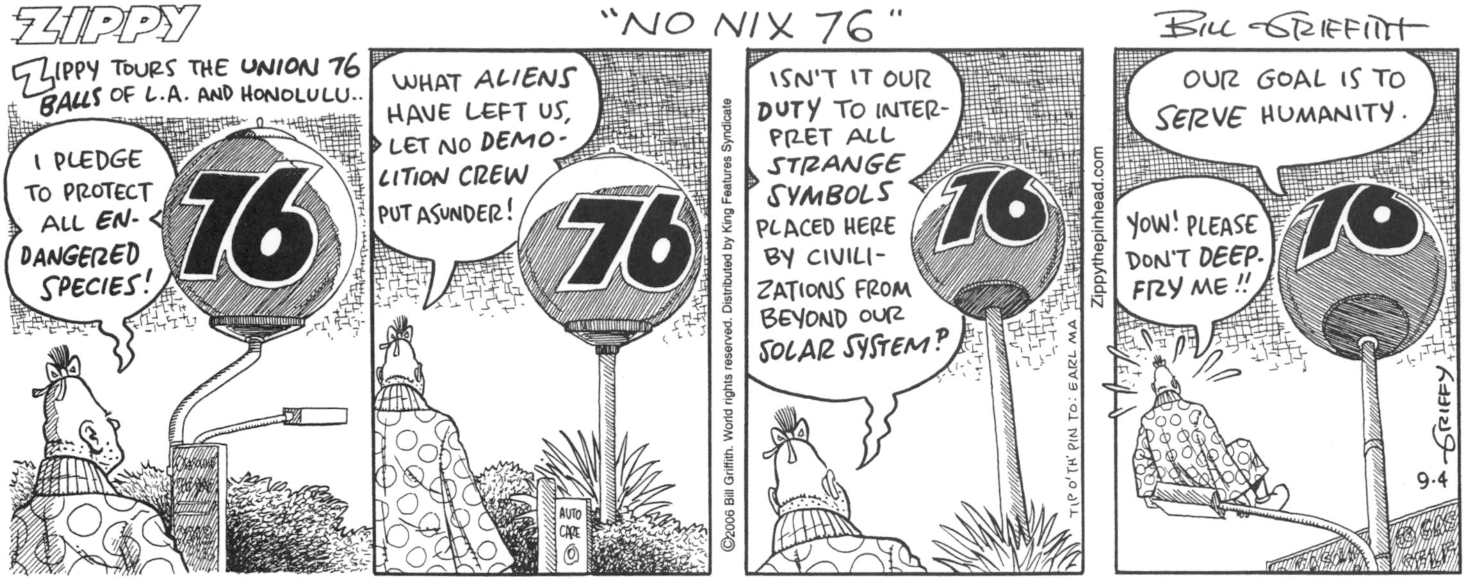
ZIPPY
"NO NIX 76"
BILL GRIFFITH
ZIPPY TOURS THE UNION 76 BALLS OF L.A. AND HONOLULU..
I PLEDGE TO PROTECT ALL ENDANGERED SPECIES!
76
WHAT ALIENS HAVE LEFT US, LET NO DEMOLITION CREW PUT ASUNDER!
76
AUTO CARE
©2006 Bill Griffith. World rights reserved. Distributed by King Features Syndicate
ISN'T IT OUR DUTY TO INTERPRET ALL STRANGE SYMBOLS PLACED HERE BY CIVILIZATIONS FROM BEYOND OUR SOLAR SYSTEM?
76
TIP O' TH' PIN TO: EARL MA
Zippythepinhead.com
OUR GOAL IS TO SERVE HUMANITY.
YOW! PLEASE DON'T DEEP-FRY ME!!
76
GRIFFY
9·4

178

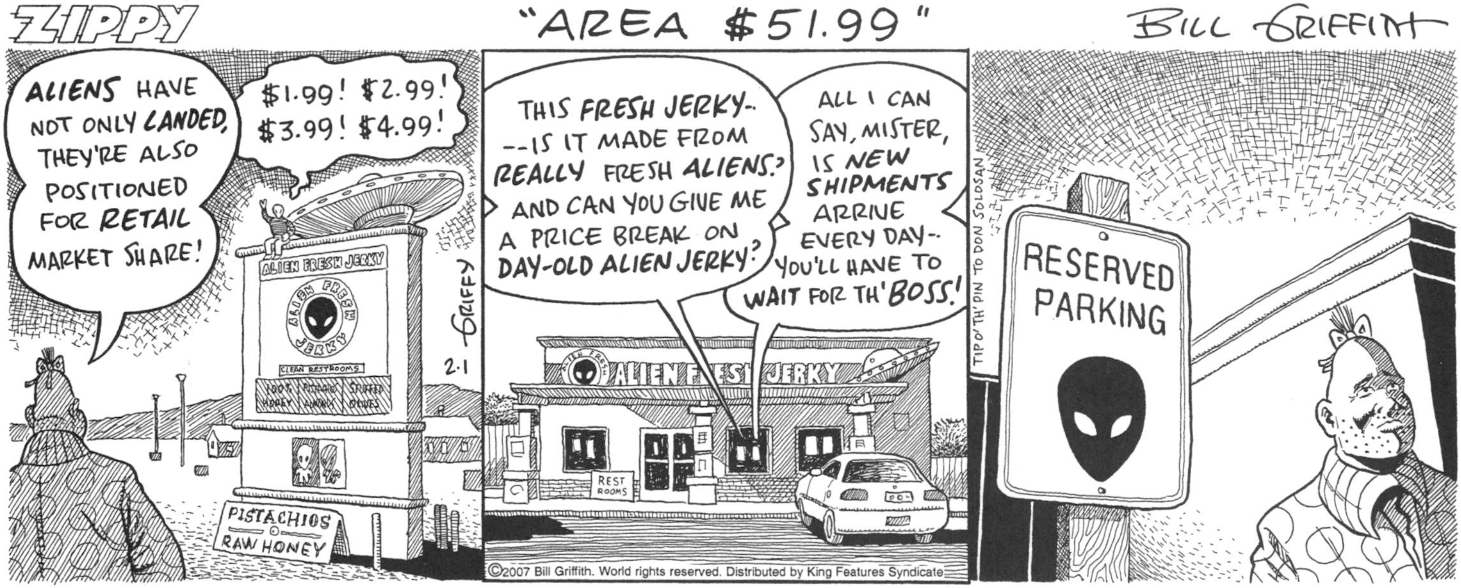
ZIPPY
"AREA $51.99"
BILL GRIFFITH
ALIENS HAVE NOT ONLY LANDED, THEY'RE ALSO POSITIONED FOR RETAIL MARKET SHARE!
$1.99! $2.99! $3.99! $4.99!
ALIEN FRESH JERKY
ALIEN FRESH JERKY
CLEAN RESTROOMS
PISTACHIOS
RAW HONEY
GRIFFY
2·1
THIS FRESH JERKY-- --IS IT MADE FROM REALLY FRESH ALIENS? AND CAN YOU GIVE ME A PRICE BREAK ON DAY-OLD ALIEN JERKY?
ALL I CAN SAY, MISTER, IS NEW SHIPMENTS ARRIVE EVERY DAY-- YOU'LL HAVE TO WAIT FOR TH' BOSS!
ALIEN FRESH JERKY
REST ROOMS
©2007 Bill Griffith. World rights reserved. Distributed by King Features Syndicate
TIP O' TH' PIN TO DON SOLOSAN
RESERVED PARKING

179

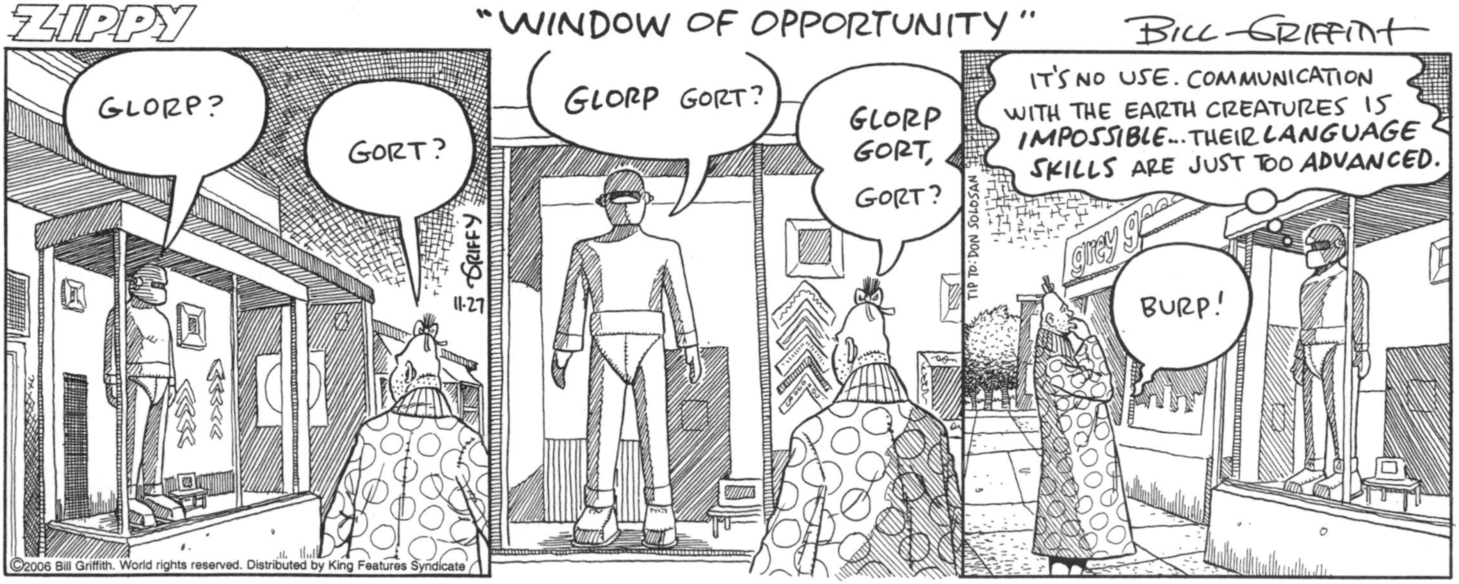
ZIPPY
"WINDOW OF OPPORTUNITY"
BILL GRIFFITH
GLORP?
GORT?
GRIFFY 11-27
GLORP GORT?
GLORP GORT, GORT?
IT'S NO USE. COMMUNICATION WITH THE EARTH CREATURES IS IMPOSSIBLE... THEIR LANGUAGE SKILLS ARE JUST TOO ADVANCED.
TIP TO: DON SOLOSAN
BURP!
grey goo
©2006 Bill Griffith. World rights reserved. Distributed by King Features Syndicate

180

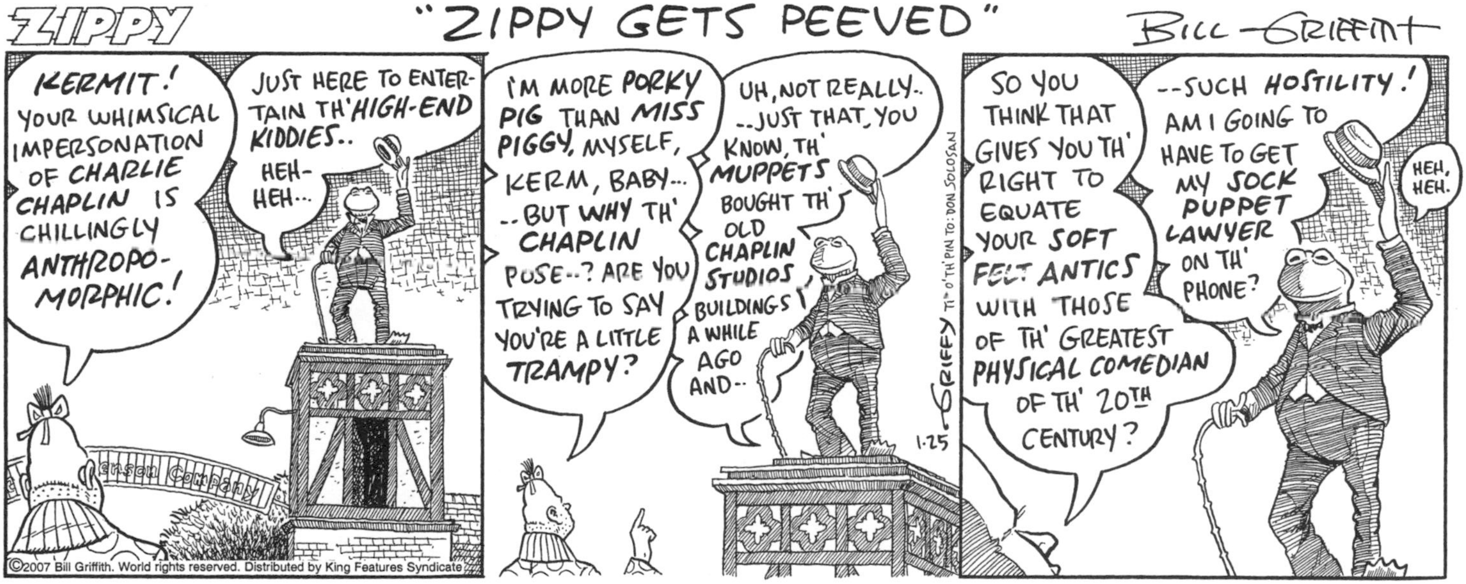
ZIPPY
"ZIPPY GETS PEEVED"
BILL GRIFFITH
KERMIT! YOUR WHIMSICAL IMPERSONATION OF CHARLIE CHAPLIN IS CHILLINGLY ANTHROPO-MORPHIC!
JUST HERE TO ENTER-TAIN TH' HIGH-END KIDDIES.. HEH-HEH...
I'M MORE PORKY PIG THAN MISS PIGGY, MYSELF, KERM, BABY... --BUT WHY TH' CHAPLIN POSE--? ARE YOU TRYING TO SAY YOU'RE A LITTLE TRAMPY?
UH, NOT REALLY.. --JUST THAT, YOU KNOW, TH' MUPPETS BOUGHT TH' OLD CHAPLIN STUDIOS BUILDINGS A WHILE AGO AND..
GRIFFY 1-25
TIP O' TH' PIN TO: DON SOLOSAN
SO YOU THINK THAT GIVES YOU TH' RIGHT TO EQUATE YOUR SOFT FELT ANTICS WITH THOSE OF TH' GREATEST PHYSICAL COMEDIAN OF TH' 20TH CENTURY?
--SUCH HOSTILITY! AM I GOING TO HAVE TO GET MY SOCK PUPPET LAWYER ON TH' PHONE?
HEH, HEH.
©2007 Bill Griffith. World rights reserved. Distributed by King Features Syndicate

181

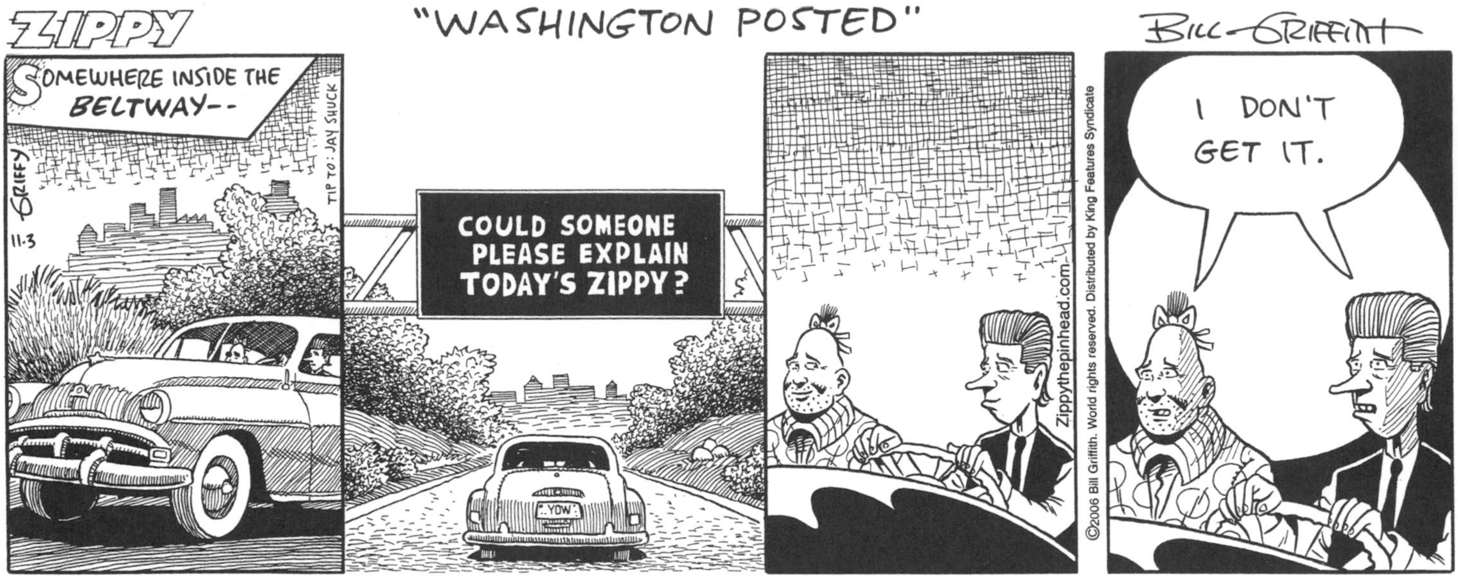
ZIPPY
"WASHINGTON POSTED"
BILL GRIFFITH
SOMEWHERE INSIDE THE BELTWAY--
GRIFFY 11-3
TIP TO: JAY SHUCK
COULD SOMEONE PLEASE EXPLAIN TODAY'S ZIPPY?
YOW
I DON'T GET IT.

182

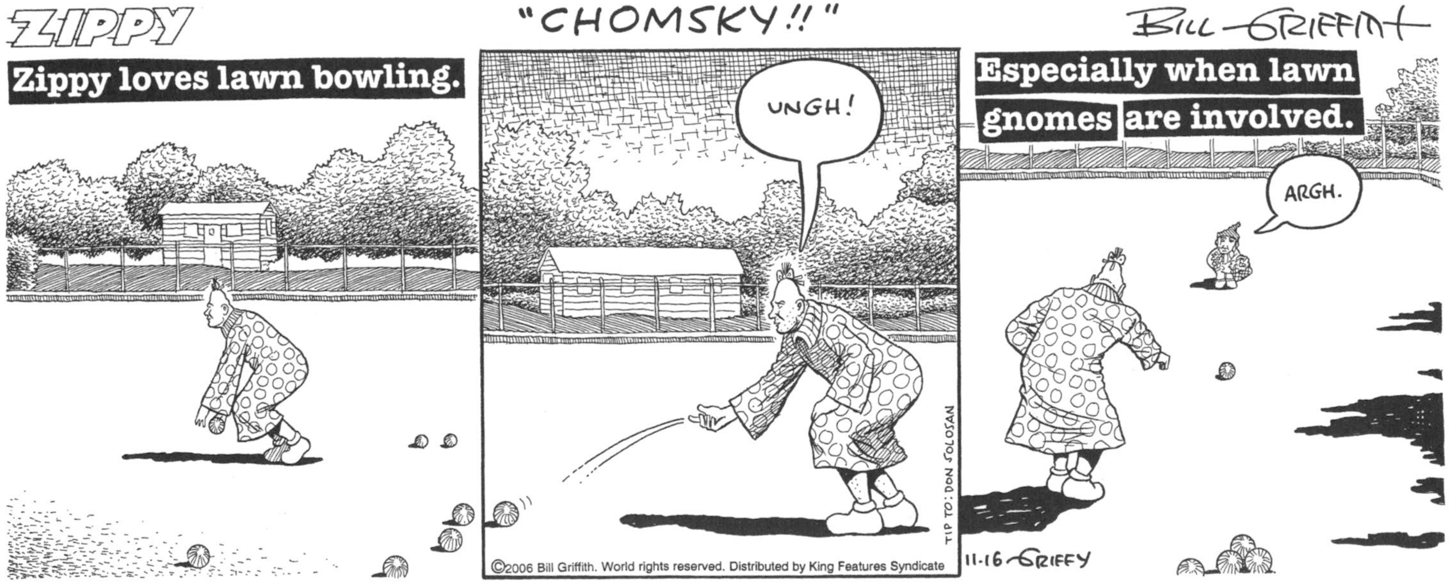
ZIPPY
"CHOMSKY!!"
BILL GRIFFITH
Zippy loves lawn bowling.
UNGH!
TIP TO: DON SOLOSAN
Especially when lawn gnomes are involved.
ARGH.
11-16 GRIFFY

183

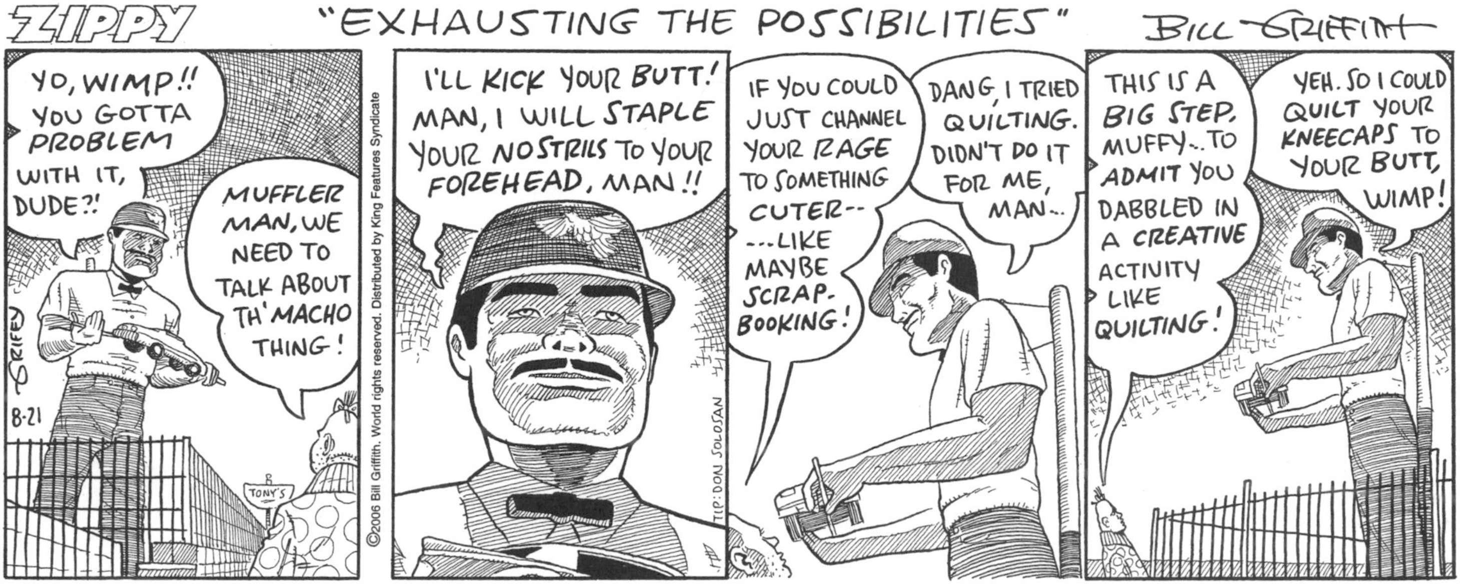

ZIPPY
"EXHAUSTING THE POSSIBILITIES"
BILL GRIFFITH
YO, WIMP!! YOU GOTTA PROBLEM WITH IT, DUDE?!
MUFFLER MAN, WE NEED TO TALK ABOUT TH' MACHO THING!
TONY'S
GRIFFY 8-21
I'LL KICK YOUR BUTT! MAN, I WILL STAPLE YOUR NOSTRILS TO YOUR FOREHEAD, MAN!!
©2006 Bill Griffith. World rights reserved. Distributed by King Features Syndicate
TIP: DON SOLOSAN
IF YOU COULD JUST CHANNEL YOUR RAGE TO SOMETHING CUTER-- --LIKE MAYBE SCRAP-BOOKING!
DANG, I TRIED QUILTING. DIDN'T DO IT FOR ME, MAN..
THIS IS A BIG STEP, MUFFY.. TO ADMIT YOU DABBLED IN A CREATIVE ACTIVITY LIKE QUILTING!
YEH. SO I COULD QUILT YOUR KNEECAPS TO YOUR BUTT, WIMP!

184

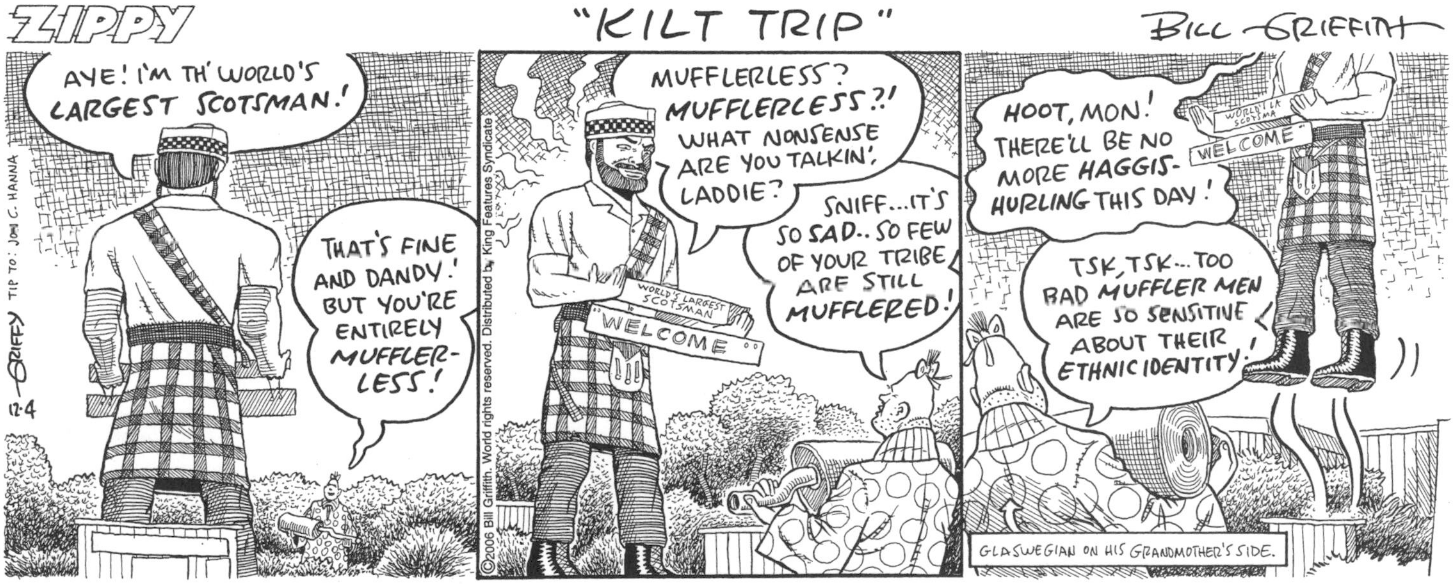

ZIPPY
"KILT TRIP"
BILL GRIFFITH
AYE! I'M TH' WORLD'S LARGEST SCOTSMAN!
THAT'S FINE AND DANDY! BUT YOU'RE ENTIRELY MUFFLER-LESS!
GRIFFY 12-4
TIP TO: JON C. HANNA
MUFFLERLESS? MUFFLERLESS?! WHAT NONSENSE ARE YOU TALKIN', LADDIE?
SNIFF...IT'S SO SAD.. SO FEW OF YOUR TRIBE ARE STILL MUFFLERED!
WORLD'S LARGEST SCOTSMAN
WELCOME
©2006 Bill Griffith. World rights reserved. Distributed by King Features Syndicate
HOOT, MON! THERE'LL BE NO MORE HAGGIS-HURLING THIS DAY!
WELCOME
TSK, TSK... TOO BAD MUFFLER MEN ARE SO SENSITIVE ABOUT THEIR ETHNIC IDENTITY!
GLASWEGIAN ON HIS GRANDMOTHER'S SIDE.

185

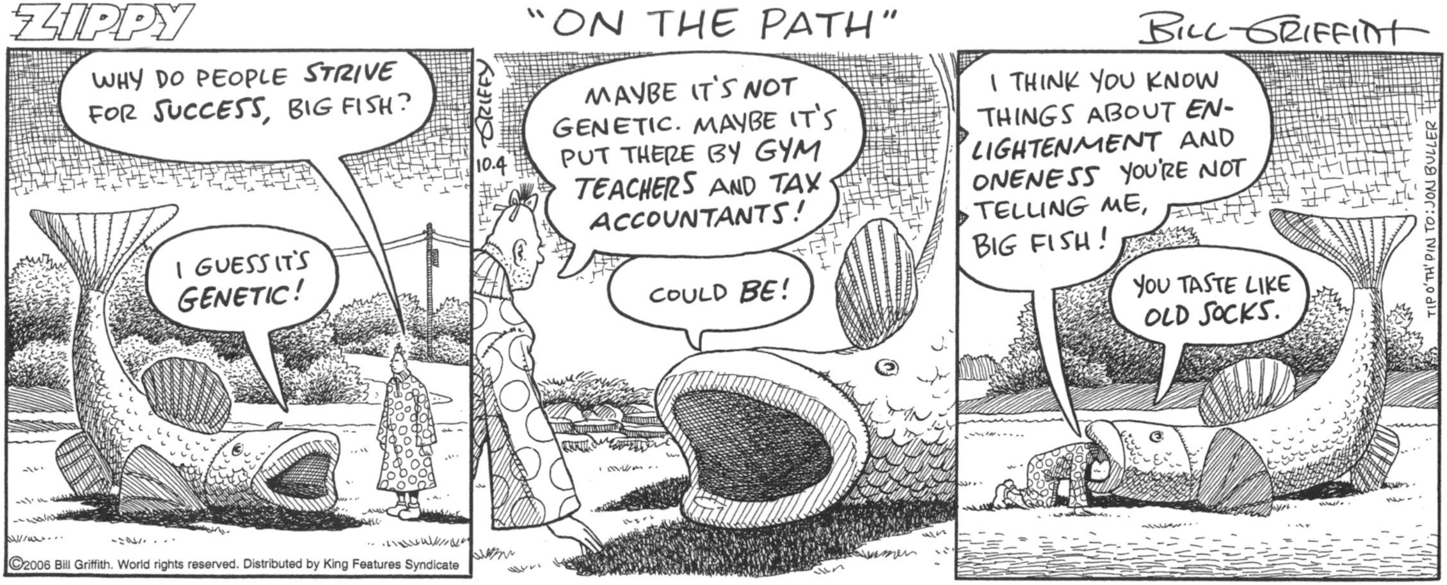
ZIPPY
"ON THE PATH"
BILL GRIFFITH
WHY DO PEOPLE STRIVE FOR SUCCESS, BIG FISH?
I GUESS IT'S GENETIC!
©2006 Bill Griffith. World rights reserved. Distributed by King Features Syndicate
GRIFFY 10.4
MAYBE IT'S NOT GENETIC. MAYBE IT'S PUT THERE BY GYM TEACHERS AND TAX ACCOUNTANTS!
COULD BE!
I THINK YOU KNOW THINGS ABOUT EN-LIGHTENMENT AND ONENESS YOU'RE NOT TELLING ME, BIG FISH!
YOU TASTE LIKE OLD SOCKS.
TIP O' TH' PIN TO: JON BULLER

186

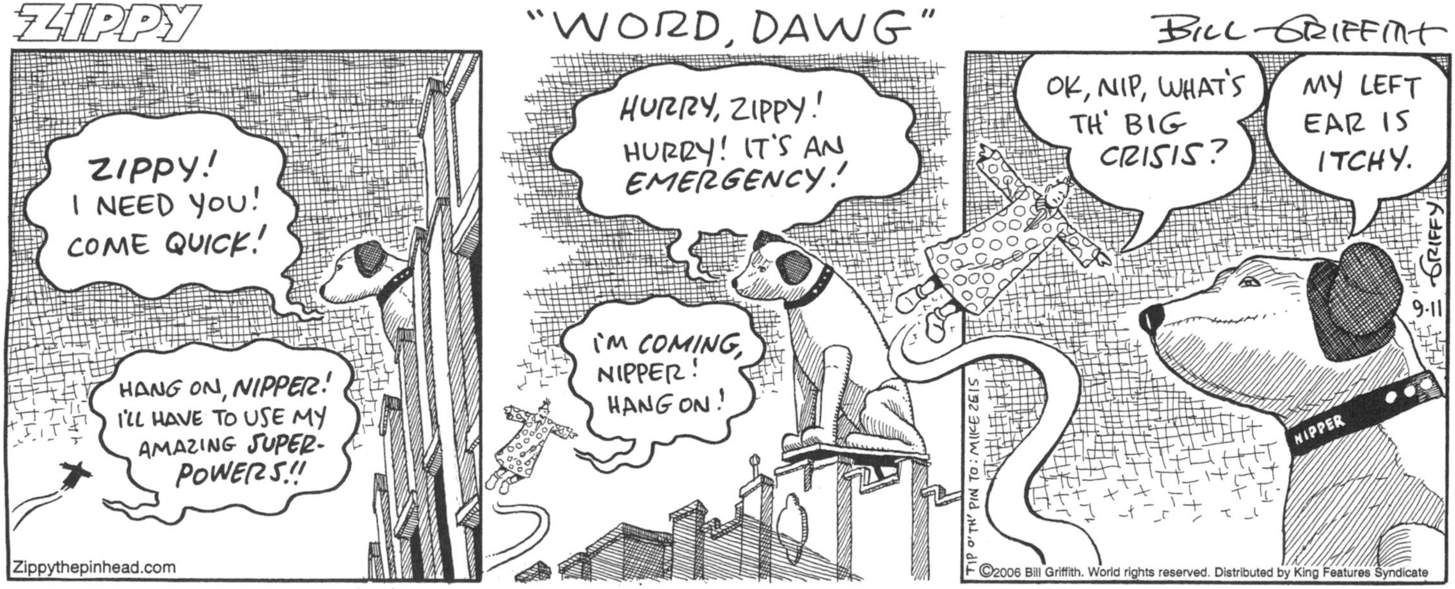
ZIPPY
"WORD, DAWG"
BILL GRIFFITH
ZIPPY! I NEED YOU! COME QUICK!
HANG ON, NIPPER! I'LL HAVE TO USE MY AMAZING SUPER-POWERS!!
Zippythepinhead.com
HURRY, ZIPPY! HURRY! IT'S AN EMERGENCY!
I'M COMING, NIPPER! HANG ON!
OK, NIP, WHAT'S TH' BIG CRISIS?
MY LEFT EAR IS ITCHY.
GRIFFY 9.11
NIPPER
TIP O' TH' PIN TO: MIKE ZEIS
©2006 Bill Griffith. World rights reserved. Distributed by King Features Syndicate

187

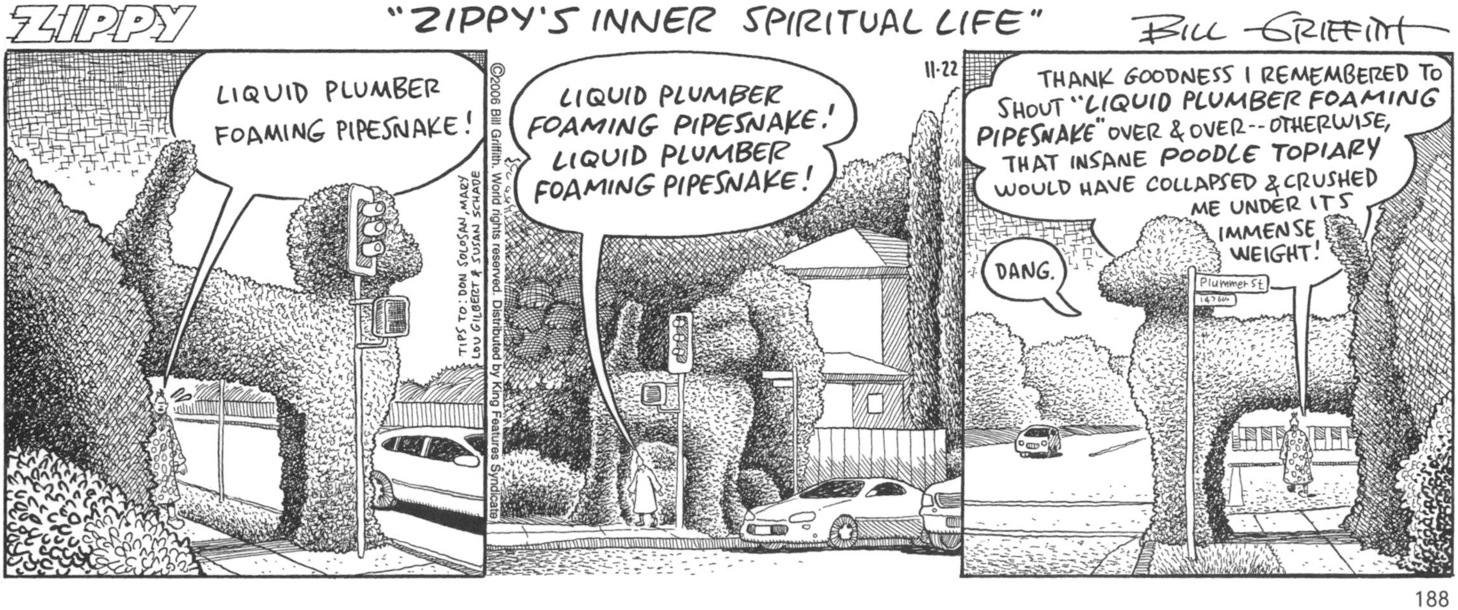
ZIPPY
"ZIPPY'S INNER SPIRITUAL LIFE"
BILL GRIFFITH
LIQUID PLUMBER FOAMING PIPESNAKE!
TIPS TO: DON SOLOSAN, MARY LOU GILBERT & SUSAN SCHADE
©2006 Bill Griffith. World rights reserved. Distributed by King Features Syndicate
11-22
LIQUID PLUMBER FOAMING PIPESNAKE! LIQUID PLUMBER FOAMING PIPESNAKE!
THANK GOODNESS I REMEMBERED TO SHOUT "LIQUID PLUMBER FOAMING PIPESNAKE" OVER & OVER -- OTHERWISE, THAT INSANE POODLE TOPIARY WOULD HAVE COLLAPSED & CRUSHED ME UNDER ITS IMMENSE WEIGHT!
DANG.
Plummer St
188

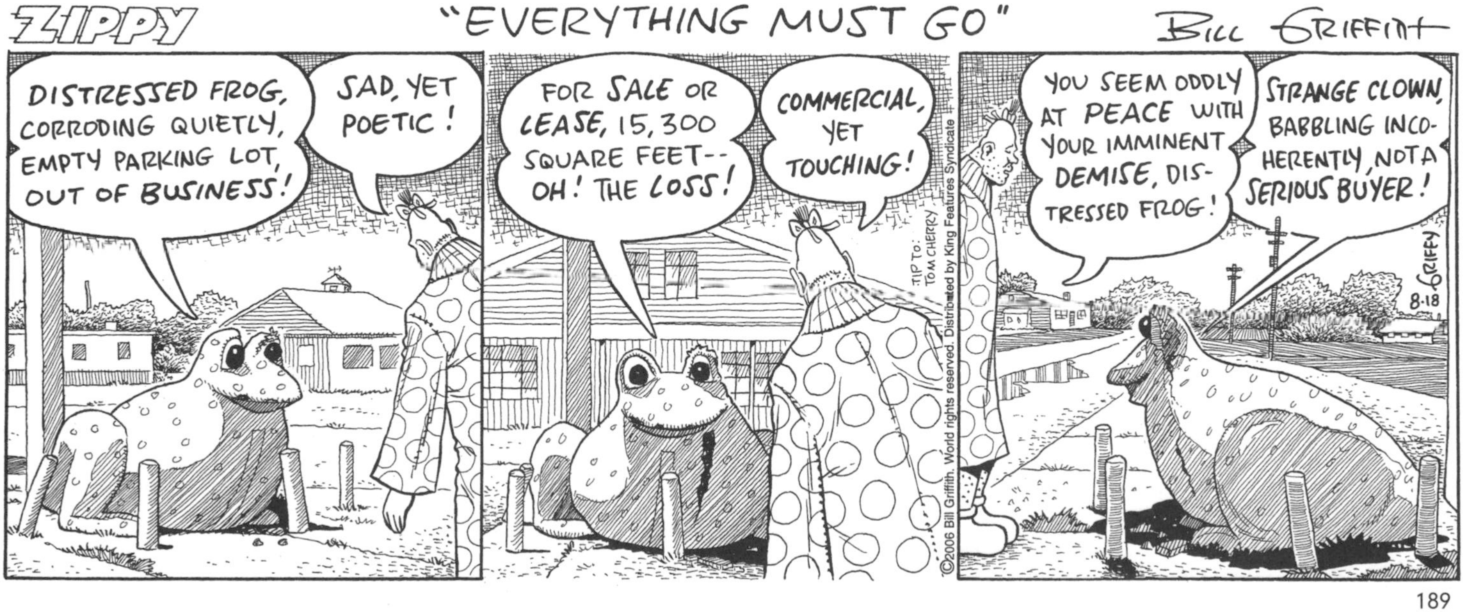
ZIPPY
"EVERYTHING MUST GO"
BILL GRIFFITH
DISTRESSED FROG, CORRODING QUIETLY, EMPTY PARKING LOT, OUT OF BUSINESS!
SAD, YET POETIC!
FOR SALE OR LEASE, 15,300 SQUARE FEET-- OH! THE LOSS!
COMMERCIAL, YET TOUCHING!
TIP TO: TOM CHERRY
©2006 Bill Griffith. World rights reserved. Distributed by King Features Syndicate
YOU SEEM ODDLY AT PEACE WITH YOUR IMMINENT DEMISE, DISTRESSED FROG!
STRANGE CLOWN, BABBLING INCOHERENTLY, NOT A SERIOUS BUYER!
GRIFFY
8-18
189

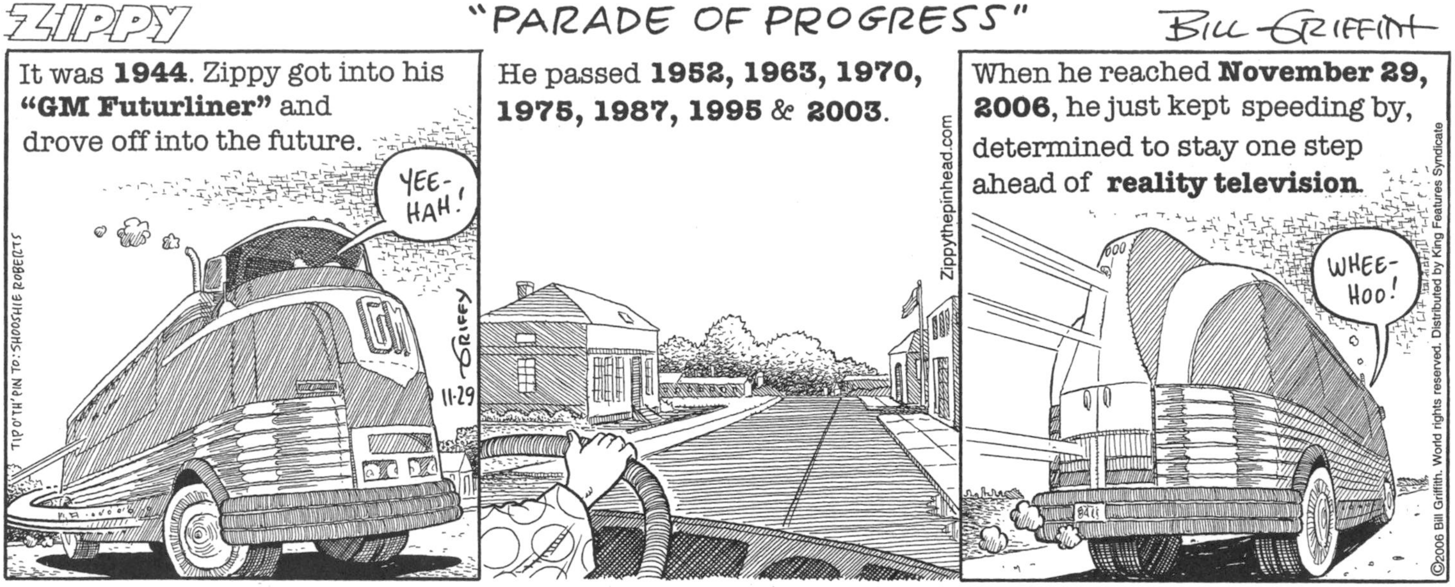
ZIPPY
"PARADE OF PROGRESS"
BILL GRIFFITH
It was **1944**. Zippy got into his **"GM Futurliner"** and drove off into the future.
YEE-HAH!
TIP O' TH' PIN TO: SHOOSHIE ROBERTS
GRIFFY 11-29
He passed **1952, 1963, 1970, 1975, 1987, 1995** & **2003**.
Zippythepinhead.com
When he reached **November 29, 2006**, he just kept speeding by, determined to stay one step ahead of **reality television**.
WHEE-HOO!
©2006 Bill Griffith. World rights reserved. Distributed by King Features Syndicate

190

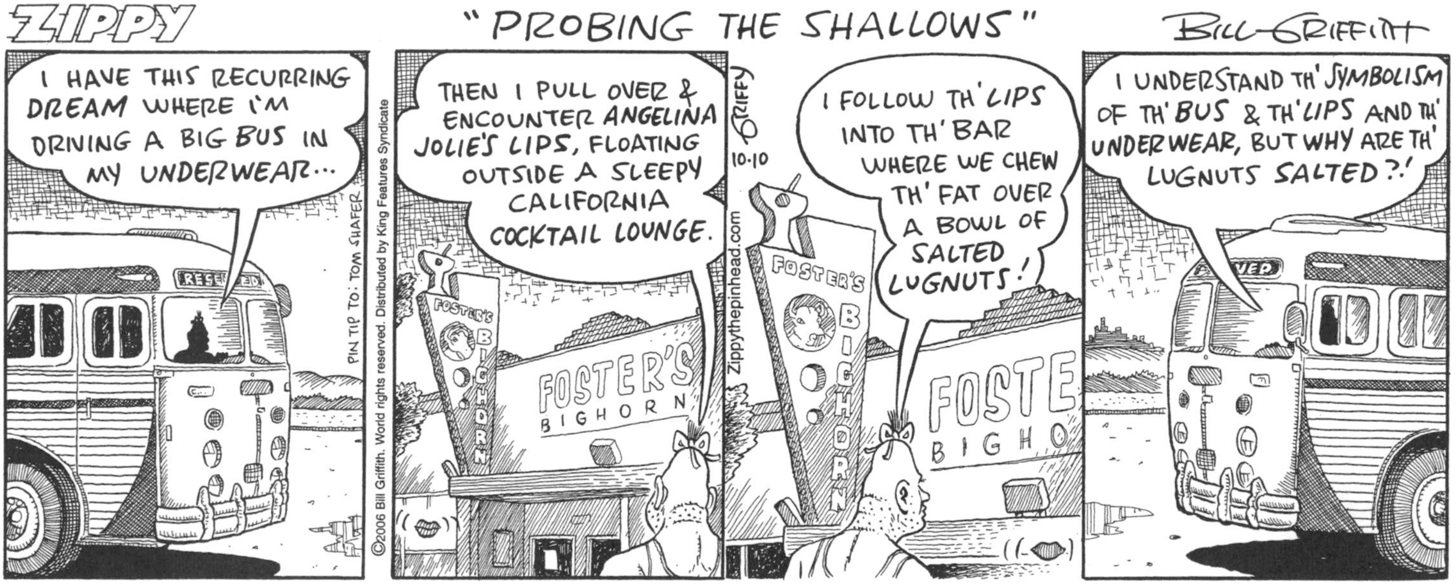
ZIPPY
"PROBING THE SHALLOWS"
BILL GRIFFITH
I HAVE THIS RECURRING DREAM WHERE I'M DRIVING A BIG BUS IN MY UNDERWEAR...
PIN TIP TO: TOM SHAFER
©2006 Bill Griffith. World rights reserved. Distributed by King Features Syndicate
THEN I PULL OVER & ENCOUNTER ANGELINA JOLIE'S LIPS, FLOATING OUTSIDE A SLEEPY CALIFORNIA COCKTAIL LOUNGE.
FOSTER'S BIGHORN
Zippythepinhead.com
GRIFFY 10-10
I FOLLOW TH' LIPS INTO TH' BAR WHERE WE CHEW TH' FAT OVER A BOWL OF SALTED LUGNUTS!
I UNDERSTAND TH' SYMBOLISM OF TH' BUS & TH' LIPS AND TH' UNDERWEAR, BUT WHY ARE TH' LUGNUTS SALTED?!

191

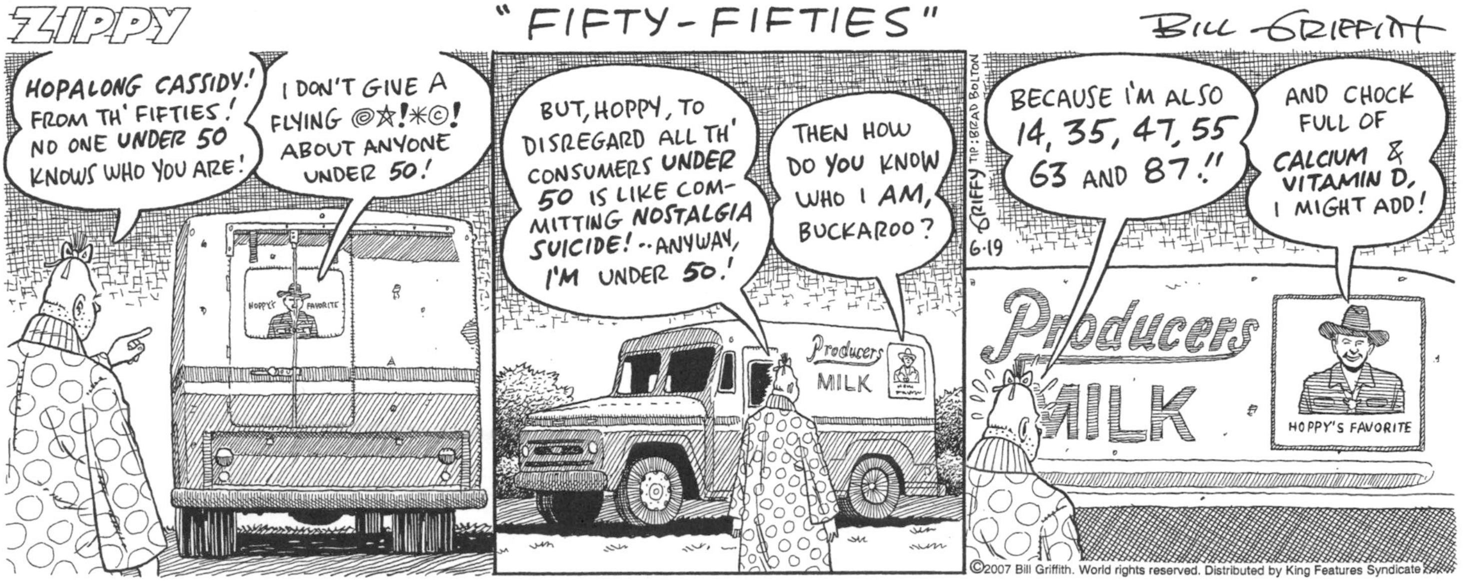
ZIPPY
"FIFTY-FIFTIES"
BILL GRIFFITH
HOPALONG CASSIDY! FROM TH' FIFTIES! NO ONE UNDER 50 KNOWS WHO YOU ARE!
I DON'T GIVE A FLYING @☆!*©! ABOUT ANYONE UNDER 50!
HOPPY'S FAVORITE
BUT, HOPPY, TO DISREGARD ALL TH' CONSUMERS UNDER 50 IS LIKE COM-MITTING NOSTALGIA SUICIDE! .. ANYWAY, I'M UNDER 50!
THEN HOW DO YOU KNOW WHO I AM, BUCKAROO?
Producers MILK
GRIFFY 6-19
TIP: BRAD BOLTON
BECAUSE I'M ALSO 14, 35, 47, 55 63 AND 87!!
AND CHOCK FULL OF CALCIUM & VITAMIN D, I MIGHT ADD!
Producers MILK
HOPPY'S FAVORITE
©2007 Bill Griffith. World rights reserved. Distributed by King Features Syndicate

192

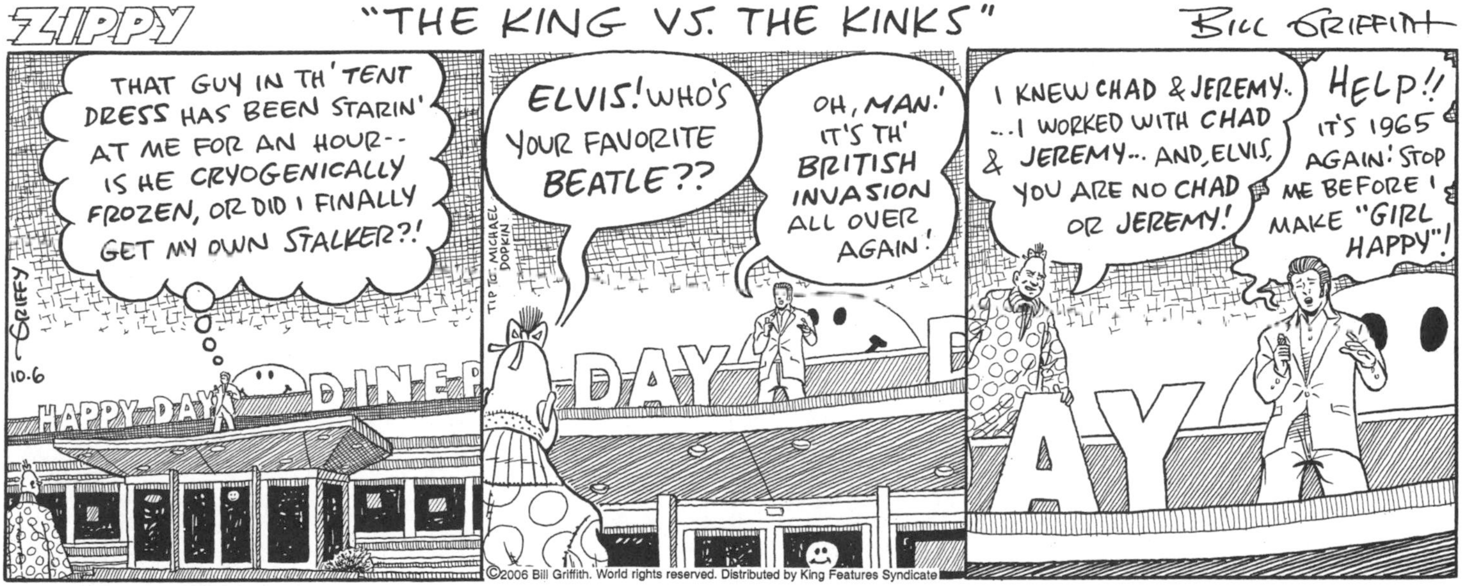
ZIPPY
"THE KING VS. THE KINKS"
BILL GRIFFITH
THAT GUY IN TH' TENT DRESS HAS BEEN STARIN' AT ME FOR AN HOUR-- IS HE CRYOGENICALLY FROZEN, OR DID I FINALLY GET MY OWN STALKER?!
GRIFFY 10-6
HAPPY DAY DINER
ELVIS! WHO'S YOUR FAVORITE BEATLE??
OH, MAN! IT'S TH' BRITISH INVASION ALL OVER AGAIN!
TIP TO: MICHAEL DOPKIN
DAY
I KNEW CHAD & JEREMY.. ..I WORKED WITH CHAD & JEREMY... AND, ELVIS, YOU ARE NO CHAD OR JEREMY!
HELP!! IT'S 1965 AGAIN! STOP ME BEFORE I MAKE "GIRL HAPPY"!
AY
©2006 Bill Griffith. World rights reserved. Distributed by King Features Syndicate

193

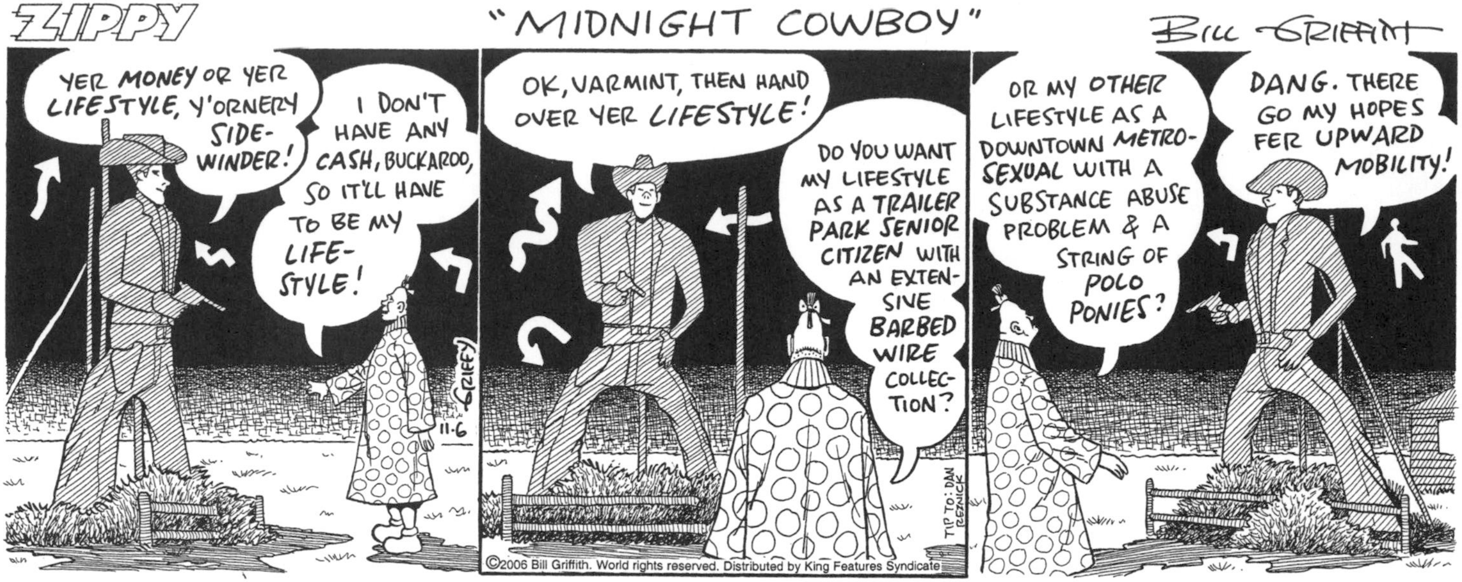
ZIPPY
"MIDNIGHT COWBOY"
BILL GRIFFITH
YER MONEY OR YER LIFESTYLE, Y'ORNERY SIDE-WINDER!
I DON'T HAVE ANY CASH, BUCKAROO, SO IT'LL HAVE TO BE MY LIFE-STYLE!
GRIFFY 11-6
OK, VARMINT, THEN HAND OVER YER LIFESTYLE!
DO YOU WANT MY LIFESTYLE AS A TRAILER PARK SENIOR CITIZEN WITH AN EXTEN-SIVE BARBED WIRE COLLEC-TION?
TIP TO: DAN REZNICK
©2006 Bill Griffith. World rights reserved. Distributed by King Features Syndicate
OR MY OTHER LIFESTYLE AS A DOWNTOWN METRO-SEXUAL WITH A SUBSTANCE ABUSE PROBLEM & A STRING OF POLO PONIES?
DANG. THERE GO MY HOPES FER UPWARD MOBILITY!

194

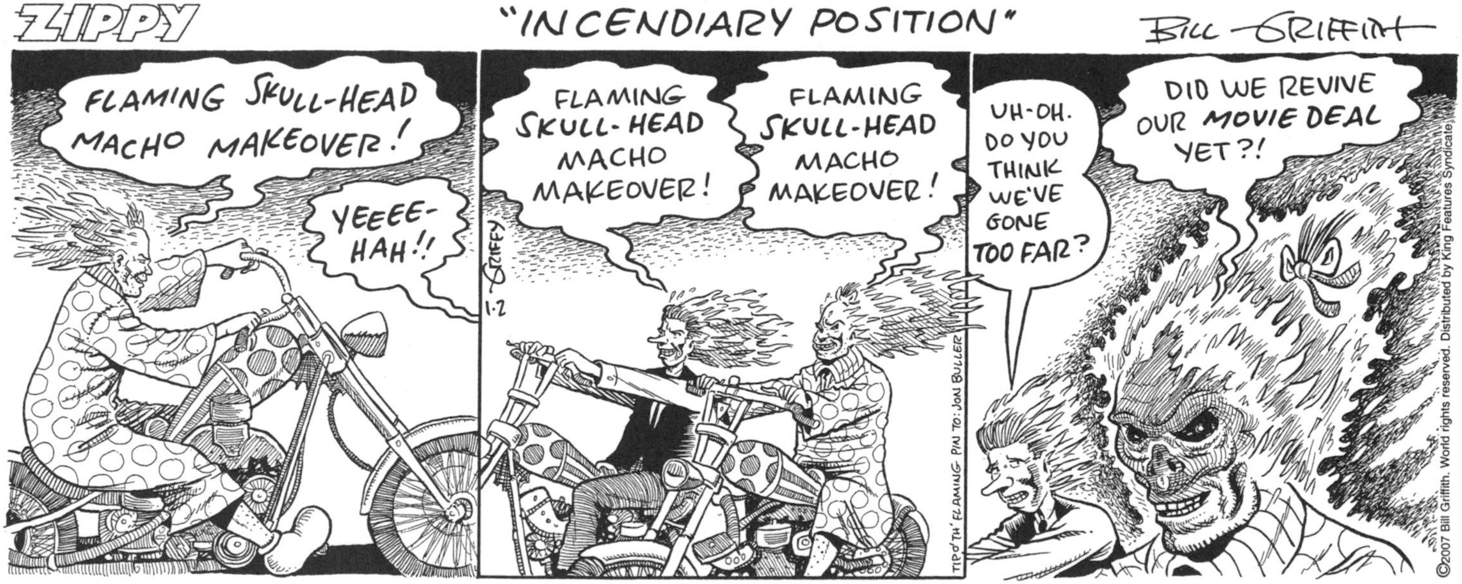
ZIPPY
"INCENDIARY POSITION"
BILL GRIFFITH
FLAMING SKULL-HEAD MACHO MAKEOVER!
YEEEE-HAH!!
GRIFFY 1-2
FLAMING SKULL-HEAD MACHO MAKEOVER!
FLAMING SKULL-HEAD MACHO MAKEOVER!
TIP O' TH' FLAMING PIN TO: JON BULLER
UH-OH. DO YOU THINK WE'VE GONE TOO FAR?
DID WE REVIVE OUR MOVIE DEAL YET?!
©2007 Bill Griffith. World rights reserved. Distributed by King Features Syndicate

195

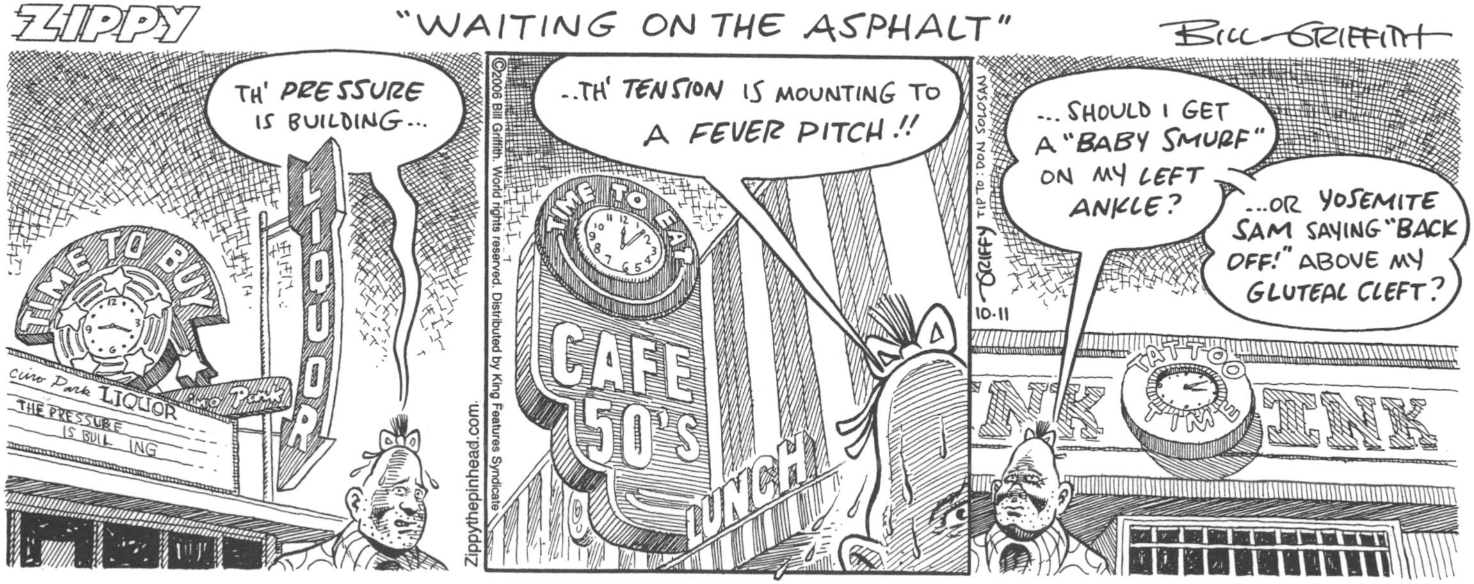
ZIPPY
"WAITING ON THE ASPHALT"
BILL GRIFFITH
TH' PRESSURE IS BUILDING...
TIME TO BUY
LIQUOR
THE PRESSURE IS BUIL ING
..TH' TENSION IS MOUNTING TO A FEVER PITCH!!
©2006 Bill Griffith. World rights reserved. Distributed by King Features Syndicate
Zippythepinhead.com
TIME TO EAT
CAFE 50'S
LUNCH
...SHOULD I GET A "BABY SMURF" ON MY LEFT ANKLE?
...OR YOSEMITE SAM SAYING "BACK OFF!" ABOVE MY GLUTEAL CLEFT?
GRIFFY TIP TO: DON SOLOSAN
10-11
TATTOO TIME
INK

196

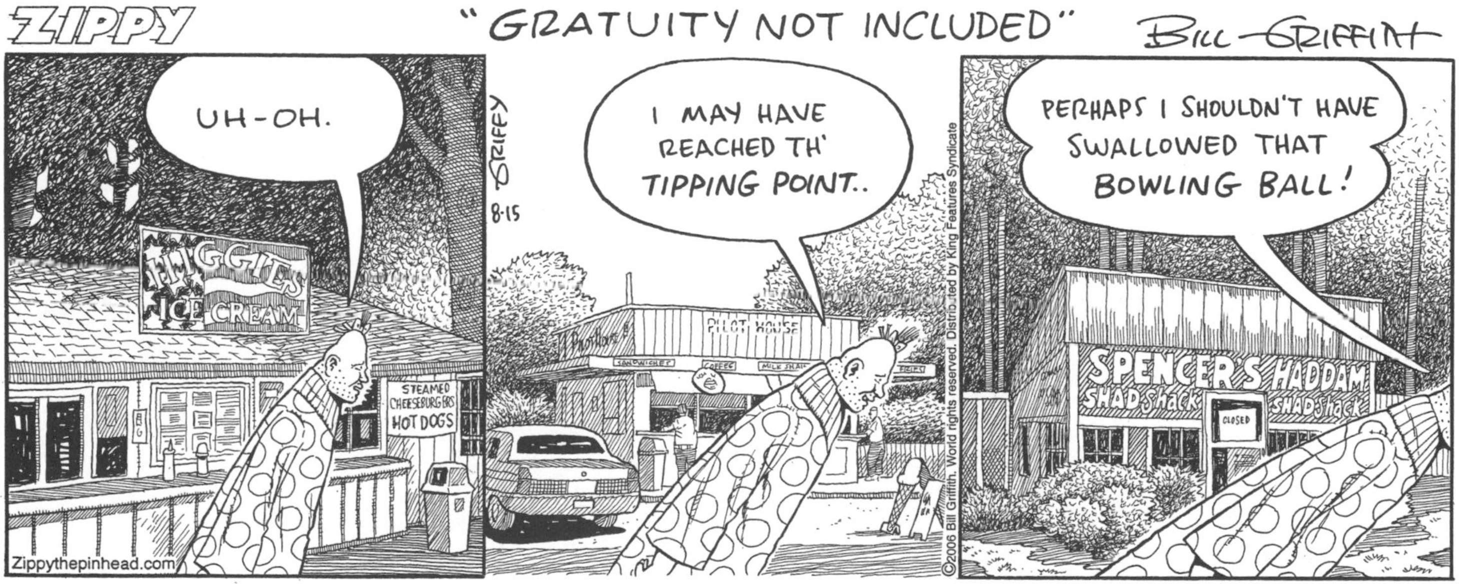
ZIPPY
"GRATUITY NOT INCLUDED"
BILL GRIFFITH
UH-OH.
ICE CREAM
STEAMED CHEESEBURGERS HOT DOGS
Zippythepinhead.com
GRIFFY
8-15
I MAY HAVE REACHED TH' TIPPING POINT..
PILOT HOUSE
PERHAPS I SHOULDN'T HAVE SWALLOWED THAT BOWLING BALL!
©2006 Bill Griffith. World rights reserved. Distributed by King Features Syndicate
SPENCER'S HADDAM SHAD SHACK
CLOSED

197

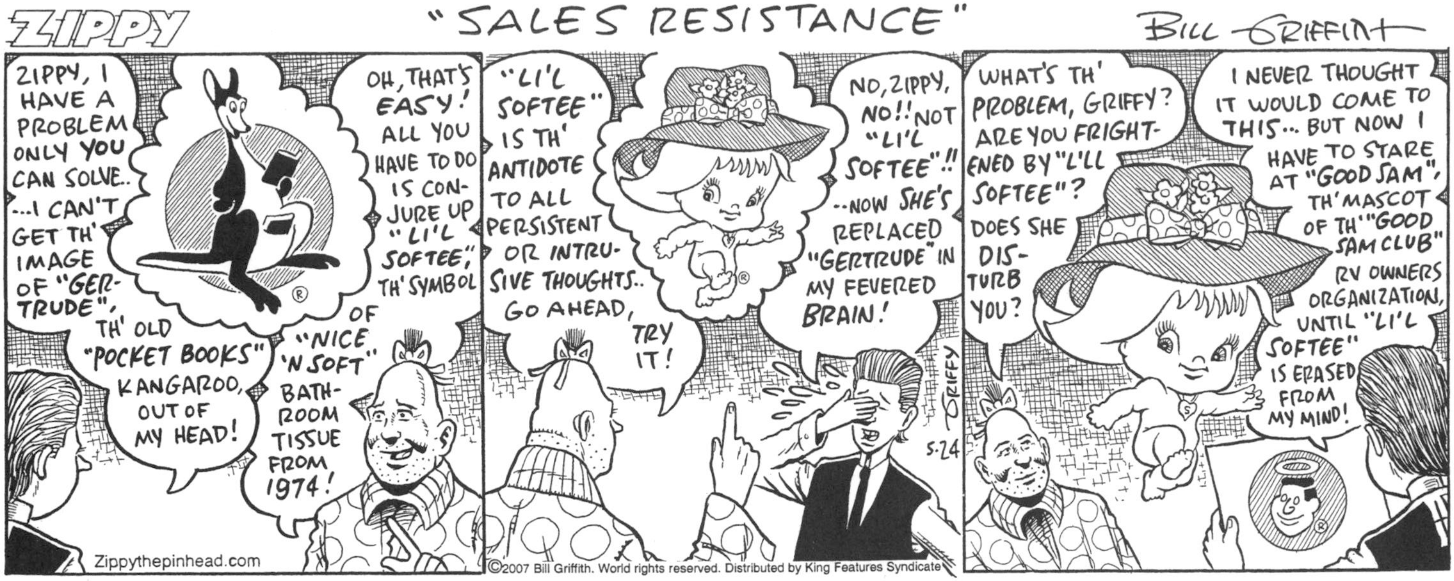
ZIPPY
"SALES RESISTANCE"
BILL GRIFFITH
ZIPPY, I HAVE A PROBLEM ONLY YOU CAN SOLVE.. ...I CAN'T GET TH' IMAGE OF "GERTRUDE", TH' OLD "POCKET BOOKS" KANGAROO, OUT OF MY HEAD!
OH, THAT'S EASY! ALL YOU HAVE TO DO IS CONJURE UP "LI'L SOFTEE", TH' SYMBOL OF "NICE 'N SOFT" BATHROOM TISSUE FROM 1974!
"LI'L SOFTEE" IS TH' ANTIDOTE TO ALL PERSISTENT OR INTRUSIVE THOUGHTS.. GO AHEAD, TRY IT!
NO, ZIPPY, NO!! NOT "LI'L SOFTEE"!! ..NOW SHE'S REPLACED "GERTRUDE" IN MY FEVERED BRAIN!
GRIFFY
5.24
WHAT'S TH' PROBLEM, GRIFFY? ARE YOU FRIGHTENED BY "L'LL SOFTEE"? DOES SHE DISTURB YOU?
I NEVER THOUGHT IT WOULD COME TO THIS... BUT NOW I HAVE TO STARE AT "GOOD SAM", TH' MASCOT OF TH' "GOOD SAM CLUB" RV OWNERS ORGANIZATION, UNTIL "LI'L SOFTEE" IS ERASED FROM MY MIND!
Zippythepinhead.com
©2007 Bill Griffith. World rights reserved. Distributed by King Features Syndicate

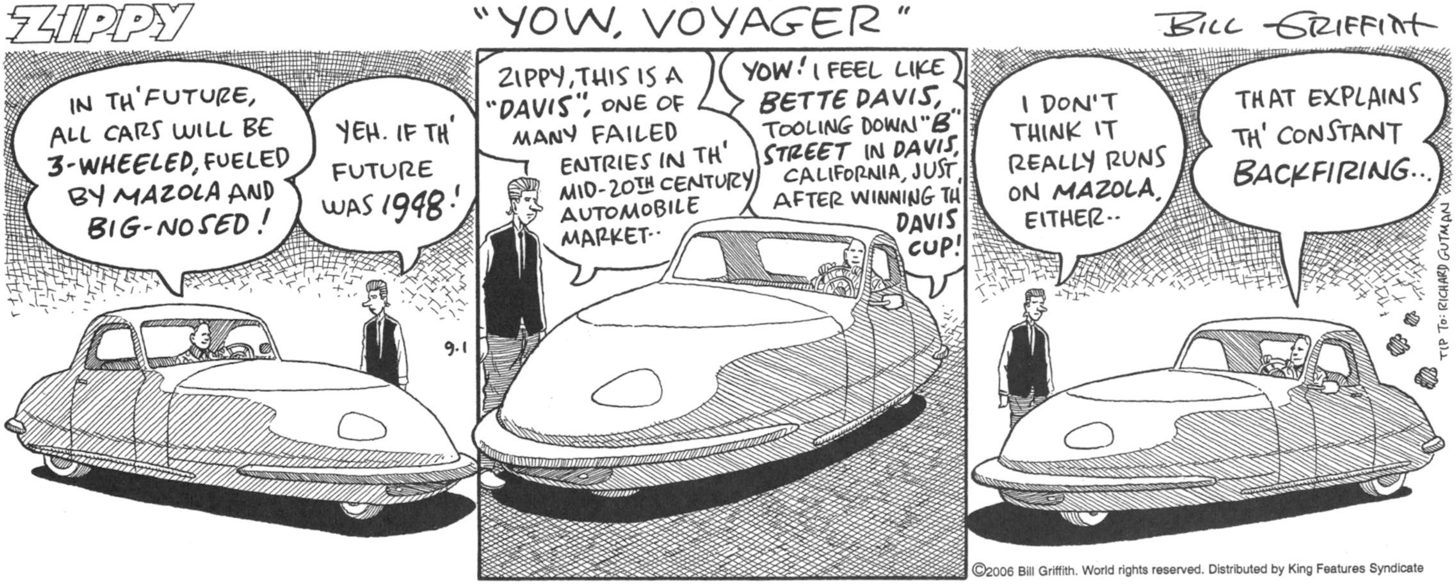
ZIPPY
"YOW, VOYAGER"
BILL GRIFFITH
IN TH' FUTURE, ALL CARS WILL BE 3-WHEELED, FUELED BY MAZOLA AND BIG-NOSED!
YEH. IF TH' FUTURE WAS 1948!
9.1
ZIPPY, THIS IS A "DAVIS", ONE OF MANY FAILED ENTRIES IN TH' MID-20TH CENTURY AUTOMOBILE MARKET..
YOW! I FEEL LIKE BETTE DAVIS, TOOLING DOWN "B" STREET IN DAVIS, CALIFORNIA, JUST AFTER WINNING TH DAVIS CUP!
I DON'T THINK IT REALLY RUNS ON MAZOLA, EITHER..
THAT EXPLAINS TH' CONSTANT BACKFIRING...
TIP TO: RICHARD GUTMAN
©2006 Bill Griffith. World rights reserved. Distributed by King Features Syndicate

198

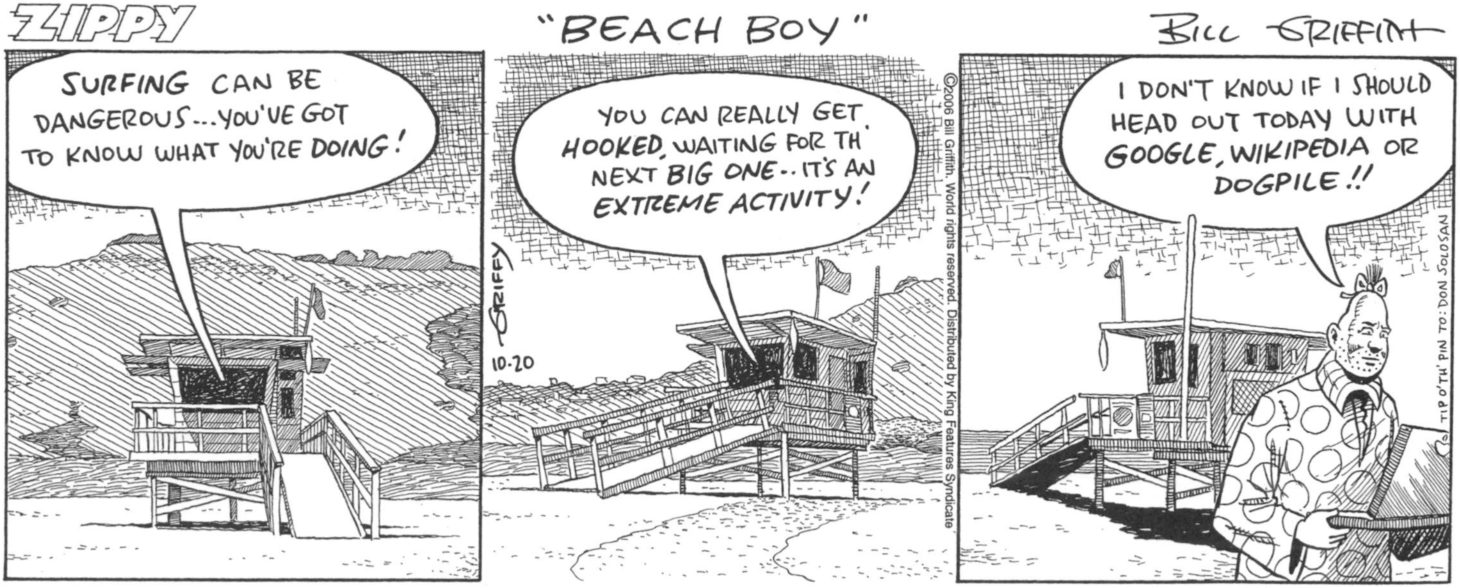
ZIPPY
"BEACH BOY"
BILL GRIFFITH
SURFING CAN BE DANGEROUS...YOU'VE GOT TO KNOW WHAT YOU'RE DOING!
YOU CAN REALLY GET HOOKED, WAITING FOR TH' NEXT BIG ONE.. IT'S AN EXTREME ACTIVITY!
GRIFFY 10-20
©2006 Bill Griffith. World rights reserved. Distributed by King Features Syndicate
I DON'T KNOW IF I SHOULD HEAD OUT TODAY WITH GOOGLE, WIKIPEDIA OR DOGPILE!!
TIP O'TH' PIN TO: DON SOLOSAN

199

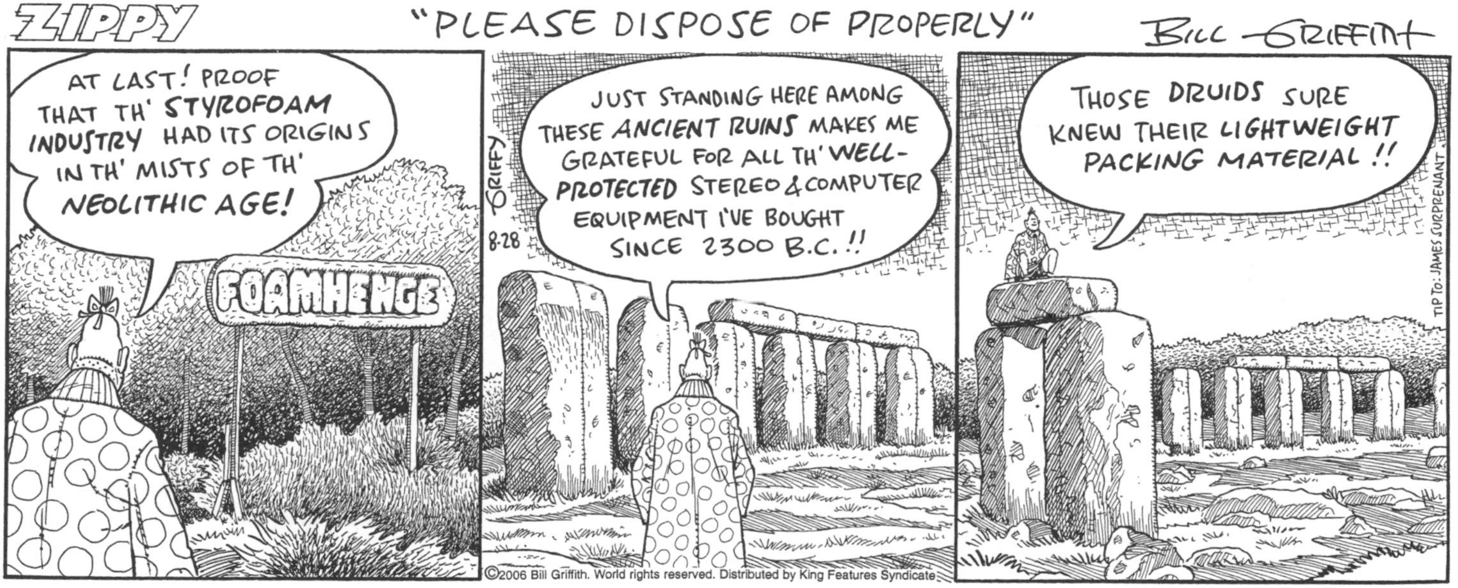
ZIPPY
"PLEASE DISPOSE OF PROPERLY"
BILL GRIFFITH
AT LAST! PROOF THAT TH' STYROFOAM INDUSTRY HAD ITS ORIGINS IN TH' MISTS OF TH' NEOLITHIC AGE!
FOAMHENGE
GRIFFY 8-28
JUST STANDING HERE AMONG THESE ANCIENT RUINS MAKES ME GRATEFUL FOR ALL TH' WELL-PROTECTED STEREO & COMPUTER EQUIPMENT I'VE BOUGHT SINCE 2300 B.C.!!
©2006 Bill Griffith. World rights reserved. Distributed by King Features Syndicate
THOSE DRUIDS SURE KNEW THEIR LIGHTWEIGHT PACKING MATERIAL!!
TIP TO: JAMES SURPRENANT

200

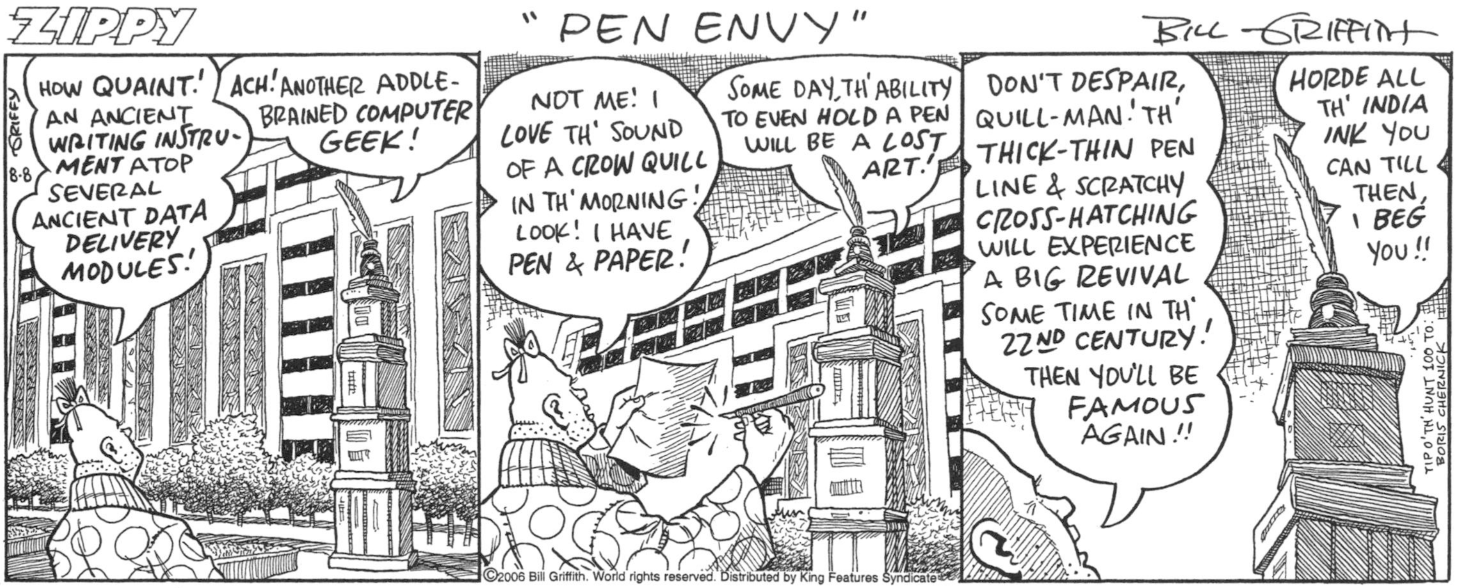
ZIPPY
"PEN ENVY"
BILL GRIFFITH
GRIFFY
8·8
HOW QUAINT! AN ANCIENT WRITING INSTRU-MENT ATOP SEVERAL ANCIENT DATA DELIVERY MODULES!
ACH! ANOTHER ADDLE-BRAINED COMPUTER GEEK!
NOT ME! I LOVE TH' SOUND OF A CROW QUILL IN TH' MORNING! LOOK! I HAVE PEN & PAPER!
SOME DAY, TH' ABILITY TO EVEN HOLD A PEN WILL BE A LOST ART!
DON'T DESPAIR, QUILL-MAN! TH' THICK-THIN PEN LINE & SCRATCHY CROSS-HATCHING WILL EXPERIENCE A BIG REVIVAL SOME TIME IN TH' 22ND CENTURY! THEN YOU'LL BE FAMOUS AGAIN!!
HORDE ALL TH' INDIA INK YOU CAN TILL THEN, I BEG YOU!!
TIP O' TH' HUNT 100 TO: BORIS CHERNICK
©2006 Bill Griffith. World rights reserved. Distributed by King Features Syndicate

201

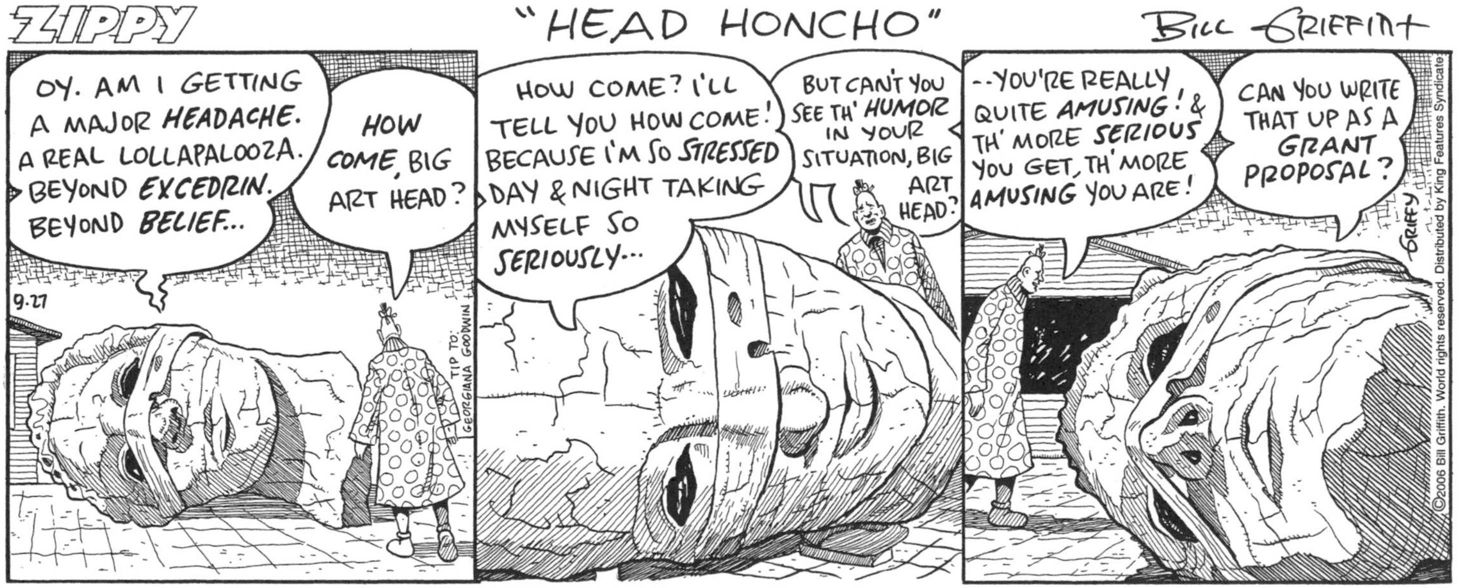
ZIPPY
"HEAD HONCHO"
BILL GRIFFITH
OY. AM I GETTING A MAJOR HEADACHE. A REAL LOLLAPALOOZA. BEYOND EXCEDRIN. BEYOND BELIEF...
HOW COME, BIG ART HEAD?
9·27
TIP TO: GEORGIANA GOODWIN
HOW COME? I'LL TELL YOU HOW COME! BECAUSE I'M SO STRESSED DAY & NIGHT TAKING MYSELF SO SERIOUSLY...
BUT CAN'T YOU SEE TH' HUMOR IN YOUR SITUATION, BIG ART HEAD?
--YOU'RE REALLY QUITE AMUSING! & TH' MORE SERIOUS YOU GET, TH' MORE AMUSING YOU ARE!
CAN YOU WRITE THAT UP AS A GRANT PROPOSAL?
GRIFFY
©2006 Bill Griffith. World rights reserved. Distributed by King Features Syndicate

202

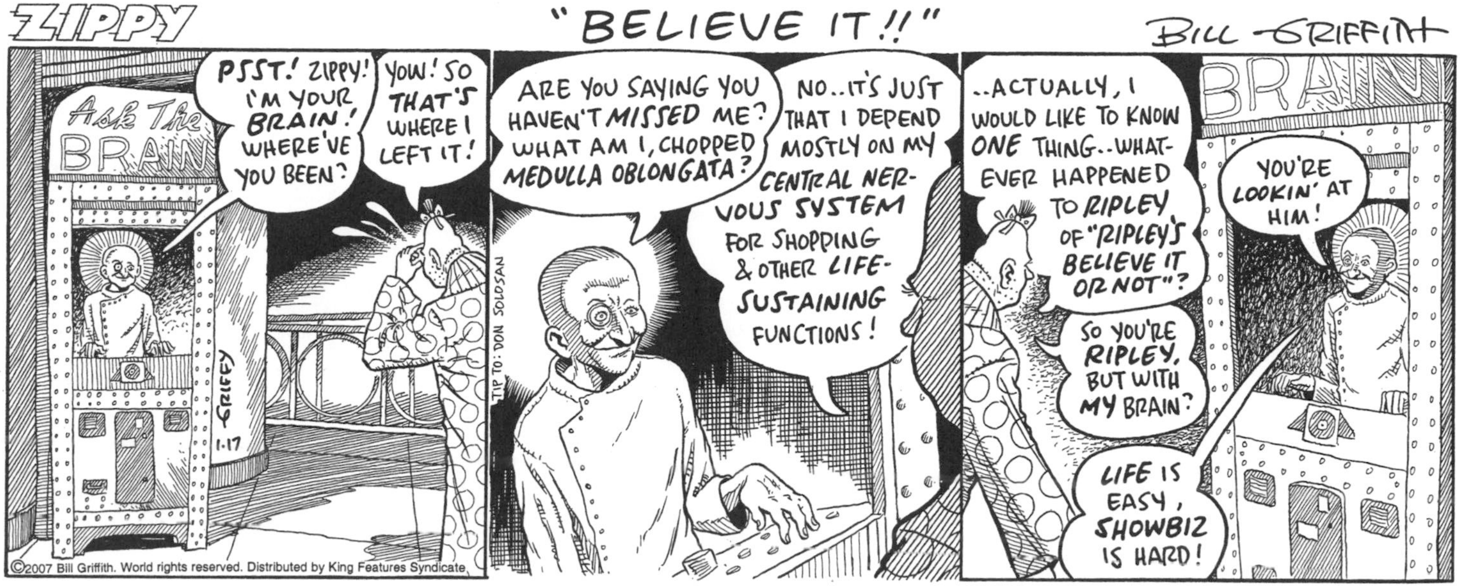
ZIPPY
"BELIEVE IT!!"
BILL GRIFFITH
Ask The BRAIN
PSST! ZIPPY! I'M YOUR BRAIN! WHERE'VE YOU BEEN?
YOW! SO THAT'S WHERE I LEFT IT!
GRIFFY 1-17
ARE YOU SAYING YOU HAVEN'T MISSED ME? WHAT AM I, CHOPPED MEDULLA OBLONGATA?
NO.. IT'S JUST THAT I DEPEND MOSTLY ON MY CENTRAL NERVOUS SYSTEM FOR SHOPPING & OTHER LIFE-SUSTAINING FUNCTIONS!
TIP TO: DON SOLOSAN
..ACTUALLY, I WOULD LIKE TO KNOW ONE THING.. WHATEVER HAPPENED TO RIPLEY OF "RIPLEY'S BELIEVE IT OR NOT"?
BRAIN
YOU'RE LOOKIN' AT HIM!
SO YOU'RE RIPLEY, BUT WITH MY BRAIN?
LIFE IS EASY, SHOWBIZ IS HARD!
©2007 Bill Griffith. World rights reserved. Distributed by King Features Syndicate

203

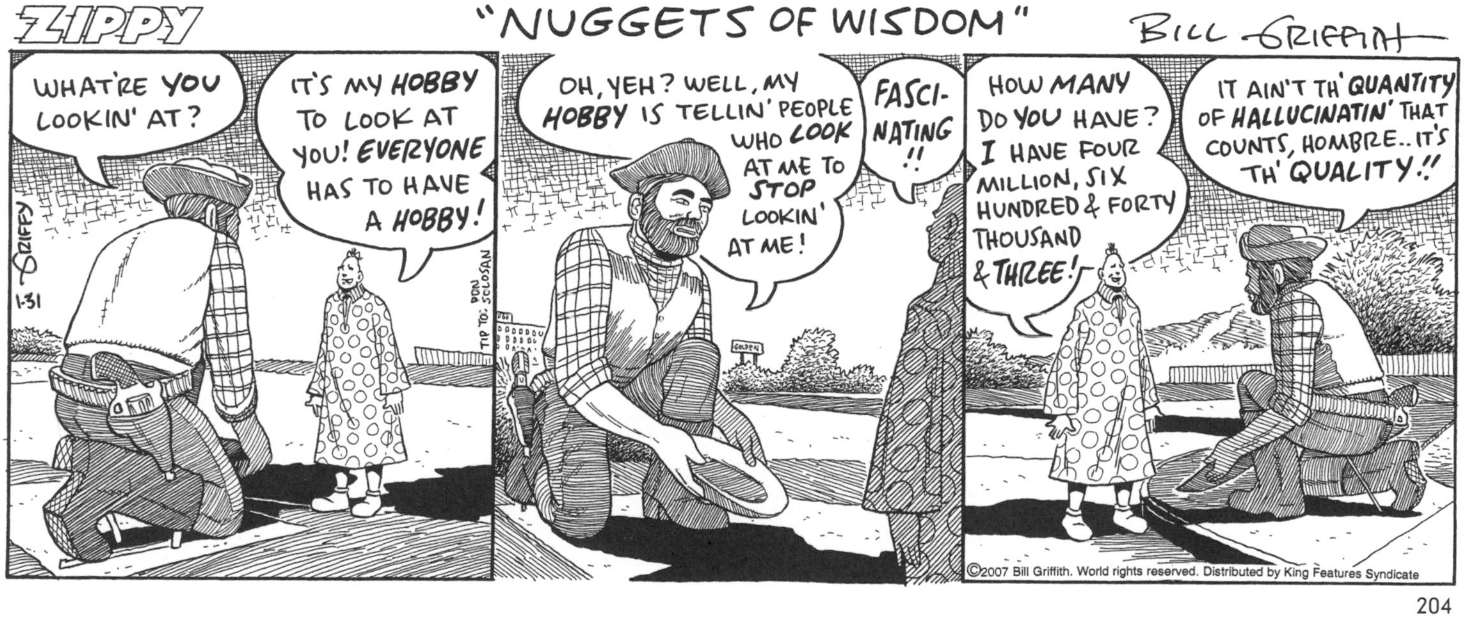
ZIPPY
"NUGGETS OF WISDOM"
BILL GRIFFITH
WHAT'RE YOU LOOKIN' AT?
IT'S MY HOBBY TO LOOK AT YOU! EVERYONE HAS TO HAVE A HOBBY!
GRIFFY 1-31
TIP TO: DON SOLOSAN
OH, YEH? WELL, MY HOBBY IS TELLIN' PEOPLE WHO LOOK AT ME TO STOP LOOKIN' AT ME!
FASCINATING!!
HOW MANY DO YOU HAVE? I HAVE FOUR MILLION, SIX HUNDRED & FORTY THOUSAND & THREE!
IT AIN'T TH' QUANTITY OF HALLUCINATIN' THAT COUNTS, HOMBRE.. IT'S TH' QUALITY!!
©2007 Bill Griffith. World rights reserved. Distributed by King Features Syndicate

204

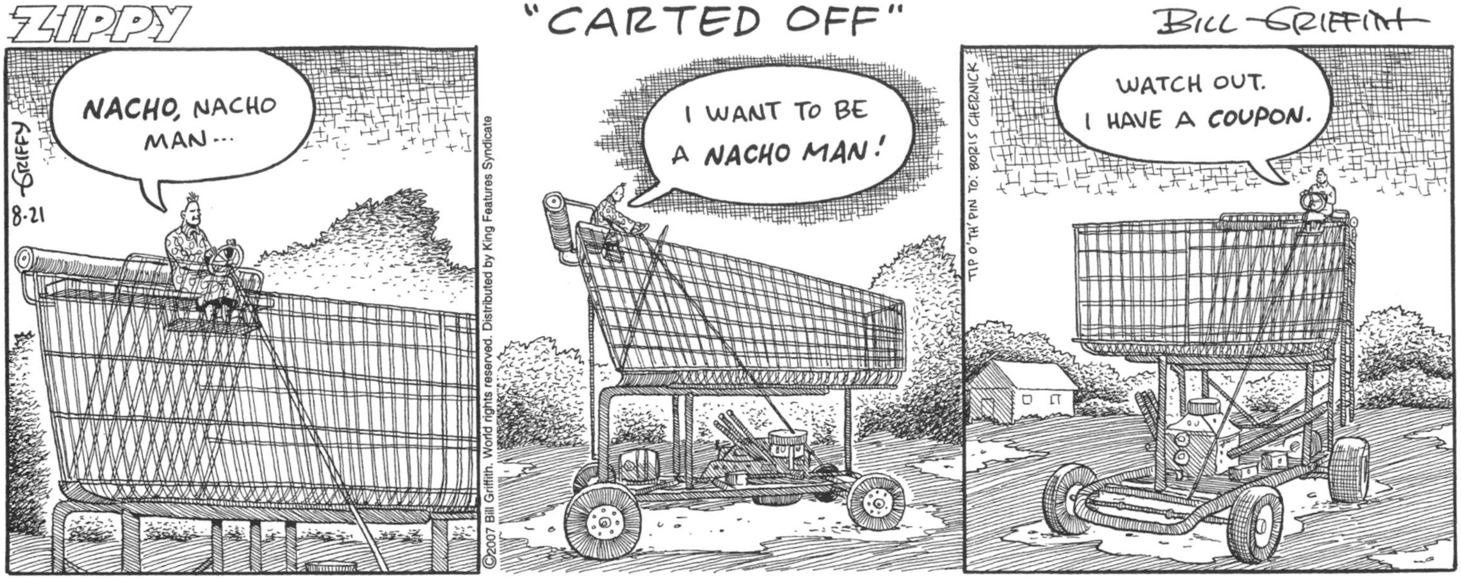
ZIPPY
"CARTED OFF"
BILL GRIFFITH
NACHO, NACHO MAN...
GRIFFY 8-21
©2007 Bill Griffith. World rights reserved. Distributed by King Features Syndicate
I WANT TO BE A NACHO MAN!
TIP O' TH' PIN TO: BORIS CHERNICK
WATCH OUT. I HAVE A COUPON.

205

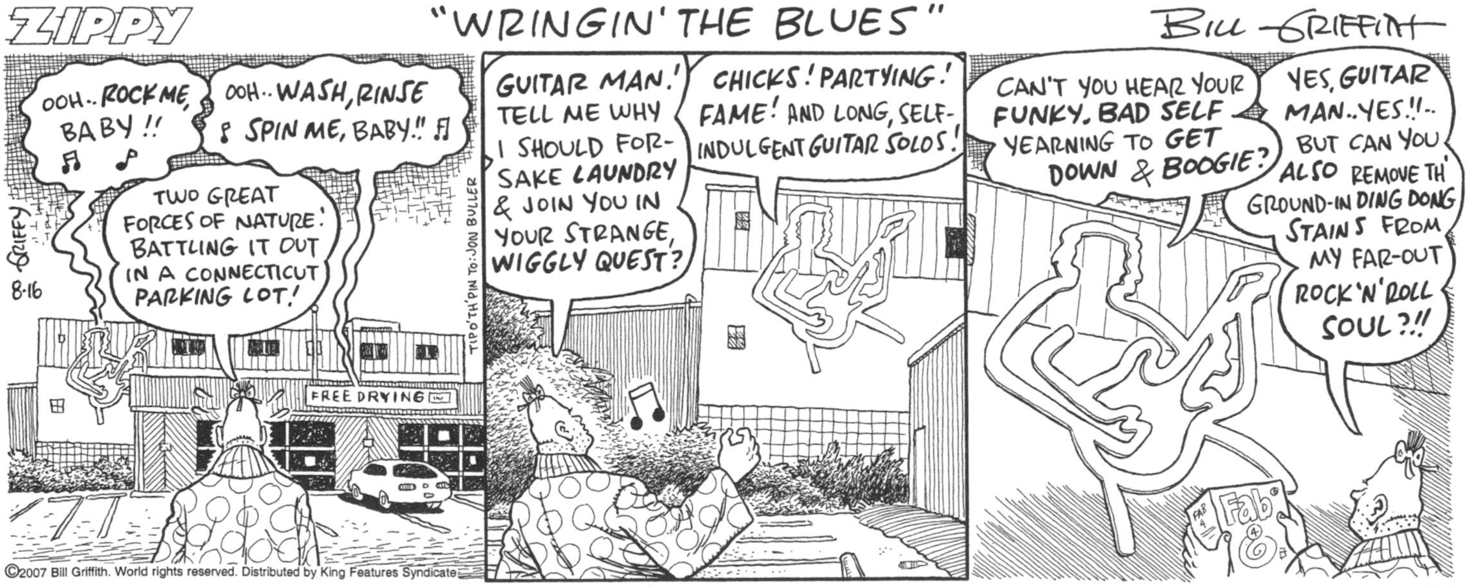
ZIPPY
"WRINGIN' THE BLUES"
BILL GRIFFITH
OOH.. ROCK ME, BABY!!
OOH.. WASH, RINSE SPIN ME, BABY!!
TWO GREAT FORCES OF NATURE! BATTLING IT OUT IN A CONNECTICUT PARKING LOT!
GRIFFY 8-16
FREE DRYING
TIP O' TH' PIN TO: JON BULLER
©2007 Bill Griffith. World rights reserved. Distributed by King Features Syndicate
GUITAR MAN! TELL ME WHY I SHOULD FORSAKE LAUNDRY & JOIN YOU IN YOUR STRANGE, WIGGLY QUEST?
CHICKS! PARTYING! FAME! AND LONG, SELF-INDULGENT GUITAR SOLOS!
CAN'T YOU HEAR YOUR FUNKY, BAD SELF YEARNING TO GET DOWN & BOOGIE?
YES, GUITAR MAN.. YES!!.. BUT CAN YOU ALSO REMOVE TH' GROUND-IN DING DONG STAINS FROM MY FAR-OUT ROCK 'N' ROLL SOUL?!!
FAB 4
Fab 4

206

COMICAL SITUATIONS

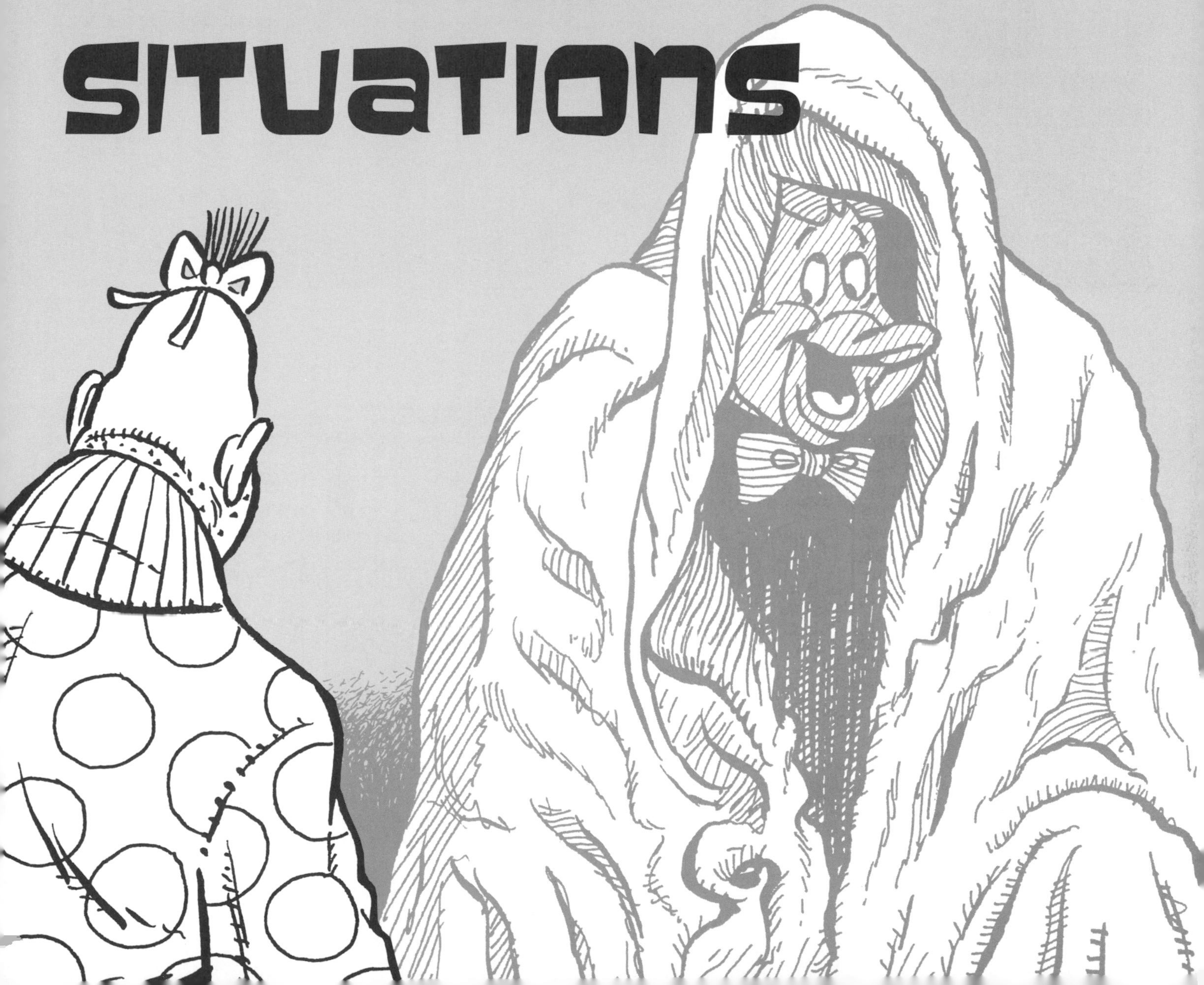

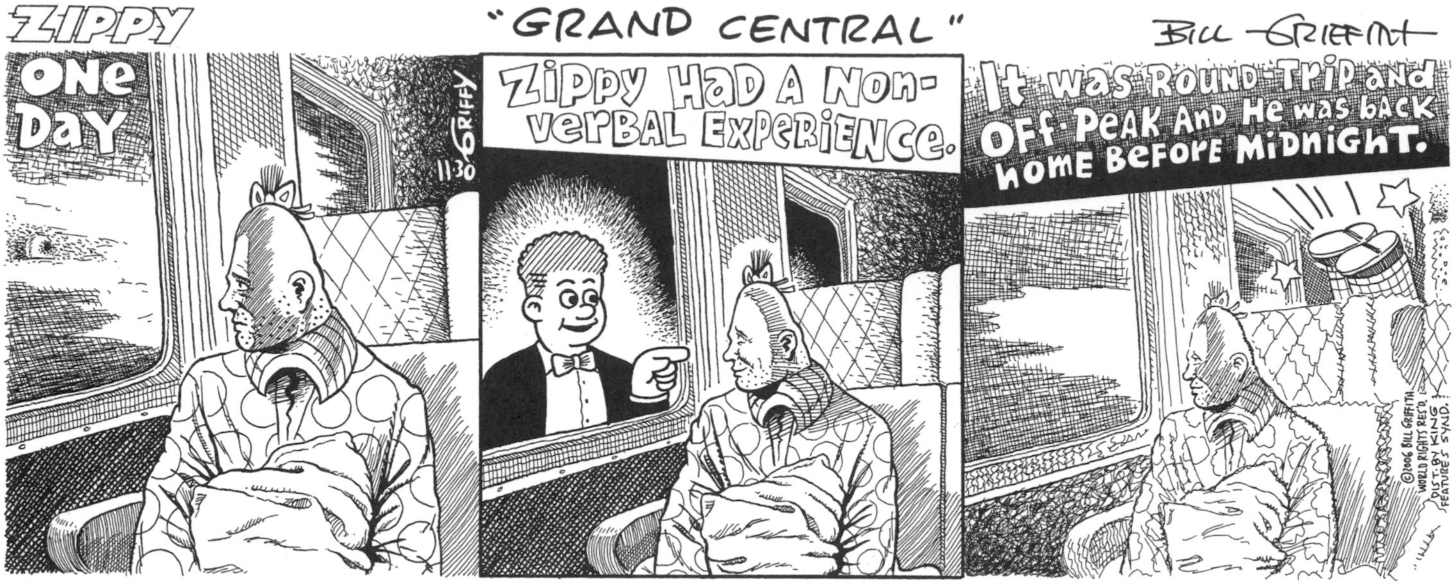
ZIPPY
"GRAND CENTRAL"
BILL GRIFFITH
ONE DAY
GRIFFY 11-30
ZIPPY HAD A NON-VERBAL EXPERIENCE.
IT WAS ROUND-TRIP AND OFF-PEAK AND HE WAS BACK HOME BEFORE MIDNIGHT.
©2006 BILL GRIFFITH WORLD RIGHTS RES'D. DIST. BY KING FEATURES SYND.

207

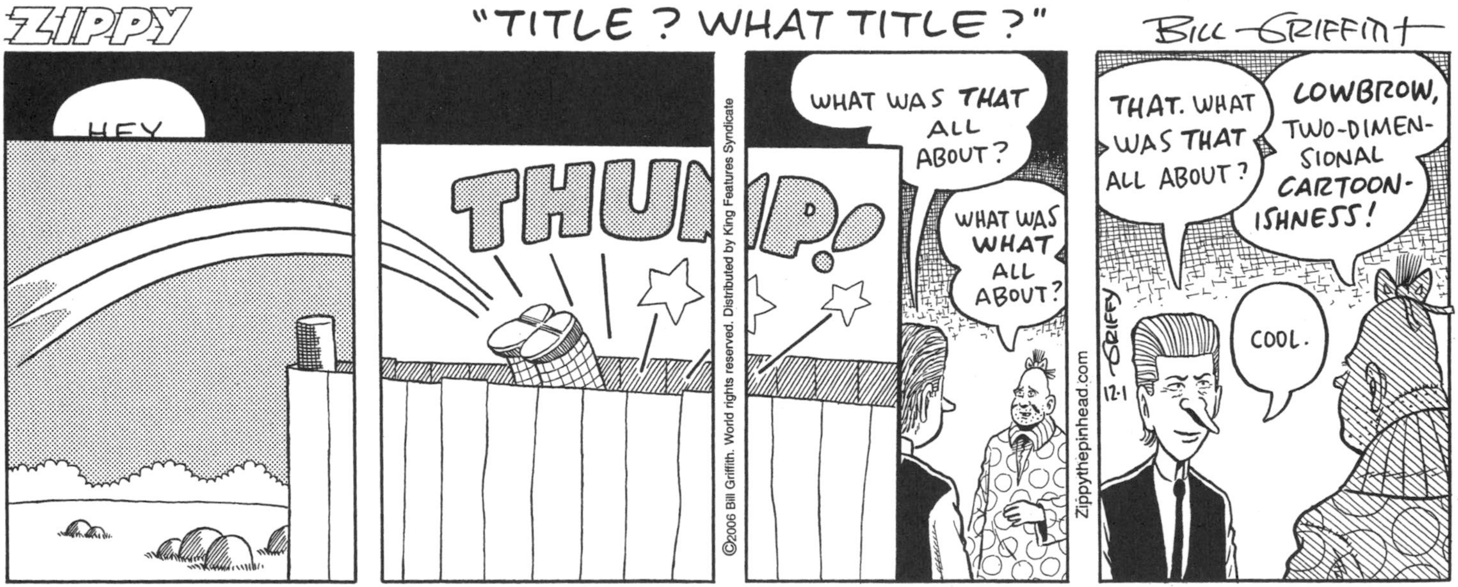
ZIPPY
"TITLE? WHAT TITLE?"
BILL GRIFFITH
HEY
THUMP!
©2006 Bill Griffith. World rights reserved. Distributed by King Features Syndicate
WHAT WAS THAT ALL ABOUT?
WHAT WAS WHAT ALL ABOUT?
Zippythepinhead.com
GRIFFY 12-1
THAT. WHAT WAS THAT ALL ABOUT?
LOWBROW, TWO-DIMENSIONAL CARTOONISHNESS!
COOL.

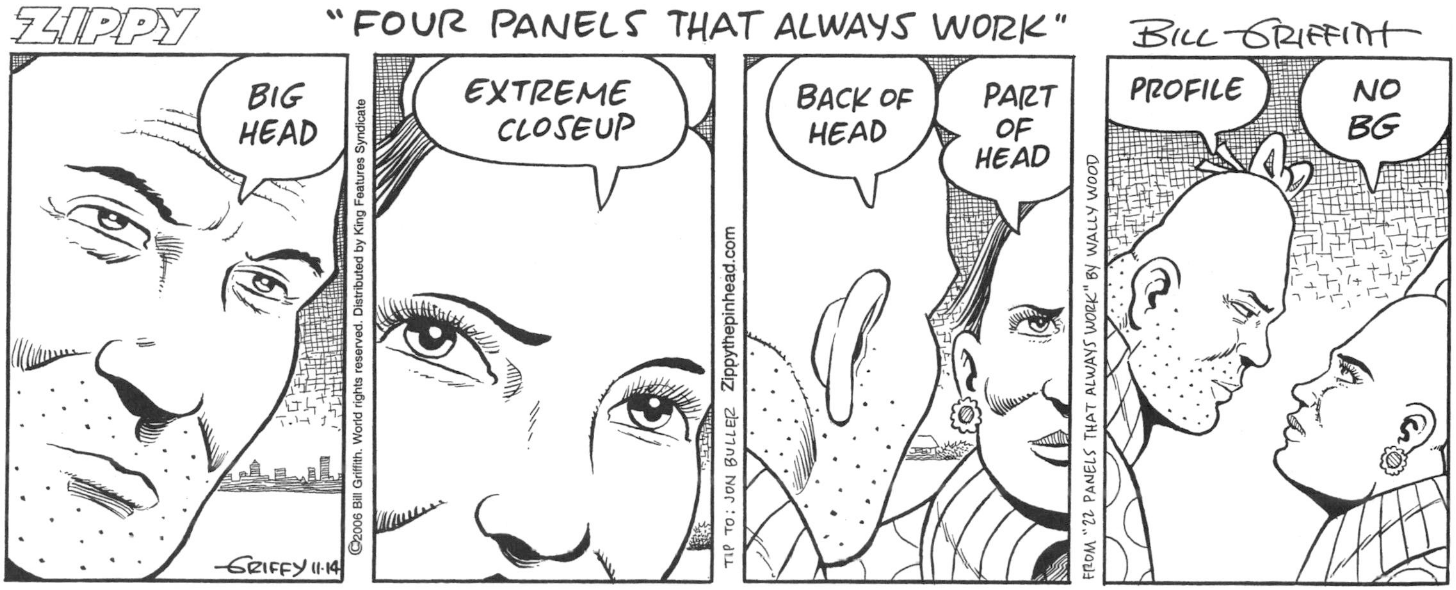
ZIPPY
"FOUR PANELS THAT ALWAYS WORK"
BILL GRIFFITH
BIG HEAD
GRIFFY 11-14
©2006 Bill Griffith. World rights reserved. Distributed by King Features Syndicate
EXTREME CLOSEUP
TIP TO: JON BULLER
Zippythepinhead.com
BACK OF HEAD
PART OF HEAD
FROM "22 PANELS THAT ALWAYS WORK" BY WALLY WOOD
PROFILE
NO BG

208

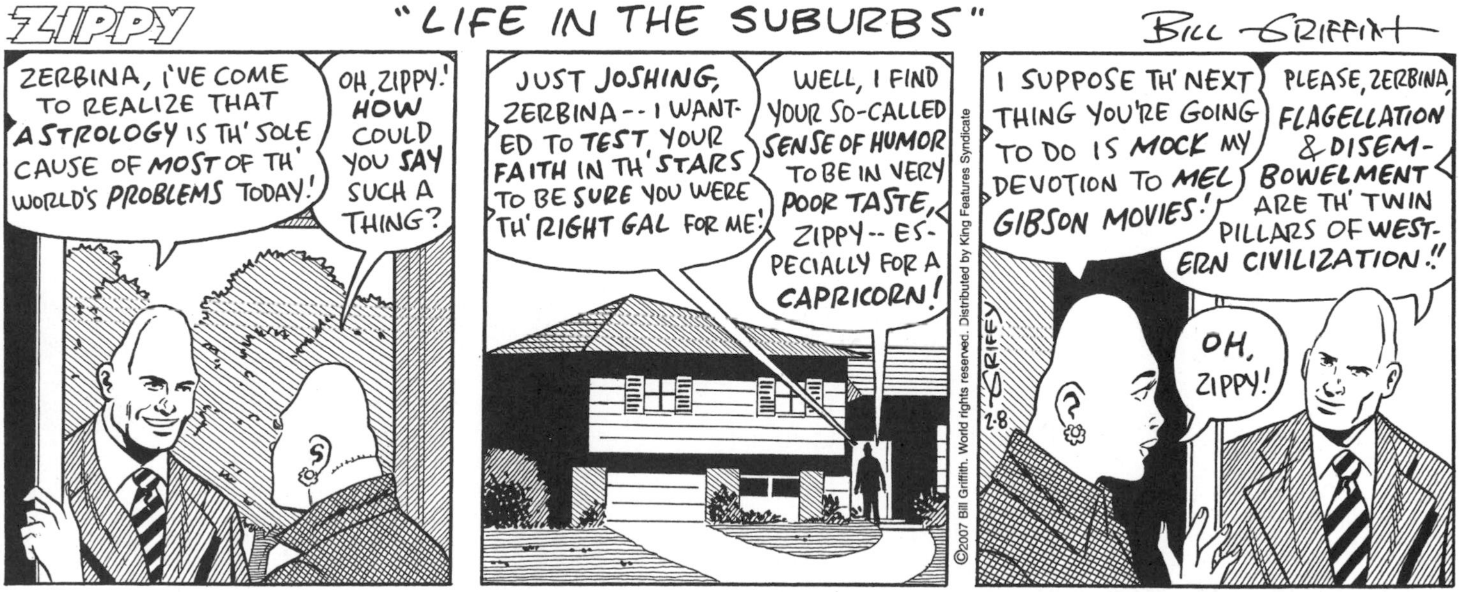
ZIPPY
"LIFE IN THE SUBURBS"
BILL GRIFFITH
ZERBINA, I'VE COME TO REALIZE THAT ASTROLOGY IS TH' SOLE CAUSE OF MOST OF TH' WORLD'S PROBLEMS TODAY!
OH, ZIPPY! HOW COULD YOU SAY SUCH A THING?
JUST JOSHING, ZERBINA -- I WANTED TO TEST YOUR FAITH IN TH' STARS TO BE SURE YOU WERE TH' RIGHT GAL FOR ME!
WELL, I FIND YOUR SO-CALLED SENSE OF HUMOR TO BE IN VERY POOR TASTE, ZIPPY -- ESPECIALLY FOR A CAPRICORN!
©2007 Bill Griffith. World rights reserved. Distributed by King Features Syndicate
GRIFFY 2-8
I SUPPOSE TH' NEXT THING YOU'RE GOING TO DO IS MOCK MY DEVOTION TO MEL GIBSON MOVIES!
PLEASE, ZERBINA, FLAGELLATION & DISEMBOWELMENT ARE TH' TWIN PILLARS OF WESTERN CIVILIZATION!!
OH, ZIPPY!

ZIPPY "THE CURVATURE OF OFFICE SPACE" BILL GRIFFITH

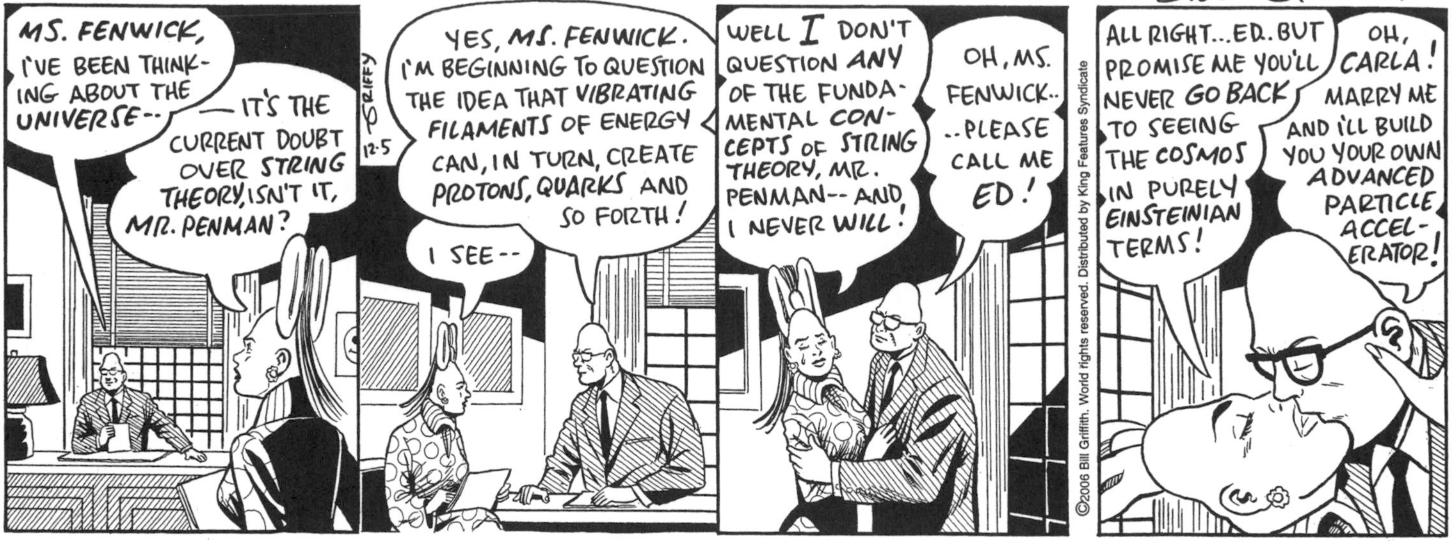
MS. FENWICK, I'VE BEEN THINKING ABOUT THE UNIVERSE--
—IT'S THE CURRENT DOUBT OVER STRING THEORY, ISN'T IT, MR. PENMAN?
YES, MS. FENWICK. I'M BEGINNING TO QUESTION THE IDEA THAT VIBRATING FILAMENTS OF ENERGY CAN, IN TURN, CREATE PROTONS, QUARKS AND SO FORTH!
I SEE--
GRIFFY 12·5
WELL I DON'T QUESTION ANY OF THE FUNDAMENTAL CONCEPTS OF STRING THEORY, MR. PENMAN-- AND I NEVER WILL!
OH, MS. FENWICK.. ..PLEASE CALL ME ED!
ALL RIGHT...ED..BUT PROMISE ME YOU'LL NEVER GO BACK TO SEEING THE COSMOS IN PURELY EINSTEINIAN TERMS!
OH, CARLA! MARRY ME AND I'LL BUILD YOU YOUR OWN ADVANCED PARTICLE ACCELERATOR!

ZIPPY "LEAPING FOR LEPTONS" BILL GRIFFITH

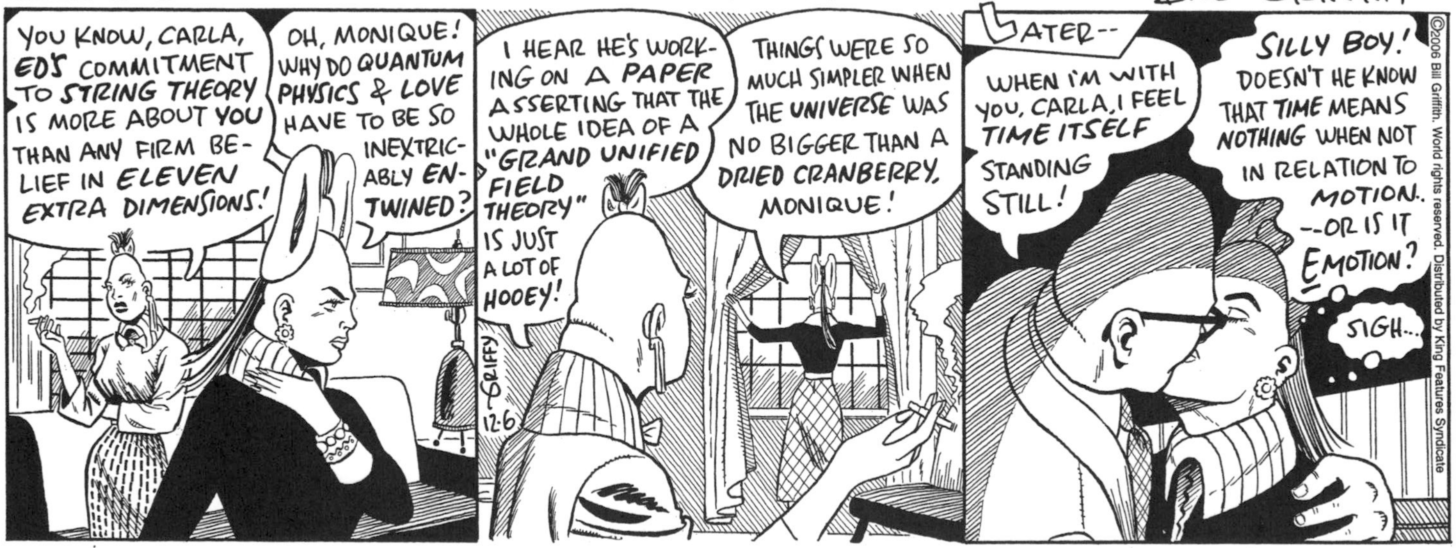
YOU KNOW, CARLA, ED'S COMMITMENT TO STRING THEORY IS MORE ABOUT YOU THAN ANY FIRM BELIEF IN ELEVEN EXTRA DIMENSIONS!
OH, MONIQUE! WHY DO QUANTUM PHYSICS & LOVE HAVE TO BE SO INEXTRICABLY ENTWINED?
I HEAR HE'S WORKING ON A PAPER ASSERTING THAT THE WHOLE IDEA OF A "GRAND UNIFIED FIELD THEORY" IS JUST A LOT OF HOOEY!
GRIFFY 12·6
THINGS WERE SO MUCH SIMPLER WHEN THE UNIVERSE WAS NO BIGGER THAN A DRIED CRANBERRY, MONIQUE!
LATER--
WHEN I'M WITH YOU, CARLA, I FEEL TIME ITSELF STANDING STILL!
SILLY BOY! DOESN'T HE KNOW THAT TIME MEANS NOTHING WHEN NOT IN RELATION TO MOTION.. --OR IS IT EMOTION?
SIGH...

ZIPPY "LEAVE IT TO BONEHEAD" BILL GRIFFITH

Uh-oh...Today's **dialogue balloons** have been mysteriously **replaced**. Let's hope this condition is **temporary**.

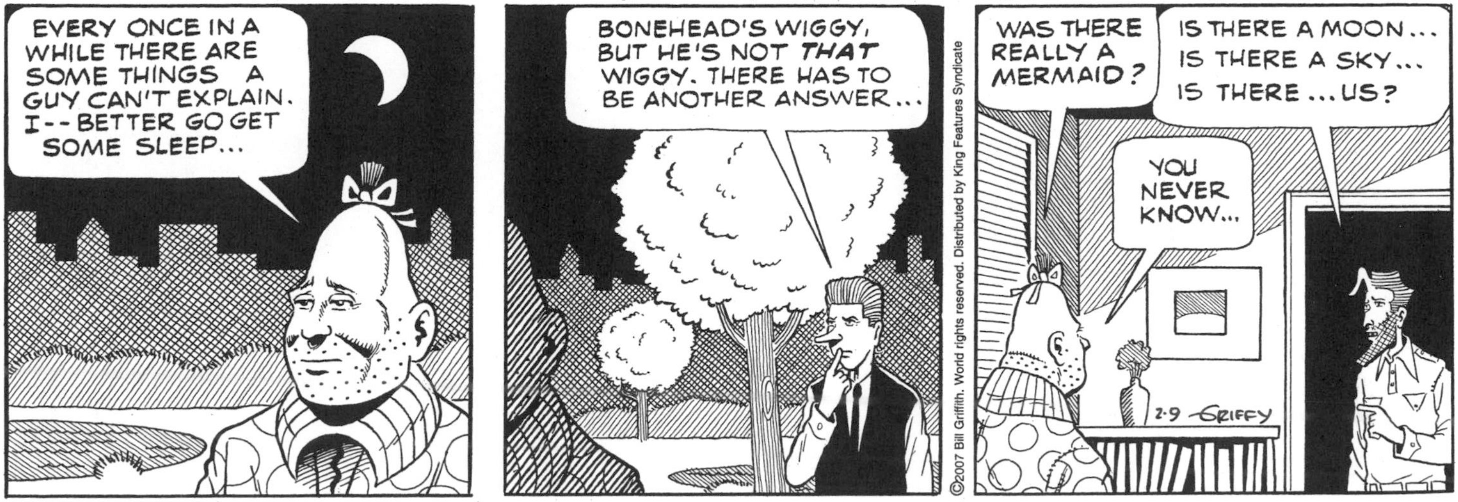
EVERY ONCE IN A WHILE THERE ARE SOME THINGS A GUY CAN'T EXPLAIN. I-- BETTER GO GET SOME SLEEP...
BONEHEAD'S WIGGY, BUT HE'S NOT THAT WIGGY. THERE HAS TO BE ANOTHER ANSWER...
©2007 Bill Griffith. World rights reserved. Distributed by King Features Syndicate
WAS THERE REALLY A MERMAID?
IS THERE A MOON... IS THERE A SKY... IS THERE... US?
YOU NEVER KNOW...
2·9 GRIFFY

209

ZIPPY "SO YOU WANT TO BE AN ELECTRICIAN" BILL GRIFFITH

Oh, no! It's happened again. Zippy's **"normal"** dialogue has been **usurped** by some unexplained **interloper**.

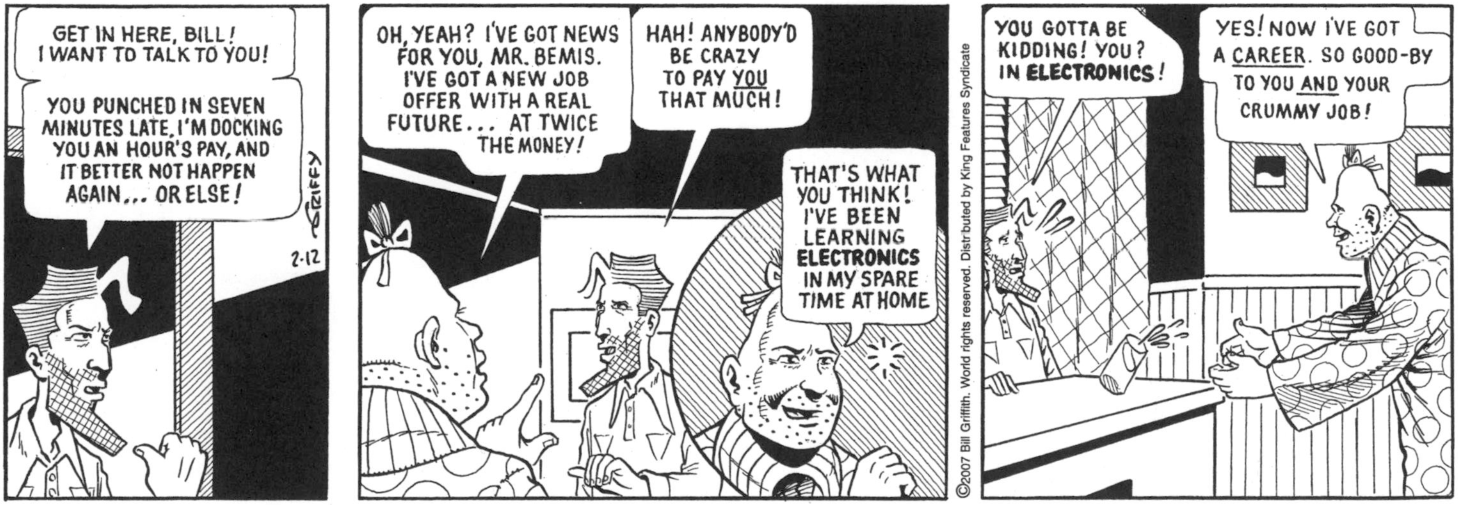
GET IN HERE, BILL! I WANT TO TALK TO YOU!
YOU PUNCHED IN SEVEN MINUTES LATE, I'M DOCKING YOU AN HOUR'S PAY, AND IT BETTER NOT HAPPEN AGAIN... OR ELSE!
GRIFFY
2·12
OH, YEAH? I'VE GOT NEWS FOR YOU, MR. BEMIS. I'VE GOT A NEW JOB OFFER WITH A REAL FUTURE... AT TWICE THE MONEY!
HAH! ANYBODY'D BE CRAZY TO PAY YOU THAT MUCH!
THAT'S WHAT YOU THINK! I'VE BEEN LEARNING ELECTRONICS IN MY SPARE TIME AT HOME
©2007 Bill Griffith. World rights reserved. Distributed by King Features Syndicate
YOU GOTTA BE KIDDING! YOU? IN ELECTRONICS!
YES! NOW I'VE GOT A CAREER. SO GOOD-BY TO YOU AND YOUR CRUMMY JOB!

210

ZIPPY "CATTLE CALL"

BILL GRIFFITH

Not again! Apparently, this **abduction** of Zippy's **regular storyline** is beyond anyone's actual **control**.

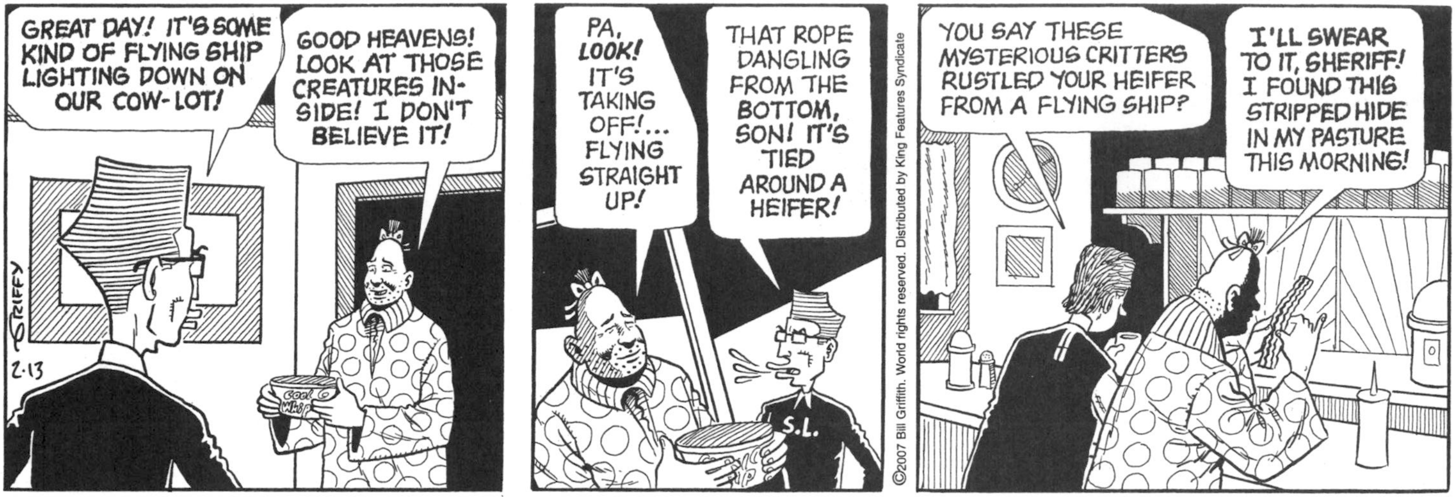
GREAT DAY! IT'S SOME KIND OF FLYING SHIP LIGHTING DOWN ON OUR COW-LOT!
GOOD HEAVENS! LOOK AT THOSE CREATURES IN-SIDE! I DON'T BELIEVE IT!
PA, LOOK! IT'S TAKING OFF!... FLYING STRAIGHT UP!
THAT ROPE DANGLING FROM THE BOTTOM, SON! IT'S TIED AROUND A HEIFER!
©2007 Bill Griffith. World rights reserved. Distributed by King Features Syndicate
YOU SAY THESE MYSTERIOUS CRITTERS RUSTLED YOUR HEIFER FROM A FLYING SHIP?
I'LL SWEAR TO IT, SHERIFF! I FOUND THIS STRIPPED HIDE IN MY PASTURE THIS MORNING!

211

ZIPPY "MISSION: AMPHIBIOUS"

BILL GRIFFITH

Once more—Zippy's **speech balloons** do not appear to be **"normal"**. It is a cause for **consternation**, indeed!

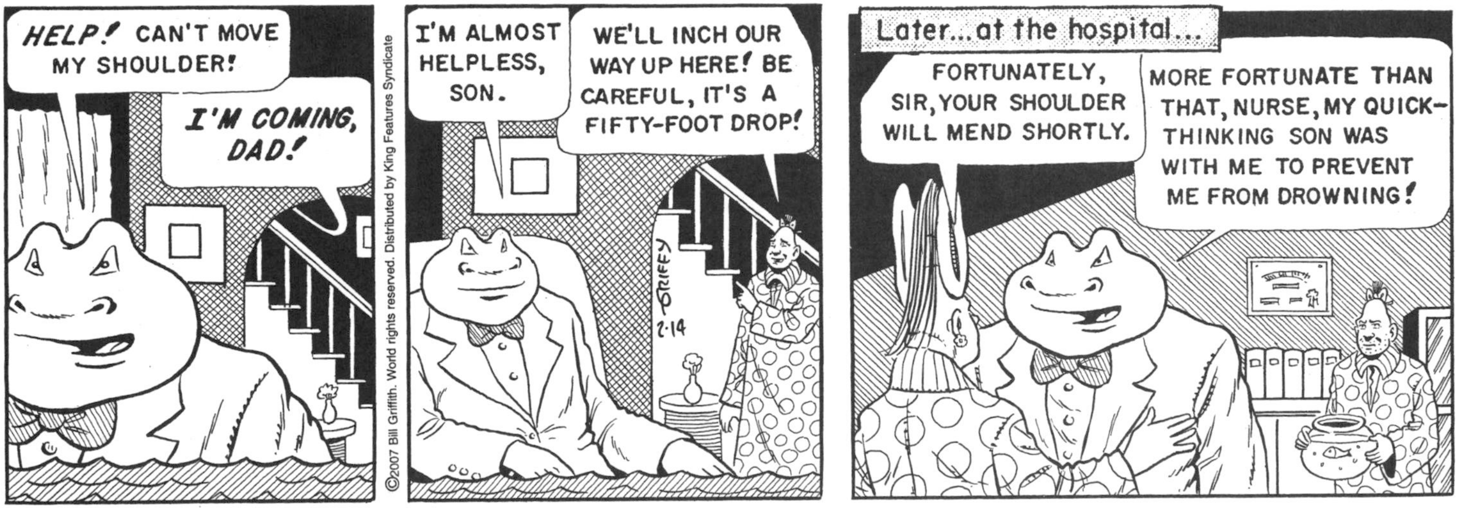
HELP! CAN'T MOVE MY SHOULDER!
I'M COMING, DAD!
©2007 Bill Griffith. World rights reserved. Distributed by King Features Syndicate
I'M ALMOST HELPLESS, SON.
WE'LL INCH OUR WAY UP HERE! BE CAREFUL, IT'S A FIFTY-FOOT DROP!
Later...at the hospital...
FORTUNATELY, SIR, YOUR SHOULDER WILL MEND SHORTLY.
MORE FORTUNATE THAN THAT, NURSE, MY QUICK-THINKING SON WAS WITH ME TO PREVENT ME FROM DROWNING!

212

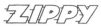

ZIPPY "AMERICAN IDYLL" BILL GRIFFITH

The **displacement** of Zippy's **dialogue** continues unabated. Perhaps tomorrow will see the **last** of this unusual **intrusion**!

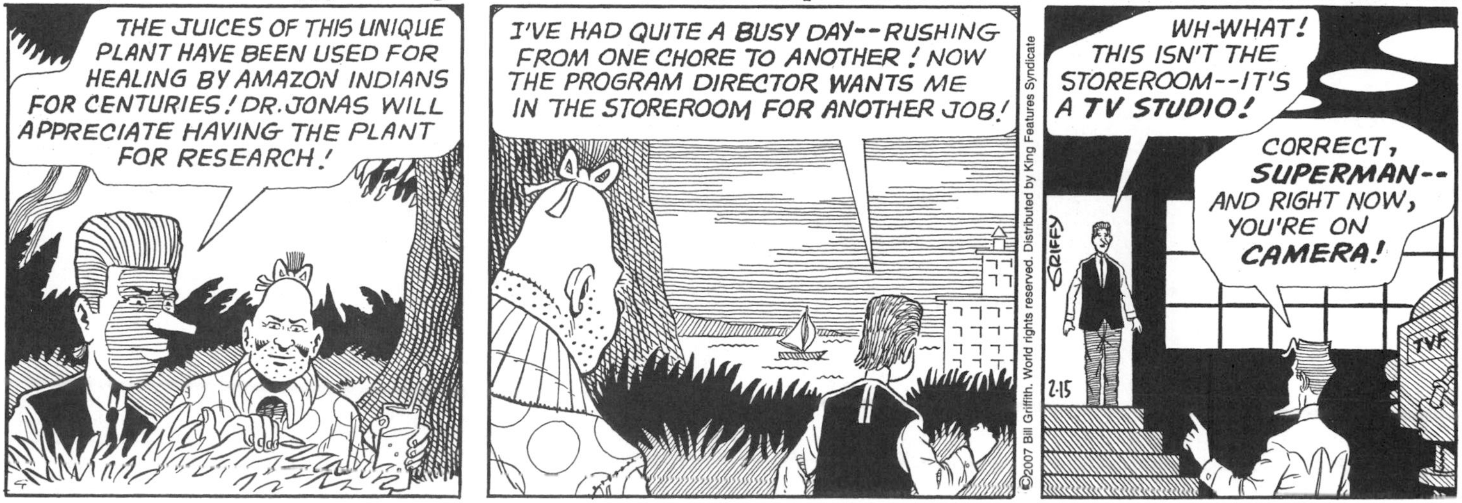
THE JUICES OF THIS UNIQUE PLANT HAVE BEEN USED FOR HEALING BY AMAZON INDIANS FOR CENTURIES! DR. JONAS WILL APPRECIATE HAVING THE PLANT FOR RESEARCH!
I'VE HAD QUITE A BUSY DAY--RUSHING FROM ONE CHORE TO ANOTHER! NOW THE PROGRAM DIRECTOR WANTS ME IN THE STOREROOM FOR ANOTHER JOB!
©2007 Bill Griffith. World rights reserved. Distributed by King Features Syndicate
WH-WHAT! THIS ISN'T THE STOREROOM--IT'S A **TV STUDIO!**
CORRECT, **SUPERMAN**-- AND RIGHT NOW, YOU'RE ON **CAMERA!**
GRIFFY
2-15
TVF

213

ZIPPY "BREVITY AND LONGEVITY" BILL GRIFFITH

The phenomenon of Zippy's **balloon usurpation** may be coming to an **end**. We hope all is **"back to abnormal"** soon!

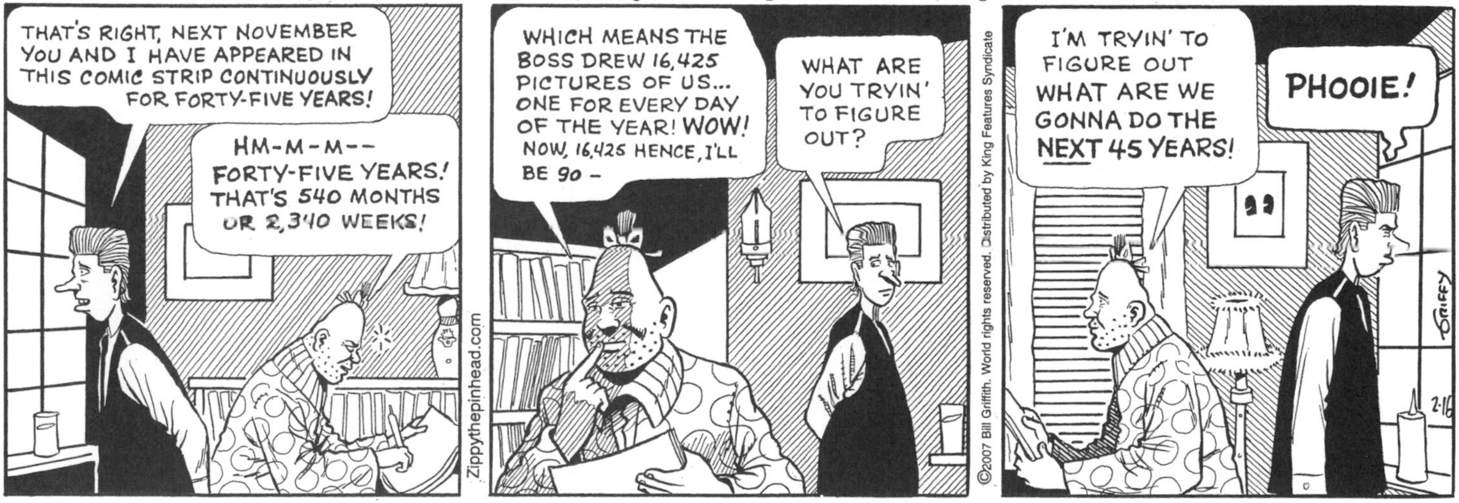
THAT'S RIGHT, NEXT NOVEMBER YOU AND I HAVE APPEARED IN THIS COMIC STRIP CONTINUOUSLY FOR FORTY-FIVE YEARS!
HM-M-M-- FORTY-FIVE YEARS! THAT'S 540 MONTHS OR 2,340 WEEKS!
Zippythepinhead.com
WHICH MEANS THE BOSS DREW 16,425 PICTURES OF US... ONE FOR EVERY DAY OF THE YEAR! WOW! NOW, 16,425 HENCE, I'LL BE 90 -
WHAT ARE YOU TRYIN' TO FIGURE OUT?
©2007 Bill Griffith. World rights reserved. Distributed by King Features Syndicate
I'M TRYIN' TO FIGURE OUT WHAT ARE WE GONNA DO THE NEXT 45 YEARS!
PHOOIE!
GRIFFY
2-16

214

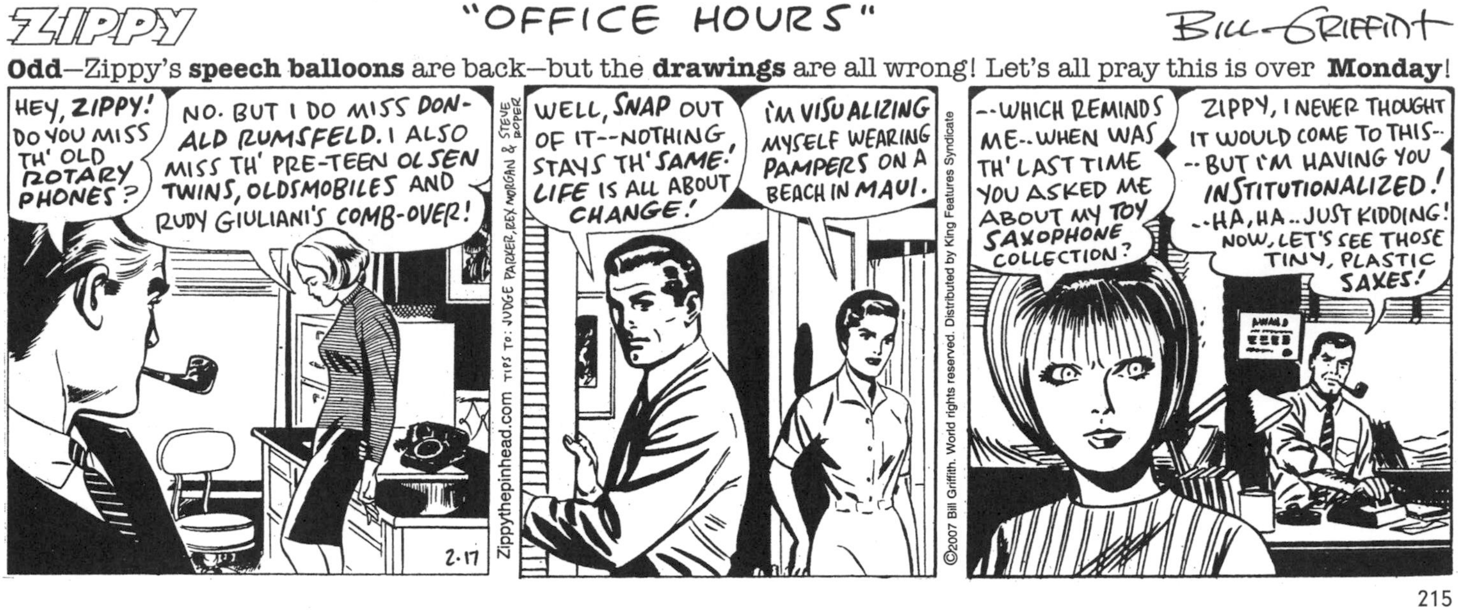
ZIPPY
"OFFICE HOURS"
BILL GRIFFITH
Odd—Zippy's speech balloons are back—but the drawings are all wrong! Let's all pray this is over Monday!
HEY, ZIPPY! DO YOU MISS TH' OLD ROTARY PHONES?
NO. BUT I DO MISS DONALD RUMSFELD. I ALSO MISS TH' PRE-TEEN OLSEN TWINS, OLDSMOBILES AND RUDY GIULIANI'S COMB-OVER!
2·17
Zippythepinhead.com TIPS TO: JUDGE PARKER, REX MORGAN & STEVE ROPER
WELL, SNAP OUT OF IT--NOTHING STAYS TH' SAME! LIFE IS ALL ABOUT CHANGE!
I'M VISUALIZING MYSELF WEARING PAMPERS ON A BEACH IN MAUI.
©2007 Bill Griffith. World rights reserved. Distributed by King Features Syndicate
--WHICH REMINDS ME--WHEN WAS TH' LAST TIME YOU ASKED ME ABOUT MY TOY SAXOPHONE COLLECTION?
ZIPPY, I NEVER THOUGHT IT WOULD COME TO THIS-- --BUT I'M HAVING YOU INSTITUTIONALIZED! --HA, HA.. JUST KIDDING! NOW, LET'S SEE THOSE TINY, PLASTIC SAXES!
215

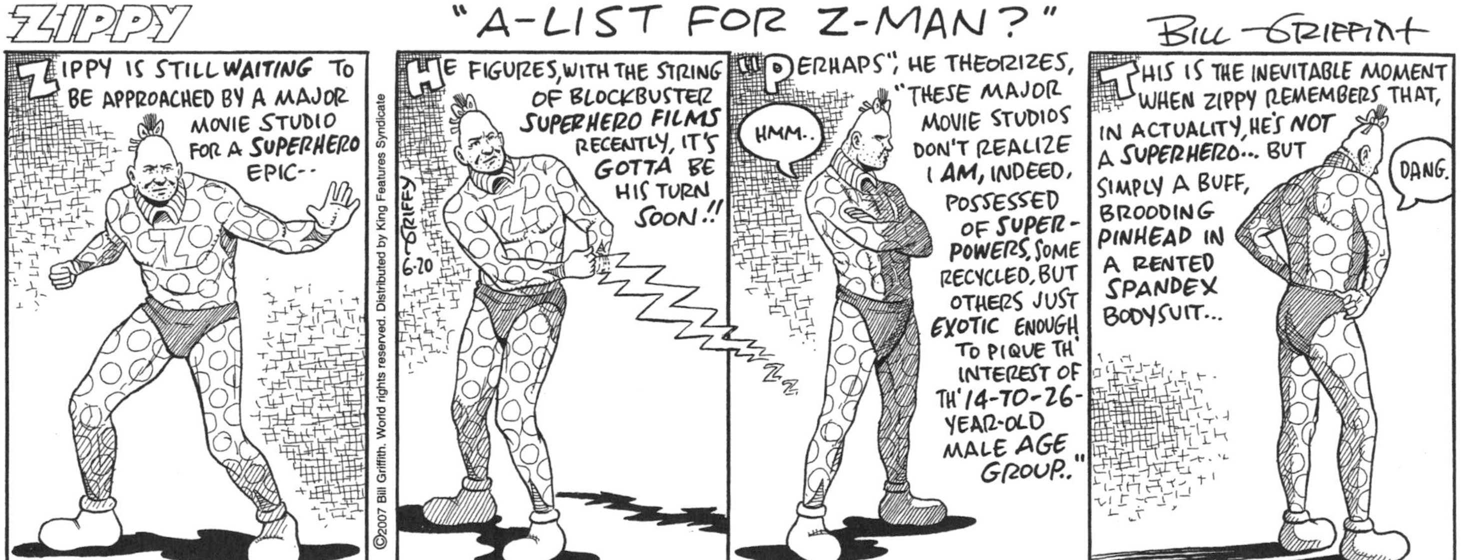
ZIPPY
"A-LIST FOR Z-MAN?"
BILL GRIFFITH
ZIPPY IS STILL WAITING TO BE APPROACHED BY A MAJOR MOVIE STUDIO FOR A SUPERHERO EPIC--
©2007 Bill Griffith. World rights reserved. Distributed by King Features Syndicate
HE FIGURES, WITH THE STRING OF BLOCKBUSTER SUPERHERO FILMS RECENTLY, IT'S GOTTA BE HIS TURN SOON!!
GRIFFY 6·20
"PERHAPS", HE THEORIZES, "THESE MAJOR MOVIE STUDIOS DON'T REALIZE I AM, INDEED, POSSESSED OF SUPER-POWERS, SOME RECYCLED, BUT OTHERS JUST EXOTIC ENOUGH TO PIQUE TH' INTEREST OF TH' 14-TO-26-YEAR-OLD MALE AGE GROUP.."
HMM..
THIS IS THE INEVITABLE MOMENT WHEN ZIPPY REMEMBERS THAT, IN ACTUALITY, HE'S NOT A SUPERHERO... BUT SIMPLY A BUFF, BROODING PINHEAD IN A RENTED SPANDEX BODYSUIT...
DANG.

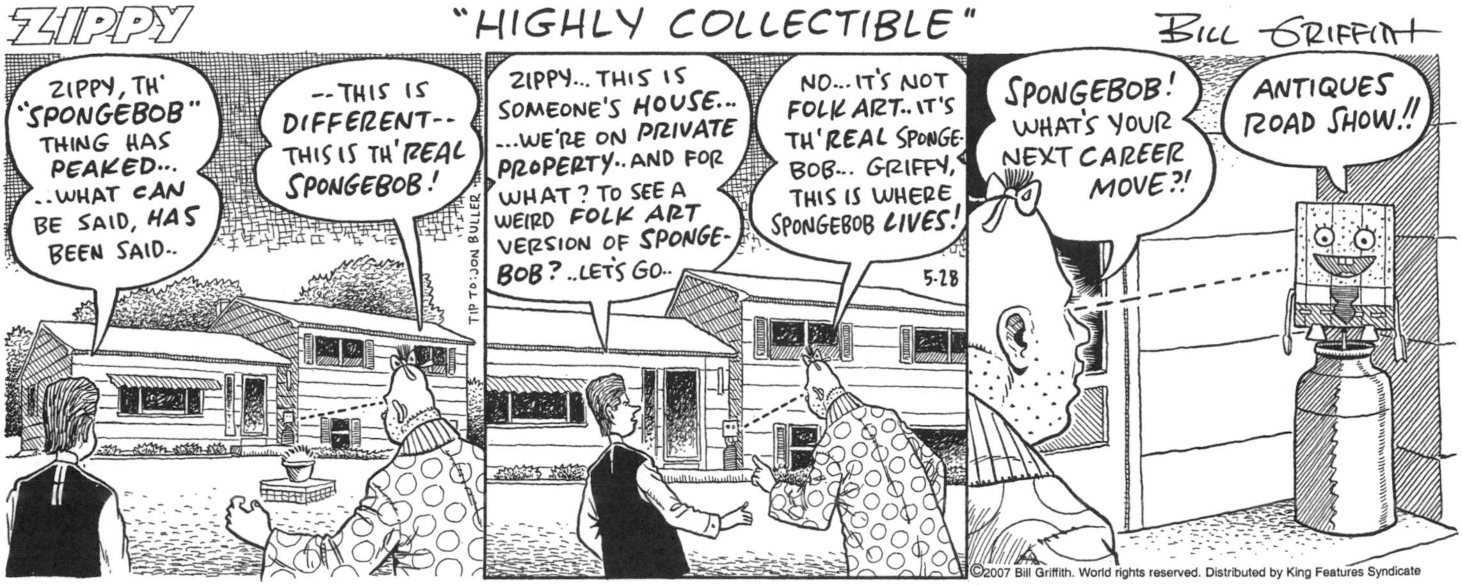
ZIPPY
"HIGHLY COLLECTIBLE"
BILL GRIFFITH
ZIPPY, TH' "SPONGEBOB" THING HAS PEAKED... ..WHAT CAN BE SAID, HAS BEEN SAID..
--THIS IS DIFFERENT-- THIS IS TH' REAL SPONGEBOB!
TIP TO: JON BULLER
ZIPPY... THIS IS SOMEONE'S HOUSE... ...WE'RE ON PRIVATE PROPERTY.. AND FOR WHAT? TO SEE A WEIRD FOLK ART VERSION OF SPONGE-BOB? ..LET'S GO..
NO... IT'S NOT FOLK ART.. IT'S TH' REAL SPONGE-BOB... GRIFFY, THIS IS WHERE SPONGEBOB LIVES!
5·28
SPONGEBOB! WHAT'S YOUR NEXT CAREER MOVE?!
ANTIQUES ROAD SHOW!!
©2007 Bill Griffith. World rights reserved. Distributed by King Features Syndicate

216

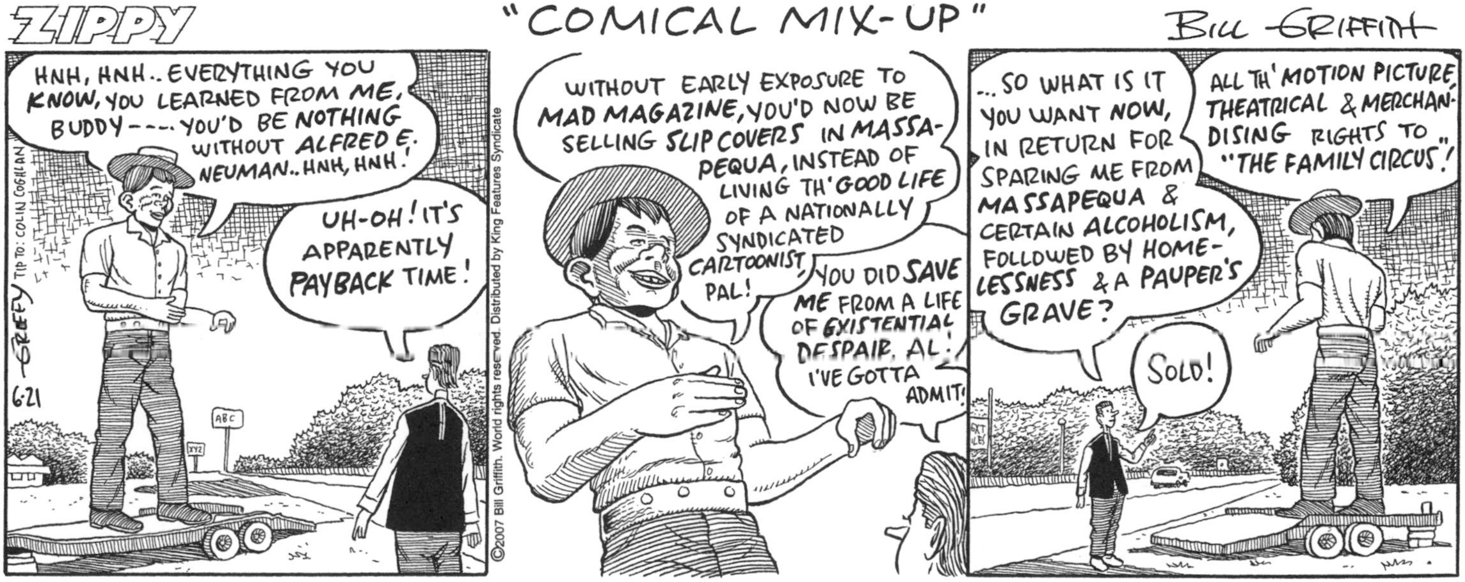
ZIPPY
"COMICAL MIX-UP"
BILL GRIFFITH
HNH, HNH.. EVERYTHING YOU KNOW, YOU LEARNED FROM ME, BUDDY--- YOU'D BE NOTHING WITHOUT ALFRED E. NEUMAN.. HNH, HNH!
UH-OH! IT'S APPARENTLY PAYBACK TIME!
TIP TO: COLIN COGHLAN
GRIFFY
6·21
ABC
©2007 Bill Griffith. World rights reserved. Distributed by King Features Syndicate
WITHOUT EARLY EXPOSURE TO MAD MAGAZINE, YOU'D NOW BE SELLING SLIP COVERS IN MASSA-PEQUA, INSTEAD OF LIVING TH' GOOD LIFE OF A NATIONALLY SYNDICATED CARTOONIST, PAL!
YOU DID SAVE ME FROM A LIFE OF EXISTENTIAL DESPAIR, AL; I'VE GOTTA ADMIT!
...SO WHAT IS IT YOU WANT NOW, IN RETURN FOR SPARING ME FROM MASSAPEQUA & CERTAIN ALCOHOLISM, FOLLOWED BY HOME-LESSNESS & A PAUPER'S GRAVE?
ALL TH' MOTION PICTURE, THEATRICAL & MERCHAN-DISING RIGHTS TO "THE FAMILY CIRCUS"!
SOLD!

217

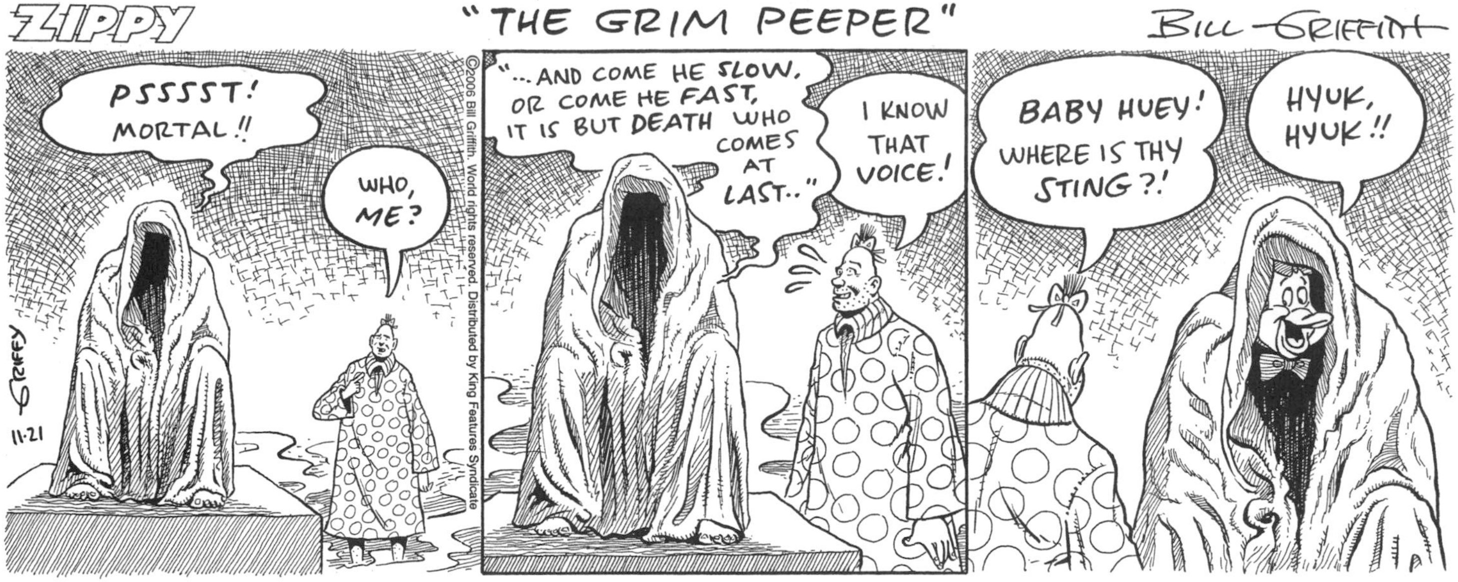
ZIPPY
"THE GRIM PEEPER"
BILL GRIFFITH
PSSSST! MORTAL!!
WHO, ME?
GRIFFY
11·21
©2006 Bill Griffith. World rights reserved. Distributed by King Features Syndicate
"...AND COME HE SLOW, OR COME HE FAST, IT IS BUT DEATH WHO COMES AT LAST.."
I KNOW THAT VOICE!
BABY HUEY! WHERE IS THY STING?!
HYUK, HYUK!!

218

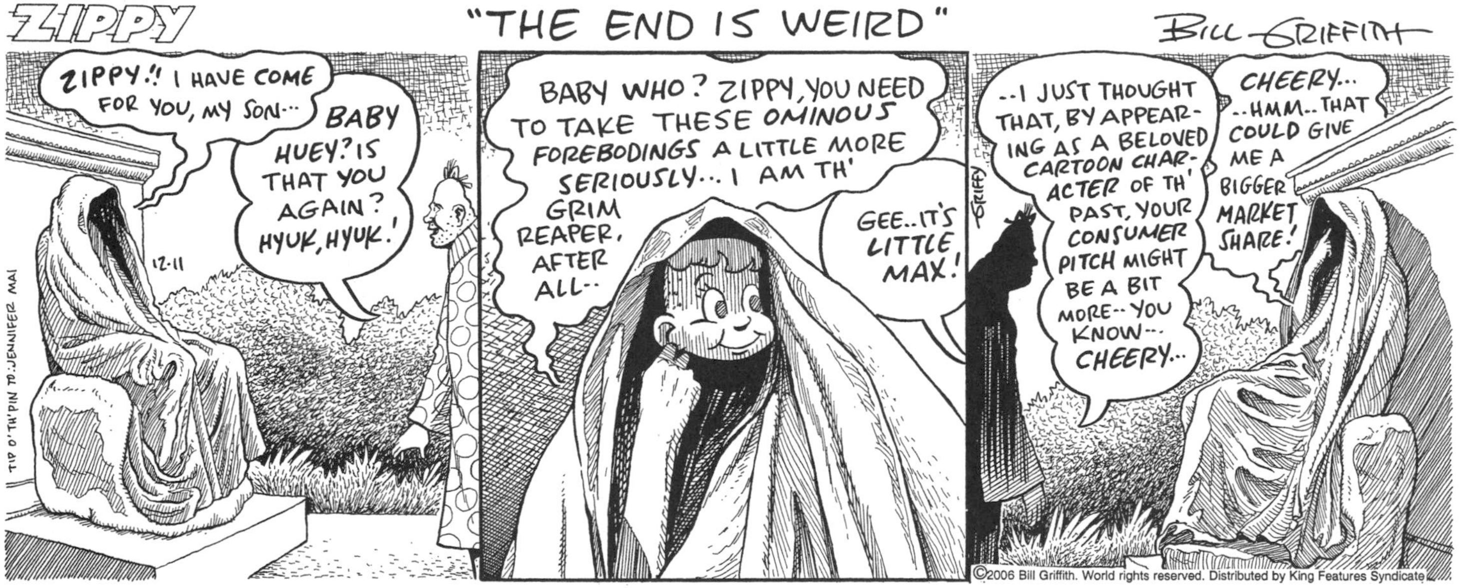
ZIPPY
"THE END IS WEIRD"
BILL GRIFFITH
ZIPPY!! I HAVE COME FOR YOU, MY SON..
BABY HUEY? IS THAT YOU AGAIN? HYUK, HYUK!
12·11
TIP O' TH' PIN TO: JENNIFER MAI
BABY WHO? ZIPPY, YOU NEED TO TAKE THESE OMINOUS FOREBODINGS A LITTLE MORE SERIOUSLY... I AM TH' GRIM REAPER, AFTER ALL..
GEE.. IT'S LITTLE MAX!
GRIFFY
..I JUST THOUGHT THAT, BY APPEARING AS A BELOVED CARTOON CHARACTER OF TH' PAST, YOUR CONSUMER PITCH MIGHT BE A BIT MORE.. YOU KNOW.. CHEERY..
CHEERY... ..HMM.. THAT COULD GIVE ME A BIGGER MARKET SHARE!
©2006 Bill Griffith. World rights reserved. Distributed by King Features Syndicate

219

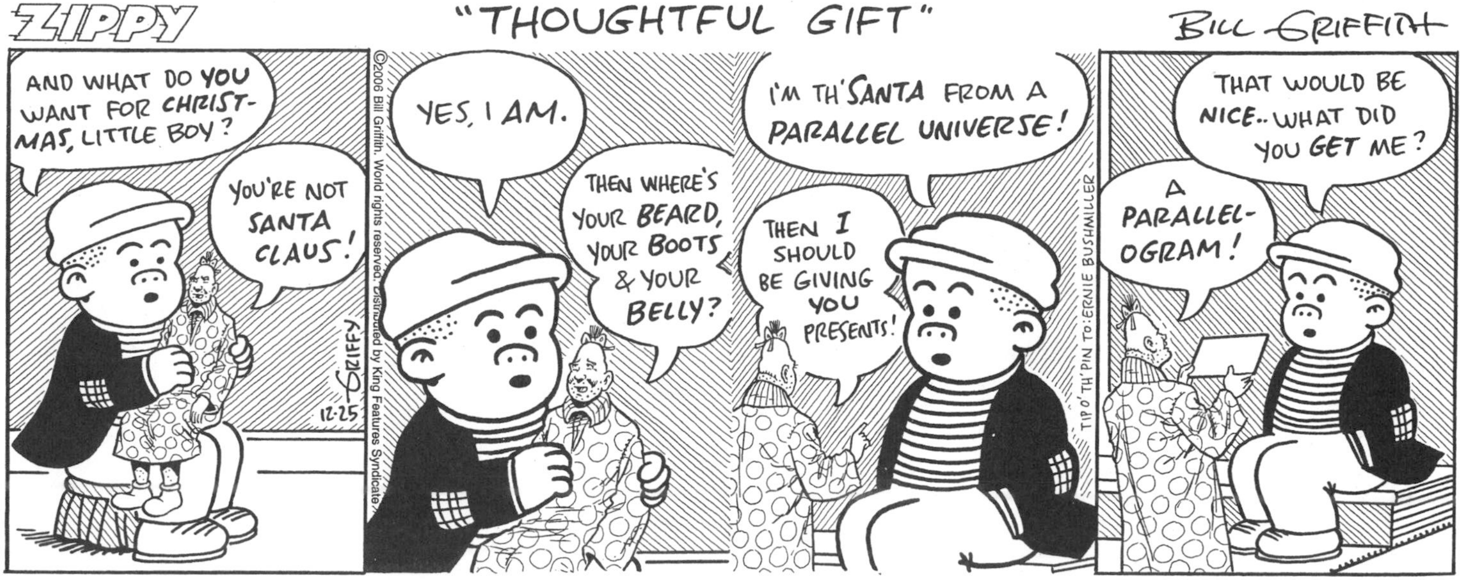
ZIPPY
"THOUGHTFUL GIFT"
BILL GRIFFITH
AND WHAT DO YOU WANT FOR CHRISTMAS, LITTLE BOY?
YOU'RE NOT SANTA CLAUS!
GRIFFY 12·25
©2006 Bill Griffith. World rights reserved. Distributed by King Features Syndicate
YES, I AM.
THEN WHERE'S YOUR BEARD, YOUR BOOTS & YOUR BELLY?
I'M TH' SANTA FROM A PARALLEL UNIVERSE!
THEN I SHOULD BE GIVING YOU PRESENTS!
TIP O' TH' PIN TO: ERNIE BUSHMILLER
THAT WOULD BE NICE.. WHAT DID YOU GET ME?
A PARALLELOGRAM!

220

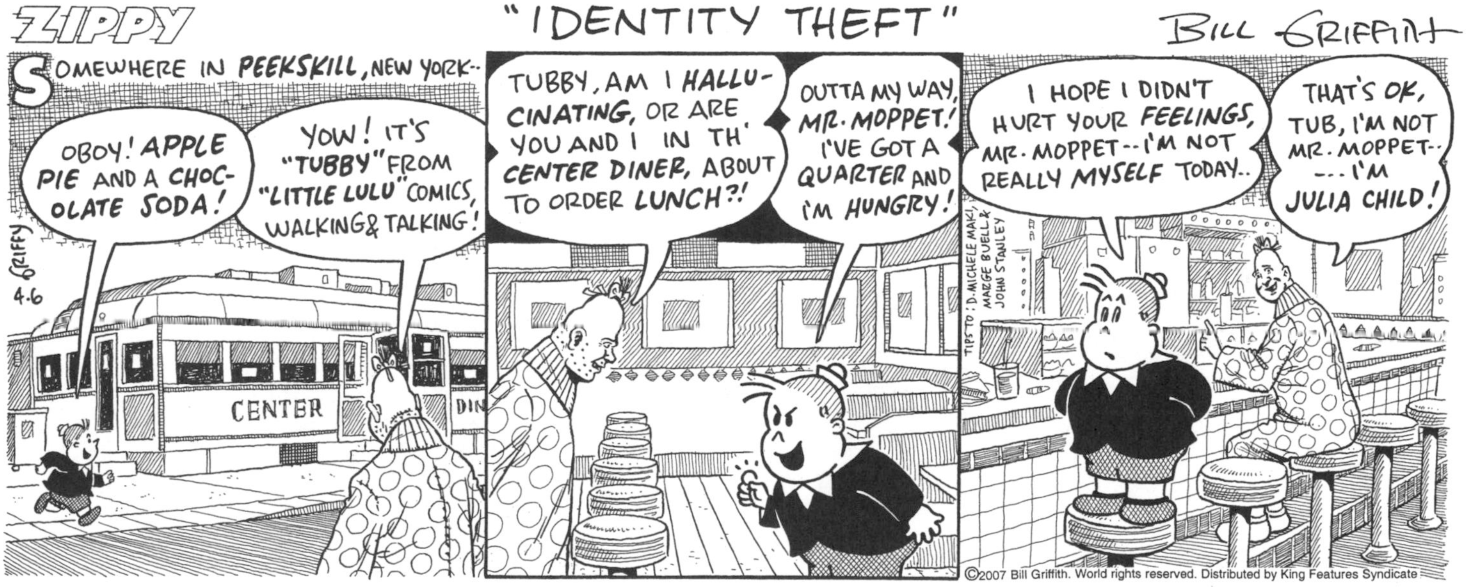
ZIPPY
"IDENTITY THEFT"
BILL GRIFFITH
SOMEWHERE IN PEEKSKILL, NEW YORK--
OBOY! APPLE PIE AND A CHOCOLATE SODA!
YOW! IT'S "TUBBY" FROM "LITTLE LULU" COMICS, WALKING & TALKING!
GRIFFY 4·6
CENTER
TUBBY, AM I HALLUCINATING, OR ARE YOU AND I IN TH' CENTER DINER, ABOUT TO ORDER LUNCH?!
OUTTA MY WAY, MR. MOPPET! I'VE GOT A QUARTER AND I'M HUNGRY!
TIPS TO: D. MICHELE MAKI, MARGE BUELL & JOHN STANLEY
I HOPE I DIDN'T HURT YOUR FEELINGS, MR. MOPPET-- I'M NOT REALLY MYSELF TODAY..
THAT'S OK, TUB, I'M NOT MR. MOPPET-- --I'M JULIA CHILD!
©2007 Bill Griffith. World rights reserved. Distributed by King Features Syndicate

221

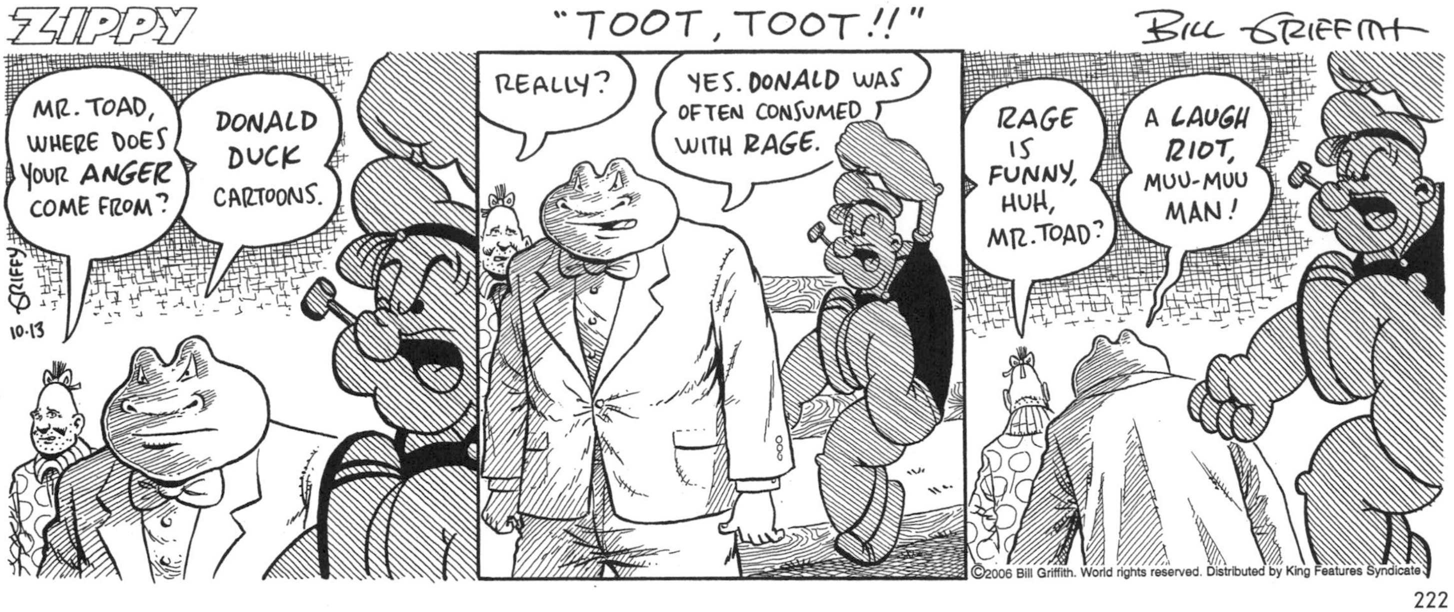
ZIPPY
"TOOT, TOOT!!"
BILL GRIFFITH
MR. TOAD, WHERE DOES YOUR ANGER COME FROM?
DONALD DUCK CARTOONS.
GRIFFY 10-13
REALLY?
YES. DONALD WAS OFTEN CONSUMED WITH RAGE.
RAGE IS FUNNY, HUH, MR. TOAD?
A LAUGH RIOT, MUU-MUU MAN!
©2006 Bill Griffith. World rights reserved. Distributed by King Features Syndicate
222

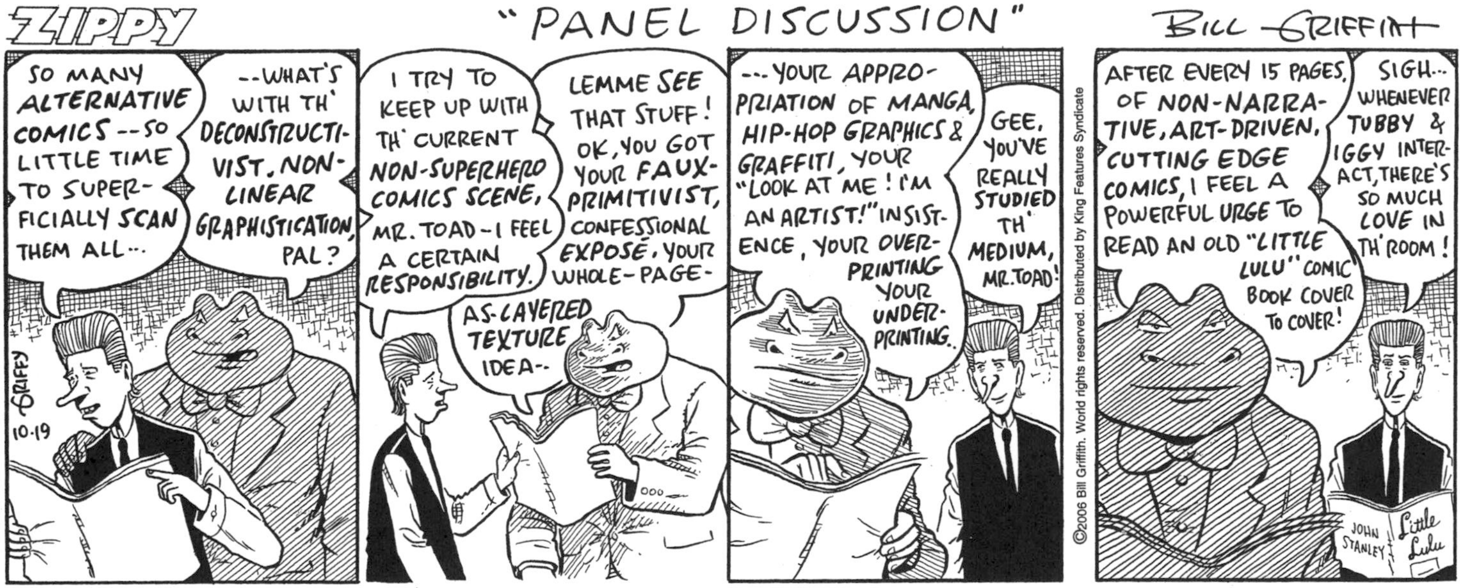
ZIPPY
"PANEL DISCUSSION"
BILL GRIFFITH
SO MANY ALTERNATIVE COMICS -- SO LITTLE TIME TO SUPERFICIALLY SCAN THEM ALL...
--WHAT'S WITH TH' DECONSTRUCTIVIST, NON-LINEAR GRAPHISTICATION, PAL?
GRIFFY 10-19
I TRY TO KEEP UP WITH TH' CURRENT NON-SUPERHERO COMICS SCENE, MR. TOAD - I FEEL A CERTAIN RESPONSIBILITY.
LEMME SEE THAT STUFF! OK, YOU GOT YOUR FAUX-PRIMITIVIST, CONFESSIONAL EXPOSÉ, YOUR WHOLE-PAGE-
AS-LAYERED TEXTURE IDEA--
--- YOUR APPROPRIATION OF MANGA, HIP-HOP GRAPHICS & GRAFFITI, YOUR "LOOK AT ME! I'M AN ARTIST!" INSISTENCE, YOUR OVER-PRINTING YOUR UNDER-PRINTING..
GEE, YOU'VE REALLY STUDIED TH' MEDIUM, MR. TOAD!
©2006 Bill Griffith. World rights reserved. Distributed by King Features Syndicate
AFTER EVERY 15 PAGES, OF NON-NARRATIVE, ART-DRIVEN, CUTTING EDGE COMICS, I FEEL A POWERFUL URGE TO READ AN OLD "LITTLE LULU" COMIC BOOK COVER TO COVER!
SIGH... WHENEVER TUBBY & IGGY INTERACT, THERE'S SO MUCH LOVE IN TH' ROOM!
JOHN STANLEY
Little Lulu

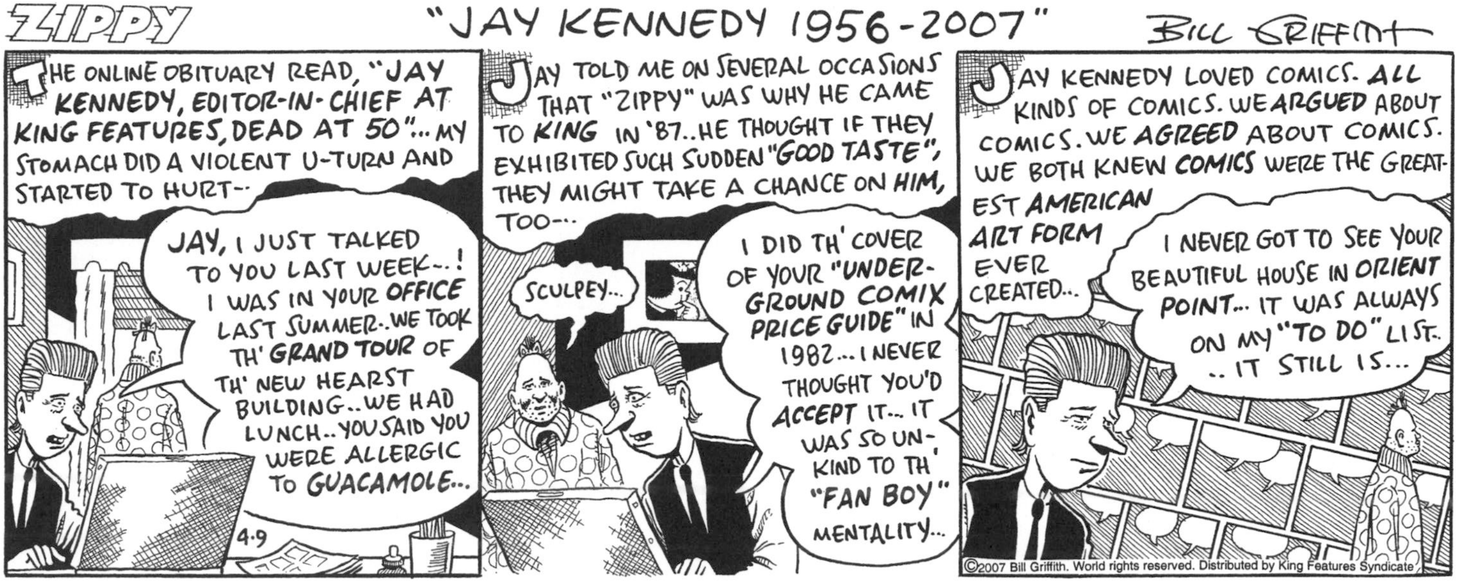
ZIPPY
"JAY KENNEDY 1956-2007"
BILL GRIFFITH
THE ONLINE OBITUARY READ, "JAY KENNEDY, EDITOR-IN-CHIEF AT KING FEATURES, DEAD AT 50"... MY STOMACH DID A VIOLENT U-TURN AND STARTED TO HURT--
JAY, I JUST TALKED TO YOU LAST WEEK--! I WAS IN YOUR OFFICE LAST SUMMER..WE TOOK TH' GRAND TOUR OF TH' NEW HEARST BUILDING..WE HAD LUNCH..YOU SAID YOU WERE ALLERGIC TO GUACAMOLE...
4·9
JAY TOLD ME ON SEVERAL OCCASIONS THAT "ZIPPY" WAS WHY HE CAME TO KING IN '87..HE THOUGHT IF THEY EXHIBITED SUCH SUDDEN "GOOD TASTE", THEY MIGHT TAKE A CHANCE ON HIM, TOO--.
SCULPEY...
I DID TH' COVER OF YOUR "UNDERGROUND COMIX PRICE GUIDE" IN 1982...I NEVER THOUGHT YOU'D ACCEPT IT... IT WAS SO UNKIND TO TH' "FAN BOY" MENTALITY...
JAY KENNEDY LOVED COMICS. ALL KINDS OF COMICS. WE ARGUED ABOUT COMICS. WE AGREED ABOUT COMICS. WE BOTH KNEW COMICS WERE THE GREATEST AMERICAN ART FORM EVER CREATED...
I NEVER GOT TO SEE YOUR BEAUTIFUL HOUSE IN ORIENT POINT... IT WAS ALWAYS ON MY "TO DO" LIST.. .. IT STILL IS...
©2007 Bill Griffith. World rights reserved. Distributed by King Features Syndicate

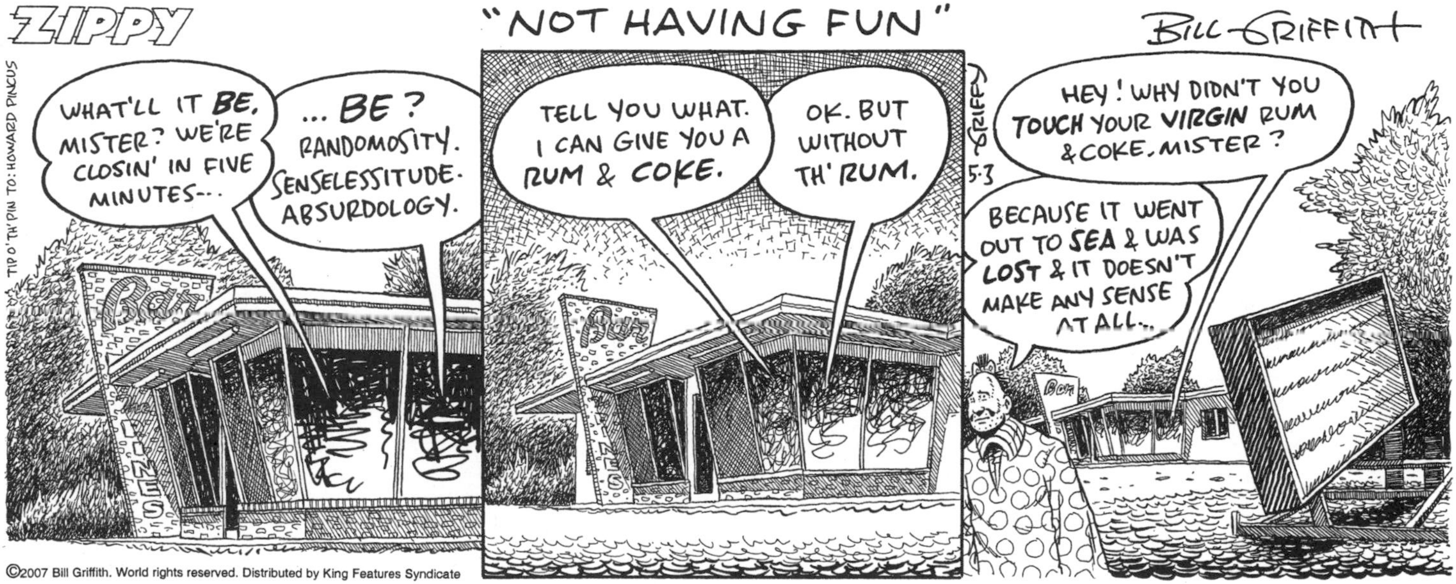
ZIPPY
"NOT HAVING FUN"
BILL GRIFFITH
TIP O' TH' PIN TO: HOWARD PINCUS
WHAT'LL IT BE, MISTER? WE'RE CLOSIN' IN FIVE MINUTES--.
... BE? RANDOMOSITY. SENSELESSITUDE. ABSURDOLOGY.
TELL YOU WHAT. I CAN GIVE YOU A RUM & COKE.
OK. BUT WITHOUT TH' RUM.
GRIFFY
5·3
HEY! WHY DIDN'T YOU TOUCH YOUR VIRGIN RUM & COKE, MISTER?
BECAUSE IT WENT OUT TO SEA & WAS LOST & IT DOESN'T MAKE ANY SENSE AT ALL..
©2007 Bill Griffith. World rights reserved. Distributed by King Features Syndicate

THE PINHEAD LIFESTYLE Chapter 1

1. Rosicrucianism is an occult Christian offshoot, founded by German Protestants around 1610. In his first screen role, actor Eugene Pallette (1899-1954) played a wounded soldier in D.W. Griffith's *Birth of a Nation* (1915). [pg. 7]

2. Indian Rocks Beach is located just north of St. Petersburg, FL. [pg. 9]

3. Wacky Packages are trading cards parodying various commercial products, first introduced by the Topps Bubblegum Company in 1967. From 1973 to 1975, Bill Griffith worked on the series, creating such memorable stickers as "Kentucky Fried Fingers" and "Generally Demented Lightbulbs." He did not create "Dr. Pooper." [pg. 10]

4. The *Mr. Ed* TV show first aired in 1961, starring Alan Young and a talking horse, originally named Bamboo Harvester. In different episodes, Mr. Ed was shown riding a surfboard, piloting a plane and wearing a Beatle wig. [pg. 11]

5. *The Partridge Family* was broadcast on ABC-TV from 1970 to 1974. An animated version titled *Partridge Family: 2200 A.D.* (1974-5) brought the characters back to life in outer space. The Barcalounger reclining armchair was first produced in 1940 by designer Edward Joel Barcolo. Zippy is still retired from show business. [pg. 11]

6. There were no Atomic Duck comic books. The closest thing was *Atomic Mouse* by Al Fago, introduced in 1953. Atomic Mouse's superpowers were a result of ingesting Uranium-235 pills. [pg. 11]

7. The Valvoline lubricating oil company was founded by Dr. John Ellis in 1886. A Black Russian contains vodka and coffee liqueur. It was created by barman Gustav Tops at the Hotel Metropole in Brussels, Belgium, in 1950. [pg.12]

8. Tom Cruise was born Thomas Cruise Mapother IV in 1962. He credits Scientology with helping him to overcome his dyslexia. [pg. 13]

9. First called Plastone, Turtle Wax was invented in 1941 by Benjamin Hirsch. In the 1950s, the Turtle Wax company branched out and created a line of dessert toppings called Party Day. [pg. 13]

10. Pizza Hut, founded in 1958 by Dan and Frank Carney, introduced a "Lasagna Pizza" in 2006. [pg. 14]

11. James Joyce (1882-1941) wrote his landmark novel, *Ulysses*, in 1922 and was an award-winning Irish tenor. Dr. Joyce Brothers (b. 1928), psychologist and advice columnist, has made cameo appearances on *The Simpsons*, *Mickey Spillane's Mike Hammer* and *Hollywood Squares*. [pg. 14]

12. The Anaheim Angels were the 2002 World Series winners. [pg. 15]

13. Hoboken, NJ, is the site of the first Blimpie restaurant, opened in 1964. A free goldfish in a bowl of colored water was given to all customers who purchased a sandwich during opening week. [pg. 16]

14. Easter Island is known as Rapa Nui in the Tahitian language. [pg. 17]

15. Abba, the Swedish pop music group, flourished from 1972 to 1982. Abba is also the name of a well-known Swedish fish-canning company. Documentary filmmaker Ken Burns (b. 1953) is sometimes accused of having a "Moe" haircut. Moe Howard (1897-1975) of The Three Stooges, was born Moses Horwitz in Brooklyn, NY. In 1925, he married Helen Schonberger, a cousin of magician Harry Houdini (1874-1926). [pg. 17]

16. Black Sabbath's *Paranoid* was released in 1970. The band was founded in England in 1966 under the name Polka Tulk Blues Company. Bess Truman (1885-1982) was the wife of Harry S. Truman, the 33rd President of the United States (1945-1953). She conducted only one press conference as First Lady and responded to most questions with "No comment." Liechtenstein is a land-locked alpine country in Western Europe. The entire country was put up for rent to business groups in 2003 to promote tourism. [pg. 18]

17. George Gershwin (1898-1937) was inducted into the Long Island Music Hall of Fame in 2006. An unconventional composer, Charles Ives (1874-1954) was largely ignored during his lifetime. Ginger Baker (b. 1939) was the drummer for the bands Cream (1966-68) and Blind Faith (1969). Wolfgang Mozart (1756-1791). One of his canons contains the lyric, "Lick me in the arse nice and clean." Johannes Brahms (1833-1897) often frequented the "Red Hedgehog" tavern in Vienna. Ipana toothpaste has been unavailable in the U. S. since the early 1970s, but is still the most popular toothpaste brand in Turkey. [pg. 19]

18. Parody of Robert Johnson's blues tune, "Stones in my Passway" (1937). [pg. 19]

19. Introduced in the U.S. in 1942, corn dogs are known as "pogos" in Canada and in Australia as "Dagwood dogs." [pg. 20]

20. "Poindexter bar bats" do not exist. [pg. 20]

21. The Guggenheim Museum in Bilbao, Spain, was designed by architect Frank Gehry (b. 1929) who said, "The randomness of the curves are designed to catch the light." [pg. 21]

22. Fraternal twins Mary-Kate and Ashley Olsen (b. 1986) got their start on the TV show *Full House* (1987-1995). Mary-Kate's new fashion line is known for its signature "homeless look." [pg. 21]

23. *The Iron Chef* TV cooking show (1993-2002) is called "Ironmen of Cooking" in Japan. According to a 2007 Gallup poll, 43% of all Americans believe that the Earth is no more than 10,000 years old. Only 14% believe the Earth is many millions of years old and that a divine intervention had no direct part in its creation. [pg. 22]

24. Jones Beach State Park on Long Island, NY, was planned and built in the 1920s by Robert Moses (1888-1981). Actors William, Daniel and Alec Baldwin were all lifeguards there. [pg. 22]

25. Mormons believe that Joseph Smith, Jr. received a set of golden plates from the angel Moroni in 1827 on a hill in upstate New York. Devoted Mormons wear a certain kind of consecrated underwear day and night, for their entire lives. So does Zippy. He hopes this does not stand in the way of his Presidential aspirations. [pg. 23]

26. Panels 1 & 3: Round Top, TX. [pg. 23]

27. The Olive Garden restaurant chain was founded in Orlando, FL in 1982. A competitive chain, Fazoli's, also offers unlimited breadsticks. "Potrzebie" is a Polish word meaning "need" which, along with "axolotl" (a Mexican salamander), was used for gag effect in the early *Mad* magazine by editor Harvey Kurtzman. Angelina Jolie (b. 1975) has four sets of geographical coordinates tattooed on her left shoulder, indicating the birthplaces of her children. Nicolas Cage (b. 1964) named his second child Kal-El, also the birth name of Superman. [pg. 24]

28. The Neolite shoe repair slogan was "Strong but oh, so gentle." The Altamont (CA) Free Concert of 1969 featured the death of Meredith Hunter, caught on film by the Maysles brothers in their documentary *Gimme Shelter* (1970). Clark Bars are made by the New England Confectionery Company (Necco). [pg. 25]

29. Lunesta is a popular prescription sleep aid. Geico is an acronym for Government Employees Insurance Company. [pg. 26]

30. Montreal, Quebec, Canada. [pg.27]

31. Holiday Lake, Bridgeboro NJ. [pg. 28]

32. Freemasonry is a membership society with roots in Scotland in the late sixteenth century. Affiliated lodges act essentially as a businessmen's club, employing secret handshakes and passwords. Both the Catholic Church and the Palestinian Islamist organization, Hamas, have condemned the Masons. The Copts are Egyptian Christians. Former Secretary-General of the United Nations Boutros-Boutros Ghali (b. 1922) is a Copt. [pg. 29]

33. Weehawken, NJ was formed in 1859. In the comic strip *Pogo*, by Walt Kelly (1913-1973), Churchy LaFemme once exclaimed "Weehawken!" as his head was unstuck from his shell by use of a bicycle pump. [pg. 29]

34. Desenex is an anti-fungal foot powder. Movie actor Dan Duryea (1907-1968) usually played a villain in his many film noir roles. His last movie was *The Bamboo Saucer* (1968) about a UFO hidden in a Red Chinese peasant village. Betty Hutton's (1921-2007) first major film role was in *The Fleet's In* (1942). Previously, she appeared in the short subject, *Public Jitterbug Number One*, in 1939. [pg. 30]

35. From a review by Frank Bruni of a New York City vegetarian restaurant in *The New York Times*, 2007. [pg.30]

36. The Stop & Shop supermarket chain was founded in Somerville, MA in 1914. In a TV episode of *The Sopranos* (1999-2007), Tony Soprano is seen shopping at a Stop & Shop in New Jersey. [pg. 31]

37. The Brunswick Corporation began its business in 1845 making horse carriages and billiard tables. A few decades later, they expanded to include bowling balls and pins and toilet seats. Dick Cheney (b. 1941) is the 46th Vice President of the United States. He occasionally requires the use of a cane for walking. (See also "THEY LAUGHED WHEN I SAT DOWN," pg. 34) [pg. 31]

38. Simone de Beauvoir (1908-1986), French author and existentialist philosopher, has a footbridge across the Seine in Paris named after her. Jolt Cola contains 143 milligrams of caffeine in its popular "battery bottle." There is also a Jolt chewing gum whose slogan is "Chew More, Do More." [pg. 32]

39. The 1954 film *Magnificent Obsession* was directed by Douglas Sirk (1900-1987). [pg. 33]

40. Franz Schubert's (1797-1828) 8th Symphony (1822) is often called the Unfinished Symphony. The Rangers are a level of the Republican fund-raising organization, the Bush Pioneers. To be a Super Ranger, one needs to gather over $300,000.00 for the Bush cause. [pg. 34]

41. French's Mustard debuted in 1904. Many people add French's French-Fried Onions to mashed potatoes and baked beans for a crispy sensation. [pg. 35]

42. On February 11, 2006, Dick Cheney accidentally shot Harry Whittington, a Texas attorney, while quail hunting. Shortly after the incident, Cheney prepared himself a cocktail. [pg. 36]

43. "Tramp stamp" is the slang term for a tattoo found above a woman's gluteal cleavage. "Met" is the Metropolitan Museum of Art, NY NY. [pg. 36]

TRANSCENDENTAL MEDICATION Chapter 2

44. Streets in Italy and Czechoslovakia. [pg. 38]

45. Baker, CA. Lyrics: Robert Johnson, "Me and the Devil Blues," 1937. [pg. 39]

46. Parody of "Howl," 1956, by Allen Ginsberg. Leona Helmsley (b. 1920) was prosecuted for federal income tax evasion in 1989 by then U.S. Attorney Rudolph Giuliani. She was portrayed by Suzanne Pleshette in a 1990 TV movie. [pg. 39]

47A-C. Near Brant Lake, NY. [pgs. 40-41]

48. Polock Johnny's Polish Sausage, Baltimore, MD. [pg. 41]

49. Beep's, Van Nuys, CA. [pg. 42]

50. 1) Montreal, Quebec, Canada 2) Near Boston, MA 3) Boston, MA. [pg. 42]

51. 1) Broken Arrow OK 2) Toronto, Ontario, Canada 3) Newmarket, Ontario, Canada. [pg. 43]

52. Santa Monica, CA. [pg. 43]

53. Santa Monica, CA. [pg. 44]

54A-B. The Nash Metropolitan automobile, originally built in England, was introduced to the U.S. and Canada in 1954. Nancy Drew's father drives a Metro in the 2007 film Nancy Drew, starring Emma Roberts, who called the car "Basically a bathtub on wheels." [pgs. 44-45]

55. Barry's Magic Shop, Wheaton, MD. [pg. 45]

56. Canterbury, England. [pg. 46]

57. "Memorial Collapse" by Ledelle Moe, Washington DC. [pg. 46]

58. Charlotte, NC. [pg. 47]

59. Scranton, PA. Joan Rivers (b. 1933) wrote and directed Rabbit Test (1978), in which the Billy Crystal character becomes pregnant and delivers a baby girl. Philosopher René Descartes (1596-1650) is the author of the famous line, "I think, therefore I am." [pg. 47]

60. Star View Diner, Somerdale, NJ. Albert Camus (1913-1960) once said, "No, I am not an Existentialist." [pg. 48]

61. Los Angeles, CA. [pg.48]

62. Lincoln, RI. "The Rapture" is prophesied by fundamentalist Christians. It describes the moment when all Christians alive on earth are suddenly transported through the air to meet Jesus in Heaven. "88 Reasons Why The Rapture is in 1988" was published in 1988 by Edgar Whisenant. [pg. 49]

63. Figueres, Spain. [pg. 49]

64. Panels 1 & 4) Arbutus, MD 2 & 3) Nice, France. [pg. 50]

FOOD FOR THOUGHT Chapter 3

65. Deep Water Diner, Carney's Point, NJ. [pg. 52]

66. Elgin Diner, Camden, NJ. [pg. 52]

67. Al's Restaurant, Chicopee, MA. [pg. 53]

68. Terminal Luncheonette, Abington, PA. [pg. 53]

69. Hollywood Diner, Baltimore, MD. [pg. 54]

70. The Gourmet Restaurant, San Bernardino, CA. [pg. 54]

71. Jennie's Diner, Ronks, PA [pg. 55]

72. The Diner, Westborough, MA. Hefty One-Zip Slider Bags are made by the Pactiv Corporation and are America's number one slider bag. [pg. 55]

73. George's Hot Dogs, Brookville, PA. "Leader of the Pack" was a 1964 pop hit by the Shangri-Las, parodied the following year by "Leader of the Laundromat" by The Detergents. "Da Doo Ron Ron" was a 1963 hit single by The Crystals, produced by Phil Spector (b. 1939). Donald Jr. (b. 1977), Ivanka (b. 1981), and Eric (b. 1984) are Donald Trump's children. They all work for the Trump Organization. Ivanka does not like being

compared to Paris Hilton (b. 1981). (See also pg. 81). Reference to Sauerkraut was first noted in ancient Rome during the first century A.D. [pg. 56]

74. Laurel Diner, Southbury, CT. Jane and Michael Stern write the "Roadfood" column for Gourmet magazine (and on their website of the same name). Reviewing the Laurel Diner, they said their "hunky home fries are not to be dissed." [pg. 56]

75. Los Angeles, CA. [pg. 57]

76. Aero Diner, N. Windham, CT. Panel 3) Los Angeles, CA. Daffy Duck first appeared in 1937 and soon developed his signature catchphrase, "You're deth-picable!" Gerald McBoing-Boing was a 1950 short animated film about a little boy who speaks in sound effects instead of words. [pg. 57]

77. New York System Weiners, Providence, RI. [pg. 58]

78. Eveready Diner, Hyde Park, NY. The name of Arby's restaurants is derived from the name of its founders, the Raffel brothers ("R.B."). Marie Callender's is a chain of 139 "home style" restaurants in the western U.S. A snickerdoodle is a soft sugar cookie, oddly unrelated to the Snickers candy bar. [pg. 58]

79. Roadside Diner, Paris, France. [pg. 59]

80. Strollo's Restaurant, Point Pleasant, NJ. [pg. 59]

81. Utamilla, OR. Actor John Wayne (1907-1979) requested that his tombstone should read "Feo, Fuerte y Formal," meaning in Spanish, "Ugly, Strong and Dignified." It was not respected. [pg. 60]

82. Bled, Slovenia. [pg. 61]

83. Donut Palace, somewhere in Louisiana. [pg. 61]

84. Los Angeles, CA. [pg. 62]

85. Frisch's Big Boy, Cincinnati, OH. (See also, pg. 95) [pg. 62]

86. Bob's Big Boy, Burbank, CA. The Big Boy Corporation demanded recently that the author "cease and desist" using their trademarked mascot in future Zippy strips. Hmmm. (See also pg. 95) [pg. 63]

87. Yocco's Hot Dogs, Allentown, PA. [pg. 63]

88. Tad's Steak House, NY, NY. [pg. 64]

89. Tastee Zone, Catonsville, MD. [pg. 64]

90. Panels 1 & 2) Sunrise, FL 3) Boboli Gardens, Florence, Italy. [pg. 65]

91. White Circle System, Bloomfield, NJ. Googleplex is name of the company headquarters for Google Inc. A googolplex is the number 10 squared to the hundredth power. Barney Google, the comic strip, was created in 1919 by Billy DeBeck (1890-1942). [pg. 65]

92. Los Angeles, CA. Architect Frank Gehry (b. 1929) is famous for his deconstructivist, warped forms, often resembling crumpled metal or paper. (See also pg. 96) [pg. 66]

93. Dublin, OH. [pg.66]

DEEP DISH Chapter 4

94. Pierce Brothers Mortuary, Los Angeles, CA. Rodney Dangerfield (1921-2004), born Jacob Cohen, Babylon L.I., NY, performed early in his career as singing waiter Jack Roy. He sold aluminum siding in New Jersey in the 1950's and had a part in the film Natural Born Killers, directed by Oliver Stone in 1994. The Tonight Show with Johnny Carson ran on NBC-TV from 1962 to 1992. In a 1973 episode, magician and psychic Uri Geller (b. 1946) was unable to telepathically bend a metal spoon as Carson watched. [pg. 68]

95A-E. Père Lachaise cemetery, Paris, France. A.) Gertrude Stein (1874-1946) B) Oscar Wilde (1854-1900) C) Honoré de Balzac (1799-1850) D) Marcel Proust (1871-1922) E) Edith Piaf (1915-1963). All quotes verified and verbatim. [pgs. 68-70]

96. Salvador Dalí (1904-1989) Museum, Figueres, Spain. Both Dalí's appearance on the TV quiz show What's My Line? (1/20/52) and Zippy's appearance on Jeopardy (4/12/06) are genuine. [pg. 71]

97. Liberace Museum, Las Vegas, NV. Lladro is a Spanish "collectible" sculpture company, founded in 1953. In one episode of The Sopranos, Carmela flung a Lladro figurine at Tony. [pg. 71]

98. Kemper Museum of Contemporary Art, Kansas City, MO. Sculpture: "The Architect's Handkerchief" by Claes Oldenburg and Coosje Van Bruggen. German architect Ludwig Mies Van Der Rohe (1886-1969) was a pioneer of the "clean" look in modern architecture, famous for the aphorism, "Less is more." [pg. 72]

99. La Criolla Restaurant, Providence, RI. Playwright David Mamet (b. 1947) is known for his clipped, overlapping dialogue in such plays and films as Glengarry Glen Ross (1984), Edmond (1982) and Wag the Dog (1997). [pg. 72]

100. Barcelona, Spain. Dadaist Marcel Duchamp (1887-1968) gave up art to play chess in 1923. [pg. 73]

101. Griff's, Albuquerque, NM. Noam Chomsky (b. 1928) calls himself a libertarian socialist and asserts that the media in the U.S. are in the business of "manufacturing consent" among the public. (See also COLOR). [pg. 73]

102. "Big Zip" is from Great Falls, VA, spotted in Annapolis, MD. *A Girl Named Zippy* (2002) is by Haven Kimmel and is subtitled "Growing up small in Mooreland, Indiana." No pinheads are involved. [pg. 74]

103. Kim Jong II (b. 1942) is the dictator of North Korea. Among his favorite films are *Rambo, Godzilla* and anything with Elizabeth Taylor. [pg. 74]

104. Los Angeles, CA. Only Santa Claus outranks Ronald McDonald in recognizability among U.S. schoolchildren. NBC-TV weatherman Willard Scott (b. 1934) claims to have created the aforesaid fast-food clown in 1963, wearing a costume featuring a "food-tray hat." [pg. 75]

105. Las Vegas, NV. Paris Hilton is related through marriage to Zsa Zsa Gabor. [pg. 75]

106. 3rd Street tunnel, Los Angeles, CA. [pg. 76]

107. L.A. Natural History Museum, Los Angeles, CA. Canadian actor William Shatner (b. 1931) is an Ashkenazi Jew, as is fellow Star Trekker Leonard Nimoy (b. 1931). [pg. 77]

108. Sculpture by Ron Mueck (b. 1958). Among the celebrities skewered by Sacha Baron Cohen (b. 1971) as his alter ego, Ali G, were Newt Gingrich, Ralph Nader and Donald Trump. [pg. 77]

109. Santa Monica, CA. Meryl Streep (b. 1949) is from New Jersey. [pg. 78]

110. Japan's Eva Air airline. The Hello Kitty jets are used on the Tokyo to Fukuoa route only. [pg. 78]

111. "Cat," 1984, by Colombian sculptor Fernando Botero (b. 1932), in front of Botero's apartment building at 900 Park Avenue, NY, NY. [pg. 79]

112. Vancouver, B.C., Canada. Mother Teresa (1910-1997) was born Agnes Gonxha Bojaxhiu. Barbra Streisand (b. 1942) sang the Irish ballad, "Mother Macree," in the TV special "The Belle of 14th Street" in 1967. [pg. 79]

113. The Nut Museum, Old Lyme, CT, now a private home. Elizabeth Tashjian, known as the "Nut Lady," (1912-2006) lived in the house for many years and composed the tune "Nuts Are Beautiful," lyrics quoted in strip. [pg. 80]

114. Girona, Spain. A Flock of Seagulls was a British synth-pop hair band formed in 1979. All of the songs on their first self-titled album are about alien abduction and invasion, with the aliens victorious at the end. [pg. 80]

SUNDAY COLOR Chapter 5

115. Piccadilly Grill, Winchester, VA. Donald Trump's children: See also "SYLVAN SETTING," pg. 56. [pg. 82]

116. Fyodor Dostoevsky's (1821-1881) *Notes From Underground* (1864) is a founding work of existentialist philosophy. [pg.83]

117. The Pulitzer prize consists of a certificate and a $10,000.00 cash award. [pg. 83]

118. The TV sitcom *Everybody Loves Raymond* (1996-2005) included an episode in which Paul Reubens ("Pee-wee Herman," b. 1952) makes a one-time appearance as an angry comic book shop owner. The word "boogie-woogie" is a doubling of "boogie," a term used to describe rent parties as early as 1913. The Weather Channel went on the air in 1982. Their first slogan was, "We take the weather seriously, but not ourselves." [pg. 85]

119. Manny, Moe and Jack—The Pep Boys—made their debut in 1921. They modeled their company name after a California dress shop named "Minnie, Maude and Mabel's." [pg. 86]

120. Jerusalem, Israel. [pg. 87]

121. East Point, GA. [pg. 88]

122. Cowtown, NJ. [pg. 88]

123. Bristol, CT. [pg. 89]

124. Parody of "What is This Thing Called Love?" (1929), by Cole Porter (1891-1964). [pg. 89]

125. Nancy's creator Ernie Bushmiller (1905-1982) would often leaf through the Sears catalog looking for gag ideas. [pg. 91]

126. The Beagle Boys appeared often in the Uncle Scrooge McDuck comic book series, first in 1951. The characters were created by Disney artist and writer Carl Barks (1901-2000). No digits other than one, six or seven ever appear on the Beagle Boys' prison ID tags, which they always wear. [pg.91]

127. Actual dialogue from the comic book *Rusty Riley, a Boy, a Horse and a Dog* #554, 1949. By Frank Goodwin. [pg. 92]

128. Definitions of all words in this strip can be found at: http://www.zippythepinhead.com/pages/aarealday.html. Scroll down to 4/29/07. [pg. 93]

129. Frisch's Big Boy, Cincinnati, OH (See also, "WISE BABY," pg. 62) [pg. 95]

130. Panel 2) Kerhonksen, NY Panel 3) Glendale, CA [pg. 95]

131. Calgary, Saskatchewan, Canada. [pg. 96]

132. Walt Disney Concert Hall, Los Angeles, CA. Gyro Gearloose was created by cartoonist Carl Barks as a character in the Scrooge McDuck series. He is Duckburg's most creative inventor and has a nephew named Newton. In 2002, Michael Moore (b. 1954) begged Oprah Winfrey (b. 1954) to run for U.S. President. [pg. 96]

133. Brooklyn Diner, 57th Street, Manhattan, NY. [pg.97]

134. Mustache Bill's Diner, Barnegat, NJ. Comics on stool: *Henry* by Carl Anderson (1865-1948). [pg. 97]

135. Calgary, Saskatchewan, Canada. Bugs Bunny first appeared in a Warner Brothers cartoon, directed by Tex Avery (1908-1980), in 1940. Elmer Fudd, Bugs' love-hate object, was first known as Egghead, introduced by Avery in a 1937 cartoon. The Hanna-Barbera animated character Huckleberry Hound debuted in his own TV show in 1958. Yogi Bear, Huckleberry Hound's sidekick, was spun off the show in 1961. [pg. 98]

136. Pennsylvania Station, Baltimore, MD. "Male/Female" sculpture (2004) by Jonathan Borofsky (b. 1942). [pg. 98]

137. Finca Miralles Gate (1902), Barcelona, Spain. The work of Catalan architect Antoni Gaudi (1852-1926) is known for its biomorphic, undulating surfaces and shapes. Among Arnold Stang's (b. 1925) many voice-over credits is that for the Honeynut Cheerios Bee in the 1980s. [pg. 99]

138. Panels 1 & 3) Skyline Diner, Front Royal, VA. Panel 2) Paris, France. [pg. 99]

139. Walt Shoaf's Barber Shop, Salisbury, NC. [pg. 100]

140. S.U.N.Y. Purchase campus, NY. [pg. 100]

141. Mr. Met, the humanoid mascot for the New York Mets baseball team, made his first appearance at New York's Shea Stadium in 1964. [pg. 101]

142. Ashland, NY. The *Partridge Family* TV sitcom (1970-1974) was loosely based on The Cowsills, a real pop-music family, famous in the late 1960s. The Cowsills were approached to star in the Partridge Family series, but refused over the deal-breaker of Shirley Jones' portrayal of their mother. Partridge Family cast member Danny Bonaduce (b. 1959) says that his current wife Gretchen Hillmer encourages him to date other women. Dutch artist Piet Mondrian (1872-1944) is known for his bold, rectangular compositions, using straight black outlines and primary colors. [pg. 101]

143. Quassy Amusement Park, Middlebury, CT. (See also "TOOT, TOOT!!" pg. 154) [pg. 102]

144. Marquette, IA. [pg. 102]

145. Las Vegas, NV. [pg. 103]

146. Times Square, NY, NY. Several of German painter Otto Dix's (1891-1969) paintings were included (and later burned) in the Nazi exhibit of "degenerate art" in 1937. [pg. 104]

147. Linbrook Bowl, Anaheim, CA. Re: Brunswick. (See also "BAG MAN," pg. 30.) [pg. 105]

148. Sauve, France. George Formby (1904-1961), English singer and comedian, played the banjo ukelele on stage and in many films, including *Let George Do It* (1940), regarded as his best. [pg. 106]

149. Doorknocker of The Museum of Jewish Art and History, Paris, France. [pg. 106]

150. Los Angeles, CA. [pg. 107]

151. Hayward, CA. [pg. 107]

POLITICS AS USUAL Chapter 6

152A-C. Kenwood Diner, Spencer, MA. A.) Captain Queeg is a paranoid U.S. Navy officer in Herman Wouk's (b. 1915) 1951 novel *The Caine Mutiny*. Shemp Howard (1895-1955) was a member of The Three Stooges comedy team. His phobias included airplanes, automobiles and water. B.) Nesselrode pie is usually made with chestnuts. A new substitute, "Nesselro," uses cauliflower. C.) Tom DeLay (b. 1947) is a former U.S. Representative from Texas. A strong supporter of the U.S. embargo against Cuba, he was photographed smoking a Cuban cigar in Israel in 2005. [pgs. 109-110]

153. Woodland Hills, CA. The Dixie Chicks country/rock group was formed in Texas in 1989. They sang "The Star-Spangled Banner" at Super Bowl XXXVII. [pg. 110]

154. Baltimore, MD. Karl Rove's (b. 1950) adoptive father was a mineral geologist. His mother owned a gift shop. [pg. 111]

155. Diamond Inn, Las Vegas, NV. [pg. 111]

156. Lodi, WI. [pg. 112]

157. Eggie's Diner, Plaiston, NH. Ned Lamont (b. 1954) ran unsuccessfully against Joe Lieberman for a Connecticut Senate seat in 2006. Marxist philosopher Corliss Lamont

158. (1902-1995) was Ned Lamont's great-uncle, Duncan Lamont (1918-1978) was a British actor. On television, he had roles on *The Texan*, *The Avengers* and *Doctor Who*. [pg. 112]

159. Glenrowan, Victoria, Australia. Ned Kelly (c. 1855-1880) was Australia's most famous bandit. He was portrayed by Sir Mick Jagger (b. 1943) in a 1970 film. [pg. 113]

160. Bob and Edith's Diner, Arlington, VA. *Hi & Lois*, created by Mort Walker and Dik Browne, debuted on the comics pages in 1954. [pg. 114]

161. Lincoln Memorial, Washington D.C. [pg. 115]

162. Anaheim, CA. [pg. 115]

163. Chappaqua, NY. Horace Greeley (1811-1872) was a newspaper editor and abolitionist and a founder of the Republican Party. Actor Keanu Reeves (b. 1964) often rides his motorcycle at night without lights in what he describes as a "demon ride." [pg. 116]

164. Eowin, SD. [pg. 116]

165. Cheshire, CT. Lord of the Dance is a touring Irish musical and dance show, produced by dancer Michael Flatley (b. 1958). Dancers complete approximately 151,200 taps per performance. [pg. 117]

166. *Dog the Bounty Hunter* is a "reality" TV show featuring Duane "Dog" Chapman's exploits capturing bail skippers. "Dog" is an avid stamp collector. [pg. 117]

167. National Portrait Gallery, Washington D.C. [pg. 118]

168. Duluth, GA. [pg. 119]

169. Seal Beach, CA. [pg. 119]

170. Ben's Chili Bowl, Washington D.C. [pg. 120]

171. Hamburger Mary's restaurant, Palm Springs, CA. [pg. 120]

AMERICA THE BEAUTIFUL Chapter 7

171. All three panels: Park Slope, Brooklyn, NY 1) 4th Avenue, 1926 2) Flatbush Avenue, 1914 3) 9th Street, 1928. Herb Alpert (b. 1935) and the Tijuana Brass had a hit in 1966 with "A Taste of Honey." Despite the name, no one in Alpert's band was Hispanic. [pg. 122]

172. Parody of "The Raven" by Edgar Allan Poe (1809-1849). Blues singer Big Mama Thornton (1926-1984) was the first to record "Hound Dog," three years before Elvis Presley, in 1953. *Hairspray* is a 1988 film directed by John Waters, Baltimore native. Waters' first film was "Hag in a Black Leather Jacket" (1964), about a white ballerina who weds a black man in a trash can on a Baltimore rooftop. [pg. 122]

173. 1 & 2) San Francisco's Portola district. 3) San Francisco's Glen Park district. [pg. 123]

174. 1) Kansas City, MO 2) Los Angeles, CA 3) Lemesa, TX. [pg. 124]

175. Lennox, CA. [pg. 125]

176. Long Beach Island, NJ. [pg. 126]

177. Sculpture by Tom Maley, Field Gallery, W. Tisbury, MA. [pg. 127]

178. The Union 76 balls that are still being removed from their poles are now being preserved, a few donated to the American Sign Museum in Cincinnati, OH. [pg. 128]

179. Baker, CA. [pg. 128]

180. Grey Goose Framing, Los Angeles, CA. "Gort" is the robot character from the film *The Day the Earth Stood Still* (1951). [pg. 129]

181. The Jim Henson Company moved into the former Charlie Chaplin Studios in Los Angeles, CA in 2002. [pg. 129]

182. Based on the results of a *Washington Post* "Style Invitational" contest from the August 20, 2006 issue. Readers were asked to compose Beltway overhead highway signs. The sign illustrated was submitted by runner-up contestant Jay Shuck. [pg. 130]

183. Douglas Park, Santa Monica, CA. (See also "JAZZERCISE," pg. 73) [pg. 130]

184. Tony's Transmissions, Los Angeles, CA. [pg. 131]

185. Crownsville, MD. Haggis is made from a variety of ingredients such as sheep's heart and oatmeal and is cooked in an animal's stomach casing. [pg. 131]

186. "Fish" by Marjorie Strider, Cornwall Bridge, CT. [pg. 132]

187. Albany, NY. "Nipper," the RCA Records mascot, was a real dog who lived in Bristol, England (1884-1895). He was painted listening to an old Edison cylinder phonograph by his owner, Francis Barraud (1856-1924). [pg. 132]

188. "Ruff-Ruff," Van Nuys, CA. "Liquid Plumber" is actually spelled Liquid Plumr, in order, we assume, to distinguish it from a professional plumber. [pg. 133]

189. Muncie, IN. [pg. 133]

190. Only 12 Futurliners were built by General Motors from 1940 through 1956. They were introduced in the "Parade of Progress" touring exhibit in 1940. One is currently owned by the Peter Pan Bus Lines of New England. [pg. 134]

191. 1 & 4) Red Skelton's 1960 "Red-eo-Tape Studio-in-a-Bus." 2 & 3) Rio Vista CA. Red Skelton (1913-1997) was a comedian and TV star. A number of his many clown paintings have sold for $80,000 each. [pg. 134]

192. Spotted in Cambridge, OH. Hopalong Cassidy was portrayed in movies and on television by William Boyd (1895-1972). [pg. 135]

193. Happy Day Diner, Rosedale, MD. Chad Stuart (b. 1941) and Jeremy Clyde (b. 1941) were a folk rock duo who had a seven top-ten hits in the U.S. from 1964-66. They appeared as "The Redcoats" in an episode of the *Dick Van Dyke Show* in 1965. [pg. 135]

194. Somewhere in Texas, near state highways 807 and 54. [pg. 136]

195. Inspired by the Marvel comic book (1973-1983) and movie *Ghost Rider* (2007). In the comic, Ghost Rider cyclist Johnny Blaze projects "hellfire" as a weapon, a skill he apparently picked up in Hell. [pg. 136]

196. 1) Encino Park, CA. 2) Santa Monica, CA. 3) Venice, CA. [pg. 137]

197. Higgie's, Pilot House and Spencer's Shad Shack, Haddam, CT. [pg. 137]

198. 1948 Davis car, created by Glen Davis, Van Nuys, CA. [pg. 138]

199. Pacific Palisades, CA. [pg. 139]

200. Natural Bridge, VA. [pg. 139]

201. Charlotte, NC. [pg. 140]

202. Venice, Italy. [pg. 140]

203. Ripley's Believe it or Not, Hollywood, CA. [pg. 141]

204. Gold Strike Casino, Jean, NV. [pg. 141]

205. Denton, NC. [pg. 142]

206. Hamden, CT. [pg. 142]

COMICAL SITUATIONS Chapter 8

207. Zippy sees Phil Fumble, Fritzi Ritz's boyfriend, by Ernie Bushmiller. The *Phil Fumble* strip ran from 1932 to 1938. [pg. 144]

208. Four of "22 Panels That Always Work," a comic art guide put together by *Mad* magazine artist Wally Wood (1927-1981). [pg. 145]

209. Dialogue appropriated from *Beach Blanket Bingo* comics, 1965. [pg. 147]

210. Dialogue appropriated from comic strip ad for the Cleveland Institute of Electronics, Inc. in *Prez* comics #1, 1973. [pg. 147]

211. Dialogue appropriated from *UFO Flying Saucers* comics #1, 1958. [pg. 148]

212. Dialogue appropriated from *New Heroic Comics* #92, 1954. [pg. 148]

213. Dialogue appropriated from *Action Comics* #309, 1964. [pg. 149]

214. Dialogue appropriated from *Mutt and Jeff* comics #62, by Bud Fisher, 1953. [pg. 149]

215. Art appropriated from: 1) *Judge Parker* by Harold LeDoux, 1970. 2) *Rex Morgan, M.D.* by Marvin Bradley, 1971. 3) *Steve Roper* by William Overgaard and Allen Saunders, 1966. [pg. 150]

216. Niantic, CT. The *Spongebob Squarepants* kid's animated TV show first aired in 1999. There are Spongebob "Happy Meals", boxer shorts and thongs. The Spongebob figure shown is clearly unauthorized. Spun off of the original British version, *Antiques Roadshow* has been broadcast on PBS-TV since 1997. Current host Mark Walberg was previously the host of the TV game show *Shop 'Til You Drop*. [pg. 151]

217. Jackson, NJ. *The Family Circus* (1960-present) by Bil Keane (b. 1922) was originally called *The Family Circle*, until objections by *Family Circle* magazine caused the name change. Previous strips by Keane include *Silly Philly* and *Channel Chuckles*. [pg. 151]

218. Stockholm, Sweden. Baby Huey began his career in 1949, created by cartoonist Martin B. Taras (1914-1994). One of Baby Huey's catch phrases was, "I think you're trying to kill me!" Quote in panel 2 is by Sir Walter Scott (1771-1832). [pg. 152]

219. Rock Creek Cemetery, Washington D.C. "Little Max" was a speechless orphan newsboy who appeared originally in the *Joe Palooka* daily comic strip (1930-1984) by Ham Fisher (1900-1955). Max had his own Harvey comic book series from 1949 to 1961. [pg. 152]

220. Sluggo by Ernie Bushmiller. [pg. 153]

221. The Center Diner in Peekskill, NY was the model for the Sunset Diner in *Little Lulu* comics, created by Marge Buell (1904-1993) and John Stanley (1914-1993). Chef Julia Child (1912-2004) played basketball for Smith College. Her last meal was a bowl of French onion soup. [pg. 153]

222. Quassy Amusement Park, Middlebury, CT. Popeye, by Elzie Segar (1894-1938), debuted in 1929. Olive Oyl's first boyfriend was named Harold Hamgravy. [pg. 154]

223. Jacksonville, FL. Like the one before it, this strip makes reference to the death of King Features comics editor-in-chief and friend of the author, Jay Kennedy. [pg. 155]

ALSO AVAILABLE FROM FANTAGRAPHICS

ZIPPY
ANNUAL
No. 1

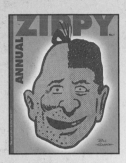

ZIPPY ANNUAL NO. 1 (2000)
160 pages, color + black and white, softcover
$22.00 postpaid

ZIPPY
ANNUAL
2001

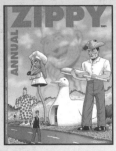

ZIPPY ANNUAL 2001
144 pages, color + black and white, softcover
$22.00 postpaid

ZIPPY
by Bill Griffith
2002

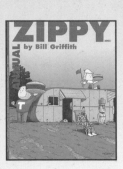

ZIPPY ANNUAL 2002
128 pages, color + black and white, softcover
$22.00 postpaid

ZIPPY
ANNUAL
2003

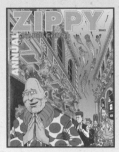

ZIPPY ANNUAL 2003
128 pages, color + black and white, softcover
$22.00 postpaid

ZIPPY
From here
to absurdity
Bill Griffith

ZIPPY: FROM HERE TO ABSURDITY (2004)
128 pages, color + black and white, softcover
$22.00 postpaid

DISCOVERING YOUR
TYPE Z PERSONALITY
DO YOU:
ZIPPY the PINHEAD
Helps you recognize
the 16 tell-tale signs
MEN, WOMEN
and CHILDREN
Need no longer feel
"PERPLEXED"
JUST FOLLOW THIS E-Z
STRIP-by-STRIP METHOD!
by Bill Griffith, P.Z.A.

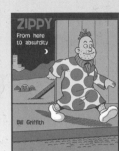

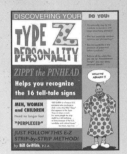

ZIPPY: TYPE Z PERSONALITY (2005)
128 pages, color + black and white, softcover
$22.00 postpaid

CONNECT THE POLKA DOTS
Zippy The Pinhead Comic Strips by BILL GRIFFITH

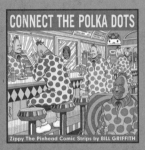

ZIPPY: CONNECT THE POLKA DOTS (2006)
144 pages, color + black and white, softcover, $22.00 postpaid

ZIPPY'S HOUSE of FUN
FULL COLOR!
54 MONTHS OF SUNDAYS
FANTAGRAPHICS BOOKS

ZIPPY'S HOUSE OF FUN
152 pages, full color, hardcover / $40.00 postpaid

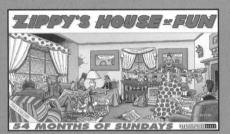

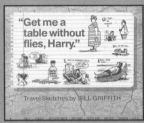

"Get me a
table without
flies, Harry."
Travel Sketches by BILL GRIFFITH

"GET ME A TABLE WITHOUT FLIES, HARRY." TRAVEL SKETCHES
160 pages, black and white, softcover / $17.00 postpaid

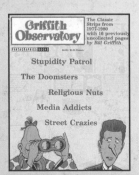

Griffith
Observatory
The Classic
Strips from
1977-1980
with 16 previously
uncollected pages
by Bill Griffith
FANTAGRAPHICS BOOKS
Stupidity Patrol
The Doomsters
Religious Nuts
Media Addicts
Street Crazies

GRIFFITH OBSERVATORY
48 pages, black and white, magazine / $6.00 postpaid

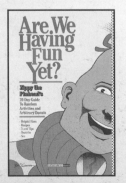

Are We
Having
Fun
Yet?
Zippy the
Pinhead's
29 Day Guide
To Random
Activities and
Arbitrary Donuts

ARE WE HAVING FUN YET?
128 pages, black and white, softcover / $15.00 postpaid

Zippy
Zippy
Zippy
No. 17
FANTAGRAPHICS BOOKS

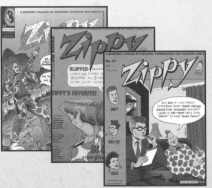

ZIPPY QUARTERLY
15 available issues (#'s 10,13 & 18 out of print), 32-48 pages, black and white, magazines / $4.50 each postpaid
Special: All available issues PLUS *Griffith Observatory* $49.95 postpaid

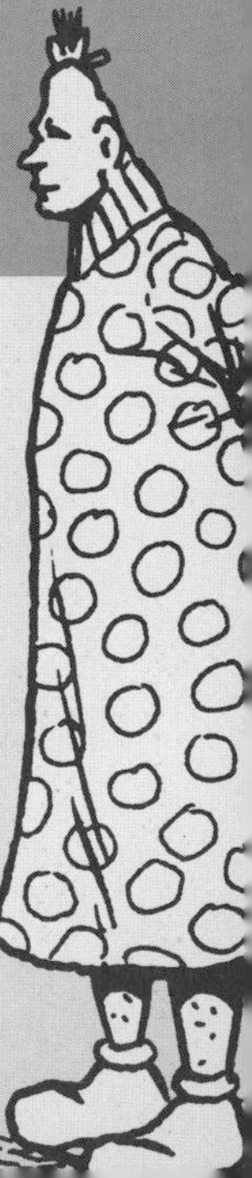

TO ORDER CALL 1-800-657-1100, WRITE FANTAGRAPHICS AT 7563 LAKE CITY WAY N.E. SEATTLE, WA 98115, OR CHECK OUR WEBSITE AT WWW.FANTAGRAPHICS.COM